The Professional Practice of Landscape Architecture

The Professional Practice of Landscape Architecture

A Complete Guide to Starting and Running Your Own Firm

WALTER ROGERS

VAN NOSTRAND REINHOLD

I(T)P® A Division of International Thomson Publishing Inc.

New York • Albany • Bonn • Boston • Detroit • London • Madrid • Melbourne
Mexico City • Paris • San Francisco • Tokyo • Toronto

I(T)P® A division of International Thomson Publishing, Inc.
The ITP logo is a registered trademark under license

Printed in the United States of America

For more information, contact:

Van Nostrand Reinhold
115 Fifth Avenue
New York, NY 10003

Chapman & Hall GmbH
Pappelallee 3
69469 Weinheim
Germany

Chapman & Hall
2-6 Boundary Row
London
SE1 8HN
United Kingdom

International Thomson Publishing Asia
221 Henderson Road #05-10
Henderson Building
Singapore 0315

Thomas Nelson Australia
102 Dodds Street
South Melbourne, 3205
Victoria, Australia

International Thomsom Publishing Japan
Hirakawacho Kyowa Building, 3F
2-2-1 Hirakawacho
Chiyoda-ku, 102 Tokyo
Japan

Nelson Canada
1120 Birchmount Road
Scarborough, Ontario
Canada MIK 5G4

International Thomson Editores
Seneca 53
Col. Polanco
11560 Mexico D.F. Mexico

1 2 3 4 5 6 7 8 9 10 COU-WF 01 00 99 98 97

Library of Congress Cataloging-in-Publication Data

Rogers, Walter.
    The professional practice of landscape architecture / Walter
Rogers.
        p.   cm.
    Includes bibliographical references (p.   ) and index.
    ISBN 0-442-01964-5
    1. Landscape architecture—Vocational guidance.   2. Landscape
architecture.   I. Title.
SB469.37.R64   1997
712'.068—dc20   96-24289
                                                    CIP

0442019645

To JL, who was with me in the beginning;
to ST, who was with me in the middle;
and to BW, who was with me in the end.
Thank you.

Contents

Introduction

In 1968 I was in the last semester of my undergraduate studies in landscape architecture at the University of Massachusetts, soon to graduate with a B.S. degree.

One of my courses in that final semester at UMass was called Professional Practice. My recollection about the course is that there was no assigned textbook. The required readings were an assembly of sections of books and photocopied articles about writing a résumé and looking for a job. The course was taught by the only faculty member who was a practicing landscape architect working in a traditionally oriented office on site planning and design projects. I think I got a B in the course, and I did write a résumé.

Two years later, after graduating with an M.L.A., I took a position on the faculty of the first of three universities I would teach at until 1981. At each university, a professional-practice course similar to the one I took in my last semester at UMass was a part of the curriculum and was taught in the last semester. A textbook was still not available, and reading materials were still a collection of parts of books and photocopied articles.

After my teaching career, I launched a private practice. The office I started, and where I still practice, flourished through the 1980s. The practice grew to include five partners and twenty-five professional, technical, and support staff. The size of the firm required us to develop administrative and management practices that allowed the firm to run smoothly and effectively.

The idea for this book grew out of the two cornerstones evident in the foregoing brief history of my professional life in landscape architecture. First, I realized in the early 1990s that a single-source textbook on the development, operation, administration, and management of a professional landscape architecture practice was still not available for the professional-practice courses taught in most college landscape architecture curriculums. Second, over the years of operating my private practice, I had developed a great number of useful tools and techniques that might be of value if passed on to aspiring landscape architects.

When I was in college, I had a burning desire to know what it would be like working in a landscape architecture office, but I didn't find out until I got my first job in a landscape architecture firm. Even then, I was aware of only a fraction of the intricacies of what went into the daily operations of the firm. This book tells the story of the wide range of strategic considerations involved in developing, operating, and managing a private practice. I intend this book to be a compendium of the professional practice of landscape architecture, and I have written it with the following groups in mind:

- Faculty teaching professional-practice and studio courses that simulate the office environment.
- Students taking professional-practice and studio courses.
- Aspiring graduates who want to know about the many facets of owning, developing, administering, and managing a private practice.
- Students and graduates who are searching for the landscape architecture career path most suited to their aims and personalities.
- Graduates who wish to start a private practice and can benefit from the methods and techniques I have developed and used effectively for almost two decades of private practice.
- Long-time practitioners who may benefit from the methods and techniques I have developed and used.
- Allied professionals who may benefit from the methods and techniques I have developed and used. (There are many similarities in practicing architecture, engineering, planning, and other environmental design professions.)

I hope you will find wisdom, honesty, integrity, and helpful methods and techniques in these pages. I hope you will enjoy reading this book as much as I enjoyed writing it.

Here's capsule of what you'll find in each chapter.

Chapter 1

A definition of the profession of landscape architecture and a brief historical overview are the core of the first chapter. Six eras of professional practice are discussed: the early park-planning era, estate design, city planning, the urban growth era, California and the West, and the environmental era.

Chapter 1 also describes the following professional career tracks:

- Private practice—design
- Private practice—design-build
- Public practice
- Academic practice
- Corporate practice
- Specialty practice

For the aspiring landscape architect, selecting a career track is an important decision that should receive a great deal of personal reflection and research of the various opportunities available. Matching one's professional career goals with financial opportunities, professional growth potential, and personal aims is one of the important decisions made at the start of one's professional career and often at other points throughout one's professional life. Professional development opportunities are discussed as a long-term, lifelong pursuit. Professional development opportunities are one of the considerations in selecting a career path and an initial employer, and in making subsequent employment decisions throughout a professional's career.

Chapter 1 also provides an overview of professional registration, the Landscape Architecture Registration Exam (LARE), and professional societies. The chapter concludes with the topic of professional ethics and values. The code of ethics of the American Society of Landscape Architects is included at the end of the chapter.

Chapter 2

Chapter 2 discusses the landscape architect's clients. The first part of the chapter focuses on the two broad categories of clients, public and private, and describes the postures, opportunities, and conditions related to developing a client mix.

A large part of the chapter discusses ten categories of projects typically carried out for private clients. Used by the American Society of Landscape Architects in its annual awards program, these categories constitute a broad definition of the private practice of landscape architecture. This chapter describes a cross section of award-winning landscape architecture projects in the following categories:

1. Community and multifamily housing development
2. Parks and outdoor recreation facilities
3. Commercial and industrial development
4. Planning and analysis projects
5. Institutional projects
6. Single-family residential and garden design projects
7. Land and water reclamation and conservation projects
8. Interior landscape architecture
9. Historic preservation and restoration projects
10. Landscape art and earth sculpture

Not-for-profit corporations and public-sector clients and projects are also discussed. A cross section of public agencies, and the client and project opportunities associated with public agencies are discussed in the last part of the chapter.

Chapter 3

This chapter presents a snapshot view of six types of landscape architecture employers:

1. Private practice: large multidisciplinary A/E firm
2. Private practice: large landscape architecture firm

3. Private practice: small landscape architecture firm
4. Private practice: design-build firm
5. Public practice
6. Corporate practice

There is no better way to evaluate career options than to compare and contrast the opportunities available among employers that represent different career tracks. Each case study provides the following information:

- History and overview of the employer
- Mission statement
- Landscape architecture opportunities with the employer, emphasizing entry-level opportunities
- Employee benefits
- Entry-level job description
- Representative examples of the employer's work and projects

Awareness of career tracks and opportunities is the first step in making appropriate career choices. Studying the practices, employment opportunities, growth opportunities, and long-term potential for job satisfaction and professional development is the key to making successful career choices.

Chapter 4

Landscape architects have four main professional relationships:

1. Landscape architect/owner
2. Landscape architect/allied professional
3. Landscape architect/contractor
4. Landscape architect/general public

Chapter 4 describes these professional relationships, which can be both contractual and noncontractual. The chapter focuses on the noncontractual relationships. Three primary types of relationships are covered: the prime consultant, multiple direct consultants, and subconsultants.

Two key elements are discussed for each of the four types of relationships: (1) the expectations of the landscape architect and (2) the expectations of the person or persons with whom the landscape architect has established a professional relationship, as well as the responsibilities of each party to the relationship.

Chapter 5

Where do landscape architects find the money to start an office and keep it going? What financing options are available, and how is the financing obtained? How are funds raised? How do lenders evaluate the landscape architect's request for financing?

Chapter 5 answers these questions by discussing the three main forms of financing:

1. Equity
2. Debt
3. Trade credit

This chapter discusses when to use debt financing versus equity financing and the pros and cons of each. Sources of funds for each type of financing are covered, as well as the concept of leveraging equity through debt.

Three phases of financing a firm are discussed:

1. Start-up financing
2. Maintenance financing
3. Continuation financing

You will also read about the differences between borrowing for capital purchases and leasing, the elements of a loan proposal, and the concept and use of trade credit as a valuable form of obtaining financing for operating a private practice.

Chapter 6

Accounting is not only for accountants. Every landscape architect who runs a private practice needs a rudimentary understanding of accounting and more specifically of financial management by using accounting information and reports. The landscape architect needs two types of information to be an effective financial manager: financial accounting information and financial management information. This chapter discusses both types of information and gives examples of each in practical applications related to the private practice of landscape architecture. Descriptions of an income statement, a balance sheet, an aged accounts receivable report, an aged accounts payable report, and a cash report, as well as examples of each, are found in this chapter.

Developing a pro forma financial statement (a projection of future income and financial condition based on present conditions) is covered. Other key financial reports of a nonaccounting nature are discussed, principally the work in progress report and workload projection. Ratio calculations are covered in depth because of their importance in evaluating the financial health of a firm. Trend ratios, liquidity ratios, such as the current ratio and the receivables turnover ratio, are covered. Equity or long-term solvency ratios and equity-to-debt ratios are also covered.

A section of this chapter deals with financial accounting systems and explains the difference between cash-basis accounting and accrual-basis accounting. Elementary accounting practices are covered, including setting up a chart of accounts for a landscape architecture firm.

Last, this chapter discusses the benefits and desirability of a computerized, integrated accounting and financial management system.

Chapter 7

The administration of the landscape architecture office; keeping track of the firm's projects; developing and maintaining filing systems; keeping financial, tax, and personnel records; and organizing business records are critical administrative tasks for successful operation of a landscape architecture office.

The key to effective office administration is using a job number to manage all of the firm's project-related information. This chapter discusses how to develop and use a job numbering system including category-of-work codes that allow the firm to study trends in the firm's procurement of work and to retrieve information for marketing purposes. Using a master roster of work in progress and work in job development phases is discussed, along with using time cards or computer time tracking systems. Using type-of-work codes and task codes for effective time card entry is another important administrative technique covered.

This chapter also includes a section on filing systems, methods, and records management, including the time requirements for keeping records and categories of the importance of information.

A section of the chapter discusses the development and use of forms in the landscape architecture office as a means to effective management of repetitive administrative tasks.

Establishing and maintaining files for both active and dead project files is another important element of office administration that results in effective retrieval of the daily information used in project work. A range of types of files necessary in the landscape architecture office is discussed, as well as record keeping for vacations, holidays, and sick leave.

A lengthy section of the chapter is devoted to the administration and record-keeping requirements for insurance needs. Descriptions of the typical insurance coverage needed by a private firm are covered in depth, including property and liability insurance, worker's compensation insurance, disability insurance, professional liability insurance, life insurance, key-person insurance, and health insurance. Retirement benefits, pensions, and programs are also discussed.

Chapter 7 explains the types of product literature files important to the landscape architecture office and how to organize a technical reference library. Office payroll administration, as well as tax administration, is also covered.

Chapter 8

Marketing is the social and business process used by landscape architects to obtain clients and projects.

Chapter 8 discusses the need for and methods of developing a strategic plan for the landscape architecture firm, including a mission statement. The strategic plan in turn sets the parameters for a marketing plan designed to analyze market opportunities, identify and select target markets, develop market strategies, and plan and implement marketing efforts. The written components of a marketing plan are spelled out.

A lengthy section of this chapter discusses marketing tools and the promotion mix. The tools discussed include

- word of mouth
- brochures
- cut sheets
- Standard Forms 254 and 255
- direct mail marketing
- direct call marketing
- cold calls
- video
- tickle files
- newspaper, magazine, radio, and TV coverage
- journal articles
- public speaking
- community service
- sponsoring community events
- trade shows and conferences
- print advertising
- slide files and photo archives
- display boards
- the physical environment of the office
- answering the telephone

Chapter 8 discusses the proposal and interview process, focusing on the response to a statement of interest, statement of qualifications, and the request for proposals.

A section of the chapter talks about market opportunities and entering new markets. A key part of this section provides techniques to assess the economic potential of new market areas.

The last section of the chapter discusses the need for the marketing staff and includes a job description for a marketing production coordinator.

Chapter 9

Chapter 9 discusses one of the most important skills needed by the practicing landscape architect—writing a contract for professional services. This chapter also discusses various other contracts the landscape architect must be familiar with and be able to understand and execute.

The chapter starts with a discussion of contract terminology and the elements of an enforceable contract.

The next section provides in-depth information on formats for professional services contracts and includes a discussion of professional association standard contracts, landscape architect–developed contracts, and client-developed contracts. The proposal process—the act of forming a contract—is also discussed. The elements of a professional services contract are outlined, and the concept of agency, where the landscape architect serves as the client's binding representative, is discussed as an important contractual element.

Sections of chapter 9 discuss contracts with allied professionals and contracts with credit agencies and lending institutions, including loan agreements. What to look for and expect in loan agreement contracts is covered in depth.

A section covers employee agreements, another contract form important for successful employer/employee relationships. A sample employee agreement is included.

A lengthy section discusses the art and skill of negotiating contracts, focusing primarily on professional services contracts. The fundamentals of negotiating postures and negotiating techniques used by both parties in the negotiating process are discussed.

The last section of this chapter includes important elements and useful clauses of a professional services contract. The elements include

- dispute resolution
- billing and terms of payment
- client's obligations
- compliance with codes and standards
- excluded services or additional services
- ownership of documents
- indemnities
- insurance
- limit of liability
- opinion of probable construction costs
- termination

Samples of contract terminology are provided for many of the elements discussed.

Chapter 10

Project management is one of the keys to successful operation of a landscape architecture firm, and the project manager approach to delivery of professional services is the most popular way to organize a landscape architecture office for completing professional services contracts.

The key elements of project management are discussed in chapter 10. They include

1. planning, organizing, and scoping the elements of a project
2. setting up tracking systems to monitor and control the flow of work
3. tracking a project and developing strategies when a project is over budget
4. managing the work flow to maximize profit for the firm on every project
5. selecting and organizing staff for successful completion of a project
6. directing and motivating staff
7. serving the client and developing a relationship that results in a satisfied client
8. providing technical supervision for the project staff
9. inspiring the professional staff and promoting professional development opportunities
10. coordinating with the firm's top management and clients
11. attaining high quality in the planning and design output of the office
12. marketing the firm by doing a good job with existing clients
13. managing the planning or design effort to meet construction cost expectations
14. taking part in performance reviews of technical staff and peers
15. assisting in writing and preparing proposals
16. closing out projects
17. managing construction observation

Throughout this chapter a wide range of tools and checklists is provided as related to successful project management.

Chapter 11

The focus of chapter 11 is the legal environment of professional practice. The chapter starts with an overview of the origins of law. One section deals with licensure law and state registration. The historical precedent of licensure laws, legal considerations, and the functioning of state boards of technical registration are covered.

A section discusses government regulatory law, agencies, and how agencies affect the practice of landscape architecture.

Another section deals with tort law and negligence, which many professionals agree may have the greatest legal consequences for private practice. Negligence is defined and the elements of law that must be proved to result in an act of negligence are discussed in detail.

Another section of chapter 11 discusses labor relations and the key laws affecting employer/employee relations. The concept of employment at will, minimum wage regulations, worker's compensation laws, OSHA and job safety, firing an employee, the Employee Retirement Income Security Act, and the Americans with Disabilities Act are discussed as related to landscape architecture practice.

A section discusses discrimination and laws involved with discrimination in the workplace. The Civil Rights Act of 1964 and subsequent amendments are discussed. Affirmative action and age discrimination are also discussed.

The last section of chapter 11 discusses the landscape architect's obligation to protect the general public, the environment, and the consumer of landscape architecture services.

The Professional Practice of Landscape Architecture

CHAPTER ONE

The Profession of Landscape Architecture and Professionalism

Joining a profession such as landscape architecture involves dedication to principles, practices, and ethics. Every profession is bound together by specific technical knowledge and skills and by a bond among its practitioners, who endeavor to advance the collective spirit of the profession. Landscape architecture is no exception.

The modern profession of landscape architecture has existed well over a century. Over the years, a body of technical knowledge has evolved that sets landscape architects apart from other professionals in related environmental disciplines. Today there are an estimated thirty thousand practicing landscape architects in the United States. These practitioners have carved an important niche among the environmental design professionals focusing on research, planning, and design of the land.

This chapter provides an overview of the history of landscape architecture, professional registration, professional development, professional societies, and ethics. It also describes the career tracks generally followed by landscape architects.

If you are reading this book, you may be thinking about a career as a professional landscape architect. Welcome aboard. You will find landscape architecture to be a rewarding occupation with its roots firmly planted in the design of public outdoor space. As the profession matures, landscape architecture today is one of the prime design professions influencing the shape of public and private outdoor environments in the United States and throughout the world. Landscape architects view themselves as stewards of the land, and they strive to achieve the highest visual quality in the built and natural landscape.

DEFINITION OF LANDSCAPE ARCHITECTURE

Landscape Architecture is the profession which applies artistic and scientific principles to the research, planning, design and management of both natural and built environments. Practitioners of this profession apply creative and technical skills and scientific, cultural and political knowledge in the planned arrangement of natural and constructed elements on the land with a concern for the stewardship and conservation of natural, constructed and human resources. The resulting environments shall serve useful, aesthetic, safe and enjoyable purposes.

Landscape architecture may, for the purposes of landscape preservation, development and enhancement, include: investigation, selection, and allocation of land and water resources for appropriate use; feasibility studies; formulation of graphic and written criteria to govern the planning and design of land construction programs; preparation, review, and analysis of master plans for land use and development; production of overall site plans, landscape grading and landscape drainage plans, irrigation plans, planting plans, and construction details; specifications; cost estimates and reports for land development; collaboration in the design of roads, bridges, and structures with respect to the functional and aesthetic requirements of the areas on which they are to be placed; negotiation and arrangement for execution of land area projects;

1

field observation and inspection of land area construction, restoration, and maintenance.

(Approved and adopted by the Board of Trustees, November 18, 1993. Source: ASLA 1993)

Brief History of the Profession

The modern profession of landscape architecture, according to Norman T. Newton, began with the design of Central Park in New York City by Frederick Law Olmsted and Calvert Vaux (Newton 1971).

May 1863 is considered by Newton to be the founding date for the profession. On May 12, 1863, Frederick Law Olmsted Sr. and Calvert Vaux resigned their positions as designers of New York's Central Park

and signed their resignation letter "Olmsted and Vaux, Landscape Architects." This is the first official use of the title *landscape architect* and "serves to establish the date, perhaps better than any other, as the birthday of the *profession* of landscape architecture" (Newton 1971, 273).

The Early Park Planning Era

After their success with New York's Central Park, Olmsted, Vaux & Co. went on to design other public park projects, including Brooklyn's Prospect Park and parks in Buffalo, Albany, Newark, Rochester, and Providence. When their partnership broke up, their work continued both individually and in collaboration until Vaux's death in 1895.

FIGURE 1-1. Bird's-eye rendering of Olmsted's plan for Central Park.
Photograph courtesy of the National Park Service, Frederick Law Olmsted National Historic Site.

FIGURE 1-2. Olmsted's 1885 plan for Boston's Franklin Park.
Photograph courtesy of the National Park Service, Frederick Law Olmsted National Historic Site.

During this early era of landscape architecture, from the 1860s to about the turn of the twentieth century, landscape architects focused on the design of public parks and open space, and Olmsted became the leading park designer in the United States. In 1878 Olmsted moved his private practice to Boston, and by 1880 he was channeling his efforts to develop a network of parks and open space in Boston's Back Bay Fens area. Critically acclaimed, Olmsted's work on the Back Bay Fens and Franklin Park resulted in one of the first urban linear park systems in America, referred to as the emerald necklace. Olmsted's approach to the plan was to solve much-needed drainage problems in the Fens while simultaneously introducing open-space and recreational land uses. This approach of tying landscape architectural improvements to drainage engineering pioneered by Olmsted in the 1880s has

been used repeatedly in American cities throughout the twentieth century and continues to be a source of landscape architecture projects.

One of Olmsted's most important projects was the World's Columbian Exposition of 1893 in Chicago. Olmsted and his partner, Henry Sargent Codman, were appointed consulting landscape architects to the exposition in 1890. These two landscape architects, in association with Daniel Burnham and John Root, the exposition's consulting architects, collaborated to develop the exposition's master plan, which was approved in December 1890 (Newton 1971).

The master plan for the World's Columbian Exposition, set in Jackson Park in Chicago, featured an axial organization. The main axis extended west from the shoreline of Lake Michigan and was bisected by the secondary north-south axis. The two axes were

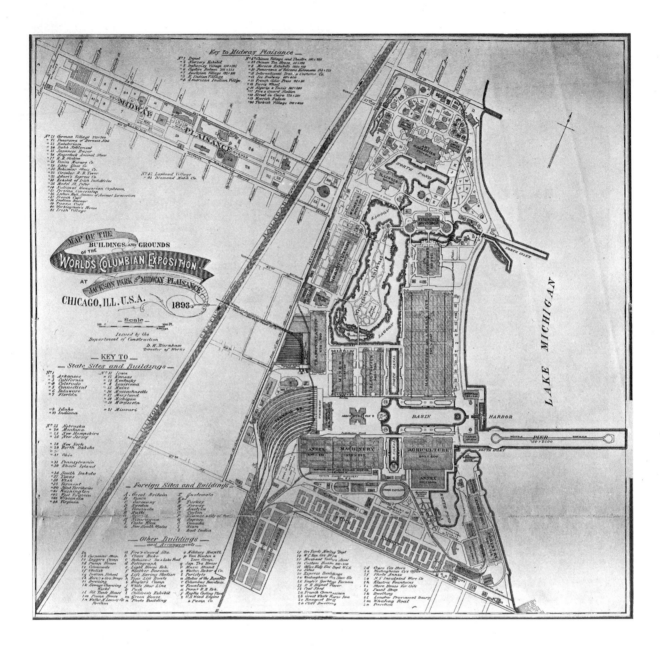

FIGURE 1-3. Plan for the World's Columbian Exposition of 1893.
Photograph courtesy of the National Park Service, Frederick Law Olmsted National Historic Site.

designed as grand pedestrian zones with basins and water features serving as focal points and the exposition's predominant buildings providing the enclosure for the spaces. The central space, named the Court of Honor, was considered to be one of the most impressive monumental spaces designed and built in the United States. The Court of Honor illustrated Olmsted's ability to understand spatial relationships, scale, and view corridors. The spatial quality was enhanced by keeping the buildings that enclosed the space to a consistent height of sixty feet and by uniformly painting the neoclassical style buildings white.

The World's Columbian Exposition served like no other previous development in America as a paradigm of interprofessional collaboration. It awakened public interest in civic design and set the stage for the City Beautiful movement of the early twentieth century.

Estate Design

Landscape architects toward the end of the nineteenth century were involved not only with parks but also

FIGURE 1-4. View looking east of the main court and great central basin of the World's Columbian Exposition of 1893.

Photograph courtesy of the Bettmann Archive.

with the design of large estate properties. The transition to estate design was natural for the early landscape architects because the large estates of this period were always developed in parklike settings. No other professionals had built up the collective experience with park design as had landscape architects.

Charles Platt, another noted landscape architect of the latter nineteenth century and early twentieth century, focused most of his work on estate design. By drawing on the principles of design he found in the formal gardens of Italian villas, Platt brought organization and structure to his estate site plans and gardens. Platt's book *Italian Gardens,* published in 1894, set a new direction in estate design trends. Led by Charles Platt, practitioners began designing formal Italianate gardens adjacent to the lavish homes of their clients. Landscape architects tried to marry the formal Italianate design with an informal landscape setting in the style of the English landscape gardening school or the picturesque school. The axis was commonly employed as the means for organizing the outdoor patios and gardens. Allées, pergolas, courtyards, and lawns were design features used to enhance views and provide interest.

Keith N. Morgan, in his wonderful reprinting of Charles Platt's *Italian Gardens,* contrasts Platt with Olmsted. Whereas Olmsted was a believer in creating the picturesque ideal, Platt deserted the picturesque for the beautiful and for the classic vocabulary of the Italian garden. Olmsted's philosophy of design

was creating naturalized landscapes after eighteenth-century English landscape gardens. He and his associates executed about three thousand design commissions using, for the most part, the naturalistic landscape concept. Morgan points out that Platt, on the other hand, emphasized the conception of the villa as a comprehensive, interrelated unit embracing the house, the flower gardens, terraces, groves, fountains, and functional landscape items such as the water system. Platt designed a large number of projects in the developing country house era during the early twentieth century (Platt, Morgan 1993).

Platt's most noted estate design may be that of the Charles Sprague estate, Faulkner Farm, in Brookline, Massachusetts. Faulkner Farm was one of Platt's early commissions. Chosen after Olmsted, Olmsted & Elliot were dismissed as designers, Platt designed Faulkner Farm with a long, straight drive terminating in a walled courtyard on axis with a large statue. A formal Italianate flower garden was designed as a main site feature and included Italian design elements such as a pool, garden sculpture, and the enclosing pergola and pavilion.

Olmsted also worked on large country estates. Like Platt and other landscape architects practicing estate design at the time, Olmsted applied formal European garden design idioms together with the softer landscape setting that had evolved in the United States out of the English landscape gardening school. Olmsted's most notable estate design achievement is

FIGURE 1-5. The flower garden at Charles Sprague's Faulkner Farm where both Olmsted and Charles Platt worked.

Photograph courtesy of the National Park Service, Frederick Law Olmsted National Historic Site.

the famed Biltmore estate owned by George Washington Vanderbilt. The estate was designed as a French château, and the formal garden design at Bilt-

more was based on precedents found at great French estates such as Vaux-le-Vicomte and Versailles.

The Biltmore estate, which was developed in 1888 on 100,000 acres of land near Asheville, North Carolina, presented Olmsted with the opportunity to develop a conservation and land management program. George Washington Vanderbilt was an ardent conservationist with interests in farming, forestry, and horticulture. Because of Vanderbilt's interests, Olmsted was able to develop not only the fashionable formal gardens, allées, and esplanades, but also a 4,000-acre tree farm and arboretum to promote advanced methods of conservation. Today, 12,000 acres of the original 100,000, including the mansion, form the core of North Carolina's Pisgah National Forest (Fabos, Milde, and Weinmeyer 1968).

City Planning

The modern profession of city planning is an offshoot of the profession of landscape architecture. The City Beautiful movement, which grew from a heightened public interest in city design after the success of the World's Columbian Exposition of 1893, gave city planning a boost in the early twentieth century.

A Rochester, New York, journalist, Charles Mulford Robinson, wrote extensively at the turn of the twentieth century about city beautification and improvements to the appearance of cities, culminating in 1901 with his milestone book *The Improvement of Towns and Cities, or The Practical Basis of Civic Aes-*

FIGURE 1-6. Detail of the flower garden pavilion at Charles Sprague's Faulkner Farm, illustrating Platt's Italianate influence.

Photograph courtesy of the National Park Service, Frederick Law Olmsted National Historic Site.

FIGURE 1-7. The Biltmore estate nearing completion in 1895.

Photograph courtesy of the National Park Service, Frederick Law Olmsted National Historic Site.

thetics. It was one of the first books written about city planning and design. Robinson's first book was received with overwhelming enthusiasm and led to a second, *Modern Civic Art, or The City Made Beautiful,* the origin of the term *City Beautiful movement.*

Robinson's books created a large market for city planning services throughout the United States. More importantly, Robinson allied himself with the landscape architecture profession. In 1913 he was appointed to a new faculty position in civic design in the Landscape Gardening Department at the University of Illinois, and became an associate member of the American Society of Landscape Architects (ASLA) in 1915.

Landscape architecture was a young, growing profession in the first two decades of the twentieth century. Moreover, city planning provided fuel for the profession's early growth. After the turn of the century, landscape architecture professionals had developed the project experience and expertise needed for working in large public outdoor places, Central Park and the World's Columbian Exposition of 1893 being prime examples. After 1909 city planning courses were offered at Harvard University in the Department of Landscape Architecture, providing educational credentials for the profession's move into city planning. By 1923 Harvard University offered a city planning option in its graduate landscape architecture program. Applying design concepts on a larger, citywide basis was a natural progression of professional development for landscape architects, and many of the earliest firms included city planning and city beautification projects in their office portfolios.

With the development in 1929 of a School of City Planning separate from the Landscape Architec-

ture Department at Harvard University, city planning shifted orientation from physical planning and city beautification toward a concern for the social, political, and economic well-being of cities. The City Beautiful movement came to an end, too, but city planning and urban design work have continued to be professional services offered by landscape architects (Newton 1971).

The Urban Growth Era

Starting about 1930 and picking up considerable momentum by 1945, the United States experienced an unprecedented growth boom that included a shift of population to the south and west and the rapid development of urban areas in growth states such as Texas, Arizona, California, Florida, and Colorado. During this era of urban growth, landscape architects were involved with a wide range of site planning for housing projects, schools, and commercial developments. Whereas landscape architecture has continued to be the profession most suited for designing parks and recreation facilities, the urban growth era provided extensive opportunities for landscape architects due to the development of highways, parkways, and public transportation systems. Parkways, in particular, have fallen under the domain of landscape architects working hand in hand with civil, structural, and electrical engineers.

The profession's work in parkway planning and design is exemplified by the work of Gilmore D. Clarke, who worked as the principal landscape architect of the Westchester County Park Commission

(WCPC) in the 1920s and 1930s. During this period, the WCPC designed a trendsetting system of parks and parkways, including the Saw Mill River Parkway, Hutchinson River Parkway, and Playland at Rye Beach, New York. The parkways were designed as connectors between major park or open-space sites. The notion that a parkway is a road in a park setting was nurtured by Clarke and his colleagues at the WCPC. The designers also solidified the parkway concepts of the variable width right-of-way, limited access, independent lane alignment, variable width medians, and soft vertical and horizontal alignment.

In 1934 Gilmore Clarke started a partnership with Michael Rapuano, forming the landscape architecture firm Clarke & Rapuano, and Clarke continued to develop parkway design concepts until his retirement in 1971. The Garden State Parkway in New Jersey, completed in 1956, is one of the firm's most notable design accomplishments.

By the early 1930s, the parkway movement was hugely successful in the heavily developed north-eastern United States. The Taconic State and the Henry Hudson Parkways in New York provided parkway designers with the opportunity to continue the development of parkway design concepts. In 1935, Skyline Drive in Virginia's Blue Ridge Mountains became the first of several important federal parkways designed by the National Park Service. Ground also was broken in 1935 for the first official national parkway—the Blue Ridge Parkway—that would ultimately continue for 470 miles, connecting Skyline Drive with Great Smokey Mountains National Park. By 1967 all but 7.5 miles of the Blue Ridge Parkway had been constructed. This final section, which skirts the rugged and rocky perimeter of Grandfather Mountain in North Carolina, presented federal and state officials a number of obstacles that were solved with perseverance and innovation. The exact route of the 7.5-mile missing link created controversy: How to build a road at 4,000 feet in remote terrain without damaging one of the world's oldest mountains?

National Park Service landscape architects and Federal Highway Administration engineers agreed the road should be elevated where possible to eliminate massive cuts and fills. Figg and Muller Engineers, Inc., developed the bridge design and construction method that made the project possible. The result was the Linn Cove Viaduct, located at milepost 304.6.

The Linn Cove Viaduct is 1,243 feet long and constructed of 153 elevated concrete segments weighing 50 tons each. Using a process of match casting, each new segment was cast against the segment preceding it in an indoor site located a few miles from the viaduct. After trucking the segments to the site, each segment was lowered into place by a stiff-leg crane and epoxied into position against the preceding segment. Steel cables threaded through the segments secured the bridge deck. This construction method eliminated the need for a construction access road on the ground, and the only construction that occurred at ground level was drilling for the foundations of seven piers.

After fifty-two years of construction, the Blue Ridge Parkway was completed in September 1987 with a ribbon-cutting ceremony that brought the Linn Cove Viaduct and other sections of the 7.5-mile missing link that skirts the perimeter of Grandfather Mountain into service.

FIGURE 1-8. 1954 photograph of the Garden State Parkway.
Photograph courtesy of the New Jersey Highway Authority.

FIGURE 1-9. The Linn Cove Viaduct on the Blue Ridge Parkway at Grandfather Mountain, North Carolina.

Photograph by Hugh Morton.

California and Growth in the West

Nowhere is the growth and urban development of the United States since 1945 more evident than in California, including the Bay Area, Los Angeles, San Diego, and Orange County. California and other western states have provided a fertile region for the most recent landscape architects to flourish. Indeed, many of the leading California firms and professional practitioners emerged to national importance due to the design opportunities available in the west.

The California practitioners who have become well known in the professional landscape architecture community include Thomas Church; Garrett Eckbo, who founded the firm Eckbo, Dean, Austin and Williams, which later became known as EDAW; Lawrence Halprin, who is most well known for Portland's downtown transit hub and Ira's Fountain; and Peter Walker, who formed Sassaki, Walker and Associates, which later became known as SWA, in San Francisco.

Thomas Church is considered an early trendsetter in the modern urban growth era of landscape architecture. His book *Gardens Are for People: How to Plan for Outdoor Living* documented his innovative approach to designing private residential gardens in California and represented a departure from the imitative design

influences of the earlier neoclassical design style. Church's approach, according to Michael Laurie (1975), recognized three sources of form for the residential garden. The first generator of form is the needs and desires of the client. The second generator includes the site conditions and the interplay of technology and materials available for site development. The third source is the orchestration of spatial experience on a site and the introduction of fine art. Church was one of the first landscape architects to espouse the value of the indoor-outdoor relationship of house to garden. Recognizing that, because of the ideal climate found in much of California, many functions of the home had spilled out into the garden and could be carried out on a regular basis outdoors, Church nurtured the concept of the outdoor room. By the 1950s, he was the dean of landscape architects in the California urban growth era. He'd been practicing for twenty-five years before *Gardens Are for People* was published in 1955 (Laurie 1975).

Garrett Eckbo continued the revolt against earlier "cookbook" schools of design, such as neoclassical and Italianate, which applied design idioms to the site regardless of functional requirements or natural site conditions. Eckbo's early work focused on site design for tract-type housing in California and culminated with his books *Landscape for Living*, published in

1950, and *The Art of Home Landscaping,* published in 1956. He also wrote *The Landscape We See,* published in 1969.

The Art of Home Landscaping is one of the first books to espouse the *process* of design and to outline the design process as a series of questions that should be answered and factors to be dealt with. The book clearly denounces the old garden design rules: "In the good old days this problem of how to shape the garden plan was made very simple for us. Dozens of garden handbooks, and every other issue of every house and garden magazine, gave us the simple lesson. Either you made it *formal*—or you made it *informal,*" (Eckbo 1956, 61). Eckbo and his California colleagues broke from the cookbook approach and asked the question *why. The Art of Home Landscaping* is a process-oriented book. It covers the general factors relevant to all home landscape problems across the country including climate, topography, vegetation, soils, context, house size and form, family composition, income, and attitudes. The book also delves into design principles such as usefulness, beauty, enclosure, and the interrelationships of design elements.

Garrett Eckbo not only advanced the profession by writing but also practiced with a number of other professionals in several offices that were setting the professional trends in landscape architecture in the San Francisco Bay Area. He teamed up with Robert Royston and Edward Williams from 1945 to 1958. When Royston left the firm to start an office with Asa Hanamoto, Francis Dean became a partner, and later in 1965, Don Austin joined the partnership, establishing the firm of Eckbo, Dean, Austin & Williams. These four partners would lay the foundation for what has arguably become the most successful and widely known modern-day landscape architecture firm—EDAW, Inc.

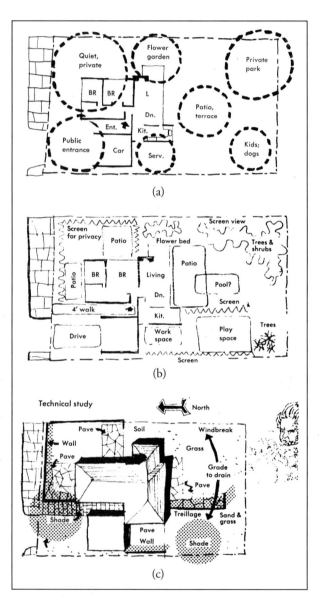

FIGURE 1-11. Key elements of Garrett Eckbo's design process in *The Art of Home Landscaping:* a., the relation study; b., the functional study; and c., the technical study.

Courtesy of Garrett Eckbo.

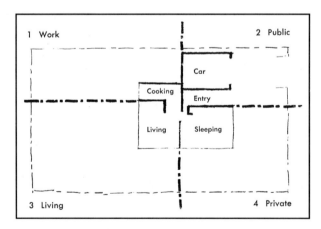

FIGURE 1-10. According to Garrett Eckbo in *The Art of Home Landscaping,* the main parts of a home are (1) **the work space,** which includes kitchen, laundry, shop, home office, sewing room, drying yard, service yard, utility garden, kids' play area, garage, and storage areas; (2) **public access,** which includes the front yard, walks, driveway, porch, and entry hall; (3) **general living space,** which includes living, dining, library, music, play, and family rooms, as well as patios, terrace, outdoor living areas, pools, courts, and gardens; and (4) **private living space,** which includes bedrooms, bathrooms, private sitting rooms, and dressing rooms.

Courtesy of Garrett Eckbo.

FIGURE 1-12. Ira's Fountain, Portland, Oregon.

No landscape architect's work embodies the spirit of the urban growth era more than that of Lawrence Halprin, who advanced the notion of design as a process, and the very process itself as an art form. Halprin has been a prolific practitioner and author. His books include *Cities, The Freeway in the City, The RSVP Cycles,* and *Notebooks.* Halprin believes that beauty can be inserted into cities by artistically designing every component of the urban fabric, from catch basin lids to streetscape and plaza. He believes that the city is "in the grandest sense, a participatory environmental art without boundaries." (Halprin 1972, 221)

Cities is a remarkably textural book that illustrates the beauty of the urban setting with photographs of its components. *The RSVP Cycles* is an attempt to explain the creative process where not one but many forces interact, and the results are emergent, not imposed. The book points out the danger of goal orientation, espousing that the process itself is the goal and the result of the process is the most desirable product (Halprin 1969).

Halprin's design work is equally as remarkable as his writing. His plan for Sea Ranch, which began in 1962, is regarded as one of the first approaches to the

FIGURE 1-13. Ira's Fountain, Portland, Oregon.

design of a planned community evolving from a study, or "ecoscore," as Halprin calls it, of the relevant environmental and cultural considerations of the site. The study included an inventory and evaluation of existing vegetation, soils, slopes, surface drainage, wind deflection, radiation impact, bioclimatic requirements, and other considerations necessary for developing a housing site in harmony with the natural balance of the site.

Halprin's plan for San Francisco's Ghirardelli Square is regarded as one of the outstanding examples of the design and linking of urban spaces. This multilevel urban shopping and eating environment was conceived by developer William Roth and visualized by Halprin as a beehive of excitement. It was fashioned out of the remains of the Ghirardelli family's chocolate factory and supplemented with underground parking, new buildings, spaces, terraces, steps, and ramps that spill down a hillside toward San Francisco Bay. The square has been one of the great people-watching environments in the United States since its completion in the late 1960s.

Halprin may be known best for his work on urban fountains, exemplified by the fountain at Embarcadero Plaza in San Francisco and by Ira's Fountain, known at first as the Civic Auditorium Forecourt Fountain, in Portland, Oregon. Ira's Fountain, which is part of an open-space network in Portland, appears to be a slice out of a natural mountain canyon with a stream and waterfalls that have been dropped into the middle of a city context. Ira's Fountain has an overpowering effect on the pedestrian, virtually placing the visitor in a misty mountain waterfall setting. It is a wonderfully interactive urban environment. Walking through Halprin's open-space network in Portland is one of the most enjoyable visual experiences that can be found in any city today. A pilgrimage to Portland to walk through Halprin's timeless creation should be a required field trip for every aspiring landscape architect.

The Environmental Era

Current directions for the profession of landscape architecture have roots in the environmental movement of the last quarter of the twentieth century. A plethora of laws and codes have been passed at all levels of government, resulting in the need for almost every project, whether public or private, to conform to environmental protection and minimum design quality standards. Today almost every city has passed a landscape ordinance or code, and these regulatory requirements have reinforced the stewardship role practiced by landscape architects. In many ways, the regulations and codes have created additional professional opportunities for landscape architects.

The environmental era was ushered in with the passage of the National Environmental Policy Act (NEPA), which was passed by Congress in 1969 and signed into law on January 1, 1970, and requires an environmental impact statement for every major federal action significantly affecting the quality of the environment. Subsequent national environmental legislation has been passed to provide for environmental and human-rights protection, including the Clean Air Act (1970 and 1977); the Clean Water Act (1972); the Comprehensive Environmental Response Compensation and Liability Act, commonly known as the Superfund (1980); and the Americans with Disabilities Act (1992).

Continued pressure on the earth's resources will result in tighter and tighter future environmental regulations. Environmental assessment and conservation of natural resources will continue to be prominent sources of professional practice opportunities for landscape architecture professionals into the twenty-first century.

Professional Career Tracks

Today, landscape architects may be found practicing in both traditional and nontraditional career tracks. A traditional career path would take one into a private or public office practicing project planning and design. A nontraditional track might find a landscape architect working as a landscape rehabilitation specialist for an international mining company. Another traditional career option is participating in a design-build company as a designer or construction crew manager.

With continued concern for the environment and human rights, the career options for landscape architects will grow. There will be less opportunity, however, in traditional private-practice options, including site planning and design. More and more, career options will fall in niche areas concerned with public participation in the planning and design process, ecosystem management, neighborhood protection, code compliance, environmental art, or historic landscape preservation.

Generally speaking, career tracks for a landscape architect fall into the following groups:

- Private practice—design
- Private practice—design-build
- Public practice
- Academic practice
- Corporate practice
- Specialty practice

Private Practice—Design

Historically, more landscape architects have followed the private-practice, design-oriented career path than any other option. Traditional private practice has focused on site planning and design of outdoor facilities, usually referred to as *project design*. There are several types of private-practice firms that a landscape architect may consider joining:

- Small firm, landscape architecture oriented
- Large firm, landscape architecture oriented
- Multidisciplinary architecture and engineering (A/E) firm that includes landscape architects
- Multidisciplinary environmental firm that includes landscape architects

Typically, a graduate or landscape architect in training will join a private-practice firm and start in an entry-level position. Duties will include hand and computer-aided drafting, production of construction documents, project-related research, and design functions in an apprentice relationship with the firm's project landscape architects or principals. As experience increases, the landscape architect will be given greater responsibility for client contact, project design, and project decision making. After several years and depending on the firm's management style, the landscape architect will be given direct responsibility for project design and direct client contact. Typically, design responsibility starts with design of construction details and subcomponents of a site design project. If the landscape architect handles the details and smaller parts of a project with skill and capability, opportunities for greater design responsibility will follow.

One of the key decisions in the private-practice design track is deciding what size of office to work in. The average private landscape architecture office em-

ploys only three design professionals, but the size of offices ranges from one or two landscape architects to one hundred or more. A large firm may present greater opportunities to the landscape architect for advancement and professional development. A smaller firm may provide opportunities for greater exposure to all phases of a design project sooner. Another important decision is whether to join a firm that employs only or predominantly landscape architects or to select a multidisciplinary firm that may be predominantly staffed with engineering professionals or architects. Multidisciplinary firms may offer access to more complex, larger-scale projects than the independent small landscape architecture office.

Private Practice—Design-Build

Many landscape architecture graduates select the design-build option as a career track. Design-build firms offer the opportunity for more control over the finished product—the built landscape. Design-build offices normally focus on residential and small-scale commercial developments, where the design-build approach is economically competitive and where the close relationship between design and construction can make a difference in the attention to detail needed for a quality finished product.

The types of construction drawings and other communication methods in the design-build office can be different from those in a traditional design-only office. Because the landscape architect in a design-build office has a direct working relationship with the construction crew, the plans may be looser and more pictorial than the construction bid documents typically produced by the design-only office. The design-build landscape architect is more likely to use sketches of construction details, three-dimensional drawings, direct verbal communication with the firm's construction superintendent, photographs of previously completed projects, and direct supervision on the job site as the methods of communication required to get the project built.

Public Practice

Federal, state, and local governments collectively employ several thousand landscape architects. In 1993, the American Society of Landscape Architects (ASLA) listed 1,070 landscape architects, 24 percent of its membership, as public practitioners. The National Park Service and state and local park departments provide the most employment opportunities in the public sector. The Denver Service Center of the National Park Service, for example, employs a large number of landscape architects to work on the planning and preservation of national parks. Federal, state, and local departments of transportation, planning, and engineering also provide a wide range of job opportunities for landscape architects.

Whereas a public practitioner may work in a design or planning capacity, he or she is more likely to work as an administrator responsible for coordinating with other government departments, managing consultant contracts, developing design guidelines, writing ordinances, and enforcing code compliance. Public practice offers a wide range of opportunities for influencing the shape of the environment and the quality of urban development through the process of developing and enforcing codes and ordinances.

Academic Practice

The academic career track includes opportunities in teaching, research, and campus planning. In most cases, advanced degrees, including a master's degree in landscape architecture and a doctorate in a related field, are required for teaching and research practice. Opportunities for academic and research practice are available, for the most part, in the university landscape architecture programs throughout the country. The 1993 ASLA handbook lists fifty institutions of higher education with programs in landscape architecture that are accredited by the Landscape Architecture Accreditation Board (LAAB). One of the best ways to begin a career path in academic practice is to serve as a teaching assistant while obtaining a landscape architecture degree.

Corporate Practice

The corporate world offers a wide range of employment options for landscape architects. One corporate practice opportunity lies with companies that develop land or recreational properties and real estate investment trusts (REITs). The Del Webb Corporation, the Fairfield Corporation, and the Summa Corporation, for example, are developers of retirement communities and other planned communities often featuring recreational themes. Walt Disney Imagineering, the planning and design group for Disney theme parks including Disneyland, has been a leading corporate employer of landscape architects.

Another type of corporate opportunity is found with companies that develop retail outlets, restaurants, hotels, or other facilities throughout the United States and the world. Although developing real estate is not the mission of the company, buildings must be developed in order for the company to sell its product or service. The list of companies is endless, but a few examples include McDonald's, Wendy's, Hyatt, Ramada, Mobil, Exxon, Home Depot, and Sears. These large corporations include real estate planning and management departments responsible for site selection, design, and management of the corporation's properties. There are considerable career opportunities for landscape architects with these corporate giants.

A third type of corporate career track is with manufacturers or suppliers of landscape industry products and construction materials. Job options include product design and development, as well as sales and management. Irrigation equipment manufacturers, such as Toro, Rain Bird, and Buckner, have employed landscape architects, as has Columbia Cascade, the maker of Timberform play equipment and site furniture.

Other corporate opportunities for landscape architects lie with companies that have a need for natural resource conservation and landscape reclamation. Mining companies, paper manufacturers, and power and utility companies normally hire in-house landscape architects and other environmental professionals to manage corporate departments dealing with conservation and reclamation. Other employment opportunities are found in the nonprofit corporate sector with organizations such as The Nature Conservancy, the Sierra Club, the Girl Scouts of the USA, and the YMCA.

The benefits usually available from large corporate employers are often the reason why a corporate landscape architecture career is chosen. Health benefits, insurance packages, a retirement program, leave benefits, a company car, promotion opportunities, and other benefits make the corporate option an inviting career path to consider.

Specialty Practice

In the last quarter of the twentieth century, a number of specialty career options have evolved, broadening the opportunities for professional practice. Landscape architecture specialty practices with the largest number of practitioners include golf course design, historic landscape preservation, irrigation design, computer applications, and environmental analysis and planning.

Most of the preparation for specialty practice occurs after graduating with the basic elements of a landscape architecture education. Although some landscape architecture programs offer courses in specialty areas, most of the training is obtained on the job after graduating. The key to a specialty career path is having a keen interest in the specialization and finding a mentor or specialty firm to work for.

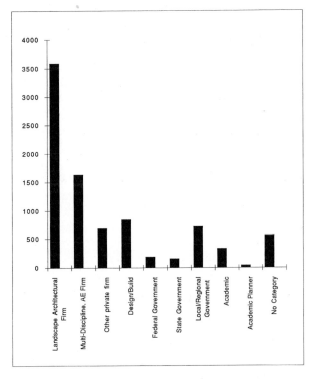

FIGURE 1-14. Members of the American Society of Landscape Architects (ASLA) by type of practice. Approximately one-third of the landscape architects in the United States are members of ASLA. This table illustrates the numbers of landscape architects by type of practice based on categories tracked for ASLA members for the year 1994.

Source: American Society of Landscape Architects 1994.

Professional Registration

In order to call oneself a landscape architect and to practice landscape architecture, state licensure is required in the United States in all but a few states and is required by provinces in Canada. Individuals wishing to practice landscape architecture must acquire a license to practice in each state or province in which they desire to practice. Licensure is based on the successful completion of education, training, apprenticeship, and formal examination requirements. Licensure, or professional registration, establishes the qualifications by which a landscape architect is deemed competent to perform work that affects the health, safety, and welfare of the general public.

There are two general types of licensure laws: *practice laws* and *title laws*. Under the requirements of a practice law, no unqualified person may perform the work of a landscape architect as the work is specified in the practice law. Under a title law, no person may call himself or herself a landscape architect unless he or she is licensed. Unlicensed persons may carry out the work of a landscape architect under a title law, but they may not call themselves a landscape architect. Registration for landscape architects began in 1954 with passage of title laws in Louisiana and California, and by 1961, five states required landscape architecture registration (CLARB 1994).

In most jurisdictions, legislation mandates the establishment of a governing board that regulates the practice of the profession. The board determines who is qualified to practice landscape architecture and enforces the registration law. In some jurisdictions—California, for example—regulatory boards are set up specifically to monitor only landscape architects. In other jurisdictions, combined boards regulate not only landscape architects but also other related design professionals such as architects and engineers. Arizona's State Board of Technical Registration, for example, governs the practice of landscape architects, architects, engineers, land surveyors, geologists, and assayers.

Each state defines the use of the title *landscape architect* or the practice of landscape architecture if the registration law is a practice law. Arizona's practice law includes the following definition of the practice of landscape architecture:

"Landscape architectural practice" means the performance of professional services such as consultations, investigation, reconnaissance, research, planning, design or responsible supervision in connection with the development of land and incidental water areas where, and to the extent that the dominant purpose of such services is the preservation, enhancement or determination of proper land uses, natural land features, ground cover and planting, naturalistic and esthetic values, the settings and approaches to buildings, structures, facilities, or other improvements, natural drainage and the consideration and the determination of inherent problems of the land relating to erosion, wear and tear, light or other hazards. This practice shall include the location and arrangement of such tangible objects and features as are incidental and necessary to the purposes outlined in this paragraph, but shall not include the making of cadastral surveys or final plats for official recording or approval, nor mandatorily include planning for governmental subdivisions (Arizona 1991).

Most states recognize the licensure of other states by a system of reciprocal registration, or *reciprocity*, where a landscape architect licensed in one state may obtain a license in a different state. A number of states, Nevada and California, for example, require the landscape architect seeking registration by reciprocity to take a short exam that usually focuses on the specific regulations of the state's registration law or on regional characteristics that affect practice in the state. Some states also have provisions in their registration law for short-term licensure in order for a landscape architect licensed in one state to carry out work and seal the plans prepared for a specific project in the state.

Professional regulatory boards join together to form organizations that work on issues of common interest such as reciprocal registration and standardization of registration exams. Landscape architecture registration boards have established the Council of Landscape Architecture Registration Boards (CLARB), a national organization through which individual member boards work to fulfill their individual missions more effectively. Although CLARB is not itself a national licensing board, the council exists to facilitate the exchange of information among its member boards and seeks to improve the regulation of landscape architecture.

CLARB, an independent nonprofit organization, is not affiliated with ASLA or the Canadian Society of Landscape Architects (CSLA). The primary service provided by CLARB to its member boards is the preparation of the Landscape Architecture Registration Examination (LARE). The LARE is used nationally and in Canada as a means for initial licensure and registration of landscape architects. Reciprocity is normally made easier if the landscape architect has obtained a license by passing the exam.

The LARE

The Landscape Architecture Registration Exam (LARE) is based on specific tasks, knowledge, skills, and abilities that are necessary to perform landscape architecture services in the best interest of the health, safety, and welfare of the general public. The exam tests whether a professional is capable of performing at a minimally competent level.

The contents of the LARE are developed by a survey of professionals, aimed at identifying the actual tasks that practitioners carry out on a regular basis. CLARB has carried out several task analysis surveys since its inception in order to update the contents of the registration exam. The most recent task analysis, completed in 1991, resulted in seven test sections:

SECTION 1: LEGAL AND ADMINISTRATIVE ASPECTS OF PRACTICE

1.1 Regulations
1.2 Contracts
1.3 Construction Administration Processes

SECTION 2: PROGRAMMING AND ENVIRONMENTAL ANALYSIS

2.1 Inventory
2.2 Analysis
2.3 Design Concepts

SECTION 3: CONCEPTUALIZATION AND COMMUNICATION

3.1 Written Communication
3.2 Conceptual Design

SECTION 4:   DESIGN SYNTHESIS

4.1   Schematic Design
4.2   Design Development

SECTION 5:   INTEGRATION OF TECHNICAL
                      AND DESIGN REQUIREMENTS

5.1   Detail Design and Materials and Methods of
       Construction

SECTION 6:   GRADING AND DRAINAGE

6.1   Grading
6.2   Drainage

SECTION 7:   IMPLEMENTATION OF DESIGN THROUGH
                      THE CONSTRUCTION PROCESS

7.1   Construction Processes
7.2   Materials and Methods of Construction
7.3   Supporting Systems
7.4   Construction Documents

The LARE is developed annually by examination committees appointed by the president of CLARB. Members are selected from various geographical areas and types of professional practice. Exam committees also represent both genders and various ethnic groups. The examination committees are responsible for developing both written exam questions and graphic parts of the exam. New multiple-choice questions are reviewed several times and tested before they are included in the LARE. The examination committee strives to develop questions that are up to date, accurate, and relevant to the knowledge, skills, and abilities required of the landscape architect. Questions are selected by the subject matter required in accordance with the exam specification and are tested and statistically analyzed to determine if they will be used on the LARE. The graphic parts of the LARE are developed in a similar manner. A number of graphic vignette problems are developed for each section of the exam. They are reviewed and tested to determine which vignette problems will actually be used on the LARE (CLARB 1994).

Professional Development

The education of a landscape architect does not end with a college degree, and professional training does not end after successfully passing the LARE or state registration exam. Education and professional development for the landscape architect is a lifelong pursuit.

Professional development is the term used to describe the landscape architect's continued honing of his or her skills and interests in the profession and the broadening of his or her professional expertise. Professional development and continuing education is so important that some states (New Mexico, for example) require their licensed professional practitioners to submit evidence of continuing education courses and other forms of updating the professional's expertise as a prerequisite for continued licensure.

Professional development can take many directions for the practicing landscape architect. For the college graduate working in an entry-level position, professional development may involve learning the methods and techniques of producing a set of construction documents in an office setting. The young professional may also be drawn toward a landscape architectural specialization, and professional development could mean focusing on acquisition of the necessary specialty skills in golf course design or environmental assessment, for example. For the experienced practitioner, professional development may mean taking college courses or training seminars to update knowledge or learning a new skill such as a specific computer software application or personnel management techniques. Serving on a committee for a professional society such as ASLA is another form of professional development that can bring meaningful personal rewards. Serving on a local design review board, planning and zoning commission, a storm water advisory committee, or a downtown development advisory commission are other forms of professional development.

Keeping up with technological advancement is one of the main reasons that professional development is necessary. Technological advancement impacts professional practice in a number of ways. New products are regularly developed for use in planning and design projects. Concrete unit pavers, for example, became widely available as alternatives to bricks, granite sets, and asphalt paving blocks. Drip irrigation products became widely available as alternatives to conventional bubbler and spray equipment. New methods of building and construction techniques are being developed regularly, resulting in the need for landscape architects to keep up to date. Moreover, the continued evolution of computer-aided design and drafting requires a constant effort to stay on top of professional development requirements.

Most firms, corporations, public agencies, and other employers support the professional development activities of their landscape architecture employees. Employers normally publish their professional development opportunities in personnel manuals. Typically, the employer's support for professional development may include some or all of the following opportunities:

- Paid leave time for taking the state registration exam and reimbursement of the cost of the exam
- Reimbursement of the recurring cost of renewing the landscape architect's state registration
- Paid time off for participating in local commissions and boards
- Full or partial reimbursement of the cost of attending professional association meetings
- Full or partial reimbursement for job-related education and training courses
- Staff retreats related to business development, goal setting, and strategic planning
- Leave time and sabbaticals for long-term professional development opportunities
- Reimbursement of expenses and paid time off for attending conferences and giving papers or presentations on the work of the firm, agency, corporate employer, or educational institution
- Providing the overhead costs, such as printing, mail, or telephone costs, related to professional development activities

Professional development is a necessary and important goal for the practicing landscape architect. A written professional development plan listing specific personal goals and objectives tied to completion dates is an effective method for focusing time and energy on expanding professional career development directions.

Professional Societies

Banding together to form associations for sharing information and advancing the collective spirit of a pro-

fession is an instinctive activity for all types of professionals. Professional organizations and societies provide a network for practitioners to exchange concepts and a forum to advance new ideas. Such organizations provide a professional home base where practitioners can obtain support, develop camaraderie with peers, and find a sympathetic ear. Professional societies provide leadership training and opportunities for every member of the organization to help in shaping the direction of the profession. Organizations can make a wide variety of materials available to help professionals succeed as leaders in their local communities. They also act as a rallying force for pro bono work carried on in communities by practicing professionals.

Professional societies are excellent vehicles for lobbying efforts intended to advance the opportunities for professional practice and job development at local, state, and national levels. Professional societies can pursue legislative programs that support the goals of practitioners, and representatives of the professional organization can meet with legislators to inform them of the views of the profession. By developing policy statements and group viewpoints, members of professional organizations take steps toward defining the broader profession in the public eye. By developing public statements on the environment, visual resources, natural resources, public lands, barrier-free design, energy conservation, water conservation, urban growth, parks, open space, and other relevant topics, these organizations educate the public about the profession of landscape architecture and its mission of stewardship of the land. Indeed, educating the public and developing public awareness is a central goal of professional societies.

Professional organizations promote and protect licensure, certification, and registration of their members. They provide a unified front that supports the need for licensure and can produce literature, displays, videos, and other materials designed to educate the general public on the values of licensure. Professional societies are particularly valuable for focusing public attention on ways that landscape architects protect the health, safety, and welfare of the general public.

Professional societies sponsor or manage the accreditation process and staff the teams that evaluate university curricula for accreditation. Accreditation by a national society provides credibility, continuity, and integrity among the educational programs that exist to train landscape architects. The Landscape Architectural Accreditation Board (LAAB), for example, the national accrediting agency for undergraduate and graduate degrees in landscape architecture, is recognized by the Council on Postsecondary Accreditation and by the United States Department of Education.

Professional societies act as disseminators of professional literature. Most professional organizations publish newsletters and journals intended to keep practitioners current on a wide variety of profession-related topics. With the continuing development of technology and computer capabilities, most professional organizations provide computer networking opportunities to their members, making a wide variety of information available for members. Professional societies also publish books relevant to the profession and act as a clearinghouse for professionally valuable literature. Many organizations sell books to members at reduced prices and publish member listings and handbooks that are very useful sources of general information about the professional practitioners.

Another valuable activity of professional societies is the recognition of professional excellence by sponsoring awards and publicizing successful professional work and cutting-edge professional activities. Professional societies sponsor national, state, and local awards programs, providing visibility for their members, as well as monetary awards for practitioners, educators, and researchers.

A few of the tangible benefits offered by professional organizations include scholarships for students; major medical, dental, and life insurance group policies; leadership seminars; technical workshops; professional liability insurance programs; and group contract documents. Organizations also sponsor annual conferences that give members opportunities to convene and renew the collective spirit of professional practice. Job referral services are another service offered by professional societies.

ASLA is the largest single organization of landscape architects. Approximately one-third of all landscape architects are members of ASLA. "The mission of the American Society of Landscape Architects 'is the advancement of the art and science of landscape architecture by leading and informing the public, by serving its members, and by leading the profession in achieving quality in the natural and built environment.' " ASLA is governed by an executive committee and a board of trustees, who draw on the exper-

tise of members to manage and direct the organization. ASLA maintains liaisons with a number of other national organizations of design, architecture, planning, engineering, environmental, and other disciplines related to the profession of landscape architecture (ASLA 1993). Joining ASLA is one of the ways that each landscape architect can be supportive of the bonds that bind professional practitioners together.

The Council of Educators in Landscape Architecture (CELA) is another national organization of professional landscape architects primarily geared to providing support for university professors and students. According to CELA's bylaws, "The purposes of The CELA shall be to encourage, support and further education in the field of landscape architecture specifically related to teaching, research, scholarship, and public service." CELA also seeks to enhance landscape architecture curricula, foster communications and the exchange of knowledge, and to facilitate interaction among the landscape architecture education community (CELA 1994).

CELA is a membership organization with three categories of institutional members and a category of corresponding, or individual, members. The three categories of institutional members include

Member Institution: schools, departments, programs, and curricula in landscape architecture that are accredited by ASLA or have three or more faculty.

Associate Member Institution: schools, departments, programs, and curricula in landscape architecture that have three or fewer faculty.

Affiliate Member Institution: educational institutions, corporations, professional societies, or other organizations concerned with or interested in landscape architecture education.

CELA is governed by a board of directors comprising CELA's six officers and seven regional directors. Each year CELA holds an annual conference to stimulate interest in landscape architecture and advance the profession. CELA publishes the proceedings of its annual conference, as well as *Landscape Journal*, published under an agreement with the University of Wisconsin Press. CELA also publishes and distributes to its membership a newsletter called *The CELA Forum on Education*.

One of CELA's activities is honoring the outstanding educators in landscape architecture curricula through an annual national awards program. Each year, CELA gives an Outstanding Educator Award, Awards of Distinction, a President's Award, and other awards recognizing excellence in landscape architecture, research, public service, administration, or service to education.

CELA AWARD WINNERS

1991   Garrett Eckbo, University of California, Berkeley
Miroslava Benes, Harvard University
Paula Horrigan, Cornell University

1990   Terence Harkness, University of Illinois
Patsy Eubanks Owens, Virginia Polytechnic University
Achva Benzinberg Stein, University of Southern California

1989   John Lyle, California State Polytechnic University, Pomona
Douglas M. Johnston, University of Illinois
Lance Neckar, University of Minnesota
David Hulse, University of Oregon

1988   Michael M. Laurie, University of California, Berkeley
Paul Groth, University of California, Berkeley
Linda Irvine, University of Illinois
John Simpson, Ohio State University

1987   John Brinckerhoff Jackson
Patrick Condon, University of Minnesota
Gary Kessler, University of Illinois
Moura Quale, University of British Columbia

1986   Bernard Niemann Jr., University of Wisconsin, Madison
Mark J. Chididter, Iowa State University
Daniel W. Krall, Cornell University
Richard N. Westmacott, University of Georgia

1985   R. Burton Litton Jr., University of California, Berkeley
Ann L. Marston, University of Massachusetts
Susan J. Hebel, University of Georgia
William L. Ramsey, University of Georgia

1984   Carl Steinitz, Harvard University
Kerry J. Dawson, University of California, Davis
Catherine M. Howett, University of Georgia
Eliza Pennypacker, Penn State University

1983   Ian J. W. Firth, University of Georgia
Van Cline, University of Minnesota
Steven Strom, Rutgers University

1982   Julius Guy Fabos, University of Massachusetts
Michael R. Hodges, Michigan State University
Warren T. Byrd, University of Virginia
Gail Elnicky, University of Minnesota
Roger D. Moore, University of Georgia
Donovan C. Wilkins, University of Arizona

1981   Roger B. Martin, University of Minnesota
Ervin H. Zube, University of Arizona
Jorg Bartels, California Polytechnic University, San Luis Obispo
Cherie Kluessing, University of Illinois, Urbana

1980   Thomas C. Hazlett, Michigan State University
Richard M. Myrick, University of Texas, Arlington
Albert J. Rutledge, University of Illinois, Urbana
Theodore Walker
Thomas A. Paulo, State University of New York, Syracuse
John S. Troy, West Virginia University
Walter M. Tryon, California Polytechnic University, San Luis Obispo
Suzanne L. Turner, Louisiana State University
David M. Vlala, University of Wisconsin, Madison

1979   Francis Dean, California State Polytechnic University, Pomona
Rodney Tapp, California State Polytechnic University, Pomona
Vincent J. Belafiore, University of Georgia
Jane Johnson, Rutgers University

1978   Harold T. Abbott, Washington State University
John J. Milliken, University of Guelph
Kenneth J. Polakowski, University of Michigan
Wiliam E. Beery, University of Georgia
Walter E. Rogers, University of Arizona

1977   Darrel G. Morrisin, University of Michigan
William H. Snyder, University of Idaho
Donald W. Girouard, Penn State University
Robert J. Hill, University of Georgia

Source: CELA 1994

Ethics

Ethics is the branch of philosophical theory concerned with morality. According to Louis P. Pojman in his 1989 text *Ethical Theory: Classical and Contemporary Readings,* morality refers to what is right and wrong, what is permissible behavior with regard to basic human values. "Moral theories differ on the scope of morality (does it include all and only human beings, or rational beings, or sentient creatures?), and they differ on the exact hierarchy of values (how does one rank survival, justice, happiness, freedom, and other good qualities?), but in general they have in common a concern to alleviate suffering and promote well being" (Pojman 1989, 2).

Most texts dealing with ethics define it as the study of what ought to be, rather than what is. Ethical theorists believe ethics and morality to be synonymous and concerned with values. They seek to understand concepts and to justify moral principles and theories. Ethics appeals to one's sense of justice (Pojman 1990).

Ethics is closely related to religion, law, and etiquette. Ethics and ethical behavior have been studied by philosophers and thinkers of all great world cultures, including both Western and Eastern philosophies. The roots of Western ethics began after 500 B.C. with the Greek philosophers Socrates, Plato, and Aristotle. Since that time, thousands of books have been written about ethics and ethical behavior. Ethical practices cut across all human activities, interpersonal relationships, and business and professional pursuits.

Ethical business decisions can affect thousands, even millions, of people, and sometimes the results of questionable ethical business decisions can cause loss of life. The most notorious ethical business decision of the twentieth century is the Ford Motor Company's decision on the Pinto gas tank. As Cullen, Maakestad, and Cavender (1987) indicate in their book *Corporate Crime Under Attack,* there has been a change in attitude in the United States toward white collar crime by media, academia, and the legal system.

The Ford Motor Company Pinto gas tank ethical decision, lawsuit, and trial played a milestone role in bringing white collar crime to the awareness of Americans, highlighting the need for ethical behavior, especially with regard to human life. After all, the real victims of a poor ethical decision are often members of the general public.

The 1971 Pinto was introduced in Ford showrooms in the fall of 1970 at a cost of $1,919. In the design of the vehicle, Ford executives made a decision not to prevent potential fuel leak problems caused by locating the gas tank six inches from the rear bumper. A means of preventing fiery accidents, a protective bladder placed between the gas tank and the passenger area of the car, would have cost the company millions of dollars. A decision to fireproof the Pinto would have removed public criticism that Ford consciously decided to manufacture cars that it knew might cause hundreds of deaths. Ford determined that it would be cheaper (and more cost-effective) to fight and settle lawsuits arising from Pinto crashes than to spend the money to fix the automobile. The now famous Ford statistical analysis indicated that it would take $49.5 million to pay for the loss of life, serious burns, injuries, and loss of vehicles, opposed to $137 million to fix the gas tank problem in the 11 million Pintos and 1.2 million Pinto trucks. Ford used this statistical analysis and other analyses to conclude that it was not cost-effective or practical to fix and recall the Pintos with the dangerous gas tank problem, suggesting that the company would willfully sacrifice human life in order to make greater profits. Ford Motor Company was not found guilty of reckless homicide charges. The attention brought to the case, however, from wide media coverage raised the consciousness level of Americans about white collar crime and ethical business behavior (Cullen, Maakestad, and Cavender 1987).

For professionals, codes of professional conduct are promulgated and upheld as statements of professionalism. What does it mean to be a professional? Some common characteristics include

- a definite field of expertise
- required education with curricula standardized among universities and colleges
- qualifications-based entry into the practice of the profession through registration, licensing, or certification
- a social conscience and an environmental ethic
- a method of self-policing with respect to negligence, and illegal and unethical behavior
- fees based on value of services
- respect for the profession

- agency relationship with clients
- fiduciary responsibility to clients
- compliance with regulations intended to protect the health, safety, and welfare of the general public
- professional practice that is honest, fair, and ethical

According to Michael Bayles in his book *Professional Ethics,* codes of ethical conduct for professionals come into play in five main ways:

1. General obligations and availability of services
2. Obligations between professional and client
3. Obligations to third parties
4. Obligations between professionals and employees
5. Obligations to the profession

General Obligations and Availability of Services

Professionals have a general obligation to prevent unauthorized and unqualified practice of their professions. Professionals are self-policing and in most cases are regulated by laws to protect the general public from incompetent performance. The practice of landscape architecture, for instance, is based on the general obligation of protecting the health, safety, and welfare of the general public.

Professionals bear an obligation to make their services available to society. Professional landscape architecture services are not as essential to the general public as medicine or law, but professional landscape architecture services should be available on equal terms for those who are able to pay for the services. According to Bayles, people have *positive* rights to health, education, and legal services, but *negative* rights to other professional services. Positive rights mean that a service, such as legal service, must be available to people. Negative rights, on the other hand, imply noninterference by society or individuals with one's right to obtain services from professionals willing to provide the services (Bayles 1989).

Obligations between Professionals and Clients

According to Bayles, the central issue in the professional-client relationship is who makes what decisions. How are the responsibility and authority for making decisions divided between professional and client? The professional-client relationship is based on one of a number of different models: agency, contractual, friendly, paternal, and fiduciary.

Under the *agency model,* the professional is hired by the client to provide services for some interest. The professional, who provides the services to achieve the client's goal, acts on behalf of the client and at the direction of the client. Under the *contractual model,* the professional and the client have mutual obligations and rights agreed to in advance, usually in the written terms of a contract. According to the *friendly model,* professionals and clients have a close relationship of mutual trust and friendship. The *paternal model* assumes that the professional has knowledge and experience lacked by the client. The professional is hired to further the client's interests and act on behalf of the client's well-being. In the *fiduciary model,* the client has more decision-making responsibility, but must rely on the professional to act on behalf of the client.

There must be a trust relationship in all good professional-client relationships. Professionals should be honest and truthful with their clients. They should deliver professional services with competency. The professional should be loyal to the client, except when loyalty may conflict with the professional's self-interest or the interests of third parties. Clients should also expect discretion and confidentiality from the professionals they hire.

Obligations to Third Parties

In addition to responsibilities to the client, professionals have a responsibility to third parties and to the effects of professional services on third parties. Third-party obligations are particularly relevant to the profession of landscape architecture. A large number of landscape architecture projects have users that are not directly the professional's client (i.e., they are a third party). A park design contract with a city parks department gives a landscape architect a huge third-party exposure and requires that the third party, park users in this case, be considered in the park design process. This client–third party–professional relationship is quite common in landscape architecture and can result in a wide range of ethical issues that must be faced by a landscape architect. In park design, for example, the landscape architect has an ethical duty to see that the equipment specified is durable, safe, and properly installed. Park development budgets need to be carefully evaluated so that compromises in safety and quality are not made if budgets are inadequate. In the worst-case scenario, lack of third-party consideration by the landscape architect may result in a third-party lawsuit brought against a landscape architect for negligence or a professional error.

Obligations between Professionals and Employers

Employees have certain obligations to their employers. Employees should have the competency level that they convey they have. The employee should warrant that he or she has the skills needed to provide the professional services requested by the employer. Employees should be honest with their employers. They should be discreet and keep employer information confidential. They should be loyal to their employers and obedient as long as the employer's needs are limited to legally and ethically permissible behavior.

Employers, on the other hand, have similar responsibilities to their employees. They too should be honest and discreet. They should not ask their employees to act unlawfully or unethically. Employers should be fair to their employees and support continuing professional development and education for their employees.

Obligations to the Profession

Most professional codes of ethics include and recognize responsibility for the public good and for conserving the environment. According to Michael Bayles (1989), there are three main facets to professional responsibility for the public good:

1. Activities of social leadership such as public service
2. Improvement of the profession and professional knowledge through research and reform
3. Preservation and enhancement of the role of the professionals

Professionals should have respect for their profession. They should hold their colleagues in high esteem. The landscape architect who respects his or her profession will make positive professional contributions.

Landscape Architecture Code of Ethics

ASLA maintains an ethics committee that develops a landscape architecture code of ethics. The most recent edition of the *ASLA Code of Professional Conduct* specifies more clearly the prohibited behavior of ASLA members and adopts as a whole the *ASLA Declaration on the Environment.* The ASLA Code of Professional Conduct includes three main canons: *professional responsibility, environmental ethics,* and *member duties.* Each canon features ethical standards, which are goals that landscape architects should strive to meet, and rules. Violation of rules might subject the ASLA member to disciplinary action. Ethical professional conduct is so important to the vitality of the profession that ASLA has given the author permission to reprint the entire code here.

ASLA CODE OF PROFESSIONAL CONDUCT

Canon 1: Professional Responsibility

Ethical Standard 1.1	Members should understand and obey laws governing their professional practice and business matters and conduct their professional duties with honesty.
Rule 1.101	Members, in the conduct of their professional practice, shall not violate the law, including any Federal, state or local laws, and particularly laws and regulations in the

ASLA CODE OF PROFESSIONAL CONDUCT

Canon 1: Professional Responsibility, continued

	areas of antitrust, employment, environment and land use planning, and those governing professional practice.
Rule 1.102	A member shall not give, lend or promise anything of value to any public official, or representative of a prospective client, in order to influence the judgment or actions in letting of contracts, of that official or representative of a prospective client. *Comment:* However, the provision of pro bono services will not violate this rule.
Rule 1.103	Government service practitioners shall not accept private practice work with anyone doing business with their agency, or with whom the member has any government contact.
Rule 1.104	Members shall recognize the contributions of others engaged in the planning, design and construction of the physical environment, and shall give them appropriate recognition and due credit for professional work, and shall not maliciously injure, or attempt to injure the reputation, prospects, practice or employment position of those persons so engaged.
Rule 1.105	Members shall not mislead existing or prospective clients about the results that can be achieved through the use of the member's services, nor shall the members state that they can achieve results by means that violate this code or the law.
Rule 1.106	Members shall not accept compensation for their services from more than one party on a project, unless the circumstances are agreed to in writing by all parties.
Rule 1.107	A member shall truthfully, without exaggeration, misleading, deceptive or false statements or claims, inform the client, employer, or public about personal qualifications, capabilities and experience. *Comment:* Members shall not take credit for work performed under the direction of a former employer beyond the limits of their personal involvement and shall give credit to the performing firm. Employers should give departing employees access to work that they performed, reproduced at cost, and a description of the employee's involvement in the work should be noted on each product, and signed by the employer.
Rule 1.108	Members shall not reveal information obtained in the course of their professional activities which they have been asked to maintain in confidence, or which could affect the interests of another adversely. Unique exceptions: To stop an act which creates harm, a significant risk to the public health, safety and welfare, which cannot otherwise be prevented, to establish claims or defense on behalf of members, or in order to comply with applicable law, regulations or with this code.
Rule 1.109	Members shall neither copy nor reproduce the copyrighted works of other landscape architects or design professionals, without prior written approval of the author.
Ethical Standard 1.2	Members should seek to make full disclosure of relevant information to the clients, public and other interested parties who rely on their advice and professional work product.
Rule 1.201	Members making public statements on landscape architectural issues shall disclose compensation other than fee, and their role and any economic interest in a project.
Rule 1.202	Members shall make full disclosure during the solicitation and conduct of a project of the roles and professional status of all project team members and consultants,

ASLA CODE OF PROFESSIONAL CONDUCT

Canon 1: Professional Responsibility, continued

	including their state licenses and professional degrees held, if any; availability of coverage of liability and errors and omissions insurance coverage; and any other material potential limitations.
Rule 1.203	Members shall make full disclosure to the client or employer of any financial or other interest which bears upon the service or project. If a client or employer objects to such association, financial interest, or other interest, the member shall either terminate such association or interest, or give up the commission or employment.
Ethical Standard 1.3	Members should endeavor to protect the interests of their clients and the public through competent performance of their work; participate in continuing education, educational research, and development and dissemination of technical information relating to planning, design, construction and management of the physical environment.
Rule 1.301	Members shall undertake to perform professional services only when they, together with those persons whom they may engage as consultants, are qualified by education, training, or experience in the specific technical areas involved.
Rule 1.302	Members shall not sign or seal drawings, specifications, reports, or other professional work for which they do not have direct professional knowledge or direct supervisory control.
Rule 1.303	Members will continually seek to raise the standards of aesthetic, ecological and cultural excellence through compliance with state requirements for continuing education.
Ethical Standard 1.4	Members should strive to promote diversity throughout the profession of landscape architecture.
Rule 1.401	Members will not conduct or participate in any employment practices or professional activities which discriminate on the basis of race, religion, gender, national origin, age, disability or sexual orientation.

Canon 2: Environmental Ethics

Ethical Standard 2.1	Members accept responsibility for the consequences of their design, planning, management and policy decisions on the health of natural systems and cultural communities and their harmony, equity and balance with one another and commit themselves to:
Ethical Standard 2.2	Generate design, planning, management strategies and policy from the basis of the cultural context and the ecosystem to which each landscape belongs at the local, regional and global scale.
Ethical Standard 2.3	Develop, use and specify products, materials, technologies and techniques which exemplify the principles of sustainable development and landscape regeneration.
Ethical Standard 2.4	Seek constant improvement in knowledge, abilities, and skills, in educational institutions, and professional practices and organizations to more effectively achieve sustainable development.
Ethical Standard 2.5	Actively engage in shaping the decisions, attitudes and values that support human health, environmental protection and sustainable development.

ASLA CODE OF PROFESSIONAL CONDUCT

Canon 3: Member Duties

Ethical Standard 3.1	Members should work to insure that they, their employees or supervisees, and other Members adhere to this code of conduct and to the Bylaws of the ASLA.
Rule 3.101	Members having information which leads to a reasonable belief that another member has committed a violation of this code, have an affirmative duty to report such information. *Comment:* Often a landscape architect can recognize that the behavior of another poses a serious question as to the other's professional integrity. It is the duty of the professional to bring the matter to the attention of the committee, which action, if done in good faith, is in some jurisdictions protected from libel or slander action. If in doubt, the member reporting under this rule, should seek counsel, prior to making such a report.
Rule 3.102	The official seal or logo of the ASLA may not be used other than as specified in the Bylaws.
Rule 3.103	Members, associates, and affiliates shall adhere to the specific applicable terms of the Bylaws regarding use of references to ASLA membership.
Ethical Standard 3.2	Members should endeavor to participate in pro bono works in the service of the public good to serve in elected and appointed capacities which improve public appreciation and understanding of Landscape Architecture, environmental systems, and the functions and responsibilities of landscape architects.

(Source: ASLA 1995)

REFERENCES

American Society of Landscape Architects. 1992. *Profiles in Landscape Architecture*. Washington, D.C.: American Society of Landscape Architects.

———. 1993, 1995. *Members Handbook*. Washington, D.C.: American Society of Landscape Architects.

Bayles, Michael D. 1989. *Professional Ethics*. 2d ed. Belmont, Calif.: Wadsworth Publishing Company.

Council of Educators in Landscape Architecture. 1994. *CELA Constitution*.

Council of Landscape Architectural Registration Boards (CLARB). 1994. *Understanding the L. A. R. E.* Vol. 3. Fairfax, Va.: CLARB.

Cullen, Francis T., William J. Maakestad, and Gray Cavender. 1987. *Corporate Crime Under Attack: The Ford Pinto Case and Beyond*. Cincinnati, Ohio: Anderson Publishing Company.

Eckbo, Garrett. *The Art of Home Landscaping*. 1956. New York: McGraw-Hill.

Fabos, Julius Gy., Gordon Milde, and V. Michael Weinmeyer. 1968. *Frederick Law Olmsted, Sr.: Founder of Landscape Architecture in America*. Amherst, Mass.: University of Massachusetts Press.

Halprin, Lawrence. 1963, 1972. *Cities*. Rev. ed. Cambridge, Mass.: MIT Press.

———. 1969. *The RSVP Cycles: Creative Process in the Human Environment*. New York: George Brazilier.

Laurie, Michael. 1975. *An Introduction to Landscape Architecture*. New York: American Elsevier Publishing Company.

Newton, Norman T. 1971. *Design on the Land: The Development of Landscape Architecture*. Cambridge, Mass.: Belknap Press of Harvard University Press.

Platt, Charles A., with Keith N. Morgan. 1894, 1993. *Italian Gardens*. Portland, Ore.: Sagapress/Timber Press.

Pojman, Louis P. 1990. *Ethics: Discovering Right and Wrong*. Belmont, Calif.: Wadsworth Publishing Company.

———. 1989. *Ethical Theory: Classical and Contemporary Readings*. Belmont, Calif.: Wadsworth Publishing Company.

State of Arizona. 1991. *Code and Rules of the State Board of Technical Registration for Architects, Assayers, Engineers, Geologists, Landscape Architects, and Land Surveyors.* Phoenix, Ariz.: State Board of Technical Registration.

STUDY QUESTIONS AND ASSIGNMENTS

1. You read the definition of landscape architecture in this chapter as approved and adopted by the board of trustees of the American Society of Landscape Architects. Write your own definition of landscape architecture based on what you've read, your educational background, and your own philosophy of what you think the profession is about or what you'd like it to be. If you are in an allied profession or related discipline, write a definition of your own profession or discipline.

2. Write an in-depth, well-researched paper about one of the landscape architecture eras discussed in this chapter:

   • The early park planning era
   • Estate planning
   • City planning
   • The urban growth era
   • California and growth in the West
   • The environmental era

3. Chapter 1 discusses six career tracks:

   • Private practice—design
   • Private practice—design-build
   • Public practice
   • Academic practice
   • Corporate practice
   • Specialty practice

   Locate and interview a landscape architect in each career track. Develop a specific set of questions to ask each landscape architect. Document your interviews and summarize your findings.

4. Chapter 1 describes four types of landscape architecture firms:

   • Small firm, landscape architecture oriented
   • Large firm, landscape architecture oriented
   • Multidisciplinary A/E firm that includes landscape architects
   • Multidisciplinary environmental firm that includes landscape architects

   Locate and interview a landscape architect in each type of firm. Develop a specific set of questions to ask each landscape architect. Document your interviews and summarize your findings.

5. Research as many corporate-practice opportunities as possible by writing or phoning corporate employers to see if they hire landscape architects and in what capacity. Document your findings.

6. Develop a comparison between the following two career tracks:

   • Private practice—design
   • Private practice—design-build

   Identify the similarities and the differences. Research salary ranges at entry level and after various higher levels of experience. Identify the daily work activities. Identify career opportunities.

7. Contrast and compare these three career tracks:

   • Private practice
   • Public practice
   • Academic practice

8. Identify and describe as many specialty-practice career options as you can. Find and document at least three examples of completed projects for each of the specialty practice options.

9. Research the professional registration law in your state or the nearest state with professional licensure. Identify wehether the law is a practice law or a title law. Obtain a copy of the rules and regulations. Develop a clear understanding of what professional activities a landscape architect is allowed to conduct. Document your findings in a paper.

10. Obtain a copy of the LARE study guide. Develop and stage a mock LARE exam with your classmates.

11. Interview landscape architects in your area to identify professional development activities they engage in. Are they involved in continuing education? Do they attend skills development

workshops and seminars? What other professional development activities do they engage in? Document your findings in a paper.

12. Write a paper on professional ethics. Research and discuss the following topics in depth:

- General obligations and availability of services
- Obligations between professionals and clients
- Obligations to third parties
- Obligations between professionals and employees
- Obligations to the profession

CHAPTER TWO

Clients and Projects

This chapter provides an overview of how a landscape architecture firm determines who its clients will be and the mix of its client base. Two broad categories of clients—*private sector* and *public sector*—are discussed in depth. The types of projects associated with different clients are discussed and examples of projects are cited. A landscape architecture firm cannot exist without a well-cultivated client base, no matter the size of the firm. Understanding the landscape architect's client opportunities, developing a client base, and nurturing the firm's clients are cornerstones of a successful business operation. Without clients to serve and projects to complete, a landscape architecture firm has no basis for being in business. With a healthy mix of private and/or public clients, however, a landscape architecture firm has the potential to flourish and prosper.

Who Are the Landscape Architect's Clients?

In the broadest sense, the landscape architect's clients are those persons or entities, such as a corporation, that need or want professional landscape architecture services and are willing to pay for the services.

The landscape architect, in general, works for two broad categories of clients: private-sector clients and public-sector clients.

Private-Sector Clients

Developers, private individuals, for-profit corporations, not-for-profit corporations, and other architecture and engineering (A/E) professionals, such as architects or civil engineers, represent most of the private-sector client opportunities for landscape architects. Whenever an individual or corporate entity seeks the expertise of the landscape architect for landscape analysis, planning, design, conservation management, or other landscape-related projects, an opportunity exists for providing private-sector professional services. The services are initiated by personal contact. Either the prospective client contacts the landscape architect, or the landscape architect seeks out a private client after identifying a potential opportunity for providing professional services. No matter how the contact comes about, developing helpful, trusting relations with clients is essential for cooperative and successful client/professional associations. Identifying and clarifying the needs of the private client and providing services that respond directly to those needs are the rewarding results of the healthy client-professional relationship.

In most cases, the client/professional relationship is successful when the client's needs are met and the landscape architect's professional capabilities are allowed to flourish in the highest ethical manner. Problems arise when the private client does not perceive the value of the services provided by the landscape architect or does not feel that the landscape architect is responsive to the client's needs. For the landscape architect, problems occur if the private client's wishes result in a project that compromises the professional's environmental-quality goals or professional ethics. In all cases, the successful private-client project is the result of a positive, mutually beneficial relationship between the client and the landscape architect built on trust, communication, and mutual goal setting.

Public-Sector Clients

The federal government, state governments, and local governments at the city, county, and metropolitan levels represent the landscape architect's client opportunities in the public sector.

In almost all cases, the landscape architect's work for a public-sector client involves a third-party user—the general public. Whereas it is also true for private-sector clients, the third-party-user relationship is generally more prevalent in public-sector work. A landscape architecture firm may also serve an architect, the firm's private client, on a public building project, but the users of the building project and its outdoor environment will be the public-servant occupants of the building, as well as the general public. The site plan and design of site improvements and plazas for a new county courthouse, for example, will be used by the public employees such as judges, attorneys, and administrative staff, as well as members of the general public having business with the court. In a large number of private-client projects, however, the client and the user are one and the same, and the landscape architect must focus on satisfying the needs of the client—the primary user. In public-sector work such as the design of a park or roadside improvements, however, the landscape architect must consider the third-party public user.

As with the private-client relationship, successful projects in the public sector result when trust and good communication exist between the landscape architect and the public-sector client and when the project is perceived to meet the needs of the third-party public user. So much emphasis is placed on meeting the needs of the public user today that almost every public project includes meetings with representatives of public-interest groups. In many cases, public meetings are even mandated by ordinances or other requirements. Resolving issues with the public constituents builds the type of trust and communication that makes a public-sector project successful.

Serving the Private or Public Client

The landscape architecture firm serves its clients in two distinct professional roles: prime consultant and subconsultant. As the owners and managers of a landscape architecture firm choose what types of clients to work for, they often find that their choices determine whether the firm's professional role will be as prime consultant or subconsultant. If the firm gravitates toward private-sector developers, there is often more opportunity to work directly for the developer as a prime consultant. If the firm's principals prefer working as part of a design team, the firm more often than not finds itself in a subconsultant role because A/E firms and architecture firms are commonly the prime consultant on development-related projects. If the firm's principals are inclined to work for public-sector clients, there may be a fifty-fifty chance that the firm will serve as a prime consultant or subconsultant. If the firm frequently works on park projects, for example, it may often work as the prime consultant because a landscape architecture firm is often in the lead consulting position on such projects. If the firm frequently works on transportation or road projects, it may be more likely to serve in a subconsultant role to a civil engineering or transportation planning firm that is serving as the prime consultant. Both prime consulting and subconsulting offer rewarding professional endeavors to the landscape architecture firm.

What Elements Determine the Landscape Architect's Clients?

The Proactive Posture for Determining the Client Mix

When a landscape architecture firm starts out, its owners, managers, or principals may take a proactive posture toward the professional orientation of the firm, the types of clients (public or private sector), and the contractual role they want the firm to play. The principals set goals for the firm and define the firm's mission in terms of the types of projects they would like to work on, the availability of clients, and the type of professional role, prime consulting or subconsulting, most likely to be available. They may decide, for example, to specialize in environmental assessment, planning, and design of open space and outdoor recreation facilities such as trail systems and wildlife refuges. Having selected this professional orientation, the firm's principals are also carving out a client niche that will be primarily public sector, and deciding by corollary that the firm will most likely serve as a prime consultant. A different firm's principals may decide to serve as support professionals to architects because a large number of architecture firms exist in the area and the principals believe they can develop a profitable niche market serving architecture firms. This proactive self-determination of the firm's professional orientation is one way that the firm's landscape architects determine its clients and the prime consulting or subconsulting role the firm will play.

The Reactive Posture for Determining the Client Mix

Another way to determine the landscape architecture firm's clientele is by hanging out the shingle and taking whatever work comes along. Of course, it helps if the projects are interesting and if the clients are good to work with and pay the firm's fees without problems. In time, the principals will find that trends emerge in the types of projects, clients, and consulting roles the firm is engaged to work on. The firm may develop one or more of the trends into office specialties and focus more and more of the firm's client-development efforts on the specialty area or areas that have evolved. Establishing a track record for specific types of projects can lead to much repeat business. The greater the reputation of the firm for its specialty work, the more likely that clients may seek out the firm—and thus define its client mix.

On the other hand, a reactive definition of the landscape architecture firm's client mix may not result in a specialization for the firm, but rather in a generalized professional practice. The firm's principals may want to maintain a healthy mix of project experience and a wide range of expertise that allow the firm to take advantage of the variety of client- and job-development opportunities presented by changing economic conditions or political, personal, or other reasons. Many landscape architecture firms intentionally maintain such a jack-of-all-trades posture. These firms develop flexible promotional materials that can be used to present the firm's experience with different orientations as needed for client- and job-development purposes.

Geographical Location of the Firm

The landscape architecture firm's clients may often be determined by the geographical location of the office, both nationally and regionally. A firm located in Bozeman, Montana, will look to the National Park Service and the National Forest Service as potential clients due to the vast amount of the land devoted to these public agencies in Montana and neighboring states. A firm located in an urban growth area of the country, such as the West and Southwest, may look to the private-sector developer, as well as individuals such as home owners, for its source of clientele. The firm that is located in a heavily populated metropolitan area, such as Boston, San Francisco, Seattle, or Atlanta, may have more opportunity to work for either private- or public-sector clients because of access to more urban growth and public works projects in general.

Where the firm is located within a regional or metropolitan area may also affect its client base. A firm specializing in planning and designing housing communities may wish to locate its office in an area of expanding suburban growth to be close to clients such as developers of housing projects, individual home owners, or architects who may be designing shopping centers or schools to accommodate the growing number of children associated with suburban growth. A firm specializing in public works projects may wish to locate its office near a government office center in order to have quick and easy access to public clients.

Professional Licensure Limitations and Opportunities

State-administered professional licensure laws, as well as the way that landscape architecture is conventionally practiced in states and regions, are two other determinants of the landscape architecture firm's clients.

In some states, the landscape architect is licensed to provide a wide range of professional services. In other states, the landscape architect's services are guided by what has been fashionable or conventional practice for many years. It is not uncommon for the landscape architect to provide site planning, grading, and drainage work in states such as New York, Washington, and Massachusetts, whereas in states such as California and Arizona, the landscape architect is often concerned with planting and irrigation design or environmental assessment and land planning. In Arizona, for example, landscape architects are not licensed to carry out drainage design; by conventional practice, however, they carry out a large amount of planting and irrigation system design, trying to mitigate the grading impacts often created by the engineering of sites.

Personal Contacts

Initially, and throughout the life of a professional office, a firm's client base is established and continues to be determined by the personal contacts of the firm's principals. When an individual or a group of partners starts a firm, one or more clients usually provide the initial opportunities for contracts. As the firm matures, personal contacts continue to play a key role in determining the firm's client base. The more contacts, the greater the opportunities for being in the right place at the right time and hearing about project opportunities. There is a direct correlation between the number of personal contacts with prospective clients in development, planning, conservation, and land management and project opportunities for the landscape architect. For the astute professional practitioner, conversations with acquaintances, friends, business associates, community leaders, professional practitioners in allied fields, and almost anyone with whom the professional comes into contact can lead to project opportunities.

After establishing a client base of personal contacts, the professional practitioner must keep in touch with his or her contacts in order to enhance the possibilities for project leads. If the client is a friend from the start, keeping in touch is usually easy. If the client is an acquaintance or a business contact, the professional practitioner may need to use specific techniques to follow up with the business contacts. Call lists, personal organizers, computer organizers, and tickle files are methods for keeping in regular contact with prior clients and with personal contacts. A tickle file is a simple method of organizing a calendar with periodic reminders to call specific contacts. No effort is required to keep in contact with present clients because regular conversations are part of the professional services. The regular contact with current clients gives each professional an edge over competitors, as well as definite opportunities for securing new projects from the existing clients. In many instances, the professional practitioner can maintain a lifelong relationship and a steady stream of contracts from clients as long as the client remains pleased with the quality, cost, and competence of the professional services. In addition, making friends with the client and taking part in social activities on a regular basis provide even greater opportunities for personal contact and job development.

Landscape architects employ other methods for developing and following up with personal contacts and to foster contacts with other professionals. Membership in professional societies, public service, social activities, breakfast clubs, and other activities can put the professional in personal contact with prospective clients. These activities are discussed in greater detail in chapter 7. Without question, developing and maintaining personal contacts is a key to job development and a successful long-term practice for the professional landscape architect.

Specialization

Developing a practice specialty may also determine the firm's client mix. The client mix of a firm that focuses on environmental assessment will be very different from that of the firm that specializes in golf course design. The environmental assessment firm is likely to have more public clients because regulatory laws, starting with the National Environmental Protection Act, require environmental clearance prior to development on public lands. State and local governments have similar environmental regulations. The firm's private clients will be developers and others who are required to deal with code compliance and the legal requirements of the national, state, and local environmental protection laws. The golf course design firm may have public clients because cities, counties, and metropolitan agencies develop public golf courses, but the firm is more likely to have a higher percentage of private clients who are developers of private, resort, and country club golf courses.

Some firms choose to specialize in one of the two broad categories of clients—public or private sector—as opposed to developing a specialty in a certain type of project. The choice is by preference. The firm's principals may enjoy working with private-sector clients or, conversely, public-sector clients. Private-sector clients demand attention to the project and relatively immediate results. For the private-sector client, time is money and projects are usually carried out on a fast-track basis. Public-sector client representatives function more as a project monitor once the scope of work and the project schedule have been developed and agreed on. Working with private-sector clients requires more attention to maintaining a friendly and closer interpersonal relationship with the client than working with public-sector clients. The personalities of the firm's principals often play a major role in the conscious choice to focus on either private- or public-sector clients.

Economic Conditions

Finally, the ebb and flow of the national economy and local economies often have a great deal of influence on the types of clients and professional roles of the landscape architecture firm. In times of national recession there will not be the breadth and depth to the client base that is found during times of national expansion. Indeed, in times of recession the firm will have to nurture its existing client base, paying particular attention to its best clients and maintaining them well. During a recession, a firm may have to adopt a survival posture, and take a close look at all client and project opportunities. In growth periods, the firm will have an expanding client base and more opportunities to set goals and strategies for positioning the firm in the most profitable and interesting markets.

The principals of a landscape architecture firm must keep abreast of trends in both local and national economies. Public spending for federal, state, and local projects, for example, often changes direction. School development and road expansion might be up, for instance, and spending for parks might be down. At another time, public funds might be available for flood-control projects and utility expansion. Firms that have the flexibility to provide the types of services for a wide range of public works projects will be able to withstand changes in the public marketplace. In the 1960s, for example, the federal Housing and Urban Development department spent hundreds of millions of dollars on urban renewal projects. In the 1990s, on the other hand, the federal government shifted a significant amount of effort and spending to preparing plans for military base closures and base realign-

ment. A local bond election might provide a large sum of money for park development. A state budget may prioritize spending on urban freeway development programs. Keeping up to date on the direction of government spending directions allows the landscape architecture firm to package its promotional materials and focus its client development efforts toward securing project work in the area of public spending that is prioritized at any given time.

Following private-sector trends also allows the firm's principals to go with the flow and focus job development efforts in local, regional, and national development areas that are hot markets. Locally, for instance, private-sector housing development often leads a growth and development trend. When enough housing is developed to create a population concentration, the housing will be followed by development of neighborhood shopping centers. As the growth area of the community continues to develop, the need for roads, schools, and parks will create public-sector opportunities. The firm that stays in tune with development trends and understands the dynamics of local development will be in a better position to project future needs and outline strategies for developing clients and penetrating market sectors in advance of when the actual work starts to appear. Daily reading of a business newspaper, subscribing to a "trends" service such as the *Dodge Report,* and keeping abreast of local politics and bond issues are a few of the many ways to keep up with economic trends. Following national and local economic trends is an important key to determining the firm's client base.

Private-Sector Clients and Projects

Private Development

Without private developers, a very large source of the landscape architect's client base would disappear. Most private developers, that is, individuals or corporations whose mission involves developing real estate projects, focus their efforts on commercial and residential development projects. Ten general areas of private development projects and private clients are discussed in the following sections. Whereas categories of private development projects could be debated and organized in many ways, the following categories are based generally on those used by ASLA for its annual national awards program.

The ten general areas of private development projects include

1. community and multifamily housing development
2. parks and outdoor recreation facilities
3. commercial and industrial development
4. planning and analysis projects
5. institutional projects
6. single-family residential and garden design projects
7. land and water reclamation and conservation projects
8. interior landscape architecture
9. historic preservation and restoration projects
10. landscape art and earth sculpture

Community and Multifamily Housing Development

From new towns and planned housing communities to condominium and apartment complexes, housing is one of the largest segments of private development opportunities for landscape architects across the United States. Landscape architects may be involved from the earliest stages of housing projects, providing site selection, environmental assessment, rezoning, code compliance, and site planning services, to the last stages of the project when the site improvements and landscaping are designed for project entries, streets, landscape buffers, visitor centers, model home complexes, open space, and site amenities.

Developers of multifamily housing projects, particularly higher-density projects such as town house and apartment projects, may provide the most valuable housing-sector client and project opportunities for the landscape architect. Multifamily housing projects include open space and outdoor recreation areas, which are key elements of the landscape architect's design domain. Open space and pathway systems for walking, jogging, and horseback riding; swimming pools and spas; beachfront development; tennis courts and golf courses; playing fields; children's play areas; and canals and waterways for boating and conservation are all facilities planned and designed by landscape architects for private-sector multifamily housing developments.

Seawatch is a 24-acre housing project of fifty-one units on the northern tip of Gasparilla Island off the southwest Florida coast. The southern end of the island and the quaint village of Boca Grande were developed in the 1920s as a railroad port. The northern area of the island, about 300 acres in size, was developed in the 1960s, and native vegetation was typically stripped and topography flattened to make way for new developments. In the early 1980s, 24 acres of the cleared land were purchased by the developer of Seawatch with the intent to develop homes in a reconstructed native landscape.

The project, which received an ASLA Design Award in 1989, was designed by landscape architects Burner & Company of Fort Myers, Florida. In collaboration with the project architect, Burner & Company carried out an extensive analysis of the island's old village and other nearby residential communities to come up with a strategy for the Seawatch master plan and to determine the elements that would give the project identity and character. The consultants attempted to create the site and architectural characteristics of the Old Florida style of development that was evident in the communities they studied in their analysis phase. Walls, tin-roofed cabanas, lattice fences, and pathways paved with crushed shells are some of the design features introduced to achieve the Old Florida look. The landscape architects altered the existing topography to create an intricate system of dunes reminiscent of natural seaside landforms. The character of a quaint seaside village was achieved by clustering the dwelling units in a radial pattern that preserved ocean views for all. Uniformity of building and plant materials was used to strengthen the identity of Seawatch. Coconut and sabal palms were used as skyline elements. Buttonwood trees were introduced as a shade tree. Sea oats and sea grape were planted to stabilize the dunes, and bougainvillea was introduced in dramatic bands of color throughout the site. The landscape architects designed recreational amenities that included tennis courts, swimming pools, and a croquet court (*Landscape Architecture* November 1989).

Blue Heron Pointe, a planned community in Northville Township, Michigan, owes its existence to the creative solution of environmental problems by the landscape architecture firm of Robert Leighton Associates, located in Ann Arbor, Michigan. The environmental liabilities that all but stopped development

FIGURE 2-1. Walks paved with crushed shells slice through dunes stabilized by plantings of sea oats and sea grape at Seawatch.

Photograph courtesy of Burner & Company.

included landslides and other safety hazards associated with erosion of an abandoned gravel pit, deposition of deep layers of silt on parts of the site, and the existence of a pristine 18-acre lake and wetland habitat that caused the Michigan Department of Natural Resources to worry about the environmental impact of a housing development and its potential for damaging the water quality of the lake and wetland. The department was particularly concerned about grading and drainage of surface runoff into the site's water resources.

Robert Leighton Associates devised a plan for grading and drainage that included capturing surface storm water in a relatively low-cost system of catch

basins and septic tanks for eventual percolation and purification through filter fabric and subsurface gravel deposits. No surface storm water is allowed to drain directly from roads into the site's water resources.

After resolving the drainage and natural-resource issues of the Michigan Department of Natural Resources, the landscape architects and other project consultants developed the plan for the residential community around the lake. The landscape architects created two fingers of water that gave all of the 144 dwelling units access to the lake. They designed an elevated boardwalk to provide limited access to the wetland area for observing the blue herons and other waterfowl. The plan also provided for slope stabilization

FIGURE 2-2. The entry point at Seawatch features large laurel figs, coconut palms, and hundreds of dwarf bougainvillea.

Photograph courtesy of Burner & Company.

and screening of an active gravel mining operation adjacent to the project. Blue Heron Pointe is a successful project because of the landscape architect's creative approach to resolving the natural resource and site issues (*Landscape Architecture* April 1991).

Located in Scottsdale, Arizona, Desert Highlands is a successful planned residential and recreational community for which Gage Davis Associates provided master planning and landscape architectural and architectural services over a period of five years. The project exemplifies a planning approach that harmoniously blends an understanding of the site with the desires of the client. The 850-acre project, located on the south slope of Pinnacle Peak, a prominent landform of the McDowell Mountains in Scottsdale, includes a dramatic golf course designed by Jack Nicklaus as the project's centerpiece. The site is characterized by lush Sonoran Desert vegetation, numerous dry desert washes, and eye-catching boulder formations.

Thoughtful integration of built elements of the project with the desert landscape has resulted in minimizing visual impact, a prime goal of the project, achieved through careful orchestration of design guidelines; codes, covenants, and restrictions (CC&Rs); and conceptual design by the planners and landscape architects. The designers laid out homesites with recommended building areas in order to preserve a goal of 50 percent or more of the natural desert vegetation on each lot. Extensive efforts to salvage and transplant giant saguaros (*Carnegiea gigantea*) and native palo verde trees supplemented the preservation efforts.

The golf course clubhouse is a good example of the efforts of Gage Davis Associates to blend architecture with the native landscape. Working with clubhouse architect William Zmistowski Associates, the firm designed exterior terraces that cascade down the slope of a large boulder formation. The lowest terrace integrates the swimming pool and spa with boulders and desert vegetation to form a cool desert retreat. Another series of pools and a meandering creek provide an oasis area adjacent to the practice putting greens, complemented by a desert interpretive trail. The organic shape and brown color of the stucco finish make the clubhouse appear to be an extension of the boulder formations. In fact, the architecture and landscape architecture are so artfully blended that visitors have to look twice to see that a major construction effort has been carried out on the clubhouse site. Merging

the natural and built environments has long been a theme in residential design by landscape architects, and the successful efforts by Gage Davis Associates at Desert Highlands were rewarded when the project received an ASLA Honor Award in 1989.

Parks and Outdoor Recreation Facilities

Mountain and seaside resorts that feature outdoor recreation amenities, golf courses, theme parks, tennis centers, water parks, family fun centers, outdoor amphitheaters, and ski areas are private parks and outdoor recreation projects that provide good sources of clientele and projects for landscape architects.

The South Cove Waterfront Park in Battery Park City at the southern tip of Manhattan, for example, is part of an open-space system in the 91-acre landfill project. The South Cove Park, designed by the landscape architecture firm Child Associates, Inc., lies adjacent to the World Trade Center and provides views of the Statue of Liberty. The 3-acre park serves residential communities in Battery Park City, as well as other nearby residential areas and Wall Street workers. The park provides a place to walk, jog, bike, or sit and take advantage of the outstanding scenery of the New York City harbor activities (*Landscape Architecture* November 1989).

The Louisville waterfront master plan developed by the landscape architecture firm Hargreaves Associates is another example of an ambitious plan for outdoor recreation and park facilities intended to reunite the people of Louisville with the city's reason for being—the Ohio River. For the people of Louisville and surrounding communities, the Ohio River is a powerful force in daily life. The city's history and present image are intertwined with commerce and industry on the river. The city's waterfront, like that of many river-oriented cities, is an industrial landscape severed from its downtown by elevated freeways, leaving the waterfront inaccessible. At the end of the twentieth century, Louisville has outgrown its dependence on its wharf and industrial waterfront. Hargreaves Associates's plan reclaims the industrial landscape and provides linkages to the waterfront.

Through an open and interactive public design process, the firm developed a flexible and powerful master plan. The plan creates a dialogue between city and river, redefining the context of the urban waterfront park and its relationship to traditional urban activity.

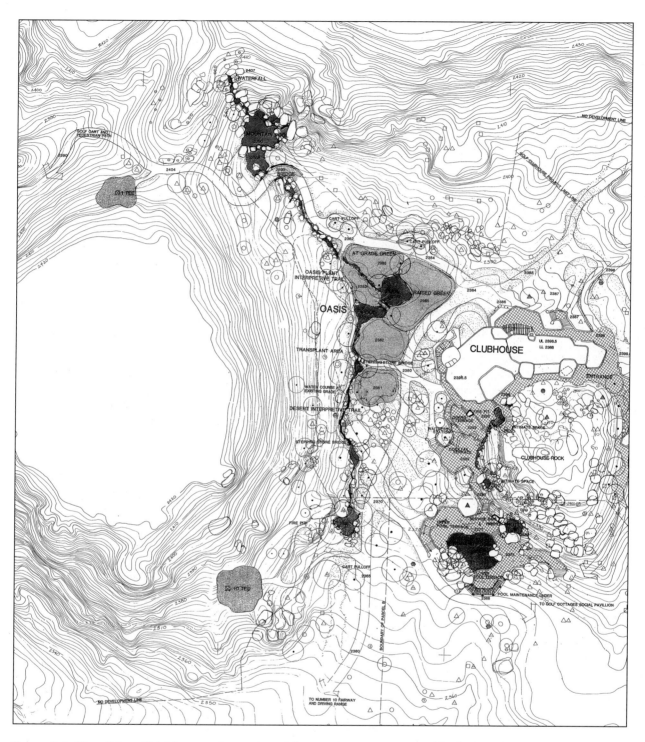

FIGURE 2-3. Plan of the golf clubhouse patios, pools, and desert oasis area at Desert Highlands planned residential and recreational community, Scottsdale, Arizona.

The plan, which won an ASLA Merit Award in 1992, features a public plaza on the riverfront for festivals and daily use and a riverboat landing. A 14-acre great lawn area flows under the freeway and provides a centerpiece for the waterfront design. It will serve as an informal amphitheater and public gathering place. Conceptually, the great lawn reenacts the original settlement of Louisville's banks as a clearing in the woods. The tilted plane of the lawn mitigates the barrier perception of the elevated freeway by lowering the

FIGURE 2-4. South Cove Waterfront Park, designed by Child Associates in Manhattan, New York.

Photograph by Cymie Payne.

ground under the freeway structure and opening views between downtown and the river.

A linear park of inlets, landforms, paths, and other features follows the waterfront edge, reflecting the flow of the river and providing opportunities for people to experience the river. The inlets provide riparian habitats for native plants and animals. The islands provide deflection barricades, protecting the shore from the wave action of barge traffic on the river and creating a safe channel for small watercraft. At one point in the linear park, an abandoned railroad bridge will be adapted to provide bicycle and pedestrian access to the Indiana side of the river.

The National Semiconductor Employee Recreational Park, according to its designers, the landscape architecture firm of Royston, Hanamoto, Alley & Abbey, offers a striking demonstration of the profession's role and importance in shaping our landscape. The project is a visionary corporate park conceived as a sanctuary for employees to enhance corporate unity and morale. The park master plan accommodates nine thousand National Semiconductor employees or three-thousand-person departmental gatherings while being an integral part of employees' daily lives.

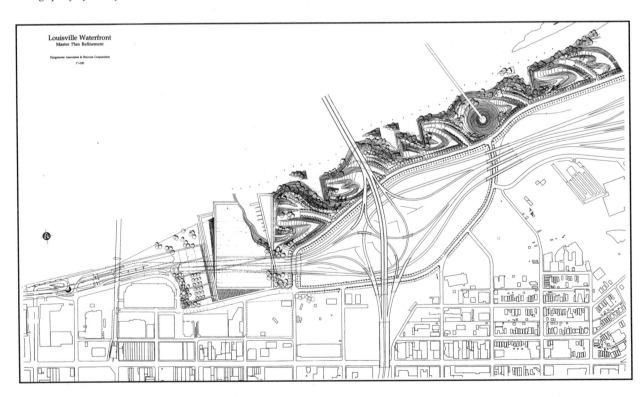

FIGURE 2-5. The Louisville Waterfront master plan.

Courtesy of Hargreaves Associates.

The 14-acre site in Santa Clara, California, a former dump and rubble field engulfed by warehouses, parking lots, and freeways, was selected to be transformed into a park for daily respite and weekend retreat for employees of the National Semiconductor Corporation. The rubble was graded into mounds that, along with jet-spray fountains, mitigate noise from the adjacent highway. A 1.5-acre irregular lake, a 1,000-seat amphitheater, a brick dance floor, quiet paths, picnic areas, ball fields, formal groves, and informal massing of trees give form to the site. A dramatic, five-story black chain-link interpretive structure, the park's centerpiece designed by landscape architect Harold N. Kobayashi, ASLA, serves as a giant picnic canopy in the park (*Landscape Architecture* November 1990).

Set within the natural vegetation of the park are diverse elements for active and passive recreation: a 1-mile jogging course located on top of the perimeter berms, large-group picnic areas, a dance and stage area, a children's play area, a 1,000-seat amphitheater,

a soccer field, ball field, open-play fields, racquetball, and many private picnic areas. Both formal public spaces and informal private niches are structured to serve diverse nodes of activity, and employees, only a few hundred yards from their work, have a place to eliminate the stresses of Silicon Valley.

This sector of private development projects offers landscape architects opportunities for specialization. In order to be effectively designed, many types of private outdoor recreation developments, such as ski areas and golf courses, require specific knowledge of the activity and how it is carried out. Knowledge of the landscape setting and the site requirements is also important. Developers are drawn to the firms that have established track records in planning and designing these specialized outdoor facilities. Because of large investments and keen competition associated with private outdoor recreation projects, the developer usually doesn't want to take a chance with an inexperienced firm. Specializing in a specific type of

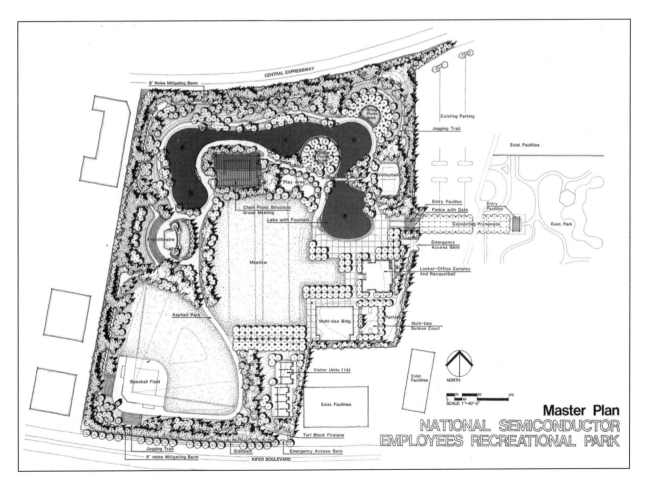

FIGURE 2-6. Master plan of the National Semiconductor Employee Recreational Park.
Courtesy of Royston, Hanamoto, Alley & Abbey.

FIGURE 2-7. Aerial photograph of the
National Semiconductor Employee
Recreational Park.
Photograph by Steve Proehl.

private outdoor recreation development can provide a
good niche market for a landscape architecture firm.

The Ventana Canyon Planned Community and
the Ventana Canyon Golf and Racquet Club in Tucson, Arizona, is one of the Southwest's outstanding
housing communities designed around a golf course
as the outdoor recreation feature of the development's
open-space system. The open-space network also features preservation of the interesting and dramatic
Sonoran Desert landscape. Design of the resort hotel's
landscape was the responsibility of the San Francisco
landscape architecture firm Perry Burr & Associates,
in conjunction with environmental consultants
Steven W. Carothers, Inc., and the Tucson landscape
architecture firm Harmony & Associates. In addition
to preserving large areas of the native vegetation,
which includes the unique giant saguaro (*Carnegiea
gigantea*) and the velvet mesquite (*Prosopis velutina*),
landscape architecture plans for the project included
salvaging and relocating large specimen plants of both
saguaros and mesquite trees on the site. The project
received an ASLA Merit Award in 1985 (*Landscape
Architecture* September/October 1985).

The golf course at the Ventana Canyon Golf and
Racquet Club, designed by Tom Fazio, has thirty-six
holes divided into the Canyon course and the Mountain course. The Ventana Canyon course has twice received the *Golf Magazine* Silver Medalist Award and
was honored by *Golf Digest* as the best resort course in
Arizona and by *Golf Week* as one of the nation's best
golf courses.

The third hole on the Mountain course at the
Ventana Golf and Racquet Club is recognized as the
signature hole of the course. According to Tom Fazio,
this hole is a good example of what he strives for in
designing a short hole. He tries to visually intimidate
the golfer, yet make the hole easier to play than it
looks. It is an excellent example of another Fazio design philosophy—he allows the golfer, wherever possible, to see the green on a par-three golf hole. Fazio
has claimed that the third hole at Ventana is the
shortest and most expensive golf hole he has ever designed. The green is surrounded by the awe-inspiring
Sonoran Desert landscape of the Santa Catalina
Mountains that border the north side of Tucson.
Preserving and dramatizing the Sonoran Desert landscape is another hallmark of the design of the golf
course.

The fairways at Ventana are planted with Bermuda
grass for its toughness and compatibility with the hot,
arid climate of Tucson. The greens are carpeted with
bent grass. Many of the golf holes have been designed
in the spirit of the target golf concept, where tees are
usually elevated and the golfer shoots over an area of
natural or enhanced desert landscape to fairway and
green targets. This concept is particularly appropriate
to desert environments because it reduces the amount
of turfed area, resulting in less water used overall. The
target concept also allows more of the natural landscape to be preserved, and in the case of the Sonoran
Desert landscape, the result is a picturesque and highly
appealing golf course.

FIGURE 2-8. The third hole, a par three, on the Mountain Course at Ventana Golf and Racquet Club, Tucson, Arizona.

FIGURE 2-9. The view from the championship tee on the fourth hole of the Mountain Course at Ventana Golf and Racquet Club illustrates the target concept of fairway design.

Commercial and Industrial Development

Another area of private-sector development that has provided a great deal of opportunity for landscape architects is commercial and industrial development projects. Shopping centers, malls, office complexes, mixed-use commercial projects, rooftop plazas, urban plazas, public transportation facilities, airport environs, industrial parks, corporate headquarters, and other corporate facilities all have public outdoor spaces associated with them. Where there is public space, there is a landscape architecture opportunity. More so than other types of private development, commercial developments may offer the landscape architecture firm the greatest opportunities for high-quality design with large construction budgets. Commercial projects and industrial parks are extremely competitive in terms of their desired market penetration. Curb appeal, project marketing, attracting shoppers, and differentiating an office complex from its competitors are some of the elements of commercial landscape architecture design that are very important to commercial developers. The setting's design, the site's amenities, and the project's visual appeal can provide an edge in the highly competitive commercial market.

A dramatic example of urban commercial design is Williams Square, designed by The SWA Group and awarded an Honor Award in 1985 by ASLA. According to *Landscape Architecture* (September/October 1985), "Williams Square is a tour de force of collaboration, a grand new open space, an urbanizing landmark for the planned community of Las Colinas."

Located in the city of Irving, Texas, between the Dallas–Fort Worth International Airport and the central business district, Williams Square serves as a focal point of Las Colinas. The centerpiece of the square is a herd of bronze mustangs, one-and-one-half times life size, conceived by artist Rob Glen and inspired by Ben Carpenter, chairman of the board and CEO of Southland Financial Corporation, the project's developer. With the aid of highly creative waterworks that splash and spray beneath the spots where the hooves of the horses touch down, the plaza takes on a unique animation and the horses take on a lifelike quality.

Project designer Jim Reeves and project architect Dan Mock wanted to achieve a real effect of hooves splashing through water. They studied the movement of horses through water and achieved a replica of the effect by designing copper emitters in the exact shape

FIGURE 2-10. The sketch plan for Williams Square designed by The SWA Group.

Photograph by Tom Fox, reprinted courtesy of The SWA Group.

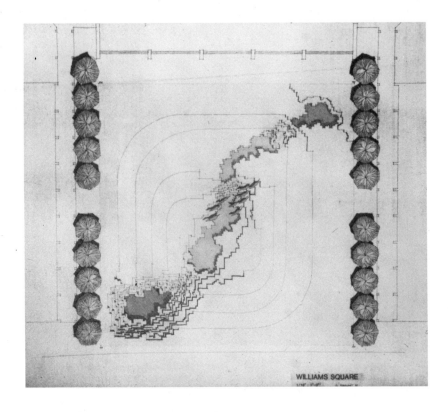

of a horse's hoof and placing the emitters beneath the strike point of the legs of each of the bronze steeds. By creating a plaza devoid of trees, benches, and other outdoor furnishings, the designers produced a neutral setting that gives the horses a life of their own. Lighting effects create a nighttime environment that heightens the water effects for people viewing the plaza after dark. This commercial design project is awe inspiring and represents one of the most creative out-door plazas designed by landscape architects in collaboration with other design and art professionals (*Landscape Architecture* September/October 1985).

Another unusual commercial project is the entry tower designed for the Pomona Auto Center by the landscape architecture design firm Land Design. The project itself is described as an auto mall, which takes the concept of the shopping mall and tailors it to automobile dealerships and related commercial activi-

FIGURE 2-11. Bronze mustangs at Williams Square.

Photograph by Tom Fox, reprinted courtesy of The SWA Group.

FIGURE 2-12. Pomona Auto Center entry tower.

ties. The Pomona Auto Center, located on a 71-acre site near Pomona, California, includes seven auto dealerships and eight related land uses. The center's entry tower won an ASLA Design Award in 1988.

According to *Landscape Architecture* (November 1988), "Individual dealerships had requested single, 100-foot-high signs to identify each of their auto sales areas from an adjacent commercial highway one-fourth mile away, and from a freeway one-half mile away. The landscape architect instead proposed a single tower bearing the insignia of each dealership, and the suggestion was accepted." The colorful and playful 85-foot tower has become a local landmark. The landscape architects also executed plans for the auto mall's planting design, irrigation system, and median improvements.

The design of corporate headquarters is one type of commercial design project that has consistently received awards from ASLA over the last several decades and is notable for high-end, upscale design due in many cases to the high visibility desired by corporate managers and boards of directors and also to the generous budgets often available. Corporate headquarters

are the plums of commercial landscape architecture design. Some of the most notable corporate facilities designed by landscape architecture firms include the Deere and Company Administrative Center, designed by Sasaki Associates, viewed by many as one of the classic design models for corporate headquarters (*Landscape Architecture* November 1991); the Shell Woodcreek Exploration and Production Headquarters in Houston, Texas, designed by The SWA Group (*Landscape Architecture* September/October 1985); PepsiCo World Headquarters in Purchase, New York, master-planned by Edward D. Stone Jr. and Associates (*Landscape Architecture* September/October 1986); and the IBM Federal Systems Division Facilities, Clearlake, Texas, designed by The Office of Peter Walker and Martha Schwartz (*Landscape Architecture* November 1989).

The IBM Federal Systems Division Facilities located in Clearlake, Texas, provide computer services to the National Air and Space Administration (NASA). The initial phase of the development includes a crescent-shaped building and grounds. A second building, which will be a mirror image of the first, will be developed to complete the project. The landscape architects, The Office of Peter Walker and Martha Schwartz, received an ASLA Merit Award in 1989 for the setting design, which mixed the regional design idioms of the southern plantation with Japanese garden influences implemented on a very large scale. Semicircular pools planted with water lilies emanate from the central axis of the postmodern building and emulate the granite and glass pattern of the building's facade. A gravel pathway system, designed as part of the semicircular pattern, ends in a stand of native pine trees that were preserved in the design process and enhanced by planting additional trees. Grading and drainage were carefully handled by gently sloping the grade away from the building, allowing percolation on the flat site without impacting the existing pine woods (*Landscape Architecture* November 1989).

Industrial projects and industrial landscape settings also provide client and project opportunities for landscape architects. Local, state, and federal regulations regularly require environmental mitigation and a good-neighbor policy from their industrial developments. These regulations and policies require environmental analyses and visual assessments during site

analysis, as well as careful site planning, environmental mitigation, and visual impact mitigation during the design stage. Industrial parks require not only site planning but also design of entry features and streetscapes because they compete with other industrial parks to attract the individual developers of development parcels. In recent years, there has been an emphasis on upscale design of industrial parks with a focus on high-tech imagery and slick design quality to bring the industrial landscapes out of the negative visual context associated with the industrial development of the last half of the nineteenth century and the first half of the twentieth century.

Visually improving industrial settings by developing and implementing design guidelines for industrial areas has provided a range of opportunities for landscape architecture firms. In the early 1980s, Johnson, Johnson and Roy, Inc., developed the Visual Improvement Plan for Downriver Industry. The aim of this plan was to strengthen the bond between heavy industrial centers and the downriver communities that surround the industrial centers along a twenty-mile stretch of the Detroit River (*Landscape Architecture* September 1981). The industries are vital to the economic viability of the region. The firm's plan provided a framework for en-

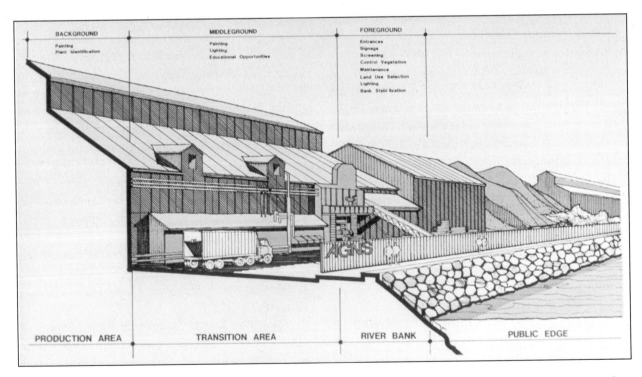

FIGURE 2-13. Visual improvement guidelines for industrial landscapes in Johnson, Johnson and Roy's plan for Downriver Industry on the Detroit River.
Courtesy of JJR.

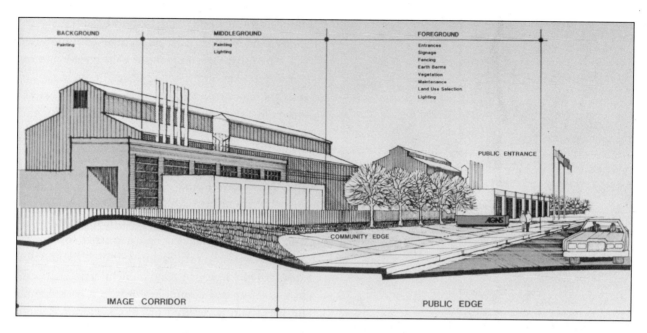

FIGURE 2-14. Visual improvement guidelines for industrial landscapes in Johnson, Johnson and Roy's plan for Downriver Industry on the Detroit River.
Courtesy of JJR.

larging the commitment of the industries from economic stability to visual quality in the industrial environment by bringing the riverfront into focus as both a corporate and a community resource. The plan provided a framework rationale for identifying visual issues and opportunities. Acceptable visual impacts were recorded and alternative levels of treatments were developed for the downriver industrial landscape setting.

Viewland Hoffman Receiving Station in Seattle, Washington, received a Merit Award in the 1981 ASLA annual professional awards program. This industrial project represents an outstanding collaboration of landscape architect, architect, and artist to integrate an electric power substation into a north Seattle neighborhood. The role of the landscape architect included responding to the Seattle City Light Company's functional requirements for the site and the concerns of the neighborhood. Public meetings resulted in a specially detailed concrete wall that mitigates visual and noise impacts of the substation. Parking was provided on one side of the site for a small commercial business and open space was located on the site for informal active play by neighborhood children. The site planning and design concept is utilitarian and functional. The plan did not try to hide the facility but rather celebrated the interesting visual characteristics of the equipment and introduced

FIGURE 2-15. Aerial view of Viewland Hoffman Receiving Station, Seattle, Washington. The informal play area and the semicircular sculpture garden are seen at the bottom of the photograph.
Photograph courtesy of Seattle City Light.

FIGURE 2-16. Emil Gerke's kinetic sculpture at Viewland Hoffman Receiving Station, Seattle, Washington.

Photograph courtesy of Seattle City Light.

public art to complement the setting. Folk artist Emil Gerke created kinetic sculpture from found objects that included electrical appliances and parts. Seattle City Light allowed the sculptures to be sited so that they would be seen together with the substation's electrical equipment. The site as a whole was integrated into the residential area by using lawns, shade trees, and flowering trees, which provide a variety of seasonal effects (*Landscape Architecture* September 1981).

Planning and Analysis Projects

Because landscape architects have excellent analytical skills developed during their educational training and sharpened in their professional practice, they naturally seek out clients that have a need for planning and analysis services. Often these types of projects have a scientific, research, or feasibility component. Many planning and analysis projects never get built. They establish criteria, provide vision, and set goals for future design and development. From 1986 to 1994, one-third of ASLA's annual professional awards were given for planning and analysis projects. In the

private sector, planning and analysis projects tend to include land planning for residential communities, large-scale urban development of a mixed-use nature, and campus planning. The public sector, on the other hand, has opportunities for planning and analysis projects focused on setting criteria and goals for the wise and sustainable use of natural and cultural resources.

Planning and analysis projects can also be carried out by quasi-private groups, such as the Gateway Economic Development Corporation of Cleveland—the client for the city's Gateway master plan project. This plan for the new Gateway sports district for downtown Cleveland was prepared in 1991 by Sasaki Associates with an impressive team of architects, engineers, and marketing and community-relations consultants. The plan, which received an ASLA Honor Award, avoided the typical stadium surrounded by acres of parking by identifying the existing parking in the central business district that could serve sporting-event spectators after business hours. The existing parking would be supplemented by a new parking garage serving loge-box and club-seat patrons, players, staff, media, and employees. The plan presented a vision that enhances the urban qualities of the downtown setting. Exits from the stadium direct people toward restaurants, bars, and retail establishments. The main entry of the stadium is the end point of a planned sequence of open spaces along a new street developed for the project (*Landscape Architecture* November 1991).

Cleveland's Gateway master plan achieved the following planning goals and urban design objectives:

- The urban design framework was established for the ballpark, arena, and parking garage so they would relate to existing buildings, create public spaces, and connect with surrounding streets and landmarks.
- Gateway's sidewalks and open spaces were integrated with downtown Cleveland's established pedestrian system.
- The concourse for the ballpark and arena was placed at street level.
- Approximately 17,000 parking spaces were identified within a ten-minute walk of the sports complex, ensuring that no surface parking would create a barrier between Gateway and the surrounding city.

FIGURE 2-17. Gateway's sidewalks and open spaces were integrated by Sasaki Associates with Cleveland's existing pedestrian systems and lead to Jacobs Field, designed by HOK Sport as the home of the Major League Cleveland Indians.

Photograph by Anne Warner.

- Traffic management, public-transit linkages, police details, special street closings, pedestrian routes, and crossings were addressed.
- Service access was planned to allow Gateway's facilities to function easily and efficiently in the tight urban setting.
- Criteria for reviewing and approving the designs of individual buildings were developed for use by the City of Cleveland and the Gateway Economic Development Corporation.

Gateway's 8.5 acres of outdoor public spaces, plazas, and sidewalks include the 2-acre Gateway Plaza and the ½-acre Indians Square. The open space was designed to create a ballpark setting, to provide outdoor gathering spots, and to accommodate programmed special activities such as lunchtime concerts and large festivals. Some of the design features include

- Cast-in-place concrete surfaces accented with 8-inch by 8-inch black pavers used as a unifying element.
- More than 6,000 inscribed pavers surrounding the 10-foot-high bronze statue of Indians baseball great Bob Feller in Indians Square recognizing the donors who contributed to the installation costs.
- Honey locusts, maples, ginkgoes, and Japanese pagoda trees, used as theme trees, were selected for their salt tolerance and resistance to air pollution.

- Trees planted in staggered double rows along Ontario and Carnegie Streets to create a strong, green edge to the project.
- Substantial electrical capacity was designed into the public spaces to accommodate events. (The public spaces have more electrical capacity than any other outdoor location in Cleveland.)
- The Sony Jumbotron Sports Marquee in Gateway Plaza was designed to complement the ballpark architecture.
- State-of-the-art intelligent highway technology manages traffic flow in the project area by using a central computer to control traffic signals and variable message signs.
- Playful, colorful signage, accented with a bouncing-ball motif, was designed to provide wayfinding and establish a unifying element for the planning area.
- The designers assisted the committee for public art in selecting and integrating a variety of artworks into the gateway's public space.

The vision established by Sasaki's Gateway master plan captures the life and spirit of traditional urban sports facilities in America, as opposed to the freestanding, isolated buildings designed in the 1960s, 1970s, and 1980s. The plan establishes strong links with downtown buildings, streets, and pedestrian ways.

Alexandria 2020 is another private-sector and public-sector partnership that sponsored a collaborative planning and analysis project headed by HOH

Associates for a 320-acre site called Potomac Yard in Alexandria, Virginia. Transportation, housing, and open space are the keystones of the plan. The site, which includes an operating rail yard, will serve as a model for state-of-the-art transportation planning including multimodal rail transit services linked to pedestrian, bicycle, bus, water taxi, and vehicular circulation. The transportation system will link existing and planned residential development. Alexandria 2020 will plan and develop neighborhoods that are in character and compatible with the layout of adjacent neighborhoods. Each of the five planned neighborhoods in Potomac Yard will include a mixed-use center and open space providing definition for the project's design and visual character. HOH Associates coordinated and managed the input of over thirty consultants, many of whom have expertise in specific transportation modes such as light-rail transit, who collaborated on this award-winning mixed-use project within view of the nation's capital (*Landscape Architecture* November 1990).

The San Francisco office of landscape architects Wallace, Roberts & Todd, in association with the Aspen, Colorado, firm Caudill, Gustafson & Ross, served as prime consultants to the Kanozan Resort Corporation, a joint venture of Tokyo Tower Company, Ltd., and Tobu Railroad, to develop a model resort community plan, The Source, located about thirty miles from Tokyo, Japan, in the western Boso Peninsula. The site contains 1,729 acres of farmland and forest in and around the village of Kanozan. The site provides far-reaching views of Tokyo, Tokyo Bay, and Mount Fuji. Ground breaking for the $100 million project occurred in 1990, and the full completion of the five phases of construction is scheduled for the year 2000.

To describe The Source merely as a resort is an oversimplification. The master plan reinvents the concept of the traditional Japanese resort, wresting from it the tendency for planners to plagiarize planning concepts of American theme parks. Although The Source is uniquely Japanese, two regional models in the

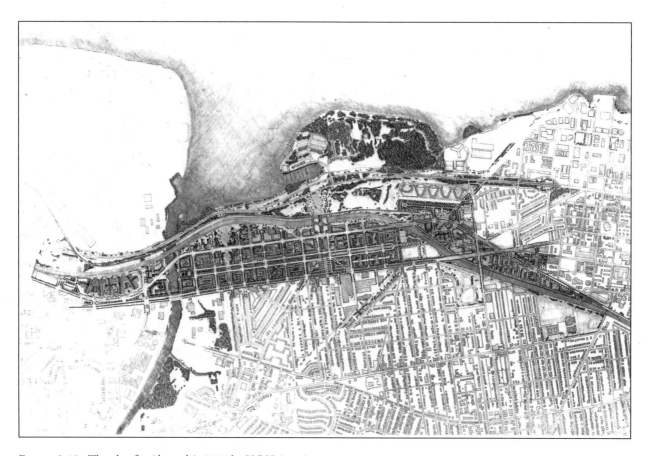

FIGURE 2-18. The plan for Alexandria 2020 by HOH Associates.

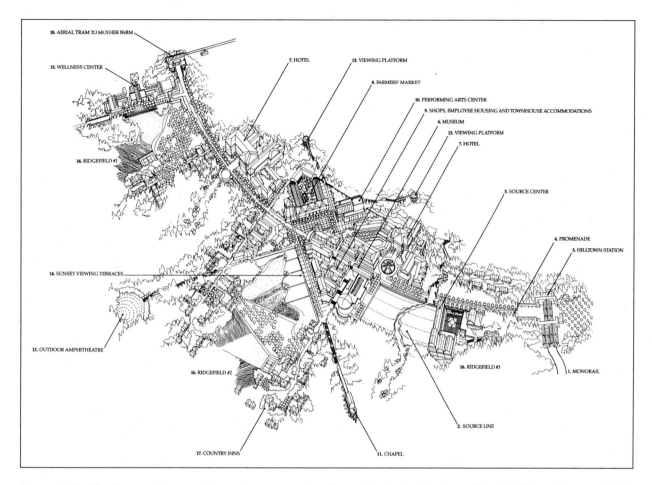

18. AERIAL TRAM TO MOTHER FARM
15. WELLNESS CENTER
7. HOTEL
13. VIEWING PLATFORM
8. FARMERS' MARKET
10. PERFORMING ARTS CENTER
9. SHOPS, EMPLOYEE HOUSING AND TOWNHOUSE ACCOMMODATIONS
6. MUSEUM
13. VIEWING PLATFORM
7. HOTEL
16. RIDGEFIELD #1
5. SOURCE CENTER
4. PROMENADE
3. HILLTOWN STATION
14. SUNSET VIEWING TERRACES
12. OUTDOOR AMPHITHEATRE
16. RIDGEFIELD #3
1. MONORAIL
16. RIDGEFIELD #2
2. SOURCE LINE
17. COUNTRY INNS
11. CHAPEL

FIGURE 2-19. The Source, a Japanese leisure resort community, planned by the San Francisco office of Wallace, Roberts & Todd.

After completing their orientation at an off-site orientation center, guests may proceed to The Source by a **monorail (1)**, which skims the ground and offers a breathtaking trip through lush green forests. Or they may walk the scenic mile-long trail called the **Source Line (2)**, where they will find works of art, gardens, and a tea house for meditation and relaxation. At the **Hilltown Station (3)**, golf carts, bicycles and shuttles wait to transport guests to their accommodations.

The **Hilltown Promenade (4)** is the circulation spine for The Source. The **Source Center (5)** is the ceremonial gateway for entering and leaving The Source. The **museum (6)** displays works of art commissioned by the Source Foundation from resident fellows. The museum forms the gateway to Hilltown, a mix of **hotels (7)**, a **farmer's market (8)**, **shops, residences, and accommodations (9)**, the heart of the resort. Arranged around a public square, Hilltown is the site for seasonal festivals, special events, and nighttime activities. It is the cultural center of The Source and includes a **performing arts center (10)**. A **chapel (11)**, an **outdoor amphitheater (12)**, and a **viewing platform (13)** are located off the square at points of the compass. A **sunset viewing terrace (14)** is located below the square.

Orchards separate Hilltown from the **Wellness Center (15)**. The center provides a complete program for physical evaluation and consultation for individuals on diet, exercise, and physical therapy programs. Swimming pools, a gymnasium, outdoor playing fields, tennis courts, and a health and beauty spa also await guests seeking physical activity and renewal.

Extending from Hilltown are **ridgefields (16)**. Crops, orchard, vineyards, flower gardens, and pastures will be organized according to the designs prepared by agronomists, horticulturists and landscape architects. The fields symbolically provide food for the guests and from the air form the outline of the flower and butterfly that embodies the resort in its logo image. Small groups of **country inns (17)** are located along the ridgefields. Cabins and tent camps for those guests desiring rustic accommodations are further afield. **Remote centers** (not pictured) are even further out from Hilltown. The remote centers offer instruction in the physical, spiritual, and environmental disciplines. The centers include an equestrian camp, an art and music camp, an observatory/planetarium, and a nature/agricultural field station.

The Mother Farm (not pictured) is separated from The Source by a pristine valley. It is accessible from Hilltown by an **aerial tram (18)**. *The Source* and the Mother Farm together provide a setting where visitors can achieve balance with nature and ponder the past, present, and future, rejoicing in the continuous celebration of rebirth.

Drawing by Donald Gibson, courtesy of Wallace, Roberts & Todd.

United States offered principles for the development: the City of Aspen, Colorado, and environs; and the agricultural regions of the Napa and Sonoma Valleys near San Francisco, California. The goals of the project include

- to create a resort environment that respects and enhances the rural, agricultural character of the Boso Peninsula and capitalizes on these characteristics and on the natural amenities of the area as tourist attractions
- to provide an environment where Japanese people can learn to renew, enrich, and expand their physical, spiritual, intellectual, and artistic well-being through the creative use of leisure time
- to establish The Source as a prototype for planning, design, and development of resorts and resort regions throughout Japan

The project design program includes the development of a community of buildings and activity areas that will provide a setting for recreation, art, music, and other educational activities. The importance of symbol in Japanese culture is expressed in the programming of The Source. The pattern of ridge-top development deemed most suitable resembles the form of a flower. The agricultural fields of the Mother

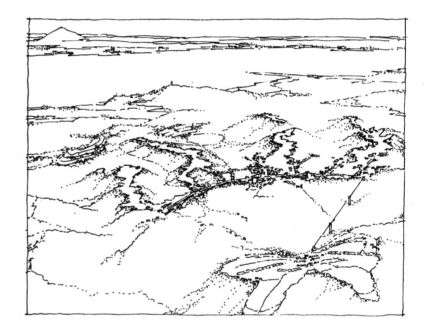

FIGURE 2-20. From the air, The Source is transformed into a tapestry of symbols. The butterfly of the Mother Farm (lower right) and the flower petal arrangement of the ridgefields development emanate from the stem of the Source Line (center). Tokyo Bay and Mount Fuji are shown in the distant horizon.

Drawing by Jim Leritz, courtesy of Wallace, Roberts & Todd.

FIGURE 2-21. The Source is centered on Hilltown, a vibrant mix of hotels, shops, restaurants, and fitness facilities. A large open-air market just off the main square (lower left) will offer fresh foods. The performing arts center (upper left) is the cultural heart of the community. The promenade (center) links Hilltown with the rest of The Source.

Drawing by Jim Leritz, courtesy of Wallace, Roberts & Todd.

FIGURE 2-22. Winding paths lead to outlying ridgefields where remote cabins and tent camps provide private, rustic accommodations. The fields will be designed and organized to provide maximum visual enjoyment.

Drawing by Jim Leritz, courtesy of Wallace, Roberts & Todd.

FIGURE 2-23. The spiritual center is one of four remote centers. An observatory/planetarium (upper left) and temple/chapel (right) encourage meditation and spiritual thought. Other remote centers offer recreation, art, music, and environmental studies.

Drawing by Jim Leritz, courtesy of Wallace, Roberts & Todd.

Farm and adjacent property owned by the developer create the shape of a butterfly. Together, butterfly and flower suggests the harmony of nature in balance, the guiding principle for the resort development. The ridge-top pattern also forms the body of a human. The ridge suggest the symbolic limbs and heart of the complex, the Mother Farm its head. Taken together, these images symbolize mankind in harmony with nature, reflecting the resort's philosophy and lifestyle.

The planning process provides a model for environmental analysis, protection, and development suitability focused on the mandate of protecting regional resources. A wide range of natural and cultural resources were analyzed to determine the development's suitability. Special factors contributed to the success of this project: "The form, symbolism and philosophy of the resort design are used in a total marketing concept and graphic identity package. The image of man, flower and butterfly will become synonymous with the resort complex. The resort planning and design process can be replicated by the owner in other recreation ventures. As such the process represents an encompassing philosophy for the owner and his corporation" (*Landscape Architecture* November 1989).

Institutional Projects

Private institutions are a good source of planning and design projects for landscape architects. Private institutions may include foundations, associations, church organizations, private social agencies, youth organizations, museums, zoos, private universities, and many other types of organizations that develop and manage environments for public use. College campus outdoor spaces, museum sculpture gardens, youth camps, and resource management plans for natural areas held by private conservation agencies such as the Audubon Society are projects that may be carried out for private institutional clients.

One of the outstanding design projects in the United States for an institutional client is the urban outdoor space created for the Christian Science Center, headquarters for the First Church of Christ, Scientist, in Boston, Massachusetts. Sasaki Associates, the project landscape architects, worked together with I. M. Pei & Partners, architects, to design the distinct, formal setting for the world headquarters complex. The design motif set by the church was to create a public outdoor space reminiscent of urban European church spaces. The landscape architectural firm and the architectural office transformed the project area from a deteriorated urban environment in the 1960s to a powerful, formal environment that

has a spiritual quality, reminding the user of the power of God.

The center includes a number of buildings that date back to the original Mother Church constructed in 1894. The Christian Science Publishing Society building, a 28-story administrative high-rise structure, a Sunday school building, and a 525-foot colonnaded administrative building are complemented by a 675-foot reflecting pool, an 80-foot-diameter fountain, planters, lawns, gardens, and urban walks and spaces. A bosquet of linden trees serves as a counterpoint to the reflecting pool. Other linden trees are used throughout the site as a unifying element. The overall quality of the complex serves as a high design standard. It is regarded as a classic urban environment that has stood the test of time (*Landscape Architecture* November/December 1987).

The San Diego Zoo's long-range master plan, completed in 1985 by the landscape architecture firm Jones & Jones, represents one type of institutional project—zoo design—significantly enhanced by the contributions of landscape architects. In the last half of the twentieth century, firms such as Jones & Jones of Seattle, Washington, have attempted to "naturalize" zoos by creating realistic habitat environments where the visitor can observe creatures in their natural setting. Wildlife parks are a direct outgrowth of this naturalistic direction in zoo design.

FIGURE 2-24. The reflecting pool and planters of the Christian Science Center, Boston, Massachusetts, designed by Sasaki Associates.

Photograph by David Akiba.

In close coordination with the staff of the San Diego Zoo, the firm of Jones & Jones reorganized the zoo into ten bioclimatic zones, including tundra, savanna, and tropical rain forest. By 1991, four of the naturalistic environments had been constructed: the East African Savanna zone, Tiger River, the Sun Bear Forest, and Gorilla Tropics.

"In Tiger River," according to *Landscape Architecture* (November 1991) "the visitor enters a misty Sumatran rain forest, encountering animals that range from fish and reptiles to web-footed fishing cats and tapirs and, finally, the Sumatran tiger. Water features evolve from mists to trickles, pools and waterfalls. Animal enclosures—made of glass, wire, moats and mesh—blend into the landscape so well that visitors often jump back at the sudden appearance of a tiger on the other side of the barrier. 'They come right down and look at you with their eyes real shiny,' said one delighted opening week visitor. 'They look like they're even going to pounce on you.' "

The profession of landscape architecture has made one of its most lasting contributions to the history of planning and design in the area of campus planning. In modern times, the standard for campus planning was set by the landscape architecture firm Sasaki Walker Associates, of San Francisco, for its plan for Foothill College in Los Altos Hills, California. The firm, with Peter Walker as the project manager, prepared a master plan that included a loop road concept, perimeter parking, site grading, pedestrian walkways, courts, plazas, terraces, and landscaping.

When ASLA awarded the Foothill College master plan a prestigious Classic Award in 1993, *Landscape Architecture* described the college as the most beautiful community college ever built:

[It] represents an early solution to pedestrian/vehicular circulation on a commuter campus. Classrooms and other facilities were located on an "acropolis" created by judicious grading of two hills joined by a

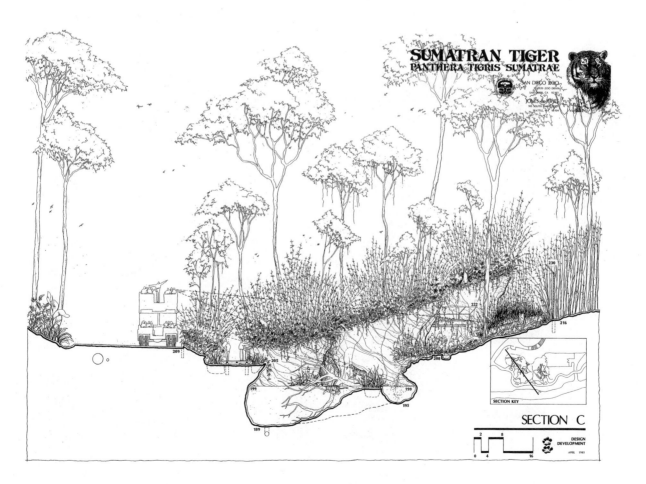

FIGURE 2-25. Illustration of the design concept for the Tiger River Trail designed by Jones & Jones for the San Diego Zoo. Visitors follow a dry-season riverbed pathway that parallels the meandering course of a stream through a tropical canyon.

massive foot bridge. Parking was located at the base of the hills, grade-separated from the pedestrian domain. . . . The acropolis features two types of pedestrian pathways. One is rectilinear, running along the base of the buildings, beneath wide, sheltering eaves that recall the Bay Area's redwood regional style. The other meanders through a series of outdoor spaces, among rolling lawns and subtly graded mounds. California sycamores and birches planted in geometric groves shade the open spaces of the academic village (*Landscape Architecture* November 1993).

The Cullen Entry for the University of Houston is campus design project that received a Merit Award from ASLA in 1989 for its designers, The SWA Group. The University of Houston wanted a new entrance to define the campus edge and create an entry statement in a visually chaotic area of commercial development parallel with an urban freeway on the eastern edge of the campus. The powerful design statement, which features an obelisk split in half and an entry sign wall, is framed by a linear planting of live oaks intended to screen the commercial area and the freeway. The exterior of each half-obelisk is clad in pink granite, and the interior faces are covered with a polished dark-gray granite that gives the illusion that the inside face is hollow, receding from the eye. The entry design combines the familiar perception of an obelisk as a focal point for terminating a view with the updated approach of creating surprise by slicing the obelisk in half. Riding or walking through the entry between the two half-obelisks creates a dynamic tension and a remembered experience for anyone arriving on the campus through this entry point (*Landscape Architecture* November 1989).

FIGURE 2-26. Aerial photograph of the Foothills College acropolis site plan concept.

Photograph copyright by Charles I. Savadelis.

FIGURE 2-27. Rectilinear paths at the base of buildings and curvilinear paths meander through shaded connecting spaces at Foothill College.

Photograph copyright by Charles I. Savadelis.

FIGURE 2-28. The Cullen Entry, showing the split obelisks, designed by The SWA Group for the University of Houston.

Photograph by Tom Fox, courtesy of The SWA Group.

FIGURE 2-29. The Cullen Entry designed by The SWA Group for the University of Houston is adjacent to an urban freeway.

Photograph by Tom Fox, courtesy of The SWA Group.

Single-Family Residential and Garden Design Projects

Many landscape architects focus their professional practice on site planning for single-family residences and garden design. Indeed, this area of professional practice is important enough to the profession of landscape architecture that ASLA publishes a magazine, *Garden Design,* devoted entirely to designing outdoor gardens. Whereas the historical roots of landscape architecture involved extensive design of estate landscapes and gardens before and after the turn of the twentieth century, a number of contemporary landscape architects, such as A. E. Bye, have devel-

oped extensive track records in site design for estates and residential gardens.

A. E. Bye is noted for a style of estate and garden design that combines three schools of landscape design: English landscape gardening, modernism, and the more recent ecological ethic. Bye's minimalist designs involve a high degree of craftsmanship, a simple palette of materials, and a sympathetic relationship to the landscape setting. In his well-known design for the Howard Stein residence in North Salem, New York, completed in the mid-1960s, Bye sliced a pathway around an existing natural bog, incorporating it as a designed feature in the residential garden setting. Bye describes his work in this way:

FIGURE 2-30. The bog landscape preserved and enhanced at the direction of landscape architect A. E. Bye for the Howard Stein residence.

Photograph by A. E. Bye.

Our bog landscape as designed by us required courageous supervision to complete. Before we could do surveys or any construction or necessary clean-up work, we had to rid the place of menacing snakes and snapping turtles, otherwise no laborers would dare enter into the thick mud and ooze. On the first day we encountered 17 snapping turtles, two copperheads, and 27 black snakes. After they were removed without injury, we pulled out tangles of fallen branches, old logs and stumps of long dead trees. Then we filled the edges of the bog with topsoil for foot paths. Little more was done except for placing some large boulders for stepping stones at visual points of interest and introducing more water tolerant plants: marsh marigolds, cattails, cinnamon ferns, winterberry holly (*Ilex verticullata*), highbush blueberry (*Vaccinium corynbosum*), arrowood (*Viburnum dentatum*), Red Osier Dogwood (*Cornus sericea*), and spicebush (*Lindera benzoin*). Also, mountain laurel clumps were planted on higher ground (Bye 1980).

Perhaps the most well known of Bye's residential projects is the Gaines residence and 500-acre Gainesway Farm in Lexington, Kentucky. Bye worked on this project for ten years and designed stables, fences, walls, roads, fountains, gardens, and a stable and barn complex for the Farm's thoroughbred stallions. The signature of the project is a 450-foot ha-ha wall that curves sinuously through a pasture adjacent to the farm buildings. The ha-ha wall is built of masonry construction using limestone field rock with deep joints that make the wall appear as if it were drylaid. Bye, who is also a master landscape photographer, conceived the wall as an intentional landscape art form. The zigzag path of large, rectilinear limestone slabs from the buildings is a contrast in form to the ha-ha wall and other strong forms in the soft, carefully graded pasture landscape.

Bye designed the stallion complex at Gainesway Farm in collaboration with architect Theodore

FIGURE 2-31. The site plan of the stallion barn complex and ha-ha wall designed by landscape architect A. E. Bye for Gainsway Farm in Lexington, Kentucky.

Illustration by A. E. Bye.

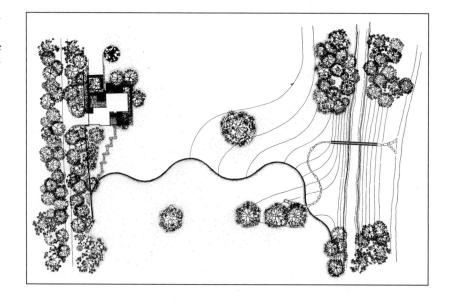

appearing to be a horse trough, serves aesthetic purposes only. The paths around the complex are paved with red brick chips that provide a color contrast to the pasture setting (Howett 1990; Johnson 1991).

Michael Van Valkenburgh Associates designed a unique residential garden, called the Black Granite Garden by *Landscape Architecture* in its 1990 awards issue. To achieve more of a Xeriscape appearance, the residential garden was updated from an existing design

FIGURE 2-32. The snow-covered winter landscape accentuates the timeless design of the ha-ha wall by landscape architect A. E. Bye at Gainsway Farm.

Photograph by A. E. Bye.

Ceraldi. The stallion complex includes eight four-horse barns, a main barn, and a lunging ring. Bye introduced a 172-foot-long water feature that slices through a group of existing oak trees. The water feature includes a number of bubblers, and although

FIGURE 2-33. The ha-ha wall where it joins the perimeter wall at Gainsway Farm.

Photograph by A. E. Bye.

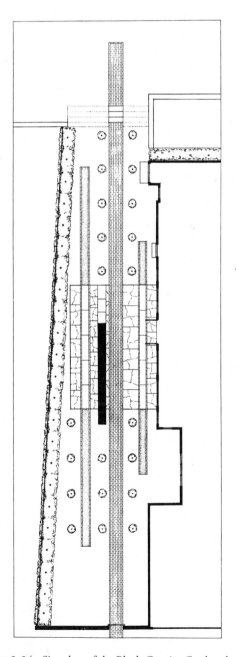

FIGURE 2-34. Site plan of the Black Granite Garden designed by landscape architect Michael Van Valkenburgh.

Plan courtesy of Michael Van Valkenburgh Associates, Inc.

that relied on lush plants. The long, narrow shape of the 2,500-square-foot garden is the foundation of the design, which encourages movement through the space and a feeling of exaggerated perspective. A long, linear path of black manganese bricks slices through the center of the space and is interrupted by a central area paved with dark granite and a water channel accented by horsetail aquatic plants at one end of the channel and a tall black-granite column at the other end. Water drizzles down the face of the black-granite column, wetting the face of the rough-cut rock and contrasting vividly with the still water in the formal channel. Italian cypress trees, planted in a linear format, are the predominant plant material used in the garden. A hedge of clipped ficus trees planted in front of a scrim of galvanized mesh for jasmine and Boston ivy to climb on forms one edge of the space, screening the neighboring house. The residence forms the opposite edge. Side paths of crushed black granite lead to sculpture niches.

Grid-based but asymmetrical, formal yet conservation-minded, the garden strives to be "understated and timeless," say the designers, while embracing "the modern tradition in landscape architecture. A spirit of calm and tranquility was pursued with attention to detail, particularly to the scale of the landscape spaces as [they] related to surface, materials and joinery."

Mentioning the "multitude of spaces, shadows and forms," the jury called the garden "the high art of landscape architecture." . . . This is the landscape architect's opportunity to be a pure artist (*Landscape Architecture* November 1990).

Many client and project opportunities for gardens, including rooftop gardens, sculpture gardens, botanical gardens, and prayer gardens, are not related to single-family residences. Gardens brighten both urban and rural landscapes and provide landscape architects with neat opportunities for professional practice.

The Phoenix Tower Roof Garden sits atop an 8-story parking garage and is viewed from the adjacent 35-story office tower of a Houston, Texas, commercial high-rise complex. The client's design program called for the space to be attractive as viewed from the office tower and also to be inviting for workers to walk into and enjoy. The project, which received an ASLA Merit Award in 1985 for The SWA Group, is viewed as an interesting graphic concept of the application of landscape architecture principles. The plan features the use of red, blue, and black tiles, as well as greens of plant materials and grass, used in geometric planes. Black tiles are used in a grid pattern in a very shallow pool to mirror the geometry of the building's glass window wall.

An open spherical framework constructed of tubular metal is the focal point of the rooftop garden and the place where users go on the walks and the red-tiled naturalistic pathway. A granite-block water feature is located in the center of the sphere and is sur-

FIGURE 2-35. The geometry and materials of the Phoenix Tower Roof Garden, designed by The SWA Group.

Photograph by Tom Fox, courtesy of The SWA Group.

FIGURE 2-36. The Phoenix Tower Roof Garden punctuates the shimmering backdrop of the mirror-glass exterior skin of the building complex.

Photograph by Tom Fox, courtesy of The SWA Group.

rounded by a circular bench. Vines cover the metal framework, which is oriented on axis to a view of the Houston skyline. The project represents a strong design concept in which the naturalistic red-tiled walkway serves as a vivid counterpoint to the geometry of the rooftop garden.

Land and Water Reclamation and Conservation Projects

Since Frederick Law Olmsted's plan for Boston's Back Bay Fens, landscape architects have always been a leading professional force in the reclamation of disturbed landscapes and conservation of open space. Marsh and riparian landscapes, beachfronts and dunes, mines and landfill operations, and logging and agricultural landscapes present a wide range of opportunities for the practice of landscape architecture. Reclamation and conservation projects draw upon the landscape architect's understanding of the interrelationships of natural resources and the dynamic forces of ecology. These projects provide opportunities for landscape architects to assemble and manage teams of ecologists, botanists, wildlife biologists, fisheries experts, archaeologists, and other professionals with expertise in natural and cultural resources to work as interdisciplinary teams so often necessary for reclamation and conservation projects. The clients for reclamation and conservation projects are usually found in the public and quasi-public sector, but private-sector opportunities may exist with mining, logging, and private landfill companies. Private conservation orga-

nizations such as the Sierra Club or The Nature Conservancy may also provide project opportunities.

Centennial Reservoir and Park in Howard County, Maryland, designed for a public-sector client, is an outstanding example of the landscape architect serving as the lead professional to develop a land and water reclamation and conservation project. Centennial Reservoir was envisioned as a flood-control project that also would meet some of the recreational needs of the county's residents. Whereas the flood-control objectives were clear from the start of the project, the recreational objectives for both active and passive recreation were less clearly defined and evolved out of the planning and design process for the park. The landscape architecture firm, LDR International, was responsible for the master plan, design development, and construction documents. The project received a Merit Award from ASLA in 1989.

The master plan for Centennial Park included five project objectives:

1. To provide, within the capacities of the site, a variety of recreational opportunities, both active and passive, for the country as a whole
2. To set aside a portion of the site as a natural reserve zone in which vegetation and wildlife communities can continue to function with as little disturbance as possible
3. To create the opportunity for establishing a nature study program, with areas set aside for field experiments, including reforestation,

FIGURE 2-37. Park users walk through knee-high grass and observe meadows that are allowed to revert back to woodlands at Centennial Park in Howard County, Maryland.

Photograph courtesy of LDR International, Inc.

FIGURE 2-38. Canoers glide through the headwaters of the reservoir at Centennial Park in Howard County, Maryland.

Photograph courtesy of LDR International, Inc.

FIGURE 2-39. The pedestrian bridge linking the north and south sides of the shoreline at the west end of the reservoir at Centennial Park in Howard County, Maryland.

Photograph courtesy of LDR International, Inc.

FIGURE 2-40. A snack shop, comfort station, and boat launch at Centennial Park in Howard County, Maryland.
Photograph courtesy of LDR International, Inc.

habitat enhancement, and water quality and erosion control

4. To establish a development program with the flexibility to change its emphasis or direction should the needs of the community change

5. To determine the role of Centennial Park as one of several regionally oriented park sites along the stream valley of the Little Patuxent River, and to explore what opportunities the stream valley, acting as a natural spine, presents for linkages with schools, residential neighborhoods, and other recreational facilities

The site for Centennial Park lies in the path of urban development that is consuming the agricultural landscape and farms of Howard County. Today Centennial Park is surrounded by urban growth, and the park's landscape architects sought to preserve the 336-acre site as a microcosm of the regional landscape, vegetation communities, and wildlife habitats. "The landscape architect designed a place where future generations of county residents would be able to walk to a meadowland habitat, to experience firsthand the succession from fields to woods, to enjoy the edge habitat between hedgerow and field and to experience the diversity of a farm pond community. . . . Farm fields are being permitted to progress through the natural succession without manipulation; reservoir design and construction emphasized habitat creation, with varying depths and edge treatments; active recreational

areas are limited to edge parcels adjacent to residential development; and community participation during the planning process and in ongoing program development has helped to assure widespread support for the park" (*Landscape Architecture* November 1989).

LDR International divided the park master plan into three theme zones: natural reserve areas, day-use sites, and organized sports fields. The park serves as a living laboratory of the transition of farmland to woodland vegetation. It also meets a wide range of active and passive recreational activities, including water-based recreation.

In 1978, a group of Ohio zoo administrators conceived an ambitious reclamation project designed to transform a 9,154-acre reclaimed coal mine into a conservation facility for endangered animals. Known as The Wilds, the site, which looks more like Africa than central Ohio, is planned to hold as many as one hundred endangered species on its rolling grasslands. The Wilds will serve two groups of users: wildlife biologists and other experts who will study the animals, and tourists. The design team, which included the Portico Group, a Seattle landscape architecture and architecture firm; Robert W. Teater & Associates, the project's senior advisor; the architecture firm of Feinknopf, Macioce, Schappa; the engineering firm of Burgess & Niple, Ltd.; and the Artist/Designer Advisory Planning Team (ADAPT) faced a challenge in developing a plan for the site. The original owner of the site, the Central Ohio Coal Company, reclaimed the coal mining operations to federal standards in the

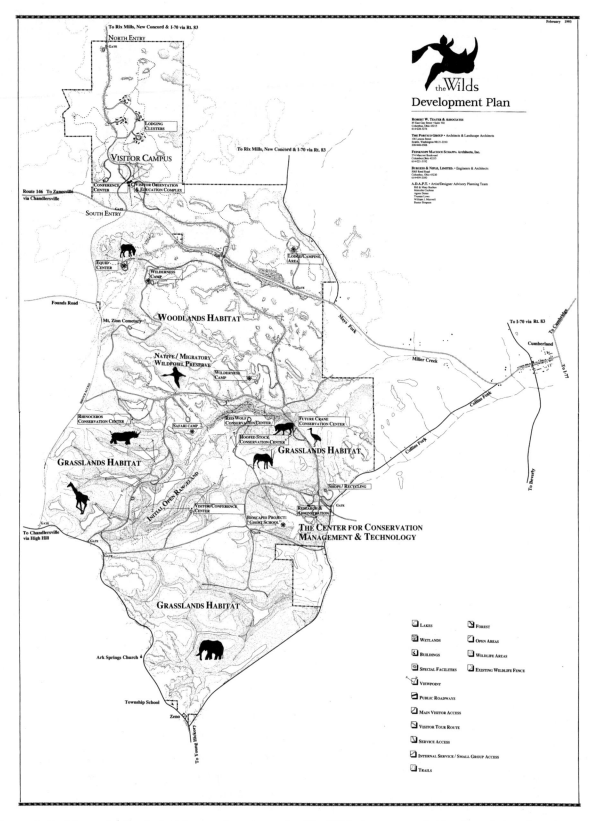

FIGURE 2-41. Master plan for the 9,154-acre reclamation project The Wilds that preserves habitat for endangered species.
Plan courtesy of The Portico Group.

1960s and 1970s. The reclamation project resulted in a contoured landscape dotted with retention ponds that was visually different from the existing terrain. The northern third of the site was revegetated with trees and the southern two-thirds are largely grasslands, creating a suitable habitat for imported grazing animals such as the scimitar-horned orix, the Hartmann mountain zebra, and Przewalski's Asian wild horse.

When the Central Ohio Coal Company gave the site to The Wilds in 1986, planners and landscape architects began developing a master plan that would ultimately be best for the animal species in terms of food and breeding. Ongoing management and development of the facility deal with the complicated issues of preserving habitat while providing access for tourists. Access roads are being sited where possible to avoid impacts on views, and problems with subsidence are causing the relocation of some of the planned facilities. Despite ongoing land management issues, The Wilds is a successful and very ambitious reclamation project (Roberts 1993).

The project increases by 60 percent the space available nationwide for breeding endangered animals. Behavioral, nutritional, and reproductive research conducted at The Wilds to enhance breeding success among endangered animals, combined with a natural, open environment, will provide the endangered species the most favorable setting in which to survive.

Interior Landscape Architecture

A small yet very visible sector of landscape architectural practice is involved with design of interior spaces and enhancement of spaces with plant materials. Firms and professionals that specialize in interior landscape architecture deal with climate-controlled spaces, natural or artificial light conditions for plant growth, and maintenance issues. Plant materials need to be selected carefully for interior plantings. They must be able to grow under artificial conditions and often need to remain a certain height or size due to interior space limitations. Atriums, lobbies, shopping malls, airports, conservatories, and indoor walkways that link buildings and building complexes all provide opportunities for interior landscape architecture.

The Fountain Court is an entry-court atrium designed by The SWA Group for a rehabilitated National Register building that once served as the headquarters of the Curtis Publishing Company in Philadelphia, Pennsylvania. This project, which received an ASLA Design Award in 1987, involved the transformation of an interior service court into a public arrival space that is rich in detail, providing a human scale to the floor level of the eleven-story interior space. The atrium features four design elements: (1) an intricate marble floor pattern, (2) a marble fountain, (3) plant materials, and (4) various plant containers.

The floor pattern emanates from the fountain and comprises six colors of polished marble pavers running at a 45-degree angle to the centerline of the space. The floor pattern continues into and through the fountain structure, which is designed as a soft, sinuous shape in 9-inch lifts altering the perception of

FIGURE 2-42. Original watercolor plan for the Fountain Court, designed by The SWA Group.

Photograph by Tom Fox, courtesy of The SWA Group.

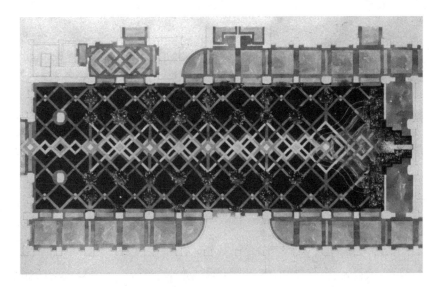

FIGURE 2-43. The Fountain Court, designed by The SWA Group.

Photograph by Tom Fox, courtesy of The SWA Group.

the marble as a hard material. The spray fountain is shaped like a slot and notched into a series of symmetrical dark-green marble planters with Chinese evergreen plants.

Three main types of plant containers are used in the space. Large pots are placed on top of 28-foot and 35-foot pedestals arranged in double rows on each side of the atrium. Dried areca palm fronds are wired into the pots, resulting in a design element that is palm-like but that will always retain its original controlled size, color, and height. Large, 5-foot-tall urns located between the palm pedestals are planted with live spathiphyllum plants. Sconces that repeat the areca palm-frond motif are mounted on the walls of the interior space (*Landscape Architecture* November/December 1987).

A 1991 ASLA award-winning interior project was completed by the San Francisco landscape architecture firm Schwartz/Smith/Meyer for a building that houses the Becton Dickinson Immunocytrometry Division in San Jose, California. The indoor site is a two-story walkway that is 25 feet wide and 475 feet long. The glass-roofed space serves as an interior connecting corridor and informal meeting space for the building's occupants. The landscape architects designed a series of geometric hedges constructed of wood lattice painted white and planted with vines. The hedges are used to enclose blue-tiled fountains in which yellow spheres called "spitting balls" serve as the source of water streamers. Orange-tiled cylindrical planters

filled with snake plant contrast with the blue fountains. A linear planting of fishtail palms reinforces movement through the space and provides a pedestrian scale element in the two-story atrium. The colors and patterns of this interior garden space create a strong design statement that relies more on hard materials than plants to attract users (*Landscape Architecture* November 1991).

The Regis Gardens conservatory in Minneapolis, Minnesota, provides an entry feature for the Walker Art Center and the adjacent Minneapolis Sculpture Garden. The landscape architecture firm Michael Van Valkenburgh Associates designed the entire garden, including paving, garden furniture, plantings, and vine scrims. The firm also provided technical support to the architect for climate control.

The topiary arches required the designers to invent a technology, which was done collaboratively with a local greenhouse. The 16-foot-tall arches were made with a stainless steel superstructure, covered with non-ultraviolet degradable plastic mesh, filled with structurally divided horizontal layers of growing medium, irrigated with an internal drip system and planted with creeping fig at four-inch staggered centers. Experiments investigating the growth response of the ficus to variations of soil mix and irrigation were conducted over a year and included testing 34 variations of soil mix (*Landscape Architecture* November 1989).

FIGURE 2-44. The "topiary arches" designed by landscape architect Michael Van Valkenburgh for the Regis Gardens' Cowles Conservatory.

Courtesy of Michael Van Valkenburgh Associates, Inc.

Historic Preservation and Restoration Projects

A specialized and growing area of landscape architecture client and project opportunities is landscape preservation and restoration. Historic landscapes are cultural resources that are important local, state, or national assets. Historical landscapes reflect the ways people have used specific sites related to occupation, subsistence, recreation, or cultural pursuits, and they reveal much about our relationship with nature. Historic landscapes include residential gardens, parks, scenic routes, explorer's routes, settler's routes, parkways, arboretums, zoos, cemeteries, residential areas, towns, villages, industrial sites, college campuses, waterfronts, and many other segments of the culturally shaped landscape. Opportunities for landscape architects include historic inventories and surveys, as well as preservation, rehabilitation, restoration, and reconstruction plans. Clients may be private or public; projects may be small or large. Whatever the size of the project, attention to detail, authenticity, and thoroughness are key elements of the successful historic landscape project.

A plan for restoration and use of Stan Hywet Hall in Akron, Ohio, was prepared by Child Associates, Inc., in 1984 and received an ASLA award for historic preservation and restoration in 1987. The estate was the vision of Frank A. Seiberling, founder of the Goodyear Rubber Company, who hired early landscape architect Warren Manning in 1911 to develop the plans for the 4,000-acre estate. Manning located the house on a ridge to take advantage of views to the rolling hills, forests, and farmlands of the surrounding rural landscape.

When Child Associates began the project, only two of Manning's extensive number of drawings for the estate were recovered, so the landscape architects had to reconstruct much of what the estate was like regarding design intent and plant materials from correspondence between Seiberling and Manning between the years of 1911 and 1928. The landscape architects were able to define the original design objectives, which included grand spatial composition, construction of long vistas, large-scale plant massing, use of native plant materials, and use of small-scale, formal outdoor rooms often introduced in natural settings on the site. The master plan's three main objectives were to (1) identify Manning's original design using the sketchy historic information that was available, (2) document existing site conditions, and (3) develop a restoration plan that featured Manning's original design intent but also accommodated the site's public use today as a cultural center for residents of the Akron area. The consultant also developed restoration priorities, funding strategies, and plans for present and future use. The successful master plan resulted in restoration of three major vistas and the intimate breakfast garden designed by Manning (*Landscape Architecture* November/December 1987).

Adaptive reuse of sites and buildings is another approach that landscape architects may take on behalf of their clients. The landscape architecture firm Johnson, Johnson & Roy, Inc., in collaboration with architects William Kessler & Associates, used adaptive reuse as their approach for the site planning and design of the Kresge Foundation headquarters in Troy, Michigan. The landscape architects retained much of the existing farm setting, including windmills and silos, and reinforced the nineteenth-century character with historically sensitive plant materials and a small orchard. A 10,000-square-foot addition to the building mass was designed to match the character of the existing structures. The new buildings, parking lots,

FIGURE 2-45. The great lawn at historic
Stan Hywet Hall.

Photograph by Alan Ward.

and current uses were introduced to the site without destroying the visual qualities of the historic site (*Landscape Architecture* September/October 1986).

Some historic landscape preservation activities are very important, serving as archival examples of the work of early landscape architects. Such is the work of Walmsley & Company (now Tourbier & Walmsley) with Charles Birnbaum in developing a plan to preserve and maintain the 20-acre Springside National Historic Landscape Site.

Springside is the central area of the Matthew Vassar Ornamental Farm, designed by Andrew Jackson Downing between 1850 and 1852. Downing is considered by many landscape historians to be the greatest American landscape theorist after Jefferson and before Olmsted. The site, outside Poughkeepsie, New York, may be the only existing authentic work of Downing's to survive today in the United States. The site was described in 1857 as a lasting monument to Downing's genius, to the management capability of its horticultur-

FIGURE 2-46. The new buildings at the
Kresge Foundation were designed to be
in character with the existing farm
buildings without overpowering them.

*Photograph courtesy of Johnson, Johnson
and Roy, Inc.*

alist, Caleb Bement, and to the vision and taste of its owner, Mathew Vassar, the founder of Vassar College. The plan for Springside's preservation and upkeep communicates the significant contribution of each man.

Preparation of the preservation plan, managed by Walmsley and Birnbaum, included specialists in architecture, horticulture, archaeology, landscape management, greenhouse operations, and history. An archaeological survey of buildings, driveways, water supply system, and vegetation revealed the extent of subsurface resources and the need for a systematic program of test pits, trenches, sonar, and infrared investigations. A horticultural analysis rated the existing vegetation by age, species, and condition. Architectural consultants examined the three surviving Downing structures, and a wood preservation specialist made proposals for immediately arresting further deterioration. The planning process included a comparison of existing site features and vegetation with historic paintings, engravings, and plant lists to determine authenticity. An important aspect of the plan is a maintenance concept intended to retain the form of the site and its details true to the work of Downing and Bement. (*Landscape Architecture* November 1989).

Landscape Art and Earth Sculpture

One of the fastest growing segments of landscape architecture practice in the last quarter of the twentieth century has been the introduction of art in the landscape and the notion that the designed outdoor environment can be art in and of itself. Landscape architects are collaborating with artists and working independently as land sculptors or using materials to paint the landscape surfaces they create as if the ground plain were a large canvas. The historical roots of this area of professional practice can be found in the work of Brazilian landscape architect Roberto Burle Marx, who gained a widespread reputation in the 1950s and 1960s by using colorful plant materials and pavements to "paint" his landscape creations. More recently the San Francisco firm Hargreaves and Associates has developed a reputation for creative collaboration with artists, resulting in projects with sculpted earth forms and colorful use of plant and paving materials. The firm also uses surprise in the environment, like the fountain at Plaza Park in downtown San Jose, California, to delight and intrigue the users of public outdoor spaces. The Plaza Park fountain is a paved surface with twenty-two jets that spout water at the intersections of a glass block grid. The entire fountain area can be walked through and has become a delightful water play area for children and adults alike (*Landscape Architecture* November 1993).

The Plaza Park project represents the rebirth of a historic urban park in the heart of a city that is itself in the midst of a commercial and cultural renaissance. The goal of the project was to reassert a public open space as the principal focus for downtown San Jose. The 3.5-acre park links together the expanded art museum, the Fairmont Hotel, and the downtown

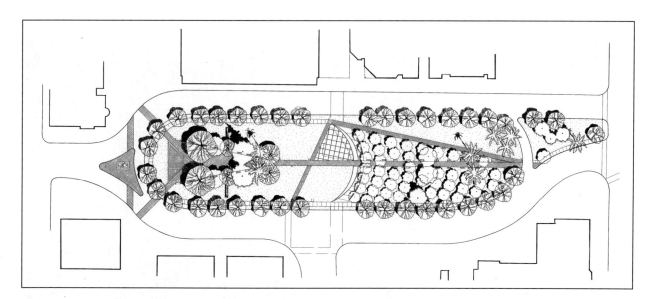

FIGURE 2-47. Site plan of San Jose's Plaza Park.

convention center. Park Plaza occupies the oldest open-space site in San Jose on ground that has been important since the city's beginning as a pueblo. Metaphorical references to the city's rich past and bright future were layered into the design of the park.

A grid of jacaranda trees recalls the almond and prune orchards of the region's rich agricultural past. The glass-block grid of the fountain alludes to the recent high-tech development of Silicon Valley. The axial central promenade traces the route of historic Monterey Road, the Camino Real that linked San Jose with the California missions. At the north end, the promenade splays into a V-shaped plaza before a granite stage. The V shape is reinforced by a stand of mature redwoods. These angled green walls create a foreshortening of perspective in the informal outdoor stage area.

Placed asymmetrically to the central spine, the fountain tells a story of San Jose's climatic, geological, and cultural history. Inspired by artesian wells discovered near the site in the 1800s, the fountain traces the water cycle through the course of a day. In the morning, the fountain produces a fine mist, like the fog that rolls onto the valley floor from the bay. As the day warms, the mist turns to a bubbling spray that slowly gives way to the grid of jets that start low and build to ample columns. The splashing jets are meant to recall the artesian wells of the pueblo era. By night the fountain's glass-block grid glows a cool green from below. The columns of water become columns of light. Throughout all hours of day and night, the fountain, which is at the same grade as the surrounding walks and lawns, provides completely unrestricted access to water.

The success of the Plaza Park project can be gauged by the overwhelming public acceptance and use of the park. On any day, the park can be found teeming with people. The fountain has become something of a local swimming hole for children and adults. On hot summer afternoons, people travel to the park from surrounding neighborhoods and beyond to cool off in its splashing columns of water. The city uses the park for numerous special events and festivals, including the transformation of the park into a wintry scene during the year-end holiday season.

Another of Hargreaves Associates landscape art pieces is Guadalupe Gardens, also in San Jose. This 4-acre courtyard garden is the first cell in a large network of public gardens totalling about 200 acres near downtown San Jose. The gardens will occupy a site within San Jose International Airport's approach zone adjacent to Guadalupe River Park. The planning and design of Guadalupe Gardens and the Guadalupe River Park are integrated and coordinated, taking advantage of the opportunity to create several hundred acres of open space within the city of San Jose. The setting, which was residential at one time, has been reclaimed for public open space due to its proximity to the airport.

The master plan for Guadalupe Gardens recognizes preexisting street grid patterns. The flowing lines of the passing river extend into the gardens from the

FIGURE 2-48. The Plaza Park fountain at day.

Courtesy of Hargreaves Associates.

FIGURE 2-49. The Plaza Park fountain at night.
Courtesy of Hargreaves Associates.

riverbank in the form of three-dimensional elements and meandering walks. The structural design concept of Guadalupe Gardens expresses the confluence of the river with the urban fabric of San Jose. The master plan includes a garden center for lectures, club meetings, and workshops; 9 acres of informal, naturalistic woodland gardens planted with wildflowers, perennials, and meadow grasses; rivulets that represent fragmented pieces of the Guadalupe River, recalling the sloughs once found on the site; play fields; and 40 acres of commercial gardens to be leased to flower and seed growers. Fifty acres of Guadalupe Gardens will be developed as courtyard gardens, following the remnants of the street grid pattern. The courtyard gardens are planned as modular cells accommodating a variety of garden styles and facilitating a variety of uses. Each courtyard can be built as a complete phase of the overall development.

In the first courtyard garden designed by Hargreaves Associates, San Jose's rich agricultural heritage, as well as natural phenomena unique to the region, are reflected metaphorically. Large earth forms mimic the surrounding foothills, stretching like fingers into the center of the garden, with flowering cherry trees and mustard drifting up the valleys. The playful pattern of the decomposed granite paths is reminiscent of the flow of the nearby river. Paths meander through the valleys, meet and intertwine like streams on a delta, spreading out in the form of an expanded fishnet across a colorful plane of native annuals and perennials. Wandering among the beds of California native

wildflowers, one can revisit the Garden City, as San Jose was once known, and encounter distinct pods of flowers planted thematically. One entrance is framed by a mass of fragrant perennials; other pods are planted with native ground covers, daylilies, roses,

FIGURE 2-50. Site plan and elevation of San Jose's Guadalupe Gardens, designed by Hargreaves Associates.
Courtesy of Hargreaves Associates.

periwinkles, statice, and spring bulbs with sweet alyssum. Smaller maintenance paths further subdivide the fishnet pattern, dividing each pod into smaller beds. Participation of community garden clubs has been a key to completing the park plantings and maintaining them.

A grass-covered cone marks the center of the courtyard. It is a focal point for passersby. The cone provides a vantage point for off-site views to San Jose, the nearby foothills, and the patterns of the courtyard plantings. This grass mound also provides exciting views of the undersides of airplanes that pass overhead, seemingly almost within reach on their descent to the runway. The courtyard garden is also a visual landmark from the air. Curving hedges frame the cone, and four concrete walks form a discontinuous cruciform, recalling the orthogonal pattern of the once-subdivided property. The gardens are meant to arouse curiosity, inviting the visitor to linger and stroll about this gentle allegory of the surrounding California landscape.

Architectural and Engineering Professionals

The architectural and engineering (A/E) community is one of the largest sources of clients and project opportunities available to landscape architecture firms. Landscape architects working for A/E firms typically work as subconsultants. The connections with A/E firms, however, may lead to opportunities for the landscape architecture firm to contract directly with a third-party client. In some cases, the A/E firm may not want the administrative responsibility and professional liability exposure associated with a subcontract and will request that the landscape architecture firm contract directly with the client.

The A/E community in general is one of the easiest client and market sectors for the landscape architecture firm to penetrate. Because collaborative professional relationships are necessary for carrying out almost all development projects, members of the A/E community, including landscape architects, enjoy professional relationships that, if maintained, are normally cooperative and beneficial. Members of the A/E community speak a similar language. Therefore developing client relationships with architects and engineers is easy. Friction may occur in crossover areas of professional services, such as site planning, because architects, landscape architects, and civil engineers all have expertise in site planning. Site grading is another

crossover area where each of these A/E professionals has expertise. Building A/E client relationships is an important part of professional practice opportunities for almost all landscape architecture offices.

Architects

For any firm of landscape architects just starting out, and usually throughout the firm's business life, architects are a major source of clients, especially for those landscape architecture firms oriented to traditional private-practice areas that include site planning, site amenity design, grading, planting design, and irrigation design. Architects not only serve directly as a landscape architect's client, but also are one of the best sources of other private- and public-sector clients. The architect may decide not to engage the landscape architect as a subconsultant on a project for which the architect is serving as prime. The architect may wish to maintain a professional working relationship with the landscape architect, directing or coordinating the landscape architect's role, but refer the landscape architect directly to the client for the contractual relationship. This allows the landscape architect to nurture a professional relationship directly with the client, who may develop future projects with or without the architecture firm that provided the initial referral of the landscape architect.

Developing architecture firms as clients is one of the easier client markets for the landscape architect to penetrate. The professional working relationship between architect and the landscape architect is well established and time tested. Architects as a client group are easy to make contact with through professional organizations. They often travel in the same professional and business circles that landscape architects do. Contact with the landscape architecture firm is frequently initiated by the architecture firm when the need for landscape architecture services occurs on a project that the architecture firm already has under contract. Once the initial contact is made by an architecture firm, the landscape architects are in a good position to nurture and develop the A/E client relationship.

Civil Engineers

Another allied profession that provides very good client opportunities for the landscape architect is civil engineering. Although civil engineers often serve in subconsulting roles, providing grading, drainage, and utility design as their part of a project design team led by an architect or a landscape architect, civil engineers also provide prime-consulting services for several types of projects, resulting in professional opportunities for landscape architects. Planning and designing roads and highways is the most important type of project where the civil engineers frequently serve as a prime consultant, and where subconsulting opportunities are available for the landscape architect. Visual and environmental assessment for corridor planning, highway beautification, landscaping, and highway impact mitigation have historically been areas of professional involvement for the landscape architect. Transportation planning, which is often carried out by civil engineers with specific training and experience in all types of transportation planning, including mass transit, provides additional subconsulting opportunities for the landscape architecture firm.

Generally speaking, civil engineers, like architects, are an easy client market for landscape architects to penetrate. The rewards can be big, too; rehabilitating our highway infrastructure and building new transit and other public transportation systems will require high levels of public spending in years to come. In the client relationship between landscape architects and civil engineers, the role of the landscape architect is usually focused on environmental assessment, urban design, planting, and irrigation design.

Structural, Electrical, and Mechanical Engineers

Although not as important as architects and civil engineers as a source of contracts for the landscape architect, structural, mechanical, and electrical engineers may provide occasional subconsulting opportunities. A structural engineer, for example, may obtain a prime contract to design a new bridge, which could lead to environmental assessment and landscape design opportunities for the landscape architecture firm. Structural, electrical, and mechanical engineers also may provide referral opportunities for the landscape architect. Landscape architects also need to develop and nurture relationships with these three engineering disciplines for those times when the landscape architect requires their services on a project.

Planners and Environmental Consultants

Another source of subconsulting and consulting opportunities can be found in professional relationships with planners and environmental consultants. Because many of the services provided by planners and environmental consultants are crossover services also provided by landscape architects, the best opportunities for client development may be in the formation of consulting teams with these allied professionals to serve private- and public-sector clients. Networking is the key to developing professional relationships with planning and environmental assessment firms.

Corporations: For-Profit and Not-for-Profit

Corporations are one of the best sources of clients and projects for landscape architecture firms. Local companies that develop buildings and physical plants, or national franchise developers such as McDonald's, Home Depot, Wal-Mart, Exxon, Hilton Hotels, or Hyatt-Regency, need landscape architecture services. A landscape architect may develop corporate clients by direct contact or by working in a subconsulting relationship with another A/E firm. Landscape architecture firms have had a wide range of opportunities to design corporate headquarters, including high-profile corporate campuses for large companies, as well as smaller facilities for local businesses. Corporate facilities frequently provide outstanding design opportunities because high-profile developments are a way for corporations to present a successful image to the community. Expensive, well-designed corporate facilities are regarded as a sign of a successful company.

Not-for-profit corporations are developers of a wide variety of facilities providing opportunities for landscape architects. Some not-for-profit corporations also focus on preservation and conservation activities providing environmental assessment opportunities for landscape architects. Direct contact by phone or in person with the executive director, property development director, or conservation director of nonprofit corporations is one of the best ways to establish a professional relationship with the nonprofit corporate client. Responding to RFPs (requests for proposals) solicited by not-for-profit corporations is another good way to develop a client relationship.

Public-Sector Clients

The public sector provides equally as much client and project opportunity as the private sector. Many landscape architecture firms have clients in both the private and the public sectors, which helps balance the firm's workload, providing stability if work in one sector is slower than the other sector.

There are three primary public-sector clients:

1. The federal government
2. State governments
3. Local governments including municipal, county, and metropolitan agencies

One of the positive and helpful aspects of securing government work and public-sector clients is that most public work today is awarded on the basis of a qualifications-based open selection process advertised through an RFP. Public works RFPs, regardless of the level of government, are announced via public notices, usually published in a newspaper or other public notification medium such as on-line computer services. The public announcement of prospective projects makes it easy for the landscape architecture firm to follow the news media and be aware of opportunities for public works projects. The downside of this public announcement process is that many projects will have large numbers of firms submitting a proposal for the work. The other aspect of the public works selection process that must be considered by the landscape architecture firm is the cost, both in time and in direct out-of-pocket expenses, associated with submitting a proposal to try to secure a public contract. The public submittal process usually involves preparing a statement of qualifications, preparing for an interview if the firm is short-listed, and conducting the actual interview and contract negotiation if the firm is selected for the project. Each of these phases can be costly, with no guarantee that the contract will be secured. Some selection processes even add further steps and additional costs, such as preparing a technical proposal.

Because the public works selection process is highly competitive, if a firm's track record is directly related to the project requirements, the odds are better for securing the work. Public servants are accountable for their decisions on hiring consultants and must ensure that the firm hired has the experience necessary to provide the best possible public services at the lowest price. The key to securing work through the RFP selection process is convincing public officials that the firm is specifically qualified and has the most related track record for the advertised project. Specialized

track records also allow a landscape architecture firm to develop relationships with the decision makers of public agencies in the firm's areas of expertise and sometimes to circumvent the selection process because no other firm may have as much experience at solving a specific design, planning, or environmental problem. The downside of specialized public-sector experience occurs when no projects are available in the firm's specialty area. The public sector offers a very large market to landscape architecture firms, and almost all firms have at one time or another developed public-sector clients.

Federal Clients

A larger number of federal agencies are sources of work for landscape architecture firms. Although this book cannot cover all of the opportunities for procuring federal public works projects, those agencies that have been the major sources of landscape architecture contracts will be discussed.

Commerce Business Daily

Procurement of federal services is publicized daily in the U.S. government publication *The Commerce Business Daily* (CBD). *The Commerce Business Daily* is ordered from the Government Printing Office and is available in daily and weekly printed versions and also through on-line computer access. The CBD is available in a wide variety of procurement codes that includes A/E services. To find out what federal project opportunities are available to the landscape architecture firm, the CBD needs to be scanned on a regular basis.

Standard Forms 254 and 255

The primary method of applying for federal work is via the Standard Form 254 (SF254) and the Standard Form 255 (SF255). These forms were introduced by the federal government to standardize the consultant selection process.

Standard Form 254 is updated by all A/E and landscape architecture firms on an annual basis and provides the federal agency an overview of each firm's capabilities and size. The form has blanks to fill in providing information on the number of employees, the types of projects completed by the firm, the location of the main office and branch offices, and the general level of revenue for the firm over the last five-year period. Standard Form 254 allows each firm to list up to thirty projects it has completed in a wide variety of project profile codes.

Standard Form 255 is used to provide specific information related to the project for which the firm is submitting its qualifications. There are ten sections of information requested in the SF255:

SECTION	INFORMATION
1–5	Blanks to write in the title of the actual project announced in the CBD, the date of the announcement, and general information such as the name of the firm.
6	Information about subconsultants that will be used by the submitting firm.
7	Résumés of the firm's key staff.
8	Up to ten examples of specifically related prior projects.
9	Current federal work in progress.
10	A statement of the firm's general capabilities and resources available to complete the work.

The combination of the SF254 for general information about the firm and the SF255 for specific project-related information are the two main submittals required for procuring federal work. As with most public works selection processes, federal selection usually includes a shortlist of firms selected from all of the submittals. The shortlisted firms will be interviewed and a final selection made by the agency. Contract negotiation occurs after the selection process is complete.

Landscape Architecture Opportunities for Federal Clients

The federal agencies or departments that have provided the most opportunities for landscape architecture firms include the following:

National Park Service
National Forest Service
Federal Highway Administration
Environmental Protection Agency
Department of Defense
Department of Housing and Urban Development
Office of Americans with Disabilities

There are many other federal agencies, too numerous to discuss in detail, that have also provided landscape architecture opportunities. Some of these agencies are:

Bureau of Reclamation
Bureau of Surface Mining Reclamation and Enforcement
United States Fish and Wildlife Service
Bureau of Indian Affairs
Department of Agriculture
Soil Conservation Service
Federal Aviation Administration
Urban Mass Transportation Administration
Department of Veterans Affairs

National Park Service

Established under the Department of the Interior in 1916, the National Park Service (NPS) administers the nation's extensive system of national parks, monuments, historic sites, and recreation areas. The NPS is charged with administering the properties under its jurisdiction for the enjoyment and education of U.S. citizens, protecting the natural environment of the parks, preserving historic sites of national importance, and assisting states, local governments, and citizens groups in the development of park areas.

The NPS has a service center in Denver, Colorado, that provides planning, architectural, engineering, and other professional services, including landscape architecture services. There are ten regional offices of the NPS and a center for the production of interpretive exhibits, audiovisual materials and publications in Harpers Ferry, West Virginia. There are more than 350 properties in the NPS, including national parks and monuments, scenic parkways, river ways, seashores, lakeshores, recreation areas, reservoirs, and historic sites.

The NPS also administers the following programs: the state portion of the Land and Water Conservation Fund, state comprehensive outdoor recreation planning, technical assistance and planning for the National Wild and Scenic Rivers Program, the National Trails Program, the National Register of Historic Places, the Historic American Buildings Survey, and interagency archaeological services. The National Park Service presides over a large number of land and water resources that provide tremendous opportunities for landscape architecture work.

EDAW, Inc., participated in a challenging project aimed at protecting Florida's Everglades National Park. This national park and the Loxahatchee National Wildlife Refuge contain world-class examples of biologically rich and unique ecosystems. The survival of these natural resources is threatened by the inflow of nutrient-laden water from a system of canals and levees managed by the Southern Florida Water Management District (SFWMD). The water that threatens the park and refuge originates as irrigation runoff from adjacent agricultural lands of 700,000 acres in size. The irrigation runoff, which drains off the fields and runs through locks and canals to the park and refuge, has impacted—perhaps irreversibly—the natural balance of the protected ecosystems.

Responding to this problem, the U.S. Department of Justice filed suit requiring the SFWMD and the Florida Department of Environmental Regulation to meet statutory water-quality standards for water entering the park and refuge. The thrust of the Department of Justice's legal arguments involved establishing cause-and-effect relationships and interpreting highly technical data and concepts from the study of biological science. EDAW was engaged to use its graphic and interpretive skills for developing courtroom exhibits to interpret and communicate the detailed and complex work of expert witnesses used by the Department of Justice. After completing extensive research on the ecosystems and watershed management issues related to the park and refuge, EDAW managed a series of workshops and one-on-one sessions with the expert witnesses to serve as the background for developing more than fifty presentation boards used to convey the scientific and technical information to a lay court. Although EDAW's client was not directly the National Park Service, the firm's work contributed significantly to the decision making for protecting the natural resource base of a precious national park (Miyakoda 1994).

U.S. Forest Service

The Forest Service was created by the Transfer Act of February 1, 1905, which transferred the federal forest reserves and the responsibility for their management from the Department of the Interior to the Department of Agriculture. The protection and development of the forest reserves are governed by the Organic Act of 1897, the Multiple Use–Sustained Yield Act of 1960, the Forest and Range Land Renewable Resources Act of 1974, and the National Forest Management Act of 1976.

The Forest Service has the federal responsibility for national leadership in forestry and stewardship of the national forests. First among the Forest Service objectives is to provide a sustained flow of renewable resources—outdoor recreation, forage, wood, water, wilderness, wildlife, and fish—in a combination that best meets the needs of society now and in the future. The Forest Service objectives have been guided by a multiple-use philosophy, and the development of plans to achieve multiple use of the national forests has provided much work for landscape architects in the twentieth century. In addition, picnic, camping, water sports, scenic drives, skiing, and other outdoor recreation areas developed by the Forest Service have led to planning and design opportunities for landscape architects.

An outstanding landscape architecture project carried out by a private consulting firm for the U.S. Forest Service is the plan for the Mount Saint Helens visitor facilities in the Gifford Pinchot National Forest in southwest Washington. The design team, closely coordinated by Forest Service staff, was led by the Seattle office of EDAW, Inc., and included the architecture firm Spencer Associates of Palo Alto, California. Design of the Coldwater Ridge Visitor Center was the first major project completed in the landscape devastated by the volcano's eruption in 1980.

The Coldwater Ridge Visitor Center is located within the landscape setting that was leveled by the blast from the nearby crater. This setting of ashes, dry mudflows, rocks hurled from the gut of the crater, and gray carcasses of trees snapped off at the base of the trunk by the more than 600-mile-per-hour winds and instantly weathered by the searing heat from the volcano resembles a lunar landscape more than any earthly counterpart. Recognizing the unprecedented opportunity to develop this site for tourism, recreation and scientific study, the Forest Service launched the design effort for access and development of visitor facilities and interpretive programs with the first visitors arriving at the Coldwater Ridge Visitor Center in 1993.

The central goal of the design team was preservation of the landscape setting while introducing the visitor center, parking areas, trails, viewing platforms, and support facilities into the fragile landscape and

FIGURE 2-51. The entrance to the
Coldwater Ridge National Volcanic
Monument.

Photograph courtesy of EDAW, Inc.

FIGURE 2-52. Arrival drive and setting
of the Coldwater Ridge National Volcanic Monument.

Photograph courtesy of EDAW, Inc.

FIGURE 2-53. Observation deck and
setting of the Coldwater Ridge National
Volcanic Monument.

Photograph courtesy of EDAW, Inc.

FIGURE 2-54. Landscape reconstruction at the Coldwater Ridge National Volcanic Monument.

Photograph courtesy of EDAW, Inc.

preserving the environment as a laboratory for scientific studies. Tree blowdowns, boulder "bombs," and ground-plane materials, including the plating of ash from the volcano eruption, were removed from the visitor-center site and replaced after construction. The aim was to make the center appear as if it had grown organically out of the pallid landscape. One hundred years from now, when it is surrounded by a majestic evergreen forest, the center will fit even more integrally with its setting. Revegetation specifications were developed from surveys of native plants growing in the area, and revegetation efforts were carried out by ecologists using hand-collected seeds and techniques developed specifically for the project. EDAW landscape architects joined Forest Service scientists to carry out transects of the construction site, identifying and cataloging all emerging flora and blast artifacts. These transects became the basis for the carefully designed landscape restoration. Blast artifacts—stumps, snags, and blowdown logs—were carefully replaced. Replanting with indigenous seeds and plant specimens collected from the immediate site area and mulching with ash residue created a seamless integration of the built project with the postblast landscape. Sustainability of the design is dynamic, not static. It will be achieved through an emphasis on site evolution and a conscious management policy of not interfering with the processes of regrowth and natural succession of the landscape.

The building architecture of the Coldwater Ridge Visitor Center was designed with a timeless quality.

The structure is integrated with the landform and emerges from it as if dropped in by helicopter. Extensive use of native rock walls further glues the structure to the volcanic setting. The green patina of the copper roof and the hexagonal central structure mimic nearby volcanic mountain peaks. The building was designed to be integrated with its setting now and in the future when conifer forests return to the site through natural revegetation processes (Leccese 1993).

At the visitor service center, the principal outdoor education and interpretive experience is the Winds of Change Trail. This looping, 2,000-foot accessible trail meanders through a large field of blowdown logs and standing snags, bringing visitors into close proximity with the aftereffects of the awesome 1980 eruption. One special section of the trail dives into the landscape, revealing cross sections of the volcanic deposition. In other sections, the paved trail becomes an elevated boardwalk, bridging sensitive planting and drainage areas. An observation deck and interspersed viewpoints along the trail route provide rest points and a setting for interpretive display panels.

An observatory, located on Johnson Ridge, is only four miles from the crater. It provides dramatic views directly into the crater and features an interpretive theater, trails, and parking. An amphitheater located east of the observatory is sited at the edge of a precipitous drop, creating the illusion that nothing exists between the visitor and the mountain except the valley floor thousands of feet below.

Federal Highway Administration

The Federal Highway Administration (FHA) became a component of the U.S. Department of Transportation in 1967 under the terms of the Department of Transportation Act. The FHA administers the highway transportation programs of the Department of Transportation and is concerned with the total operation and environment of highway systems. In administering its highway programs, the FHA gives full consideration to the impacts of highway development and travel; transportation needs; engineering and safety; social, economic, and environmental effects; and highway project costs. The FHA ensures balanced treatment of these factors by utilizing a systematic approach in providing for safe and efficient highway transportation.

The FHA manages the federal aid highway program of financial assistance to states for highway construction. This program provided for construction and preservation of the 42,500-mile national system of interstate highways, financed on a 90-percent federal, 10-percent state basis, as well as the improvement of approximately 800,000 miles of other federal-aid primary, secondary, and urban roads and streets on a 75-percent federal and 25-percent state basis. The FHA also administers the Highway Bridge Replacement and Rehabilitation Program and emergency programs to assist states in the repair or reconstruction of federal-aid highways that have suffered severe damage from natural disasters.

Funds for federal aid to highways are administered by the states, which are responsible for the planning, design, and construction of federal-aid improvements. Revenue derived from highway-user taxes is deposited into the general funds of the U.S. Treasury and credited to the Highway Trust Fund to meet, through the congressional authorization and appropriation processes, the federal share of highway program costs. Federal Highway Trust Fund moneys have provided many opportunities for landscape architecture projects in highway-impact mitigation, highway beautification, and preservation of natural, cultural, and visual resources.

The Interstate 90 project in Seattle, Washington, is one of the most ambitious achievements completed under a cooperative effort between the Federal Highway Administration, the Washington State Department of Transportation, the City of Seattle, and the City of Mercer Island. The 7-mile multimodal transportation corridor includes 200 acres of park and roadside beautification, 4 acres of new wetland, 12 miles of urban multiuse trails, and 31 acres of park and recreation amenities on lid structures within three urban communities—Seattle, Mercer Island, and Bellevue. The project is a significant achievement, the result of perseverance and design excellence of landscape architects, architects, artists, engineers, and much public input in a planning process that took thirty years from start to completion of the transportation improvement.

FIGURE 2-55. Aerial photograph of the first lid park over I-90 on Mercer Island looking east. The lid concept spans the freeway, connecting neighborhoods with parks and providing recreation opportunities.

Photograph by Denton Vander Poel, courtesy of Washington State Department of Transportation.

The old Interstate 90 freeway separated communities with a broad expanse of pavement, noise, and vehicular pollution. The new project protects the communities by lowering the roadway to reduce visual and noise impacts. It joins adjacent neighborhoods by using lid structures to provide the real estate for landscaping and parks. The entire project was designed to create a coordinated corridor for pedestrian, bicycle, and vehicular movement.

Three lid structures and seven widened bridge structures span the depressed highway. The structures provide active and passive recreation opportunities in an aesthetically pleasing environment for local street and trail users. Active recreation facilities include baseball diamonds, soccer fields, practice fields, boat launching facilities, and basketball and tennis courts. Other amenities designed with the transportation improvements include children's play areas, restroom facilities, viewing points, a picnic shelter, picnic tables,

barbecues, benches, bike racks, drinking fountains, lighting, and public art. The bicycle and pedestrian trails connect with Bellevue's trail system to downtown Seattle.

The portals of the lid structures were designed structurally to include substantial plantings of large evergreen trees at the entrances to the tunnels. The masses of evergreen trees darken the area surrounding the tunnel entrances, easing the driver's eyesight adjustment to the lower light level within the tunnels. The east portal of the tunnel at Mount Baker Ridge, known as the Portal to the Pacific, accommodates a viewing point providing spectacular views of the city's floating bridges on Lake Washington and the distant Cascade Mountains. The viewing point complements the historic character of the Lake Washington Boulevard Parkway, originally designed by the Olmsted brothers.

The project is a model of local government cooperation, public involvement, technical knowledge,

FIGURE 2-56. Bike path on the Mercer Island lid park.

FIGURE 2-57. A tot lot, parking areas, and open play fields on the Mercer Island lid park.

FIGURE 2-58. Tennis courts and a path on the Mercer Island lid park.

FIGURE 2-59. Picnic tables and barbecues amid ventilation stacks on the Mercer Island lid park.

FIGURE 2-60. The portals of the lid structure are heavily planted with evergreen trees, easing the driver's eyesight adjustment at the entrance to the tunnels.

and teamwork of allied professionals brought together to reach a common goal. The project exemplifies the vision and the mission of the Federal Highway Administration, exceeding the expectations of all of those involved with its completion.

In 1991, a new federal law, the Intermodal Surface Transportation Efficiency Act (ISTEA), was passed and has become the FHA's largest program for funding highway-related infrastructure projects. ISTEA is aimed at reducing the emphasis on cars and focusing on alternative modes of transportation and giving local governments more authority over how funds are spent. ISTEA also mandates public participation in transportation planning. ISTEA has provided significant opportunities for landscape architects because the law is focused on mitigating the impact of freeways. Part of ISTEA's funds are slated for mass transit programs, and another part of the funding is authorized for highways. The Surface Transportation Program of the highway funds requires at least 10 percent of each state's share of the program be targeted for enhancements that increase the environmental, historic, or aesthetic attributes of highway projects. These funds provide excellent opportunities for landscape architects.

The Squaw Peak Parkway in Phoenix, Arizona, is one highway project that has benefited from the FHA's emphasis on enhancements intended to increase the aesthetics of freeways. The Squaw Peak Parkway includes some of the heaviest plantings found on any stretch of freeway in the Phoenix metropolitan area. It also includes a 5-mile stretch of more than thirty huge pots on and beside the 12-foot-high sound walls on both sides of the freeway. The pots are the creation of artists Mag Harries and Lajos Heder. The pots may be considered successful in one sense

FIGURE 2-61. Landscaping on the Squaw Peak Parkway in Phoenix, Arizona.

FIGURE 2-62. Giant pots in the Squaw Peak Parkway right-of-way.

because they have been a source of much conversation and criticism. The landscaping of the freeway has been regarded as a model of the color and diversity that is achievable through Xeriscape design and the use of new drought-tolerant plant materials introduced to the region in the 1980s. The plants are plentiful and used in extensive drifts throughout the right-of-way and medians.

Environmental Protection Agency

The Environmental Protection Agency (EPA) was established under the National Environmental Policy Act of 1960 and became an independent agency in the executive branch of the federal government pursuant to the Reorganization Plan of 1970.

The EPA was created to permit coordinated and effective governmental action on behalf of the environment. The EPA protects and enhances our environment to the fullest possible extent under the laws enacted by Congress. The agency's mission is to control and abate pollution in the areas of air, water, solid waste, pesticides, radiation, and toxic substances. Its mandate is to mount an integrated, coordinated attack on environmental pollution in cooperation with state and local governments. The agency works through ten regional offices throughout the United States.

The preparation of environmental impact statements (EIS), regulated by the EPA, has been a big source of landscape architecture work since the creation of the EPA in 1960. Undoubtedly, the EPA will continue to provide opportunities for landscape architects in years to come.

Department of Defense

The Department of Defense (DOD), comprising all branches of the military, is the largest federal agency. Every state has some defense activities and some defense establishments. The DOD is one of the largest developers and users of facilities in the country and a tremendous source of work for landscape architects and other A/E design professionals. Indeed, many of the opportunities for landscape architects at DOD facilities are through subconsulting relationships with other A/E professionals.

The United States Army Corps of Engineers has been an ongoing provider of opportunities for landscape architecture firms. The commanding general of the Corps of Engineers serves as the army's real-property manager. Under the overall supervision of the commanding general, the Corps of Engineers determines the requirements for real property; carries out programming and planning functions; and acquires, operates, and maintains the real property for the army and the air force.

The U.S. Army Corps of Engineers also executes civil works programs. The civil works programs include research and development, planning, design, construction, operation, and maintenance related to rivers, harbors, and waterways, as well as administration of laws for the protection and preservation of navigable waters and related resources such as wetlands. The Corps of Engineers also assists in recovery from natural disasters.

The Commerce Business Daily, the government's main outlet for advertising the procurement of professional services, is packed daily with requests for qualifications for planning and design services on military bases, forts, and naval stations.

Department of Housing and Urban Development (HUD)

In 1965, the Department of Housing and Urban Development Act became effective and HUD was created to serve as the principal federal agency responsible for programs concerned with the nation's housing opportunities, as well as improvement and development of the nation's communities. HUD functions through ten regional offices and administers a wide variety of programs. Germane to the landscape architect are HUD's programs aimed at aiding community and neighborhood development and preservation and encouraging a strong private-sector housing industry that can produce affordable housing by stimulating public-private partnerships.

HUD is administered under the supervision and direction of a cabinet-level secretary who formulates recommendations for basic policies in housing and community development. Since its inception, HUD has indirectly and directly provided a wide range of opportunities for landscape architects. Indirectly, HUD has nurtured housing development opportunities through its Federal Housing and Administration (FHA) and Government National Mortgage Association (GNMA) mortgage programs. Directly, HUD has provided development funds for thousands of housing development projects that resulted in design opportunities for the A/E community.

Office of Americans with Disabilities

The Americans with Disabilities Act (ADA) of 1991, which went into effect on January 26, 1992, prohibits discrimination on the basis of disability and requires that all new public places and commercial facilities be designed and constructed to accommodate people with disabilities. Places of public accommodation, for instance, include over five million private establishments such as restaurants, hotels, theaters, convention centers,• retail stores, shopping centers, dry cleaners, laundromats, doctors' offices, museums, parks, libraries, zoos, amusement parks, schools, day-care centers, and health spas. The law also calls for the removal of architectural barriers in existing facilities where readily achievable or the provisions of alternative measures to make goods and services accessible.

The ADA has created both indirect and direct opportunities for landscape architects. Many facilities such as college campuses and city school districts have carried out ADA compliance reviews of their facilities and developed long-range plans, pending funding, for bringing the facilities into ADA compliance. Once funding becomes available, planning and designing improvements to the facilities provides additional opportunities for landscape architects.

State, County, Metropolitan and Municipal Government

The majority of public works projects for landscape architecture firms come from the state and local levels of government. In particular, parks and recreation departments, transportation and highway departments, flood-control districts, and departments of environmental quality provide a great number of public works opportunities for landscape architects. Many landscape architecture firms specialize in park planning and design, as well as transportation and highway beautification, with a large percentage of the firm's workload consistently coming from projects focused in these areas. One reason that some landscape architecture firms develop a public works focus is due to specific requirements of the public agencies for design, preparation of construction documents, reporting, invoicing, and other administrative procedures. Every state highway department, for example, has specific design criteria for highway right-of-way landscaping and roadside beautification. Departments also have specific require-

ments for production of design plans and construction documents. The design objectives and the requirements for producing documents are often described in manuals and department directives. Specific formulas and methods for calculating overhead and profit are used. Some states require that fees be developed based upon an approved estimate of hours and using a fee formula that is based on direct hourly pay rates multiplied by the office overhead rate plus an allowed percentage for profit. Required reporting formats that include regular administrative updates describing the amount of work completed and the percentage complete are frequently required. Landscape architects who are successful in procuring state highway department work will find that they will need to make a large time investment in familiarizing themselves with the design and administrative requirements, but once this education process is complete, they will have an advantage over others wishing to obtain future highway work. The investment in time to become familiar with the agency requirements has a value that is recognized by the state agency and will pay dividends in terms of future work as long as the landscape architecture firm provides friendly, competent, and error-free services.

As with other market sectors, developing state and local public-agency clients involves nurturing friendly, long-term relationships with the staff members of the state and local government departments. Developing long-term relationships can give one firm a slight edge over another firm in procuring public work. Good relations with public agency staff might also result in contracts being awarded directly to a firm rather than going through a public selection process if the agency staff have reasons to justify the direct selection. Direct selection results when there is a time crunch and the desired professional services are needed immediately, or when agency staff can justify selection of the firm because the firm has specific qualifications that no other local office has.

Landscape architects are selected for most state and local public works projects through a qualifications-based, open selection process. This process mirrors the federal procurement process and typically includes these steps:

1. Advertisement of the desired professional services
2. Submittal of qualification materials or a proposal

3. Short-listing for interviews or for preparation of a detailed proposal
4. Interviewing or discussing the detailed proposal with a selection committee
5. Selection
6. Contract negotiation
7. Ratification of selection and contract negotiation by an elected body, such as a city council, or by the top administrative appointee of a public agency

Every step of the process is important. In the first step, the landscape architecture firm must make the decision whether to submit for an advertised public works project. The decision should be made on a wide variety of criteria including the following:

1. Are members of the firm interested in the type of professional work advertised?
2. Is the firm competitive? Does it have a track record that will set the firm out from other offices likely to submit qualifications?
3. Does the firm have established relationships with the agency staff or members of the selection committee, giving the firm an edge over competitors?
4. Does the firm need the work?
5. Is the project interesting and challenging?
6. Does the firm have uncommitted and qualified staff available to work on the project if selected?
7. How costly will it be to prepare the qualifications statement and go through with the interview if the firm is short-listed?
8. Are the advertised fees commensurate with the scope of services desired?
9. Will the project add to the firm's visibility and future promotional capability?

If the answers to these questions and others the firm may have are positive, and the firm decides to pursue the project, the next important consideration is acquiring background information about the project, determining the professional expertise and subconsultants that will be required, and touching base with agency staff and decision makers to find out their perceptions and hidden agendas, as well as showing interest in the work. After the background information is obtained, a go or no-go decision should be revisited. If the background information indicates the firm will have difficulty with the selection process, the firm may be wise to shelve the RFP and go on to the next client or job-development opportunity. If the background information and contact with agency representatives indicate a green light, the firm will go on to preparing its statement of qualifications.

Writing a well-conceived statement of qualifications or proposal that is thoroughly researched and offers a balanced team of the consultant's staff and any subconsultants that may be required is the key to advancing in the public-works selection process. If the firm doesn't get to the interview or detailed proposal step of the process, no work will result from its efforts. Learning how to write and present an effective statement of qualifications is one of the most important aspects of landscape architecture practice and essential for securing state and local government work. Preparation of proposals and statements of qualifications, as well as preparation for interviews, is covered in chapter 7.

State and Local Government Opportunities

The state and local government departments, agencies, and offices that have opportunities for the professional practice of landscape architecture vary widely but include the following:

Transportation and engineering
Environmental quality
Parks and recreation
Fish and wildlife
Land and real estate
Environmental protection
Architecture and facility
Historic preservation
Planning and zoning
Natural resources
Tourism and promotion
Wetlands and water resource

Generally speaking, state and local government agencies mirror federal agencies. Obtaining state and local public works projects depends upon hearing about the opportunities. Specific activities necessary to keep informed about public works opportunities include the following.

State and Local Procurement Offices. Many states and local public agencies have branches or departments that exist specifically for procuring outside services.

Sometimes the purchasing department is used. Sometimes the specific department handles its own procurement. In any event, landscape architects must make sure they are registered with the appropriate procurement agency in order to receive notification of pending public works procurement.

Annual Information Forms.   Most procurement agencies update their files annually. Landscape architects must be sure to complete annual information updates and remain current in procurement agency files.

Business Newspapers.   Most public agencies that use a public selection process advertise in a business or other local newspaper. Subscribing to these sources of public advertisements is a very good way to keep up with public works solicitations and requests for proposals.

Personal Contact.   Landscape architects must maintain personal contact with representatives of state and local agencies in order to be aware of public works opportunities.

Additional methods, including newsletters, promotional pieces, and public speaking, are discussed in chapter 7.

Most landscape architecture firms will include some state, county, metropolitan, or municipal government clients and projects in their portfolio, and developing these clients is an important part of professional practice. Learning how to find the work and establish client relationships at the local government level is necessary for a well-rounded basis of continuing practice opportunities. The main consideration to remember is that, without clients and projects, no landscape architecture practice will remain viable.

REFERENCES

Bye, A. E. 1980. The Bog—A Landscape That Maintains Itself. *Landscape Architecture* 70 (March): 186–189.

Henderson, Gwendolyn J., ed. 1991. *The United States Government Manual 1991/92.* Washington, D.C.: Government Printing Office.

Howett, Catherine, ed. 1990. *Abstracting the Landscape—The Artistry of Landscape Architect A. E. Bye.* University Park, Pa.: Department of Landscape Architecture, University of Pennsylvania.

Johnson, Jory. 1991. Two by Bye. *Landscape Architecture* 81 (June): 66–69.

Landscape Architecture. 1981 ASLA Awards (September 1981); 1985 ASLA Awards (September/October 1985); 1986 ASLA Awards (September/October 1986); 1987 ASLA Awards (November/December 1987); 1988 ASLA Awards (November 1988); 1989 ASLA Awards (November 1989); 1990 ASLA Awards (November 1990); 1991 ASLA Awards (November 1991); 1992 ASLA Awards (November 1992); 1993 ASLA Awards (November 1993); 1994 ASLA Awards (November 1994). Ed. Grady Clay, Susan Rademacher Frey, and James G. Truelove. Washington, D.C.: American Society of Landscape Architects.

Leccese, Michael. 1993. Volcanic Adventures Where the Clear-Cut Ends. *Landscape Architecture* 83 (February): 38–43.

Miyakoda, Tooru, ed. 1994. EDAW: The Integrated World, Landscape Design and Sustaining Environments. *Process: Architecture* 120. Tokyo: Process Architecture Co.

Roberts, Paul. 1993. The Practice of the Wilds. *Landscape Architecture* 83 (October): 88–89.

Woodbridge, Sally B. 1991. Building on Collaboration. *Landscape Architecture* 81 (April): 56–63.

STUDY QUESTIONS AND ASSIGNMENTS

1. Interview landscape architects in your area and develop a broad list and short description of clients served by landscape architects in both the private sector and the public sector. Include examples of the types of projects completed for the clients.

2. Interview principals of landscape architecture firms in your area to identify what elements are the main determinants of their client mix. Do they take a proactive or reactive posture for obtaining clients? Is the client mix determined by geography? How does professional licensure influence the mix of clients? What role does personal contact play in securing clients and developing a client mix? Does the firm have a specialization that influences its client mix? What role do the ebb and flow of national and local economics play in the firm's client mix?

3. Locate, photograph, and document the design concept of three examples of landscape architec-

ture projects in your area for each of the ten general areas of private practice:

- Community and multifamily housing development
- Parks and outdoor recreation facilities
- Commercial and industrial development
- Planning and analysis projects
- Institutional projects
- Single-family residential and garden design projects
- Land and water reclamation and conservation projects
- Interior landscape architecture
- Landscape art and earth sculpture

4. Interview principals of architecture firms in your area. Identify the types of projects in which they use landscape architects as subconsultants. Identify as many examples as possible in order to develop a wide cross section of the types of work landscape architects engage under contract to architecture firms. Summarize your findings and draw conclusions from your research.

5. Interview principals of civil engineering firms in your area. Identify the types of projects in which they use landscape architects as subconsultants. Identify as many examples as possible in order to develop a wide cross section of the types of work landscape architects engage under contract to civil engineering firms. Summarize your findings and draw conclusions from your research.

6. Interview principals of planning and environmental firms in your area. Identify the types of projects landscape architects engage with planning and environmental firms. Identify as many examples as possible in order to develop a wide cross secion of the types of work landscape architects engage with planning and environmental firms. Summarize your findings and draw conclusions from your research.

7. Identify not-for-profit organizations in your area. Interview executives of the not-for-profit organizations to see if they use landscape architecture firms and for what types of projects. Document your findings in a paper.

8. Locate, photograph, and document five landscape architecture projects in your area for each of the three main levels of public-sector clients:

- Federal government
- State government
- Local municipal, county, and metropolitan government

9. Obtain a copy of *The Commerce Business Daily* and find an advertisement for a landscape architecture project. Using the SF255 and SF254 forms, as well as responding to the requirements addressed in the advertisement, prepare a proposal as if you were submitting for the project.

10. Identify and document at least one example of a project carried out for each of the following federal agencies:

- National Park Service
- National Forest Service
- Federal Highway Administration
- Environmental Protection Agency
- Department of Defense
- Department of Housing and Urban Development
- Bureau of Reclamation
- Bureau of Surface Mining Reclamation and Enforcement
- Unites States Fish and Wildlife Service
- Department of Agriculture
- Soil Conservation Service
- Urban Mass Transportation Administration
- Department of Veterans Affairs

CHAPTER THREE

Case Studies

One of the best ways to understand the professional practice of landscape architecture is to look at different private- and public-practice options. A difficult decision faced by most aspiring landscape architects is what professional-practice direction should be taken to best meet the individual's goals. Should one enter the private sector or the public sector? Should one launch a career in education and research? Should one work for a small design firm, a large design firm, or a design-build firm? Career decisions are not unique to the entry-level professional, either. Many landscape architects start out in one area of professional practice and later make a professional course correction. Some professionals have started in private practice working for a large firm and later moved into a small firm of their own. Some have started in a small firm that has grown to be a large firm. Others start in education and later move into private practice. Still others start in private practice, move into public practice, and then go back to private practice. And some start in private practice with a large incorporated firm and stay with the firm for their entire professional life, working their way up the firm's personnel ladder to become project managers, principals, and owners of the firm.

Professional career choices are highly individual. Choosing a career option depends on exposure to opportunities, personal goals, energy, life cycles, and income and security objectives. Selecting an employer may be based on the region or city where an individual wants to live and the work opportunities there. The decision may be affected by the health of the general economy and the availability of jobs. It may come about because an individual has developed a specialization that is only available for practicing in the public sector or in a niche field of private practice.

Clearly, however, an entry-level professional and graduate of a landscape architecture program will try to make the best match between his or her goals, both professional and personal, and the initial career direction. Writing specific goals and objectives can help to identify the best professional-practice direction. Having a vision of some of the options available also helps. This chapter provides that vision by taking a look at six different professional practice directions:

1. Private practice: large multidisciplinary A/E firm
2. Private practice: large landscape architecture firm
3. Private practice: small landscape architecture firm
4. Private practice: design-build firm
5. Public practice
6. Corporate practice

A case study will illustrate each professional career option. The examples are practice oriented because that is the emphasis of this book. Education or research career tracks are not included because they are specialized careers that require an advanced landscape architecture degree and often a doctorate. The case studies present similar information for each professional option so that comparisons may be made.

Before the case studies, pros and cons of each professional practice option have been itemized in table

TABLE 3.1 **Career Track Opportunities**

Career Track Considerations	Large Landscape Architecture Firm	Large A/E Firm	Small Landscape Architecture Firm	Design-Build Firm	Public Practice	Corporate Practice
1. Opportunity to interface with allied professionals	H	H	M	M	H	H
2. Variety of projects	H	H	M	M	H	M
3. Complexity of projects	H	H	M/L	M/L	H	H
4. Degree of project responsibility	M	M	L	M	L	M
5. Travel opportunities	H/M	H/M	L	L	H/M	H/M
6. Company benefits	AA	AA	A	A	AA	AA
7. Starting salary	AA	A	BA	BA	A	AA
8. Income potential	AA	AA	A	A	A	AA
9. Availability of and access to resources	H	H	M/L	M/L	H	H
10. Responsibility for project decisions	M	M/L	H/M	H/M	M/L	M/L
11. Contact with clients	M	M/L	H/M	H	M	M
12. Professional development opportunities	H/M	H/M	M/L	M/L	H/M	M

High = H, High to Medium = H/M, Medium = M, Medium to Low = M/L, Low = L Above Average = AA, Average = A, Below Average = BA

3.1. They should be viewed as generalizations and used only as a guide to evaluating the differences between the career opportunities. There are many times when the pros of working for a larger firm can also be found in a smaller firm and when aspects of private practice are also found in public practice. The individual should evaluate each and every employment opportunity on its own terms and relate it to his or her personal and professional goals.

HNTB Corporation: Large Multidisciplinary A/E Firm

History and Overview

Since its founding in 1914 as a partnership, HNTB's architects, engineers, planners, and landscape architects have helped shape communities throughout the United States. In the beginning, the firm focused on bridge design and quickly emerged as one of the nation's leading bridge designers.

HNTB's bridge work provided a natural progression into toll road and highway design projects. Today, the firm is a recognized leader in toll facilities, having completed projects in Maine, Florida, Kentucky, West Virginia, Oklahoma, Massachusetts, New York, Texas, Kansas, and California. HNTB continues to be a leader in the industry in the application of advanced technologies for this market, including intelligent transportation systems and electronic toll and traffic management systems.

HNTB also designs aviation facilities and airports of all sizes, from small commuter facilities to major hubs. The firm's aviation portfolio includes planning and design services for airport master planning, runway design, airport technical design, heliports, and cargo facilities.

HNTB's entry into architecture was accomplished by acquiring established architectural practices or by starting an architecture practice in one of the firm's existing offices. Today the firm's architects, interior designers, urban planners, and landscape architects provide design services for a variety of commercial and institutional facilities including office buildings, sports venues, convention centers, hotels, resorts, golf courses, as well as transportation, schools, health care, and recreation facilities.

The firm also provides environmental engineering services, focusing primarily on water and waste water resources. The firm's projects include water distribution systems, waste water treatment plants, and water reclamation facilities.

In 1993 HNTB Corporation was established to more efficiently meet the needs of public- and private-sector clients. The new structure enables key personnel to devote more time to the management of the firm and to major projects. The firm is governed by a board of directors, and management responsibilities are developed and implemented under the direction of a three-member office of the chairman. Members of the HNTB board of directors and the office of the chairman are executive officers within the firm. The firm's offices are grouped into five geographic divisions and corporate business services. Each division is headed by a division president. Service groups, based on technical disciplines, are responsible for developing strategic marketing plans, guiding business development, and overseeing technical quality and development.

In 1994 the firm formed two new companies—The Infrastructure Management Group (IMG) and The Alcyone Group, Incorporated (AGI). IMG focuses on assisting public and private clients with financial consulting and project funding. AGI is HNTB's design-build firm, specializing in commercial, educational, and manufacturing facilities.

MISSION STATEMENT

To provide both public and private sector clients around the world with effective and cost efficient solutions to their infrastructure problems through the application of high quality technical and management talent and skills. In providing solutions to clients, HNTB provides a challenging and rewarding environment for employees.

VISION

Our vision will change as we accomplish our goals, but the element of our vision that will not change is that HNTB will aspire to be the BEST in our chosen markets and services, and that we will attract and retain the BEST people to be part of our organization.

1. We envision creating a cadre of project managers who are the best trained and skilled in what clients want—superior communication, leadership, interpersonal skills, innovative technical solutions.
2. We envision being a leader in providing exemplary levels of service, exceeding what clients are accustomed to receiving from others and responding in ways that communicate consistent concern for their needs.
3. We envision creating a marketing system that marshals the resources of the firm.
4. We envision forming strategic alliances in the form of mergers, acquisitions, joint ventures, and others that will strengthen our competitive advantage.
5. We envision developing attitudes, systems, and skills throughout the firm to manage the business more profitably so that HNTB is among the industry leaders in financial return to shareholders and employees.
6. We envision becoming the leader in the use and application of new information technology.
7. We envision continuing to lead the industry in finding and applying new technologies to solve client problems.
8. We envision creating a work environment that encourages innovation and creativity.

Landscape Architecture in HNTB

Since the early 1970s, landscape architecture has been an integral part of HNTB's practice. The firm's landscape architects have contributed significantly to HNTB's growth and have provided important planning and design services to public and private clients throughout the United States.

HNTB's landscape architects have engaged a portfolio of projects that is varied in both type and complexity. The firm's landscape architects have worked on a variety of building projects, including resorts, residential developments, office parks, schools, health-care facilities, recreational developments, golf courses, theme parks, museums, sculpture gardens, waterfront developments, and airports. Services include master planning for both new and existing developments and design services to maximize the economic and aesthetic qualities of each property.

The Intermodal Surface Transportation Efficiency Act (ISTEA) provides important financial resources for landscape architectural design on transportation-related projects and new opportunities for HNTB's landscape architects to work closely with the firm's engineers. Working together, HNTB's landscape architects and engineers collaborate to enhance the aesthetic qualities of bridges, highways, tollways, and urban corridors. HNTB's landscape architects have developed an impressive portfolio of work on bikeways, a growing transportation mode.

The firm's project diversity provides many career experiences for landscape architects and the opportunity to work directly with allied professionals within the firm. Each employee has opportunities to work on a wide variety of projects, advancing personal and professional growth. HNTB has a meaningful professional development program that provides employees the opportunity for additional training as designers, technicians, and managers. The firm's continuing education program provides support to each employee seeking advanced degrees in his or her chosen profession or related field.

Employee Benefits

HNTB provides a valuable and comprehensive employee benefits program to help protect employees and their families from financial hardship; to assist with medical expenses; to provide paid time off for rest and relaxation; and to assist employees in growth through training, certification, and tuition programs.

The firm provides health-care and dental coverage under three deductible plans. The employee may choose the plan best suited to his or her needs. The firm provides the opportunity for eligible employees to pay for out-of-pocket medical and dental expenses with pre-tax dollars under provisions of Section 125 of the Internal Revenue Service Code.

Group life and accidental death insurance equal to two times annual earnings are provided at no cost for eligible employees. Supplemental life insurance coverage and dependent life insurance are available to employees at group premium rates. While traveling on company business, employees are covered at no cost with business travel accident insurance up to $100,000.

HNTB uses a policy of paid time off (PTO) to provide employees with time off for rest and relaxation. PTO is also used for the first eight hours of each illness. Full-time employees are entitled to immediately use their accrued PTO. Part-time employees must work at least twenty hours per week and have completed one year of service before they are eligible to use accrued PTO.

Full-time employees who have worked less than nine years for the company and who work forty hours per week accrue PTO at a rate of fifteen working days per year. PTO accrues to the new employee at the start of full-time employment.

Employees with more than nine years of service, but less than twenty-four years, accrue PTO at the rate of twenty working days per year. Up to forty total working days may be accrued.

Employees with more than twenty-four years of service accrue PTO at the rate of twenty-five working days per year. PTO may be accrued to a total of fifty working days.

Full-time employees working thirty-five hours per week accrue PTO at seven-eighths of the rate for those working forty hours per week. Carryover time is also prorated at seven-eighths the rate of the forty-hour-per-week worker.

Part-time employees working more than twenty hours per week accrue PTO at a rate of one hour for every twenty-six hours worked. The maximum amount of time allowed for carryover is two weeks.

PTO accrued in excess of the maximum amounts allowed by employee category is paid on the last payroll of each year. Advances of PTO are not authorized by company policy. Terminating employees are paid for unused PTO at the time the employee leaves the company. An employee transferring between HNTB offices, however, is not paid for unused PTO. It is carried over to the new office location.

Employees are requested to schedule PTO absences throughout the calendar year so that adequate staff is available in the office at all times. PTO absences are subject to getting bumped if workload requires the employee to be in the office. Employees may utilize PTO in one-hour increments.

The following rules apply to HNTB's employees incurring a short-term disability:

1. The first eight hours of the disability absence will be charged to PTO. Subsequent days of absence will be charged to sick leave and/or to

short-term disability (STD) benefits as appropriate.

2. Employees eligible for short-term disability benefits may expend accrued PTO in lieu of short-term disability benefits.

3. Employees on short-term disability status will accrue additional PTO credit, but will have no vested right to credits accrued until they return to full-time employment.

4. Employees unable to return to active work upon completion of 180 calendar days of disability will be terminated and will receive payment for unused PTO in the same week in which they complete the 180-day period.

5. Procedures for charging PTO in cases involving rehabilitative partial-day or rehabilitative intermittent absences are resolved by contacting the director of human resources.

HNTB's sick-leave policy compensates employees for absence from regular duties due to personal illness. Paid sick leave is available to all full-time employees and accrues at the rate of four hours per month of service. The first eight hours of each absence (even if for illness) is charged against paid time off (PTO). Thereafter, HNTB pays eligible employees at their regular basic salary for sick-leave absences to the limit of the employee's accumulated sick-leave balance. Employees may utilize sick leave in one-hour increments. Holidays falling within or adjacent to sick leave are not counted as sick leave. Upon written request, submitted prior to the end of each week, employees may substitute PTO for sick leave.

Employees may carry over unused sick leave from one calendar year to another. Advance sick leave, however, is not authorized. Unused sick leave is not vested, and all sick-leave credit is forfeited upon the employee's termination or death.

The following eligibility requirements apply to paid sick leave:

1. Employees absent on scheduled work days are required to notify their supervisor(s) each day they are unable to work, unless the severity of the illness precludes such notification. HNTB may require a physician's statement to verify illness. Failure to notify the supervisor(s) or provide a physician's statement may void a claim for sick-leave pay, constitute vol-

untary resignation of employment, or result in termination.

2. Upon expiration of ten consecutive work days of absence due to illness (including the first eight hours charged to PTO), employees will be automatically placed on medical leave of absence, retroactive to the first day of absence. Employees will be required to provide a physician's statement at the time they begin a medical leave of absence and monthly physician's statements thereafter while receiving sick-leave pay. Failure to provide a physician's statement will void the claim for sick-leave pay and may result in termination. A physician's release for return to work must be presented the day the employee returns to work after medical leave of absence, hospitalization, or surgery.

The following regulations apply to sick-leave absence:

1. Sick leave will not be used for any purpose other than personal illness. Abuse of sick leave will be considered grounds for immediate termination of employment.

2. Sick leave can be substituted for PTO pay only if an employee is hospitalized while on a scheduled PTO. The first eight hours of such period of absence must still be charged to PTO.

3. Sick-leave pay will be paid only for approved and documented absences and for times when the employee would normally be scheduled to work.

4. Notice of an employee's intent to return to work after prolonged illness will be given to the supervisor not less than twenty-four hours in advance so that work scheduling adjustments can be made.

5. To become eligible for short-term disability benefits, an employee must have completed ninety days of full-time employment and must have exhausted accrued sick leave. Allowable leave under the Family Medical Leave Act is deemed to be used concurrently by an employee using short-term or long-term disability benefits. The terms and conditions applicable to short- and long-term

disability benefits are stated in HNTB's Employee Handbook.

An employee receiving worker's compensation will receive full pay for a maximum of 180 calendar days. The combined worker's compensation benefits and payroll will not exceed the employee's basic salary. After 180 days, the employee is eligible to apply for long-term disability benefits.

Each employee is immediately eligible on the first day of employment to participate in the firm's 401(k) retirement and savings plan. Each participant may elect to have a percentage of pay withheld on a pre-tax basis and contributed to his or her account in the plan. The maximum contribution is 15 percent of annual earnings up to the maximum dollar limit allowed by the IRS. Participants may allocate their account balances among five investment fund options. HNTB matches fifty cents for every dollar an employee contributes up to the first 4 percent of salary, with a maximum amount limited to $400. In addition to this contribution, HNTB normally makes an annual contribution to the plan based on the profit of the company.

The firm has two programs geared directly for personal growth and professional development. Educational assistance is available to all full-time employees. HNTB pays tuition fees for approved courses that are successfully completed with a grade of C or better. To be approved, the course must benefit the employee and the company. Employees are encouraged to become registered in their technical discipline, such as landscape architecture. Employees receive their normal rate of compensation for any time required within regular working hours to prepare applications and to appear before the registration board or licensing or certification authority. Employees acquiring their first professional registration or license are eligible for a one-time lump-sum bonus.

Last, HNTB is affiliated with a credit union, and membership to the credit union is open to all HNTB employees.

Entry-Level Job Description— Landscape Architect

Reports to: Project manager
Summary Description: Assists in producing and completing design documents through gathering information, organizing data, and applying results.

Functional Duties and Responsibilities:
1. Assists in producing the design of construction documents.
2. Assists in developing presentation material.

Performance Standards:
1. Quality and timeliness of design solutions.
2. Responds appropriately to direction.
3. Personal growth and development.

Minimum Required Education:
B.A. or B.S. in Landscape Architecture

Minimum Required Experience:
1. Total: none
2. Within HNTB: none

Minimum Required Certification: None

Managerial Scope: Nonsupervisory

Freedom to Act: Closely supervised; assignments require diversified work procedures.

Judgment and Initiative: Routine work within established procedures, requiring use of some judgment and initiative to occasionally plan or alter the sequence of work.

Magnitude of Decisions: Decisions are primarily internal with little potential for time lost.

Accountability of Results: Primarily contributes directly to projects.

Environmental Relationships:
1. External Contacts: obtaining information for internal use.
2. Internal Contacts: meeting on uncomplicated matters; receiving or exchanging information.

Special Skills Required: Good graphic, oral, and written communication skills.

Working Conditions:
1. Overtime may be required.
2. May perform other duties as dictated by office workload and staffing requirements.

Representative Examples of HNTB's Landscape Architecture, Planning, and Urban Design Projects

- Nelson Atkins Museum of Art, Henry Moore Sculpture Garden, Kansas City, Missouri
- Washington National Airport landscape master plan, Washington, D.C.
- Renaissance Office Park master plan, Overland Park, Kansas

FIGURES 3-1, 3-2, and 3-3. HNTB's deck park over a depressed section of I-10 in Phoenix, Arizona, has been named the Margaret T. Hance Park. The park is divided into three sections: a neighborhood park, an urban plaza, and a cultural park. Photo (A) is the urban plaza with the cultural park in the background. Photo (B) is an overview of the neighborhood park. Photo (C) is the playground and sculpture in the neighborhood park.

(A)

(B)

(C)

- New Hanover County Airport landscape master plan, Wilmington, North Carolina
- Kellogg Avenue design, Wichita, Kansas
- The Deck Park at Central Avenue, Phoenix, Arizona
- I-10 West Papago Inner Loop, Phoenix, Arizona

- Manhattan comprehensive land use plan, Manhattan, Kansas
- Rockhurst College master plan, Kansas City, Missouri
- Lisbon/North Avenue study, Milwaukee, Wisconsin
- Town Center strategic plan, Fishers, Indiana

FIGURE 3-4. Glenwood Canyon, on the western slope of the Rocky Mountains, is a scenic attraction for motorists of U.S. Route 6 and 24.

Photograph courtesy of HNTB, Inc.

FIGURE 3-5. HNTB's design sketches for I-70 through Colorado's Glenwood Canyon minimized environmental impacts on fir and aspen plant communities and reduced visual impacts by locating the highway largely to one side of the canyon and close to the White River. Terraced roadways and cantilevered structures were part of the firm's design proposals to enhance the route's scenic value for motorists. The structures also provide unrestricted wildlife access to the river.

Illustration courtesy of HNTB, Inc.

FIGURE 3-5. Continued.

FIGURE 3-6. Aerial view of HNTB's Visitor Center for the Indiana Dunes National Lakeshore Park.

Photograph courtesy of HNTB, Inc.

- Downtown streetscape and Rialto Plaza improvements, Joliet, Illinois
- Downtown revitalization plan, Seymour, Indiana
- Adams Dairy Parkway Corridor study, Blue Springs, Missouri
- Comprehensive plan update, Carmel, Indiana
- Princeton comprehensive plan, Princeton, Indiana
- Rio Salado Recreation Area, Tempe, Arizona
- Fox River Upper Flats development opportunities, Appleton, Wisconsin
- State Capital Complex master plan, Phoenix, Arizona

FIGURE 3-7. Design of the Indiana
Dunes National Lakeshore Visitor
Center solved the problem of building
over a constantly shifting base of dune
sand by raising the building on piles.
Photograph by Orlando R. Cabanan.

FIGURE 3-8. Design perspective of
HNTB's Bellevue Transit Center.
Illustration courtesy of HNTB, Inc.

- Marion Laboratories Headquarters master plan, Kansas City, Missouri
- Hartford Pedestrian Plaza, Hartford, Connecticut
- Anchor Center, Phoenix, Arizona
- Brightman Street Bridge bicycle and pedestrian amenities, Fall River, Massachusetts
- T. F. Green Airport landscape master plan, Providence, Rhode Island

- Indiana State University plan, Terre Haute, Indiana
- Rose-Hulman Institute of Technology master plan, Terre Haute, Indiana
- Arsenal Technical High School campus plan, Indianapolis, Indiana
- Comprehensive plan, Oak Lawn, Illinois
- Eli Lily & Company, Northwest Quadrant plan, Indianapolis, Indiana

- National Advocacy Center landscape design, Columbia, South Carolina
- Urban waterfront canal design, Menasha, Wisconsin
- Downtown Manitowoc urban design and traffic study, Manitowoc, Wisconsin
- Downtown planning and design, Wausau, Wisconsin
- Port Plaza Mall expansion, Green Bay, Wisconsin
- Main Street streetscape, Oconto Falls, Wisconsin
- Architectural design guidelines, Madison, Wisconsin
- Historic Building Survey, Sioux City, Iowa
- Town center strategic plan, Fishers, Indiana
- Fond du Lac downtown and riverfront revitalization, Fond du Lac, Wisconsin
- Lafayette growth management program, Lafayette, Louisiana
- Historic District plan, Madison, Indiana
- Downtown revitalization plan, Seymour, Indiana
- Downtown revitalization plan, Greenburg, Indiana
- Downtown revitalization plan, Franklin, Indiana
- Downtown revitalization plan, Greenfield, Indiana
- I-70/I-470 Interchange, Topeka, Kansas
- Route 146, Worcester/Millbury, Massachusetts
- Kellogg Avenue design, Wichita, Kansas
- Environmental review guidelines, Texas Turnpike Authority
- Bridge aesthetic guidelines, Minnesota Department of Transportation
- Aesthetic guidelines, Orange County tollroads, Orange County, California
- Boulder Highway improvement project, Henderson, Nevada
- South Riverfront Expressway study, Jackson County, Missouri
- Arkansas Rails to Trails, Little Rock, Arkansas
- Himeji Friendship Garden, Phoenix, Arizona
- Fountain Hills Jr./Sr. High School, Fountain Hills, Arizona
- Bloomington parks plan, Bloomington, Indiana
- Swope Park master plan, Kansas City, Missouri
- White River Park, Indianapolis, Indiana

- St. Joseph riverfront, St. Joseph, Missouri
- Indiana Dunes National Park, Indiana
- Topeka Sports Complex, Topeka, Kansas
- Osceola Spring Training Facility, Osceola, Florida
- Port Charlotte Spring Training Facility, Port Charlotte, Florida
- Ohio River Greenway, Southern Illinois
- International Bluegrass Festival site, Owensboro, Kentucky
- Arizona National Memorial Cemetery, Phoenix, Arizona
- Old Cross Cut Canal Park, Phoenix, Arizona
- Swope Park Golf Academy, Kansas City, Missouri
- Shawnee Bend Resort, Lake Ozark, Missouri
- Casa Grande High School, Casa Grande, Arizona
- Swope Memorial Golf Course, Kansas City, Missouri
- Hillcrest Country Club, Kansas City, Missouri
- Camp Zama Golf Course, Camp Zama, Japan
- Whispering Firs Golf Course, McChord AFB, Seattle, Washington
- Manhattan Woods Golf Club, Orangetown, New York
- Geneva National Golf Club, Geneva, Wisconsin
- Aqua Fria Resort Center, Phoenix, Arizona
- Holbrook Country Club, Tennis Center, and Pool Complex, Leawood, Kansas
- Princess Hotel Tennis Complex, Scottsdale, Arizona
- Country Club Plaza Tennis Complex, Kansas City, Missouri
- Hilton Pointe Tapatio Water Park, Phoenix, Arizona
- Camp Ponderosa Ranch, Heber, Arizona

EDAW, Inc.: Large Landscape Architecture Firm

History and Overview

In 1940, Garrett Eckbo started a partnership with Ed Williams to practice landscape architecture in San Francisco, California. At the end of World War II,

Robert Royston joined the partnership, and Eckbo went to Los Angeles to establish the firm's second office. By 1965 Francis Dean and Don Austin had joined the firm, and Robert Royston had left. In 1965 the four partners decided to incorporate, primarily for the legal protection provided to professional practitioners through the corporate shield. The firm prospered and grew due to the design and business capability of the founding partners and to the surge of growth that occurred in California and the other western states after 1950. Garrett Eckbo left the firm in 1973, followed by Don Austin in 1974, and Francis Dean in 1978. After the founding partners, Eckbo, Dean, Austin, and Williams, left the firm, the new ownership adopted the acronym EDAW for the name of the firm. The new owners began developing the multioffice, national, and then international organization that has become one of the premiere landscape architecture firms in the world. The talented and capable owners that inherited the firm from the original four partners began the transition into a corporate landscape architecture giant that in 1994 employed several hundred people, had eight offices in the United States, seven offices overseas, and a total company revenue over $29 million (Miyakoda 1994).

The firm provides a full range of professional services that includes landscape architecture, planning, urban design, environmental analysis, site engineering, and graphic design. Professional services are focused on ten broad categories of clients and projects: community revitalization; federal facilities; parks, recreation, and public gardens; resource management; transportation; corporate and office projects; institutional projects; residential and planned communities; resorts and theme attractions; and public utility planning.

EDAW, Inc., has been a prominent force in the fields of landscape architecture, urban design, and environmental planning for more than a half century. EDAW's emphasis on the broad and increasingly complex issues of land-use planning and design encourages the appropriate use of resources. The firm is involved with every aspect of environmental planning, design, and management. EDAW espouses a philosophy that views planning, policy making, environmental analysis, physical design, and implementation as a continuum of related professional services. The firm's professional staff and management seek to improve the quality of the relationship between people and their environment throughout the world.

MISSION

In 1992, EDAW, Inc., produced a vision statement called *EDAW VISION: EDAW in the Year 2002.* The mission of the firm is derived from this vision statement prepared by the firm's owners.

A vision is a product of the imagination, a picture of the future that exhibits foresight. Since it is futuristic, it is inevitably lacking in detail but it can be strong in concept, memorable, stimulating . . . even inspiring.

A vision is something to pursue. However, unlike a plan, it contains no process, schedule or means of achievement. Like a plan, it can change and should be reviewed from time to time, but since it is clearly futuristic or long-term, it should not be reviewed too often.

Purpose. EDAW's vision statement serves a number of purposes: It serves to communicate our values among ourselves, clients and potential employees; it should motivate all our staff, give direction and be an incentive for everyone to strive for excellence. Our vision should anticipate the future to the best of our abilities, which, combined with its values, enables it to be the reference for major decisions and strategic planning.

The Company. EDAW, Inc. is an internationally renowned firm, preeminent in land-based analysis, planning and design. EDAW, Inc. is a member of EDAW Group, an affiliation of allied companies bound together by common ownership and through synergistic contributions toward the preservation of common values. This vision of EDAW, Inc. is portrayed as a snapshot of what the company might look like ten years from now.

Philosophy. The firm is greatly concerned with every aspect of environmental management and its integration. We see planning and policy-making, environmental analysis, physical design and implementation as a continuum of related professional activities. As discreet functions they have identity, but their integration adds meaning. Through the application of these professional skills we strive to improve the quality of the relationship between people and their environment.

The firm wishes to be renowned for its good judgement, professional integrity, technical competence and the innovation of new products. We support our constituent professions but are not limited by their need for definition and therefore often step outside these confines and push the state of the art and the profession forward.

Our most distinguishing philosophy is the integration of planning and design. In addition, our work is characterized by the following:

- Our design is always appropriate, pastoral and contemplative or energetic and stimulating thematic as befits the situation
- Our work is contemporary or timeless, artistic with an intellectual basis that is respectful of the responsibility of a public art
- Our work is socially responsible, regionally responsive
- We are problem solvers who delight in the satisfaction of service to our clients.

Ethics. EDAW is dedicated to being a leader in the professions of its services. As such, we abide by their codes of ethics and professional conduct. We are also in business and we conduct our business with honesty and in an honorable way. We make every effort to avoid conflicts of interest wherever the potential for conflict is discovered.

Geographic Reach. EDAW is U.S. based with a truly national presence from which it addresses the full global markets—America, Europe and Asia. The firm has offices in major cities in the U.S. and some overseas, positioned to market and produce the most significant national and international projects.

People. Our identity attracts the best and brightest, but it is also structured to keep them (10 percent turnover per year). Our people are rewarded and recognized with human resources programs and professional incentives and benefits. Our Profit Sharing Plan contains $5 million; we reward our people at the top of the scale, but most importantly, it is "the" place to work—exciting, fun, dynamic, energetic, creative.

The firm employs approximately 400 people of diverse backgrounds and origins, but all of exceptional talent and enhanced with a team spirit. We are an equal opportunity employer with an affirmative action plan.

Our geographical spread provides unusual opportunities, both professional and personal,

for our people. They have the opportunity to work out of these different locations as their skills and experience match with project needs. Our work with the environment engenders respect for individuals and nurtures their professional development, helping them to help themselves.

Services and Product. Our essential services are the same today as when the firm started, plus a better balance so that graphic design and site civil are represented evenly throughout the offices. In all the services we offer we seek excellence, and we are the preeminent landscape design and urban planning firm.

The development and marketing of our professional skills is the responsibility of everyone. The Executive Committee provides leadership both inside and outside the company in this regard. It also coordinates our product development, sets priorities and coordinates programs within EDAW.

In order to effectively integrate our services, we need to keep a certain balance. At the same time, reality requires occasional shifts in response to the market. Fifty percent of our work is typically for private clients; the balance for public clients. New services are added according to our vision and their ability to be integrated in the continuum of services in a supportive and expanding way.

We are a professionally based company and our work must always have the potential to improve this planet for man's long-term habitation. Our product seeks innovation through a collaborative or team approach. We are also dedicated to client satisfaction and contributing to a project in the broadest sense, going beyond the "brief" where knowledge and situation permit.

Marketing. Marketing is critical to the continuing existence of the firm. In addition, it is a catalyst to make projects happen. We are a market- and client-driven organization, but are practice based. As such, we understand our clients and our clients' problems so that better than 50 percent of our work is from repeat clients.

EDAW's style and image is cerebral, innovative, problem-solving, and service-oriented. We are particularly known for our ability to be responsive by understanding a client's needs and generating products on short notice with quick turnaround.

EDAW has published extensively and is known to be at the forefront of its profession through its publications as well as realized plans, processes and built projects. Much of the work that comes to us from previously unknown clients is triggered from our published works and from referrals.

The firm's growth is deliberate and carefully strategized towards this vision. We are driven not by growth goals but rather by market, product and service. Growth is one way in which we measure the excellence of our product and service.

We are collaborative, forming alliances with allied professionals to achieve our global objectives.

Ownership and Governance. The firm is owned by approximately 30 principals and is governed by a nine-member Board with two to three members outside the company.

Principalship is the highest professional recognition the firm can make. As such, it is not only appropriate that principals own the company, but that they answer to each other in terms of professional product, quality and conduct.

Management. EDAW has a decentralized or regional structure to optimize service and product.

A small corporate staff provides the ties that bind the firm together through leadership, service and control functions. It leads the firm and services the offices, assisting them in serving clients and moving the company towards its desired future. Efficiency characterizes its operations, and it is recognized as the single best source of firmwide data, analysis and collective learning. Corporate energizes the firm through directing the constructive communications and pursuit of this common vision and supportive strategies.

Each office is managed by an officer of the corporation and coordinated through a committee of these officers. Decisions of each management group are made on a majority basis.

Operations. EDAW is a technology- or capital-intensive firm with the use of CADD, GIS and other similar technological applications at the cutting edge and pervasive throughout the cor-

poration. Word and data processing and CADD are routine functions of most of the staff.

The firm invests annually in a research-and-development unit that responds to the direction of the markets in which we are active to develop new products and technologies.

Technological exchange among offices, regions and other entities is considered one of the firm's greatest assets and occurs frequently on both a formal and informal basis. This goal overrides provincial office issues to create a true firm without walls.

Internal communications abound, with clear mechanics and channels as well as informal and spontaneous ones.

Landscape Architecture in EDAW

Landscape architecture is the profession of the firm's progenitors and continues to be the core of the professional services provided by EDAW. By most calculations, EDAW is one of the two or three largest private employers of landscape architects in the world. EDAW's landscape architects work shoulder to shoulder with other allied professionals in the firm, creating a client-driven, multioffice, strategic-thinking professional-practice firm that also advances professional standards, wins awards, and receives critical acclaim. The client list and the zeal of the firm's staff suggests a successor to Olmsted as steward of the world's definitive landscapes.

EDAW's Summer Student Program is a key to attracting and cultivating the best landscape architecture graduates as future employees. Each summer, ten to twelve student interns, selected from a pool of candidates provided by their landscape architecture and planning professors, take part in the program, adding candor and energy to the firm's corporate culture. The goals of the summer student program include making the schools and the profession more aware of the firm, attracting top design talent to the firm, and providing an opportunity for EDAW's professional staff to explore new ideas. Many of the summer interns later join the firm.

The program consists of a two-week retreat and a ten-week office internship. The program is hosted each year by a different EDAW office. The retreat tackles a problem of regional or national significance in the context of a real project. EDAW staff, including principals, work together as a team to develop a plan that is presented to the real project client.

After the two-week retreat, the summer interns are assigned to an EDAW office of their choice, where they take part in day-to-day activities and work on actual projects. Whereas the interns are paid for their participation, many find the most important benefit of the internship to be the doors it opens for their future careers. Many of the EDAW staff say that the summer intern program is the finest thing that EDAW does (Miyakoda 1994).

Employee Benefits

Each EDAW employee receives a valuable range of benefits designed to protect employees and their families. The benefits include medical and hospital insurance; dental care; life and accidental death and dismemberment insurance; business travel insurance; pre-tax reimbursement of health and dependent care; sick pay; short- and long-term disability insurance; profit sharing; retirement plan; vacation time; paid holidays; bonuses; special achievement awards; payment of professional license fees; professional memberships; license exam leave; educational assistance; worker's compensation; and social security.

EDAW provides medical insurance coverage on the first day of the month following the date of hire. The employee may choose a preferred provider organization (PPO) plan or an NPP plan. The PPO plan includes a 90 percent, 80 percent, or 70 percent benefit based on the employee's projected medical needs. Deductibles are $250 per individual or $750 per family. The NPP plan has a $10 copay for doctors office visits with no deductible, a $50 emergency room charge, 100 percent co-insurance, and $10 prescriptions. The firm's dental insurance, provided on the first day of the month following the date of hire, includes 100 percent coverage for preventive dentistry with no deductible; $50 deductible per year for general and major services up to a maximum of $1,500; and 50 percent for major restorative work. The firm has a flex-spending program that allows employees to pay for health care as well as dependent care with pre-tax dollars under provisions of Section 125 of the Internal Revenue Service Code.

Life insurance and accidental death and dismemberment insurance with a $25,000 benefit are provided on the first day of the month following the date of hire. Employees may also purchase supplemental life insurance at 50 percent or 100 percent of their annual salary or wage. Business travel accident insurance is a benefit for all employees on the first day of hire. Officers and principals receive $100,000, and other employees receive $50,000 of travel accident insurance.

Long-term disability insurance is provided on the first day of the month after an employee's hire date. The plan covers 60 percent of basic earnings integrated with other disability payments that the employee may receive. Employees are covered by short-term disability insurance after one full year of employment with the firm. The short-term disability insurance, which provides for two-thirds of basic earnings integrated with other disability payments, kicks in after sick pay is used. Sick pay is granted at a rate of ten days per year, and employees are eligible at time of hire, but sick pay may not be taken in advance of accrual. Sick pay is prorated for part-time employees.

EDAW has a profit-sharing plan that is based on the firm's profitability. Employees are eligible to receive profit sharing one year after being hired with a minimum of 1,000 hours of work required per year. Contributions are deposited in a retirement account for the employee. Allocations are based on a percentage of each employee's salary. EDAW also administers a 401(k) retirement plan and employees may make optional contributions of up to 15 percent of salary to the plan.

Employees are eligible to accrue paid vacation at the time of hire. EDAW pays ten days of paid vacation per year for each employee. Vacation time may not be taken in advance of accrual. Senior associates and employees with five years of service to the company receive fifteen days of paid vacation per year. Principals and employees with ten years of service to the company receive twenty days of paid vacation per year. Vacation pay is prorated for regular part-time employees. EDAW pays for eight holidays per year for full-time employees. Holiday leave is prorated for regular part-time employees.

Upon appointment to associate, senior associate, or principal, EDAW employees are eligible to receive incentive compensation based on company or office profitability. Associates and nontitled staff are eligible to receive special achievement awards and spot bonuses for outstanding performance from the date of initial hire.

EDAW pays for a portion of employee license fees after an introductory period with the company. The firm pays for 50 percent of first-time examination fees and 50 percent of license renewal fees for the state in which the office is located. After six months of employment, employees may take up to five days of leave with full pay to take professional licensing exams for the first time. When an employee is appointed to title status in the firm, EDAW pays 100 percent of the cost of one professional association membership for principals and senior associates and 50 percent of one membership for associates.

EDAW has an educational assistance program that pays for 50 percent of educational expenses up to a maximum of $500 per twelve-month period. Educational assistance is available after an introductory period.

Entry-Level Job Description— Landscape Architect

According to EDAW's director of development, the firm does not have formalized job descriptions for entry-level landscape architects. Instead, the firm looks for certain qualities in its new hires. EDAW seeks the following qualities:

- Broad interests in and sensitivity to both design and planning
- Originality
- Intelligence
- Flexibility
- Diversity
- Energy and self-motivation
- Strong conceptual and communication skills
- Creative thinking and problem-solving abilities
- Demonstrated expertise in CADD and proficiency with software generally applicable for use in a planning and design firm, including word processing, page layout, and spreadsheet applications
- Familiarity with various scales of projects from large land planning to construction documents

- Interest in sustainability, new urbanism, and rural by design

Representative Examples of EDAW's Projects

COMMUNITY REVITALIZATION

- Asia and Pacific Trade Center, Osaka, Japan
- Clarke Quay restoration and redevelopment plan, Singapore
- Colorado Springs downtown plan, Colorado Springs, Colorado
- Kobe West inner-city plan, Kobe, Japan
- Louisville West Main Street, Louisville, Kentucky
- Mission Bay plan, San Francisco, California
- Ross's Landing (Tennessee Aquarium), Chattanooga, Tennessee
- Windsor Waterfront plan, City of Windsor, Ontario, Canada

FEDERAL FACILITIES

- Castle AFB reuse plan, Atwater, California
- Fitzsimmons Army Medical Center, Denver, Colorado
- Myrtle Beach AFB reuse plan, Myrtle Beach, South Carolina
- National Renewable Energy Laboratory, Golden, Colorado
- Native American Indian Museum, Washington, D.C.
- U.S. Capitol East Plaza, Washington, D.C.
- U.S. Embassy, Lima, Peru
- Williams AFB reuse plan, Mesa, Arizona

PARKS, RECREATION, AND PUBLIC GARDENS

- Ameriflora '92 Exposition Entrance, Columbus, Ohio
- Baylands Park, Sunnyvale, California
- Cape Hatteras Lighthouse relocation, Cape Hatteras, North Carolina
- Historic Bathhouse Row, Hot Springs, Arkansas
- Mount St. Helens National Volcanic Monument, Washington

FIGURE 3-9. EDAW's long-range plan for the Monumental Core in Washington, D.C. The plan is meant to guide development through the year 2050.
Photograph courtesy of EDAW, Inc.

- National Capitol Columns, Washington, D.C.
- Sutro Baths Historic District, San Francisco, California
- Upper Newport Bay Regional Park, Newport Beach, California

RESOURCE MANAGEMENT

- Amfac strategic land plan, Oahu, Maui, Hawaii
- Everglades National Park, Everglades, Florida
- Land and Reservoir Management Plans, Idaho, Oregon, Washington; U.S. Bureau of Reclamation
- Mono Lake visual resource analysis, Mono Lake, Florida
- Mount Vernon viewshed analysis, Mount Vernon, Virginia
- San Francisco/Alameda watershed management plans, San Francisco, California

TRANSPORTATION

- Atlantic Avenue streetscape, Virginia Beach, Virginia
- Central Platte Valley transportation project, Denver, Colorado
- Interstate 25 corridor study, Colorado Springs, Colorado

FIGURE 3-10. Washington Harbour is 6-acre urban mixed use development designed by EDAW. The landscape design responded to strict limitations resulting from the project's on-structure location. Shade trees are planted in individual planters connected by continuous soil trenches beneath the pavement.
Photograph courtesy of EDAW, Inc.

FIGURE 3-11. The Australian town of Robina is a planned community situated on the Gold Coast in southeastern Queensland. The Robina Land Corporation commissioned EDAW to develop the detail plans for the town center. A series of water features will link the town square to a large circular lake.

Photograph courtesy of EDAW, Inc.

- Forty miles of interstate highway landscape and irrigation, Los Angeles, California
- Mount Vernon Memorial Highway, Washington, D.C.
- Route 87 freeway design study, San Jose, California

CORPORATE/OFFICE

- Advanced Cardiovascular Systems, Temecula, California
- Carlson Center, Minnetonka, Minnesota
- Dulles Corner, Fairfax County, Virginia
- Eleven Hundred Peachtree, Atlanta, Georgia
- Kia Motors Headquarters, Seoul, Korea
- Main Street Concourse, Santa Ana, California
- Toyota Regional Sales Headquarters, Irvine, California

INSTITUTIONAL

- Cook/Fort Worth Children's Medical Center, Fort Worth, Texas
- Penn State University Research Park, State College, Pennsylvania
- St. Joseph's Medical Plaza, Orange, California
- St. Jude's Children's Hospital, Memphis, Tennessee
- University of Colorado Health Sciences Center, Denver, Colorado
- University of Missouri—Francis/Southern Quads, Columbia, Missouri

FIGURE 3-12. EDAW provided comprehensive landscape architecture services for the Asia and Pacific Trade Center in Osaka, Japan. The project goals include transforming harsh climatic conditions into a desirable waterfront setting. EDAW's design incorporates a dramatic 25-foot grade change over the 1,800-foot waterfront. From the upper terraces to the waterfront, a step-and-ramp system provides distinctive overlooks, gardens, fountains, eating areas, pavilions, and an amphitheater.

Photograph courtesy of EDAW, Inc.

FIGURE 3-12. EDAW's design team was responsible for the $4.5 million, 36-acre land and waterscape development of the Scottsdale Princess Hotel in the heart of a spectacular Sonoran Desert site in Arizona. Plant materials included 350 palms, hundreds of shade trees, and thousands of shrubs and cacti. (A) The formal promenade courtyard of the Princess Hotel looking from the entry point. (B) The formal promenade courtyard of the Princess Hotel looking toward the entry point with the water feature in the foreground. (C) The pool patio of the Princess Hotel.

(B)

(A)

(C)

FIGURE 3-13. EDAW provided master planning, landscape architecture and site engineering services for the 30-acre Carter Presidential Center in Atlanta, Georgia.

Photograph courtesy of EDAW, Inc.

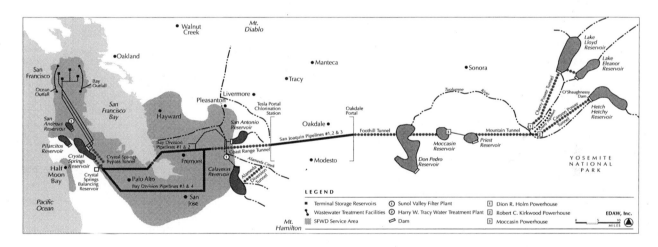

FIGURE 3-14. EDAW led a team of consultants in a four-year comprehensive planning process to identify a sustainable approach for the East Bay Municipal Utility District to supply water to its 1.2 million customers on the east side of San Francisco Bay over a thirty-year period. EDAW focused on six alternative solutions that incorporated both supply-side and demand-side management considerations. The selected plan focuses on recharging an existing groundwater storage basin instead of constructing a new reservoir for water storage. A groundwater conjunctive use program is proposed in the plan to raise the water table by recharging in wet years. In dry years, farmers in the area would draw from groundwater rather than from surface water resources.

Courtesy of EDAW, Inc.

- University of Virginia Central Grounds, Charlottesville, Virginia

RESIDENTIAL AND PLANNED COMMUNITIES

- Avenal Farm, Potomac, Maryland
- Desert Mountain, Scottsdale, Arizona
- Eco City, Chib Prefecture, Japan
- Puerto Azul, Philippines
- Robina Town Center, Brisbane, Australia
- Rock Creek, Superior, Colorado
- Techwood Homes, Atlanta, Georgia

RESORTS AND THEMED ATTRACTIONS

- Baie des Citrons, Noumea, New Caledonia
- Disney's Dixie Landings, Orlando, Florida
- EuroDisney Resort District, Marne-la-Valee, France
- Lao Lao Bay Resort, Saipan
- Palmilla Resort, Cabo San Lucas, Mexico
- Pricia Takehara, Hiroshima Prefecture, Japan
- Princeville, Kauai, Hawaii
- Santa Barbara at Spanish Waters, Curaçao, Netherlands Antilles
- Woobang Cultural Park, Taegu, Korea

UTILITY PLANNING

- Long-range water supply program, Northern California
- GIS implementation program, Boise, Idaho
- Historic hydroelectric study, Georgia
- Cutler Hydro Project, Logan, Utah
- North Umpqua Hydro Project, Oregon
- Jocassee Fold tie-In siting and EIS, South Carolina
- Victorville transmission line, California

The Acacia Group, Inc.: Small Landscape Architecture Firm

History and Overview

The firm was founded in Tucson, Arizona, in 1979 as a sole proprietorship by Walt Rogers. It grew in the 1980s, first becoming a partnership when Robert Gladwin joined the firm and next a corporation in 1983. The firm grew by merger to include a third principal, Rosina Harmony, in 1984, and by expan-

sion to include a Phoenix office managed by another principal, Brian Rothman, in 1985. Practicing under the names of its first three principals, Rogers, Gladwin & Harmony, Inc., for much of the 1980s, the firm became a leading landscape architecture office in Arizona and the Southwest. On January 1, 1989, the firm changed its name to The Acacia Group, Inc., after one of the principals left. The main reason for the new name was to make changes easier when principals departed, were hired, or were promoted from within. The firm's remaining partners agreed that establishing name recognition for the firm that didn't include the owners' names would give long-term stability to the name of the firm.

Beginning in 1989, the firm, which employed a staff of about twenty-five at the time, began to downsize due to the demise of the savings and loan industry in the United States and its impact on construction funding. Further hardship occurred with the 1991–1992 recession and a nationally depressed development and construction industry. The Acacia Group, which leveled off in 1991 at a small office staff of four or five people, is still guided by Walt Rogers. He and his partner, John Hucko, are considered to be experts in Xeriscape design for arid region site planning, landscape architecture, and irrigation design.

The firm's primary areas of professional practice have included

landscape architecture
site planning
park and recreation planning
urban design
environmental assessment
irrigation design
water conservation planning
desert revegetation programs
historic landscape preservation

The Acacia Group has been the recipient of over thirty local awards and three national awards for excellence in design, research, and resource planning. A recent award for Sunnyslope Transit Center in Phoenix came from the United States Energy Department for the firm's innovative use of cooling towers on the project. The Acacia Group served as the prime planning and design consultant on this project. In 1991, Walt Rogers, representing the firm, received a Landscape Visionary Award for his work on the

Sunrise Drive Arterial in Pima County, Arizona. Sunrise Drive was described by the architectural critic of the *Tucson Citizen* newspaper as the most aesthetic arterial road in Pima County.

MISSION STATEMENT

The Acacia Group seeks to provide the highest quality landscape architecture services in Tucson, Arizona, the Southwest, and other arid environments by serving its clients with honesty, integrity and the highest professional ethics. The firm seeks to provide the best professional effort on behalf of its clients, both public and private, and respond to the needs of all users of the built and natural world.

Members of the firm take great pride in their work and believe they are stewards of our land, sustaining it for future generations. We strive always to improve the relationship between people and the world they live in. And, we set an example by personal commitment to a way of life centered on spiritual values.

We believe that people are our greatest resource. We strive to create a working environment that is people-friendly and supportive of the personal and professional goals of all of those that work for The Acacia Group. For, it is the collective goals of all of our individual employees, past, present, and future, that creates the heart and soul—the corporate culture—of The Acacia Group.

The Acacia Group is committed to landscape architectural solutions that are fiscally feasible, socially responsible, and sensitive to a sustainable future for our natural and cultural resources. We strive to be recognized for our professional expertise and technical competence. Our mission is achieved by satisfied clients who believe they have gained value from our professional services.

Landscape Architecture in The Acacia Group, Inc.

Because the firm has always focused on landscape architectural project design, the role of the landscape architect has been paramount. All professional staff, whether entry level or advanced, are encouraged to be problem solvers and to take on as much responsibility as they are willing to assume. Entry-level landscape architects are encouraged to challenge themselves. The management style of the firm's principals is focused on

providing opportunities for personal and professional development. Landscape architects are given responsibility for all phases of project design, for production of the instruments of our service, and for interpersonal, interprofessional, and client relationships at the earliest possible time after employment with the firm.

The work of the firm is normally carried out by the line staff under the direction of the firm's seasoned professionals, who guide the staff as mentors rather than dictating the outcome of any given project. The firm's principals believe that junior staff best learn how to provide professional services when individuals are allowed to make their own mistakes and cherish their own successes. Because the firm is a business operation, it sensitizes all employees to the need to provide professional landscape architectural services in a profitable manner. The firm emphasizes project time management and completion of contracted professional services within the hours allotted for each project. The stability and reputation of the firm are a direct result of individual effort and close cooperation between all of the firm's professional and administrative staff. The firm encourages its landscape architects most of all to enjoy their work. The Acacia Group strives for a happy and professionally fulfilled landscape architecture staff.

Employee Benefits and Personnel Policies

Each employee of The Acacia Group receives benefits provided by the firm as a measure of the firm's gratitude for the employee's service. The firm has established personnel policies and company benefits to promote fair and equitable treatment of all employees.

Employees of The Acacia Group are hired as full-time, part-time, or temporary staff. A twelve-week probation period is applicable for all full-time and part-time staff. Employees are not eligible for company benefits, except those required by law, until satisfactory completion of the probation period. Managers of the firm have the option to shorten or extend the probation period.

Each employee signs an employment agreement with the following terms:

1. The Acacia Group, Inc., the company, will employ the undersigned in the initial position of _____ and at the initial wage rate of _____.

2. The employee's future wage rate and position(s) shall be determined by the company in its sole discretion.

3. The employee's employment with the company is not for any specified term and may be terminated by the employee or by the company at any time for any reason, with or without cause.

4. Paragraphs 1, 2, and 3 above constitute the complete agreement between the employee and the company regarding matters referred to in said paragraphs and supersede any and all prior written or oral agreements or understandings on such matters. The employee understands that no representative of the company has been authorized to enter into any agreement or commitment with the employee that is inconsistent in any way with the terms of paragraphs 2 and 3 above.

5. The terms set forth in paragraphs 2 and 3 above may not be modified in any way except by a written agreement signed by the employee and by an authorized representative of the company that expressly states the intention of the parties to modify the terms of the agreement.

Signed: _____

Other personnel policies cover office hours, the work week, overtime, time cards, and pay periods.

Holidays

The firm provides paid holidays for New Year's Day, Memorial Day, Fourth of July, Labor Day, Thanksgiving Day, Christmas, and a floating holiday that may be used any time by each eligible employee. Full-time employees are paid for eight hours. Part-time employees are paid on a prorated basis of time worked.

Leave Time

The firm lumps together all leave time, whether for illness or for personal leave such as vacations or other personal time off. The firm emphasizes the importance of leave time for rest and relaxation, as well as for sickness or personal reasons. All employees are encouraged to take leave time to the maximum amount earned. The firm tries to arrange that all requests for leave time fit the individual needs of each employee. All personnel are requested to advise their supervisor of leave time preferences as far in advance as possible.

Paid leave time is available to all full-time and part-time personnel starting on the employee's anniversary date when the probation period has been completed. The first year's leave time is prorated from the anniversary date to December 31 of the same year. Thereafter, leave time is calculated on a calendar basis. Leave time for part-time employees is paid on a prorated basis of time worked. Paid leave time is not available to employees on probation. Staff are informed by monthly printouts of the leave time they have accumulated, the leave time they have used, and the leave time they have remaining for each calendar year.

An employee may borrow up to five paid leave days in addition to those earned up to the maximum amount owed by the company. If an employee terminates employment prior to repayment of the borrowed days, the balance of the advanced leave time is deducted from the employee's termination pay. All leave must be used within the calendar year and cannot be carried over to the following year unless approved in advance by an authorized representative of the company. If an employee is requested by an authorized representative of the company to delay taking leave time, or is prevented from doing so by compelling circumstances, payment may be authorized for leave time not taken.

Leave Time Schedule

Length of Employment	Paid Leave Time
Year 1	40 hours/year
Year 2	64 hours/year
Year 3	80 hours/year
Year 4	96 hours/year
Year 5 and 5+	120 hours/year

Disability Leave

If an employee becomes disabled on the job or becomes pregnant, the employee may take up to four months unpaid leave time. Every effort will be made to return the employee to his or her previous position and compensation level upon return to the company; however, this is not guaranteed. The employee is responsible for notifying the company and developing a mutually acceptable disability leave schedule. During this time, health insurance benefits will continue at the employee's cost according to the prevailing benefit policy in effect at the time.

Absence and Tardiness

Absence and tardiness are detrimental to the operation of the company. All personnel are expected to be at work during the normal business hours, Monday through Friday. Scheduled leave time and all other unscheduled time off from work must be charged to the available leave time accrued by the individual in accordance with leave-time policy. Employees may elect to take time off for absence without pay. Making up time is not permitted unless circumstances require absence from work and the absence is approved in advance by an authorized representative of the company. When an employee must be absent from work because of illness or other unscheduled need for time off, he or she must notify an authorized representative of the company. Excessive absence or tardiness may be cause for reprimand or dismissal.

Reimbursable Expenses and Expense Accounts

Employees required to spend personal money for approved company business expenditures, such as travel or supplies, will be reimbursed by the firm. Receipts, invoices, or other forms of verification of expense must be submitted with time cards. The employee will submit a job number to bill the expense to with the request for reimbursement. Upon approval, petty cash held at the office can be used to pay for purchases. Employees may also request a corporate check or the use of a corporate credit card for payment of business expenditures in advance of the purchase.

The use of personal cars for business purposes will be reimbursed at the prevailing IRS rate (currently $.30 per mile). The employee must submit mileage reports with the project number for billing to the client.

Out-of-Town Travel

All project related out-of-town travel must be approved by the managing principal. Employees will submit an expense report form with attached receipts to that principal within two days of return. All salaried employees will receive their regular salary while traveling in a project-related capacity. All hourly employees will be paid for actual hours spent en route and in directly billable capacity.

Airline reservations, ticket charges, and rental cars will be handled in advance in most cases. Employees will receive a per diem of $65 per night for lodging and $35 per day for meals. These limits apply to every employee of the company, but may be extended upon approval by an authorized representative of the company. A travel advance may be obtained upon twenty-four hours notice with preparation of a written expense budget estimate. The spending of reasonable travel-related expenses is a professional responsibility.

Employee Insurance Benefits.

The firm desires to provide adequate personal and family benefits and optional insurance programs so that concern with these issues will be reduced to a minimum. The firm's insurance benefits, as well as related federal and state programs, include the following:

1. Worker's Compensation Insurance
   All employees are insured in accordance with state and federal laws for accidents or injuries incurred during the course of performing work for the company. Each employee is responsible for promptly reporting to the office any on-the-job injury. The firm pays one hundred percent of these insurance premiums.

2. Group Health Insurance
   The firm offers a group health insurance plan (HMO) to all eligible employees. At this time, the firm pays for 50 percent of the employee's individual premium. The employee pays for 50 percent of the individual premium and 100 percent of premiums for any dependent or family coverage. A deduction is made from the employee's paycheck to cover the employee's share of the premium. The coverage is available at the earliest possible date allowed by the insurance provider. Employees are responsible for 100 percent of the cost of health insurance during the probationary period.

3. COBRA (Consolidated Omnibus Budget Reconciliation Act)
   Federal law requires most employers having certain group health plans to offer employees and their families the opportunity for a temporary extension of health coverage at group

rates if the employee would otherwise lose coverage because of a "qualifying event." One hundred percent of the premium plus administrative charges will be paid by the employee if he or she elects to continue coverage.

Professional Registration, Organizations, and Education

The firm will pay professional registration fees for principals, associates, and others as deemed necessary for the operation of the company.

The firm will pay for one-half of the cost of membership in one professional organization as long as the individual is active in that organization. *Active* is defined as participating regularly in meetings, holding office, and representing the company on committees. Membership must be approved by a principal in advance of the request for reimbursement of the membership costs.

Payment or reimbursement of expenses by the firm for employee education, seminars, workshops, or conferences is made on a case-by-case basis at the discretion of the company. The employee must make a request for assistance. The firm welcomes all requests and encourages employees to advance their educational pursuits.

Work Area

A clean, orderly desk and work area reflect each employee's quality of workmanship. Each individual is expected at the end of each day to leave his or her work area in a neat and tidy condition. This daily cleanup minimizes fire hazard, promotes general office aesthetics, and safeguards office and personal equipment.

Telephone Calls

Employees making long-distance business calls are required to list each call and a project number for billing. Personal long-distance calls during business hours are discouraged except in an emergency or for compelling personal reasons. Personal long-distance calls should be noted on the form provided or charged to the employee's home phone number or personal calling card. The charge for personal long-distance calls will be deducted from the employee's paycheck. Personal local calls should be made with discretion and for important reasons.

Resignation

Employees who intend to resign for any reason are asked to give at least two weeks' notice. Termination pay will be through the effective date of resignation plus accrued leave. Termination pay is paid on regular pay dates and at the discretion of the company.

Disciplinary Action and Dismissal

The company will not tolerate any behavior by an employee that is unprofessional, unproductive, or disruptive to the work of others. The following policy outlines the procedure by which such actions or behavior will be handled:

1. A verbal warning (first warning) will be given to the employee. The circumstances of the offense and warning will be noted in the employee's personnel file.
2. A written warning (second warning) will be prepared, signed by the employee and the supervisor, and placed in the employee's personnel file.
3. Another verbal and written warning (third warning) will be prepared, signed by the employee and the supervisor, and placed in the employee's personnel file. Disciplinary actions or restrictions may be issued.
4. If the behavior continues, the employee may be dismissed from employment.

Equal Employment Opportunities and Harassment

The Acacia Group is an EEO firm and has always been committed to its equal opportunity program. The written program is available for review by any employee. All employees have the right to work in an environment that is free of discrimination and harassment. In particular, conduct that has the purpose or effect of substantially interfering with an individual's work performance or creating an intimidating, hostile, or offensive work environment is not permitted.

If any employee encounters conduct that is inconsistent with this policy, the conduct should be reported to a principal of the firm. The company maintains detailed procedures for resolving such conflicts. All claims will be investigated. If the company determines that harassment has occurred in violation of this policy, appropriate disciplinary action will be taken.

Compliance with the firm's legal obligations regarding equal employment opportunity and harassment shall be taken very seriously by all employees. Please help us preserve mutual respect for all employees of the firm.

Outside Employment

Outside employment is discouraged. Full mental and physical capabilities are hampered by holding more than one job. Involvement in additional employment using company equipment or creating a conflict of interest for either the firm or its clients may be cause for dismissal.

Merit Raises, Performance Reviews, and Promotion

Merit raises and promotions are based on performance and merit. During annual reviews, employees set their own professional goals for growth and development within the company. Achieving these goals is an important factor in assessing performance and awarding merit raises and promotions. The employee's fulfillment of assigned professional responsibilities during the year is another important consideration.

The first performance review occurs at the end of the probation period, usually twelve weeks after beginning employment with the firm. Thereafter, formal performance reviews are held on an annual basis on the employee's anniversary date. Informal reviews may be held on a case-by-case basis and when requested by an employee. Performance reviews are normally carried out by a principal most familiar with an employee's work and one or more of the firm's management staff.

Raises are based on four main considerations, including the employee's profitability to the firm:

1. Achievement of professional goals set at the annual review.
2. Positive feedback from clients, supervisors, and co-workers.
3. Completing contracted work within the hours and fee scheduled for the projects. An employee's performance on all projects worked on during the period covered by the review will be considered. Profitability will be rewarded.
4. Attitude and happiness of the employee.

Jury Duty

Recognizing that jury duty is an important civic responsibility, the company will pay the employee's normal full-time salary or wage for participating on a jury for up to five days. The employee must transfer his or her jury stipend to the company. Benefits will continue without interruption. Expenses for travel or meals are not reimbursed.

Stamping of Plans

Employees who have obtained registration and are directly supervising the preparation of plans may stamp documents prepared by themselves or employees working under their direction. The documents must be reviewed by a principal and be reviewed under the procedures established for quality control in the office.

Confidentiality

All employees will respect proprietary and confidential information concerning company business. Personnel policies, compensation, billing rates, project fees, marketing prospects, and company financial condition are key areas where confidentiality must be respected. Outside requests for corporate or project information should be directed to a principal.

Entry-Level Job Description— Landscape Architect

Occupational Classification:
　　Project designer, project planner
Organizational Relationships:
　　1. Reports to: principals, project managers, senior designers, or planners
　　2. Coordinates with: project managers, senior designers or planners
Primary Job Summary: Responsible for design or planning functions and assignments under the direction of senior design or planning staff, project managers, or principals.
Work Performed:
　　1. Executes assigned design or planning tasks.
　　2. Produces drawings and performs drafting functions manually or by computer.

3. Executes assigned research and investigation tasks such as site analyses.
4. Performs construction field observation and site measurements under the direction of a project manager or senior designer.
5. Executes quantity takeoffs and construction cost projections under the direction of a project manager or senior designer.
6. Assists in writing specifications or reports under the direction of a project manager or senior designer.
7. Manages work and time for individually assigned tasks.
8. Performs tasks normally associated with the practice of landscape architecture under the direction of a project manager or senior designer.
9. Performs tasks related to the operations of the office as requested.

Education and Experience: Landscape architecture degree and experience; planning degree and experience; other design degree such as architecture or engineering; Landscape Architect in Training (LAIT) certification desired; 1–2 years experience in design and planning desired.

Personal Qualities:

1. Good organization skills, self-discipline, creativity, and motivation.
2. Interpersonal communication skills.
3. Adaptability and flexibility.
4. Even temperament, self-confidence, and ability to deal with criticism or disappointment.
5. Innovative and open to new ideas.
6. Good written and oral communication skills.
7. Sensitive to people and listens well.

Measurement of Performance:

1. Effective self-management relative to time and budget constraints on individual projects.
2. Timely and accurate submittals of work products such as plans, drawings, and reports.
3. Harmony, happiness, and productivity among co-workers.
4. Dedication to achieving highest design quality and high quality of workmanship.
5. Others as set by the individual in consultation with principals and supervisors.

Representative Examples of The Acacia Group's Projects

- Morris K. Udall Regional Park master plan
- Morris K. Udall Regional Park Recreation Center and Park Facilities
- Rillito Riverpark, Flowing Wells to Campbell Avenue (3 miles) feasibility analysis of converting the potable irrigation system to effluent, Tucson, Arizona
- Santa Cruz County Courthouse and Park Site master plan, Nogales, Arizona
- Arrowhead Park master plan, Chandler, Arizona
- Charreria, Mexican Rodeo and Fiesta facilities design program, Tucson, Arizona
- Memorial Park master plan update, El Paso, Texas
- Eastland Park and Neighborhood Center, Casa Grande, Arizona
- 13-mile Santa Cruz Riverpark master plan update, Tucson, Arizona
- University of Arizona Campus Farm master plan, Tucson, Arizona
- Pima County Flood Control District (PCFCD) "as needed" landscape architecture service contract, 1991–1993, Pima County, Arizona

FIGURE 3-15. The Acacia Group received an ASLA Merit Award in 1984 for its inventory and analysis of the health and transplant ability of 8,056 giant saguaros on the site of the La Paloma planned residential community in Tucson, Arizona.

Photograph courtesy of The Acacia Group, Inc.

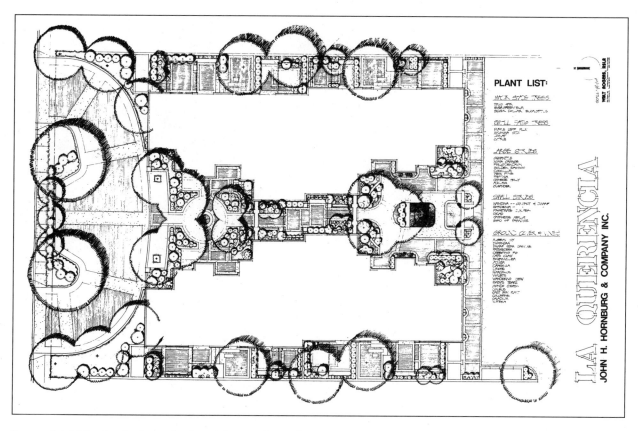

FIGURE 3-16. The Acacia Group developed the site plan and carried out landscape architecture services for La Querencia, an eight-unit town home project in Tucson, Arizona.

Illustration courtesy of The Acacia Group, Inc.

FIGURE 3-17. Automobile entry court and gated access point for La Querencia town homes.

Photograph courtesy of The Acacia Group, Inc.

FIGURE 3-18. The front entry for
the $6.4 million recreation center at
Morris K. Udall Regional Park in
Tucson, Arizona, where The Acacia
Group was responsible for designing
$1.5 million in park facilities and land-
scaping.

Photograph courtesy of The Acacia Group, Inc.

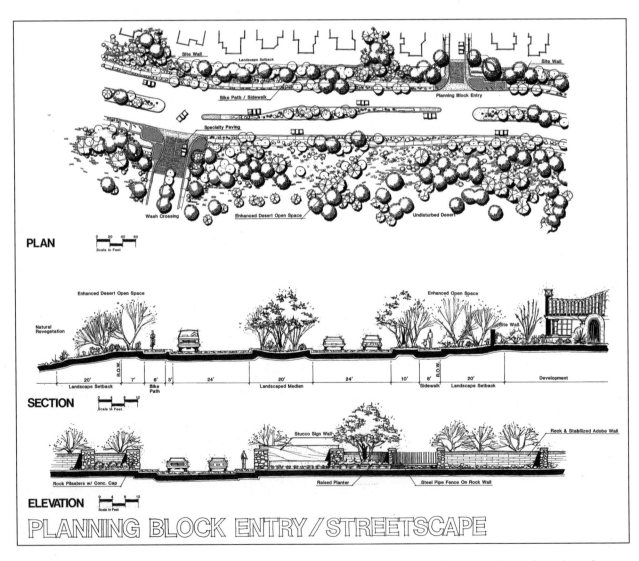

FIGURE 3-19. Desert revegetation, street right-of-way, and entry-wall plans developed by The Acacia Group for a planned community in Pima County, Arizona.

Illustration courtesy of The Acacia Group, Inc.

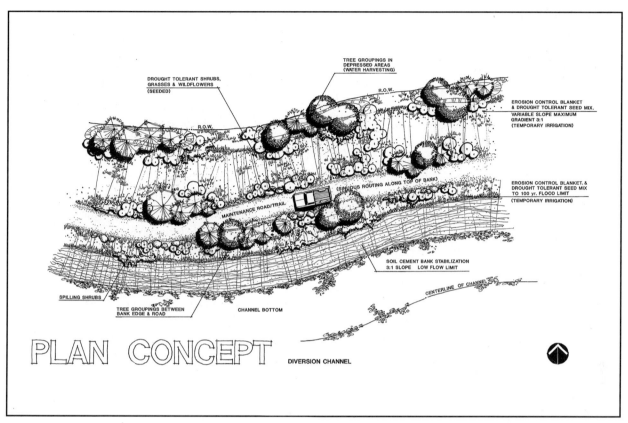

(A)

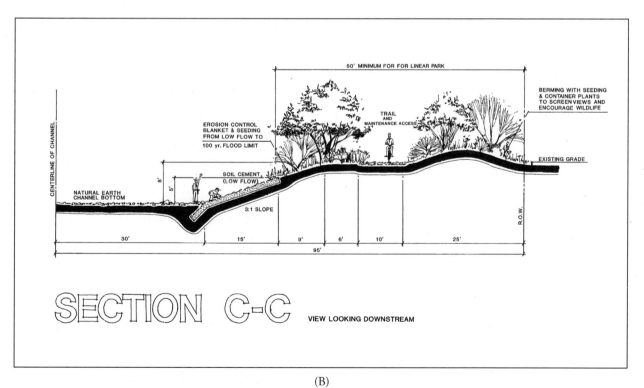

(B)

3-20. The Acacia Group's mitigation plan (A) and elevation (B) for a naturalized flood control channel and linear park using native and drought-tolerant plant materials introduced by seeding and by planting container-grown plant materials.

Illustrations courtesy of The Acacia Group, Inc.

- Balboa Park, Sepulveda Drainage Basin, U.S. Army Corps of Engineers, Los Angeles District, Los Angeles, California
- University of Arizona, Hillenbrand Stadium, Women's Intercollegiate NCAA Softball Stadium, Tucson, Arizona
- Desert West Park, recreational facility improvements, Phoenix, Arizona
- Dave White Regional Park and Golf Course improvements, Casa Grande, Arizona
- Lincoln Regional Park Softball Complex, Tucson, Arizona
- Playground for the Visually Handicapped, Arizona School for the Deaf and the Blind, Tucson, Arizona
- Kennedy Regional Park Fiesta Area and Amphitheater Park improvements, Tucson, Arizona
- University of Arizona, Central Refrigeration Plant Park Buffer, Tucson, Arizona
- Desert Sky Pavilion landscape and irrigation improvements, Phoenix, Arizona
- Colinas del Sol Apartments site improvements, El Paso, Texas
- Starrview Apartments at Starr Pass planned community site improvements, Tucson, Arizona
- B'Nai B'Rith Apartments site improvements HUD project, Tucson, Arizona
- Moonrise Apartments at Starr Pass planned community site improvements, Tucson, Arizona
- The Pyramids Apartments site improvements, Las Vegas, Nevada
- The Islander Apartments site improvements, Las Vegas, Nevada
- La Posada Congregate Nursing Care Facility, Green Valley, Arizona
- Paloma del Sol Patio Home streetscape, Pool and Recreation Center, and Model Home Complex, La Paloma planned community, Tucson, Arizona
- Las Palomitas Townhome Project streetscape, Pool and Recreation Center, and Model Home Complex, La Paloma planned community, Tucson, Arizona
- Olive Square Townhouse project site improvements, Peoria, Arizona
- La Querencia Townhomes site improvements, Tucson, Arizona
- Meso Environmental Quadraplex Underground Housing landscaping and irrigation design, Yuma, Arizona
- Foothills Ridge Townhomes streetscape and pool recreation area, Tucson, Arizona
- Fairfield in the Foothills rezoning, Pima County, Arizona
- Fairfield Sunrise East Townhomes streetscape, entry, and pool recreation complex, Pima County, Arizona
- Tanque Verde Inn site improvements, landscape and irrigation design, Tucson, Arizona
- Quality Inn Green Valley site improvements, landscape and irrigation design, Arizona
- Hotel Pitic site rehabilitation plan, Hermosillo, Mexico
- Gran Hotel de Hermosillo, Hermosillo, Mexico
- Tucson Country Club New Golf Clubhouse, Tucson, Arizona
- Sunnyslope Transit Center Site Improvements, Phoenix, Arizona
- Ronstadt Transit Center landscape and irrigation design, Tucson, Arizona
- Aviation Parkway bike path, urban nodes, landscape and irrigation design, Tucson, Arizona
- Golf Links Road landscape and irrigation design, Tucson, Arizona
- City Center Plaza, Norwest Bank Tower, Tucson, Arizona
- Historic Florence, Arizona, town center concept plan, Florence, Arizona
- Tovrea Castle landscape preservation plan, Phoenix, Arizona
- Old Las Vegas Mormon Fort Historic State Park landscape preservation master plan, Las Vegas, Nevada
- Old Towne Artisans Historic Courtyard adaptive reuse plan in the historic El Presidio neighborhood, Tucson, Arizona
- El Membrillo historic neighborhood plan, Tucson, Arizona
- Two parking lots on Main Street in historic Old Town Cottonwood, Arizona
- Conservation potential analysis for turf facilities in Arizona: criteria for the second management period 1990–2000, Arizona Groundwater Management Act, Arizona

Department of Water Resources, State of Arizona

- Inventory and evaluation of 8,056 giant saguaros on the site of La Paloma planned community, Tucson, Arizona
- Colorado Aqueduct Project (CAP) Water Treatment Plant, desert revegetation program, landscape and irrigation design, Pima County, Arizona

Adsit Landscape and Design Firm, Inc.: Landscape Architecture Design-Build Firm*

History and Overview

Russ Adsit started his design-build landscape architecture firm in 1976 in Memphis, Tennessee. A graduate with a degree in landscape architecture from the School of Environmental Design, University of Georgia, Adsit started in the design-build area of private practice immediately after leaving college. He worked for the Landscape Services company in Birmingham, Alabama, for a year before relocating to Memphis and starting his own company. He started small, working at first on maintenance projects and small landscape installations. In 1977 Adsit hired a University of Georgia landscape architecture graduate, Charles Fahrenkopf, who later became Adsit's partner. By 1978, in response to market trends, Adsit stopped doing maintenance and focused on landscape design and installation. His ability to adjust to market trends has since become a hallmark of Adsit's management of the growth and development of the firm.

By the mid 1980s, Adsit was aware of the growing demand for irrigation. His clients wanted to know that the money they spent on landscaping would be a good investment. Irrigation became an insurance policy of sorts for protecting the landscaping. Finding a lack of qualified and responsible irrigation installers, Adsit decided to offer design and installation of irrigation

systems as a central part of the firm's services. After four or five years, a number of other qualified irrigation firms opened up in Memphis, and competition was keen. By the late 1980s, Adsit realized the firm had lost money on irrigation work over a two-year period. Once again, Adsit made an adjustment and closed the irrigation division. Two of the firm's employees bought different parts of the irrigation operation and started firms that Adsit began using as subcontractors. One of the firms focused on irrigation inspection and management. The other firm focused on installation. Adsit found that subcontracting irrigation installation provided a more responsible service to his clients because the other firms had lower overhead and were focused on a specific landscape-related activity, allowing them to keep current with the technological advances in irrigation equipment. Meanwhile, Adsit was able to focus on landscape design and installation, providing a better service and product rather than trying to be all things to all people.

In the late 1980s, Adsit Landscape and Design was doing design, installation, interior landscape, and also had returned to landscape maintenance. By this time, the firm was getting major clients and larger commercial projects. The owners of the commercial projects were willing to pay profitable fees for maintenance, and this area of the firm made sense again. Memphis had become a competitive environment for leasing office space. Owners and managers of office and commercial developments rapidly became aware that the curb appeal of well-maintained projects provided a competitive edge.

Also by the late 1980s, Adsit noticed that the interiorscape business had fallen off. Again not fearing a change in direction, Adsit sold the interiors part of his business to a friend and began referring this service. By 1990 Adsit was focusing on design, installation, and maintenance of outdoor landscaping, and the firm continued winning awards. The firm won the Memphis City Beautiful Commission's Beautiful Business Award in 1989, 1990, and 1991. In 1988 Russ Adsit was named Outstanding Business Volunteer by the Memphis Botanic Garden Foundation, a tribute to his business interest.

When asked about the reasons for the success of the firm, Adsit points to the emphasis on service. He gives much credit to the early implementation of computer capabilities in the company. The firm started using computers in the 1970s for word processing and

---

*The assets of Adsit Landscape and Design Firm, Inc., were sold by Russ Adsit to Robert Pyeatt on November 18, 1994. The company now operates as The Pyeatt Company LLC dba Adsit Landscape and Design Firm.

presenting proposals in order to make an impression on clients. While continuing to use word processing for proposals, the firm has added scheduling capabilities for budgeting, billing, receivables, payables, and job costing. More recently the firm has added computer imaging to its technological repertoire.

Adsit also highlights his association with other professionals as a secret of his success, along with hard work, which he points out is a given in the landscape industry. He sets his own standards, rather than following the crowd. Maintenance has become another key to the firm's success. About 60 percent of the firm's work is maintenance, 35 percent is installation, and 5 percent is design fees. Maintenance provides the long-term continuity to the firm's landscape design and installation. Maintenance is an element of visual control of a landscape setting that a purely design-oriented firm normally does not have control over.

Russ Adsit has always been management intensive in the operation of the firm. He is concerned about people—the firm's customers and its employees. He treats them well. He's fair and honest. While focusing on people and business management, he has never been afraid of making a strategic change in the business when the need for change has appeared. He has always been willing to assess where the firm is and where it is going. He has been willing to make a change in direction if his business sense tells him it's needed.

Adsit Landscape and Design Firm, Inc., is recognized as one of the best-quality landscape design-build-maintenance firms in the Memphis and the Mid-South area. The firm has worked in Tennessee, Arkansas, and Mississippi, and has designed work in Texas, Georgia, Alabama, and South Carolina. The work is primarily commercial, residential, and industrial. The firm's services include

LANDSCAPE ARCHITECTURAL DESIGN

    Planting plans and details
    Construction details
    Irrigation plans and details
    Residential and commercial design
    Interior planting design and details
    Construction specifications
    Maintenance specifications

LANDSCAPE CONSTRUCTION

    Planting
    Irrigation
    Drainage
    Low-voltage lighting
    Retaining walls
    Patios and decks
    Brick and concrete work
    Special features
    Cross-tie work

EXTERIOR LANDSCAPE MAINTENANCE

    Quarterly programs
    Weekly mowing
    Fertilizer programs
    Preventive maintenance
    Mulching and cleanup
    Pruning and shaping
    Pre- and post-emergent herbicides
    Seasonal color (annuals and perennials)
    Pest control

MISSION STATEMENT

We are a team of landscape management professionals dedicated to and empowered by the strength of our people. We seek challenges to create innovative solutions which demonstrate our commitment to quality and a sincere desire for total customer satisfaction and profitability at a fair price. Our future growth lies in our ability to anticipate the needs of our clients and employees through communication and understanding to develop a quality environment.

Landscape Architecture in the Adsit Landscape and Design Firm, Inc.

The role of the landscape architect at Adsit Landscape and Design has always been one of salesperson, project manager, designer, and customer service representative. The staff landscape architects work directly with the client. The landscape architects assist their clients and help them achieve their landscape development goals.

The staff landscape architect has hands-on control of the project from start to finish and sees each part of the project come together from conceptualization to construction to use of the finished project by the client. The landscape architect builds a base of experience that is enriched by involvement in construction as well as design. The experience gained from overseeing the construction activities is carried forward to succeeding projects.

Evidence of the significance of landscape architects in Adsit Landscape and Design is the importance placed on professional registration and on membership in ASLA. Russ Adsit maintains professional registration as a landscape architect in six states—Alabama, Arkansas, Georgia, Mississippi, South Carolina, and Tennessee. He was elected as a Fellow in the American Society of Landscape Architects in 1992. A Fellow must have at least ten years standing as a member. Fellows are recognized for their outstanding contributions to the profession, for excellence in executed works of landscape architecture, and for direct service to the society.

Employee Benefits

The employee handbook for Adsit Landscape and Design Firm, Inc., covers the qualifications for employment and the company benefits for all employees. The purpose of the employee handbook is to communicate with employees, promote fair and equitable employment practices, encourage a high level of commitment to the goals of the company, and to familiarize new employees with the company's organization, office procedures, and employment benefits. The manual is not a contract for employment and is not the final authority on the relationship between the employer and the employee.

The handbook includes a wide range of company policies related to employment conditions, work hours, probation, salary, organization, rules, regulations, vehicle use, equipment use, and disciplinary policies. The following summary includes only those sections of the handbook related to employee benefits.

Joining the Firm

To effectively serve the firm's clients, each employee must exhibit the highest professional standards. All positions within the company are made on the basis of qualifications, experience, and competence of the individual for that particular position. Employees must pass a drug test before joining the company.

The firm does not tolerate discrimination because of age, race, creed, color, national origin, religion, economic status, or political affiliation. Employees believing that a discriminatory problem exists should report such beliefs to the owner or the persons designated to handle discriminatory problems.

The company has a policy of providing a positive work environment for employees, including freedom from sexual harassment.

The firm's policy regarding sexual harassment is as follows:

1. The company prohibits sexual harassment of its employees in any form. Such conduct may result in disciplinary action up to and including dismissal.
2. Specifically, no supervisor shall threaten or insinuate, either explicitly or implicitly, that an employee's refusal to submit to sexual advances will adversely affect the employee's employment, evaluation, wages, advancement, assigned duties, shifts, or any other condition of employment or career development.
3. Other sexually harassing conduct in the workplace, whether committed by supervisory or nonsupervisory personnel, is also prohibited. This includes offensive sexual flirtations, advances, or propositions; verbal abuse of a sexual nature; graphic verbal comments about an individual's body; sexually degrading words used to describe an individual; and the display in the workplace of sexually suggestive objects or pictures.

The firm accepts cards of interest at any time from individuals who wish to be considered for employment during the year, regardless of the season or need for workers. Applications are accepted, if there is an opening, from those individuals who the company feels meet the initial qualifications for the job. An individual must have a recently completed and signed application to be considered an active candidate for work.

A *regular employee* is defined as any employee who has completed seven months of continuous service, which includes any probationary period. Regular employees are employees who work at least 35 hours per week and 1,400 hours per year. Should a regular employee be laid off and then be recalled, that employee will continue to be considered a regular employee. The employee does not continue to accumulate benefits during a period of layoff.

A *seasonal employee* is one hired for a limited or defined period to perform a specific task at the convenience of the company. Once the particular job is completed, the seasonal position will be eliminated and the employment terminated.

Employee records are kept as required by state and federal laws.

Where practical, job openings will be announced for hiring within the company before consideration is given to hiring from outside the company.

Employees who choose to leave the company are requested to give written notice as follows:

1. Foreman: ten working days
2. Secretary: ten working days
3. Managers: twenty working days
4. Regular employees: ten working days
5. Seasonal employees: five working days

Notice is to include a reason for resignation and a forwarding address.

The dates of employment and the position held are the only items of information that will be given to anyone regarding the employee's file. Requests for recommendations will be handled on a case-by-case basis.

There are no provisions for severance pay.

Evaluations, Wages, and Probation

Employee appraisals are made on both an informal and a formal basis. Performance reviews are made after the first three months of employment and thereafter on the anniversary of the employee's date of employment. Salary reviews are made on a company-wide basis during April of each year.

If an employee is on probation, the following restrictions apply:

1. No raises or consideration of raises.
2. No paid time off.
3. No paid holidays.
4. No sick pay.
5. If any incident occurs, employment of the individual on probation will be terminated

with no consideration for unemployment benefits.

Salary

Employees of the company whose duties are professional, administrative, or managerial will normally be salaried. Salaried employees will be paid their salary irrespective of the number of hours worked per week and will receive all fringe benefits as outlined in the employee handbook.

Employees not classified as salaried will be paid on the basis of the number of hours worked. Regular employees will receive all fringe benefits outlined in the employee handbook unless otherwise indicated. Seasonal employees are ineligible for benefits.

Each employee is responsible for keeping an accurate record of actual hours worked. Failure to show an entry on the time record will result in not getting paid for that time until the time worked has been proven. The paycheck will be processed during the period immediately following receipt of a properly completed time record. Anyone caught using another person's time record or attempting to get paid for time not worked or punching the time record of another will be dismissed immediately.

Payroll checks are issued each week. The company's work week is Monday morning to Sunday night. Checks are available every Tuesday after 5:00 P.M. If Tuesday is a holiday, checks will be available the following Wednesday morning.

Bonuses are discretionary and always subject to current economic conditions, the employee's contribution to the company goals, and a supervisor's evaluation.

Promotions are based on positions open, the ability of the employee to perform the work, and a past record of good attendance, diligence on the job, and a desire to contribute to the overall goals of the company.

Whenever specific wage or labor requirements are a part of a contract project, they will be posted and brought to the attention of employees on that project.

Expenses for which employees will not be reimbursed include, but are not limited to, items of a purely personal nature, replacement of lost or stolen articles, clothing or repairs required by extreme climatic conditions, the cost of family care services, commuting travel expenses, and the cost of personal tools or equipment.

Pay advances are not a company policy. Only in proven cases of emergency will an advance of wages earned be authorized. If authorization is granted, the office must be notified one day in advance. Advances are available only to regular employees who have been employed for at least one full year. All advances are deducted in full from the next regular paycheck.

Work Considerations

The company employs a point system for tardiness and absenteeism. Points are assigned depending on the amount of notice given and the degree of lateness.

Over 15 minutes late, no call	½ point
Over 15 minutes late, call 30 minutes prior to starting time	½ point
Absent, no call	2 points
Absent, call 30 minutes prior to starting time	1 point
Absent, call or notice at least 48 hours prior to starting time	½ point

An employee who misses two consecutive days without calling or giving notice is presumed to have quit.

If an employee is in the hospital or being seen by a doctor, no points will be charged if a note from the physician is brought in.

The tardiness and absenteeism policy covers jail time, personal days, illness, hangovers, car breakdowns, ride problems, bus wrecks, and oversleeping.

Employees are allowed one unpaid, excused absence each calendar quarter without assignment of points. An excused absence must be approved 48 hours in advance.

Accumulated points for tardiness and absenteeism shall result in the following actions:

Monthly, over 2 points	counseling
Monthly, over 3½ points	dismissal
Quarterly, over 3 points	counseling
Quarterly, over 6 points	dismissal

When an employee has been counseled, the employee is considered to be on probation and subject to the terms and conditions of probation until the points fall below the monthly or quarterly minimum.

Employees required to serve on jury duty will receive pay in accordance with state law. Currently employees receive normal salary less jury compensation. Employees must give twenty-four hours' notice and present the summons for jury duty.

Employees are asked to report for work, rain or shine. Employees that report for work on rain days have the option of staying and doing tasks assigned, or may leave. Employees who leave will receive $3 for that day to cover the cost of transportation. The employee must arrive at the assigned time and clock in and out to qualify for the $3 transportation pay. Employees who receive monthly bus passes are not eligible for the $3 transportation pay. If an employee is late on a rain day, points will be assessed and no pay will be received. If an employee receives specific instructions from a supervisor not to report to work on a particular day, the employee will not receive points or be paid.

Time Off

The company allows eight hours sick pay every month, paid at the regular rate of pay. Time from normal office hours related to dental or doctor's appointments will not be considered sick leave unless prior written notice is given. Employees will be paid two sick days per calendar year without a doctor's note. Additional sick leave will only be paid after the third day out sick if a letter is received from the employee's doctor prior to the third day out of work. Sick pay will then commence from the date of the doctor's visit. A maximum of 160 hours may be accumulated. Payment in lieu of time will not be considered. Sick pay will not be paid if the employee fails to give prior notice.

Regular full-time employees will have the following holidays off with eight hours pay at the regular rate, providing the employee works regular scheduled working days before and after the holiday. If the holiday falls on a Saturday or Sunday, no pay will be allowed for that holiday. If an alternate day is allowed as the holiday, pay will be allowed for that day, but not in addition to any other pay.

Holiday	Day
New Year's Day	January 1
Independence Day	July 4
Labor Day	September legal day
Thanksgiving Day	November legal day
Christmas Day	December 25

Employees in the military forces reserve program or National Guard will receive a leave of absence without pay for their two-week training camp, or as allowed by applicable law. Supervisors should be informed as soon as possible about the schedule for the military training. Persons called up for longer active service should inform their supervisor.

All maternity leave will be treated as sick leave.

Layoffs or slowdowns normally occur during the hottest part of the summer and about December or January during the winter. The management will attempt to give as much notice as possible for these periods of time.

Vacations with pay are a benefit for regular employees actively working at the time the employee takes vacation time. Vacations with pay are not compensation for previous work performed, but a benefit granted to company employees so that they may spend time with their families and then return to work. The company may extend vacation with pay to an employee at time of layoff in November or December of each year.

To be eligible for vacation with pay, the employee must meet the following requirements:

1. The employee must work a minimum of 1,400 hours in a calendar year.
2. The employee must actively be on the company's payroll at the time the employee wants to take scheduled vacation. Any employee who quits or is terminated before taking scheduled vacation will not receive vacation pay even though the employee may have worked a minimum of 1,400 hours.
3. Vacation for regular employees will be scheduled in November or December in conjunction with layoff, unless the employee makes arrangements prior to layoff for time off within the time frame allowed the following year. If for some reason an employee does not return to work from layoff, pay in lieu of time off will not be considered.
4. Vacation may be scheduled after completion of 1,400 hours of service in a calendar year. Time off will be considered on a first-come-first-serve, seniority basis. No vacation may be scheduled March 1 through June 15, or August 15 through October 31.
5. Forms to request time off are available in the office. Only written requests for time off will be considered and must be submitted at least thirty days prior to the scheduled time off.
6. Vacation with pay will be paid at the employee's current hourly rate of pay excluding overtime rates.
Paid vacation time is as follows:
   A. One to five years of continuous service — 3 days
   B. Six to ten years of continuous service — 8 days
   C. Eleven years or more — 12 days

Out-of-Town Work

Employees assigned to work out of the normal working area will be reimbursed a daily expense of not more than $14 for each full day on the job, and the cost of all overnight lodging will be paid by the company. The compensation breakdown is as follows: breakfast, $2; lunch, $4; and dinner, $8. All expenses must be documented and turned in for reimbursement.

Company Benefits

The company offers payroll deductions for credit-union deposits. After three months of employment, an employee is eligible to join the credit union.

The company participates in the Federal Social Security Plan (FICA). Employee benefits payable under this plan are (1) monthly retirement payments at age sixty-five to the insured and dependent spouse, (2) monthly survivor's payments to the employee's family in the event of death, and (3) lump-sum death payment to the spouse of the insured or to the person who pays the funeral expenses.

The currently available insurance program will be offered to eligible employees. This benefit changes as market and underwriting conditions change.

The company provides worker's compensation insurance for its employees. If an employee is injured at work, medical treatment is guaranteed and paid for by this insurance. Should an employee be unable to work due to an injury suffered at work, the insurance will pay the employee for loss of salary as specified by the policy. Exceptions to worker's compensation insurance are as specified by law and the insurance policy.

An employee injured on the job must complete an incident report, as well as the first report of injury required by the insurance company. Failure to complete the reports may make the employee personally responsible for the expense of the injury.

An employee injured on the job will be paid for eight hours that day at the employee's regular rate of pay. Regular employees will be compensated for missed days upon notification by the treating physician for a maximum of ten days. Seasonal employees will not receive further compensation except as the worker's compensation policy allows.

The company contributes to the State of Tennessee Department of Employment Security Trust Fund as required by law. This money is available under current law to compensate any employee discharged for lack of work or without cause. Specific details of this program are available from the local Office of Employment Security.

An employee discount is available for employees. The company allows purchases of items at cost plus 15 percent. The employee must pay sales tax. Someone other than the employee/purchaser must write up the sale. A discount is not available on delivery charges when charging for delivery is necessary. Employees must pay for purchases within ten days. Items that are not stocked by the company must be paid for upon receiving the merchandise.

In addition to professional affiliation, all employees are encouraged to engage in various forms of continuing education, which may include conferences, seminars, short courses, professional society meetings, and conventions. The company pays tuition for approved continuing education programs. All such activities will be coordinated with the workload and schedule of the office.

Job Description—Landscape Designer/Salesperson

Summary: Prepares landscape designs and sells work to clients by performing the following duties:

Essential Duties and Responsibilities: The duties of the job are listed below. Other duties may be assigned.

- Greets customer on the phone and determines customer's needs prior to setting appointment on site.
- Suggests ideas that meet client's needs and emphasizes selling points of company such as quality, design, and utility.
- Visits client's home or office by appointment to sell design, installation, and maintenance services.

- Prepares design documents from fieldwork, sketches, plans, and specifications to finalized drawings in a timely fashion.
- Prepares sales and design contracts.
- Receives payment or obtains credit authorization.
- Requisitions drafting room and resource room supplies.

Supervisory Responsibilities: Coordinates 2 to 4 subordinate supervisors who supervise a total of 6 to 15 employees in the landscape division and maintenance division. Is responsible for the coordination of these units as they relate to the client's needs.

Responsibilities include planning, assigning, and directing work, addressing complaints, and resolving problems.

Qualification Requirements: To perform this job successfully, an individual must be able to perform each essential duty satisfactorily. The requirements listed below are representative of the knowledge, skill, and ability required. Reasonable accommodations may be made to enable individuals with disabilities to perform the essential functions.

Education and/or Experience: Bachelor's degree (B.L.A.) from a four-year college or university. One to two years sales-related experience or equivalent combination of education and experience is desired.

Language Skills: Ability to read and interpret documents such as safety rules, procedure manuals, and operating and maintenance instructions. Ability to write routine reports and correspondence. Ability to speak effectively before groups of customers or employees of organizations.

Mathematic Skills: Ability to calculate figures and amounts such as discounts, interest, commissions, proportions, percentages, area, circumference, and volume. Ability to apply concepts of basic algebra and geometry.

Reasoning Ability: Ability to solve practical problems and deal with a variety of concrete variables in situations where limited standardization exists. Ability to interpret a variety of instructions furnished in written, oral, diagram, or schedule form.

Certificates, Licenses, Registrations: Tennessee or home state valid driver's license. Acceptable driving record for the last three years with no drug or alcohol convictions. Pest control certification is a plus, but is not required.

Physical Demands: The physical demands described here are representative of those that must be met by an employee to successfully perform the essential functions of this job. Reasonable accommodations may be made to enable individuals with disabilities to perform the essential functions.

While performing the duties of this job, the employee is regularly required to walk and to reach with arms and hands. The employee is frequently required to sit; to use hands and fingers to handle or feel objects, tools, or controls; and to talk or to listen. The employee is occasionally required to stand, climb, or balance; to stoop, kneel, crouch, or crawl; and to taste or smell.

The employee must regularly lift or move up to 25 pounds, frequently lift or move up to 50 pounds, and occasionally lift or move up to 100 pounds. Vision requirements of this job include close vision, peripheral vision, depth perception, and the ability to adjust focus.

Work Environment: The work environment characteristics described here are representative of those an employee encounters while performing the essential functions of this job. Reasonable accommodations may be made to enable individuals with disabilities to perform the essential functions.

While performing the duties of this job, the employee regularly works in outside weather conditions. The employee occasionally works near moving mechanical parts and is occasionally exposed to fumes or airborne particles and toxic or caustic chemicals.

The noise level in the work environment is usually moderate.

Representative Examples of Adsit Landscape and Design Firm Projects

The firm specializes in residential and commercial landscape design, installation, and maintenance. Completed projects are found primarily in Memphis and the Mid-South area. By not publishing a list of the firm's residential projects, anonymity of these clients has been respected. Table 3.2, which lists some of the firm's commercial clients in the Memphis area, indicates the design, build, and maintenance services provided.

FIGURE 3-21. Residential design plan by Adsit Landscape and Design Firm for a home in Germantown, Tennessee.
Illustration courtesy of Adsit Landscape and Design Firm, Inc.

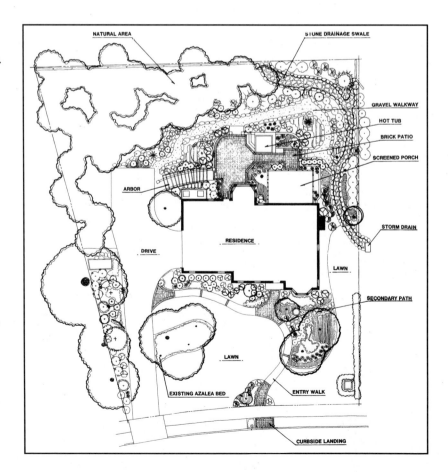

FIGURE 3-22. Driveway, front entry court, and landscaping designed and constructed by Adsit Landscape and Design Firm for a residence in Memphis, Tennessee.

Photograph courtesy of Adsit Landscape and Design Firm, Inc.

FIGURE 3-23. Landscaping designed, constructed, and maintained by Adsit Landscape and Design Firm for the Southwind Office Center.

Photograph courtesy of Adsit Landscape and Design Firm, Inc.

FIGURE 3-24. Grounds of the International Paper Computer Center where the landscaping was constructed and is maintained by Adsit Landscape and Design Firm.

Photograph courtesy of Adsit Landscape and Design Firm, Inc.

TABLE 3.2 **Memphis-Area Adsit Commercial Clients**

Client	Design	Build	Maintenance
Clark Center	X	X	X
Church of the Holy Spirit	X	X	X
Church of the Holy Communion	X	X	X
Sonic Drive-In	X	X	
Christian Brothers High School	X	X	X
Colonial Rubber Works	X	X	X
Community Bank of Germantown	X	X	
Cordova Creek Apartments	X		
International Paper Computer Center		X	X
International Place	X	X	X
Southwind Office Center	X	X	X
Federal Express	X	X	X
Gulf Oil		X	X
Memphis State University		X	X
Park Place Mall	X	X	X
Promus Companies	X	X	X
Holiday Inn		X	X
Asbury United Methodist Church	X	X	X
Bonanza Steak House	X	X	
Baddour, Inc., Headquarters	X	X	
Baddour Memorial Center		X	
Batesville Casket	X		
Weston Companies	X	X	X
Harding Academy	X	X	
Memphis Botanic Garden	X	X	X
Germantown Baptist Church		X	
Heritage Place	X	X	
Hanover Square	X	X	
Ideal Chemical	X	X	X
Infiniti of Memphis	X	X	
Kappa Delta Sorority Headquarters	X	X	X
Chi Omega Sorority Headquarters	X	X	X
Methodist Hospital		X	
Nissan Motor Corporation	X	X	X
Michelin Tire Corporation	X	X	
Memphis Belle Museum	X	X	
Mud Island	X	X	
Penn Marc Center	X	X	X

Denver Service Center, National Park Service: Public Practice

History and Overview

The National Park Service has valued the contributions of environmental design professionals from its inception. Design services were handled through regional centers until the 1950s, when the Park Service centralized planning, design, and construction services into two centers—the Western Office of Design and Construction, in San Francisco, and the Eastern Office of Design and Construction (Eastern Service Center), in Philadelphia and later in Washington, D.C. These centers provided professional services to field areas until the early 1970s, when a single, central location was selected and the Denver Service Center was born. The reason for centralizing design services was to better serve the

National Park System through a critical mass of individuals. Located under one roof, the design professionals created a synergy as they worked together to develop sensitive and appropriate solutions for the nation's heritage of unique natural, cultural, and historical sites—the U.S. national parks.

The Denver Service Center (DSC) continues to be the principal office to carry out the planning, design, and construction program of the National Park Service (NPS). The center offers professional services to all park managers in the National Park System. The DSC provides the concepts, documentation, and technical expertise allowing NPS decision-makers to implement proposals for the best management and use of the national parks.

To carry out its mission, the DSC employs a staff of landscape architects, architects, historians, engineers, natural resource specialists, sociologists, and other experts. The DSC balances the fluctuations in workload and the needs for additional expertise not available in the center by using private-sector architectural and engineering firms. Approximately one-third of the work carried out by the center is accomplished with outside consulting assistance.

Because of the range of talents required to execute the planning, design, and construction program, the DSC has the greatest aggregation of professional and technical expertise in the National Park Service. The center also houses a number of specialized services. It is a source of information and support in these areas. The DSC develops and implements life-cycle costing and value engineering for NPS projects. It provides a wide range of services through a sophisticated graphics operation, including land mapping, graphic design, and information storage and retrieval in its Technical Information Center. DSC employees often represent the National Park Service in relations with other federal agencies, universities, international organizations, and foreign governments.

Decisions to involve the DSC in a national park project are made jointly by park managers and field directors. Planning for a specific park includes a general approach followed by specific actions. The most comprehensive plan is the *general management plan.* Each park must have an approved general management plan that sets the groundwork for specific planning, design, and construction needs.

Once the broad concepts for visitor use, resource management, and park operations are established in an approved general management plan, they are explored in more detail in *specific plans* for resource management, interpretation, and development. Specific plans related to facility development or preservation are normally carried out in the DSC as part of the *design phase.*

The design process has five phases: (1) pre-design, (2) preliminary design, which consists of schematic design and design development, (3) construction documents, (4) construction, and (5) postconstruction. Construction work is normally contracted to a private company and is overseen by a DSC construction supervisor. The construction supervisors ensure that designs are carried out as specified in the construction documents so that the federal government and the National Park Service get the quality of product that was designed. The DSC also has a postconstruction evaluation program to assess completed work. Within the first year that a completed park facility is in use, the DSC is alerted to and addresses any construction problems noticed by the park manager.

The overall planning, design, cultural resource preservation, and construction program of the DSC addresses a large number of independent projects simultaneously in an efficient and management-responsive manner. Because the DSC has a finite staff and funds that are authorized in an annual budgeting process, and because all requested projects compete for the services available from the DSC, the center uses a system of servicewide assessment and priority setting to prioritize and schedule projects.

Park planning and design priorities are updated every three to five years. The director can change a priority or add a new priority at any time based on considerations such as a field director's request, congressional concern, or an emergency. Hurricane Andrew's damage to Everglades National Park is an example of how an emergency can require funding and change priorities. Shifts in priorities are determined by evaluating new projects against the ongoing program. Fluctuations in appropriations can raise the funding cutoff line for priority projects in a given year, causing a scheduled project to be delayed until funding levels are increased or higher priority projects are completed. Congressional initiatives also affect priorities and projects that are in line for funding. Reprioritization can dramatically affect the DSC's work from year to year.

The Denver Service Center functions as a project matrix organization. Project managers are the leaders in accomplishing the center's work. They are the single point of contact for the client. They are selected based on the management needs for the project and the professional discipline best suited to the client's needs. Project managers select from a discipline pool of professionals to assemble a project team. The client, or a representative of the client, is a full member of the project team. A project agreement serves as the contract between interests on each job.

The office hierarchy of the DSC comprises a leadership team made up of the director, chief of operations, chief project manager, and the chiefs of architecture, landscape architecture, engineering, contract administration, resource planning, and management services. The leadership team also includes an executive assistant and a communications specialist. Quality leaders provide direction and professional guidance to employees. Technical experts contribute specialized expertise in various aspects of the disciplines at the DSC.

Mission Statement

The Denver Service Center created the following vision statement in 1995 as part of an intensive effort to re-engineer its organization and its delivery of services:

> National Park Service Employees at the Denver Service Center are committed to providing quality planning, design, and construction services for parks and the public that treasures them. We share a commitment with our National Park Service partners within the National Park Service to protect our natural and cultural heritage while providing our services in a timely and cost-effective manner.

The Role of the Landscape Architect in the Denver Service Center

Landscape architects have enjoyed enormous flexibility for advancement in the National Park Service and the Denver Service Center. They can stay in a design role or move into management positions as park superintendents, field directors, park chiefs of maintenance, administrators, project managers, and construction supervisors. Landscape architects have an impressive record of rising to top management positions in the NPS. At least two directors of the

National Park Service were trained as landscape architects.

If a landscape architect wishes to stay within the career track of professional practice, the Denver Service Center offers a rich interdisciplinary work environment. In many ways, the DSC resembles a large multidisciplinary planning and design firm that specializes in park and recreation projects. The office size varies. It has ranged between 500 and 800 employees. In addition to landscape architects, the staff includes architects, natural scientists, archaeologists, and planners, as well as structural, civil, mechanical, environmental, electrical, and geotechnical engineers. The DSC offers an excellent opportunity for entry-level landscape architects to learn from experienced professionals of all disciplines.

Professional-practice career tracks for landscape architects include planning, design, and construction. Typical planning projects consist of evaluating sites for inclusion in the National Park System; preparing large-scale general management plans (master plans that address land-use management and policy issues); and preparing conceptual development plans, transportation plans, parkwide trail plans, and resource-management plans. The planning process requires evaluating and documenting environmental impacts by preparing environmental impact statements. Landscape architects often assume the lead role in preparing these documents. Public involvement is an important aspect of the planning and design process. Landscape architects with effective presentation skills, as well as diplomacy and conflict mediation talents, often play leadership roles in public meetings.

The bulk of the design work consists of doing site development plans for small-scale projects such as park roads, parking areas, visitor centers, maintenance complexes, campgrounds, trailheads, trails, boating facilities, and concession facilities. There are challenges associated with designing facilities in remote settings, often with severe climatic constraints, and designing facilities that are sustainable, easily maintained, durable, and vandal proof. Landscape architects spend time preparing the project scope of work in conjunction with other design-team members, park staff, and regional administrators. Landscape architects develop schematic design alternatives, design development drawings, presentation graphics, construction cost projections, and construction drawings and specifications.

The DSC's designers use a combination of Auto-trol, AutoCADD, and Intergraph computer programs. Landscape architects also have a variety of visual simulation and geographic information system (GIS) software available for their use.

In addition to design work, the landscape architect has opportunities to serve as a project supervisor on the construction site, ensuring that the contractor performs the work in accordance with the design intent and the construction documents. Project supervisors act as liaison between the contractor and the designers, as well as between the contractor and the NPS contracting office responsible for paying the contractor. Project supervisors spend much of their time watching the construction activity, poring over plans and specifications, doing daily and weekly reports, meeting with the contractor to resolve anticipated problems, interpreting the construction documents, discussing safety issues, and writing and negotiating contract modifications and change orders. Opportunities exist for the landscape architect to design a project, move into the field to supervise construction, and return to the office for more design work. Overall, opportunities for the landscape architect in the Denver Service Center are limited only by an individual's interest and enthusiasm.

Employee Benefits

The National Park Service offers DSC employees a comprehensive benefits package available to all federal employees.

Leave Time

Employees earn sick leave and annual leave time based on the time of service. Annual leave increases with the time of service. Sick leave remains the same throughout an employee's time in government service. Leave is earned as follows:

- Four hours of sick leave are earned for each eighty hours worked.
- Four hours of annual leave earned for each eighty hours worked during the first three years of service
- Six hours of annual leave earned for each eighty hours worked after three years of service

- Eight hours of annual leave earned for each eighty hours worked after fifteen years of service
- Ten paid holidays per year

Health Benefits

One of the benefits of working for the government is the protection against the cost of medical care. A range of health plan options are available under the Federal Employees Health Benefits program (FEHB). Participation in FEHB is voluntary, but enrollment is encouraged. The government pays 60 percent of the average high option premium of the six largest health benefits plans in its program, but not more than 75 percent of the total premium for any plan. After the government contribution is deducted from the total cost, the employee pays the remainder of the premium through salary withholdings.

Two basic types of plans are available: fee-for-service plans and prepaid plans. Fee-for-service plans reimburse the employee for covered services. The employee enrolled in a fee-for-service health plan may choose the physician, the hospital, and other health care providers. The Blue Cross and Blue Shield plan is an example of a fee-for-service health plan. Prepaid plans include the comprehensive medical plan (CMP) and health maintenance organization (HMO) plan. These plans provide or arrange for health care by designated physicians, hospitals, and other providers in specific locations. Coverage under each basic plan may be elected for the individual or for the family. Specific regulations cover the time of enrollment and effective dates for coverage.

Life Insurance

Life insurance can be purchased at the employee's option through the Federal Employees' Group Life Insurance (FEGLI) program. The program offers low rates and the convenience of payment through a payroll deduction. The government pays one-third of the cost of the basic insurance. Employees are automatically covered unless the coverage is waived by the employee. The program includes the basic life insurance plan with three options: standard, additional, and family.

Under the basic plan, life insurance coverage is equal to the employee's actual rate of annual basic pay (rounded to the next $1,000) plus $2,000, or

$10,000, whichever is greater. The basic plan includes an extra benefit of double the amount of the life insurance benefit until age thirty-six, decreasing at 10 percent per year until age forty-five at which time the extra coverage ends. The basic plan also includes accidental death and dismemberment coverage, but the extra benefit does not apply to this coverage.

The standard option increases the coverage by $10,000. If the employee's basic pay is higher than the basic coverage plus $10,000, the standard option may be increased to the actual salary amount rounded to the next $1,000. Coverage for accidental death and dismemberment may be increased up to the actual face value of the standard option. The employee pays the full cost of the standard option to the basic plan.

The additional option, which is elective and fully paid by the employee, allows the employee to elect additional coverage in the amount of one, two, three, four, or five times annual basic pay.

The family option allows the employee to cover eligible family members: $5,000 for spouse and $2,500 for dependent children. The employee pays the full cost of coverage under this option.

Retirement Benefits

Employees earn retirement benefits based on the Federal Employees Retirement System (FERS). The FERS is a three-tiered program that includes social security benefits, a basic benefit plan, and a thrift savings plan. Each employee of the National Park Service pays full social security taxes and a small contribution to the basic benefit plan. In addition, the NPS contributes an amount equal to 1 percent of the employee's basic pay each pay period into the employee's thrift savings plan. The three components of FERS work together to give each employee of the Denver Service Center a financial foundation for retirement years.

Savings Plan

A thrift savings plan (TSP) allows employees to contribute up to 10 percent of their salary to a savings plan. The DSC contributes an additional 1 percent automatically to the savings plan and up to an additional 4 percent based on the amount contributed by the employee. If the employee contributes 5 percent, for example, the DSC is automatically required to contribute an additional 1 percent and makes a matching contribution of 4 percent, for a total of 10 percent. The intent of the TSP is to be the third part of the retirement savings plan. Employees may not withdraw money from the TSP while still employed by the federal government. Loans may be made, however, from the funds for certain purposes such as purchasing a house, education expenses, medical expenses, and financial hardships. All participants may choose from one or more of the three TSP funds for investment opportunities. The three funds are the Government Securities Investment Fund, the Common Stock Index Investment Fund, and the Fixed Income Index Investment Fund.

Entry-Level Job Description— Landscape Architect

The entry-level job description for landscape architects seeking employment with the Denver Service Center falls under the government service rank of GS-807-05.

Position: Official Title: Landscape Architect

Summary of Duties: Assists professional landscape architects to relieve them of routine tasks in the design function.

Performs landscape architectural design work on a single aspect of a broader project designed by a higher-level professional or may be required to design sites for which functional layout of similar sites can be adapted. Discusses with higher-grade landscape architects the data needed to accomplish the job and the proper approach to the problem.

Collects data for design work by researching existing files, previous designs, consultation with higher graded landscape architects, and by field observation.

Utilizing data, under close supervision, completes preliminary drawings, construction drawings, and specifications.

Prepares scale models, including landscape architectural, architectural, and engineering aspects of work in the Branch of Planning, primarily of work assigned to the Landscape Architectural Section.

Factor 1—Knowledge Required by Position:

Knowledge of professional landscape architectural principles and concepts, as well as the ability to apply standard practices, methods, and techniques to perform design work of limited scope. Familiarity with allied architectural, civil engineering, planning, and biological science fields as these relate to landscape architecture.

Factor 2—Supervisory Controls:

Supervisor makes assignments together with specific instructions as to objectives, scope, anticipated problems, and procedures to be used. Work of a repetitive nature is performed independently. Any deviations, problems, or unusual situations are referred by the employee to the supervisor or higher-grade professional. Work is reviewed upon completion for accuracy and adherence to standard practices and to assure conformance with requirements.

Factor 3—Guidelines:

Guidelines include technical manuals, directives, precedents, standards, texts, specifications, and established practices. Such guidelines are detailed and are usually directly applicable to individual assignments. The employee exercises judgment in selecting appropriate guidelines and deciding among alternative approaches. Situations where existing guidelines are inadequate are referred to supervisor or higher grade landscape architect.

Factor 4—Complexity:

Assignments consist of varied projects intended to provide diversified experience as a foundation for future project responsibility of greater scope, difficulty, or magnitude. Assignments are typically screened to eliminate difficult or unusual problems. Assignments require familiarity with and use of standard principles, methods, and practices to solve relatively limited professional problems. Assignments may also be made to provide assistance to higher-grade professionals in the allied design professions of engineering and architecture for the purpose of broadening an understanding of the interrelationship between the professions. Work of this nature is closely supervised as a learning process by responsible higher-grade professionals.

Factor 5—Scope and Effect:

Personal contacts are with other landscape architects and other professionals such as architects, engineers, planners, natural resource specialists and cultural resources specialists within the immediate office.

Factor 6—Purpose of Contacts:

Contacts are chiefly to obtain advice or assistance, to report on status or results of work, and to obtain information on condition of existing facilities and systems.

Factor 7—Physical Demands:

Work is essentially sedentary except for occasional walking, bending, and climbing during facility or construction site visits.

Factor 8—Work Environment:

Work is usually performed in an office setting, although there are occasional visits to facility or construction sites.

Representative Examples of Denver Service Center Projects

- Aztec Ruins National Monument preservation plan, New Mexico
- Arkansas Post National Memorial Visitor Center, Arkansas
- Andersonville National Historic Site Visitor Center, Museum and Entry Drive, Georgia
- East Broad Top Railroad protection management and interpretive plan, Pennsylvania
- Bent's Old Fort National Historic Site reconstruction plan, Colorado
- Biscayne National Park Convoy Point site plan, Florida
- Blue Ridge Music Interpretive Center site plan and environmental assessment, Virginia and North Carolina
- Buffalo National River preservation plan, Arkansas
- Cambria Iron Company historic resource study, Pennsylvania
- Delaware Water Gap National Recreation Area Day-Use Pavilion, Pennsylvania and New Jersey
- Grand Canyon National Park waterline replacement, Arizona
- Grand Canyon National Park Entrance Station facility, Arizona
- Grand Teton National Park plan for Colter Village, Wyoming
- Indiana Dunes National Lakeshore Environmental Education Center, Indiana
- Jean Lafitte National Historic Park and Preserve restoration, Louisiana
- Jean Lafitte National Historic Park and Preserve Interpretive and Operations Center, Louisiana

FIGURE 3-25. Denver Service Center landscape architects and architects carried out the site planning and architectural design for the Rainy Lake visitor center, marina, and operations offices, the first facilities in Voyageurs National Park, Minnesota.
Photograph courtesy of National Park Service, U.S. Department of Interior.

FIGURE 3-26. Site design details for the Rainy Lake visitor center, Voyageurs National Park, include carefully detailed wood and battered rock walls seen in this photograph of the entry walk.
Photograph courtesy of National Park Service, U.S. Department of Interior.

- Johnstown Flood National Memorial Visitor Center, Pennsylvania
- Johnstown Flood National Memorial Historic Unger House adaptive reuse for offices, Pennsylvania
- Klondike Gold Rush National Historical Park historic structures rehabilitation, Alaska
- Lincoln Home National Historic Site restoration, Illinois

FIGURE 3-27. Denver Service Center staff were responsible for project planning at Ellis Island, New York, a part of the Statue of Liberty National Monument.

Photograph courtesy of National Park Service, U.S. Department of Interior.

FIGURE 3-28. Denver Service Center staff prepared plans and technical specifications for the restoration of the ornamental copper domes on the main structure at Ellis Island.

Photograph courtesy of National Park Service, U.S. Department of Interior.

FIGURE 3-29. Denver Service Center staff designed the boardwalk trail through a sensitive resource area at Sandstone Falls in the New River National River, West Virginia.

Photograph courtesy of National Park Service, U.S. Department of Interior.

FIGURE 3-30. Overlooks on the Sandstone Falls boardwalk provide interpretive and educational points as the trail meanders through various plant communities.

Photograph courtesy of National Park Service, U.S. Department of Interior.

FIGURE 3-31. In the 1950s, Colter Bay Village was developed at Grand Teton National Park. The village includes a visitor center, marina, lodging, restaurants, a store, service stations, campgrounds, a picnic area, and employee housing. In the 1980s, significant user pressure on the facilities gave rise to proposals for rehabilitating the existing facilities and adding new facilities.

Photograph courtesy of National Park Service, U.S. Department of Interior.

- Mesa Verde National Park plan for structures to shelter surface ruins, Colorado
- New River Gorge National Park high-use trail plan, West Virginia
- Redwood National Park Information Center, California
- Statue of Liberty National Monument rehabilitation plan, New York
- Steamtown National Historic Site plan, Pennsylvania

- Voyageurs National Park Rainy Lake Visitor Center, Minnesota
- Yellowstone National Monument design and restoration of Old Faithful Inn, Wyoming, Idaho, Montana
- Yosemite National Park employee housing, California
- Yosemite National Park Waste Water Treatment Plant, California

FIGURE 3-32. The Denver Service Center planning team used computer simulation to analyze development alternatives at Colter Bay Village, Grand Teton National Park.

Photograph courtesy of National Park Service, U.S. Department of Interior.

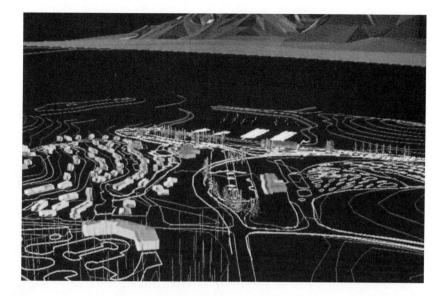

FIGURE 3-33. Reconstruction plans for Bent's Old Fort National Historic Site, built in 1829 along the Santa Fe Trail, were carried out by a Denver Service Center planning team.

Photograph courtesy of National Park Service, U.S. Department of Interior.

FIGURE 3-34. Bent's Old Fort was reconstructed of readily available materials including mud adobe bricks, mud plaster, viga beams from local cottonwood and pine trees, and millwork and hardware fashioned at the fort's blacksmith shop.

Photograph courtesy of National Park Service, U.S. Department of Interior.

FIGURE 3-35. Original Rain Bird sprinkler profile overlaid on agricultural field.

Courtesy of Rain Bird Sprinkler Mfg. Corp.

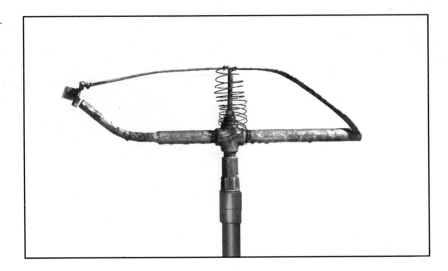

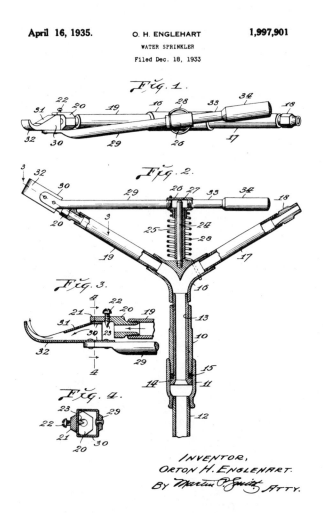

April 16, 1935.   O. H. ENGLEHART   1,997,901
WATER SPRINKLER
Filed Dec. 18, 1933

Fig. 1.

Fig. 2.

Fig. 3.

Fig. 4.

INVENTOR,
ORTON H. ENGLEHART.
BY *Martin O. Smith* ATTY.

FIGURE 3-36. Rain Bird water sprinkler patent drawing.
Courtesy of Rain Bird Sprinkler Mfg. Corp.

Rain Bird: Corporate Practice

History and Overview

Rain Bird started in the summer of 1933 when Orton Englehardt, a citrus farmer, inventor, and friend of Clement and Mary LaFetra, showed the LaFetras a new device for watering his lemon grove in Glendora, California. The device, a new impact sprinkler, offered slow-rotation watering that irrigated the trees slowly, evenly, and by itself.

Mr. LaFetra was impressed with the sprinkler and began selling it for Mr. Englehardt. The new sprinkler was patented and produced on an individual-order basis. One of the first big orders came after a demonstration of the sprinkler at the Los Angeles Country Club. The greens keeper thought high water pressure of 150 psi would blow up LaFetra's contraption, as it was thought of in those early days. When the impact sprinkler worked and other gardeners saw the device in operation, the country club ordered twelve. Soon after, a big order for 100 sprinklers came when a professor at the University of California–Davis demonstrated the new method of watering plants. The development of the impact sprinkler head led to irrigated lands that now exceed 50 million acres worldwide.

Eventually, Orton Englehardt decided he preferred farming to manufacturing and sold the rights to his invention to Clement and Mary LaFetra. The

FIGURE 3-37. Rain Bird pop-up spray head over turf.

Courtesy of Rain Bird Sprinkler Mfg. Corp.

FIGURE 3-38. Rain Bird pop-up spray heads over a large turf area.

Courtesy of Rain Bird Sprinkler Mfg. Corp.

LaFetras began manufacturing the new irrigation product in their barn on October 13, 1935.

The name for the invention was drawn from American Indian lore by a teacher at a Glendora school. Indian tradition held that a bird brought rain to the parched Southern California land. The LaFetras began using the name "Rain Bird" for the irrigation sprinkler and registered the name as a brand trademark.

The company continued to develop innovative irrigation equipment and introduced lightweight aluminum pipe to the product line in 1946. The new pipe revolutionized the irrigation industry and catapulted growth based on unprecedented demand for agricultural irrigation in Southern California.

The original patent has now expired, and there are many impulse-driven sprinklers today, but the trademarked name has stayed with the company to serve as its logo since the early days in California. Rain Bird's design efforts have resulted in more than 130 patents since 1933. Some of the company's innovations include computer-controlled irrigation systems; the Precision Jet tube, which eliminates side splash, conserving water; and pressure-regulating spray heads that maintain water pressure equally for optimum performance.

In 1964, the LaFetra's son Anthony joined the company. He held several positions and has served as the president since 1977.

Since its modest beginning in LaFetra's lemon grove in Glendora, the Rain Bird company has grown into the largest manufacturer of irrigation systems in the world. The company offers over 4,000 irrigation products, including rotors, valves, spray heads, moisture sensors, controllers, drip irrigation emitters and tape, as well as computer irrigation control systems.

Rain Bird now operates under five strategic business units (SBUs) and an international division. Each unit is responsible for engineering, manufacturing, testing, and selling products designed with a specific user or market in mind.

Contractor Division

The Contractor strategic business unit delivers irrigation products to landscape and irrigation contractors who design and install irrigation systems in residential and light-commercial facilities, including single-family private homes. Most of the products are manufactured at the Anthony Manufacturing–Residential Division plant located in Azusa, California, and at the Hyson plant in Tijuana, Mexico.

Commercial Division

Headquartered in Tucson, Arizona, the company's Commercial strategic business unit targets contractors, landscape architects, and irrigation system designers. The products are installed at commercial projects, public works facilities, shopping centers, schools, industrial centers, parks, and athletic fields. The products distributed by this business unit are manufactured at the Anthony Manufacturing Division commercial plant.

Consumer Products Division

The Consumer Products strategic business unit, headquartered in San Diego, California, sells its products through retail stores such as home-improvement centers, hardware stores, and lawn and garden shops. The products are sold directly to home owners and other consumers. This business unit offers hose-end lawn and garden products as well as drip and underground watering products easily installed by the home owner. A large number of these products are manufactured in Tijuana, Mexico.

Golf Division

The Golf strategic business unit offers complete irrigation systems for golf courses to superintendents, landscape architects, golf course designers, and irrigation consultants. The division provides thorough site-analysis services as a design aid, as well as training and after-sales service. The products distributed by this business unit are produced at the Anthony Industrial Plant in Azusa, California.

Agri-Products Division

The Agri-Products strategic business unit delivers irrigation products to farmers and agribusiness through a network of wholesale distributors and independent dealers. This division's products include sprinkler systems and low-flow systems designed to save water and energy while achieving superior crop production. Agri-products are produced at the Rain Bird Sprinkler Manufacturing facilities located in Glendora, California, and in Tijuana, Mexico.

International Division

As Rain Bird's overseas marketing and sales arm, the International strategic business unit delivers a complete line of Rain Bird products to more than 120 countries around the world. This division's product line is drawn from each of the other four strategic business units.

Other Companies

Rain Bird also has other companies that service the strategic business units. The T.H. Molding Company supplies molded plastic parts. Rain Bird Corporate Services provides administrative services. Rain Bird Distribution Corporation distributes all of the company's products worldwide. Clemar Manufacturing makes electronic controllers for the various divisions, and the Ceres Product Corporation distributes the company's Lawnlife product line.

Through the years, Rain Bird has grown and changed while maintaining its position as the world's leading manufacturer of irrigation products.

Rain Bird was built on the goal of providing the best quality sprinkler on the market. Our job is to help Rain Bird "be the customer's best choice." We continue to emphasize the quality of our products and services and realize that the concern for and care of all employees toward this goal is the best assurance that Rain Bird remains number one.

Rain Bird's overall mission is to be the industry leader by:

- Profitably providing defect-free, high-value water-conserving products for worldwide irrigation applications.
- Achieving customer satisfaction by meeting or exceeding customer expectations.
- Being a responsible employer respected by employees and the community.

Landscape Architecture at Rain Bird

Landscape architects work primarily in Rain Bird's sales force as area specifications managers and district managers. Degreed landscape architects also work as product managers in Rain Bird's marketing departments. The company relies on landscape architects in two primary ways. First, landscape architects understand the needs of the company's landscape architecture and irrigation consultant customers. Second, they understand the technical aspects of landscape design and irrigation applied to planting design and the healthy growth and maintenance of plant materials. The training of landscape architects provides excellent background needed for sales and customer support. Landscape architects serving as sales representatives for Rain Bird speak the language of the landscape architectural consultants and irrigation designers who specify the company's products. Although there are no design-related career tracks for the landscape architect in Rain Bird, the opportunities in sales and customer support offer a different type of career track for the landscape architect inclined to succeed in a corporate environment.

Employee Benefits

At Rain Bird the first ninety days of employment are a time for company-sponsored orientation. The new employee attends meetings to learn about the company, the benefits offered to employees, and other company-sponsored programs.

Employee relations are a cornerstone of Rain Bird's corporate philosophy. The company strives for strong, rewarding relationships between employees and their managers. Open communication is a goal. Employees are encouraged to discuss problems openly and directly with their supervisors. Third-party communication is discouraged. The company, which is not unionized, believes in policies and practices designed to quickly resolve day-to-day problems that may occur in the workplace. By working together, all employees make Rain Bird a viable and healthy organization and a satisfying place to work. Management accepts responsibility for providing favorable working conditions with competitive pay and benefits. The company believes that each individual has the right to speak for himself or herself.

At Rain Bird, each plant, department, or strategic business unit has a human resources consultant available to work with each employee on employee-relations issues, questions, and concerns. The consultants assist employees with insurance and benefits questions and help employees interpret Rain Bird's policies and procedures. The human resource consultants serve as objective third-party counselors, helping employees and supervisors resolve problems or conflict in the work environment.

The company wants each newly hired employee to become one of the company's team, to respond with the appropriate behavior expected of a regular employee. Occasionally the company and a new employee discover that the job, the company, or performance is not what both wanted. If this situation, develops, the company urges all new employees to discuss the matter with their supervisor.

The company's compensation policy is to pay competitively in the geographical area where employees work. Each year the human resources department researches what other companies are paying for similar jobs. Based on the research, pay scales are adjusted on or around October 1 for all of the hourly paid positions. Salaried employees are reviewed once each year prior to January 1. Overtime is voluntary, except under unusual circumstances. Supervisors attempt to distribute available overtime equitably among employees.

Rain Bird has a set number of holidays and scheduled floating holidays normally used to provide employees with long weekends throughout the year. Vacation time is two weeks after one year of employment, three weeks after seven years of employment, and four weeks after fifteen years of employment. Employees who work less than 1,600 hours in a given year earn prorated vacation time. No vacation time or pay may be taken until the first anniversary of employment.

For jury duty, Rain Bird pays the difference between the employee's normal daily pay and jury duty compensation for up to ten days in a three-year period for subpoenaed witness duty, if the employee is not a party to the litigation.

Rain Bird allows up to three days off with pay for time needed for traveling to and attending a funeral of a member of the employee's immediate family, which includes a spouse, child, parent, brother, sister, grandparents, parents-in-law, brother-in-law, sister-in-law, grandparents-in-law, and children-in-law.

Company benefits include medical, dental, and life insurance; a 401(k) retirement program; individual benefit accounts; educational reimbursement; employee activities; cost savings on the purchase of Rain Bird products; and a credit union benefit.

The company's benefits program philosophy is to maintain a benefits package that is competitive within the geographic area where employees are located. Rain Bird regularly surveys the benefits offered by other similar companies in order to keep its program up to date. Benefits begin ninety days after the start of employment. Each year, the company has an open enrollment period when each employee has the opportunity to make changes in benefits.

Rain Bird provides a variety of insurance options for each employee and the employee's family. The company's medical plans cover doctor visits, prescription drugs, hospitalization, and dental and mental health benefits. Several choices of plans may be available depending upon the employee's location among the company's employment centers. Rain Bird pays for most of the premium, and the employee contributes a portion of the costs. Life insurance is provided at no cost to employees.

Employees who want to supplement their retirement savings may contribute a portion of their pay to the company's 401(k) savings and investment plan. The employee may select from a variety of investment alternatives with different risk levels.

Rain Bird has an internal program of individual benefits accounts (IBA) that enables employees to pay, with nontaxable money, health-related expenses not covered by group health insurance. The company's insurance premiums are automatically paid through funds in the IBA. Each employee may elect to reduce his or her pay and put the money in the IBA, providing a tax-free fund for medical expenses and child care.

The company encourages employees to further their education and reimburses regular full-time employees as follows:

- Tuition and parking fees are reimbursable at 100 percent. Books and lab fees are reimbursed at 80 percent. The company pays the first $500 and half of the amount over $500 per calendar year.
- Courses must be approved in advance of enrollment. Employees must enroll in degree programs that have a direct bearing on the employee's present performance at the company or on a reasonably attainable future capacity at the company.
- Requests for approval of a course or program and for reimbursement are made through each employee's supervisor, appropriate director, or vice president.
- The employee must attain a grade of C or better and be employed and working full time at Rain Bird at the beginning and end of the course to receive reimbursement.

Each year, Rain Bird sponsors various group activities in which employees may participate for fun and enjoyment. Attendance is voluntary.

Employees may purchase most Rain Bird products at about 50 percent off the retail list price.

Entry-Level Job Description

Position: Area specifications manager
Division/Departments: Rain Bird Sales, Inc., Turf Products
Reports to: Regional sales manager
Job Latitude: Operates with substantial independence to accomplish objectives, referring to the regional sales manager when variations from established policy or marketing philosophy are required.

Position Responsibilities: Area specifications managers operate as consultants to our turf market customers by developing a thorough understanding of their business and of the industry so that managers can recognize the customers' needs and recommend the Rain Bird products or systems that best fill those needs.

Area specifications managers operate with a great deal of autonomy, work independently in their assigned territory, and interface daily with irrigation consultants, landscape architects, irrigation contractors, developers, government agents, distributor personnel, and other irrigation users. This position is responsible for developing and implementing sales objectives, analyzing sales results, training irrigation users, and working as an essential member of the sales team. In addition, area specifications managers serve as the voice of the customer for Rain Bird sales, marketing, engineering, and manufacturing staffs.

Minimum Qualifications:
- B.S. degree
- Excellent general business skills
- Strong selling and communication skills with three years previous sales experience
- Skills in problem-solving and thinking
- Familiarity with word processing, spreadsheets, and database applications

Desirable Qualifications:
- A postgraduate degree
- Irrigation industry knowledge and thinking
- Working knowledge of commercial and residential irrigation design, installation, repair, and product application

Representative Examples of Projects Using Rain Bird's Products

- EPCOT, Walt Disney World, and EuroDisney. EPCOT and Walt Disney World have one of the largest MAXICOM computer central control installations in existence.
- Simplot Feeders, Idaho, use Rain Bird controllers and rotors to control dust on twenty feedlots.
- National Wildflower Research Center, Texas
- The Smithsonian Institute, Washington, D.C.

- Nike, Inc., Corporate Headquarters, Beaverton, Oregon
- Microsoft Corporation, Corporate Headquarters, Redmond, Washington
- State Farm Insurance Company, Texas
- Electronic Data Systems, Corporate Headquarters, Texas
- GTE, Corporate Headquarters, Texas
- City of Paris, France, reduced irrigation water consumption 40 percent by changing from hand watering to Rain Bird systems controlled by the company's Urbacom Central Controller.
- City of Bakersfield, California, was the first nonagricultural winner of the State of California's Landscape Water Conservation Management Award in 1995. The city saved over eight million gallons of water from 1993 to 1995 after installing Rain Bird systems on 65 acres of parks.
- Rain Bird systems are used on seven of the top ten golf courses in the United States according to *Golf Digest* in 1993. Rain Bird systems are used at Pebble Beach Golf Links in California and at Shinnecock Hills Golf Club, site of the 1995 U.S. Open.
- Rain Bird equipment is used at Arizona State University's Sun Devil Stadium, site of the 1996 Super Bowl. The Baseball Hall of Fame in Cooperstown, New York, uses Rain Bird irrigation equipment. Rain Bird rotors are approved by the World Soccer Federation.

REFERENCES

Gregory, James. 1991. Adsit Adjusts to Ebb and Flow of the Landscape Industry. *Landscape & Irrigation* 15 no. 9, 10, 12, 14, 16, 52, 53.

Miller, Robert L. 1994. From San Francisco to Sydney: The Integrated World of EDAW. *Process: Architecture* 120: 5–9. Ed. Miyakoda Tooru. Tokyo: Murotani Bunji, Process Architecture Co.

Miyakoda, Tooru. 1994. From Partnership to Corporation: History of the Transition of the Eckbo, Dean, Austin and Williams Partnership to EDAW. *Process: Architecture* 120: 5–9. Ed. Miyakoda Tooru. Tokyo: Murotani Bunji, Process Architecture Co.

STUDY QUESTIONS AND ASSIGNMENTS

1. Divide your class into three-to-five person teams. Each team is to function as a design office and develop a mission statement for your office. Refer to the mission statements in the six case studies.

2. Compare, analyze, and contrast the benefits offered by each of the case study companies. Develop an ideal benefits package that you would like to receive from a prospective employer. You will be able to use this ideal benefits package as a way to evaluate what is offered to you when you interview for future employment.

3. Compare, analyze, and contrast the differences between the types of employment opportunities offered by the six companies in the case studies. Focus on the role of the landscape architect. Summarize the key differences and opportunities.

4. Write an ideal job description for an entry-level landscape architect. Refer to the job descriptions in the case studies and additional research to develop your ideal job description.

CHAPTER FOUR

Professional-Practice Relationships

Landscape architects have four main professional-practice relationships:

1. Landscape architect/owner
2. Landscape architect/allied professional
3. Landscape architect/contractor
4. Landscape architect/general public

The relationships are both contractual and noncontractual. Contractual relationships are bound by the requirements of completing the scope of services agreed upon with the client and by the other legal obligations of a contract for professional services. Noncontractual relationships involve taking professional responsibility for complying with codes such as the Uniform National Building Code, applying professional judgment, adhering to standards of care, practicing within one's professional capability, taking responsibility for environmental stewardship, and incorporating quality control in the preparation of the landscape architect's instruments of service. Noncontractual relationships can become contractual if specific elements of the relationship are written into the agreement with the owner as terms of the contract. Whether contractual or not, all professional-practice relationships have ethical and moral obligations that should be carried out with honesty and integrity.

A landscape architect's client may be an owner who is also the user of the completed project or plan, an owner who is not the user, or a party with a vested interest, such as an allied professional or a government agent. A landscape architect serves the owner in one of three ways:

1. As the *prime consultant* having direct contact with the owner and responsible for managing and directing the services of subconsultants that may be necessary.
2. As one of a number of consultants, or *multiple direct consultants,* hired by the owner. Each consultant has direct contact with the owner and has responsibility for coordinating as necessary to successfully complete the project.
3. As a *subconsultant* to a prime consultant, usually an allied professional. There may not be, and frequently is not, direct contact with the owner. The subconsultant is responsible for communicating through the prime consultant and coordinating with the prime consultant and the other subconsultants.

These professional-practice relationships are guided by conventional lines of communication. The prime consultant always communicates directly with the owner. A subconsultant communicates with the prime consultant and only with the owner when requested by the owner or when authorized by the prime consultant. A subconsultant hired by a subconsultant creates another level of communication, one step further removed from the owner. The levels of communication create a ladder of authority for decisions and coordination on every project. The highest rung of the communication ladder is between the owner and the prime consultant. The next rung below is communication between the prime consultant and the prime's subconsultants. Below that is communication between a subconsultant and lower-level subconsultants.

If the owner is not the user, communicating with users of the project results in another line of communication. Sometimes an owner will act on behalf of the users to develop a design program with the prime consultant and some or all of the subconsultants based on prior experience, professional judgment, established standards, and interviews with potential users. The design program for market-driven projects, such as apartment complexes, is usually developed by the owner and the consultants acting on behalf of the user. The design program for a public works project almost always includes public input in the design process. The public input is obtained through direct interaction with users, questionnaires implemented in public meetings, media outlets, and individual meetings with interest groups. Whether a market-responsive project or a public project, a user profile is vital to the success of all projects. Because the landscape architect is a shaper of the environment, a prime consultant usually involves the landscape architect in developing the user profile when the landscape architect is a subconsultant.

Prime-Consulting Relationships

When a landscape architect serves a client as the prime consultant, direct access to the owner exists. As the prime consultant, the landscape architect takes an active role in making decisions that affect the outcome of the project. The two *L* words—*listening* and *leading*—are important to the success of the prime-consulting relationship. If the owner has a clear idea of the goals of the project and states the goals in a design program that includes specific functional, aesthetic, and financial parameters, the landscape architect serves best by being a good listener. The landscape architect may assist the owner by refining the project's parameters where acceptable to the owner during the programming or schematic design phase of the project. When the owner's needs and goals are not well defined, the landscape architect's leadership qualities are essential to the success of the project. The ability to ask questions is important, drawing out the goals from the owner in a give-and-take process of developing the design program. Prior experience with similar projects provides the background for the landscape architect to help the owner focus on key design issues while developing the program. Knowing when to listen and when to lead is a hallmark of successful landscape architects.

In a prime-consulting relationship, the landscape architect often engages subconsultants that have subordinate relationships with the landscape architect and work on the project at the direction of the landscape architect. The subconsultants include allied professionals who are responsible for various elements of the project. The landscape architect is responsible for scheduling and managing the input of each subconsultant and clearly communicating the owner's goals and the design requirements of the project. When serving as a prime consultant, the landscape architect maintains a professional, legal, business, and social relationship with all those involved in the successful completion of the project.

Multiple Direct-Consulting Relationships

In some cases, an owner will hire a number of allied professionals to serve in a direct capacity. Each consultant has direct access to and communicates with the owner. In effect, the owner maintains a number of prime-consulting relationships.

In multiple direct-consulting relationships, the landscape architect has direct access to the owner and must coordinate with each of the other allied consultants. The success of this type of owner-and-consultant relationship is grounded in good communication.

Multiple direct-consulting relationships have become increasingly popular with owners seeking more control and greater involvement in the outcome of the project. Many consultants serving as primes are not interested in administering subcontracts and bearing the professional liability of subconsultants. Such consultants encourage owners to consider using multiple direct-consulting arrangements. Fees are also a consideration. The costs associated with managing the input of the various consultants are borne by the owner rather than paying a markup on subconsultants commonly charged by the prime consultant. The multiple direct-consulting approach also facilitates communication between the owner and the consultants, mitigating the problem of misinformation that can be associated with a prime consultant's interpretation of the owner's goals.

Subconsulting Relationships

When a landscape architect serves an allied professional as a subconsultant, the owner is one level above the landscape architect and usually removed from direct communication. The direction given to the landscape architect is the prime consultant's interpretation of the owner's goals. Information can be lost in the translation of the owner's goals by the prime, and the landscape architect must take care to ensure that clear direction is received. Time and income is lost when inadequate information or unclear direction is given to the landscape architect.

In the subconsulting relationship, the landscape architect must be responsive to the direction of the prime consultant. If clear direction is not provided, the landscape architect must ask the prime as many questions as necessary to define the landscape architectural requirements of the project.

The main benefit of working as a subconsultant is that liability and responsibility are limited to the specific subconsulting tasks. There is less coordination and management responsibility than serving as a prime. The main constraint is caused by limited access and communication with the owner or the user. The landscape architect's client, for example, may be an architecture firm serving as the prime consultant. The owner may be a public housing authority represented by the agency's staff. The users of the project will be future residents of the housing project. The prime may choose to limit the landscape architect's contact with the owner. User needs and design direction may be based on information drawn from prior experience with the design of public housing projects and professional judgment. This secondhand information is likely to result in competent design work and a project that functions adequately and is safe. Limited access to the owner and user, however, usually results in a built project that is ordinary rather than exemplary.

Landscape Architect/Owner Relationship

Expectations in the Landscape Architect/Owner Relationship

There are expectations in every relationship. Unfulfilled expectations may lead to resentments, and resentments in the landscape architect/owner relationship will result in an unsatisfied client or an unhappy consultant. When expectations are identified up front and satisfied through the course of the relationship between the professional and the nonprofessional, harmony exists and the relationship is rewarding. In the landscape architect/owner relationship, the landscape architect must understand the owner's expectations, and the owner or client needs to know the landscape architect's expectations. Getting to know each other's expectations can be expedited by paying attention to the following:

- Have at least one and possibly several meetings prior to making a commitment to engage in a consulting relationship with an owner who will be the client. Ask a lot of questions. Make sure the relationship feels comfortable and communication is easy.
- Check out the background and history of the prospective client.
- Clearly identify landscape architectural expectations in conversations with the owner. Is the project a possible award winner? Is the project ordinary, but interesting for some specific professional challenge? Is there a need to fast-track the project in order to meet the owner's schedule? Does the landscape architect want to try out a new plant material that does not have a proven track record? Are there environmental issues that may cause problems?
- Query the owner and determine the owner's expectations. Document the understanding of the owner's expectations in a follow-up letter. Does the owner want to develop more of a project than the budget realistically allows? Does the owner want to use a questionable material or construction technique? Is the project so large that it will stress the market availability of certain plant materials? Does the owner expect more services from the firm's principals than are permitted under the proposed fee using the firm's standard billing rates?
- Walk the site with the owner. Discuss expectations in a give-and-take conversation.
- Visit other projects with the owner. Discuss pros and cons in a give-and-take conversation.
- Prepare a drafted written scope of services and review it with the owner prior to finalizing the scope in the formal agreement for professional services.

- Give the owner literature, such as that available from ASLA, describing the kinds of services provided by landscape architects.

Owner's Expectations

Although every landscape architect/owner relationship may be different, there are some general expectations that most owners have about their landscape architecture consultants. Owners hire landscape architects because the owners do not have the technical training to design a garden, create a site plan for a shopping center, develop a plan for an urban waterfront, or prepare a visual impact assessment of logging operations or a power line corridor. Above all else, owners expect their landscape architect to be technically competent. As a measure of technical competence, owners look at prior projects completed by the landscape architect and evaluate similarities between the landscape architect's experience on prior projects and the technical requirements of the present project. Owners ask the landscape architect questions about the technical aspects of their project. An owner needs to establish a comfort level with the technical capability of the landscape architect for the landscape architect/owner relationship to get off to a good start and end successfully.

The owner also expects the landscape architect to be creative. The owner expects the design plan, the built project, the planning document, or any other product of the landscape architect's services to be more creative than if completed by the owner. Owners measure design and planning creativity by reviewing the landscape architect's completed projects. Some owners have a higher expectation of the landscape architect's design skills than other owners. They are looking for world-class, upscale design and have the financial capability to carry out a world-class project. Some owners—indeed, the majority of owners—want quality design within the constraints of a moderate yet realistic budget. There are also owners who want quality design on a low budget.

Professional services are an intangible product. Evidence of the quality of the professional services is evident in the visual appeal and creativity displayed in the final product or built environment. All owners want to feel there is value to the creativity provided through the professional services. Owners want to feel

that the completed project looks better than it would have if they had not used the services of the professional landscape architect.

Owners want the landscape architect to be responsive to their needs, desires, goals, and objectives, which are stated in the design program, the list of planning parameters, or a project goal statement. Responsiveness is a key to the landscape architect's success, and the way the landscape architect responds to the owner's needs, desires, goals, and objectives should be evident in the plan. The landscape architect should be able to walk the owner through the plan, discussing and pointing out how the plan responds to each of the owner's needs, desires, goals, and objectives. Walking the owner or client through a plan for the first time can result in a terrific rush of adrenaline for the landscape architect. This experience of explaining how the plan responds to the owner's design program and describing the creative nuances of the plan is an exhilarating moment in the day-to-day professional practice of landscape architecture.

The bottom line of the landscape architect/owner relationship is satisfaction. The landscape architect should have the ability to translate the functional, aesthetic, and environmental goals into an acceptable plan that satisfies the client and the owner. Satisfied owners are vital to the long-term success of every landscape architecture firm. A satisfied owner pays off in repeat work, referrals, and good references for future clients. Owner satisfaction is a primary aim of every landscape architecture office.

Landscape Architect's Expectations

Every landscape architect expects the owner will allow, or even encourage, the landscape architect to be genuinely creative and free to express the greatest degree of creative opportunity allowed within the constraints of the owner's budget. Working for an owner who wants to control every line put down on a plan or every word written in a planning document will inhibit the professional's creative freedom. The owner who hires the professional and lets the landscape architect loose to ply the creative talents learned through educational training and honed through professional practice is the most rewarding client to work for. The landscape architect expects each professional experience to be rewarding, providing opportunities that will be challenging and allowing opportunities for professional growth and development.

Another of the professional's expectations is that the project will get built or the plan will be implemented. No one enjoys working on a project only to see it not be implemented. Circumstances sometimes dictate that a project can't be constructed: the owner may lose financing, or the political climate may change during the process of completing a landscape management plan. One of the rewards for the landscape architect, however, is seeing the results of the design process come to fruition.

In the landscape architect/owner relationship, the landscape architect also expects the owner to be cooperative and communicative, sharing the needs, desires, goals, and objectives that will make the project successful. The landscape architect expects the owner to be responsive to questions aimed at refining the owner's needs and getting input to successfully complete the professional services. The landscape architect will seldom be successful without the owner's cooperation.

Last, the landscape architect expects to get paid. Notwithstanding the legal requirements of the contract for professional services, the landscape architect expects to receive compensation for the services rendered because the landscape architect *and* the owner believe there is a value to the services. If the landscape architect suspects that an owner is not willing or able to pay for the services rendered during the course of working on a project, the relationship will be quickly undermined. The landscape architect may wish to stop working on the project and pursue options available through the contract and other legal alternatives to recover the professional fees.

Budgets

The owner's budget drives every project. Some owners are interested in upscale, or "high," design and have the funding to develop a high-end project. They want to engage the services of a landscape architecture firm with the experience and capability to deliver a high-end project, and they are willing to pay the fees necessary to develop a professional relationship with the firm. Some owners seek the lowest fees possible and go through a process of obtaining competitive fee quotes from a number of firms. Such projects are bottom-line oriented and commonly referred to as *production proj-*

ects. The owners want to achieve a good-quality service at the lowest possible fee, resulting in a competently designed, but not overdesigned, project. They want their projects to be in budget or under budget.

Many owners fall somewhere in between having a high-end, unlimited budget and a low-end, restrictive budget, and one of the first things a landscape architect should do when engaged by an owner is to verify whether the budget is adequate for the design program and if a funding source exists to implement a planning project. The landscape architect can alleviate stress on the relationship by resolving budget shortfalls before engaging the development of the design plan. Problems occur when the landscape architect designs a plan that meets the needs and desires of an owner, only to find out that the construction cost is substantially higher than the owner's available funding. The owner's heart becomes set on the plan artfully crafted by the professional, but funds are not available to construct the plan as shown. If additional funding can not be obtained, the owner and the landscape architect must undertake the emotionally difficult process of reducing the costs by cutting out parts of the project, reducing quantities and sizes, lowering quality of materials, and taking other cost-cutting measures.

The best landscape architect/owner relationship exists when the budget is known, is adequate, and the design meets the owner's needs and objectives. Sometimes the budget is known and is not adequate, but the landscape architect is able to successfully meet the owner's needs and objectives by coming up with a clever solution or using a unique material that costs less but works as well as the desired material. In other situations, the budget is not known, but the landscape architect's design solution meets the owner's needs and the owner happily constructs the project because funding is available. These situations usually result in a satisfied owner from the budgetary standpoint.

Difficulty arises in the landscape architect/owner relationship when the budget is known, is inadequate, and the landscape architect is neither able to convince the owner that the budget is too low nor able to come up with a plan that meets the owner's needs by holding to the budget. If the landscape architect verifies the budget before developing the plan, and the budget appears to be too low but the owner insists on proceeding with the established design program, something will have to give later in the process. Phasing may be used to implement only a part of the design plan that can be constructed with available funds. Add alternates may be used as part of the construction documents so that as much of the project as possible can be constructed. Or the project may be put on hold until additional funds can be obtained to build the project as designed. The landscape architect may also resent the owner if the fee is based on an inadequate budget, but the design is executed for a substantially greater amount of construction. Because fees are based partly on the construction costs, the owner will receive more services from the landscape architect because the project scope and design program are greater than the project budget. In this situation, the landscape architect needs to negotiate an increase in fees if there are additional costs of designing a substantially larger project than the owner has budgeted.

Whether the budget is adequate or inadequate, the landscape architect should approach each project by trying to maximize the quality and extent of what can be built for the available funds. A useful professional skill is a knack for stretching the dollar. Budget maximizing skills are obtained by experience, understanding the local construction climate, reviewing as many alternatives as possible for every design decision, and being sensitive with the client's money as if it were the landscape architect's personal money. Without question, owners will have greater satisfaction if they feel that they are getting more for their budget from their professional landscape architect.

Working with an Owner

Involving the owner in the planning and design process is one of the keys to successful professional practice. Patience is a virtue because many owners and clients are not accustomed to working with professional landscape architects. Knowing where and when to involve the owner can make the process more comfortable for the owner and more pleasant for the professional. The key times for involving the owner are

1. during the development of the design program or setting the planning goals and objectives;
2. during design development of the project;
3. during the design of construction details and selection of materials;
4. when reviewing the plans at the preliminary plan or schematic design stage;
5. when reviewing design development plans;
6. when reviewing and approving the final plans.

Owners tend to have more useful input in the design process when asked to comment on detail design and on the selection of materials. Because owners are usually not trained as designers, their input in the site planning process should be focused on whether functional relationships appear to be correctly laid out, distances and sizes appear be correct, and quantities seem to be what the owner wants. Before reviewing a site plan with an owner, the landscape architect should prepare questions related to how the owner will use the project. The questions can be asked when walking the owner through the plan. The answers will help the landscape architect evaluate the plan to see if it is correctly designed to match the owner's needs. Some landscape architects will actually design the preliminary or schematic plan for projects that are not overly complicated at a table with the owner present. The landscape architect can talk through the development of the plan with the owner and ask him or her questions that confirm whether the basic layout and structure of the plan appear to be what the owner has in mind. This process of developing a conceptual plan in the presence of the owner can build confidence in the professional, save time, and get a design project off to a successful start. Surprises are minimized as the plan is developed in further detail. Because the owner approves the concept before extensive work is put into developing the plan, the landscape architect can pay more attention to developing the plan to a finer level and to developing the details of the plan.

Checklists are very useful in working with an owner. Checklists can be developed to include questions to ask a client or owner at every stage of the design process from initial contact to postconstruction evaluation. Checklists may be most beneficial during the programming of a design project to ensure that all of the owner's needs, desires, goals, objectives are hashed out.

Determining the owner's motives can be useful, too. The owner's motives will color the landscape architect/owner relationship and affect the way the landscape architect approaches the project. The developer of a 450-unit production apartment complex may have a single, overriding motive: to develop the project at the least cost and flip it to a new owner at a 15 percent profit over costs and fees. The developer is not likely to approve any site expenses not considered normal development costs for competing projects unless the site improvements heighten the ability to sell the completed project.

Last of all, the landscape architect must be able to handle rejection. The practicing landscape architect is not going to hit it off with every owner. That is perfectly natural. There will be some relationships where the landscape architect will have a personality difference that will prevent an effective give-and-take in the planning and design process. There will be times when communication seems impossible. There will be times when the owner aborts the project for no apparent reason. There will also be times when the landscape architect recommends a design direction or a specific construction material and the owner flatly rejects the recommendation with or without a reason. On the other hand, there will be many times when the landscape architect/owner relationship is rich, rewarding, and enjoyable—communication is easy and the project is a success.

Each landscape architect must remember that he or she has the right to decide whether to work for an owner and potential client. Deciding who to work for is one of the important decisions facing the professional practitioner. It's okay to say no to a potential client if there is a reason why the landscape architect decides not to work for the person. It's also okay to end a relationship with an owner during the design process if the working conditions are unpleasant or adversarial.

The Landscape Architect's Responsibilities in the Landscape Architect/Owner Relationship

Scope of Services

The landscape architect makes a commitment to a scope of services in the agreement for professional services. Carrying out the scope of services is the foundation of the professional relationship between the landscape architect and the owner. The landscape architect must develop a specific, written scope of services that both the landscape architect and the owner agree adequately meets the owner's needs. If the owner

develops the scope of services, however, the landscape architect should review it and agree that it will adequately serve the needs of the owner. Once agreed to, the written scope of services becomes part of the contract and will guide the relationship between the landscape architect and owner.

The landscape architect is responsible for carrying out the scope of services with interest and with the level of professional effort consistent with the standard of practice for landscape architects. Under normal circumstances, the scope is adequate for completing the project. In some cases, however, additional services are necessary to effectively represent the owner. The need for additional services may arise due to unanticipated site conditions, changes in government regulations, or the contractor's activities on the site. As a safeguard, the landscape architect should make it clear that the initial scope of services is based on assumptions made before starting the project. The owner needs to accept that unanticipated additional services may be needed and that the owner is expected to pay for them.

Code Compliance

A very important technical responsibility of the landscape architect is confirming that codes are met. There are generally two levels of codes: national and local. The Uniform National Building Code (UNBC) is the most well-known national code, and is referred to by all levels of government. Design and construction projects must conform to the UNBC. The Americans with Disabilities Act (ADA) has resulted in additional national-level regulations that landscape architects must respond to. There is a plethora of local codes, such as zoning ordinances, floodplain regulations, subdivision standards, water conservation ordinances, and others too numerous to mention, that affect the landscape architect's work and must be addressed by the landscape architect. Planned communities and industrial and commerce parks may have design guidelines, CC&Rs, and planning regulations prepared by the master developer that need to be adhered to. Sometimes it seems that every direction a landscape architect turns there is another law, code, or ordinance to contend with. Indeed, much of the day-to-day practice of landscape architecture project design deals with verifying that the design of a project complies with the various levels of applicable codes. Every owner and client expects that the landscape architect will deliver construction or planning documents that comply with applicable codes.

Safe Design

The landscape architect is obligated to prepare a plan for the owner that results in a safe environment with low risk of injury. Safety issues surround all levels of design decisions. Gradients of walks, driveways, and parking areas must be designed for safety, especially in areas that have wet or freezing climatic conditions. Edges with drop-offs must have safety railings. Steep walkways should have surfaces finished with nonslip treatments, such as a heavy broom finish on concrete surfaces. Handrails need to be designed at the correct height. Lighting that is designed for visibility and security is vital to safe sites. Placement of outdoor furniture so that users feel safe from criminal harm has become a more important consideration for designers of outdoor public spaces.

Creating safe landscape architecture requires professionals to scrutinize their plans for safety glitches. Removing unsafe conditions found in plans is one of the preventative measures that can be taken. Landscape architects need to have a good working knowledge of the UNBC, as well as other national and local codes developed to protect the health, safety, and welfare of the general public. Applicable sections of the UNBC should be required reading for every student and practitioner of landscape architecture to develop a general familiarity with safety guidelines for steps, ramps, drop-offs, and other safety aspects of site planning and project design.

No matter how much attention is placed on safety in the design process, there may be instances where a professional landscape architect is named in a lawsuit that claims negligence. In today's litigious world, the odds are likely that many practicing landscape architects will be impacted in some way by third-party lawsuits. I once heard of a lawsuit filed because a tree limb fell off a shade tree adjacent to a picnic table, injuring someone sitting at the picnic table. When developing the design of the park, the landscape architect surely thought mostly about the comfort that the shade would bring to the picnicker. The possibility that a branch would fall off the tree and injure someone might never have crossed the landscape architect's mind. The case was ultimately settled in favor of the picnicker, and the landscape architect's professional liability insurance company paid the claim. The point

is that even when a landscape architect has the best intentions of designing a safe and functional plan, there are reasons to review even the least-suspect design conditions for safety considerations.

Risk and Professional Liability

Every time a landscape architect is engaged by a client, exposure to risk occurs and professional liability results. Liability in professional design services is governed by civil, or tort, law. Risk in the design process is associated with the possibility that a claim may be made charging that the professional services resulted in a negligent act, and that the negligence caused injury or damage to others. The concept of negligence centers on the general notion that every member of society has a duty to conduct his or her affairs so that unreasonable risk of harm to others is avoided. Under the terms of civil law, the landscape architect will be liable to the injured party if the injured party can prove that a negligent act should have been anticipated and avoided.

In the landscape architect/owner relationship, the landscape architect also has risk exposure directly related to the owner as a result of the contract for professional services and contract law. If the landscape architect or a subconsultant to the landscape architect omits something from the drawings, an electrical line, for example, and the omission is discovered during construction, the contractor will seek a change order to install the electric line. The owner may request that the landscape architect pay for some or all of the cost for installing the electric line because it was omitted from the plans. One of the best ways to limit contract risk is to develop clear, precise contracts that clearly spell out the professional's responsibility and the owner's. A clear and specific agreement on the scope of services goes a long way toward preventing misunderstandings. Risk may of course be limited by securing professional liability insurance, commonly referred to as *errors and omissions insurance*. Thorough checking of the contract documents by more than one experienced professional in the firm is another way to minimize risk caused by errors or omissions in the plans.

The landscape architect and the owner also have risk associated with the possibility of future third-party lawsuits. Third-party suits may also involve others, such as the contractor. The best ways to mitigate the possibility of future third-party lawsuits based on claims of negligence are to carry professional liability insurance and to thoroughly review and check contract documents to minimize exposure. Sometimes a risky situation is not foreseen during design and becomes evident during construction. Resolving risky situations that occur during construction is in everyone's best interest, even if an additional cost is required. The owner should be warned in advance that unforeseen conditions may occur although the landscape architect tries to identify all of them in the design phase. The owner needs to understand that identifying risky situations during construction observation is one of the useful services provided by the landscape architect. This service should not be viewed as a flaw in the plans but rather as an integral part of the professional design services contract.

Another way for the landscape architect to mitigate risk in the relationship with the owner is to identify unpreventable risks, such as hazardous environmental conditions, and exclude responsibility for these from the contract for professional services. The landscape architect can ask the owner to bear the consequences of unpreventable risks if the landscape architect agrees to accept the project assignment. The risks should be clearly identified in the contract for professional services (Dixon and Crowell 1993).

The Contract Guide, published by the Design Professionals Insurance Company (DPIC), is one of the best resources available for dealing with the risks associated with providing professional services. This guide recommends the following eight ways for the professional design consultant to manage risk:

1. Minimize risk by offering to provide more extensive professional services that allow the landscape architect to thoroughly address all aspects of the project. Quality-oriented clients will see the benefits of comprehensive services and be more likely to authorize and pay for them. The landscape architect's initial proposal should include a comprehensive scope of services, including services during construction, so that the owner will have a chance to say yes or modify the services to conform with his or her expectations and budget.

2. Transfer risk by obtaining professional liability insurance.

3. Educate the owner about the owner's responsibility for risks within the owner's control.

Develop an agreement that requires the owner to cover a fair share of costs associated with risk and liability. Reasonable owners will accept some forms of risk allocation, such as an indemnification clause. Unreasonable owners want the landscape architect to indemnify them against any and all future claims.

4. Identify potential problems that neither the landscape architect nor the owner may be able to prevent. If the contractor's work results in an error in construction, the contractor may bring a suit naming the landscape architect at fault due to an omission in the plans. The owner may also be brought into the suit. The landscape architect can avoid significant losses by including a limit-of-liability clause in the agreement with the owner.

5. The landscape architect can identify risks that are so significant or catastrophic that the landscape architect is not willing to accept the risk under any circumstances. These identified risks, such as those that may occur due to the discovery of hazardous underground material on the site, can be excluded from the landscape architect's responsibility by using appropriate language in the agreement with the owner.

6. Send a letter to the owner with a list of the services that the owner declined to accept in the contract. The list may exonerate the landscape architect and prevent the owner from holding the landscape architect liable for failing to perform services that were recommended but the owner decided to forgo. This action effectively transfers the liability to the owner.

7. Establish conditions in the agreement with the owner intended to reduce risk, as well as the costs associated with a liability problem that may arise. Agreeing on a less costly method than litigation or arbitration for resolving disputes is an example of a way to reduce risks and costs. Limiting the owner's ability to sue the landscape architect for consequential damages, such as the loss of the use of a facility, is another way to reduce risk and costs.

8. Develop a clear and precise contract with the owner that prevents misunderstandings and

makes the provisions of the agreement easily understood by a judge or jury if the problem becomes a legal issue. Ambiguous contracts make lawsuits more likely if a problem occurs because there is more leeway in developing an argument for a marginal claim (Dixon and Crowell 1993).

Functional and Aesthetic Design

Every landscape architect strives to achieve a functional and aesthetically designed environment. The owner expects the project and its component parts to function appropriately for the intended use or uses and to be distinguished by the aesthetic attributes of a well-designed environment. The landscape architect has a responsibility to identify the owner's needs during the program-development phase of the project in order to meet all functional and aesthetic requirements. The landscape architect needs to place the appropriate level of emphasis on both the functional and the aesthetic development of the project. Sometimes the functional side of the project requires more weight than the aesthetic; sometimes the aesthetic requires more. Both receive at least some attention in developing the landscape architecture project.

Environmentally Sound Design

The landscape architect has a responsibility for environmentally sound site planning and design that is nonpolluting and free of hazardous materials. The very nature of landscape architecture education focuses on planning and design using environmentally sound principles and incorporating the concept of sustainability. The techniques of site and resource analysis taught in virtually every landscape architecture program today give the landscape architect the tools for developing environmentally sound plans, as well as maintaining an environmental ethic. Inventory and analysis of natural vegetation, habitat, climate, soil conditions, topography, slope, aspect, subsurface conditions, water resources, and other environmental components provide the basis for a plan that is environmentally sensitive.

A landscape architect would not knowingly develop a plan that results in environmental pollution. The landscape architect has a responsibility to the owner to develop a plan that does not create a source of pollution and also is not affected by any known off-site sources of pollution. Some areas of the landscape

architect's responsibility are more likely to trigger pollution than others. Grading, drainage, and storm water runoff present possibilities for pollution due to sediment discharge or chemicals and metals that are carried by runoff from streets and parking areas into watercourses. In the site planning process, the landscape architect must consider the water table and presence of deep underground aquifers to avoid negatively impacting groundwater through runoff and percolation.

Visual pollution is an area of regional, urban, and site planning that landscape architects are not only trained to avoid in their work but also to mitigate if observed as an existing environmental problem. Landscape architects also have an obligation to identify possible sources of noise pollution that should be mitigated in the planning process. Commonly associated with transportation improvements, visual and noise impacts of a freeway on adjacent land uses can be mitigated by grade changes, mounds, walls, vegetation, and other treatments that screen views of the freeway and soften or deflect sound transmission.

Hazardous materials cause a different kind of problem for the landscape architect. Hazardous materials are being discovered at alarming rates in locations where they are not anticipated. Landscape architects work on large sites that may be affected by transmission of hazardous chemicals in the groundwater resources. Landscape architects work on urban sites where hazardous materials such as asbestos may have been used in past construction or chemicals such as TCE may be present in the existing soil matrix. In waterfront projects, hazardous materials or heavy metals may be evident in the water resource. The discovery of unanticipated hazardous materials can result in substantial exposure to risk and liability for the landscape architect. Adding to the element of risk is the fact that professional liability insurance companies generally do not insure damages caused by exposure to hazardous materials. If discovery of hazardous materials is anticipated on a project, the landscape architect should have contractual protection, such as indemnification, to prevent a significant loss.

If subsurface hazardous material is suspected or encountered, the landscape architect should notify the owner immediately and recommend the services of a geotechnical consultant. The owner needs to know that immediate measures may be necessary to protect human health and safety. The landscape architect should enjoy a relationship with the owner that allows the professional the freedom to act with impunity and to take necessary measures to protect the public health and safety. The landscape architect needs to feel comfortable that the owner will compensate the consultant for actions taken. Geotechnical experts are in a position to identify the hazardous condition, notify the appropriate environmental regulatory agencies, and develop a mitigation plan. The owner should make decisions about hazardous materials based on the best advice available from the landscape architect, geotechnical consultant, and other experts. Regardless of the relationship between a landscape architect and owner, the contract should contain a clause that covers discovery of hazardous materials.

Budgets

The landscape architect is obligated to design a project that can be built within the owner's budget. There are very few instances where a landscape architect is given carte blanche and is able to design a project with an unlimited budget. In most cases, particularly in the case of public works projects, the owner sets a budget and the landscape architect fashions a plan that conforms to the available funds. There are times when—no matter how diligent the efforts of the landscape architect—he or she cannot match the design work to the budgeted construction funds. When the budget is just impossible to meet, the landscape architect may have to notify the owner and discuss a reduction in the scope of work or request that the budget be increased. There are also times when the landscape architect can meet the budget but may wish to present an alternative solution that is more expensive because he or she feels the alternative will better meet the owner's needs. If the solution is superior, the landscape architect may petition the owner to consider increasing the construction funding.

When I first started out as a private practitioner, I found that matching the design plan to the available construction budget was one of the most difficult tasks to achieve in my consulting design practice. Almost always, the owner's needs and desires did not match his or her pocketbook. I would design what I thought I heard the owner say he or she wanted, only to find that my estimate of probable construction costs was higher than the available construction funds. To my dismay, cost-cutting measures often impacted the design so much that I ended up not liking what

was constructed due to the compromises that were made. I found that taking the time to review the program and verify that the budget was adequate was a good way to avoid disappointment later on. At the start of each project, my firm now regularly includes a budget verification task that emphasizes developing a realistic design program matched more closely with the owner's available construction funds. This budget verification step in the design process has resulted in design plans that more accurately reflect the construction budget. We avoid the gut-wrenching process of cutting elements from the plan or reducing the quality, amount, or size of materials to bring the design in line with the budget. Both the owner and my design firm have a comfort level that what we have designed can be constructed within the budget.

Confidentiality

Owners expect and often require confidentiality in relationships with landscape architects. They expect the professional not to disclose any information whatsoever about their intent. The landscape architect is not allowed to discuss any data, conclusions, or results of the planning and design services without permission from the owner.

Problems can arise when confidentiality on behalf of the owner conflicts with existing laws, particularly those relating to environmental protection, pollution, and hazardous materials. If the landscape architect upholds the owner's desire for confidentiality, the law may be violated. The landscape architect also has a fundamental responsibility to protect the health, safety, and welfare of the general public. If underground hazardous material is discovered, and requirements for confidentiality compromise the landscape architect's legal responsibility, he or she should seek legal advice. The landscape architect must approach the owner and recommend that the issue be dealt with above board, legally, and with the highest degree of integrity. The landscape architect can work with the owner to resolve the problem if all parties concerned with the issues meet the intent of environmental laws. In the worst case, confidentiality could be construed as a cover-up. If the issues are not dealt with above board, the landscape architect must have a paper trail that proves that he or she acted in accordance with the law.

When the owner insists on confidentiality and requires a confidentiality clause in the contract between the landscape architect and the owner, the landscape architect has the opportunity to clarify confidentiality issues. The landscape architect can stipulate in the agreement for professional services that confidentiality does not apply if complying with orders from courts or requirements of government agencies. The landscape architect also wants to retain the right to communicate freely with professional staff in the firm and subconsultants concerning project information.

Quality Control

The landscape architect is responsible for controlling the quality of workmanship and accuracy of the plans, drawings, specifications, reports, and all other instruments of service prepared under the terms of the agreement with the owner. The owner expects quality control.

Landscape architecture firms should have quality-assurance programs in place. Many firms develop quality-control manuals and written procedures. Some clients, such as public agencies, request that the written procedures be submitted with the landscape architect's proposal and require the written procedures to be included as part of the terms of the contract. Quality-control programs include the following elements:

- Check all documents before they leave the office.
- Designate a single point of contact with the owner.
- Involve all of the necessary professional disciplines and follow all legal requirements of the state board of technical registration.
- Require that a responsible member of the firm checks all documents and that a second responsible member of the firm checks them again (back checks) before they are stamped.
- Establish a clear chain of command for each project.
- Require that all staff working on the project share in the responsibility for quality control.
- Involve the owner in reviewing and checking the documents.
- Employ a checklist to see that all documents meet applicable codes, ordinances, and laws.
- Utilize a peer review process for complex projects.

The owner may want the landscape architect to adhere to quality-control measures that are explicitly included in the contract for professional services.

Excluding written quality-control procedures from the contract, however, is the best approach to this request. Explain to the owner that as a practicing professional you are obligated to provide quality services consistent with the standard of care practiced by other competent, licensed landscape architects. You rely on professional skill and training to execute the professional services to the best of your ability. If specific quality-control measures are written into the agreement, binding the landscape architect to use them, they may not fit the needs of the project as it unfolds. The procedures should be included only if contractual provisions allow the landscape architect to use professional judgment in the application of the procedures and to adjust the procedures if the project requires other quality-control measures that are more appropriate (Dixon and Crowell 1993).

Timeliness

Owners expect landscape architects to render their services in a timely manner. A project schedule is often one of the first documents produced by a landscape architect. Meeting the schedule is important, and timeliness may become one of the yardsticks by which the owner evaluates the landscape architect's professional services. When the schedule becomes a part of the actual agreement between the landscape architect and the owner, the schedule must include provisions that relieve the landscape architect from schedule delays not under the landscape architect's control. Delays caused by the owner, government agencies, or private reviewing agents such as design professionals who review plans for conformance with CC&Rs, can be excluded from the landscape architect's responsibility.

Timeliness is important to the landscape architect, as well as the owner. The professional's fees are normally based on an estimated amount of time that will be required to perform the services. If delays are caused by the owner or by reviewing agencies, the project will continue longer than the landscape architect anticipated. The firm will spend additional time on the project, and the firm will lose money. Arrangements with the owner and contractual language should allow the landscape architect to recoup any additional fees that result from delays that are out of the consultant's control.

Standard of Care

In the landscape architect/owner relationship, the doctrine of *standard of care* creates an important legal foundation if the issue of negligence should arise. Owners may interpret *standard of care* to mean perfection, and they may expect perfection from the landscape architect. The professional's documents, for instance, should be perfect in every respect. What is actually expected of a landscape architect is that he or she provides professional services consistent with the ordinary level of skill and care practiced by other reasonably competent landscape architects. The legal test for standard of care according to *The Contract Guide* is that the design professional's actions are reasonable, normal, and prudent under the given circumstances. Although landscape architects strive for perfection in their work, perfection is impossible to achieve. In reality, the perfect set of plans has never been produced. In order to set realistic expectations with the owner, the landscape architect can take the following steps:

- Inform the client that plans will be prepared in the best professional manner consistent with the standard of care.
- Insist that the owner have realistic expectations of the professional services.
- Prepare promotional literature that accurately portrays the landscape architect's capabilities.
- Offer to correct defective instruments of professional services at no additional cost to the owner.
- Define the standard of care in the agreement with the owner. Make the definition realistic and avoid expanding it beyond the expected level of the standard of care exercised by professionals practicing under similar circumstances.
- Ask the owner to agree in the contract between the owner and the contractor to a contingency fund that covers costs that may occur due to discrepancies or omissions in the construction documents.
- Ask the owner to include language in the agreement between the owner and the contractor making it clear that the construction documents may include discrepancies, conflicts, errors, or omissions, and that the remedy for these will be covered by the contingency fund (Dixon and Crowell 1993).

Warranties

Owners expect the landscape architect to guarantee the professional services. Owners may even expect the landscape architect to guarantee or certify that a project has been constructed exactly according to the construction documents.

In the first case, the landscape architect can agree to perform professional services consistent with the standard of care and make corrections at no additional cost to the owner if the services are found to be defective.

In the second case, the landscape architect can not realistically guarantee or certify that a project has been constructed in strict accordance with the plans. The landscape architect is simply not able to know if the contractor has built every detail of the project in conformance with the plans. During the construction services phase of the work, the landscape architect may be engaged to provide construction observation services. The consultant can certify that the construction site was visited at specific dates and times and that certain observations were made. The landscape architect can report on the placement of bedding material in the sections of irrigation line observed on a specific visit to the site. The landscape architect cannot, however, certify that all of the bedding material was placed in all of the irrigation trenches exactly as shown on the plans. By certifying or warranting that construction of the irrigation line was carried out in conformance with the plans, the landscape architect would be assuming liability beyond the standard of care and assuming liability that actually belongs to the contractor.

The Contract Guide includes a number of suggestions to avoid establishing a relationship with the owner where the landscape architect warrants, certifies, or guarantees anything except adhering to the standard of care practiced by the profession:

- Explain the concept of *standard of care* and avoid establishing a relationship or contractual agreement that expands professional liability by warranties, guarantees, or certifications.
- If the owner insists on inappropriate warranties or certification, consider walking away from the project and not engaging a contract with inappropriate language.
- Add language to the agreement that prevents the owner from requiring warranties or certifications.
- Tell the owner that warranties or certifications nullify the firm's professional liability insurance coverage.

- Be willing to accept the owner's expectations that you certify facts that you observe to be true about the construction of the project (Dixon and Crowell 1993).

Documentation and Record Keeping

The owner has a right to expect that the landscape architect will keep accurate and thorough records of the design and correspondence documents related to the work. Landscape architecture firms commonly interpret the length of time for keeping documents as the duration of the statute of limitations. The statute of limitations is a specified length of time in which a person can bring a lawsuit, and varies from state to state. Many states have different statutes of limitations for written contracts and oral contracts. Consulting the landscape architecture firm's attorney will provide helpful direction in determining the appropriate length of time for keeping documents related to the statute of limitations law of the state.

Some landscape architecture firms keep documents indefinitely or forever, providing a useful archive of the firm's project history. The archive is a helpful resource for developing promotional information about the firm. Another good reason to keep documents is that owners often need follow-up work on their projects or additional services well after completion of a project. If documents are readily available, the landscape architecture firm will be able to get a head start on responding to the owner's follow-up needs. When a project involves a number of phases of development, the firm should keep documents for an indefinite period of time.

Capability

Owners expect landscape architects to be able to do what they say they can do. Landscape architecture firms should steer clear of inflating their promotional literature to give the impression that the firm can do more than it has actually been responsible for. Sometimes landscape architects in a firm consider submitting a proposal for a project that may be stretching the firm's capability. Trying to advance the professional capability of a firm is a good idea. Creating opportunity to challenge the firm's professionals is one of the motivations of private practice. In such situations, the design professionals need to develop a detailed proposal that works through accomplishing those tasks that they may not have had direct experience with before. Involving the necessary subconsultants is typically a part of the proposal. With a clear understanding of how to go about providing a service level not previously engaged, the firm is on stable ground with the owner. The landscape architects should clearly make the owner aware, however, that they will be providing the specific services or the expanded service level for the first time.

The landscape architect also has a responsibility to the owner to provide services that fall within the area of professional responsibility governed by technical registration laws. These laws allow the landscape architect to provide a broader range of professional design services, such as engineering and architecture, by serving as a prime consultant and subcontracting the services of architecture and engineering firms.

Sealing the Work

One of the landscape architect's responsibilities is sealing the drawings, specifications, reports, and other products of the professional's service to the owner. State registration laws require stamping of construction documents and reports by a licensed professional. Failure to stamp the instruments of service is breaking the law, and can result in censure, fines, and the loss of the license to practice. By stamping the plans, the landscape architect is legally confirming that he or she prepared the plans or that they were prepared under the direct supervision of the landscape architect. The sealed drawings are part of the owner's insurance that the work has been carried out by a technically competent professional.

The Owner's Responsibilities in the Landscape Architect/Owner Relationship

Information

With the exception of paying the landscape architect for the professional services, the most important responsibility of the owner in the landscape architect/owner relationship is providing information regarding the requirements of the project. The owner must provide the landscape architect with a design program or a set of planning goals and objectives. Without a program, the landscape architect has no way to approach the project. If the owner does not have a program, the landscape architect's first task is to work with the owner to generate a program.

In addition to a design program, the owner has a responsibility to provide the practitioner with other information pertinent to the professional services. The landscape architect needs to know the owner's schedule. The design professional needs to be aware of any constraints, hidden agendas, and things the owner definitely does not like or want. The owner must transmit any site-specific criteria that will influence the way the landscape architect develops the site plan or designs the elements of the plan. The owner must let the landscape architect know if there is a need for special equipment, flexibility, multiple-use, or expandability in the plan. The owner must clearly communicate his or her functional and aesthetic requirements to the consultant.

The landscape architect will have great difficulty working for an owner who is reluctant to provide the information necessary to the practitioner to carry out the professional services. Sometimes an owner will give out enough information for the professional to develop a preliminary plan and then reveal more information during the process of reviewing the plan. If the owner reveals information to the professional in limited amounts at each stage of the design process, the landscape architect will have to spend more time than anticipated developing a satisfactory plan and lose money on the project. Landscape architects must inform owners of their obligation to provide information. The success of the project is directly dependent on the information the professional receives.

Budget and Finance Information

The owner has a responsibility to provide the landscape architect with a budget for the project, including construction costs and any other budget-related costs. The owner should provide evidence that he or she has funding to pay for the professional services and to build the project if it is a construction-type project or implement the plan if it is a planning project. The landscape architect needs to ensure that the owner is able to fulfill the payment obligations of the design services contract and has a vested interest in seeing the labor of the landscape architect's efforts actually come to fruition.

Designated Representative

The owner has an obligation to designate a representative authorized to act on behalf of the owner if the owner is not the professional's direct contact. The designated representative should have the authority to make decisions and legally bind the owner. When working with a corporation, the representative should be an officer of the corporation. If the landscape architect has any doubt about the authority of the owner's designated representative, the professional can ask the owner to specify in writing which agent or agents are authorized to act on the owner's behalf and legally bind the owner.

Surveys and Legal Information

In the landscape architect/owner relationship, the owner is obligated to furnish a survey and legal description of the project site, usually submitted to the landscape architect in the form of a boundary and topographic survey. The survey also includes accurate information on the location of utilities and other site culture. The landscape architect frequently arranges for the survey to be carried out by a surveyor working as a subconsultant. The survey and legal description are vital to successfully developing a site plan. Without accurate information, components of the site plan might be located off the property, utilities that need to remain accessible might be paved over, a zoning mistake might occur, an on-site sewer line might not match the invert of an off-site sewer line, or any number of other disastrous mistakes can occur.

Geotechnical and Consultant Services

The owner is responsible for providing the services of a geotechnical engineer, either directly or at the request of the landscape architect. The services of a geotechnical consultant are recommended on virtually every project that includes the development of site improvements such as structures, pads, pavements, and walls, especially retaining walls. The geotechnical analysis will provide specific recommendations for the depth of footings, subgrade preparation, and provisions for handling subsurface water. The structural engineer will need the geotechnical consultant's report to carry out structural calculations and design the structural approach necessary for each specific project. Geotechnical services may include, but are not limited to, soil testing, subgrade analysis, percolation analysis, fertility analysis, chemical analysis, determination of soil-bearing capacity, soil corrosion analysis, discovery of hazardous materials, and professional recommendations regarding the soil conditions related to the land-use and development program for a specific site.

In addition to geotechnical services, the owner is obligated to furnish the services of other consultants that may be necessary. In many cases, such as public works projects, the services of subconsultants including structural, electrical, mechanical, civil, and environmental engineers are required by law. In private projects, the need for subconsultants is guided by the complexity of the project; professional judgment; liability consequences; and health, safety, and welfare concerns. An uncomplicated residential project may not require a civil engineer to assist the landscape architect with grading and drainage requirements, nor would this type of project necessarily require an electrical engineer for lighting design. A complex project such as an amusement park may require a wide range of consulting engineers and specialists.

The owner may be more inclined to agree with the landscape architect's request for engineering and specialty consultants if the landscape architect identifies the need for their services during initial discussions and if the landscape architect presents the scope and cost of the consultants' work in the proposal. Owners are more likely to balk when the need for engineering or specialty consultants is identified during the course of the project. The landscape architect has the right to request the services of the needed consultants, nevertheless, and should usually not proceed with the work until the owner approves the request.

Accounting and legal services may also be needed for a landscape architecture project. Accounting services may come into play in relation to audits of the contractor's applications for payment and payment of subcontractors. Legal services are necessary in many ways, including drafting of CC&Rs, recording of an easement, and applying for a rezoning.

The important thing to remember is that the landscape architect strives to provide the best possible services to the owner while maintaining the health, safety, and welfare of the general public. When the best professional judgment of the landscape architect indicates that a consultant is needed, there should never be a question about approaching the owner to request involving the necessary consultant.

Suspension or Abandonment

The owner should notify the landscape architect in writing as soon as possible and at least within seven days if the project is to be suspended or abandoned. The owner has a responsibility to compensate the landscape architect for services performed prior to the notice of suspension or abandonment. If the project is suspended and resumed, the owner should compensate the landscape architect for expenses incurred during the interruption and for the costs of gearing up and starting work again. If the owner abandons the project, the landscape architect may want to request reimbursement for services and costs associated with terminating work on the project.

Landscape Architect/Allied Professional Relationship

Expectations in the Landscape Architect/Allied Professional Relationship

As with landscape architects and owners, a rewarding relationship between professionals ensues when they identify expectations up front and work to satisfy them throughout the course of a project. Many of the owner's expectations and responsibilities discussed earlier apply to an allied professional when the landscape architect serves as a consultant to the allied professional. Conversely, they apply to the landscape architect when the landscape architect is the prime consultant.

Because the relationship between the landscape architect and an allied professional depends upon which professional is the prime consultant, the following section discusses expectations and responsibilities first when the allied professional is the prime consultant and second when the allied professional is a subconsultant to the landscape architect.

Expectations of Allied Professionals as Prime Consultant

By the very fact that the allied professional has engaged the landscape architect as a subconsultant, the allied professional has determined that the landscape architect has technical capability important to the success of the project. The allied professional expects the landscape architect to perform the services accurately and competently. In representing themselves, landscape architects should be careful not to enlarge their professional capability; they should offer services that adhere to the standard of practice ordinarily expected of members of the landscape architecture profession currently practicing in the same geographic region under similar conditions.

Allied professionals serving as the prime consultant on a project also expect the landscape architect serving as a subconsultant to adhere to lines of communication set up with the owner and the other subconsultants working on the project. The allied professional does not want information to be incorrectly communicated to the owner, nor does the allied professional want the landscape architect to present a plan that has not been reviewed by the allied professional. To effectively manage the project, the allied professional needs to know that everything being communicated with the owner and with other consultants is filtered through the allied professional.

The allied professional expects the landscape architect to keep all of the information about the project confidential until that information is made public by the owner. The allied professional should not, however, expect the landscape architect to withhold information from government agencies when the landscape architect and the allied professional have a public responsibility to report the discovery of hazardous materials or other environmental contaminants regulated by the government. The allied professional must accept the landscape architect's responsibility to preserve the health, safety, and welfare of the general public. The allied professional has the right, however, to expect to be notified by the landscape architect in order to coordinate with the owner before notifying a public agency.

The allied professional serving as the prime consultant expects the landscape architect to be punctual in meeting due dates established for the project. Missing a due date is likely to irritate the allied professional and cause stress on the relationship between the landscape architect and the allied professional.

Last, allied professionals expect the landscape architect to make recommendations for surveying, testing, or providing other data necessary for successfully completing the project in the eyes of the landscape architect. The allied professional relies on the landscape architect to bring up and deal with information needs in the course of the project. The allied professional will be angry at the landscape architect if a problem occurs during construction, for example, and the problem could have been avoided if the landscape architect had alerted the allied professional earlier in the design process. A landscape architect should never hesitate to recommend any type of testing or data that may avert problems, particularly construction problems. The allied professional serving as prime consultant may also expect the landscape architect to be aware of the project as a whole as it unfolds in the design process and to anticipate the need for landscape architectural input where the prime consultant may fail to recognize the need.

Expectations of Allied Professionals as Subconsultant

When the landscape architect serves as the prime consultant, allied professionals have different expectations. First and foremost, the allied professional expects to be paid by the landscape architect. Second, the allied professional expects the landscape architect to communicate in full the needs of the owner and the requirements of the project the allied professional will be responsible for. The allied professional also expects the landscape architect to appoint a representative of the firm to serve as a direct point of communication with the allied professional.

Budgets and Design Sensitivity

When the allied professional is the prime consultant, he or she expects the landscape architect to design to the budget. When the allied professional is a subconsultant working at the direction of the landscape architect, the allied professional is expected to design to the budget. In either case, if the budget is so low that the public health, safety, or welfare may be threatened, the consultant is obligated to notify the client. When the landscape architect is working as a subconsultant to an allied professional, and the landscape architect considers the landscape budget inadequate for the allied professional's acceptable level of design quality, the landscape architect should notify the allied professional. The landscape architect should strive for a level of design quality commensurate with the level of quality that the allied professional is trying to achieve. The landscape architect should also see that the allied professional's budget is adequate to achieve the desired level of design quality.

Working with an Architect

Landscape architects work with architects more than any other professional discipline. Because architects are design professionals, they expect the landscape architect to be design conscious, too. Likewise, the landscape architect expects the architect to bring creativity to the design of the project. Under the best conditions, pairing these two professionals results in a better project with a higher design quality because of the synergy that can occur. For example, a building is likely to be located sympathetically on the site and be enhanced by the site features and topography. The designed features of building, hardscape, and softscape combine to create a project that is visually appealing as a whole. In the worst case, the input of one of the professionals outweighs the other, and the dominance is evident in the visual appearance of the project.

In working with an architect, either as a prime consultant or subconsultant, I have found that complementing or supplementing the building results in a solution appreciated by the architect. During the site-planning process, carefully locating the structure to blend naturally with the site and minimize grading usually complements the architecture. Accentuating the physical attributes of the site by incorporating them into the architectural solution also complements the architecture. Using materials that are the same as, similar to, or that enhance the building materials is likely to complement the architecture. I have never found a reason to compete with the architecture and have always sought to achieve a blending of site and structure. When I have shown a desire to work with the architect, a good relationship almost always results.

Working with a Civil Engineer

After architects, landscape architects work the most with civil engineers. Civil engineers are technically oriented and tend to expect the landscape architect's involvement in a project to be technically sound. Generally, civil engineers also appreciate the softening that landscape architects can bring to a project. When the landscape architect is the prime consultant, the civil engineer is engaged for specific technical expertise often related to designing utility or drainage improvements. When the civil engineer is the prime, the landscape architect is involved to mitigate the impacts of grading operations, drainage improvements such as regional retention basins, or utility construction such as the location and construction of power line corridors. Many excellent public works projects have benefited by involving landscape architects to mitigate environmental impacts and beautify the civil-engineering improvements. Likewise, landscape projects often need the technical input of a civil engineer to be safe and sound.

The civil engineers I have worked with have appreciated the landscape architectural input in projects. From hardscape and landscape improvements that beautify a transportation project to landscape recovery plans intended to mitigate the destruction of natural environments, the landscape architect's expertise can be a valuable service when coordinated with the civil engineer's expertise.

The Landscape Architect's Responsibilities in the Landscape Architect/Allied Professional Relationship

Allied Professional as Prime Consultant

When the landscape architect serves as a subconsultant to an allied professional, the landscape architect has similar responsibilities as when serving the owner. The landscape architect has a responsibility to complete the scope of services in a timely manner and to meet the schedule set by the allied professional. The landscape architect must comply with codes, ordinances, and laws. The design plans should result in a safe project that minimizes risks to the health, safety, and welfare of the users. The landscape architect is responsible for avoiding unreasonable risk to others and completing the work with the standard of care ordinarily practiced by other landscape architects. The landscape architect's work should be aesthetic, functional, and environmentally sound. The landscape architect is responsible for quality control and accuracy of plans, drawings, specifications, reports, and other instruments of service. In addition, the allied professional expects the landscape architect to guarantee the workmanship in the preparation of the instruments of service and to seal the instruments of service upon final delivery to the allied professional. The allied professional also expects the landscape architect to keep proper records of the work for at least the duration of the statute of limitations.

Landscape Architect as Prime Consultant

Allied professionals expect the landscape architect to pay for the subconsulting services and to provide the information needed to carry out the services. The landscape architect is responsible for providing budget information, surveys, legal descriptions, geotechnical data, tests, and the services of subconsultants that may be needed by the allied professional. The landscape architect must designate a contact person, normally a principal or project manager of the landscape architecture firm, to serve as a point of contact with the allied professional. Last, the landscape architect must notify the allied professional if the owner has suspended work on the project or abandoned it.

Landscape Architect/Contractor Relationship

Expectations in the Landscape Architect/ Contractor Relationship

In dealing with the contractor, the landscape architect serves as the owner's agent and has the authority to act on behalf of the owner. The consequences of the landscape architect's actions, whether the owner agrees with the actions, are the responsibility of the owner. The contractor has expectations of both the landscape architect and the owner while executing the contract for construction.

Contractor's Expectations

The contractor expects the landscape architect's construction documents to be accurate, thorough, and complete. The contractor also expects the landscape architect to provide clarification of the construction documents at the request of the contractor. The landscape architect has a responsibility to visit the site on a regular basis while carrying out construction administration services on behalf of the owner and to keep the owner informed of the progress of construction. The contractor expects the landscape architect to be fair and responsive while carrying out the construction administration services. The contractor has the following expectations related to the landscape architect's facilitating the administration of the construction contract:

- The landscape architect will communicate the contractor's concerns to the owner.
- Communication with the landscape architect's subconsultants will be through the landscape architect.
- Communication with the contractor's subcontractors will be through the contractor.
- The landscape architect will review and approve the contractor's applications for payment.
- The landscape architect will review and approve the contractor's submittals required by the contract documents, including shop drawings, product information, and samples.
- The contractor expects the landscape architect's review of submittals to be carried out in a timely manner, causing no delay in the work.
- The landscape architect will prepare and submit approved change orders to the owner.
- The landscape architect will inspect the completed project to determine the dates of completion or substantial completion, and submit to the owner the contractor's request for final payment.
- The landscape architect will interpret questions of the contractor's performance at the request of the contractor or the owner.
- The landscape architect will interpret and act on disputes or claims made by the contractor or the owner, including claims for unknown subsurface conditions, where an adjustment is requested for payment or for a time extension. If the landscape architect's decision cannot resolve such claims, he or she may recommend legal methods of dispute resolution including mediation, arbitration, and litigation.
- The contractor expects the landscape architect to review and approve minor changes in the

work that do not change the intent of the design and do not involve adjustments to the contract sum or time but that may facilitate the contractor's work on the project.

- The contractor expects the landscape architect to be fair in reviewing completed work that does not conform to the construction documents but that may be acceptable to the owner and the landscape architect instead of requiring removal and replacement of the completed work for strict compliance with the construction documents.

Landscape Architect's Expectations

The landscape architect expects the contractor to respect the established lines of communication and communicate with the owner through the landscape architect. The landscape architect's expectations include forming a productive, cooperative, and non-adversarial relationship with the contractor. The landscape architect expects the contractor to protect the safety of persons and property at the job site. The landscape architect has the following expectations related to the landscape architect's facilitating the administration of the construction contract:

- The landscape architect expects the contractor to provide all of the labor and materials, obtain and pay for permits and fees, pay taxes, and provide insurance coverage required for carrying out the construction of the project.
- The landscape architect expects the contractor to review the construction documents and the field conditions and report to the landscape architect any discrepancies, errors, or omissions.
- The landscape architect expects the contractor to employ a competent job superintendent who will be on the job site for the duration of the construction.
- The contractor must maintain safety on the job site.
- The contractor must submit to the landscape architect a construction schedule before commencing work on the project.
- The contractor must maintain a copy of the construction documents on the site and make as-built changes on them.

- The landscape architect expects the contractor to submit shop drawings, product data, and samples with adequate leeway for the time required for review and approval.
- The landscape architect's review of the contractor's submittals is intended to be limited to checking for conformance with the construction documents and the intent of the design.
- The landscape architect has the authority to reject work that does not conform to the construction documents and expects the contractor to remedy the rejected work.
- The landscape architect expects the contractor to fix any damage caused by construction activities at no additional cost to the owner.
- The landscape architect expects the contractor to keep the job site clean and to clean up the site after completing the work.
- The contractor must provide the landscape architect and the owner access to the work at all times while the work is in progress.
- The landscape architect expects the contractor to follow the same lines of communication expected of the landscape architect.
- The landscape architect expects the contractor to submit cost proposals for change orders in a timely fashion.
- The landscape architect expects the contractor to submit requests for payment in a timely fashion.
- The contractor must notify the landscape architect immediately if the contractor encounters hazardous materials on the site.
- The landscape architect expects the contractor to observe all government regulations related to hiring practices while carrying out the construction activities.
- The landscape architect expects the contractor to have a plan for emergencies that may conceivably occur during construction.
- The landscape architect expects the contractor to uncover work that the landscape architect has requested to review prior to backfilling. If the landscape architect rejects the work, the contractor must remedy the work in conformance with the construction documents. The contractor will pay the cost of uncovering work.
- The landscape architect expects the contractor to carry out materials testing during construc-

tion and coordinate with authorities for inspections required by government agencies.

Working with the Contractor

Developing forms used during construction administration is one way that landscape architects can enhance the working relationship with the contractor. Computerized forms for submittal reviews, field reports, and meeting summaries allow the landscape architect to expedite construction administration work. Contractors usually appreciate quick turnaround of submittal reviews and timely notification of issues that are written up in field reports. When the landscape architect completes reports in a timely manner, the contractor develops admiration and respect for the consultant.

A regular meeting at the job site, at least once per week, is another way to develop a good working relationship with the contractor. The regular meeting can be attended by the landscape architect, the superintendent, subcontractors whose work is going on at the time, and the owner or owner's representative. The regular meeting fosters communication and serves as a vehicle for following the progress of the construction. A written summary of the weekly meeting is an excellent way to make project progress reports to the owner.

Giving proper consideration to the contractor's proposals for changes that save the owner money is another way to develop trust in the relationship with the contractor. The landscape architect's approval will serve to involve the contractor in a meaningful way, as long as the proposals do not compromise the integrity of the design or the health, safety, and welfare of the users.

Last, if a problem occurs with respect to an error, omission, or faulty construction, the landscape architect can act as a leader and work toward resolving the problem without pointing fingers or acting disgruntled, even if the fault may be his or hers. To the owner, completing the project is usually paramount, and completing the project should be the focus of the landscape architect and the contractor. The resolution of fault will be determined later by the dispute resolution methods set in place in the contract for construction between the owner and the consultant.

Landscape Architect/General Public Relationship

Expectations in the Landscape Architect/General Public Relationship

The relationship between the landscape architect and the public is veiled when compared to the clear relationship that develops, aided by contracts, between a landscape architect and the owner, allied professionals, or the contractor. For the landscape architect, the term *general public* refers to all of those people who may use the project designed by the professional or who in some way may be affected by it. In a larger sense, the general public means all of civilization relative to the stewardship ethic professed by landscape architects. A landscape architect's vow to be a steward of the land applies not just to those people residing in the region where the landscape architect practices, but for all people everywhere.

Expectations of the General Public

Code compliance is one of the most prominent expectations of the landscape architect in the eyes of the general public. Public agencies create laws, ordinances, and codes intended to protect the health, safety, and welfare of the general public, and consultants must be aware of such regulations and comply with them.

The general public also expects the practitioners of all professions to be self-regulating and to develop and uphold a code of ethics. Landscape architecture is no exception.

The landscape architect is expected to abide by the standard of care or standard of practice for landscape architects and to adhere to the professional registration law. The general public also expects landscape architects to develop plans and designs that are environmentally sound, safe, and as risk-free as possible.

Last, landscape architects are expected more and more to involve the user in the design process for public works projects (parks, for example) and in private projects that have high exposure to members of the general public (such as residents that live adjacent to a proposed development). Public involvement in the planning and design process has come of age in the last quarter of the twentieth century and is likely to be expected of consultants for many years into the future. The public also expects the consultants to listen to them and to hear what they are saying. Resentment occurs when the public is asked for its input and the consultants do not respond by making an appropriate change in the plan. In addition to involving the users in the planning and design process, landscape architects are expected to carry out research, review the literature, and use the best professional judgment available in designing public works projects. Experience and professional judgment become more and more important as projects increase in sophistication.

Landscape Architect's Expectations

Landscape architects expect the public to be responsive when asked to become involved in the planning and design process. They expect the general public to respond with a positive attitude. The consultant can become frustrated if public participants are quiet, shy, or unhelpful. Frustration also occurs if the public participants are negative, belligerent, or uncooperative. One of the best ways to convince the public that its input has been received is to make the graphic and written changes in the plan proposed by the public participants.

Landscape architects also hope that people enjoy using the public environments developed, managed, or protected as a result of the landscape architects' professional efforts. Seeing children having fun in a play area, commuters relaxing in a public transit center, waterfowl flourishing in a preserved wetland, or kayakers enjoying a white-water run, made possible by multiple-use management guidelines on public lands, are examples of the satisfaction that landscape architects can expect from the general public.

REFERENCES

Dixon, Sheila A., and Richard D. Crowell. 1993. *The Contract Guide: DPIC's Risk Management Handbook for Architects and Engineers.* Monterey, Calif.: DPIC Companies.

Karner, Gary A. 1989. *Contracting Design Services.* Washington, D.C.: American Society of Landscape Architects.

STUDY QUESTIONS AND ASSIGNMENTS

1. Pair off in twos. One person should play the role of landscape architect. The other should play the role of an owner. Each role player should develop questions to ask the other aimed at identifying expectations in the landscape architect/owner relationship.

2. Compare and contrast the similarities and differences between the three main consulting relationships discussed in this chapter:

   • Prime-consulting relationships
   • Multiple direct-consulting relationships
   • Subconsulting relationships

3. There are a number of key times to involve the owner in the planning and design process:

   • During the development of the design program or setting the planning goals and objectives.
   • During design development of the project.
   • During the design of construction details and selection of materials.
   • When reviewing the plans at the preliminary plan or schematic design stage.
   • When reviewing design development plans.
   • When reviewing and approve the final plans.

   Develop a checklist of questions that can be used to prompt a client's input for each of these key times in the design process.

4. Research the codes and regulations affecting landscape architects in your community. Obtain copies of the codes and prepare a paper identifying the code obligations. Summarize the key elements covered by each code in a paper.

5. Select three to five spaces or places in your community and evaluate the designs in terms of safety. Document in writing and graphics the safe and unsafe conditions. Refer to the codes and regulations you studied in question 4.

6. Locate an example of a landscape architecture project in your community or by talking to a practicing professional. Identify what professional-liability risks are related to the project. How might some or all of the risks be avoided?

7. Establish a realistic budget for one of your design studio projects. Carry out a construction cost projection to see if you have designed the project within the budget.

8. Develop a quality-control procedure that can be used as a checklist for project quality. Refer to the items discussed in this chapter and interview landscape architects in your community to see what quality-control procedures they use. Combine all of your results into a quality-control checklist that you can use on your projects.

9. Research the definition of the *standard of care* as practiced by landscape architects. Write a paper that explains and defines the standard of care practiced by landscape architects.

10. Research the statute of limitations and other criteria for keeping various documents in the landscape architect's files. Include project documents, contracts, legal documents, personnel information, insurance files, and other documents.

11. Write a paper on the owner's responsibilities in the design process. Include the responsibility to provide project program information to the landscape architect, budget information, responsibility to designate a representative to work with the landscape architect, surveys and legal information, geotechnical and environmental information, and all other information that an owner is obligated to provide to the landscape architect in order for the design services to be executed.

12. Write a paper on the landscape architect's expectations of allied professionals and owners in the professional consulting relationships.

13. Write a paper on the landscape architect's expectations of contractors in professional relationships.

14. What are the expectations of the landscape architect in the broad relationship with the general public? What are the general public's expectations of the landscape architect? Write a paper discussing these relationships.

CHAPTER FIVE

Finance

Where do landscape architects find the money to start an office and keep it going? What financing options are available? How is financing obtained? What are the main considerations in raising funds? How do lenders evaluate a request for financing? What does the firm use for collateral?

This chapter will answer these questions and provide an overview of the three major forms of financing:

1. Equity
2. Debt
3. Trade credit

This chapter will also discuss the main considerations for raising funds, as well as the three phases of financing that a firm may face.

Every landscape architecture firm will need to use some or all of the forms of financing to start and maintain a firm. The financing vehicles used depend upon the personal wealth of the founders and how much of their personal finances the founders are willing to risk. The founders of every landscape architecture firm must decide what balance to strike between using personal funds and using financing available from outside sources. How the funds are obtained is not only a start-up issue but also a recurring fact of business life as long as the firm remains viable. Familiarity with funding sources and finance options is one of the most important elements of the successful business practice of landscape architecture.

Five Considerations for Raising Funds

The landscape architecture firm that is considering raising funds must ask five main questions:

1. What is the amount of the funds needed?
2. When are the funds needed?
3. What purpose are the funds needed for?
4. What form of financing will be used?
5. Who will provide the funds?

The amount of financing required is determined by calculating the amount of money required for a capital investment, for example, or estimating the projected costs of starting the office, financing an expansion, or the maximum amount needed for an operating line of credit. When the funding requirements are based on a projection, overestimating the need is a better approach than underestimating. If the firm's estimates are too low, a shortage of funds is likely to jeopardize the venture. Underestimating a need for capital is embarrassing, and the firm may have difficulty in going back to the source of funds, or to another source, to raise the shortfall.

Timing relates directly to the firm's business planning and external factors such as the direction that interest rates are trending or the general availability of capital. The firm's business plan will have a time line that indicates a date when the funds are needed. The timing can be critical. The source that controls the funds may have a use for the money that ties it up until the landscape architecture firm needs it, or the funds may be earning interest that will be lost to the source when the funds are delivered to the landscape architecture firm. If the landscape architecture firm borrows the funds from a lending institution, the firm will begin paying interest on the money when it is deposited in the firm's account. Waiting until the funds are absolutely needed will save interest costs for the landscape architecture firm.

The purpose of the funds determines the type of financing the firm selects. If the need for the funding is not immediate and can be covered by the firm's current profits, the firm may be able to wait until accounts are received to fund the need. If the need is immediate, such as making a payroll or tax deposit, the firm will need access to a short-term credit source if it is available. If the need is for capital equipment, the firm will want to know when the equipment is needed and plan ahead to obtain a long-term note if savings or retained earnings or another liquid form of funding is not available. If the firm needs the funds for operating materials, the firm may have a readily available source of funds by relying on trade credit.

Determining what form of financing will be used depends upon the equity, or retained earnings, in the firm, the financial health of the firm and its owners, and the amount of debt already incurred by the firm. Short-term money needs are usually funded by the profits and equity in the firm. Immediate short-term needs can be funded by an operating line of credit or a revolving line of credit for which creditors usually require payment in the near future. Long-term funds used for equipment and real estate funding are almost always provided from loan capital.

Start-up financing decisions are influenced by the form of the business. Sole proprietors and partnerships are financed initially by personal contributions of funds, loans, venture capital by a silent partner, or bringing in another owner or partner. Corporations have the legal ability to raise funds by selling stock either to members of the firm or outside investors. Large corporations that have the possibility of revenue growth may consider selling stock to the general public to raise funds. Investors buy the stock because they believe the firm has the potential to provide them with a good return on their investment.

Once the firm has an established operating and credit track record, the sources of financing will vary. Private financing from friends or family is one of the first sources to explore when the need for capital arises. Financial institutions, banks, private investors, and governments are the other sources. Leasing has grown in popularity as a funding method for equipment and vehicles. Selling stock to members of the firm or the public raises funds but dilutes the ownership of the firm at the same time. Government-sponsored tax relief and incentive programs are often overlooked as a source of financing. The landscape architecture firm's analysis of all sources of financing should always include such programs.

The bottom line when the firm needs to raise funds is to review all of the options available and make a sound decision based on the cost to the firm, the terms of the financing, and the relationship with the provider of the funds (Bates 1982).

Three Phases of Financing a Firm

Landscape architecture firms may go through one, two, or three phases of financial needs:

1. Start-up financing
2. Maintenance financing
3. Continuation financing

The initial need for financing is to start the firm. Start-up financing provides money for

- purchasing equipment
- leasing an office space
- investing in stationery
- covering deposits required for utility service
- covering operating expenses such as phone service, utilities, and printing
- buying supplies
- covering tax obligations
- obtaining a business license
- covering the cost of vehicle use and maintenance
- providing insurance coverage
- paying oneself and one's employees

The initial investment in the firm is made by the individual founder or founding partners. If the firm is started as a sole proprietorship or a partnership, the initial investment is the contributed capital. If the firm begins life as a corporation, the initial funding is used to purchase shares of stock.

Initial funding comes from personal savings and in the form of gifts or loans from family, friends, or other investors. Other sources for initially capitalizing the firm are banks and lending institutions. Loans made at the start of a firm are often tied to the personal wealth and personal collateral of the founders because the firm has little or no collateral of its own.

Sweat equity is a vehicle that can help in the initial financing of the firm. Sweat equity means working for no pay until cash flow is available to pay a regular salary for the owner or owners. If the firm is started as a corporation, and stock is obtained by the firm's founders in lieu of a salary, tax laws require that income is recognized for the dollar value of the sweat equity exchanged for stock.

Leasing companies are a very good source of start-up capital because they allow the founders to obtain the use of equipment for a small initial outlay of capital. The U.S. Small Business Administration and other government agencies are another source of start-up financing.

Some firms have started by obtaining a government grant or other government-sponsored project that effectively guarantees a source of funding for the length of the grant. Starting a firm with a sure source of revenue provides a comfortable cushion while the founders develop market share and clients in the public and private sector of the economy.

Another start-up method is moonlighting, where the founder or founders maintain regular jobs and work at night and on weekends to start developing their own client base and the funds necessary for start-up financing. When enough capital is raised, the founders break away from their regular jobs to go full time with their start-up firm.

Start-up funds are used to build the firm's organization and establish a share of the landscape architecture market that will sustain the firm.

Maintenance financing is the next stage in the financial life of a firm. In the maintenance phase, the firm is already established. A steady stream of accounts receivable is available to use for collateral. Equipment and furniture assets are in place, and the firm possibly owns real estate assets. Financing requirements are focused on replacing assets as they are depreciated and on growth. Cash-flow management is an ongoing responsibility of the firm's managers and plays an important role in maintenance financing. The owners of the firm no longer have the capability, or in many cases the desire, to finance the firm's investments during the maintenance phase of financing.

In the maintenance phase of development, the firm looks to leasing and lending institutions for financing day-to-day operations and acquiring new equipment and furniture. If the firm is a corporation, it may look at selling stock to employees as a vehicle for financing growth and for stabilizing the financial interests of the firm by spreading ownership among a greater number of investors buying into the closely held corporation. Private investors and venture capitalists are outside sources of expansion financing.

Merger or acquisition may be a vehicle used for financing growth. Merging with another firm may create an opportunity to borrow funds using the higher amount of accounts receivable of the combined firms as collateral. The larger size of the new firm formed by the merger may be more appealing to private financiers or lending institutions, making sources of funds more readily available. A smaller firm may be acquired by a larger firm, providing equity financing for the business goals of the smaller firm.

Financial stability is a primary goal of financing approaches used during the maintenance period of a firm's business life.

The final phase of financing a landscape architecture firm is continuation financing. In this phase, lengthening the life of the firm or major expansion are primary objectives. The original owners may be at the age of retirement and wish to see the firm continue under the guidance of more youthful management and new owners. If the firm is large enough, it may have the opportunity to raise continuation financing through a public offering of stock. Major expansion may be a goal during the continuation phase of financing a firm and may involve large merger/acquisition moves or penetrating new market sectors either geographically or by type of service.

One source of continuation financing used by landscape architecture firms is the employee stock ownership plan (ESOP). Under an ESOP, the future of the firm is financed by making ownership available to a broad range of the employees who invest in the firm by purchasing its stock through direct cash purchase or payroll reductions.

Debt or Equity?

In all phases of financing the landscape architecture firm, managers must continually ask themselves whether it is better to use equity or debt to finance the operations and expansion of the firm.

Debt capital is normally easier to find, quicker to obtain, and does not dilute the ownership of the firm. With debt capital, however, there is debt service. Regular payments of interest and principal must be made regardless of the profitability of the firm.

In most cases, obtaining debt capital requires some form of collateral. For the landscape architecture firm, debt capital may not be readily available until the firm has developed a steady flow of revenue. The accounts receivable that come with the revenue stream are the main source of collateral for most landscape architecture firms. One of the negative aspects of debt capital is the personal guarantee, which many owners of landscape architecture firms are reluctant to agree to. Most lending institutions, banks, and leasing companies now require personal guarantees of the firm's owners in order to consummate a loan.

If the firm is financed with debt, and if the firm is successful, everything left over after repaying the debt belongs to the owner or owners of the firm.

Equity financing requires the owner or owners to risk personal capital. The greater the number of equity partners or stockholders, the greater the financing potential. In fact, one of the nagging questions that faces the founders of a landscape architecture firm is how many partners or stockholders are needed to finance the firm. The more the financing is spread among partners or stockholders, the more the profits are spread among them. When financing a firm through equity capital, the founders must ask themselves if they would rather own 20 percent of a highly successful and profitable firm or 100 percent of a would-be highly successful and profitable firm.

In the final analysis, the best approach is the one that fits the need, personality, desires, and wherewithal of the founders or financial managers of the firm.

Landscape architects should consider the following questions when deciding between debt and equity financing of the firm:

DEBT

- Can the firm qualify for debt financing?
- What terms and conditions will be placed on the debt financing?
- What is the current level of the prime rate and prevailing interest rates? Is the prime rate trending up or down?
- How many sources of debt financing are available in order to take advantage of competition for the loan terms?
- Are the owners of the firm willing to make personal guarantees in order to secure the loan?
- Does the firm have assets to pledge as collateral?
- Has the firm made workload and cash-flow projections to verify that a revenue stream will be available to service the debt?
- Do current interest rates make debt financing undesirable?
- What is the urgency of the financing need?
- What is the after-tax cost of borrowing funds?
- What financial reports will the lender require? Does the firm already prepare them, or will preparing financial reports require additional administrative effort or require costly outside services?
- What is the present debt load of the firm?
- Will acquiring new debt increase the firm's leverage beyond its ability to comfortably carry the debt or secure additional debt financing if emergency funding is needed?
- Can the firm secure enough debt financing to meet its financial goals?
- Will debt financing need to be supplemented with equity financing?
- Has the firm looked at equity financing as an option to funding the need?
- What is the best balance between debt and equity financing for the firm?

EQUITY

- What are the financial resources of the firm's owners? Are the resources adequate, and are the owners willing to use their resources to finance the firm's needs?
- Is the financial strength of the partners or stockholders more or less equal?

- How many equity partners or investors are needed to raise the desired amount of financing?
- Does the firm have enough owners or investors available with the financial resources to meet the financial need?
- Are the firm's founders willing to share control with others?
- Are the firm's owners willing to share confidential personal financial information with other investors?
- Are the firm's owners willing to share profits with other partners or stockholders?
- Will equity financing provide enough capital for the financial need?
- What financial information and reports will be needed to keep partners, stockholders, and investors informed about the use of the funds?
- Will equity financing need to be supplemented with debt financing? (Lister 1995)

Equity Financing

The financial definition of *equity* is the residual value of a business beyond any liabilities owed by the business. Equity is the capital contributions to the firm and the total of the firm's profits year after year—its retained earnings. If the owner or partners of a landscape architecture firm contribute funds for the initial capitalization of the firm, or for capital or operating needs as the firm matures, they are building ownership, or equity, in the firm. If the firm is organized as a sole proprietorship, the individual owns 100 percent of the equity in the firm. If the firm is organized as a partnership, each partner's equity is based on the percent of contributed capital at start-up or on an agreed-upon formula or percent of ownership. If the firm is organized as a corporation, personal funds are invested to purchase stock in the firm. The number of shares of stock relative to the total number of shares outstanding determines the investor's proportionate ownership of the firm.

The goal of equity financing is to obtain a return on the invested money. The return for a sole proprietor or the partners in a firm is growth in profits and an increase in the retained earnings of the firm and in the growth of the firm's asset value as reflected in the firm's financial statement. As retained earnings and assets increase, the individual owner or partners see the value of their investment in the firm increase.

The return on investment for the corporate investor comes in the form of dividends paid on the shares of stock owned and on the increase in the face value of the stock. The increase in the firm's asset value and in retained earnings reflected in the profitability of the firm results in an increase in equity and in the per-share value of the firm's stock.

The corporate structure of a landscape architecture firm is attractive for raising capital because the value of each share is easy to determine at any time and the corporate structure protects the investor from personal liability. By contrast, the unlimited liability of the sole proprietorship and the general partnership is a deterrent to raising equity capital. The marketability of shares of stock is superior to the marketability of an interest in a partnership or a sole proprietorship, which automatically becomes a partnership if equity ownership is sold to another.

The form of the business is not cast in stone for the entire life of the landscape architecture firm. The business form can be changed to accommodate the financial requirements at different times in the life of the firm. Many landscape architecture firms start life as a sole proprietorship or general partnership. In the beginning, the firm is small and the contributed start-up capital is relatively easy to accumulate from personal savings and from relatives or friends who put few restrictions on the use of their money except that the principal be returned. As time goes on, financing needs increase beyond the investment capability of the firm's owners, family, and friends, and changing to a corporate structure becomes very appealing as a vehicle for raising funds and for limiting the greater liability associated with the larger financial operations.

The landscape architecture firm has a number of equity financing options available:

- Sweat equity
- Personal savings
- Family and friends
- Partners: general or limited
- Venture capital investors
- The landscape architect's present employer

Sweat Equity

When an individual, partners, or stockholders start a landscape architecture firm and elect to forgo their salary, the resulting increase in the firm's financial condition is due to the profit made by not paying salaries. The accumulated profit shows up as retained earnings on the firm's financial statement. The value of the retained earnings is the value of the sweat equity. Forgoing salary may be used as a financing mechanism at any time in the life of the firm.

Using sweat equity financing is a common practice for landscape architecture firms and other types of professional-practice firms. If the owner, partners, or stockholders elect to use this form of financing, they must realistically remember where the money created in the firm is coming from. If one forgoes a salary, one must draw the money needed for personal expenses from personal savings or some other source of personal income. One must put food on the table and pay the rent or the home mortgage. The money must come from somewhere.

Sweat equity financing in the corporation can result in friction between stockholders if the terms of forgoing salaries are not discussed and understood beforehand. If different salary levels exist among stockholders, and if different amounts of stock are owned, forgoing salaries will result in different economic returns to the stockholders. Therefore, sweat equity as a corporate financing vehicle should be well thought out before forgoing salaries, as illustrated by the following example.

A firm has two stockholders, owner A and owner B. Owner A owns 75 percent of the common stock. Owner B owns 25 percent. Both owners have equal salaries of $1,500 per week. They have an existing line of credit with an outstanding balance of $15,000 and decide that they want to create the financing to pay off the balance on the line of credit by each forgoing salaries for five weeks. The savings in salaries will create $15,000 of equity in the company and finance the repayment of the line of credit. The net effect of the sweat equity increases the firm's retained earnings by $15,000, effectively increasing the value of the firm's stock by $15,000. The stockholders must recognize that stockholder A will benefit by the sweat equity financing to a greater extent than stockholder B because of the 75 percent/25 percent split in ownership. Whereas the per-share value of the firm's stock will increase equally for both stockholders, the dollar value of the sweat equity and the return on investment is greater for owner A because of the equal salary contributions. Owner A realizes an increase in stock value

of $11,250 on an investment of $7,500 in salary, a 150 percent return on investment. Owner B realizes an increase in stock value of $3,750 on the $7,500 salary investment, a 50 percent return on investment.

Personal Savings

Many aspiring professional practitioners start their firm using personal savings for start-up capital and operating expenses until a revenue stream is available to cover the costs of operating. Using personal savings is the chosen way that most entrepreneurs start a business. Personal savings may come from more sources than one's savings account in a bank or other savings institution.

If a landscape architect works for a firm or a government agency and wants to start his or her own private practice, the retirement funds vested in the firm or government retirement program are a good source of savings that can be reinvested in starting the new private practice. Another source of personal savings may come from an inheritance or a trust fund that becomes available at a time when an individual has the desire to start or expand a firm.

Insurance policies offer good sources of capital to start a firm or finance a capital funding need in the mature firm. The cash value of the insurance policy may be obtained or a loan may be made using the policy as collateral.

Equity in one's home is another good source of money to fund the start-up or continued financial needs of a firm. The equity in the home is taken out by remortgaging the house or taking out a home equity loan. The equity from the home is transferred into equity in the new landscape architecture firm. As long as the landscape architect feels that the new firm will be profitable, the equity will not be lost. Using home equity as a way to raise capital also has tax advantages. The interest on home mortgage loans is one of the last remaining personal tax deductions in the federal tax code.

Family and Friends

If an aspiring professional practitioner has no personal savings, no home to mortgage, or is looking for funds to supplement personal savings, family and friends are a convenient source of financing. The main value of using family and friends as a source of investment capital is that the terms of the loan are often more favorable than from a commercial loan institution. Family and friends may even make the money available as a gift. Family and friends usually are sympathetic to the goals of the aspiring private practitioner, and moral support can be a side benefit of securing financing from them.

The negative aspect of using family and friends as a source of financing is bad blood. If problems occur with the start-up of the firm or its continuation, the funds may be lost, causing emotional pain and resentment between the landscape architect, family, and friends. There is nothing worse than being saddled with a family member's "I told you so." The possibility of losing a friend is another emotional setback that one may choose not to risk just for the sake of tapping into a source of financing.

When obtaining financing from family and friends, the best rule of thumb is to treat family or friends with the same serious approach used with a commercial lender. Prepare actual loan documents. Pay interest when it comes due. Provide financial statements and other reports on the health of the family member's investment. Strive to separate the business obligations from the enjoyment of the relationships and activities carried out with family and friends. If money is accepted from family or friends, make the same hard decisions about protecting the investment as if it had come from personal savings or from a financial institution that will have legal documents to protect its investment.

Partners

Starting a firm with one or more partners has one main financial benefit: the costs for starting the firm and maintaining its financial health are spread out among the partners. The greater the number of partners, the more the financial burden is spread out. The financial reward is spread out, too.

Partnerships can enhance the growth potential of a landscape architecture firm because partners not only spread out the financing of the firm but also bring different knowledge and business interests. Partnerships fall into two broad categories: *general* and *limited*.

General partnerships are formed by working partners, and all of the partners are active participants in the business of the office and in generating revenue. Decisions are made based on the concurrence of the partners. Expenses are borne and profits are distributed based on the proportionate share of the firm owned by each partner. In most cases in a general partnership, the percentage of ownership is based on dividing 100 percent by the number of owners.

Limited partnerships, comprising one or more silent partners and one or more controlling partners, provide a form of financing in which the silent partner contributes funding and the controlling, or general, partner manages the operations of the firm. The silent partner receives a percent of the profits and other considerations for financing the start-up and operations of the firm.

Structuring a limited partnership is an effective method for involving family or friends in the financing of a firm. The family members or friends contribute financing and remain in the background, while the private practitioner maintains control of the firm, handling day-to-day business operations. The limited partnership should be based on appropriate legal documents and spell out the terms of the return on investment and repayment of the principal.

Partnerships can be formed between all types of entities. An A/E firm or another landscape architecture firm may be a source of partnership financing when the partnership responds to a niche market or complements the business direction of the A/E firm or another landscape architecture firm (Heath 1995).

Venture Capital Investors

Venture capital is money invested in a landscape architecture firm, usually in the form of an equity investment, with the anticipation that the investment will result in a handsome return on investment. Venture capitalists fit a wide variety of descriptions—wealthy individuals, another company, or a group of investors that come together to finance promising companies. Venture capitalists typically seek a 20 percent to 30 percent return on their investment, and here lies the main problem for landscape architecture firms in obtaining financing from venture capitalists. In a good year, a landscape architecture firm may make a profit of between 5 percent and 10 percent, not enough to attract financing by most venture capitalists. This form of financing may have more merit for side businesses, such as a manufacturing company started by a landscape architecture firm. The side business may benefit directly from the association with the landscape architecture firm. Profit projections from this business association may be the incentive that a venture capitalist needs to commit financing to the new company.

The Landscape Architect's Present Employer

A good source of start-up capital and financing is the landscape architect's present employer.

If an employee of a landscape architecture firm gets the urge to start his or her own office, one of the first places to turn for financing the start-up costs is the firm where the employee presently works. Many landscape architecture firms are always looking for ways to expand into new geographic markets or into different areas of professional services. Firms also don't want to lose good employees, especially those employees that have the discipline and drive needed to launch a private practice. If the employer's firm is profitable and has retained earnings available or another source of financing, it may be willing to capitalize the start-up of a new firm by one or more of its employees for an equity position.

Leveraging Equity through Debt

Using start-up capital to leverage equity through debt is an important concept for the landscape architectural entrepreneur to understand. *Leverage* is the extent to which the entrepreneur substitutes long-term debt for start-up money. The goal of leverage is to make the start-up financing go further by making initial capital purchases with borrowed money. Here's an example of how it works:

A landscape architect decides to start a new office with $10,000 in savings. Capital items that will be needed immediately include:

Computer	$2,500
Printer	1,000
Furniture	1,000
Phone system	500
Total capital costs	$5,000

If the capital items are bought outright, half of the initial capital will be used, possibly causing financial stress on the start-up operation of the firm. If the landscape architect can use debt to finance the purchase of the capital items, and if 80 percent financing can be obtained, only $1,000 instead of the $5,000 total will be required from the initial start-up costs to obtain the capital items. Of course, the landscape architect must factor the monthly debt service, or loan payments, into his or her business plan and into the projected costs of doing business.

The actual amount of equity investment in the firm remains $10,000. Substituting debt for part of the initial equity financing makes the start-up funds go further by leveraging them. One consideration to keep in mind is the ratio used by some lenders as a guide to the amount of leverage a firm should engage. The leverage ratio is the debt-to-worth ratio and represents the level of capital contributed by creditors to capital contributed by owners. Lenders like the leverage ratio to be 3:1 or lower; that is, they want to be sure that the landscape architecture firm has financed its assets with at least one dollar of contributed capital for every three dollars of borrowed funds (Lister 1995).

Debt Financing

Debt is incurred when the landscape architecture firm borrows money as a method of obtaining capital or operating finances. Debt is a liability. It results in the obligation of the landscape architecture firm to return the principal amount of money borrowed from a lender at a specific time in the future. The lender charges an interest fee for the use of the money. The borrower must pay the interest, usually on a regular basis such as monthly, and almost always in advance of repaying the principal amount owed.

Loans are structured where an amount of money is borrowed for a specific length of time (the term) at a designated interest rate. The amount, the term, and the interest rate are the three main elements that are negotiated in the process of borrowing money from a lender. Sometimes fees are added, such as percentage points and late payment fees, which are also negotiable.

The art of negotiating a loan is making trade-offs between the three elements. If you give the lender the interest rate the lender desires, you should try to get the lender to give you the length of time that you desire. If you need a specific amount of financing, $10,000, for example, and no other amount will do, you will need to hold out for that amount and may need to be willing to accept the lender's terms on interest rate and length of time. Another negotiating axiom is if you set the amount higher than you need and the interest rate lower than you're willing to pay, the lender will grant terms longer than you expect—giving you some negotiating room. You may end up acquiescing to the lender's terms, but if nothing is ventured, nothing is gained.

When borrowing money, shopping for the most favorable terms and interest rate is important. Think of the process as similar to buying a pair of shoes, only you are buying debt. You wouldn't buy the first pair of shoes that you saw without trying them on, checking out how well they are manufactured, and waiting until you checked one or more stores to see which store has the best price. Likewise, finding the best source of money involves reviewing the debt financing options and shopping for the best terms.

The landscape architecture firm has a wide range of alternatives available for debt financing of the firm's monetary needs:

- Short- and long-term commercial loan
- Mortgage
- Personal loan
- Noncommercial loan
- Line of credit
- Lease
- Government-backed loan

Short- and Long-Term Commercial Loans

Banks and commercial lending institutions supply the bulk of loans to businesses, including landscape architecture firms. Banks and commercial lending institutions use money deposited with them as the source of their funds for making commercial loans. The difference between the interest that banks pay their depositors and the interest they charge their borrowers covers their cost of operating and provides them with a profit.

As a result of the failure of savings and loan institutions in the late 1980s and early 1990s, federal reg-

ulators strengthened the rules and performance standards used in the banking industry for commercial loans. Banks and commercial lenders are more cautious than ever about lending to businesses that lack the demonstrated ability to repay the borrowed funds. The cost of loans, or the points paid to a bank, have increased. Service and document-preparation fees have been introduced and increased if already existing. Collateral requirements have been strengthened. The performance of the borrower is scrutinized more carefully and the cash flow necessary to service the debt has become a very important element of analyzing the credit-worthiness of a borrower. Trends in the length of loans are shorter and shorter. Banks are not willing to loan money at a fixed interest rate for long periods (five years or longer) because they are unable to predict whether the interest rates they must pay to depositors will increase above the rates they charge borrowers and severely impact their income.

Banks vary in the types of loans they offer, the terms of the loans, and the level of risk their management is willing to accept. Most loans secured by small and medium-size landscape architecture firms are secured with liens on the firm's assets. As a standard operating procedure, banks and commercial lending institutions also require personal guarantees from owners of 20 percent or more of the firm (Lister 1995).

Short-term loans are funded for twelve months or less. The main concern of a bank that grants a short-term loan is repayment of the principal. Interest income is secondary. Short-term notes are typically written as a demand note, which means that the banker can demand repayment at any time up to and including the due date. The bank is likely to ask that some or all of the firm's assets that are readily converted to cash, such as the landscape architecture firm's accounts receivable, be used as collateral for a short-term loan.

Short-term loans are normally used as a source of operating capital. For example, when a landscape architecture firm is awarded a very large contract and must purchase or rent equipment and hire additional staff to start the project, short-term financing can bridge the gap between the immediate financial need and future cash flow. If a firm has a contract in place providing a substantial increase in annual revenue, a lender will be more inclined to make a short-term loan. The lender will have a comfort level that the money can be repaid.

All loans over twelve months in length are considered long-term debt. One of the most common forms of long-term debt taken on by landscape architecture firms is the installment loan.

When a landscape architecture firm buys vehicles, computers, office equipment, and furniture, the firm frequently finances such purchases with an installment loan. The loan is structured for equal payments of principal and interest over the length of the loan. The amount of the payment is calculated based on the total of the interest and the principal divided by the number of monthly payments. The interest on installment loans is typically front loaded and is costly to the borrower. The interest for the full length of the installment loan is calculated at the start of the loan, added to the principal amount borrowed, and the total is divided by the number of payments. Here's an example:

Financed cost of computer and printer	$10,000
Interest rate = 13%	
Term = 5 years	
Total interest on the loan =	
$10,000 × 13% × 5 years	$ 6,500
60 payments at	$275 Ea.

Compare the cost of the installment loan to the cost of a loan computed at a rate of 13 percent using simple interest:

	Installment Loan	Simple Interest Loan
Amount of loan	$10,000	$10,000
Interest rate	13%	13%
Term	60 months	60 months
Total interest paid	$6,500	$3,304

Obviously, negotiating a simple interest installment loan, if possible, is a better business decision for the landscape architecture firm and front-loaded installments loans should be avoided (Tuller 1991).

Long-term commercial loans secured from banks vary in length from one to twenty years; loans with a period of three to five years are common. Some long-term loans are amortized. The loan amount is divided by the number of months in the term, and the monthly interest is calculated on the amount of total principal remaining after each monthly amount of principal is subtracted from the total principal due. Under the typical amortized payment schedule, the amount of principal reduction is less in the beginning and more at the end of the scheduled number of loan payments, and the amount of interest paid is greater in the beginning and less at the end of the scheduled number of loan payments. The amount of interest paid is less with each payment because it is calculated on a constantly decreasing principal amount. Amortization calculations can result in equal monthly payments or in unequal monthly payments with equal principal amounts, decreasing interest amounts, and a decreasing total payment amount over the length of the loan (Lister 1995).

Long-term loans also are structured as interest-only loans where the interest is set at a specified annual rate and charged to the borrower on a monthly basis until the loan balance is repaid in full.

Mortgage loans are another form of long-term debt secured by real estate. A mortgage is normally amortized over fifteen, twenty, or thirty years. Real estate mortgages can contribute to the financial picture of the landscape architecture firm by adding significantly to the total assets owned by the firm, making the firm look good on paper.

Mortgages require a significant outlay of money up front in the form of a down payment, points, fees, and other costs associated with closing the mortgage loan. Due to the need for up-front capital, mortgages may not be a part of the start-up financing picture of most landscape architecture firms. Purchasing real estate when retained earnings provide enough capital for a down payment is a way for the landscape architecture firm to increase equity by paying off the mortgage and by benefiting from a possible increase in property value.

Sources of short- and long-term loans are banks, savings and loan institutions, finance companies, consumer lenders, credit unions, venture capitalists, mortgage companies, and governments.

Personal Loans

Some people have personal or family wealth. Others have an excellent credit history, strong earnings, and money in the bank. These people may qualify for an uncollateralized personal loan, a signature loan often made available as a line of credit. These loans are granted based on the financial strength of the borrower. The terms of these loans vary. They are frequently made for terms similar to those of credit cards or overdraft protection with quick approvals and high interest rates. The stronger the financial condition of the individual, the better the terms of the loan are likely to be.

Noncommercial Loans

Loans from relatives and friends are noncommercial loans. These loans are very useful in the financing picture of a landscape architecture office. They are negotiated in a friendly environment and usually carry more favorable terms than commercial loans. If family or friends have money available to lend, the landscape architect should approach them in a professional manner, with a loan proposal, as if he or she were approaching a bank or other commercial lender.

Loans from family and friends should have proper documentation that specifies agreed-upon terms and interest rates. Relatives and friends are likely to be mostly concerned about the return of the principal borrowed from them. One way to structure a loan from a noncommercial lender is to repay the principal before paying interest.

Lines of Credit

Lines of credit are used mostly for temporary and intermittent financial needs. The professional landscape architecture firm uses lines of credit mostly for managing the regular shortfall of operating capital caused by the lag between invoicing for services rendered and receiving the actual revenue. In the ideal business world, the landscape architecture firm would collect the cash it needs to operate from its clients shortly after invoicing them at the time when the cash is needed to pay for operating expenses. But because the business world seldom—if ever—works that way, the firm needs a line of credit to fill the gap between the time when the money is earned and when the client pays the bill. A line of credit is indispensable for maintaining stability in day-to-day operations, making regular payroll commitments, and withholding tax deposits.

There are several types of lines of credit: overdraft protection, operating lines of credit, revolving lines of credit, and bridge or swing loans.

Overdraft protection covers a shortfall in the firm's commercial checking account. The protection is commonly linked to a credit card. Overdraft protection is a service provided by the firm's commercial banker to protect the firm's creditors from insufficient funds in the firm's commercial checking account. The protection covers the amount of checks written against an overdrawn account.

Overdraft protection is particularly useful when the firm uses a general checking account and a different payroll checking account. Sometimes transfers of funds into the payroll account from the general checking account can lag, and overdraft protection avoids an embarrassing situation when employees cash their paychecks and the transfers have not been completed.

An *operating line of credit* allows the firm to borrow needed funds when it has a cash shortfall and repay the borrowed funds when cash is available. The firm uses an operating line of credit for temporary cash-flow problems and is required to pay at least the interest amount on a monthly basis.

Lenders typically set up an operating line of credit due and payable in a one-year period. Lenders usually require that the line of credit is reduced to a zero balance during the year the line of credit is provided. They often allow the zero balance to be achieved at the time when the line of credit is renewed each year. If the firm's financial condition remains healthy at the time of the annual renewal, the lender renews the line of credit, and the amount necessary to pay the line down to a zero balance is borrowed from the renewed line of credit. The annual renewal process allows the borrower and the lender to adjust interest rates, the cap amount on the line, and any other terms desired at the renewal date. Borrowers can expect fees or points to be charged by a lender each year when the line of credit is renewed.

The interest rate of a typical line of credit, as well as many other commercial loans, is frequently tied to the prime rate. The prime rate is the prevailing interest rate charged by large money center banks in the United States. It acts as a benchmark for lenders and is based on their cost of doing business. It is derived from their cost of money or the interest they pay on deposits plus overhead and profit.

Loan interest rates are stated as the prime rate plus additional points, or interest. If the prime rate is 7 percent, for example, the rate for an operating line of credit or other commercial loan would be stated as prime plus 2, resulting in a loan rate of 9 percent. Good customers (firms that have an established loan repayment record, good credit worthiness, capability of personally guaranteeing repayment of the loan, and an established relationship with the bank) may obtain a loan with a low rate of .75 percent (.75 points) above prime. Firms that represent a higher risk to the bank are more likely to have a rate of as much as 3.75 percent (3.75 points) above prime rate. The higher rates result in substantially higher costs to the borrower.

Armed with a clearer understanding of the rate structure, a firm can negotiate on a level playing field with banks and other lenders. The firm may end up paying what it feels is a high interest rate, but the bankers will know the firm's negotiators understand the lending jargon and the structure of the lending process. Knowing that rates are negotiable and banks are competing with each other allows the borrower to negotiate with some leverage.

Once an operating line of credit is in place, it may function as a quasi–long-term loan if the line of credit is collateralized by accounts receivable and renewed year after year. Unless the landscape architecture firm is extraordinarily profitable, there may not be a convenient way to eliminate the operating line of credit. It becomes an operating fact of life as long as the interest is paid regularly, the firm's credit remains good, and the line of credit is renewed each year at generally favorable terms. The interest is viewed as an annual cost of doing business. The firm focuses on preventing large fluctuations and significant reductions in its accounts receivable. The firm wants to avoid a major dip in receivables that would require a large pay-down of the operating line of credit, severely impacting cash-flow management.

A *revolving line of credit* is similar to an operating line of credit. A revolving line of credit may be extended for as much as three years and does not require annual payment down to a zero balance. During the period that the loan acts like an operating line of credit, the firm can draw against it and pay down the principal as cash flow allows, paying at least the interest on a monthly basis. At the end of the term of the revolving line, the principal must be paid or converted to a term loan.

Landscape architecture firms use revolving lines of credit to finance expansion when the exact amount needed to finance the growth can't be determined.

The expansion plan should illustrate a solid return on investment to ensure that the lender will be comfortable that the loan can be repaid (Lister 1995).

A *swing loan* is a short-term line of credit that is used to finance a need where a delay in receiving the revenue is forecast. For example, the firm may be purchasing a new office, and the closing date is October 1, but the closing date on the sale of the old office is not until November 15. In this case, the firm could approach a lender for a forty-five-day swing loan to cover the need for the closing funds for the new office until the funds are received from the sale of the old office.

A landscape architecture firm might also use a swing loan to mitigate profits near the end of the fiscal year. If a firm realizes that it is having a good year and will be extraordinarily profitable, but profits are tied up in a large amount of accounts receivable toward the end of the fiscal year, the firm may use a short-term loan collateralized by the outstanding receivables to pay bonuses to its owners and employees in order to mitigate the tax bite on its profits. The firm can pay back the short-term loan thirty to sixty days later in the new fiscal year when the accounts receivable are received.

Leasing

One method of acquiring assets such as vehicles, equipment, and furniture is *leasing*. This method of financing capital expenses catapulted into popularity in the 1980s due to favorable tax credits and depreciation allowances. When interest rates are high and bank financing is hard to obtain, leasing may be viewed more favorably than purchasing. When interest rates are moderate to low and debt financing is readily available, leasing loses some of its glamour. However, making a definitive statement of what circumstances make leasing more favorable than purchasing or vice versa is very difficult.

Leasing usually provides the following advantages over purchasing an asset:

- Leasing requires a lower initial cash outlay.
- Leasing allows the asset to be treated in one of two ways for financial management purposes: (1) as an operating expense, or (2) as a capital asset.

- The administrative process of leasing many items such as computers, equipment, or furniture is quick and easy and avoids the lengthy and uncertain process of applying for a loan. The asset is obtained and put to use quickly.
- Once a track record is established with a leasing company, the process of obtaining new lease financing is very easy.
- The lease can be structured so that the asset may be purchased at the end of the lease for one dollar or for a price below the probable market value.
- When a firm's borrowing capacity is low or a loan request is turned down by a bank, leasing companies may be a willing financial partner. Leasing companies or equipment vendors are more interested in packaging an attractive deal than a third party such as a bank.
- Leasing-company personnel tend to be easy to work with and accommodating.
- A firm may be able to negotiate a master lease, like a leasing line of credit. When equipment or furniture is needed, it is added to the lease without going through the process of negotiating a lease agreement again. The monthly payment will be adjusted to cover the new assets.
- The leasing company usually bears the impact of obsolescence, if the risk of obsolescence is high.

There are two basic types of leases:

1. The operating lease
2. The capital lease

An operating lease allows the landscape architecture firm to report the lease payment as an operating expense on the firm's financial statement. The asset is expensed and not depreciated. The firm is not required to show an asset or liability on its financial statement. The operating lease transaction preserves the firm's ability to obtain debt financing because the operating lease doesn't increase the firm's reported debt load or its debt-to-equity ratio.

A capital lease, on the other hand, treats the asset as if it were purchased with funds from a loan and financed by debt. The dollar amount of the lease appears as an asset on the firm's balance sheet. The asset is depreciated, and the dollar amount of the lease is shown as a liability on the balance sheet.

The common criteria used to determine if a lease is considered a capital lease for accounting purposes are

1. if ownership of the asset is transferred to the firm at the end of the lease payments,
2. if the lease contract allows the firm to purchase the asset for less than fair market value at the end of the lease term,
3. if the lease amount is equal to or greater than 75 percent of the economic life of the leased asset.

One of the confusing issues related to leasing is how the IRS views the lease. Both the lessor and the lessee must agree on who will report the lease as an asset and take advantage of the depreciation and tax benefits. If the leasing company treats the asset as if they own it, the landscape architecture firm will show the lease payment as an expensed item for tax purposes. Automobiles, for example, are normally leased this way, with the lessor depreciating the vehicle and the landscape architecture firm expensing it.

If a lease meets the following guidelines, the leasing company, not the landscape architecture firm, will show the asset on its balance sheet and include depreciation of the asset as a cost on its income statement:

- The term of the lease is less than 80 percent of the useful life of the asset.
- The value of the asset at the end of the lease (its residual value) must be 20 percent or more of its original cost.
- The landscape architecture firm must have purchased the asset for at least its fair market value.
- The leasing company has not paid or guaranteed payment of any part of the original cost of the asset.
- The leased equipment must not be so specialized that no one except the landscape architecture firm may use it when the leasing term is complete (Lister 1995).

One other type of lease arrangement—the purchase and lease back of equipment—can benefit the owners of the landscape architecture firm. This method of financing the capital needs of a landscape architecture firm depends upon the owners having financial strength. In this approach, the owners purchase the equipment, furniture, or other capital asset and then lease the asset back to the firm. In this way, the firm obtains the equipment or furniture it needs and the owners benefit from the depreciation write-off and the income earned on the lease.

Another application of a purchase-and-lease-back arrangement involves a third party. For example, a landscape architecture firm owns its office building and has depreciated all or most of it over thirty years. The firm's owners decide they don't want to move from the building, but they would like to capture the equity in the real estate. They seek a third party to buy the building and negotiate with the new owner to lease back the building so the firm can stay in it. The owners use the funds from the sale to fund a recapitalization of the firm or to make a large contribution to their retirement program.

Government-Backed Loans

Although many federal grant and loan programs exist, small businesses such as landscape architecture firms often look first to the Small Business Administration (SBA) for loan assistance. The SBA, which is established under the Department of Commerce, assists small businesses by providing advisory services, education, and financing. The SBA facilitates borrowing for small firms that otherwise cannot obtain funds from banks or other lending institutions on reasonable terms. Most of the SBA's financial assistance comes in the form of loan guarantees made to a bank or a lending institution.

The SBA has a wide variety of loan programs. The most well known is the 7(a) Loan Guaranty Program. The 7(a) program provides for a federal guarantee on 90 percent of loan amounts up to $155,000, and 85 percent on loan amounts over $155,000, made by a bank or lending institution. The maximum amount is $750,000. There are limitations on the term of the loan and on the amount of interest that a bank can charge over the prime rate.

Other SBA loan programs include a low-documentation loan program, loan programs for economically or socially disadvantaged borrowers, loans to assist handicapped individuals, loans for Vietnam-era and disabled veterans, disaster loans, and loans for companies that have been injured or displaced by a government act. The small business set-aside program and programs of financial assistance to women and minorities that are funded by the SBA may be particularly relevant to many small landscape architecture firms. The SBA has developed many programs that are targeted at women who want to own their own firm. Another funding program particularly suited to landscape architecture firms is the SBA-backed mortgage, which allows the purchase of an office building with a 10 percent down payment and a 90 percent mortgage.

The SBA-backed mortgage is one way for some firms to purchase their office space when the 20 percent to 25 percent down payment for a typical mortgage on commercial property is not available. The SBA-guaranteed commercial mortgage loans also allow many of the closing costs to be financed further reducing the out-of-pocket costs to the firm.

The SBA programs, qualification criteria, loan requirements, and availability of funds change with the ebb and flow of politics in Washington. The best advice for a landscape architecture firm contemplating the pursuit of SBA-backed financing is to make contact with the nearest SBA office and let the government representatives provide assistance in matching the best current loan program to the needs of the firm.

How Lenders Evaluate a Loan Request

The Five Cs

According to Kate Lister and Tom Harnish in their excellent book *Finding Money: The Small Business Guide to Financing,* the five Cs are still the bottom-line standards that lenders use to evaluate whether a borrower is creditworthy. The landscape architecture firm and its principals will be evaluated on "Character, Capacity, Collateral, Capital, and Conditions—the five Cs of credit" (Lister 1995).

The character of the firm's owners is at the top of the credit evaluation list. Lenders will examine whether a landscape architecture firm and its owners have received credit in the past and have paid their bills. The lender will run a credit check on the firm and on its owners. Past credit patterns of use and abuse indicate how debt will be managed in the future. Poor money management, excessive consumer credit, late payments, and missed payments by the owners of a firm in either their personal finances or the finances of a previous business are likely to influence the way owners run the business of the landscape architecture firm.

The lender will request a credit report from one of several local or national credit agencies that track the lending history of individuals and firms. Local credit agencies are listed in the yellow pages. The three largest national credit reporting agencies are

- TRW
  Box 2350
  Chatsworth, California 91313
- TransUnion
  Box 7000
  N. Olmstead, Ohio 44070
- Equifax
  Box 105873
  Atlanta, Georgia 30348

The main business credit reporting agency is

- Dun & Bradstreet
  899 Eaton Avenue
  Bethlehem, Pennsylvania 18025

Knowing what credit reporting companies have to say about the firm and its owners is vital information to have at hand when attempting to secure a loan.

The best advice regarding credit reports is to keep them as clean as possible. By obtaining a credit report from each of the major national credit bureaus, unfavorable or incorrect information may be corrected. In 1970, Congress passed the Fair Credit Reporting Act, which requires credit bureaus to delete information from a credit history that is inaccurate or that cannot be verified as truthful by the bureau. There is also a statute of limitations on the length of time credit agencies may keep adverse information on a credit report.

In order to have negative credit information removed from a credit report, the landscape architecture firm must notify the credit reporting agency and submit a dispute letter. If the credit bureau cannot verify the accuracy of the information from the creditor, the bureau is obligated to remove the information

from the credit report. The firm should obtain credit reports from all of the local agencies and from the big three credit reporting companies to verify that each report contains only accurate information. If a problem exists on one agency's report, the firm should check the reports of the other major agencies to see if the credit problem also exists on their reports. If the dispute cannot be resolved, the firm can have the credit agency include a summary of the firm's version of the disputed information in its file and in future reports requested by creditors.

If credit problems exist and cannot be removed from the report, be honest with the prospective lender. Try to avoid having a credit problem become an issue by addressing it up front. In addition to having the credit bureau report your version of the dispute, prepare a written statement of any extenuating circumstances and how the conditions that led to the credit problem have been resolved so they are less likely to occur now and in the future. The fact that you are aware of a previous credit problem and have taken honest steps to correct it may be enough for a prospective lender to discount the problem.

References and what people have to say about the character of the firm and its owners are very important to the prospective lender. Select several people who can provide a positive reference for the firm and its owners. Provide the names, addresses, and phone numbers to the lender and encourage the lender to contact the references.

The second of the five Cs is capacity. Can the landscape architecture firm and its owners pay off the debt?

Lenders will examine the actual and projected growth rate of the firm's revenue and profits. They will examine financial statements carefully, looking for stability in income and expenses. They will ascertain whether the firm has the cash flow available to service the loan. They will look at the relationship between the firm's debt and equity (the debt-to-equity ratio). They will ask about expected revenue, work in progress, contracts received, and future workload outlook.

Lenders are likely to reconfigure the firm's financial statements and look at various business ratios that serve as a barometer of the firm's financial condition. The main ratios reviewed by lenders include liquidity ratios, such as the current ratio, and leverage ratios, such as debt to net worth. Calculating these ratios from the firm's financial accounting information is covered in the next chapter.

Lenders will examine the firm's aging reports of accounts receivable and accounts payable. They will examine the firm's profitability, gross profit and net profit as a percent of revenue. They will examine operating expenses as a percent of revenue, and they will ascertain the accounts receivable turnover ratio, also discussed in chapter 6. Lenders may also convert financial statements to cash-flow projections.

Assessing the firm's capacity using ratio and direct analysis of financial statements before approaching a lender can identify problems with the firm's financial performance. The firm can take corrective measures before approaching the lending institution, or prepare explanations of corrective measures based on forecasts of future workload and profits to use in negotiating with a prospective lender. Workload projections and financial projections are extremely useful in negotiating with a lender. Projections must be part of the firm's planning tools. Not only are they useful in presenting materials to a lender, but they allow the firm to accurately determine its ability to generate revenue and profits to service the debt obligations. Workload and financial projections are also covered in chapter 6.

Collateral, the third of the five Cs, is the cash equivalent used by a lender as a guarantee of funds to pay back the debt. Here landscape architecture firms have a small advantage over manufacturing, wholesale, and retail operations. Lenders prefer accounts receivable as collateral over machinery, equipment, and inventory. The personal assets of the firm's owners and personal guarantees on business loans are also important.

Cash is the supreme form of collateral. A landscape architecture firm that is cash rich will have little trouble securing a loan if cash is the primary source of collateral. Accounts receivable are next in line. Typically, lenders will loan up to 80 percent of the value of accounts receivable under ninety days old. Equity on real estate owned by the landscape architecture firm is also a good source of collateral. Typically, a lender will loan 75 percent to 80 percent of the value of equity on real estate. Furniture and equipment such as computers command a lower percentage of collateral value, typically 10 percent to 50 percent.

The fourth of the five Cs is capital. How much capital is the landscape architecture firm risking? Firms that carry a higher debt load have a higher risk of financial failure than firms that carry less debt.

Lenders traditionally examine the firm's debt-to-equity ratio as an indicator of risk. Generally speaking, lending institutions and banks prefer granting loans to firms when owners have a large stake in the business. Red flags go up for lenders when they see a firm's total debt is more than three times the owner's or shareholder's equity, or when the debt-to-worth ratio is greater than 3:1.

The debt-to-equity ratio, for which the calculations are illustrated in chapter 6, is based on information taken directly from the firm's balance sheet. The information on the balance sheet should be reviewed to discover if any existing conditions will allow recasting the balance sheet in order to improve a debt-to-equity ratio higher than 3:1. The firm's accountant can be very helpful by looking for items such as undervalued assets that are highly depreciated and friendly debt, such as loans by owners, that may be subordinated to a new loan by a bank or other lender.

For example, Ace Landscape Architects has a balance sheet that shows assets of $100,000. One of the assets is a building that has been depreciated to a value of $50,000 carried on the books but is now worth $150,000. The balance sheet also shows outstanding loans to the owners of $30,000. These loans have been carried on the balance sheet for many years and are not being repaid. The balance sheet shows owner's equity of $45,000 and liabilities of $180,000, a debt-to-equity ratio of 4:1. If the asset value is adjusted to $150,000 based on the market value of the office building, and the $30,000 debt to the owners is subordinated to the loan being requested, the assets are recast for a total of $200,000, increasing the owner's equity to $145,000, and effectively removing $30,000 in liabilities. The new debt-to-equity ratio is 1.03:1, or $150,000 to $145,000.

The message in this scenario is to understand the true value of a firm's assets and liabilities in calculating the worth of the firm and its borrowing potential based on the debt-to-equity ratio.

The last of the five Cs is the conditions under which the firm is requesting a loan. The lender will examine the economy, both national and regional, the state of the landscape architecture market, and any other conditions that might impact the firm's ability to repay the debt.

Workload and job-development projections that indicate rosy expectations of future revenue are very helpful for convincing a lender that economic and market conditions are healthy. Knowledge of current events in the national and regional economy can impress a lender, too. If the landscape architect can quote local economic forecasters with facts and figures that indicate a housing, commercial, or industrial boom, the lender will be reassured that future revenue opportunities for the firm are optimistic. If the landscape architect can point to a large bond issue that will result in a huge increase in public works opportunities or school spending, a lender may feel comfortable that the firm will capture a projected part of the fees. If the national and local economy are depressed, on the other hand, the landscape architect will have considerably greater difficulty in persuading a lender to make a loan.

Personal Guarantees

Most landscape architecture firms are small businesses owned by one or a few individuals. Whether the firm is structured as a sole proprietorship, partnership, or corporation, the principals and owners *are* the business. Regardless of the structure of the firm, even if the structure is a corporation intended to shield the individual owners, a lender will look to the owners to personally guarantee repayment of borrowed funds.

Personal guarantees have proliferated since the savings-and-loan crash of the late 1980s and are now a common practice. They are required not only by banks and lending institutions, but also often in consumer loan documents and leases.

Lenders subscribe to the school of thought that if the owner or owners of a landscape architecture firm are not willing to risk their personal assets, then neither should the lender. Lenders typically use a *joint and several clause* for personal guarantees. A joint and several clause makes each of the guarantors responsible for the entire loan, even if the borrower is a corporation or if there are three partners who sign the loan documents and each has only one-third of the financial responsibility of the firm.

A personal guarantee set up as a joint and several clause for a lease agreement is typically worded as follows:

The undersigned, jointly and severally, guarantee payment of all amounts owing under this Lease Agreement and the payment upon demand of the amount owing on said lease in the event of default by the Lessee, Ace Landscape Architects. Under-signed waives notice of default, notice of performance, demand for performance, notice of nonperformance, protest, notice of protest, and any and all other notices to which the undersigned would be otherwise entitled by law. Undersigned agrees to pay all amounts owing upon demand without requiring any action or proceeding against the Lessee and specifically waives any right to require action against Lessee or undersigned as of any indebtedness, liability, or obligation of the Lessee under the terms of this Lease. The undersigned, jointly and severally, agree to pay Lessor a reasonable attorney's fee should Lessor retain an attorney to enforce any of the terms and conditions of this Guaranty or this Lease.

The Loan Proposal

Many people approach obtaining a loan with their hat in their hands. The lender has the money they need, and the best way to get the money is to do anything and everything the lender requests of them. The lender strives to keep the lending process mysterious. Unless the borrower appears to have some financial savvy, the lender provides only enough information to execute the loan process, usually on the lender's terms. The more a borrower knows about the lending process and finance in general, or at least appears to know because the borrower has done some homework, the more likely the borrower will be to obtain a loan with terms that are as favorable as possible.

There are two schools of thought on how to go about making a request for a loan from a bank or other lending institution.

The first approach is to call up a bank or another lender and ask what information they will require. Assemble the information. Meet with the lender (hat in hand) and negotiate the terms of the loan. There is nothing wrong with this approach, and with the busy schedule of many professionals, it may be the only practical approach. This call-up-the-lender approach will have more favorable results if the borrower has some knowledge of banking, accounting, and finance and is capable of answering the lender's questions and reacting to terms as they are offered by the lender.

The second approach is to prepare a written loan proposal illustrating that the borrower understands the loan process, has a good grasp of the business of landscape architecture, and has the necessary financial information about the firm for a lender to make a loan decision. The bottom line of a loan proposal is to request the amount of financing and spell out the terms that the firm would like to achieve. The proposal doesn't have to be slick, but it should be organized and complete. A clear loan proposal with an up-to-date financial statement and other financial documents will go a long way toward impressing a lender and greasing the skids of the loan process.

A loan proposal might include the following:

A. An executive summary of up to four pages that includes the following information:
   1. A brief overview of the firm, how long the firm has been in business, and its major clients and projects
   2. The amount of money the firm wants to borrow
   3. The type of loan desired (long- or short-term, operating line of credit, or swing loan)
   4. The purpose of the loan
   5. How the firm plans to generate the funds to repay the loan
   6. A description of available collateral
   7. A summary of the firm's current financial status, profitability, and key financial ratios
B. Supporting information can be included in the form of attachments:
   1. Three years of financial statements
   2. Three years previous federal tax returns
   3. Current work in progress and workload projections
   4. Aged accounts receivable report
   5. Aged accounts payable report
   6. Table of collateral values
   7. Personal financial statements for the firm's owners
   8. Sample of the firm's project cut sheets

Impressing a lender with a well-constructed loan proposal has the added benefit of speeding up the approval process, which may be important if the firm needs the finances quickly (Lister 1995).

Trade Credit

One of the most valuable forms of credit available to the landscape architecture firm is trade credit—the unsecured financing offered to a firm by its suppliers.

The landscape architecture firm relies on a variety of suppliers of services and products to carry on the business of providing professional services. Landscape architecture firms typically use some of the following suppliers and vendors:

- Blueprinting companies
- Photocopy businesses
- Drawing and drafting materials supplier
- Stationery supplier
- Photographic processing companies and film suppliers
- Office products businesses
- Office equipment suppliers
- Office cleaning companies
- Long-distance phone service companies
- Phone service
- Utility companies
- Insurance companies
- Gasoline companies
- Computer technicians
- Allied professionals such as architects, engineers, and graphics professionals

Because vendors and suppliers of services want to do business with the landscape architecture firm, their terms are more lenient than those of a bank or lending institution. They are likely to extend credit without asking a lot of questions, and they won't ask to see the firm's financial statement or other business information. They may have an application form, which usually asks for the names of other trade references used by the firm. In effect, they become trade partners, and the success of their business is tied to the success of the landscape architecture firm's business. Realistically, a landscape architecture firm would probably elect to find another business trade partner if a vendor or supplier is not willing to extend trade credit to the firm.

Trade credit may be extended for fifteen, thirty, forty-five, sixty, and even ninety days. The money the firm spends with trade credit partners is effectively an interest-free loan for the amount of time the trade credit is extended. If the trade credit is not abused by the landscape architecture firm, it is a valuable source of operating finances.

The amount of trade credit and the length of the terms vary with suppliers. The phone company and utilities are likely to provide only fifteen to thirty days of credit before service is threatened. Office supply businesses and blueprinting companies may provide up to ninety days of trade credit before they demand payment. Insurance companies may set up quarterly or semiannual payment terms.

Whereas trade credit is used throughout the business life of a landscape architecture firm, it is also a vital component of starting a firm. The following scenario illustrates how much financing might be provided over a 90-day period for a small firm. Table 5-1 shows the level of spending for services and supplies that might occur in a small landscape architecture office over a 90-day period. The amount that is "borrowed" by using trade credit, including the interest saved, is $22,372.23. Although the business world doesn't work exactly like this scenario, the table does point out the value of trade credit in financing the everyday operations of a landscape architecture firm. By the end of 120 days, assuming the firm is accruing about $7,000 per month in trade credit, the firm will have borrowed almost $30,000 with no interest, and is obligated to pay only the oldest accounts of 90 days and those accounts that will grant the firm only 15 to 30 days credit, a total of $8,835.00.

The landscape architecture firm should never abuse trade credit. Suppliers of services and products can put the firm on COD if accounts become excessively overdue, and COD terms will cause a hardship on day-to-day operations. Taking advantage of trade credit, nevertheless, should be a standard operating procedure to the extent that the firm's owners are comfortable with the practice. A good rule to follow is to pay up trade credit totals when the firm is cash rich. Paying off trade credit balances periodically will improve the relations with the firm's trade credit partners.

The firm may use a number of approaches to increase trade credit opportunities, leading to improved cash flow through managing the firm's accounts payable.

- Establish exclusive business agreements with the firm's key vendors and suppliers of services in exchange for longer payment terms. You scratch my back, I'll scratch yours. Sometimes exclusive trade arrangements will even result in discounts for the landscape architecture firm.
- Use a lag time from when an invoice is received until it is entered into the firm's payables sys-

TABLE 5-1   The Financing Value of Trade Credit

Product or Service	15–30 Days	60 Days	90 Days
Utility service	$200.00		
Phone service	200.00		
Long-distance phone service	100.00		
Health insurance	900.00		
General and liability insurance		$350.00	
Automobile insurance		100.00	
Errors and omissions insurance	400.00		
Office cleaning company	75.00	75.00	$75.00
Office products supplier	25.00	125.00	50.00
Drawing and drafting supplier	150.00	175.00	200.00
Photographic processing and film supplier	50.00	25.00	50.00
Blueprints and printing supplier	750.00	1,200.00	800.00
Stationery supplier			125.00
Copy service	60.00	80.00	75.00
Gasoline credit card	60.00	60.00	60.00
Computer technician	150.00	250.00	100.00
Office equipment supplier	60.00	75.00	
Architect	1,500.00	2,500.00	1,000.00
Engineer	3,000.00	2,000.00	2,500.00
Model builder			2,000.00
Total	7,680.00	7,015.00	7,035.00
Interest saved @ 1.5% per month	115.20	210.45	316.58
Total 90-day trade credit and interest saved			22,372.23

tem. This float period can add up to another month of time to the aging of each account payable.

- Let vendors know that you are willing to personally guarantee payment of accounts.
- Set up a special interest-bearing account for accounts payable. The interest earned on the account after ninety days, for example, will result in additional revenue available to make payments, a self-created discount.
- Agree to pay higher prices for supplies and services if the longer payment terms are granted.
- Let suppliers know when you've found more competitive prices. They might match the lower prices.
- Offer to trade services in payment of accounts, thereby preserving cash.
- Communicate with suppliers and vendors when the firm's payments will be late. Creditors appreciate the honesty and will often grant a longer grace period. Keeping trade credit partners in the dark tends to make them nervous about the firm's ability to pay. Letting them know the firm has a short-term cash-flow problem quiets the nerves.
- Refuse to pay interest to trade partners if they attempt to charge interest on overdue accounts.

Summary—Planning, Action, Adjustment

Financing a landscape architecture firm is a business fact of life. In today's world, it is unrealistic for the landscape architectural entrepreneur to expect clients to pay COD for professional services as they are performed. Timely collecting and up-front retainers may be used to put cash in the hands of the landscape architect sooner rather than later, but financing the operations of the firm through the lag time between invoicing and receiving payment for services is a necessity. Purchasing equipment, computers, furniture, and supplies is a necessity. Travel may be a necessity. Without a business plan to obtain the financing needed to start, maintain, and continue the operation of the landscape architecture firm, success is doubtful.

To effectively manage the financing of the landscape architecture firm, the owners and principals must embrace two activities:

1. Planning
2. Action and adjustment

Planning

If you don't know where you're headed, you won't know what kind of financing or how much money will be needed.

Writing a business plan forces the owners of the firm to focus on business strategy, financial goals, and the financing needed to implement the strategy and achieve the goals. Why start a business to begin with if financial goals are not one of the primary motivations?

The process of working through a business plan is as important as the actual document. Although elements of a written business plan vary, the following topics are usually considered in most plans:

- *Executive Summary.* This is the entire business plan in a nutshell. Keep it to three pages or less. Start with a draft of the executive summary, then go through the planning process and document the entire plan. After the process is completed, go back and finalize the executive summary.
- *Description of the Firm and the Services.* Start with a history of the firm and the main achievements of the principals. Describe the services offered by the firm and give examples of major projects.
- *Organizational and Management Structure.* Describe how the business is set up. Is it a sole proprietorship, a partnership, or a corporation? Who owns what percent? Who is accountable? How is responsibility shared and delegated? How is the firm managed? What is the design and business philosophy of the firm?
- *Competition and Market.* How many other firms provide landscape architecture services in the region? How large is the market? What is your market share? What is your work in progress status? What is your job-development outlook? (See chapter 8 for more information of what

might be included in this section of the business plan.)

- *Growth Projection.* Every lender wants to know how and in what way the firm intends to grow. Growth provides a comfort zone and an indication that the firm will be able to repay debt. What revenue projections are associated with the anticipated growth of the firm? How will the costs associated with growth increase the firm's operating costs? Does the firm need to purchase capital equipment related to growth projections? Do the costs of anticipated growth cover the costs of expansion?
- *Risks.* Discuss the risks and impediments to the firm's operations. What will happen to the firm's operations, revenue, and profits if growth does not occur? What external factors, nationally and regionally, may impact operations? What is the worst-case scenario, and what are the firm's contingency plans to deal with it?
- *Financial Information.* Include past, current, and projected revenue and past, current, and projected financial statements for two to three years. Include a projection of accounts receivable showing how an increase will be available to offset the finance costs. Identify the amount of equity in the firm and if any additional equity contributions or sources are planned.
- *Supporting Information.* In this section, which can be set up as an appendix, include information that supports the business plan, such as résumés and job descriptions of owners, principals, and key staff and copies of significant contracts. Also include the firm's strategic plan and marketing plan, or excerpts from them.

When the business plan is worked through and written, use it with lenders. It would be part, for example, of a loan request, or the information would be used to develop a loan proposal. Review the business plan at regular intervals. Rehash it. Rewrite it so that it is always current.

Action and Adjustment

One element of a successful landscape architecture practice is keeping current with market conditions and tracking the success of the firm measured against the market and the success of other firms. If the firm provides a good service, keep it going. If the firm consistently underperforms, and revenue does not meet projections and expectations, ask yourself why. If there is a reason and it can be resolved, develop and implement an action plan to solve underperformance. If the firm consistently underperforms expectations, on the other hand, have the courage to close it and find a new employer. Constantly evaluate the level of debt taken on by the firm in terms of the benefit achieved by incurring the debt or by contributing additional equity financing.

If the firm has a consistent track record of stability and sustainability, determine why so that successful actions may be continued. For the established firm with a history of business stability, there is nothing wrong whatsoever with a business goal of continuing the stability.

If analysis indicates that capital financing may solve underperformance or may achieve superior performance, develop an action plan to secure the necessary financing. Get out and find the money. Be willing to take the risk necessary, because the rewards can be exhilarating.

Action and adjustment related to business trends are the key to successful financial management and the financial success of the firm. Every landscape architecture firm can be financially successful, but its owners must do everything in their power to assure the financing of the firm. Remember the old adage, "You need money to make money." The financing is out there if you act and adjust.

REFERENCES

Bates, James, and Desmond L. Hally. 1982. *The Financing of Small Business.* London: Sweet & Maxwell.

Federal Trade Commission. 1992. *Facts for Consumers: Fair Credit Reporting.* Washington, D.C.: Office of Consumer/Business Education, Bureau of Consumer Protection.

Heath, Gibson. 1995. *Getting the Money You Need: Practical Solutions for Financing Your Small Business.* Homewood, Ill.: Irwin Professional Publishing.

Hermanson, Roger H., James Don Edwards, and L. Gayle Rayburn. 1989. *Financial Accounting.* Homewood, Ill.: Irwin Professional Publishing.

Levin, Dick. 1983. *Buy Low, Sell High, Collect Early and Pay Late: The Manager's Guide to Financial Survival.* Englewood Cliffs, N.J.: Prentice Hall.

Lister, Kate, and Tom Harnish. 1995. *Finding Money: The Small Business Guide to Financing.* New York: John Wiley & Sons.

Scott, David F., John D. Martin, J. William Petty, and Arthur J. Keown. 1988. *Basic Financial Management.* Englewood Cliffs, N.J.: Prentice Hall.

Silver, David A. 1988. *Up Front Financing: The Entrepreneur's Guide.* New York: John Wiley & Sons.

Tuller, Lawrence W. 1991. *When the Bank Says No! Creative Financing for Closely Held Businesses.* Blue Ridge Summit, Pa.: Liberty Hall Press.

STUDY QUESTIONS AND ASSIGNMENTS

1. Where do landscape architects find the money to start an office and keep it going? Answer this question using this book and other sources of information on finance.

2. Chapter 5 discusses three phases of financing:
   - Start-up financing
   - Maintenance financing
   - Continuation financing

   Write a paper discussing the options for financing in each of the phases.

3. Discuss the differences between debt and equity financing. When is debt financing a better choice than equity financing? When is equity financing a better choice than debt financing?

4. Discuss the equity financing options available to landscape architects. Include the following and any other options you may uncover in your library research.
   - Sweat equity
   - Personal savings
   - Family and friends
   - Partners: general or limited
   - Venture capital investors
   - The landscape architect's present employer

5. Discuss the debt-financing options available to landscape architects. Include the following and any other options you may uncover in your library research.
   - Short- and long-term commercial loan
   - Mortgage
   - Personal loan
   - Noncommercial loan
   - Line of credit
   - Lease
   - Government-backed loan

6. *Part A:* Discuss the types of short- and long-term loans used by landscape architects and the typical purposes they are used for. *Part B:* Identify all of the start-up costs for starting a landscape architecture firm and operating it for one year. How would you use loans to finance the start-up and operations costs?

7. What are the advantages of leasing over purchasing assets?

8. Assume that you are a practicing landscape architect. Using the information in this chapter and additional research, put together a loan proposal that would provide for a $25,000 operating line of credit and a three-year loan of $20,000 for a new computer system.

9. Write a paper that shows you understand the way trade credit is used as a financing mechanism in a landscape architecture office.

10. Writing a business plan forces the owners of a firm to focus on business strategy, financial goals, and the financing needed to implement the strategy and achieve the goals. Divide your class into three-to-five-person teams. Each team is to function as a design office and develop a business plan for its office.

CHAPTER SIX

Accounting

The Landscape Architect as Financial Manager

If you start a landscape architecture firm, or go to work for one, staying in business will be one of the firm's main goals. Staying in business requires paying attention to business, and paying attention to business depends on having a reasonable understanding of financial management and accounting.

Staying in business requires enough revenue to cover the cost of operating and maintaining at least a break-even financial condition in which expenses do not exceed income over a given period of time. Accounting, which is called the language of business, provides the basic information necessary to know if the business is breaking even or operating at a profit or at a loss. Accounting provides information needed for analyzing the firm's financial condition, studying trends, and making projections about the firm's future financial condition. Accounting also provides the information for analyzing the effects of alternative financial decisions, such as different ways to expand operations of the firm, on the future financial condition of the firm.

A goal of this book is to sensitize the professional landscape architect to the advantages of successful financial management and the need for at least a rudimentary knowledge of accounting. Many professionals have started private practices with a single financial goal: to make as much money as possible. This goal motivates many private practitioners. Making money, however, is only half of the financial equation for success. The other half is managing the money.

Many practitioners who start firms pay the rent, the utilities, the reproduction bills, and if any money is left after the bills are paid, they pay themselves a draw or salary. Some practitioners continue operating in this mode indefinitely. Their income grows if the number of commissions and revenues increase. When there is more work than the practitioner can handle, he or she may expand the firm and hire one or more employees. Employee salary expenses and additional costs for equipment, furniture, and supplies often mean that less money is available to cover the salary of the private practitioner. If work continues to come in, there may soon be enough revenue to match the salary of the practitioner prior to the expansion. Profits may increase. If commissions become sporadic, however, and the revenue stream is inconsistent, the private practitioner will face difficult decisions. Should hours be cut back for the new employees? Should they be laid off? Can the firm cover the costs of submitting a proposal for a project that will stabilize the revenue stream if the firm is successful in competing for the project? Without accounting procedures to provide an informed basis for making a decision, the answers to these and many other questions will be hit or miss, and hit-or-miss financial decisions will eventually impact the business health of the private practice. If a monthly profit-and-loss statement and a balance sheet, along with other helpful financial accounting reports, are available from the inception of the landscape architecture firm, the practitioner will have the data available for making informed decisions about either the growth or the downsizing of the firm. When the landscape architect has historical financial data available about the operating costs, revenue, and profitability of the firm, he or she can base decisions about how to manage the future on actual statistics and trends rather than hunches and whims.

Profitability is a financial goal of every firm. At the discretion of the firm's owners, profits are used to reward employees, to expand the firm, or to provide a cushion for future slow periods. A profitable firm remains solvent. Its owners have funds to invest in the future and to continue to do what they like to do best—practice landscape architecture. If a firm incurs losses and is unprofitable, it may become insolvent and face the possibility of going out of business.

The landscape architect needs two types of financial information to be an effective financial manager: *financial accounting* information and *financial management* information. Both are interrelated, and much financial management information is derived from the financial accounting information.

Financial accounting provides historical information that recapitulates the firm's monetary events that have already happened. Accounting provides orderly records of the firm's financial events, as well as records necessary for tax purposes. Financial accounting information serves as a barometer of the financial health and well-being of the firm.

As a financial manager, the landscape architect is interested in the past financial performance of the firm to serve as a guide for the future and as a means for monitoring the profitability of the firm. The *income statement* and the *balance sheet* are the two most important financial accounting reports used by the landscape architect. Together, the reports make up the firm's *financial statement*. As a firm grows and revenue increases, different types of financial accounting reports with more detail may become necessary. However, the financial statement will always be the core of the firm's financial accounting reports.

The aged accounts receivable report, the aged accounts payable report, and the cash report, or checkbook register, are three other indispensable financial accounting reports. These three reports are the tools needed for day-to-day cash management. The aged receivables report tells how much revenue has been billed and how long the billed amounts have been outstanding. The aged payables report tells how much the firm owes to its creditors and vendors and how long each debt has been outstanding. The cash report, usually showing the amount of funds available in the firm's checkbook, tells the manager how much cash is on hand to cover the cost of operations. The cash report may include other readily available sources of cash, such as funds set aside in a savings deposit. The cash report might also include the amount of funds the firm has available for borrowing immediately on its operating line of credit.

Financial management information results from using the financial accounting information as a source of data and carrying out financial analyses to evaluate the financial health of the firm or to provide answers to what-if questions. Some financial management information uses other direct sources of financial data to make projections of future financial conditions.

If the landscape architectural financial manager wants to know how two different courses of action for expanding the firm will affect the bottom-line profitability of the firm, he or she can use a future projection of the firm's income statement and balance sheet to illustrate in black and white the financial effect of each alternative. The projected financial statement, or *pro forma statement,* is a highly effective aid in financial decision making. Regularly calculating a number of key *financial ratios* is another type of financial management activity very helpful in managing the landscape architecture firm. Last, one of the most overlooked pieces of financial management information is the report of *work in progress* and a *workload projection.*

Financial Accounting Information

Income Statement

The bottom line of the income statement, sometimes called a profit-and-loss statement or an earnings report, indicates the profitability of the landscape architecture firm for a stated period of time, such as a month or a year. The income statement enumerates revenues and operating expenses. Revenues are the inflows of assets, such as cash, that result from the firm's rendering its services. Expenses are the costs incurred to produce revenues. The difference between revenues and operating expenses is the net profit or loss. If revenues exceed operating expenses, a profit occurs; if operating expenses exceed revenues, a loss occurs.

Income statements are made up of line items that represent categories of the firm's income, such as billed revenue or interest income, and expenses, such as salaries, insurance, rent, telephone, and entertainment. Categories are individualized for each firm, but virtually all income statements will have a number of similar entries. All firms have telephone and utility expenses, for example, and these line items typically appear on all financial statements. Finding the right level of detail is the key to developing the list of line items in the income statement. Some firms may want the detail of having a line item for each utility service, including telephone, gas service, electric service, water, sewer, on-line computer service, and others. Other firms find that lumping all utilities together as a single line item provides sufficient information. The objective is to develop on the income statement a list of line items that provides management with the most useful snapshot of the firm's financial business activities.

Income statements include the revenues and expenses for the current period, usually a month, and also for the year to date. Percentages are commonly shown for each line item and for totals in the income statement. The percentage for each monthly line item can be compared at a glance to the year-to-date percentage, highlighting whether the monthly income or expense line item is higher or lower than the year-to-date average. The percentages provide very useful historical information for financial management of the firm. Changes in percentages will highlight where the firm's financial managers need to monitor operations to determine why they are generating more or less income, or whether overspending or underspending is occurring. Figure 6-1 is an example of an income statement for the fictional landscape architecture firm Ace Landscape Architects.

What information can be gleaned by looking at the income statement of Ace Landscape Architects? First, looking at the income statement, one can see the amount of revenue generated in the month of December ($37,255.34) and for the entire year ($400,083.77). The monthly expense for each line item of expenses can be compared to the year-to-date expense to see if overspending or underspending occurred. Almost 2.5 times the average monthly expense, for example, was spent for office supplies, 1.73 percent in the month versus .65 percent in the year-to-date column. This high expense item was expected, however, by the firm's management. They had made a financial decision to increase expenses at the end of the year in order to offset profits made by the firm and reduce taxable income. Stocking up the firm's office supply cabinet was one of the ways the firm increased expenses in December.

Monitoring monthly expenses against year-to-date expenses by percentage of spending is a good way to use financial statements as a management tool. When a financial budget is created at the beginning of the fiscal year, the tool is even more effective. Some firms carry a third column in the income statement in order to itemize the annual budgeted amounts for revenue and for line item expenses. The actual monthly revenue and expense figures can then be compared to the budgeted monthly amount, and the percent columns for all three—budgeted, current, and year-to-date revenue and expenses—can be compared.

Another way to use the income statement is to target expense items for reduction if the item increases on a year-over-year basis both in terms of actual expenses and percentage of year-to-date expenses. Financial managers frequently target insurance expenses, for example, because they have a way of always increasing and becoming a larger and larger percentage of annual expenses. Looking at Ace's income statement, a total of $12,996.84, or 3.5 percent, of the firm's revenue was spent for worker's compensation, health, professional liability, general liability, and auto insurance. The firm's financial managers can attempt to reduce the actual dollar cost of insurance expenses as a goal and decide not to exceed 3.5 percent of the total annual expenses for insurance.

Income statement data for the previous five years of operation can be most helpful in analyzing the current income statement and for targeting expense items to reduce costs or to increase spending for discretionary expense items. Trend data can point out where current spending is high or low in relation to the way the firm has typically operated in the recent past. Including more than five years of average expense data is not necessary to get a pretty good picture of the firm's operating history and how it relates to current spending.

The net profit or loss is the bottom line of the income statement. Graphically tracking profit and loss for the month and for the year-end income statement is a good way to provide a visual picture of how well the firm is doing. With the graphing capability of spreadsheet software, visualizing monthly and year-

FIGURE 6-1. Ace Landscape Architects income statement for the twelve months ended December 31, 1996.

	CURRENT MONTH (DECEMBER)		YEAR TO DATE	
	($)	(%)	($)	(%)
Income				
Billed revenue	$37,255.34	99.79%	$396,813.20	99.18%
Miscellaneous income	79.00	0.21	3,270.57	0.82
Total income	37,334.34	100.00	400,083.77	100.00
Operating Expenses				
Outside consultants	6,240.00	20.32	79,490.92	21.37
Reimbursable expenses	852.75	2.78	13,845.36	3.72
Direct salaries—principals	6,735.20	21.93	91,226.03	24.53
Direct salaries—employees	1,461.53	4.76	23,493.18	6.32
Administrative salaries—principals	4,384.80	14.28	50,317.72	13.53
Administrative salaries—employees	2,250.11	7.33	19,712.07	5.30
FICA expense	966.10	3.15	12,348.78	3.32
Unemployment insurance	82.24	0.27	587.98	0.16
Worker's compensation insurance	45.15	0.15	556.54	0.15
Health insurance	259.70	0.85	2,782.80	0.75
Professional liability insurance	496.76	1.62	5,117.56	1.38
General liability and auto insurance	531.83	1.73	4,539.94	1.22
Professional registration and fees	310.00	1.01	2,210.35	0.59
Education and seminars	0.00	0.00	1,275.00	0.34
Dues and subscriptions	60.00	0.20	967.80	0.26
Rent	1,171.50	3.81	13,525.50	3.64
Utilities	197.98	0.64	2,117.48	0.57
Telephone	243.29	0.79	3,351.77	0.90
Postage and shipping	29.00	0.09	685.66	0.18
Office supplies	531.87	1.73	2,424.60	0.65
Auto leases	985.04	3.21	4,947.19	1.33
Auto expenses and maintenance	506.92	1.65	5,837.86	1.57
Mileage expense, travel, and lodging	236.57	0.77	5,456.59	1.47
Taxes, licenses, and fees	69.29	0.23	2,365.36	0.64
Meals and entertainment	808.58	2.63	1,825.35	0.49
Gifts and charitable contributions	550.00	1.79	1,105.24	0.30
Promotion and advertising	25.00	0.08	300.00	0.08
Storage expense	49.52	0.16	594.24	0.16
Depreciation expense	321.90	1.05	13,372.01	3.60
Amortization expense	88.92	0.29	1,067.04	0.29
Interest	220.44	0.72	4,470.46	1.20
Total operating expenses	30,711.99	100.00	371,918.38	100.00
Net Profit or (Loss)	6,622.35	21.56	28,165.39	7.57

over-year profitability has become an easy task for financial managers of landscape architecture firms.

Balance Sheet

The balance sheet is a report that represents a statement of the firm's financial condition at a specific point in time, at the end of a month or year, for example. It consists of two sections. The first section shows the assets, which are the financial resources of the firm. The second section shows the liabilities and the owner's equity. The liabilities are the financial obligations of the firm to outside creditors. The owners' equity is the financial value of the firm to its owners. The difference between the assets and liabilities is the owners' equity and represents the basic accounting equation:

$$\text{Assets} = \text{liabilities} + \text{owners' equity}$$

A firm's assets are anything it owns that has monetary value. A firm's cash, as well as cash equivalents such as refundable deposits, is an asset. Accounts receivable, furniture, equipment, computers, buildings, and investments are also assets. A balance sheet usually includes the following broad categories of assets:

current assets (cash, checkbook balance, prepaid rent, refundable deposits, and payroll advances)
accounts receivable (invoiced amounts)
fixed assets (furniture, equipment, capital leases, accumulated depreciation)
investments (long-term securities)
intangible assets (organizational costs, goodwill)

Liabilities are the claims of creditors on the firm's assets. Liabilities are the debts of the firm. Accounts payable, allowances for taxes, and notes payable are examples of liabilities. A balance sheet usually includes the following broad categories of liabilities and equity:

liabilities (current debts, including current portions of long-term debts; loans to owners or stockholders; salaries payable; and long-term liabilities such as notes and capital leases)
owners' or stockholders' equity (contributed capital, retained earnings, value of treasury stock, accumulated profit or loss)

As the basic accounting equation indicates, the assets of a firm minus its liabilities equal the owners' equity. Equity is the investment of the owner or owners plus any profits that accumulate over the years the firm is in business. Conversely, any losses that accumulate over the years the firm is in business reduce the equity in the same way that accumulated profits increase the equity.

The balance sheet provides information about the firm's solvency. The income statement and the balance sheet together are the two most important financial accounting statements. They are usually produced at the same time and generally referred to as the firm's financial statement. Figure 6-2 is an example of a balance sheet for Ace Landscape Architects.

What can be determined by looking at the balance sheet of Ace Landscape Architects? In the assets column, one can see the current total amount of accounts receivable ($87,443.54), which are the primary asset of a landscape architecture firm. One can also add the value of the fixed assets, which include furniture, fixtures, and equipment, plus capital leases, and get a total of $39,798.04. If the accumulated depreciation is divided by the total value of fixed assets, one can see that a considerable part of the fixed assets, or 78.6 percent, has been depreciated and that the value of the fixed assets to the firm is almost used up.

In the liabilities side of the balance sheet, the current amount of money owed on the firm's operating line of credit, $20,000, is seen at the top of the column. The operating line of credit is considered a current liability because it is collateralized by the firm's accounts receivable (which are considered current assets) and because the line of credit is due in less than one year. The total long-term debt owed is the second key figure seen in the liabilities column. The amount owed for each of the specific long-term notes is listed under the long-term debt column. The promissory notes are debts owed to former stockholders to purchase their stock after they left the firm.

The owners' equity is the bottom line of the balance sheet, just as net profit is the bottom line of the income statement. Owners' equity is referred to as the *book value* of the firm. For a corporation, such as Ace Landscape Architects, the owners' equity is the shareholders' equity and is used to determine the value of a share of the firm's stock by dividing the shareholders' equity by the number of shares of stock the firm has issued. If Ace's three stockholders, for example, each own 10,000 shares of stock for a total of 30,000 shares, the value of each share will be $1.30 ($39,120.97 ÷ 30,000).

The book value is the value of the firm as reported in the books kept by the firm's accountant and illustrated on the balance sheet as owners' or stockholders' equity. It implies the amount of money that would be available to the owners if the firm were liquidated. Liquidating the firm would involve collecting all of the accounts receivable, converting all of the firm's other assets to available cash, including selling its fixed assets for at least the value of the assets less depreciation, and using the total of cash assets to pay off all of the current and long-term liabilities. Another frequent use of the book value is determining the price of the firm during a merger or a sale of the firm.

Taken together, the liabilities and the owners' equity represent the way the firm is funded. The firm

FIGURE 6-2. Ace Landscape Architects balance sheet for the twelve months ended December 31, 1996.

Assets		
Current assets		
Petty cash	$82.02	
General checking account	2,592.96	
Payroll account	50.00	
Payroll advances	500.00	
Total cash		$3,224.98
Accounts receivable		
From clients	87,443.54	
Total receivables		87,443.54
Investments		
Money market account	2,500.00	
Total investments		2,500.00
Other current assets		
Refundable deposit	475.00	
Security deposit, equipment	600.00	
Total other current assets		1,075.00
Total current assets		94,243.52
Fixed assets		
Furniture, fixtures, and equipment	16,915.95	
Capital leases	22,882.09	
Accumulated depreciation	(31,293.14)	
Total fixed assets		8,504.90
Total assets		102,748.42
Liabilities and Owners' Equity		
Current Liabilities		
Operating line of credit	20,000.00	
Accounts payable	1,050.00	
Visa cards payable	1,481.81	
Total current liabilities		22,531.81
Long-term debt		
Notes payable	1,014.28	
Loan payable—National Bank	9,583.34	
Capital lease, auto	5,355.45	
Capital lease, auto	3,978.91	
Promissory note 1	1,091.36	
Promissory note 2	7,041.89	
Promissory note 3	7,030.41	
Shareholder's note	3,600.00	
Shareholder's note	2,400.00	
Total long-term debt		41,095.64
Total liabilities		63,627.45
Stockholders' equity		
Common stock	30,000.00	
Treasury stock	(27,000.00)	
Retained earnings	7,955.58	
1996 profit or loss	28,165.39	
Total owners' equity		39,120.97
Total liabilities and stockholders' equity		102,748.42

can fund its operations by using debt, or borrowed money, such as the operating line of credit and the long-term notes. The firm can also fund its operations by increasing its equity by selling stock, for example, to a prospective stockholder or by retaining greater amounts of its profits. If the firm becomes exceptionally profitable, it could retain all profits and fund operations by the value of its stock and by retained earnings. In this case, no liabilities would be listed on the balance sheet, and the firm's per-share stock value, using Ace's balance sheet as an example, would be $3.42 ($102,748.42 ÷ 30,000). If the firm were not profitable, however, and losses reduced the value of the firm's retained earnings, the firm would use borrowed funds to equalize the balance sheet equation.

Aged Accounts Payable

Accounts payable are amounts owed by the firm to others such as landlords, vendors, and subconsultants. When an invoice is received or when a regular monthly bill, such as rent, comes due, an account payable is established. An aging of the accounts payable refers to a listing of the invoices classified according to length of time each has been due and payable. The aging is normally classified by thirty, sixty, ninety, and over ninety days outstanding. Over thirty days outstanding is normally considered past due. The aged payables report is essential for managing and prioritizing the payment of bills. Figure 6-3 shows a sample of an aged accounts payables report for Ace Landscape Architects.

Managing the payment of accounts payable in relation to available cash is easy when the firm is profitable and when the firm receives payment for its services in a timely fashion. When clients are slow with their payments and profits are low, payment of accounts payable can become a stressful task, a management juggling act of prioritizing which bills to pay before others. The following suggestions are helpful when cash flow is tight:

- Make collection calls for all accounts and track the dates that clients say they will make payments and the amounts they will pay. Knowing when income will be available for payables is essential for managing when bills will be paid.
- Develop a priority list of payables so that essential bills such as rent, utilities, and installment-loan payments are paid first.

- Call vendors and subconsultants that are owed money and tell them that cash flow is slow. Give them an expected date for payment.
- Institute short-term cost-saving measures so that all available cash can be used for payables.
- Borrow from the firm's operating line of credit if one is available. If an operating line of credit is not available, consider negotiating for one with a lending institution. The loan can be negotiated for a long term so that it is available for future times of cash shortage; or it can be negotiated for a short term, such as thirty or ninety days, to handle the immediate cash shortage. The firm's accounts receivable are frequently used as collateral for an operating line of credit.

Aged Accounts Receivable

The dollar amounts of invoices sent to clients, representing the firm's billings for services rendered, are called *accounts receivable*. An aging of accounts receivable, like an aging of accounts payable, is a listing of invoices to be collected classified by thirty, sixty, ninety, and over ninety days outstanding. Over thirty days outstanding is considered past due. Over ninety days past due may be considered uncollectable by lending institutions. If the firm's receivables are used as the collateral for a loan, such as an operating line of credit, banks will usually not lend money on the accounts that are over ninety days outstanding. Figure 6-4 shows a sample of an aged accounts receivable report for Ace Landscape Architects.

Prompt collection of receivables is an obvious key to the financial health of the landscape architecture firm. The receivables turnover ratio and the average age of receivables are commonly used as indicators of the firm's collection efficiency.

The receivables turnover ratio indicates how many times during the year the landscape architecture firm's receivables are generated and actually collected. To calculate the receivables turnover ratio, divide the total billed revenue by the average accounts receivable balance:

Receivables turnover ratio

$$= \frac{\text{Total billed revenue}}{\text{Average receivables balance}}$$

FIGURE 6-3. Ace Landscape Architects aged payables report, July 1, 1996.

Name	Due Date	Total Due	Current Under 30 Days	31–60 Days	61–90 Days	Over 90 Days
Auto Leasing Specialists	7/1/96	$497.35	$497.35			
Alan Smith (reimbursable exp.)	6/30/96	$58.29	$58.29			
American Leasing	7/1/96	$501.53	$501.53			
CADD/Print, Inc.	4/10/96				$195.25	
	5/10/96			$250.50		
	6/10/96		$125.25			
Total		$571.00				
Collaborative Design Group	3/12/96					$200.00
	4/10/96				$1,000.00	
	5/10/96			$500.00		
		$1,700.00				
Copier Brothers	6/17/96	$55.00	$55.00			
Deluxe Business Forms	4/20/96	$90.00			$90.00	
City Electric	7/1/95	$258.34	$258.34			
Federal Express	4/15/96				$35.00	
	5/15/96			$15.00		
	6/15/96		$20.00			
Total		$70.00				
Land Design Civil Engineers, Inc.	1/12/96					$200.00
	2/10/96					300.00
	3/10/96					300.00
Total		$800.00				
LDC (long distance phone)	7/1/96	$76.44	$76.44			
Mary Jones (reimbursable exp.)	6/30/96	$29.95	$29.95			
National Bank Chargecard	7/1/96	$250.00	$250.00			
Paychex, Inc.	6/10/96	$55.00	$55.00			
State Compensation Fund	6/1/96	$127.93		$127.93		
Structural Concept Engineers, Inc.	2/15/96	$400.00				$400.00
Rent	7/1/96	$1,150.00	$1,150.00			
Reproductions, Inc.	3/12/96					$350.00
	4/10/96				$783.95	
	5/10/96			$985.27		
	6/10/96		$879.21			
Total		$2,998.43				
U.S. West (phone)	7/1/96	$187.45	$187.45			
Grand Total		$9,876.71	$4,143.81	$1878.70	$2,104.20	$1,750.00
Aging Percent			41.96%	19.02%	21.30%	17.72%

FIGURE 6-4. Ace Landscape Architects aged receivables report, July 1, 1996.

Name	Invoice Number	Due Date	Total Due	Under 30 Days	31–60 Days	61–90 Days	Over 90 Days
American Land Development, Inc.	960701	7/1/96	$2,500.00	$2,500.00			
Anderson Residence	960601	6/1/96			$1,500.00		
	960702	7/1/96		$500.00			
Total			$2,000.00				
BMOC Developers, Inc.	960104	1/1/96					$200.00
	960204	2/1/96					500.00
	960305	3/1/96					300.00
Total			$1,000.00				
Kennedy Park— Phase 4	960305	3/1/95					$927.34
	960404	4/1/95					548.95
	960504	5/1/96				$329.99	
	960605	6/1/96			$327.81		
	960703	7/1/96		$2,275.87			
Total			$3,482.62				
Devine Developers & Builders Co.	960404	4/1/96					$150.00
	960504	5/1/96				$550.00	
	960605	6/1/96			$600.00		
	960704	7/1/96		$3,500.00			
Total			$4,800.00				
Exxon, Inc.	960504	5/1/96				$7,500.00	
	960605	6/1/96			$7,000.00		
	960705	7/1/96		$300.00			
Total			$14,800.00				
Home Depot, Inc. (Rte. 66)	960504	5/1/96				$1,009.29	
	960605	6/1/96			$2,653.67		
Total			$3,662.96				
Home Depot, Inc. (Bilby Road)	960706	7/1/96	$2,405.59	$2,405.59			
Land Design Civil Engineers, Inc.	960109	1/1/96					$250.00
	960208	2/1/96					575.00
	960310	3/1/96					225.00
	960707	7/1/96		$2,500.00			
Total			$3,550.00				
Meyers residence	960708	7/1/96	$1,500.00	$1,500.00			
City Unified School District	960510	5/1/96				$250.00	
	960610	6/1/96			$4,509.08		
	960708	7/1/96		$3,997.31			
Total			$8,756.39				
University Historic Study	960511	5/1/96				$3,000.00	
	960611	6/1/96			$4,500.00		
	960709	7/1/96		$1,500.00			
Total			$9,000.00				
VORTEX, Inc.	960710	7/1/96	$2,500.00	$2,500.00			
Grand Total			$59,957.56	$23,478.77	$21,090.56	$12,639.28	$3,676.29
Aging Percent				39.16%	35.18%	21.08%	6.13%

The average accounts receivable balance is determined by adding the accounts receivable at the beginning of the year to the accounts receivable at the end of the year and dividing by two. Using Ace Landscape Architects' year-end balance sheet (figure 6-2) as an example, the average accounts receivable is $87,443.54 (year-end balance shown on the balance sheet) plus $79,330.97 (beginning year receivables balance not shown on the balance sheet) divided by two, or $83,387.26. The turnover ratio, therefore, is the 1996 total billed revenue of $396,813.20 divided by $83,387.26, which equals 4.76.

By itself, this number is not very meaningful. It could be compared to the turnover ratio of other firms or to the turnover ratio of Ace Landscape Architects for prior years. The turnover ratio is more useful to the landscape architecture financial manager if converted to the average number of days that receivables are outstanding, or the average age of receivables. To obtain the average age of the firm's receivables, divide the number of days in a year by the receivables turnover ratio:

$$\text{Average age of receivables} = \frac{365}{\text{Receivables turnover ratio}}$$

For Ace Landscape Architects, the average age of receivables is 76.7 days. This means that it takes the firm approximately two and one-half months to collect its money after invoices are sent out. Obviously, lowering the average age of receivables should be a financial management goal of the landscape architecture firm.

The average age of receivables can be calculated from monthly income statements by using the end-of-month receivables for the specific month from the preceding year and the current end of month receivable. If the average age of receivables is calculated and graphed each month, trends in collection time will be available for the firm's financial managers. When the average age of receivables increases, the firm can reinforce collection efforts. When the average age of receivables decreases, money may be readily available for discretionary use by the firm's managers.

Cash Report

The statement of cash or cash on hand is an easy financial accounting report to prepare—it is usually the current balance showing in the firm's checkbook register. Most firms now keep the checkbook register by using a spreadsheet computer program. The firm's checkbook balance may also be automatically updated if the firm is using an integrated accounting software package.

When the firm has been profitable and excess cash is deposited in accounts other than the checkbook, such as savings accounts or short-term CDs, a separate summary report listing the checkbook balance and the other readily available sources of cash will be useful to the firm's financial managers.

Financial Management Information

Pro Forma Financial Statements

A pro forma income statement, balance sheet, and cash flow statement are accounting terms for a projection of future income, financial condition, and cash flow based upon the present financial position. Pro forma statements are useful for visualizing the future financial condition of the landscape architecture firm under different scenarios and answering what-if financial questions. The following hypothetical situation illustrates a pro forma financial statement for Ace Landscape Architects.

At the end of 1996, Ace learned they were awarded the largest contract in the history of the firm, $200,000 in fees for a public park project. The parks department required that design and construction documents be completed within twelve months by December 31, 1997. The owners of the firm expected the workload in addition to the park project to remain at the same level as in 1996. They were optimistic that the firm could achieve a record $600,000 in income. They wanted to see the effect of their expectations on their future profits and the firm's income statement and balance sheet. They wanted to study the difference in their financial position using two alternative ways of managing the expansion of the firm that would be necessary to accommodate the expected steady stream of work and the big park design commission. The owners decided to make a projection of their financial condition in the form of pro forma financial statements that would help them make the best financial decision for managing the growth. The two expansion alternatives they studied are as follows:

EXPANSION ALTERNATIVE 1

Hire two additional junior-level designer/drafters at a salary cost of $54,000 per year.

EXPANSION ALTERNATIVE 2

Hire one experienced CAD technician at a salary of $28,000 per year, one part-time entry-level drafter at a salary of $11,000 per year, and purchase a new CAD station at a cost of $15,000.

On the surface, each expansion alternative appears to cost the firm a total of $54,000. After

FIGURE 6-5.   Ace Landscape Architects pro forma income statement.

	1996 Year End		1997 Pro Forma Alternative 1		1997 Pro Forma Alternative 2	
	Actual	Percent	Actual	Percent	Actual	Percent
Income						
Billed revenue	$396,813.20	99.18%	$596,000.00	99.33%	$596,000.00	99.33%
Miscellaneous income	3,270.57	0.82	4,000.00	0.67	4,000.00	0.67
Total income	400,083.77	100.00	600,000.00	100.00	600,000.00	100.00
Operating Expenses						
Outside consultants	79,490.92	21.37	125,000.00	24.81	125,000.00	25.40
Reimbursable expenses	13,845.36	3.72	22,500.00	4.47	21,000.00	4.27
Direct salaries—principals	91,226.03	24.53	98,000.00	19.45	98,000.00	19.91
Direct salaries—employees	23,493.18	6.32	74,500.00	14.79	61,500.00	12.50
Administrative salaries—principals	50,317.72	13.53	52,000.00	10.32	52,000.00	10.57
Administrative salaries—employees	19,712.07	5.30	23,000.00	4.56	22,000.00	4.47
FICA expense	12,348.78	3.32	16,583.00	3.29	15,611.00	3.17
Unemployment insurance	587.98	0.16	674.00	0.13	650.00	0.13
Worker's compensation insurance	556.54	0.15	750.00	0.15	650.00	0.13
Health insurance	2,782.80	0.75	4,765.00	0.95	3,773.00	0.77
Liability insurance	5,117.56	1.38	7,500.00	1.49	7,500.00	1.52
General liability and auto insurance	4,539.94	1.22	4,700.00	0.93	4,700.00	0.95
Professional registration and fees	2,210.35	0.59	2,400.00	0.48	2,400.00	0.49
Education and seminars	1,275.00	0.34	1,500.00	0.30	1,500.00	0.30
Dues and subscriptions	967.80	0.26	1,000.00	0.20	1,000.00	0.20
Rent	13,525.50	3.64	14,200.00	2.82	14,200.00	2.89
Utilities	2,117.48	0.57	2,550.00	0.51	2,550.00	0.52
Telephone	3,351.77	0.90	5,100.00	1.01	4,800.00	0.98
Postage and shipping	685.66	0.18	950.00	0.19	950.00	0.19
Office supplies	2,424.60	0.65	3,500.00	0.69	3,500.00	0.71
Auto leases	4,947.19	1.33	4,947.00	0.98	4,947.00	1.01
Auto expenses and maintenance	5,837.86	1.57	7,000.00	1.39	7,000.00	1.42
Taxes, licenses, and fees	2,365.36	0.64	2,100.00	0.42	2,100.00	0.43
Mileage expense, travel and lodging	5,456.59	1.47	6,500.00	1.29	6,500.00	1.32
Meals and entertainment	1,825.35	0.49	2,700.00	0.54	2,700.00	0.55
Gifts and charitable contributions	1,105.24	0.30	1,750.00	0.35	1,750.00	0.36
Storage expense	594.24	0.16	594.00	0.12	594.00	0.12
Depreciation expense	13,372.01	3.60	11,000.00	2.18	16,000.00	3.25
Amortization expense	1,067.04	0.29	1,100.00	0.22	1,100.00	0.22
Interest	4,470.46	1.20	4,400.00	0.87	5,600.00	1.14
Promotion and advertising	300.00	0.08	600.00	0.12	600.00	0.12
Total operating expenses	371,918.38	100.00	503,863.00	100.00	492,175.00	100.00
Net Profit or (Loss)	28,165.39	7.57	96,137.00	19.08	107,825.00	21.91

reviewing the results of the 1997 pro forma financial statements, including the pro forma income statement shown in figure 6-5 and the pro forma balance sheet shown in figure 6-6, the owners of the firm selected alternative 2. This alternative resulted in an almost 3 percent higher projected net profit, $12,188 greater owner's equity, and $27,188 more in assets than alternative 1.

In order to develop the pro forma comparison of the two financial alternatives, the owners must try to predict the firm's future operating expenses. Where possible, keeping expense items at the same spending level is recommended for each alternative unless there is a good justification for differences. In the pro forma statements, the salary line item is obviously going to be different because alternative 1 has $54,000 in additional salary expenses whereas alternative 2 has $39,000 in additional salary expenses. The different salaries also affect the costs of salary-related insurance expenses such as FICA and unemployment insurance.

Line items such as rent will stay the same in both projections because no expansion of the office floor space is anticipated. Note, however, that the telephone line item is slightly different because more telephone usage is expected with two designer/drafters on the staff than with the CAD technician and a part-time drafter. Items such as postage and shipping are projected to increase over the 1996 expense level, but there is no reason to show these line items at a different spending level. Interest and depreciation expenses, however, are dramatically different in alternative 2 due to the purchase of the new computer.

Work in Progress and Workload Projection

Knowing how much work in progress the firm has under contract and the revenue that may be expected from the work is very useful for the financial managers of a landscape architecture firm. Work in progress is

FIGURE 6-6. Ace Landscape Architects pro forma balance sheet for alternatives 1 and 2.

	1996	Alternative 1 1997	Alternative 2 1997
Assets			
Current assets			
Petty cash	$82.02	$100.00	$100.00
General checking account	2,592.96	7,818.00	7,818.00
Payroll account	50.00	50.00	50.00
Payroll advances	500.00	0.00	0.00
Total cash	3,224.98	7,968.00	7,968.00
Accounts receivable			
From clients	87,443.54	188,121.95	205,309.95
Total receivables	87,443.54	188,121.95	205,309.95
Investments			
Money market account	2,500.00	12,500.00	12,500.00
Total investments	2,500.00	12,500.00	12,500.00
Other current assets			
Refundable deposit	475.00	275.00	275.00
Security deposit, equipment	600.00	600.00	600.00
Total other current assets	1,075.00	875.00	875.00
Total current assets	94,243.52	209,464.95	226,652.95
Fixed Assets			
Furniture, fixtures, and equipment	16,915.95	16,915.95	31,915.95
Capital leases	22,882.09	22,882.09	22,882.09
Accumulated depreciation	(31,293.14)	(33,000.00)	(38,000.00)
Total fixed assets	8,504.90	6,798.04	16,798.04
Total assets	102,748.42	216,262.99	243,450.99

FIGURE 6-6. (*Cont'd.*)   Ace Landscape Architects pro forma balance sheet for alternatives 1 and 2.

	1996	Alternative 1 1997	Alternative 2 1997
Liabilities & Owners' Equity			
Current liabilities			
Line of credit	20,000.00	10,000.00	10,000.00
Accounts payable	1,050.00	32,000.00	32,000.00
Visa cards payable	1,481.81	2,000.00	2,000.00
Total current liabilities	22,531.81	44,000.00	44,000.00
Long-term debt			
Notes payable	1,014.28	507.00	507.00
Loan payable—National Bank	9,583.34	6,000.00	6,000.00
Capital lease, auto	5,355.45	5,355.45	5,355.45
Capital lease, auto	3,978.91	3,978.91	3,978.91
Promissory note 1	1,091.36	1,091.36	1,091.36
Promissory note 2	7,041.89	7,041.89	7,041.89
Promissory note 3	7,030.41	7,030.41	7,030.41
Shareholder's note	3,600.00	3,600.00	3,600.00
Shareholder's note	2,400.00	2,400.00	2,400.00
New computer		0.00	15,000.00
Total long-term debt	41,095.64	37,005.02	52,005.02
Total liabilities	63,627.45	81,005.02	96,005.02
Owners' equity			
Common stock	30,000.00	30,000.00	30,000.00
Treasury stock	(27,000.00)	(27,000.00)	(27,000.00)
Retained earnings	7,955.58	36,120.97	36,120.97
1996 profit or loss	28,165.39	96,137.00	108,325.00
Total owners' equity:	39,120.97	135,257.97	147,445.97
Total liabilities and capital	$102,748.42	$216,262.99	$243,450.99

the total amount of contracted fees less the amount of work already completed on the contracts and invoiced. If the revenue from work in progress is projected over the future, such as six months in advance, the firm's financial managers will have a good idea of the likely revenue stream and when the income will be factored into the firm's financial picture. If the high job-development opportunities are added to the work in progress, an expected workload projection will be available not only for managing the firm's financial activities but also for making other decisions such as whether or not employees will need to be added or laid off, or whether overtime is needed or hours should be cut back. A workload projection is easy to develop using spreadsheet software. It is an invaluable tool for managing the financial stability of a landscape architecture firm. See figure 6-7 for an example of a workload projection for Ace Landscape Architects.

Financial Ratios

A ratio is a comparison of one number to another. The ratio is obtained by dividing one of the numbers by the other. Ratios are widely used to analyze financial statements (income statement and balance sheet) and to understand the financial health of the landscape architecture firm—its financial strengths and weaknesses. Ratios determined using information from a financial accounting report can be compared to a benchmark ratio to indicate the landscape architecture firm's financial condition in relation to its condition at the time of the benchmark. The firm will be doing the same, better, or worse than the benchmark. If a landscape architecture firm has revenue of $100,000 in its first year of operation, and it cost $80,000 to produce the revenue, the firm would have $20,000 profit and a 20 percent profit ratio ($20,000

FIGURE 6-7.   Ace Landscape Architects workload projection.

			BILLING PERIOD						
Work in Progress									
Project No.	Project Name	Rem. Fee	7 7/1–8/1	8 8/1–9/1	9 9/1–10/1	10 10/1–11/1	11 11/1–12/1	12 12/1–1/1	Future
94115-10	PV water audit	14.7							14.7
94122-19	Vista de Sierras constr. admin.	0.5	0.1	0.1	0.1	0.1	0.1		0.0
95101-11	Kennedy Park—phase 4	8.0	2.00	2.00	1.00	0.50	0.50	0.50	1.5
95135-13	University Historical Study	6.0	0.50	4.50	1.00				0.0
95152-19	Campus Apartments constr. admin.	2.5	1.00	0.50	0.50	0.50			0.0
95199-19	Devine PRC	8.0	1.5	0.5					6.0
95201-14	Exxon, Inc.	10.0	3.0	1.0					6.0
96102-12	Big Fork wetlands study	40.0	0.5	7.5	9.0	7.5	5.0	4	6.5
96107-19	Anderson residence	1.0		0.2	0.3	0.3	0.2		0.0
96110-17	Home Depot, Inc. (Rte. 66) constr. admin.	6.3	1.0	0.5	0.5	0.5	0.5	0.5	2.8
96128-19	Meyers residence	2.0	1.0				0.2	0.2	0.6
96141-14	Canyon Elementary School	6.0	2.0					1.0	3.0
96150-18	La Posada Hotel (VORTEX, Inc.)	12.5	5.0	5.0	2.5				0.0
96151-17	Home Depot, Inc. (Bilby Road)	6.6	2.6	0.5	2.0	0.5			1.0
96168-11	Big Sky Park	20.0		1.0	3.0		4.0	4.0	8.0
96175-19	Cooper residence	5.0				2.5	1.5		1.0
		Rem. Fee	7 7/1–8/1	8 8/1–9/1	9 9/1–10/1	10 10/1–11/1	11 11/1–12/1	12 12/1–1/1	Future
	Subtotal WIP	149.10	20.20	23.30	19.90	12.40	12.00	10.20	51.10
	Capacity corp.		27.00	27.00	27.00	27.00	27.00	27.00	
	Cost	20.00	20.00	20.00	20.00	20.00	20.00	20.00	
	Surplus or shortfall (–) over cost		0.20	3.30	–0.10	–7.60	–8.00	–9.80	
Very High Job Development									
Project No.	Project Name	Rem. Fee	7 7/1–8/1	8 8/1–9/1	9 9/1–10/1	10 10/1–11/1	11 11/1–12/1	12 12/1–1/1	Future
95180-00	North Boulevard medians	12.4		0.4	3.0	4.0	4.0		1.0
96182-00	Wayside Apartments	29.0			5.0	8.0	8.0	1.0	7.0
96197-00	Central High School rehab	18.0				1	4	4	9.0
	Subtotal	59.40	0.00	0.40	8.00	13.00	16.00	5.00	17.00
		Rem. Fee	7 7/1–8/1	8 8/1–9/1	9 9/1–10/1	10 10/1–11/1	11 11/1–12/1	12 12/1–1/1	Future
	Total WIP and JD	208.50	20.20	23.70	27.90	25.40	28.00	15.20	68.10
	Capacity corp.		27.00	27.00	27.00	27.00	27.00	27.00	
	Cost		20.00	20.00	20.00	20.00	20.00	20.00	
	Surplus or shortfall(–) over cost		0.20	3.70	7.90	5.40	8.00	–4.80	

÷ $100,000). If the second year of operation resulted in $200,000 in revenue with costs of $180,000, the firm would again realize a profit of $20,000, but the profit ratio would be 10 percent ($20,000 ÷ $200,000). By comparison, the firm's profit ratio in the second year is one-half that of the first year. With this knowledge, the firm's financial managers could take corrective actions, such as reducing the cost of operation or increasing fees, in order to achieve a consistent profit ratio of 20 percent.

Three types of ratios are important to the landscape architecture firm: trend ratios, liquidity ratios, and equity ratios.

Trend Ratios

Trend ratios result from comparing a current number to a base year index number or to an average ratio of similar firms to evaluate how the firm is doing in relation to the index number or to other firms. If a firm increases its profits by 10 percent per year for five years, its profits would be 50 percent above the base year index number. If information available for other similar landscape architecture firms indicates that 5 percent profit is the normal trend, the firm will know that its profits are 50 percent higher than the industry trend.

Virtually every accounting number or any ratio that can be calculated can be compared to an index number. Landscape architecture firms commonly compare trend ratios for the following accounting numbers:

- Total annual revenue
- Average monthly revenue
- Percentage of net profit to revenue
- Cost of reimbursable expenses in relation to total costs
- Average age of receivables
- Percentage of receivables over and under ninety days
- Cost of subconsultants as a percent of total revenue
- Overhead multiplier ratio
- Income tax as a percent of total revenue
- Billable versus nonbillable time
- Costs of various expense categories such as utilities and telephone
- Depreciation as a percent of fixed assets
- Per-share value of common stock
- Liquidity ratios
- Solvency ratios

Liquidity Ratios

These ratios indicate a firm's ability to pay its short-term debts with its available capital, referred to as *working capital* in accounting language. Liquidity ratios are used on a regular basis to show interested parties, such as a bank the firm is trying to secure credit from or the firm's financial managers, the firm's solvency and capacity to meet maturing current liabilities. These ratios are the most basic indicator of a firm's financial health.

The *current ratio* is the most widely used liquidity ratio. It is computed by dividing the total current assets by the total current liabilities:

$$\text{Current ratio} = \frac{\text{Current assets}}{\text{Current liabilities}}$$

If a firm has $100,000 in current assets, such as cash on hand and accounts receivable, and $50,000 in current liabilities (bills), then it has a current ratio of 2:1 and twice as much money as it needs to pay its current bills. If the ratio were reversed, the firm would obviously be in a precarious financial position with respect to current financial conditions. It would have only one-half the funds necessary to pay its current bills. The firm may be insolvent. Any ratio less than 1:1 is cause for financial management concern.

As another example, the current ratio for Ace Landscape Architects using the 1996 balance sheet data is 4.18 ($94,243.52 ÷ $22,531.81).

The *receivables turnover ratio* and the *average age of receivables* discussed earlier are two other ratios used to evaluate the firm's liquidity. These ratios measure the usefulness of a landscape architecture firm's main asset—its accounts receivable. The correlation here is that even though a firm might have a good current ratio of 2:1, if the firm's turnover ratio is a low 2.0, six months will be needed to collect the income and its current usefulness is low.

Equity or Long-Term Solvency Ratios

These ratios show the relationship between the firm's debt and the firm's equity financing. The *equity ratio* shows how much of a firm's total assets are provided by its owners, or stockholders in the case of a corporation:

$$\text{Equity ratio} = \frac{\text{Stockholders' equity}}{\text{Total assets}}$$

In the case of Ace Landscape Architects, the equity ratio is .38 ($39,120.97 ÷ $102,748.42). In other words, about 40 percent of the firm's equity is funded by the owners through stock and retained earnings.

The equity ratio has an inverse relationship for owners versus creditors. From the creditor's side of the fence, the higher the proportion of stockholders' equity, the better. A high equity ratio indicates that the firm has a financial cushion to pay back creditors in the event of a business downturn. Some banks may insist that the landscape architecture firm maintain a minimum equity ratio in order for the bank to lend the firm funds. From the stockholders' viewpoint, debt financing may be preferable to equity financing because the interest cost of the debt financing will reduce net income and the corresponding income tax liability. Debt financing has its negative side effects, too. In a period of slow business activity, such as a recession, the firm's revenue may shrink along with its accounts receivable, impacting the firm's ability to service its debt load.

The equity-to-debt ratio is another long-term solvency ratio often reviewed by financial institutions such as banks. The equity-to-debt ratio is computed as follows:

$$\text{Equity-to-debt ratio} = \frac{\text{Stockholders' equity}}{\text{Total debt}}$$

For example, if the owner's equity in a firm were $300,000, and the firm owed a bank $100,000, the debt-to-equity ratio would be 3:1. This means that there is enough equity in the firm, three times the amount needed, to easily pay off the long-term debt should the owners decide to liquidate the firm.

In the case of Ace Landscape Architects, the debt-to-equity ratio is .95:1. The stockholders' equity is $39,120.97, and the long-term debt is $41,095.64. Only the long-term debt is used in this example because the line of credit is considered current short-term debit that is collateralized by the current accounts receivable.

One other equity ratio, the *times interest earned ratio,* may be used by both a landscape architecture firm's financial managers and lending institutions. This ratio indicates to creditors and the firm's financial managers whether the firm can meet required interest payments when they are due. The times interest earned ratio is expressed as follows:

Times interest earned ratio

$$= \frac{\text{Income before interest and taxes}}{\text{Interest expense}}$$

Ace Landscape Architects' times interest earned ratio for its 1996 income statement is 6.3 ($28,165.39 ÷ $4,470.46).

Financial ratios are one of the primary tools that financial managers of landscape architecture firms and lending institutions such as banks use to evaluate a firm's ability to take on long-term debt and service the debt load of principal and interest. Ratios are particularly helpful as guidelines when compared to profession-wide standards for similar firms. If the profession-wide receivables turnover ratio is known to be 3.9, which means that the average length of time required for collection of receivables is ninety-five days, the financial manager of a landscape architecture firm can evaluate the firm's performance in terms of the national average and make financial management adjustments as necessary.

Financial Accounting Systems

There are two generally accepted systems for keeping financial accounting records—the *cash-basis* system and the *accrual* system. From a business perspective, the first decision to make about a landscape architecture practice is what type of entity it will be—a corporation, a partnership, or a sole proprietorship. The second business decision is what type of accounting system the firm will use—cash-basis accounting or accrual-basis accounting. In almost all cases, a landscape architecture firm will select the accrual system.

Cash-Basis Accounting System

Cash-basis accounting deals only with transactions involving money. Accounting records are made only when money is actually received or paid out. Revenue and expenses are recorded only at the time when cash actually changes hands.

There are two main advantages for using the cash-basis system of accounting. First, it is easy to understand and to maintain cash-basis accounting records. Any documents that provide evidence of cash changing hands, such as receipts, canceled checks, and bank deposit slips, are the records of the cash-basis accounting system. Second, in contrast to the accrual system, the firm does not pay taxes on the income it earns until the actual cash is collected. Thus, no taxable income arises from either unbilled professional services, such as income earned but not invoiced, or from accounts receivable, which include income earned and invoiced but for which the cash has not yet been collected.

There are three disadvantages of using the cash-basis accounting system. First, the firm does not deduct its business expenses until they are actually paid. Second, the firm's accounting records do not match its revenue earned during the accounting period, one month, for example, with the expenses incurred during the same period. Matching revenue with expenses is essential for an accurate picture of the financial condition of the firm. Third, the forms, procedures, and reports used in the cash system become difficult to manage as the size of the firm and the number of employees increase.

Accrual-Basis Accounting System

Accrual-basis accounting recognizes income earned and expenses incurred without regard to when the actual cash is received or paid out. The revenue is recognized as the amount of money represented by the percentage of work in progress that has been completed at the end of the accounting period, such as one month, and invoiced for that period. The accrued revenue represents the amount of income a firm is entitled to during the accounting period, and is determined by the number of hours worked on the project or the percentage of the work completed during the accounting period.

Expenses, on the other hand, are recognized (accrued) when they are incurred during the accounting period. These expenses, for supplies or subconsultant's services, for example, represent debt obligations that the firm takes on without regard to when the actual cash is paid out for the debts incurred. In the accrual system, expenses and income are, in a sense, "paper money." The income and expenses, and subsequent profit or loss, occur only on paper as the product of the flow of work and the accrual accounting system.

The major advantage of accrual-basis accounting is that the revenue earned and the expenses required to earn the revenue are matched up at a point in time. The difference between the revenue and the expenses is the profit or loss. By providing a running picture of income versus the expenses required to produce the income, the accrual method allows the firm's owners or managers to have timely awareness of the firm's profitability during each accounting period.

The main disadvantage of accrual accounting is that it is more complex than cash-basis accounting. It is fairly safe to say, however, that landscape architecture firms that grow in size, revenue, and complexity will, out of necessity, use the accrual method of accounting. Computer software has taken a great deal of the mystery and difficulty out of accrual-basis accounting. Accrual-basis accounting also requires greater emphasis on the financial management of the firm because taxes may be paid on income for which the cash may not have been received. Indeed, cash flow management is an essential component of managing a more financially complex firm using accrual accounting. The firm must keep enough cash on hand on a regular basis to cover payroll, operating expenses, meet withholding tax obligations, and pay federal and state income taxes.

Landscape architecture firms using the accrual method of accounting must convert to a cash basis at the end of the firm's fiscal year in order to determine the firm's income-tax obligations. Managing the firm's cash position after converting from accrual accounting records is one of the most important functions of the firm's financial managers in order to mitigate the firm's income tax obligations to the greatest extent.

The firm's financial managers may want to begin making tax conversion calculations as early as six months prior to the end of the firm's tax year (December 31 for most firms). By calculating the cash position starting in July and making projections of the probable income, the firm's managers will have as much time as possible to take corrective action if it appears the firm will have extraordinarily high profits and corresponding income-tax obligations.

Converting to cash from accrual accounting records is easy. The year-to-date accounts receivable (AR) total is subtracted from the previous year-end accounts receivable total. A negative amount decreases cash profits; a positive amount increases cash profits. The year-to-date accounts payable (AP) total is subtracted from the previous year-end total. A positive number reduces cash profits; a negative number increases cash profits. The current year-to-date accrued profit or loss is then added to the net accounts receivable and payable to determine the net cash profit. If the calculations indicate a loss, there is no income tax liability. If there is a net cash profit, however, the firm will owe income taxes unless there are losses from previous years that can be used to offset the profits.

Figure 6-8 illustrates the process of converting from accrual to cash profits. The cash conversion, made after nine months of operation in the tax year, indicates a net cash profit of $15,000 would be realized if everything stayed the same through the end of the year. The profit would result in an income-tax obligation of $5,100 at a 34 percent tax rate. The firm's managers were concerned because they predicted that accrued profits would double to $20,000 by the end of the year. They were confident, nonetheless, that the financial operation of the firm could be managed to eliminate the income-tax burden. They predicted accounts receivable would increase to $60,000. Based on the profitable outlook, they were able to negotiate a short-term loan, borrowing against future revenue, to obtain $5,000 needed to pay down their accounts payable. The result illustrated in the second half of figure 6-8 shows no cash profit and no income-tax obligation when the accrual numbers are converted to cash.

Figure 6-9 illustrates the 1996 year-end cash conversion for Ace Landscape Architects. The firm has a net loss of $3,522.50. Cash projections are also illustrated for the two 1997 expansion alternatives based on the pro forma financial statements. The projection indicates a cash profit for both alternatives, but the cash profit for alternative 2 is $4,450 less than alternative 1—another good reason for selecting the second alternative for expanding the firm.

Recording Financial Information— Elementary Accounting

Double Entry and the Accounting Equation

In performing financial accounting, the landscape architecture firm's accountant keeps track of each event that will have any bearing on the firm's financial condition. These events include actions such as the receipt of funds from a new partner who buys stock in the firm, increasing the firm's assets, as well as the firm's stockholder's equity; billing a client for $10,000 in professional services, increasing the firm's assets; or receiving a bill for $200 for blueprints, increasing the firm's liabilities. By keeping track of financial events as they happen, the accountant is able to present a financial picture of the firm using the language of accounting.

FIGURE 6-8.   Converting from accrual accounting to cash.

Cash Conversion after Nine Months of Tax Year			
Income	Previous Year-End Total	Current Year-to-Date Total	Cash
Accounts receivable	$50,000.00	$40,000.00	$10,000.00
Accounts payable	25,000.00	20,000.00	(5,000.00)
Current year accrued profit			10,000.00
Net cash/taxable income			15,000.00
Income tax at 34%			5,100.00

Cash Conversion at End of Tax Year			
Income	Previous Year-End Total	Current Year-End Total	Cash
Accounts receivable	$50,000.00	$60,000.00	($10,000.00)
Accounts payable	25,000.00	15,000.00	(10,000.00)
Current year accrued profit			20,000.00
Net cash			0.00
Income tax at 34%			0.00

FIGURE 6-9.   Ace Landscape Architects 1996 conversion from accrual accounting to cash and 1997 pro forma conversions for alternatives 1 and 2.

Cash Conversion 1996 Tax Year End

Income	1995 Year-End Total	1996 Year-End Total	Cash
Accounts receivable	$79,330.97	$87,443.54	($8,112.57)
Accounts payable	24,575.34	1,050.00	(23,525.34)
Accrued profit			28,165.39
Net cash/taxable income			(3,472.52)
Income tax at 34%			0

Cash Conversion Pro Forma 1997 Year-End Alternative 1

Income	Previous Year-End Total	Current Year-End Total	Cash
Accounts receivable	$87,443.54	$188,121.95	($100,678.41)
Accounts payable	1,050.00	32,000.00	30,950.00
Accrued profit			96,137.00
Net cash			26,408.59
Income tax at 34%			8,978.92

Cash Conversion Pro Forma 1997 Year-End Alternative 2

Income	Previous Year-End Total	Current Year-End Total	Cash
Accounts receivable	$87,443.54	$205,309.95	($117,866.41)
Accounts payable	1,050.00	32,000.00	30,950.00
Accrued profit			108,325.00
Net cash			21,408.59
Income tax at 34%			7,278.92

In order to keep track of the firm's financial picture, the accountant uses a journal to record the financial events. To ensure that all financial transactions are properly recorded, the accountant uses a system called *double-entry bookkeeping*.

In order to understand the double-entry, think of it in terms of the basic equation of accounting:

$$\text{Assets} = \text{liabilities} + \text{owners' equity}$$

Any event having a financial bearing on the firm will affect the basic accounting equation because the equation summarizes the entire financial position of the firm. By definition, the basic accounting equation must always remain in balance. Absolutely nothing can take place financially that would cause the basic accounting equation to become out of balance.

A change in any one of the elements of the equation must change at least one other element of the equation. For example, let's begin with a basic accounting equation that looks like this:

$$\text{Assets} = \text{liabilities} + \text{stockholders' equity}$$

$$\$500,000 = \$400,000 + \$100,000$$

If the firm were to borrow $100,000 from a bank, the firm would have an infusion of cash. Assets would increase by $100,000. Likewise, the firm would owe money to the bank, and its liabilities would increase by $100,000. Now the equation would look like this:

$$\text{Assets} = \text{liabilities} + \text{stockholders' equity}$$

$$\$600,000 = \$500,000 + \$100,000$$

The basic accounting equation is in balance. If one compares the second equation to the first, two numbers have changed. The term *double entry* simply means that it is not possible to change one number in the basic accounting equation without changing at least one other.

The two numbers that are changed, however, need not be on opposite sides of the equation. What if the firm used a part of the $100,000 loan to purchase a new CAD system for a price of $15,000 and paid for the system with cash? The firm's asset of cash would decrease by $15,000, while its asset of equipment would increase by $15,000. The equation would remain as:

Assets = liabilities + stockholders' equity

$600,000 = $500,000 + $100,00

Although the basic accounting equation does not appear to have changed, it really has. The left side of the equation has both increased and decreased by $15,000. Although the totals on either side of the equation have remained the same, the firm's accountant would have recorded the specific parts of the double-entry system that have occurred on the left side of the equation. Just remember that every entry must have a corresponding entry that results in keeping the basic accounting equation in balance.

Bookkeeping

The terms *debit* and *credit* are mechanical tools used by financial accountants to carry out the double-entry system of bookkeeping. The use of debits and credits can be confusing to the person not trained in bookkeeping. Prior to actually using the debits and credits to balance a firm's accounting records, bookkeepers modify the accounting equation.

First, stockholders' equity is broken into the two elements that contribute to it: contributed capital plus retained earnings. So the basic accounting equation becomes:

Assets (A) = liabilities (L) + contributed capital (CC) + retained earnings (RE)

More specifically, the change in assets equals the change in liabilities plus the change in contributed capital plus the change in retained earnings. Therefore, letting the change in each element of the equation be represented by the symbol *delta* (Δ), the equation can be shortened to:

$$\Delta A = \Delta L + \Delta CC + \Delta RE$$

Moving further, retained earnings increase by adding net income and decrease when dividends are paid. Net income is revenue (R) minus expenses (E). Revenues increase a firm's assets, and expenses decrease a firm's assets. Dividends (D) are a distribution of some of the firm's profits to its owners. Therefore, the basic accounting equation can now be stated as the change in assets equals the change in liabilities plus the change in contributed capital and revenues minus the change in expenses and dividends:

$$\Delta A = \Delta L + \Delta CC + \Delta R - \Delta E - \Delta D$$

Using algebraic functions, the basic accounting equation can be manipulated to reflect all positive functions:

$$\Delta A + \Delta E + \Delta D = \Delta L + \Delta CC + \Delta R$$

This last equation is manipulated by bookkeepers using debits and credits. Debits are increases in anything on the left side of this equation, and credits are increases in anything on the right side. If anything on the left side decreases, it is credited. If anything on the right side decreases, it is debited. The bookkeeping process is one of debiting or crediting the appropriate side of the equation. For example, if cash, which is an asset, is increased because a partner purchases stock in the firm, assets (on the left side of the equation) would be debited. At the same time, contributed capital (on the right side of the equation) would increase so it would be credited, keeping the basic accounting equation in balance.

If you find debits and credits confusing, don't be alarmed. A bookkeeper for the typical landscape architecture firm uses computer software to keep the firm's accounting records and its basic accounting equation in balance. The equation for each journal entry made by the bookkeeper must be in balance in order for the overall equation for the firm to remain in balance. The result is the firm's balance sheet, one of the key accounting documents that is most meaningful to the firm's financial manager.

Chart of Accounts

The complete collection of all the accounts of a firm is the *general ledger*. The accounts are classified into balance sheet accounts (assets, liabilities, and stockholders' equity) and income statement accounts (revenues and expenses). A complete listing of all of the accounts by number and title is the landscape architecture firm's chart of accounts. The chart of accounts is analogous to a table of contents for the business of the firm. Each account typically has an identifying number and a title. Over time, accounting practices have adopted the following account numbers and titles as conventional practice: asset accounts, 100–199; liability accounts, 200–299; stockholders' equity and dividend accounts, 300–399; revenue accounts, 400–499; and expense account, 500–599.

A chart of accounts may be lengthy and very detailed, or it may be general and include only a few account titles. As an example, let's examine a liability account. A firm might decide to have a single account number called *utility expenses,* or the firm might decide to break down these expenses into several headings or accounts, each with its own number, including single accounts for telephone, electricity, gas, water and sewer, and so on. The chart of accounts should be fine-tuned to provide the level of detail necessary for understanding and evaluating the income and expenses of the firm and the balance sheet. The income statement and balance sheet for Ace Landscape Architects (figures 6-1 and 6-2) illustrate the chart of accounts for a small-sized landscape architecture firm.

Selecting an Accountant

A firm will require some or all of the following accounting services:

1. Bookkeeping
2. Regular reporting of financial statements, usually monthly
3. Tax preparation
4. Financial advising
5. Financial representation, such as for a tax audit.
6. Preparation of special financial reports, such as those requested by a bank or financial institution.

All of these services may be found in a single full-service accounting firm, or the services might be provided by more than one firm. Some firms use a bookkeeping firm for financial record-keeping services and a certified public accountant (CPA) for their tax and financial advisory needs. The availability of easy-to-use accounting and financial management software has allowed landscape architecture firms to do some or all of the bookkeeping and accounting work in house.

Even if some of the firm's bookkeeping work is carried out by a bookkeeping firm or internally using accounting software, the firm will need an accountant at some time during its business life. Selecting an accountant is important to the long-term business health of the firm. Use the following criteria when selecting an accountant:

1. Credentials. All accountants are educated in accounting processes and rules. A certified public accountant (CPA), however, has passed the examination given by the American Institute of Certified Public Accountants. The examination requires not only accounting knowledge but also knowledge of business law and tax regulations.
2. Experience with professional-service firms. Accounting for professional-service firms is different from accounting for manufacturing firms or retail companies.
3. Willingness to work with the firm's owners and business managers.
4. Personality and comfort level with the personal working relationship.
5. Cost and method of contracting for the services desired.
6. Willingness to work with other firms, such as a bookkeeping firm, if all the accounting services are not procured from the CPA.

Accounting Software

The wide range of accounting application software available for personal and business computers has made bookkeeping, accounting, and financial management for the design firm easy and effective for the nonaccountant. These accounting programs have made it possible for landscape architecture professionals to have greater control over in-house generation of financial reports, providing more readily available data for managing the firm. These software programs are effective because they use a few key data entries to integrate the component operations of the accounting and financial management process with project management.

Typical accounting software includes the following integrated modules:

1. *Payroll.* The design firm can calculate regular payroll and tax deductions, as well as make quarterly tax reports, usually based on the single entry of time from the employees' time cards.
2. *Receivables.* The firm can enter income when it is generated and produce an aging report of accounts receivable. The entries posted in the receivables module are automatically entered as revenue in the general ledger module.
3. *Payables.* Amounts for materials, services, and items such as rent and utilities are entered when invoices are received by the design firm or regular monthly payments come due. After invoice amounts are entered, aged payable reports are automatically produced for the firm's owners or financial managers. The entries are automatically entered as expenses in the general ledger module.
4. *General Ledger.* The general ledger module lets the design firm prepare its own income and expense statement and balance sheet in house. Due to the integrated nature of the software, data that have already been entered in this module are supplemented by additional accounting information to produce these key reports that indicate the profitability of the firm.
5. *Checkbook.* The accounting software makes keeping a checkbook a relatively easy chore. Checks written are automatically accounted for as cash disbursements.

Many small landscape architecture firms take advantage of the easy-to-use accounting software packages to carry out their own in-house accounting and produce their own in-house business reports. These in-house documents are then double-checked by the firm's accountant, reducing the overall cost of accounting services. Larger design firms of twenty-five or more landscape architects may employ a full-time bookkeeper or controller, who may use more sophisticated software and often produce all of the firm's accounting needs in house.

Some of the integrated accounting programs available on the retail market, such as Quicken and M. Y. O. B., are inexpensive and easy to use. These programs provide excellent in-house accounting capability for small landscape architecture firms. Other programs, such as Peachtree Accounting, Sema 4, and Timberline, provide advanced accounting software designed specifically to meet the needs of larger firms that require a wider range of financial management reports, such as job costing and project progress reports.

Quicken is one of the most popular personal and small business financial software programs available. It is simple to use and includes checking, savings, credit card, investment, and loan elements. It also includes a financial calendar and a tax planner. New versions even include a stock quotation feature. Quicken can be combined with its sister software, Quickbooks, to form a very useful software package for a small landscape architecture office.

M. Y. O. B. is a complete integrated accounting program that includes general ledger, checkbook, invoicing, cash-flow forecasting, accounts receivable, accounts payable, and payroll components. The software is capable of printing over 100 financial management reports. The payroll function has automatic tax calculations.

The by-product of using in-house accounting software is a variety of other financial and project management reports that can be very useful to the practicing landscape architect. Project cost accounting reports, which indicate how profitable a design firm is on an individual project, are extremely useful in managing the flow of work and developing fees for similar future projects. The project cost accounting report is derived from the hours entered for each employee in the accounting software. Analyzing the project cost accounting report will indicate, for example, if too much time has been spent in the schematic phase of the project or the construction documents phase, or if too much time has been spent by principal-level employees versus drafting-level employees.

Summary reports that are produced from the regularly-entered time card information and financial data are very useful to both financial and project managers of the landscape architecture firm. Some of the types of summary reports that can be prepared include:

1. *Percent of work in progress completed.* If a high percent of the firm's total work in progress, 80 percent, for example, has been completed, and few or no new projects are in the job-development pipeline, the firm's managers will need to focus on job development or face a reduction in workforce.
2. *Percent of billable hours.* Effective financial management and profitability depend upon keeping the number of billable hours versus the nonbillable hours to a maximum. A landscape architecture firm may have a goal of 85 percent billable time for all of its employees, for example. The percent of billable hours report will indicate if that goal is being achieved.
3. *Profit and loss trend reports.* A summary report of the design firm's profitability by week or month over a given time period is another interesting and useful management tool. Many of the accounting software packages also allow easy graphic depiction of the profit and loss trend line of the firm.

Overview of Accounting: Six Integrated Components

The easiest way for the professional landscape architect to develop a grasp of managing the accounting process is to view it as six primary integrated components:

1. Time records
2. Payroll
3. Receivables
4. Payables
5. Cash receipts and disbursements
6. Project cost accounting

Time Records

Keeping time records is the cornerstone of the private practice of landscape architecture. In the accounting process, time records have a direct bearing on the payroll, receivables, and project cost accounting components. Every employee of the landscape architecture office, including principals and administrative staff, should keep an accurate record of the billable time spent working on specific projects, as well as nonbillable time spent on overhead or administrative tasks. Timekeeping records are used by the firm to

1. pay employees,
2. produce invoices,
3. analyze the time spent to complete work on projects and the costs to the firm.

Payroll

The labor costs for completing the firm's landscape architecture projects and carrying out the administrative functions of the firm represent the single largest percent of the firm's cost of doing business. Each employee is assigned a labor rate, hourly wage, or salary, and is paid at a regular interval such as weekly, biweekly, or on the fifteenth and last day of each month. The labor rate times the number of hours worked in the payroll period or the salary per payroll period for each employee represents the gross payroll amount. After gross payroll is calculated, deductions must be made for FICA (Federal Insurance Contribution Act), which is a combined payment for old-age, survivors, and disability insurance (formerly called social security), and medicare. The federal government sets the percentage and maximum amount each year. The employer pays the tax through payroll deductions and is required by federal law to match the amount paid by the employee. In addition to FICA, the employer must account for FUTA (Federal Unemployment Tax) deductions. The federal government also annually sets the percentage and maximum compensation to which the FUTA tax rate is applied. Deductions are also made for federal, state, and local income tax obligations (withholding taxes), and for voluntary deductions such as medical insurance, disability insurance, payroll savings plans, and retirement plans.

Receivables

The firm's income or revenue is achieved through submitting invoices to its clients for services rendered.

Compensation is based on the type of agreement with the client, fixed fee, hourly, or hourly with a not-to-exceed maximum amount, for example. Progress billings, which reflect the percentage of the project that has been completed, are commonly made on a monthly basis. The progress billings include amounts for labor, reimbursable expenses, and outside services such as subconsultants. Receivables create the revenue component of the integrated accounting process. The receivables are illustrated in an aged accounts receivable report, which is one of the most needed reports for financial management of the firm's cash flow.

Payables

Requests for payment by subconsultants, vendors, and other firms providing goods or services to the landscape architecture office comprise the accounts payable of the firm. They are illustrated in an aged payables report, another of the reports necessary for the firm's financial and cash-flow management.

Cash Receipts and Disbursements

The actual income (cash) received and the actual money paid out by the firm is recorded in the checkbook and is the basis for managing the cash flow of the firm. Cash-flow management is often the most critical day-to-day problem for the firm's financial managers. It is directly tied to receivables and payables. A short-term line of credit or source of funds from savings or investments is an important element required for the successful management of cash flow because the cash disbursements required for payroll and payables almost never match up with the cash on hand from receivables.

Project Cost Accounting

Project cost accounting involves tracking and analyzing the costs associated with rendering services on each project versus the revenue earned for each project. Project cost accounting involves analyzing the time spent, who is spending it, and how it is being spent on each project. It also involves analyzing the cost of direct expenses, such as reproductions, travel, or subconsultants' expenses, required for the project. Project cost progress

reports during the course of the project are absolutely necessary for effectively understanding profitability and the effectiveness of the project manager. Final project cost printouts are very useful tools for estimating future project costs and setting up future project cost accounting reports and reporting procedures.

REFERENCES

Finkler, Steven A. 1983. *The Complete Guide to Finance and Accounting for Nonfinancial Managers.* Englewood Cliffs, N.J.: Prentice Hall.

Hermanson, Roger H., James Don Edwards, and L. Gayle Rayburn. 1989. *Financial Accounting.* Homewood, Ill.: BPI/Irwin.

Livingstone, John Leslie. 1992. *The Portable MBA in Finance and Accounting.* New York: John Wiley & Sons.

Mattox, Robert F. 1982. *Standardized Accounting for Architects, Third Edition: A Guide to Understanding, Developing and Implementing Accounting Procedures.* Washington, D.C.: The American Institute of Architects.

Spurga, Ronald C. 1986. *Balance Sheet Basics: Financial Management for Nonfinancial Managers.* New York: Franklin Watts.

STUDY QUESTIONS AND ASSIGNMENTS

1. Research national statistics and other reference sources to find information on the profitability trends over ten to twenty years for landscape architecture firms and other A/E firms throughout the country. Present your findings in a paper.

2. Develop a chart of accounts for a landscape architecture office income statement in two ways: Develop one chart that is simple and uses only broad categories of operating expenses. Develop another that is made up of very detailed categories of expenses. Refer to figure 6-1.

3. Using this chapter and other financial and accounting references, write a paper that discusses money and cash-flow management. Develop a list of methods and techniques for money and cash-flow management in a landscape architecture firm.

4. Using this chapter and other financial and accounting references, write a paper that explains your understanding of the basic accounting equation:

Assets = liabilities + owner's equity

5. Research the receivable turnover ratio and average age of receivables for landscape architecture firms and other A/E firms. Write a paper summarizing the twenty-year trends for the average amount of time it takes for landscape architecture and A/E firms to collect revenue after invoices are sent out.

6. A landscape architecture firm receives a resource planning contract for $350,000 in fees. The contract is to be completed over a two-year period. The owners of the firm expect their income from other contracts to remain at a constant level of $500,000 per year for the two-year period. The firm must expand to be able to handle the added workload. The owners have identified two alternative expansion plans:

   1. Hire a project manager and a junior-level landscape architect at a total salary cost of $65,000 per year.
   2. Purchase a GIS computer-mapping system at a cost of $20,000 and hire a professional experienced in GIS at an annual salary of $40,000 per year to work with existing staff.

   Using this chapter and figure 6-5 as a reference, set up an income statement for the firm using a year-end revenue of $500,000. Make operating expenses such that the firm's profit at year end is 8 percent. Develop a pro forma income statement projected for two years of operations for each alternative expansion option. Make a recommendation on which expansion alternative to implement. Base your recommendation on the financial and accounting decisions.

7. Using this chapter and other financial and accounting references, write a paper that illustrates your understanding of financial ratios. Include trend ratios, liquidity ratios, and equity ratios.

8. Using this chapter and other financial and accounting references, write a paper that explains your understanding of the accrual accounting system. Discuss its advantages and disadvantages.

CHAPTER SEVEN

Business Administration and Record Keeping

In spite of the most well-conceived administrative systems, the following words can all too often be heard in landscape architecture offices: "If I had a dollar for every time I couldn't find something in this office, I'd be a millionaire," spoken by a principal or project manager when a critical piece of project data can't be found in the office files.

The administration of the landscape architecture office, from keeping track of the firm's projects to developing and maintaining filing systems to keeping up with the requirements of tax laws, is the hub of the business-management wheel. Without an efficient and easily-used filing system, the office staff may be doomed to endless hours of lost time spent looking for information needed to run the business.

A landscape architecture office of fifteen to twenty people, for example, will produce a tremendous amount of material that needs to be filed:

- Project records
    Original reproducible drawings
    Project design drawings
    Project data
    Correspondence and transmittals
    Phone conversation records
    Construction administration records
    Contracts
    Invoices and billing history
- Financial information for the current and prior years
- Personnel records
- Tax information
- Insurance information

- Bookkeeping files
- Leases, long-term notes, and mortgages
- Marketing and promotional materials
- Information files for specialty subconsultants
- Product literature and technical reference files
- Dead files and project archives

Computerization of the landscape architecture office has made office administration easier and more organized, but it has not reduced the amount of paper generated in the design office. In fact, computers allow more information to be processed, which in turn generates even greater amounts of hard copy to be filed. Using computers has also created additional administrative tasks such as managing computer files and storing floppy disks, which have their own filing requirements. Trying to remember where something is filed on a floppy disk or a section of a hard drive can be time consuming without a good electronic information filing system.

The landscape architecture graduate will be surprised by the amount of materials that need to be filed and stored in a design office. The landscape architect in training or a new employee will have to learn to use the project filing system and the product literature files when he or she begins employment with a new firm. As project administrative responsibilities increase, all of the office files will be used by the design firm employee. If the landscape architect is starting a new firm, he or she should plan on spending a considerable amount of time developing the administrative systems, filing methods, and business forms that will be used in the office.

Job Number—The Key to Office Administration

The project filing system in most landscape architecture offices revolves around the project number. Every project gets a number, and the number goes on everything related to that project—every letter, note, phone memo, drawing, invoice, or photocopy of a product literature cut sheet associated with the project. The project number should be located in a prominently visible place on the document to aid in easy filing and retrieval.

A variety of job-numbering systems are used in landscape architecture offices. Figure 7-1 shows an example of a job number. The first five numbers are a general reference; the last two numbers are a specific code. The job number in figure 7-1 tells the user the year the job number was issued, the sequential number of that job during the year, and the general category of work the job falls under. A variation on the job number will normally be used to denote those projects that are in the job-development phase rather than work in progress. Most firms give a prospective project a job number so that they can track time spent in job development. Job-development time contributes to the overhead of running the office, which affects the office overhead rate or overhead multiplier. Some firms try to recoup time spent in job development, especially when a fixed fee is negotiated for the project.

Category-of-Work Code

In the example job number shown in figure 7-1, the last two digits are a code for the type of work category. A type-of-work code is useful for studying the trends in the office's procurement of work and in sorting out projects and retrieving project information for marketing purposes. The following lists is an example of work categories for a typical landscape architecture office:

CODE	CATEGORY OF WORK
00	Job development
10	Landscaping, revegetation, and irrigation
12	Commercial and retail
13	Roadside and transportation
14	Parks and recreation
15	Hotels and leisure facilities
16	Environmental assessment, resource analysis, and resource planning
17	Historic preservation
18	Land planning and urban planning
19	Industrial parks and corporate headquarters
20	Water conservation and irrigation
21	Multifamily residential
23	Single-family residential
24	Graphics, models, and exhibits

This system of codes uses fourteen numbers, but as many numbered codes as desired may be used. Using too many categories makes the system overly complex. Staff will have trouble deciding which category a job fits into if there are too many options to choose from. The key is to use enough categories to clearly differentiate the types of projects the firm works on without excessive detail that makes the system unwieldy.

The code 00 for projects in the job development phase is changed to an active code once the project is actually secured and a contract is signed. Some job numbering systems have numbers to identify cities, states, or regions where the project is located so that a firm can track its geographic market penetration. Large multioffice firms use numbers to identify which office the project belongs to.

Another reason for adding category-of-work codes to the job number is for tracking projects to fill out the federal government's SF254 and SF255 forms. The

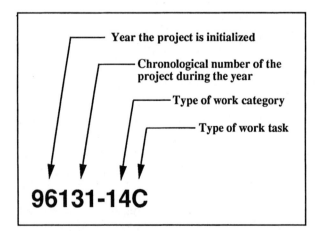

Year the project is initialized

Chronological number of the project during the year

Type of work category

Type of work task

96131-14C

FIGURE 7-1. Example of a job number.

SF254 needs to be updated on an annual basis, and the landscape architecture firm must add to the form the number of jobs in the SF254 categories that the firm executed in the previous year. At the same time, the firm must calculate and track the number of jobs by category over the last five years. Using a job numbering system with category-of-work codes makes the annual updating chore reasonably easy. Indeed, a landscape architecture firm may even decide to use the SF254 code numbers for its own category-of-work codes. SF254 standard codes are illustrated in figure 7-2. Most landscape architecture firms using SF254 codes for the office job numbering system would use the following codes:

059   Landscape architecture
056   Irrigation; drainage

033   Environmental impact studies, assessments, or statements
078   Planning (community, regional, areawide and state)
079   Planning (site, installation, and project)
117   Zoning and land-use studies

Once a job numbering system is implemented in an office, the project filing system is a straightforward process of filing all project-related materials by the job number. The job-related files, however, may be found in various places in the office, including general files for project data and correspondence, contract and billing files, active files for drawings and work in progress, dead files for project data, and dead files for drawings of completed projects.

Experience Profile Code Numbers for use with questions 10 and 11

001 Acoustics; Noise Abatement
002 Aerial Photogrammetry
003 Agricultural Development; Grain Storage; Farm Mechanization
004 Air Pollution Control
005 Airports; Navaids; Airport Lighting; Aircraft Fueling
006 Airports; Terminals & Hangars; Freight Handling
007 Arctic Facilities
008 Auditoriums & Theatres
009 Automation; Controls; Instrumentation
010 Barracks; Dormitories
011 Bridges
012 Cemeteries (Planning & Relocation)
013 Chemical Processing & Storage
014 Churches; Chapels
015 Codes; Standards; Ordinances
016 Cold Storage; Refrigeration; Fast Freeze
017 Commercial Buildings (low rise); Shopping Centers
018 Communications Systems; TV; Microwave
019 Computer Facilities; Computer Service
020 Conservation and Resource Management
021 Construction Management
022 Corrosion Control; Cathodic Protection; Electrolysis
023 Cost Estimating
024 Dams (Concrete; Arch)
025 Dams (Earth; Rock); Dikes; Levees
026 Desalinization (Process & Facilities)
027 Dining Halls; Clubs; Restaurants
028 Ecological & Archeological Investigations
029 Educational Facilities; Classrooms
030 Electronics
031 Elevators; Escalators; People-Movers
032 Energy Conservation; New Energy Sources
033 Environmental Impact Studies, Assessments or Statements
034 Fallout Shelters; Blast-Resistant Design
035 Field Houses; Gyms; Stadiums
036 Fire Protection
037 Fisheries; Fish Ladders
038 Forestry & Forest Products
039 Garages; Vehicle Maintenance Facilities; Parking Decks
040 Gas Systems (Propane; Natural, Etc.)
041 Graphic Design

042 Harbors; Jetties; Piers; Ship Terminal Facilities
043 Heating; Ventilating; Air Conditioning
044 Health Systems Planning
045 Highrise; Air-Rights-Type Buildings
046 Highways; Streets; Airfield Paving; Parking Lots
047 Historical Preservation
048 Hospital & Medical Facilities
049 Hotels; Models
050 Housing (Residential, Multi-Family; Apartments; Condominiums)
051 Hydraulics & Pneumatics
052 Industrial Buildings; Manufacturing Plants
053 Industrial Processes; Quality Control
054 Industrial Waste Treatment
055 Interior Design; Space Planning
056 Irrigation; Drainage
057 Judicial and Courtroom Facilities
058 Laboratories; Medical Research Facilities
059 Landscape Architecture
060 Libraries; Museums; Galleries
061 Lighting (Interiors; Display; Theatre, Etc.)
062 Lighting (Exteriors; Streets; Memorials; Athletic Fields, Etc.)
063 Materials Handling Systems; Conveyors; Sorters
064 Metallurgy
065 Microclimatology; Tropical Engineering
066 Military Design Standards
067 Mining & Mineralogy
068 Missile Facilities (Silos; Fuels; Transport)
069 Modular Systems Design; Pre-Fabricated Structures or Components
070 Naval Architecture; Off-Shore Platforms
071 Nuclear Facilities; Nuclear Shielding
072 Office Buildings; Industrial Parks
073 Oceanographic Engineering
074 Ordnance; Munitions; Special Weapons
075 Petroleum Exploration; Refining
076 Petroleum and Fuel (Storage and Distribution)
077 Pipelines (Cross-Country—Liquid & Gas)
078 Planning (Community, Regional, Areawide and State)
079 Planning (Site, Installation, and Project)
080 Plumbing & Piping Design
081 Pneumatic Structures; Air-Support Buildings
082 Postal Facilities
083 Power Generation, Transmission, Distribution
084 Prisons & Correctional Facilities
085 Product, Machine & Equipment Design

086 Radar; Sonar; Radio & Radar Telescopes
087 Railroad; Rapid Transit
088 Recreation Facilities (Parks, Marinas, Etc.)
089 Rehabilitation (Buildings; Structures; Facilities)
090 Resource Recovery; Recycling
091 Radio Frequency Systems & Shieldings
092 Rivers; Canals; Waterways; Flood Control
093 Safety Engineering; Accident Studies; OSHA Studies
094 Security Systems; Intruder & Smoke Detection
095 Seismic Designs & Studies
096 Sewage Collection, Treatment and Disposal
097 Soils & Geologic Studies; Foundations
098 Solar Energy Utilization
099 Solid Wastes; Incineration; Land Fill
100 Special Environments; Clean Rooms, Etc.
101 Structural Design; Special Structures
102 Surveying; Platting; Mapping; Flood Plain Studies
103 Swimming Pools
104 Storm Water Handling & Facilities
105 Telephone Systems (Rural; Mobile; Intercom, Etc.)
106 Testing & Inspection Services
107 Traffic & Transportation Engineering
108 Towers (Self-Supporting & Guyed Systems)
109 Tunnels & Subways
110 Urban Renewals; Community Development
111 Utilities (Gas & Steam)
112 Value Analysis; Life-Cycle Costing
113 Warehouses & Depots
114 Water Resources; Hydrology; Ground Water
115 Water Supply, Treatment and Distribution
116 Wind Tunnels; Research/Testing Facilities Design
117 Zoning; Land Use Studies
201 _____
202 _____
203 _____
204 _____
205 _____

STANDARD FORM 254 (REV 10-83)

FIGURE 7-2a. SF254 experience profile code numbers.

STANDARD FORM (SF) **254** Architect-Engineer and Related Services Questionnaire	1. Firm Name / Business Address:		2. Year Present Firm Established:	3. Date Prepared:
			4. Specify type of ownership *and* check below, if applicable.	
	1a. Submittal is for ☐ Parent Company ☐ Branch or Subsidiary Office		A. Small Business B. Small Disadvantaged Business C. Woman-owned Business	

5. Name of Parent Company, if any:	5a. Former Parent Company Name(s), if any, and Year(s) Established:

6. Names of not more than Two Principals to Contact: Title / Telephone
1)
2)

7. Present Offices: City / State / Telephone / No. Personnel Each Office   7a. Total Personnel _____

8. Personnel by Discipline: *(List each person only once, by primary function.)*

____ Administrative	____ Electrical Engineers	____ Oceanographers	____ _____
____ Architects	____ Estimators	____ Planners: Urban / Regional	____ _____
____ Chemical Engineers	____ Geologists	____ Sanitary Engineers	____ _____
____ Civil Engineers	____ Hydrologists	____ Soils Engineers	____ _____
____ Construction Inspectors	____ Interior Designers	____ Specification Writers	____ _____
____ Draftsmen	____ Landscape Architects	____ Structural Engineers	____ _____
____ Ecologists	____ Mechanical Engineers	____ Surveyors	____ _____
____ Economists	____ Mining Engineers	____ Transportation Engineers	____ _____

9. Summary of Professional Services Fees
   Received: (Insert index number)   Last 5 Years (most recent year first)

                                    19_____ 19_____ 19_____ 19_____ 19_____

Direct Federal contract work, including overseas   _____ _____ _____ _____ _____
All other domestic work   _____ _____ _____ _____ _____
All other foreign work*   _____ _____ _____ _____ _____
*Firms interested in foreign work, but without such experience, check here: ☐.

Ranges of Professional Services Fees
INDEX
1   Less than $100,000
2   $100,000 to $250,000
3   $250,000 to $500,000
4   $500,000 to $1 million
5   $1 million to $2 million
6   $2 million to $5 million
7   $5 million to $10 million
8   $10 million or greater

FIGURE 7-2b. First page of the SF254 form.

By implementing a job numbering system, all project-related materials can be filed by job number including electronic files and discs. Storing all the electronic data for a project on a single floppy disk is an effective way to organize electronic data files where the disks can be filed in order by job number. Remember to make backup copies of the disks.

Master Roster

An important use of the project numbering system is organizing the firm's work in progress and work in job-development status into a total list of the firm's projects for reference by all employees. The project list, or project master roster, is updated regularly and used by all staff members on a daily basis to mark time cards and to organize their work. Design office staff are often working on multiple projects at one time and will find it helpful to have a master roster close by to refer to.

Jobs organized in a master roster provide a list that can be used for other administrative tasks, such as estimating the amount of fees remaining on a project in relation to the remaining amount of work required to complete the project, resulting in a workload projection described in chapter 6.

Time Cards

Keeping track of the time spent on projects is the basis for managing projects and invoicing clients for the firm's professional services. Time cards, either hard copy or electronic media, are used by virtually every landscape architecture office. Project staff fill out their time cards on a regular basis, using the job numbering system and a work task code that identifies the specific type of task carried out by general categories. Office administrative staff enter time card information into the office time management and invoicing system to create project time reports, project progress reports, and reports used to prepare invoices.

Tracking the type of work tasks completed by office staff is necessary for producing accurate project time reports so that office staff and project managers will know not only how much time has been spent on a project but also what tasks the time is spent on. Numbers or letters are used to designate the different types of work tasks carried out by the office staff. The numbers or letters are entered on time cards and turned in at the end of a one-week or two-week period for data entry into the office's timekeeping system. A typical letter system for a design-oriented landscape architecture office would include the following letters and work task codes. This letter system would be treated as the firm's default system of work tasks.

CODE	TYPE OF WORK TASK
A	Job development and precontract work
B	Research, data collection, start-up, site reconnaissance, fieldwork, base plans
C	Site analysis and schematic design
D	Design development
E	Construction documents
F	Services during construction
G	Graphics and renderings
H	Report preparation
I	Project management and administration
J	Additional services

The type-of-work task codes can be adapted to a specific project by changing the task descriptions or adding new tasks and letter codes in order to create task codes only for that project. The project manager would be responsible for developing the project-specific task codes and making the list available to each employee working on the project. The project manager also would make the project-specific task codes known to the office administrative staff because the codes would need to be set up properly in the office computer systems for time tracking and invoic-

ing. The following is an example of a project-specific task code for an environmental assessment project.

CODE	TYPE OF WORK TASK
A	Job development
B	Site reconnaissance, fieldwork, data gathering
C	GIS base plan
D	GIS data entry
E	GIS data analysis and site analysis
F	Set up public interest group database
G	Public interest group input meetings
H	Develop and prepare draft report
I	Public interest group feedback meetings
J	Prepare final report
K	Project administration

Type-of-work task codes can be very specific. Again, the rule of thumb is not to make the work of timekeeping so complicated and tedious that employees balk at the process. The following is an example of a coding system that uses letters and numbers to provide greater detail on employee work activities by phase and task codes. This system would result in more detail information available to project managers in project progress reports.

A   PRE-CONTRACT AND JOB DEVELOPMENT

A1	Client contact/job development meetings
A2	Job development tasks and project research
A3	Proposal writing
A4	Contract negotiation

B   PROJECT ADMINISTRATION

B1	Project initialization and file setup
B2	Internal accounting, administration, and billing
B3	Project progress meetings
B4	Quality-control plan
B5	Management reports
B6	Subconsultant management
B7	General project administration

C   SCHEMATIC DESIGN (30 PERCENT)

C1	Site reconnaissance
C2	Site analysis
C3	Quantity takeoff, budget analysis, and cost projection

C4   Base plans
C5   Schematic design

D   Design Development (60 Percent)

D1   Design development
D2   Planting design
D3   Irrigation design
D4   Grading design
D5   Product and materials research
D6   Construction detail design
D7   Quantity takeoff and cost projection
D8   Outline specifications

E   Final Design and Construction Documents (90 Percent)

E1   Layout plans
E2   Grading plans
E3   Planting plans
E4   Irrigation plans
E5   Construction details
E6   Quantity takeoff and cost projection
E7   Specifications

F   Final Design and Construction Documents (100 Percent)

F1   Checking and revisions
F2   Quantity takeoff and cost projection
F3   Project design closeout

G   Construction administration

G1   Pre-bid meeting
G2   Bid analysis
G3   Preconstruction meeting
G4   Construction observation and field reports
G5   Weekly progress meetings and reports
G6   Review submittals and shop drawings, reports
G7   Review and approve change orders
G8   Review and approve pay requests
G9   Final inspection and punch list
G10   General construction administration
G11   Project closeout

In addition to tracking time spent on project tasks by codes, the landscape architecture office should track time spent on various overhead tasks by letter codes on the time cards. Landscape architecture firms have a number of overhead tasks that are not billable to a client. Job-development time, vacation time, sick time off, and general overhead and other nonbillable time must be tracked on time cards and entered into the office timekeeping system. A sample of overhead tasks and letter codes is shown below. When combined with the project default tasks, these overhead tasks provide the complete listing of the firm's work tasks that are typically entered on employee time cards.

CODE	TYPE OF WORK TASK
O	General overhead, project planning, and management
L	General leave
S	Sick leave
H	Holiday
P	Professional societies and community service

An example of a time card and entries is shown in figure 7-3. Note the entry of information for each line item of work includes the project number, the type-of-work task code, a brief description of the work carried out, and the amount of time worked on the task. The brief description provides further detail about the work task completed by the employee. The description is useful if the invoicing for the project is on an hourly basis and the client wants to see a description of the actual tasks carried out by the employee.

Office practices vary on the smallest breakdown of time that employees are required to report on their time cards. The smallest unit of time commonly used by firms for timekeeping purposes is one tenth of an hour, or six minutes. One quarter of an hour is also commonly used. Using half hours or full hours may not provide enough of a breakdown to fairly keep track of time. The smallest unit of timekeeping is established as a general operating procedure by each firm. The size of the fee and the duration of the project may affect the timekeeping process. Employees working on a project with a very large fee and a long duration may know in advance that 100 percent of their time for the week will be spent in data collection on the project. The time card entry will be simple. Forty hours will be entered under the project number and code for data collection. The need for more detailed breakdown of time entries occurs when the project has a small fee and a full scope of work.

Employee No.: WA64   **Month:** October   **Year:** 1996

Employee Name: William Anderson

Job No. and Work Code:	Project Name:	Work Done:	14 M	15 T	16 W	17 T	18 F	19 S	20 S	Total Hours
O	Office overhead	General office administration	0.5	0.1	1.3	0.3				2.2
96131-14 C	Foothills Middle School	Schematic design	7.5	2.9						10.4
96172-18D	Ramada Inn	Design development		4.0						4.0
96172-14D	Ramada Inn	Project administration		1.0			0.5			6.0
95163-15E	Aviation Parkway	Construction documents			0.7		1.0			1.7
96153-15E	Aviation Parkway	Project administration			2.0		1.5			3.5
96202-00A	Highlands Park	Job development, draft proposal			0.5	5.0	2.0	3.0		10.5
95187-13B	3467 E. Broadway Rezoning	Meet w/ City staff			2.0					2.0
96206-00A	Foothills Park	Pre-proposal meeting			1.5					1.5
94136-11F	River Park	Field work for punch list				2.0				2.0
94136-11F	River Park	Punch list and project admin.				0.7	0.6			1.3
96157-10B	Downtown Hotel	Site reconaissance					2.4			2.4
P	ASLA	Attend monthly Chapter meeting				2.0				2.0
		Total Regular Time:	8.0	8.0	8.0	8.0	8.0			40.0
		Total Overtime:				2.0		3.0		5.0
		Total time:								45.0

Signature:

FIGURE 7-3. Completed time card.

Filing and Records Management

Every landscape architecture office has a need to file information and manage records. The need is no less important in a small firm of one to twenty employees than it is in a large firm that may employ several hundred or thousands of employees. An effective filing and record management system is important for any size landscape architecture firm and includes the following attributes:

1. It is efficient, expandable, and easy to use.
2. It is uniform and has a method of organization.
3. It protects the firm's vital records.
4. It includes both current files and archives.
5. It includes the development and management of forms.

Efficient, Expandable, and Easy to Use

An effective filing and records management system allows for the routine handling of information, documents, and records. Every filing system will grow in size and must have expandability in its method of organization. It also must have the physical room for expansion. Many highly organized filing systems have come unglued when the need for expansion caused by growth in the sheer volume of materials was not preplanned.

Complementing expandability is the need to eliminate filed materials that are outdated, useless, or exceed the time requirements for records retention. Regular and planned weeding out of files is very important to the success of an efficient filing system. A client's going out of business may eliminate the need for the landscape architecture office to keep information on the client. The statute of limitations for each state provides a guide for the recommended retention time of legal documents and information. The *Guide to Record Retention Requirements* in the code of federal regulations, last revised in 1989, is another source of information for making decisions about how long to keep documents.

The following general guidelines for retaining information and records may help administrators of most landscape architecture offices develop a policy for what material may be weeded out and when:

PERMANENT RETENTION

All vital records, corporate charters, incorporation records, minutes of corporate meetings, stock ledger, stock sales or transfer records, corporate resolutions, partnership documents, tax returns and related documents, tax audit records and related tax bills, depreciation schedules, annual reports, contracts, capital leases, claims regarding any tort cases, records of arbitration, records of mediation, trade name or trademark registrations, patents, copyrights, annual financial statements, executive correspondence, directives from owners or corporate officers, the personnel manual, office procedures, the administrative manual, file copies of the firm's forms, employee personnel files.

PERIOD RETENTION

3 years: Payroll checks, monthly financial statements, accounts payable invoices, bank deposits, bank statements, expense reports, payroll registers, petty cash records, travel expense reports, time cards, accounting and audit work papers

5 years: Employee withholding records, accounts receivable invoices, equipment repair and maintenance records

7 years: Office equipment records, cash receipts records, one copy of all project-related data (Gill 1988).

Filing cabinets should be accessible. File drawers should not be overstuffed, causing difficulty in removing or inserting paper. The system itself should be as simple as possible. Using the job number as a numerical filing system is a simple way to file all of the firm's project-related information. Filing everything by its job number is the single filing directive that all employees must obey. If a filing system is too cumbersome and physically inaccessible, it will be self-defeating. A filing system that is difficult to use causes employees to pigeonhole information and develop a plethora of wildcat personal filing systems. Pigeonholed information leads to inefficiency and lost project data.

An effective filing and records management system will have some or all of these characteristics:

- Reduce or eliminate countless hours of staff time spent searching through useless volumes of information in search of needed documents or information.
- Provide for the security of vital, sensitive, or confidential information.
- Enhance overall efficiency of the landscape architecture office and increase the potential for office billable time.
- Mitigate the proliferation of costly filing cabinets that require expensive office floor space.
- Save money on expensive filing supplies and equipment.
- Minimize office clutter.

Uniformity and Organization

There are four ways to arrange or classify files adaptable to the requirements of a landscape architecture office: alphabetically, numerically, by subject, or by color. Whichever method is used, the key to organization is labeling every record with the number, letter, color, or subject code.

Alphabetic systems use the letters of the alphabet, A through Z, as the general file identifiers. The specific items, such as persons names and manufacturers' names or addresses, are arranged alphabetically. Alphabetical systems are useful for personnel files, office administrative files, subconsultant files, and product literature files. Alphabetical organization is the most commonly used method for organizing the material actually filed within a file. The default system on computers normally organizes electronic files alphabetically.

Numeric systems are most often set up with the numbers arranged consecutively. Numeric systems work well for arranging files chronologically. Filing by dates is a numeric system. Numeric systems are excellent filing methods when the records are prenumbered, such as check registers and invoices, or when documents receive an assigned number, such as a job number.

Subject filing is used to arrange records according to what they are about. Subject filing is difficult to administer and is frequently combined with a numeric or alphabetic system. The subjects are first arranged in meaningful topics, and then a number or letter is assigned to each topic heading.

Color coding is usually combined with a numeric or alphabetic system, providing a dual or overlay function to the filing system. Colors of files can serve as references, for example, to very large categories of information. Business administrative files can be red; personnel files can be orange; accounting files, blue; project files, white; and so on. Colors also work well as a way to subdivide a recurring file category. If project data are filed by job numbers, color file folders can be used to identify different subfiles. In every project file, contract information is always found in the red files, invoicing information is always found in orange files, correspondence is always found in blue files, project data are always found in green files, and so on (Gill 1988 and Lundgren 1989).

No matter what method of classifying and managing files is used, the filing system must be applied in a uniform fashion for the system to be organized and efficient.

Vital Records

Those records that are necessary to reconstruct the landscape architecture firm in the event of a disaster are considered vital records. These records include the corporate charter and corporate minutes, and the number of stockholders and the amount of stock held by each stockholder. Vital records include the firm's main contracts in progress and the project information files and billing records for work in progress. All legal documents, such as leases and deeds of trust, are considered vital records. Original copies of office procedures memorandums and manuals, as well as office forms, should be kept with vital records. Some records are considered vital due to the sentimental value attached to them, such as the original copy of an ASLA Honor Award.

The loss of essential documents and information on work in progress can cause serious financial hardship and legal difficulty for a landscape architecture firm. The loss of vital records may even cause the firm to go out of business. In the event of a disaster, valuable papers insurance coverage has saved many firms from total loss and going out of business.

A landscape architecture firm should have a plan for recovery from disaster and loss of vital records. Off-site storage of vital electronic and hard-copy records is part of most disaster recovery plans. Here are several steps that every landscape architecture firm should take in order to develop a disaster recovery plan:

- Assess the risk associated with the loss of office records and rank each record or type of record on a risk value scale such as from one to ten or from low to high risk.
- Determine the amount of time that would be needed to recover critical office functions in the event of a disaster and develop ways to minimize the time.
- Develop a specific plan for storing and recovering vital records that includes elements such as off-site storage of vital records, computer backup policies, and a reciprocal agreement with another firm to use space, equipment, and records in the event of a disaster.
- Define specific roles of the firm's officers, responsible senior staff, and employees in the event of a significant loss or disaster.
- Establish firm-wide procedures for continually updating and maintaining the disaster recovery procedures. Include the procedures, in detail and step by step, in a firm disaster-recovery manual.
- At regular time intervals, test the disaster recovery plan with a dry run.

Forms

Every landscape architecture office uses a number of forms in the day-to-day work and administration of the office. Forms are used for repetitive administrative and project management activities. When appropriately designed, forms are a helpful resource, reducing repetitive work and increasing the productivity and efficiency of office staff.

Developing, refining, and managing the use of forms is a time-consuming task for managers and office administrative staff. Some of the considerations include

- developing only necessary forms for truly repetitive tasks where time savings will be realized;
- designing forms for maximum effectiveness;
- refining forms over time so they continue to work better;
- eliminating unnecessary forms;
- simplifying forms for easy use;
- consolidating forms that have overlapping purposes;
- reproducing, stocking, and distributing forms.

Landscape architecture firms obtain forms both by ordering them from suppliers that specialize in developing and distributing a wide range of forms for business use, and by developing the forms in house. Page layout and design software and laser printers have made the task of developing and designing in-house forms easier. The following administrative forms are commonly used by landscape architecture offices:

- Time cards
- Phone message forms
- Call records forms
- Photocopy records
- Blueprint records
- Travel report forms
- Transmittal letter forms
- Fax transmittal forms
- Reimbursable expense forms
- Mileage report forms
- Petty cash forms
- Supply requisition forms
- Routing forms

Developing and designing a form is best accomplished by first recognizing the need for a form and second by utilizing a forms content and usage checklist. The following content and usage checklist for a landscape architecture office is adapted from Donald B. Tweedy's checklist in his book *Office Records Systems and Space Management*.

1. What is the purpose of the form?
2. Is there a clearly established need for the form?
3. Could the purpose of the form be served by a different type of document?
4. Are there any legal questions related to the use of the form?
5. Have all of the office staff been consulted about the use and design of the form?
6. Have office staff been asked to review drafts of the form prior to final production? Has the form been tested under all expected working conditions?
7. Has the form been used on a trial basis to work out the kinks prior to formally introducing the form?
8. Who fills out the form?
9. How is the form used?
10. Is the form to be mailed? How does it relate to envelope sizes?
11. Will the form require multiple copies to be filed?
12. Does the form require instructions for its use?
13. What is the source of errors expected in using the form?
14. How frequently will changes to the form be required? Monthly? Annually? Never?
15. Is folding required?
16. Does the form require sorting?
17. Does using the form require any special devices or equipment?
18. Is the size or layout of the form limited by available equipment or business machines?
19. Can the form be purchased from a supplier at less cost than developing it in house?
20. Is there an existing format that can be adapted for developing and designing the form?
21. Is information on the form copied onto other documents?
22. If information is copied onto other documents, how does the process influence the design of the form?
23. Is the sequence of data on the form convenient for copying onto other documents?

Job No.: _____
Date: _____

Ace Landscape Architects A

LETTER OF TRANSMITTAL

TO: _____
_____
_____

Attn: _____
RE: _____

We are sending you

☐ Attached   ☐ Under separate cover via: _____
☐ Prints   ☐ Plans   ☐ Specifications   ☐ Reports   ☐ Copy of letter
☐ Other _____

These are transmitted as checked below

☐ for approval   ☐ for your use   ☐ as requested   ☐ for review and comment
☐ Other _____

Remarks: _____
_____
_____
_____
_____
_____
_____
_____
_____

Signed: _____

Copy to: _____

If enclosures are not as noted, kindly notify us at once.
PHONE NUMBER (520) 622-2302 FAX: (520) 622-8270

ADDRESS: 2440 E. Broadway Blvd., Tucson, AZ 85719

FIGURE 7-4. Example of a letter of transmittal form.

Ace Landscape Architects

Landscape Architecture
Site Planning
Park & Recreation Planning
Urban Design
Environmental Assessment
Irrigation Design
Water Conservation Planning
Desert Revegetation Programs

FAX TRANSMITTAL

ACE Job No.: _____

Number of pages including cover:_____

Date:_____

To:_____

Company:_____

FAX No.:_____

☐ FAX Transmittal Only
☐ FAX Transmittal. Hard copy to follow by mail.
☐ FAX Transmittal. Hard copy to be delivered by
   messenger.

Sender:_____

RE.:_____

NOTE: _____
_____
_____
_____
_____
_____
_____
_____
_____
_____

2440 E. Broadway Blvd.
Tucson, AZ 85719
(520) 622-2302
FAX (520) 622-8270

FIGURE 7-5. Example of a fax transmittal form.

Travel Expense Report

Name: _____ Nature of
Job Number: _____ Business: _____
Destination: _____ Travel Dates: _____

Expenses:	Day 1 Date:	Day 2 Date:	Day 3 Date:	Day 4 Date:	Day 5 Date:	Day 6 Date:	Totals
A. Company Expenses:							
Airfare							
Rental Car							
Other Transportation							
Lodging							
Meals							
Miscellaneous							
A. Subtotal Company Expenses:							
B. Employee Reimbursables:							
Airfare							
Rental Car							
Other Transportation							
Lodging							
Meals							
Miscellaneous							
B. Subtotal Employee Reimbursables:							
C. Daily Total Expenses:							

NOTE: Attach receipts for all expenses.

Less advances: _____
Less company charge receipt: _____
Amount due employee: _____
Ammount due company: _____

Employee Signature: _____
Date: _____
Authorized by: _____

FIGURE 7-6. Example of a travel expense report form.

24. Is the form to be filled out by hand, by type-writer, or computer printer? Does the form require both electronic and hard-copy formats?

25. How is the form to be filed?

26. Does the form have a specific space requirement for filing?

27. Does the form require a special paper for handling, permanence, or writing?

28. How long is the form to be kept?

29. Have the working conditions for filling out the form been considered? Will the form be filled out while the user is outdoors on a site, for instance?

30. Can the form be designed with the firm's logo or other identifying element on it?

31. What can be done to simplify the form?

32. What can be done to reduce the cost of the form?

33. What type of writing instrument is likely to be used to fill out the form?

34. Does the form need to be bound in a loose-leaf folder? Can it be made up in tablet format with a gummed edge?

35. Is the size appropriate for related business machines, filing cabinets, or printers?

36. Does the heading or title make the purpose of the form clear?

37. Can the title be made briefer?

38. Will the use of color, shading, or stippling aid the usefulness of the form?

39. Is the wording of questions concise and clear?

FIGURE 7-7. Example of an office
routing form.

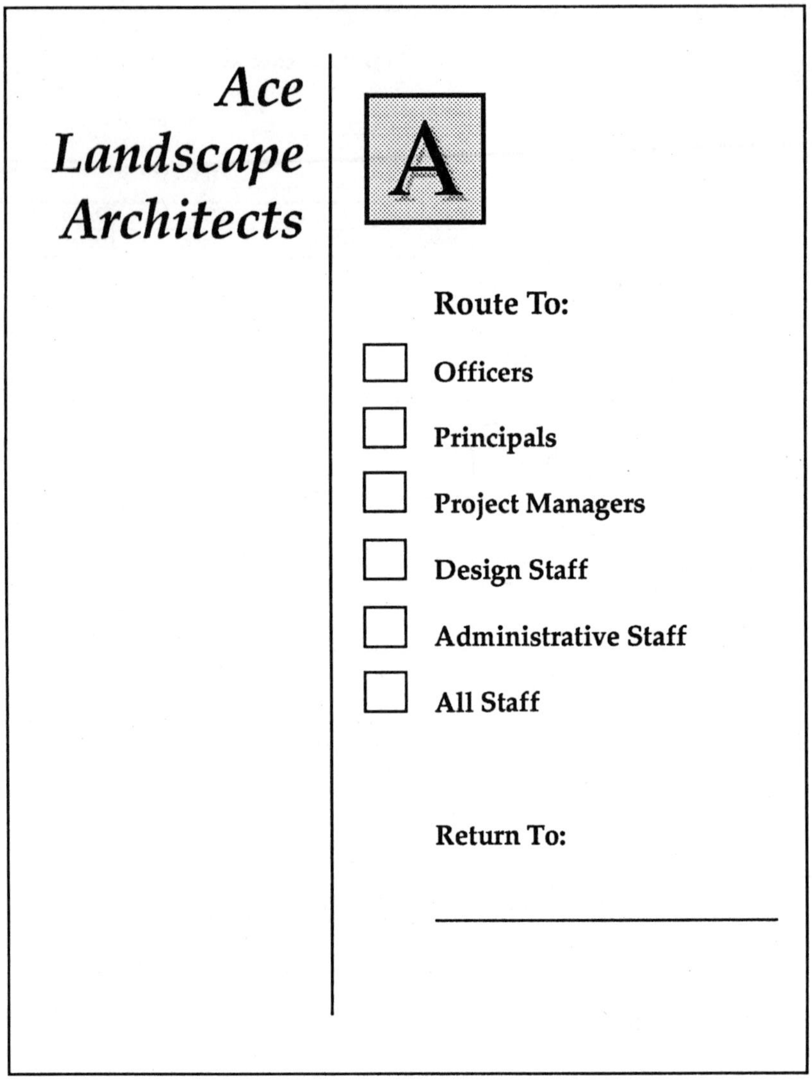

Ace Landscape Architects

A

Route To:

☐ Officers

☐ Principals

☐ Project Managers

☐ Design Staff

☐ Administrative Staff

☐ All Staff

Return To:

_____

40. Would preprinting likely entries help?
41. Are type style, boldface, italics, and other typographic techniques used to give the appropriate emphasis?
42. Is the layout convenient for entering information? Does it facilitate a logical sequence of thought?
43. Does the form require mathematical computations? Is the design logically set up for the mathematical computations?
44. Does the form have to be designed to work with a window opening in an envelope?
45. Have folding marks or instructions been provided if the form requires folding (Tweedy 1986)?

Landscape Architecture Office Files and Records Management

Project Data and Project Information Files

There are two general types of project filing requirements in the landscape architecture office: active projects files and dead project files.

Active Project Files

Active project files, used for active project data, contracts, and active filing needs, are accessed by all of the office administrative and professional staff on a daily basis. Small offices may have several filing cabinets, organized by job numbers, that are open and accessible by all of the firm's staff. Sometimes the office secretary is assigned the task of retrieving and refiling files in order to have central control over the ongoing retrieval and refiling of project materials. Larger offices may have a file checkout system controlled by a filing clerk, and all retrieval and filing of project files will go through the clerk. Active project computer files may also be accessed by professional staff through computer network systems or floppy disks shared by the project staff. The larger the office, the greater the control procedures required for shared computer files to prevent data from accidentally being lost and to guard against glitches and computer viruses.

All of the information and data related to the execution of a design project should be in an active project file—filed under the project's job number. Some projects may be very small and have little information to file. In these cases, there may be a single file folder and/or computer folder for project-related materials. Many projects, however, tend to build up large quantities of paper materials and electronic data that need to be filed, and breaking the project records into subfiles is helpful. Typical project file subfiles may include the following:

- correspondence
- transmittals
- project data and notes
- phone memorandums
- contracts and contractual matters such as insurance records
- subconsultant records
- billing
- construction administration, including
  field notes
  weekly progress meeting reports
  submittals and approvals
  meeting notes
  correspondence and transmittals
  change orders
  pay applications
  telephone memos

All project-related materials should be filed no matter how insignificant they may seem, and all project-related materials should have the job number inscribed on them. It is always surprising to design office staff how often materials in a project file need to

be found and referenced, not only for working on that specific project, but also for working on other projects.

Construction administration files are often filed in a loose-leaf binder under the headings cited above. A loose-leaf file can be kept by the professional staff member who is carrying out the construction administration services. This system works well because of the regular need for the construction administrator to refer back to memos, phone records, pay requests, change order requests, submittal approvals, and all other information generated during the construction process. After construction is completed, the loose-leaf record of project construction can be transferred to filing cabinets for archiving, or it can be left in the loose-leaf file itself and placed on a shelf with other completed construction administration files.

Dead Project Files

Dead files, or project archives, may not be accessed on a daily basis, but there is a recurring need to access archived project materials. Completed project files, or dead files, contain project data that are often very useful because it applies to similar situations in current project work. Dead file information may need to be accessed to fulfill requests for information by a former client or for problems related to completed work such as third-party lawsuits or claims made on professional liability insurance. Whereas dead files do not require the regular access that active project files do, the information in dead files is usually quite important when the need for the information occurs.

Dead project files and project archives are a headache for office administrative managers. The typical landscape architecture office generates a very large quantity of hard copy, drawings, and other project-related information such as photographs and negatives. The storage space requirements, even the actual storage techniques, such as how the drawings and reproducible plans are filed, present a constant challenge to landscape architecture office administrators. Sometimes archive storage requirements are large enough and office space so limited that the firm will need to use off-site locations. Flat files and hanging files are used for archiving project drawings and reproducibles. Storage cartons and round storage tubes are other methods used for long-term filing of drawings. Filing cabinets are used for hard-copy and photo morgues. Cardboard files are often used for older archived projects in an attempt to keep down the cost of storing

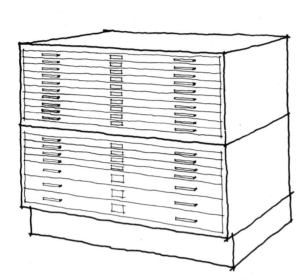
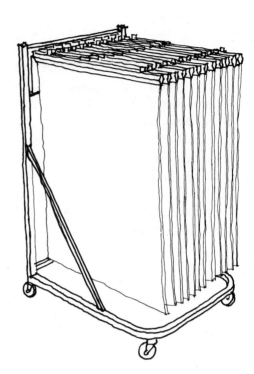

FIGURE 7-8. Flat files and hanging files are very useful for filing drawings in progress and archiving drawings.

completed project information. Microfiche is a very useful method for archiving project information and reducing physical storage costs. Microfiche is expensive, however, and many owners do not want to pay for the cost of the photography and the viewing equipment necessary for information retrieval. Other newer electronic filing systems, such as computerized scanners, are also available and used when cost is not a factor.

The simplest and most economical method of storing dead project files is the system adopted by the typical landscape architecture office. This usually entails moving active hard-copy files and drawings to archive storage areas. If this system is used, hard-copy project files and drawings should be cleaned out before putting the material in dead project files. Only the absolutely essential project materials should be archived, and duplicate materials should be weeded out of the files. Computer files should be cleaned up and moved to floppy-disk files, magnetic tapes, or storage hard drives that are physically located in computer archives.

Some offices keep all of their archived project files covering every project completed by the office from day one. Keeping all project records from day one, however,

will ultimately result in overwhelming storage requirements. If storage space is not costly, storing all of an office's project records will provide a valuable historical perspective on the planning and design output of the office. Just think, for instance, how little we would know about Frederick Law Olmsted if he had not kept the records of most of his work. In most offices, however, the dead project files should be cleaned out periodically, and the oldest project files may be eliminated from the office archives. There is one time when the need to reduce and clean out project archives becomes most important—when the office moves or merges with another office. Moving provides a very good incentive to lighten the load of dead project files.

General Design Files

Landscape architecture offices have a need for filing general design data, standard specifications, and construction details. The general design information is used over and over again on projects, but adapted specifically to the needs of each project. These general design files may be hard-copy files and electronic files. Most offices keep a hard-copy file and an electronic file of graphic symbols, notes, and construction details, which can be accessed by the firm's landscape architects and tailored to project-specific conditions. Internet tie-ins to on-line design services, such as LandNET, offered by ASLA, are becoming more readily accessible and can provide construction details, specifications, and other design information.

Personnel Records

A personal file for every person hired by the landscape architecture office is a necessity for keeping track of the personnel information required for every employee. Personnel records for each employee include the following information:

1. Home address, phone number, and whom to notify in case of an emergency
2. Information on federal and state withholding taxes (e.g., W-2 forms)
3. Completed job application form
4. Employment agreement
5. Résumé
6. Work review records
7. Personnel memos and records
8. Records of pay increases
9. Information about the employee's achievements while employed at the firm
10. Reprimands
11. Record of termination of employment
12. Any other information, such as newspaper clippings, related to the employee's activities while employed by the firm

The personnel file is important not only while the employee is actively working for the landscape architecture office but also after the employee leaves the firm. Requests for information are common long after the departure of the employee. Requests for references from future employers, verification of employment dates for mortgage companies, requests for information by the IRS and state boards of technical registration, and requests by the former employee for information relative to the period he or she worked for the firm or for recommendation letters are some of the reasons why access to personnel records continue after the employee has left the firm.

Financial Records

Administrative staff and owners of the firm need to access the office financial files on a daily basis. These files contain all of the data and information necessary to keep the financial records of the company and provide information for bookkeeping. The best time to update many of these financial files is at the beginning of each new calendar or fiscal year. Because many of the financial records are kept on a monthly basis, the files will be ready to be used if each month is set up at the beginning of the year. Information normally kept in financial files includes

- monthly records of payables and copies of checks written for the payables
- monthly records of revenue
- deposit slips
- vendor payable files
- subconsultant payable files
- monthly P&L statement and balance sheet
- checking account balance and records of checks written
- travel report records
- records of long-term notes and amortization schedules

Payables Records. During the course of each month, the landscape architecture office receives numerous invoices from suppliers of goods and services to the firm, as well as invoices for rent, utilities, telephone, and the like. These invoices and copies of checks written to pay these invoices are kept in a monthly file because the information is normally received on a monthly basis and the records are used to create monthly financial statements.

Office administrative and financial computer systems also allow the printing of a monthly payables report that is included as a part of the monthly payables records.

Revenue Records. Invoices are usually sent to clients on a monthly basis. Copies of invoices are filed in a billing file that provides a running account of billings to the client—a billing history. Revenue is received primarily in the form of checks. Copies of the checks and the invoices the clients are paying are kept in files. The firm's bookkeeper or accountant uses these monthly records of income in preparing the monthly financial statements.

Vendor Files. Each landscape architecture office uses a variety of vendors that provide goods and services to the firm and usually bill for those goods and services on a monthly basis. A file should be set up for each vendor in order to track the copies of bills of sale and merchandise received against future invoices and statements. Copies of checks made out to the vendors may also be kept in the files.

Subconsultant Files. If a landscape architecture firm is active as a prime consultant, it will employ a number of specialty subconsultants such as structural engineers, electrical engineers, archaeologists, botanists, habitat consultants, and others on a regular basis. Information should be kept in the project's contract or billing file, usually filed by the name of each subconsultant, for all of the contract and financial activity related to subconsultants serving on each project. These files should contain copies of invoices, copies of checks used to pay these invoices, and information relating to any adjustments made in amounts owed to the subconsultant. The information not only is used in preparing monthly financial statements and project progress reports, but also provides the data for annual tax-related tasks such as preparing federal 1099 forms.

Another area of subconsultant information associated with marketing and job development is the data, résumés, and materials kept on file for the firms that the landscape architecture office uses for subconsulting activities. The subconsultants information file may be kept up to date and administered by clerical staff, but the principals of the firm and those who assemble and produce proposals are the main users of the information. Generally the best ways to keep subconsultant's information on file is alphabetically by discipline or name of the firm. Materials may include the subconsultant's SF254, SF255, résumés, firm qualifications, cut sheets, and brochures.

Developing a computer database filing system is a good way to organize subconsultant files by discipline if the landscape architecture firm has deep files of a wide range of subconsultants. Preliminary screening of firms by discipline can be made before sifting through their filed hard-copy materials or before making contact with a possible subconsultant the firm wishes to include in a proposal.

Monthly P&L Statement and Balance Sheet. The financial information filed on a monthly basis culminates in the preparation of the monthly financial statement and other financial reports. The completed financial reports are filed in the respective monthly financial files. The financial managers and owners of the firm may want to keep a copy of the monthly P&L statement and the balance sheet handy in a loose-leaf file at their own desks because these summaries of the financial condition of the firm are frequently referred to by managers.

Checking Account. Today's landscape architecture office normally keeps records of checks written and deposits into checking accounts as computer files. Integrated computer financial software or spreadsheets are used to track deposits and checks. Most firms keep hard copies of monthly reports.

Travel Reports. Most landscape architecture firms today involve travel as part of the business practice. Records of business travel costs and reimbursement to office staff should be kept on both electronic and hard-copy files. These records are filed on a monthly basis, and copies are filed in the project billing files so the travel costs may be invoiced to the client.

Records of Long-Term Notes and Amortization Schedules. Long-term notes for each piece of equipment, vehicle, printer, computer, or copier, as well as other long-term notes for loans to corporate officers and stock purchase programs, should have an amortization schedule prepared for them and filed. These amortization records may be generated by in-house financial managers and kept in computer files. Financial managers and owners frequently refer to the amortization schedules in their work of managing the firm's short- and long-term finances.

Governmental Requirements

Local, state, and federal levels of government have a plethora of requirements that landscape architecture offices need to comply with in order to do business.

Local governments, for example, require a business license, have purchasing departments with annual reporting requirements, and may require that an affirmative action report be completed and updated on an annual basis.

State governments also have requirements for annually updating information with the state's procurement office. State departments of transportation, environmental quality, water resources, or parks and recreation may also have specific rules or requirements for doing business with them.

The federal requirements include annual updating of SF254 forms used in procuring federal consulting work and tax records, which will be discussed in greater depth later in this chapter.

Information for each of the governmental agencies and their requirements for doing business should be kept on file. If an agency requires an annual report, keeping last year's report and other materials in the file will simplify the annual update.

Marketing Information

Marketing staff, principals, and project managers engaged in marketing and job development in the landscape architecture office will have a wide variety of materials to keep on file. Company brochures, project cut sheets, slide files, videotapes, copies of old proposals, presentation boards, and supplies and materials used in putting proposals together are some of the marketing materials that require administration and filing in the professional landscape architecture office.

Project cut sheets can be conveniently filed by type-of-work category. Much of the marketing materials are best filed or located in a separate marketing area, office, or studio geared toward marketing and sales. The marketing section of the office may have lots of storage space for the materials mentioned in the preceding paragraph, as well as other equipment such as computers equipped with the types of software helpful in proposal preparation and a hole puncher for spiral binding. A separate area in the office for marketing functions provides space for developing and producing much of the firm's marketing materials. Many firms now produce their own cut sheets, brochures, and proposals in house using word processing and page layout software.

Drawings in Progress

Flat files, vertical hanging files, desk drawers, and side throw tables are some of the most commonly used methods of filing drawings in progress. For projects with a large number of sheets, a flat file in which plans in progress can be laid flat after working on them is a necessity. CADD files will also have to be maintained for work in progress, but the reproducible original

drawings that take up the greatest amount of space cause the filing headache. Periodically cleaning out filing drawers that hold drawings of completed projects and moving these drawings to project archives is an important housekeeping procedure. If the office uses a photo storage system, this is the time that the plans should be sent to be photographed for the microfiche archive files.

Secretarial Information and Supplies

There is a wide variety of business equipment, office supplies, and administrative paraphernalia, such as a mail scale or boxes of labels, used by office administrative staff in running the day-to-day business of the office. No office can run without these materials and supplies, and they need to be filed and stored.

Vacations, Holidays, and Sick Leave

An established office with a number of employees will have a fair amount of record keeping associated with administering vacations, holidays, and sick leave. Regular reporting on the available days each employee has remaining for leave time or sick pay is very important for employees to manage their time off from work.

Vacation time may change with the number of years each staff person has been employed based on company policy. Keeping track of vacation time earned and vacation time used is an administrative task important to employees. Time should be calculated and the information should be filed in office computer data files. Hard copies should regularly be made available to employees. Vacation, leave time, sick days, and holidays taken should be read from time cards by administrative staff and subtracted from time available. Using spreadsheet software can simplify record keeping if this timekeeping function is not a part of an integrated timekeeping and financial software program.

Insurance

Office-management staff frequently refer to insurance policies. The filing system for policies should be well

ACE LANDSCAPE ARCHITECTS

MONTHLY LEAVE TIME UPDATE   ACCRUAL THROUGH SEPTEMBER 1, 1996
UPDATE: 9/30/96   UTILIZATION THROUGH SEPTEMBER 30, 1996

EMPLOYEE BY NUMBER	ANNIVERSARY DATE	MONTHS	MONTHLY ACCRUAL	HOURS ACCRUED	HOURS BORROWED	HOURS TAKEN	HOURS REMAINING
01WR	May-80	JAN-SEPT	10	90	0	51.6	38.4
04JH	Jun-82	JAN-SEPT	10	90	0	76	14
76JH	May-90	JAN-SEPT	5.33	49.97	0	26.5	23.47

LEAVE TIME CRITERIA:			
	YEAR 1	40 HOURS/YEAR	(3.33/MONTH)
	YEAR 2	64 HOURS/YEAR	(5.33/MONTH)
	YEAR 3	80 HOURS/YEAR	(6.67/MONTH)
	YEAR 4	96 HOURS/YEAR	(8.00/MONTH)
	YEAR 5+	120 HOURS/YEAR	(10.00/MONTH)

FIGURE 7-9. Example of leave time calculations carried out on a spreadsheet program for a small three-person landscape architecture office.

organized and complete, because they are often consulted during a time of stress due to loss or pending loss.

The main types of insurance required by a professional landscape architecture office are as follows:

- property insurance
- property liability insurance
- worker's compensation insurance
- disability insurance
- professional liability (errors and omissions) insurance
- life insurance and key-person insurance
- unemployment insurance
- health insurance

Property Insurance

All of the real property owned by the landscape architecture office, including real estate, vehicles, equipment, and valuable papers, should be insured for its replacement value. The firm's insurance agent will have a great deal of input on the insurance valuation of the real property owned by the landscape architecture office.

Purchasing property insurance requires attention to detail to ensure that all of the firm's property is covered. There are a large number of extensions, endorsements, and options available from insurance companies. Such options, which should be carefully considered, includes debris removal, collapse of buildings, water damage, loss due to fire, payment of extra expenses if business is interrupted, pollutant cleanup and removal, arson coverage, accounts receivable, valuable papers and records, insurance of property while off the insured premises, property in transit, property of others, damage from burglary, and employee dishonesty (stealing from the company). Insurance policies may also carry a wide range of exclusions and legal liabilities. The office insurance administrator must review all of the endorsements, options, and exclusions to see that the landscape architecture firm is purchasing the insurance coverage it needs. Automobile insurance is usually sold with the property insurance and liability coverage.

Property Liability Insurance

If a person is injured while on the firm's property or is hurt while using equipment in the firm's office, that person is covered by liability insurance purchased by the landscape architecture firm. The general liability insurance policy is often sold in tandem with property insurance and is sometimes referred to as casualty insurance.

In addition to the insurance goals of the design firm, the dollar-limit requirements for property and liability insurance may be determined by the public agencies the firm consults with. Most local, state, and federal contracting agencies have set limits of property and liability requirements. Many governmental agencies require a minimum of $1,000,000 in general liability insurance coverage.

Worker's Compensation Insurance

Employers are required by state laws to insure workers against work-related injuries. Worker's compensation insurance is provided by private insurance companies or state-authorized agencies. Most states also allow a firm to be self insured, but the firm must adhere to strict regulations.

Worker's compensation insurance premium rates are based on the amount of remuneration paid to employees times a rating factor for various job classifications. A registered landscape architect, such as a principal in a firm, will be classified at a higher rate than a draftsperson, for example. Staff who regularly go out to job sites for construction surveillance will be classified at a higher rate. The National Council on Compensation Insurance (NCCI) collects data on job-related accidents and classifies all jobs on a uniform basis. Most states adhere to the NCCI's job classification and rates reflecting the relative hazards of each job. Landscape architecture firms pay worker's compensation insurance premiums on a quarterly basis.

In the event of an accident, claims on worker's compensation policies should be made promptly. Laws require that the employer immediately tell an injured worker the name and address of the insurance carrier, the policy number, and the expiration date. Most worker's compensation insurance laws require the employer to complete a report about the injury within ten days.

Worker's compensation insurance laws cover medical treatment of the work-related injury, disability benefits, and benefits, including burial expenses, for dependents in the event of fatal injury or death caused by a work-related accident.

Workers injured on the job may experience a period of anxiety about the extent of their injury, the treatment, and potential adverse impacts on their job, their economic status, and their family's well-being. The proper handling of a worker's compensation claim by the administrative managers of the landscape architecture office, as well as the insurance carrier and state agencies, beginning at the time of the injury, can be a significant factor in promoting an early recovery, return to work, and a reduction in claim losses.

Disability Insurance

If an employee of the landscape architecture office becomes disabled and cannot return to work because of the injury, disability insurance will provide for the well-being of the insured. *Disabled* means that because of injury or sickness one cannot perform the material duties of one's gainful occupation for which one is reasonably trained or educated. Disability benefits are normally paid as a percentage of base monthly earnings. The benefit may be stated as an amount equal to the lesser of (1) 60 percent of one's basic monthly earnings, or (2) 70 percent of your basic monthly earnings less other income benefits, or (3) the maximum monthly benefit.

When the insurance administrator of a landscape architecture firm negotiates and renews disability insurance coverage, he or she must resolve many questions about the terms of the coverage:

- When do disability benefits become payable? Is there an elimination or waiting period? How is the benefit calculated?
- Will the paid benefits have exclusions of other income benefits (e.g., social security benefits or worker's compensation insurance)?
- What happens if one tries to return to work and becomes disabled again (recurrent disability)?

- What happens to the benefit upon the employee's death?
- What disabilities, if any, are not covered by the plan?
- Are there exclusions for preexisting conditions?
- Are there limitations due to mental illness, alcoholism, and drug addiction?
- Is one covered if one is not in active employment due to injury or sickness?
- If one's employment ends, can the disability policy be converted to individual coverage?
- When must the insurance carrier be notified of a claim? Must proof of claim be given?
- What happens if facts are misstated during the application period?

Disability insurance is a reasonably inexpensive and valuable company benefit. It should be provided by the landscape architecture firm, perhaps jointly sharing costs with eligible employees. One last thing to remember about disability insurance is to pick a policy or plan that has a good track record and is easy to administrate. Call references and talk to representatives of firms that have made disability claims to see how easy and hassle free the claim process is.

Professional Liability Insurance

Insuring the firm's landscape architects against damages arising from the conduct of professional practice, including third-party claims made years after a project has been constructed, is the reason for professional liability insurance, sometimes called errors and omissions (E&O) insurance.

Professional liability insurance companies indemnify insured policyholders for errors, omissions, or negligent acts. A professional liability insurance policy usually provides coverage to defend the insured policyholder by providing legal counsel until limits set by the policy are exhausted. The professional liability insurance business commonly writes E&O policies in such a manner as to spell out the exclusions of the policy, or what is not covered by the insurance, rather than what is covered by the insurance.

There are a number of reasons why an E&O policy uses exclusions rather than describing in detail what the coverage includes. First, E&O insurance providers do not want to provide coverage that is found in other types of insurance policies such as liability insurance, worker's compensation insurance, and disability insurance. Second, some kinds of risks, such as joint ventures, are not easy to define. Third, some risks, such as insuring activities dealing with toxic materials, are just too risky. Finally, E&O insurance providers are not interested in insuring dishonest, fraudulent, or criminal acts. Typical exclusions include worker's compensation, asbestos, joint ventures, computer errors, design-build coverage, punitive damages, quantity takeoffs, and cost estimates.

Most professional liability insurance policies are "claims-made policies." They cover claims made during the period of coverage. However, one policy might define a claim as "knowledge of circumstances" that might lead to a demand for money to remedy the error. Another policy might define a claim as the actual "demand for the remedy." Both of these definitions have problems associated with professional practice. In the first, a landscape architecture firm might have knowledge of a possible E&O claim while its deductible on its E&O policy is $25,000. Because the firm's insurance administrator is concerned, he or she notifies the insurance company. Subsequently, the E&O insurance comes up for renewal and the deductible is reduced to $5,000. After the renewal, the claim is actually made against the E&O policy, leaving the firm with the larger deductible because the firm notified the insurance carrier based on the "knowledge of the circumstances" that could possibly have led to the claim rather than waiting until the actual claim was made. In the second definition, the firm's insurance administrator may not want to change E&O insurance providers if the administrator "knows of circumstances" that might lead to a claim. A new insurer will ask about situations about which the administrator "has knowledge of circumstances," which could lead to a claim. Such circumstances are not likely to be covered.

Another issue when procuring professional liability insurance coverage is the retroactive date of the coverage. A claims-made policy usually applies to errors or omissions made prior to the first day of coverage. This prior-acts coverage is an important part of negotiating the E&O coverage. The prior-acts coverage is triggered by a retroactive date. Coverage is provided after this date. Before the retroactive date, prior acts are not covered. Obviously, an older retroactive date is more desirable to the landscape architecture firm.

Needless to say, the landscape architecture office administrator in charge of insurance has a difficult task evaluating the coverage of prospective E&O policies. The administrator should obtain annual quotes from a number of professional liability insurers. The administrator should evaluate the exclusions in each policy in detail to truly understand the impact that coverage, or excluded coverage, has on the exposure of the firm. Costs should also be carefully evaluated. Costs can vary as much as 200 percent among various companies. Office insurance administrators should work with an insurance agent who has a special interest and experience in working with design firms and who specializes in professional liability insurance. Using an experienced agent does not cost more and may save the firm a large amount of premium costs in the long run. Obtaining quotes from more than one E&O insurance company results in a backup if the firm's E&O insurance carrier raises premiums, goes out of business, or reduces or refuses coverage.

Life Insurance and Key-Person Insurance

Most landscape architecture firms provide and pay for life insurance for the key people in the office. This is done primarily to ensure that the loss of a key person does not cause significant disruption to the operations of the firm. For example, a firm has two key partners. One partner is the firm's lead marketer and is very effective at client development and maintenance. The second partner provides the lead in design and production of construction documents. If one or the other unexpectedly dies, the firm's ability to function might be seriously disrupted. If both partners maintain life insurance policies with each other as the beneficiary, the death benefit can be used as the capital needed to reorganize the firm to carry on business again.

Life insurance policies are also available for many of the firm's employees through add-ons to other policies such as disability insurance, which often includes a small life insurance benefit as part of the policy. In addition, most credit card companies also provide for life insurance benefits with the use of the credit card.

Unemployment Insurance

One of the most useful insurance coverages, especially for young professionals and new hires in a landscape architecture office, is unemployment insurance. The federal government and state governments insure employees against loss of employment. This insurance coverage is paid for by the employer. Most employers pay both a state and federal unemployment tax. Federal unemployment tax, or FUTA, is paid entirely by the employer and is due annually. Employers use form 940 for reporting purposes and pay taxes on the first $7,000 in wages paid to each employee.

If you are an employee and have lost your job, filing for unemployment insurance is usually handled through the state department of economic security. If you decide to file for unemployment insurance benefits, do it soon after employment is terminated, because most benefits are paid only after filing and are not paid for any time out of work before the unemployment claim is actually filed.

States have eligibility requirements and a base period of time that an employee must work in the year prior to making the claim for unemployment insurance. The benefit is usually figured as a percentage of the wages paid during the base period with a maximum cap such as $165 per week. The maximum amount depends upon the total amount of wages reported in the last base period.

The unemployment insurance claimant must meet a considerable number of responsibilities in order to collect the unemployment insurance benefits. The claimant must register for work in the state work-referral system and must be ready to accept work if offered. The claimant must make an active, serious, and continuing effort to seek work. If the claimant has performed any work or has earned money or has received money from pension, annuity, or retirement plan while collecting unemployment insurance, he or she must report any such income. Employees who have lost their job can normally collect unemployment benefits for one year.

Health Insurance

Providing cost-effective health insurance coverage for the landscape architecture firm is one of the most time-consuming activities for the office business administrator. Health insurance is the one type of insurance used most often by the staff of the landscape architecture office. Therefore, making an informed decision about coverage for the firm's employees is important. The benefits offered by the health plan and the amount the firm's employees must pay out of pocket for medical care and prescriptions differ substantially from plan to plan.

In general, there are two broad categories of health-care options:

1. fee-for-service plans
2. managed-care options

Fee-for-Service Plans

Fee-for-service health plans are the most traditional form of commercial health insurance available. Under these plans, the insured chooses his or her own doctors and hospitals. Many of these plans require deductible amounts and coinsurance payments. The insurer pays claims for reasonable and customary medical charges for physician and hospital care. Major medical plans are the most common type of fee-for-service coverage provided by employers.

Fee-for-service health plans are characterized by three major features:

1. Employer and employees share the cost of health insurance premiums.
2. Employees have complete freedom to select the medical care providers of their choice.
3. The insurance company pays only the allowable claim.

Fee-for-service health plans have long been an important type of employee benefit because of their flexibility and the freedom of the insured to choose health coverage providers.

Managed-Care Plans

A managed health-care plan integrates the delivery of health-care services with how the services are paid for. There are significant financial incentives integrated in the plan for the participants to use the doctors, health-care providers, and procedures associated with the plan. The two most common types of managed-care options are preferred provider organizations (PPOs) and health maintenance organizations (HMOs). Most managed-care plans share the following basic characteristics:

1. The provider organization arranges for physicians, hospitals, clinics, and other providers to supply a comprehensive set of health-care services to insured members of the plan.
2. The provider organization sets up formal programs for the selection of medical practitioners and for quality assurance.
3. The provider organization establishes incentives for the insured participants to use the services and procedures associated with the plan.

Preferred Provider Organizations (PPO).   Typically, a PPO consists of groups of physicians and hospitals that contract with employers or third-party administrators to provide health-care services to the insured persons. The providers accept pre-negotiated fees and payment for services provided. The PPO may be sponsored by a group of hospitals, a group of doctors, a third-party administrator such as Blue Cross and Blue Shield, or any other insurance entrepreneur.

Health Maintenance Organizations (HMO). The name *health maintenance organization* was coined in the early 1970s and was given to the 1973 federal legislation that promoted the development of the HMO concept. Basically, an HMO is an organized system for providing health care, usually in a certain geographic area. An HMO provides an agreed-upon set of health maintenance services, as well as illness and injury treatment services, to the enrolled participants in exchange for a set premium. Nonparticipants are excluded from any services, even if they can pay full value for the services. These plans provide services that are agreed upon in advance and generally require no deductible payments. Some plans may require a nominal co-payment for doctor visits and prescriptions. In recent years, many HMOs have offered plan options that feature higher co-payments in efforts to contain the overall costs of employer-provided health-care plans.

Choosing a Health Insurance Plan

Selecting health coverage and a health insurance company is a time-consuming and important task for the landscape architecture office. The firm's administrator must develop a good working relationship with an insurance agent who specializes in health insurance plans, and work with the agent to determine the type of plan (HMO, PPO, or major medical, for example) most suitable to the landscape architecture office. The plan must be acceptable to the firm's owners and principals, as well as the employees. The best way to find out what type of plan coverage the firm's employees want is to ask them. Accessibility of services, costs, and the range of coverage will be the key concerns of most employees.

Once the type of plan desired by the firm is decided, the agent will be very helpful in assisting the firm's insurance administrator in selecting the actual provider company. The insurance administrator should evaluate how easy it is to make a claim, as well as how willing the provider company is to pay claims. Checking references on a prospective health insurance company is also a good idea. Most states have an insurance department that regulates insurance companies and receives complaints about insurance companies. Checking with the state department during the process of selecting a health insurance company is a good idea (Health Insurance Association of America 1991).

Price should not be the primary consideration in selecting a health insurance company. The service provided and the help you receive from the company's agent are also important. The following checklist is a starting place for determining the firm's needs and comparing health insurance plans and services:

HEALTH INSURANCE COMPANY COMPARISON CHECKLIST

1. What are the needs of the landscape architecture firm's employees?
   Number of employees _____
   Number of employees
      with dependents _____
   Age of employees _____
   Sex of employees _____
   Employees and dependents
      of childbearing age _____
   Employees and dependents with
      preexisting medical conditions _____
   Employees with high-risk
      health problems _____
   Employees with health insurance available
      from other sources _____
2. What percentage of coverage will be paid for by the landscape architecture firm, by the employee?
3. What medical services does the firm want to have covered (yes or no)
   Inpatient hospital services

   Outpatient services
   Psychiatric and mental-health coverage
   Drug and alcohol abuse treatment
   Nursing care
   Home health care
   Hospice care
   Dental provisions
   Maternity care
   Prescription drugs
   Eye care and coverage
   Preventative care and checkups
   Chiropractic care
   Medical tests and X-rays
   Mammograms
   Cancer coverage
4. Does the plan contain exclusions for preexisting conditions that will affect employees?
5. Are there service limitations or exclusions that will affect employees?
6. What are the cost-reduction options available to the firm (i.e., higher co-payment, higher deductible)?
7. What is the total cost of the policy?
8. Is the cost equal for each employee?
9. Is the employer required to pay for a certain percentage of the coverage?
10. What is the deductible rate structure?
11. Is the premium rate guaranteed? If it is guaranteed, for how long?
12. What has been the rate increase history for the company?
13. What will happen to premiums if one of the firm's employees has a major claim?
14. What is the process for handling individual claims?
15. How often will the landscape architecture firm be billed? Monthly? Quarterly?
16. How much administrative time and effort will be required of the landscape architecture firm?
17. Will the agent be available to meet with the employees of the landscape architecture firm?
18. How long will it take to process a claim?
19. What do references say about the insurance company?
20. What do the landscape architecture firm's employees say about the insurance company after listening to the explanation of services provided (Health Insurance Association of America 1991).

COBRA Requirements

In 1986, the federal government passed Public Law 99-272, Title X, which requires that most employers with fifteen or more employees offer temporary health insurance coverage when an employee loses group health coverage due to a reduction in hours of employment, termination of employment, or because the firm has filed for reorganization protection under Chapter 11 of the federal bankruptcy laws. The spouse of an employer also has the right to protection under the law if health insurance coverage is lost due to death of the spouse, termination of the spouse's employment, divorce, legal separation, filing for Chapter 11 bankruptcy protection by the firm, or if the spouse becomes eligible for medicare. A dependent child of the employee also has rights to coverage under the law.

The law requires a landscape architecture firm to notify an employee who has lost coverage, or the employee's spouse or dependent children, of the employee's rights for access to continued health insurance coverage. Under the terms of the law, the employee who has lost coverage has up to sixty days from the date of lost coverage to notify the landscape architecture firm's plan administrator of the desire for continuing health-care coverage.

If the employee elects the continuing coverage, the landscape architecture firm is required to provide equal coverage for up to thirty-six months unless the employee is terminated or hours are reduced, in which case the required coverage must be afforded for a period of up to eighteen months. The law does not require that the landscape architecture firm pay for the coverage. The employee is responsible for payment. The law does require that the landscape architecture firm administer the cost of the coverage. The law also provides that the employee be allowed to enroll in an "individual plan" provided by the health insurance company after the eighteen-month or three-year period. Evidence of the notification of the employee of his or her rights under the law must be filed in the employee's personnel file (Health Insurance Association of America 1991).

Retirement Benefits

Landscape architecture firms use revenue and profits to provide retirement benefits for owners and employ-

ees of the firm. Whether a landscape architect works for a firm or starts his or her own firm, provisions for a pension plan or retirement benefits are an important consideration for employment. If a professional is interviewing several firms and public agencies for possible employment, the retirement benefits provided by each prospective employer should be one of the main evaluation criteria used in deciding which employer to go with. If the professional is starting a firm, providing retirement benefits or a pension plan should be one of the firm's financial goals.

Retirement benefits can help the landscape architecture firm promote the following employer and employee goals:

- *Assisting employees with retirement savings.* The foremost reason that pension plans and retirement benefits are provided is because most people find personal saving difficult to carry out of their own volition. Personal saving requires discipline. Moreover, our tax system and economy are oriented toward consumption rather than savings.
- *Providing tax deferral for owners and highly compensated employees of the firm.* Owners and highly compensated members of the firm can often benefit by sheltering a substantial part of their pre-tax income through the firm's pension plan or retirement benefits.
- *Recruiting, retaining, and rewarding employees.* All things being equal when comparing firms for employment, a prospective employee is more likely to work for the firm that has the best pension plan. A firm's retirement benefits can help recruit new employees by matching or bettering benefits offered by competitors. The firm can reward employees by tying benefits to productivity and profitability. Employees can be retained by tying maximum retirement benefits to longevity with the firm.
- *Retiring employees with dignity.* A pension plan will allow professionals who have spent a lifetime with the firm to retire with dignity without suffering a huge drop in their standard of living.
- *Encouraging productivity.* Retirement benefits that are tied to the productivity and profitability of the firm can provide employee incentives. Employee stock ownership plans are one

of the methods used to encourage productivity (Leimberg 1990).

Qualified and Nonqualified Plans

Retirement programs and pension plans are either qualified or nonqualified. Qualified plans generally receive more favorable tax benefits, but are subject to strict government regulations. Qualified plans include the Section 401(k) plans, the Simplified Employee Pension (SEP) and various profit-sharing or savings plans. Most firms that implement a pension plan or retirement benefits use a qualified plan option that is available to all employees as the firm's basic retirement benefit.

Nonqualified plans are used to provide retirement benefits to a select group of employees such as owners, principals, or key senior staff. A nonqualified plan provides benefits in addition to or instead of the firm's qualified retirement plan. Nonqualified plans do not provide the same tax benefits as qualified plans. In the nonqualified plan, the employer is not allowed to take the income-tax deduction at the time of the contribution to the savings plan. The firm must wait until the year when the employee withdraws from the savings account and actually reports income from the deferred compensation plan. Nonqualified plans are very useful to the owners of a landscape architecture firm when they want to provide deferred income to themselves or to a select group of principals, but the cost of implementing a qualified plan might be too high because a large number of the firm's employees would also have to be covered. The nonqualified plan is ideal for firms that want to provide owners and key employees with retirement income but cannot afford to implement a qualified plan, or that want to provide different or additional benefits to key employees already receiving the maximum benefits under the firm's qualified plan. One useful method of funding a nonqualified pension plan is to fund the plan through life insurance that is held by the landscape architecture firm but that benefits the employee.

Because the majority of pension plans or retirement programs sponsored by landscape architecture firms are qualified plans, the remainder of this section will be devoted to these valuable methods of saving for future security (Leimberg 1990).

Types of Qualified Pension Plans

Qualified retirement plans receive tax benefits that are not available to nonqualified plans. Payments into the qualified plan in the form of employer contributions and employee salary deductions are exempt from being taxed in the year in which they are paid. Being tax-free, the funds deposited in the pension plan account will accumulate to greater amounts over time than money saved privately, for which taxes are due on the interest earned.

Qualified retirement plans are defined either by the *contribution,* where the employer specifies an amount to be contributed, or by the *benefit,* where the employer guarantees a predetermined benefit level.

In a defined-contribution plan, the landscape architecture firm starts and maintains an account for each employee who participates in the retirement program. Benefits are paid to each employee when he or she retires or leaves the firm. The amount of the benefit is based on the amount contributed by the employer, the employee, and earnings on the account over the time the employee has participated. The employer does not guarantee that a certain amount will be in the account or a specified benefit will be available, only that a specified amount will be deposited. Typical defined-contribution plans include specific contributions based on a percentage of the employee's annual compensation, such as 10 percent, or profit-sharing plans where the employer determines the amount contributed each year based on the profitability of the firm.

In a defined-benefit plan, the landscape architecture firm starts and maintains an account for each employee who participates in the retirement program. The plan is designed to provide a specific amount of income to each participant at the normal age of retirement. These plans are difficult to design and implement because they provide adequate levels of benefits for all employees regardless of their age at the time of entry into the plan. Defined-benefit plans are actuarial. Employers must fund the plan with regular deposits determined actuarially to ensure that the plan will have sufficient funds available to pay the benefits promised to all participants. Such plans are very useful, however, for small landscape architecture firms where an older controlling employee wants to maximize tax-deferred retirement benefits, and there are a number of younger employees in the firm to help balance out the cost of the required regular deposits. Defined-benefit plans are also useful for a group of young professionals about the same age who start an office and want to have known future retirement benefits while keeping the costs to a set amount for the duration of the plan. Because the professionals are young, they will have a longer time to make the required periodic deposits, and costs will be lower in proportion to the payout at the time of retirement.

There are many ways to determine the benefits of a defined-benefit retirement plan. Common formulas are the flat amount, the percentage of salary, and the unit of time served.

Under the flat-amount formula, the plan provides a specified amount of income (such as $1,000 per month) to each participant beginning at a set retirement age (age sixty-five, for example). The plan usually requires the employee to work a minimum number of years for the firm (fifteen to twenty years is common) in order to receive the benefit, and the benefit may be prorated if he or she has worked fewer years for the firm. The flat-amount formula does not differentiate between employees with different compensation levels. This formula is appropriate when salaries are more or less equal.

Another formula provides a retirement benefit that is a percentage of the employee's salary or earnings. The formula might provide a retirement benefit of 50 percent, 65 percent, or 80 percent of the employee's annual earnings at the time of retirement. If an employee is making $80,000 at retirement and the retirement benefit is 80 percent of the salary at retirement, the benefit would be $64,000 per year. Like the flat-amount formula, percentage plans usually require the employee to work a minimum number of years for the firm (again, fifteen to twenty is common) in order to receive the full benefit, or receive prorated benefits for fewer years with the firm.

The unit-of-time-served method bases the benefit on the length of time the employee works for the firm. The formula might provide 2 percent of earnings for each year of service, and the cumulative percentage would be applied to the employee's salary when he or she retires. An employee who retires after thirty years of service with a salary of $100,000 would receive a retirement benefit of $60,000, computed by multiplying 2 percent by thirty years of service by the salary at retirement, or 60 percent of $100,000.

Defined-Contribution Plans

Defined-contribution retirement plans are the most common, and developing a defined-contribution plan for a landscape architecture firm can be stressful. There are many plan options to choose from and many alternatives for investing the funds. Selecting a plan that the firm's employees will perceive as valuable is difficult. The larger the number of employees, the greater the difficulty due to age differences and personal priorities for spending disposable income. The defined-contribution plans include

- Employee stock ownership plans (ESOPs)
- Direct contribution plan
- Profit sharing
- Savings plan
- Section 401(k)
- Simplified Employee Pension (SEP)

Employee Stock Ownership Plans

Under an ESOP, employees receive ownership in the firm in the form of stock. Obviously, the firm must be set up as a corporation under this type of qualified plan, and the corporation must be a C type. ESOPs are not permitted for Sub S corporations.

Participants' retirement account balances are stated in terms of the number of shares of stock owned. In addition to contributed shares, which are typically calculated based on a profit-sharing formula, dividends may be reinvested to purchase additional shares of stock. The plan must be nondiscriminatory, and cannot favor highly compensated members of the firm. All of the qualifications, such as vesting, funding, reporting, and disclosure, required by law must be met. In a landscape architecture firm, where the stock is typically closely held and not traded publicly, employees taking part in the plan must have the right to vote on corporate issues that include mergers and changes in corporate structure, liquidation, dissolution, and sale of substantial amounts of assets. In a closely held corporation, stock valuations must be made regularly by an independent appraiser. ESOPs are a good way to transfer ownership to employees when the owners of a landscape architecture firm are nearing retirement and wish to retain the value of the firm.

Direct Contribution Plan

One of the simplest of qualified plans, the direct contribution plan allows employers to make contributions of money to each employee's individual account under the terms of a nondiscriminatory formula. Annual contributions are usually set up as a specific percentage of each employee's salary. The plan benefits from all of the tax-deferred elements of qualified plans. Direct contribution plans are exceptionally useful when most of the landscape architecture firm's employees are young and have a long time to accumulate benefits. The plan is ideal for a new firm that is being formed by a group of associates that are young and all around the same age. The plan rewards longevity with the firm and could be one of the elements that binds the members of the firm together. In addition to the regular reporting and other qualifications that must by law be met, the plan must meet minimum annual funding requirements and is subject to penalties if the minimum is not met.

Profit Sharing

When a landscape architecture firm's profits are likely to vary from year to year, a profit-sharing pension plan should be considered. Under a profit-sharing plan, employer's contributions may be flexible. They are discretionary and based on annual profits. A specific formula is used to make contributions to each employee's individual account. The profit-sharing retirement program provides incentives for employees because account deposits theoretically increase with greater profitability of the firm. The plan is simple, easy to administer, and easy to explain to employees of the firm. One disadvantage is that the total amount of annual contributions is limited to 15 percent of the firm's total payroll. Other plans allow up to 25 percent of the annual payroll amount. Another disadvantage to employees is the unpredictability of the contributions made by the firm because the amount of the owner's contribution is discretionary. A profit-sharing plan provides for tax-deferred income if all of the qualifications, such as vesting, funding, reporting, and disclosure, required by law are met.

Savings Plan

A savings retirement plan is set up to allow the employee to make voluntary after-tax contributions that will be matched by contributions made by the landscape architecture firm. The plan allows employees to determine the funding level at which they choose to participate, but for the plan to be effective, employees must have the discipline necessary to make after-tax contributions. If the employee does not contribute sufficient funds, he or she jeopardizes an adequate retirement income. There are limitations on the amounts that may be contributed by highly paid employees.

The after-tax nature of the savings retirement plan is a disadvantage to this method of pension funding. Since the introduction of the 401(k), which allows pre-tax contributions, the popularity of the savings retirement plan has been preempted. Today, the savings plan is often provided as an add-on to the 401(k) plan (Leimberg 1990).

Section 401(k)

Through a Section 401(k) employer-sponsored pension plan, an employee of a landscape architecture firm can make contributions of up to $7,000 indexed annually in the form of tax-deferred savings. The plan must be tested annually to ensure that it does not discriminate in favor of highly compensated members of the firm. The plan may be funded entirely by salary deductions at a level elected by the employee and supplemented by the employer. However, deductions are limited to 15 percent of the employee's compensation. Employer funding is normally made on a matching-contribution basis or by a discretionary amount frequently tied to the firm's profitability.

One of the attractive provisions of the 401(k) retirement plan is the possibility of withdrawing money for a personal hardship including death, disability, funeral expenses, medical expenses, eviction from the employee's residence, and payment of tuition for the employee's family members. Withdrawal for a hardship carries a 10 percent early-distribution tax penalty. Loans, subject to a number of limitations, may also be made against the 401(k) funds.

As with all qualified pension plans, vesting, funding, reporting, and disclosure requirements must be met. One of the attractive advantages of a 401(k) plan is that each employee can choose his or her own level of funding and is not tied to a prescribed amount. As part of the administration of the plan, employees normally complete a deduction form on an annual basis.

Another attribute of the plan that benefits employees is 100 percent vesting immediately. Even if an employee leaves a firm shortly after starting work and making contributions to the plan, the funds must be transferred to the employee. The funds may be paid as a cash lump sum and are typically rolled over into another retirement account administered by a new employer or into the employee's individual retirement account (Spencer 1991).

Simplified Employee Pension (SEP)

A Simplified Employee Pension (SEP) is a retirement plan that allows self-employed individuals and employers to make contributions under an easily administered qualified plan. The employer makes the contributions to the employee's individual retirement account (IRA). A single government form (5305-SEP) can be used to satisfy the written requirements of the SEP. An employer who signs a SEP agreement with employees is not required to make contributions to the SEP-IRAs that are set up. If the employer does make contributions, however, they must be based on a written allocation formula, and they must not discriminate in favor of the highly compensated members of the firm. Up to 15 percent of each employee's annual compensation or $30,000, whichever is less, may be contributed to the SEP-IRA. Salary deductions may be used to implement the contributions.

A key benefit of the SEP program is that each employee has individual control over the investment vehicle for the account. Young professionals may choose more aggressive stock accounts for their deposits, and older employees may elect more conservative investment vehicles.

Individual Retirement Account (IRA)

An individual retirement account is a personal savings plan that offers an individual tax advantages to set aside money for retirement. IRAs can be set up and contributed to by an employer, such as a landscape architecture firm, but almost all IRAs are set up by an individual. IRAs may be set up with several types of organizations including banks, savings institutions, stock brokerage firms, mutual funds, and insurance companies, as long as the organization meets the Internal Revenue Code.

Individuals may contribute up to $2,000 or 100 percent of the individual's taxable income, whichever is less, to the IRA each year. The contributions may or may not be deductible based on the individual's total income for the year and whether the individual is also covered by an employer's retirement plan. The investment vehicle for IRA contributions is entirely controlled by the individual. Income earned in the IRA account is not taxed until the time of withdrawal after the age of fifty-nine and one-half. Early withdrawal may be made at the individual's discretion, but a 10 percent penalty will apply to the funds that are withdrawn early (IRS 1994).

No matter what type of retirement plan is provided by the landscape architecture firm, everyone should consider an IRA for funding retirement. An IRA probably will not provide for all of the long-term funds needed, but it is a retirement vehicle that should not be overlooked.

Product Literature Files and the Technical Library

Of all the files found in the landscape architecture office, the product literature files and technical reference library are the most useful to the office design and drafting staff.

Technical reference files can be sophisticated and highly developed like a general reference library, or they can be organized around a system of categories developed by the landscape architecture office staff. A well-planned filing system, however, should be user-friendly, efficient in terms of minimizing the time required to find a particular product or type of equipment, and expandable. The quantity of technical reference material and files of product literature grows as an office develops over time. Filing alphabetically by subject is an effective method for organizing technical reference files.

One very helpful file that should be maintained by the landscape architecture office is a hard copy and computer file of the firm's general construction details that are used and adapted project after project. Typically, a construction detail file is organized by types of landscape construction. Planting details, irrigation details, pavement details, walls, footings, drainage, fountains, curbs, benches, lighting, erosion control, and shade structures are common construction detail file headings.

Manufacturer's product literature should also be filed by categories. A system of loose-leaf binders works well. The firm's landscape architects will need to reference the product literature files for virtually every project that has a modest degree of difficulty or challenging design requirements. A well-organized system for filing product literature will cut down on the time required to access the files of manufacturer's information. Time saved will mean more time spent on design development, solving the problems associated with the project, and generating revenues and profits. The following categories are a starting point for organizing a landscape architecture office's product literature files:

- Alternative energy products and solar controllers
- Barbeques
- Bridges and decks
- Concrete technical information
- Docks and marinas
- Doors and gates
- Drains and drainage products
- Drinking fountains
- Exercise equipment and exercise courses
- Fences
- Fertilizers technical information
- Fountains and garden pools
- Garden ornaments
- Geotextiles and erosion control
- Handrails and railings
- Irrigation controllers
- Irrigation products, piping, and heads
- Irrigation pumps
- Landscaping products
- Lighting
- Nursery catalogs: bulbs and flowers
- Nursery catalogs: grasses
- Nursery catalogs: hydromulching products
- Nursery catalogs: nonregional
- Nursery catalogs: regional
- Nursery catalogs: seeds and seed mixes
- Outdoor art and artists
- Outdoor furniture
- Paving materials
- Planters
- Plant maintenance and growth, fertilizers
- Plants technical information
- Play structures and equipment
- Recreation surfaces

- Restrooms
- Root barriers and weed barriers
- Shelters and shade structures
- Signage and graphics
- Site furniture: bike racks and bike lockers
- Site furniture: concrete
- Site furniture: metal
- Site furniture: plastic and fiberglass
- Site furniture: wood
- Soil stabilization
- Spas and hot tubs
- Sport surfaces
- Swimming pools and equipment
- Surfaces: asphalt, concrete, gunnite
- Surfaces: stone
- Surfaces: unit pavers and brick
- Tree equipment and tree grates

Payroll Administration

Two general approaches are available for administering the landscape architecture office payroll: in-house or outside-service payroll administration.

In-House Payroll Administration

The in-house administration of office payroll normally appeals to the small firm with only a few paychecks to prepare per payroll period and the large firm that can afford to employ a full-time payroll manager or controller to administer the payroll preparation process. In-house payroll preparation is aided today by any one of a large number of computer payroll software applications. As discussed in other parts of this book, integrated business management software systems usually provide a payroll module as part of the system. If payroll administration is handled in house, tax deposits and quarterly reports must also be administered. These functions and other reporting and tax requirements add time to payroll administration over the time required for the task of making out payroll checks.

Outside Payroll Service

There are many nationally franchised and local payroll services that prepare payroll checks for a fee. In most cases the fee is reasonable, and the cost of the outside payroll service should be regularly evaluated in relation to the costs of the landscape architecture office providing payroll services in house. One of the positive qualities of using a payroll service is that the service will calculate the tax deposit requirements of the landscape architecture office. The payroll service assumes the liability for the accuracy of the tax calculations. The firm's payroll administrator merely has to deposit the appropriate funds in the firm's checking account to cover the tax requirement.

Whether payroll is calculated in house or by a contracted payroll service, the decision rests with the firm's managers. There are pros and cons for each method, and the managers and owners of each firm will decide for themselves which method is best for them.

Payroll Periods

An important decision about the administration of the landscape architecture firm's payroll is how frequently the paychecks are written. Should paychecks be issued once each week, every other week, twice monthly, or monthly? Bimonthly and every two weeks are the most frequently used payroll periods because they put money in the hands of employees at a fairly frequent rate and require less time to administer. Weekly paychecks require too much administrative effort and higher administrative costs. Monthly paychecks (check with labor laws for legality) substantially reduce administrative costs and effort, but may cause undue hardship on employees in terms of personal cash-flow requirements and personal financial management.

For other payroll administration related to bonuses and reimbursements, there is a wider variety of plans. Typically, bonuses are paid quarterly or annually. Travel expenses, mileage for personal use of employees' vehicles, and personal out-of-pocket expenses are typically reimbursed on a monthly basis.

Employer's Tax Administration

The administration of the landscape architecture firm's federal and state tax obligations is an important and time-consuming task required for the successful business management of the firm. The Internal Revenue Service (IRS) requires that an employer must withhold federal income taxes and other taxes, such as social security tax, for each employee by payroll period. States also require withholding taxes to be collected and prepaid; the methods and systems of state departments of revenue are related to the IRS's systems. The amount of taxes to be withheld for each employee is based on the gross wages paid and the withholding allowances claimed by each employee.

Landscape architecture firms also pay supplemental wages such as bonuses and overtime pay. Withholding for supplemental pay may be taken out at a flat rate of 28 percent as long as the supplemental pay is specifically identified by the employer and the appropriate withholding is made for the regular pay.

Withholding taxes must be withheld by every employer and must be paid in a timely fashion. If taxes are withheld but not deposited in a timely manner, the employer will face a penalty of 2 percent to 15 percent of the unpaid taxes. Unpaid taxes are also assessed interest. Not complying with federal and state withholding tax obligations can result in severe criminal penalties. If a firm decides to administer its own payroll and withholding-tax obligations, the firm should review the federal and state tax guides that are available and updated each year to ensure that the requirements are being met.

The administration of employer tax obligations requires excellent record keeping and can be carried out by the firm's bookkeeper, accountant, or one of many local and national payroll service companies. Using a payroll service can be one of the smartest management decisions made by the administrators of a landscape architecture firm. The payroll service not only will correctly calculate the employer's tax withholding obligations, but also will calculate the employer's tax contributions, complete the necessary tax forms (by payroll period and quarterly), and make the actual deposits. Employer tax obligations are an administrative headache that can be efficiently discharged to a payroll service, probably at less cost than they can be handled in house. In many cases, the payroll service will also assume complete responsibility for the accuracy of the tax withholding and filing of required forms. The remainder of this section will describe the main responsibilities and considerations of employer tax obligations.

Taxpayer Identification Number

All partnerships, corporations (including S corporations), and certain sole proprietors must have a federal employer identification number (EIN) to use as a taxpayer identification number. Sole proprietors may use their social security number, but must apply for and use an EIN if they pay wages to one or more employees or if they must file pension or excise tax returns. To apply for an EIN, the firm's office administrator should use Federal Form SS-5 available from the IRS. If the business form of the landscape architecture firm changes from partnership to corporation, for example, a new EIN may be required.

Employee Records

Each employer is required by law to keep all records of employment taxes (income-tax withholding, social security, medicare, and federal unemployment taxes) for at least five years. Records should contain the employer identification number, copies of the filed returns, and dates and amounts of withholding deposits made. The firm's income tax withholding records should include at least the following information:

1. Each employee's name, address, and social security number.
2. The total amount and date of each wage payment and the period of time the payment covers.
3. The amount subject to withholding tax, social security tax, and medicare tax paid on each payment date.
4. The amount of withholding, social security, and medicare tax collected on each payment and the date it was collected.
5. Copies of statements by any employee relating to residence in a foreign country, Puerto Rico, or the Virgin Islands.
6. Information about the amount of each payment made for health plans.
7. The withholding statement for each employee—Federal Form W-4.
8. Any agreement between the firm and the employee for the voluntary withholding of additional amounts of taxes.
9. Federal Form W-5 for any employees eligible for earned income credit and who wish to re-

ceive their payment in advance rather than when their income-tax return is filed.

For federal unemployment tax, the firm is required to keep the following records:

1. The total amount paid to the firm's employees during the calendar year.
2. The amount of compensation subject to the unemployment tax.
3. The amount the firm paid into the state unemployment fund.
4. Any other information required on Form 940.

Withholding Tax

Although there are a number of ways to calculate the amount of federal withholding required per pay period, the two most commonly used are the *percentage method* and the *wage bracket* tables.

Using the percentage method requires the employer to first calculate the amount of employee income for the pay period that is subject to withholding. This is determined by multiplying a single withholding allowance, specified by the federal government for each type of payroll period, by the number of allowances that the employee claims on the W-4 and subtracting this amount from the gross payroll amount. This amount is multiplied by specified percentage tables produced by the IRS for each category of payroll period. The percentage tables for one withholding allowance result in the following deductions:

Daily	$9.04
Weekly	$45.19
Biweekly	$90.38
Bimonthly	$97.72
Monthly	$195.03
Quarterly	$587.50
Semiannually	$1,175.00
Annually	$2,350.00

Withholding Example

A married employee is paid $450 per week. The employee has claimed two allowances on Form W-4. Using the percentage method, the income-tax withholding is figured as follows:

1. Total wages paid $450.00
2. One allowance = $45.19
3. Allowances claimed on W-4 =   2
4. Multiply line 2 by line 3 $90.38
5. Amount subject to withholding tax
     (subtract line 4 from line 1) $359.62
6. Tax to be withheld determined from
     the IRS tax table for married person $36.09

Using the wage bracket method requires a reasonably simple process of finding the proper IRS table for the type of payroll period and the filing status of the employee (unmarried or married).

Using the preceding example, referencing the proper tax table, the employee's withholding tax falls between $35 and $37 and can be rounded to $36.

Once the federal withholding tax requirement is calculated, the state requirement is figured as a percentage of the federal obligation.

Social Security Tax

The Federal Insurance Contribution Act (FICA) provides for a federal system of old-age, survivors, disability, and hospital insurance. The old age, survivors, and disability insurance part is financed by the social security tax. The hospital insurance part is financed by the medicare tax. Beginning in 1991, each of these taxes began being reported separately. The FICA tax is paid in equal matching amounts by both employers and employees. The employer must collect and pay the employee's part of the tax and the employer must also pay an equal matching amount of tax. For 1995, the 6.2 percent old-age, survivors, and disability insurance tax is levied on the first $61,200 of wages paid to the employee. There is no income restriction for the 1.45 percent hospital insurance (medicare) tax. In effect, the FICA tax is 7.65 percent of the first $61,200 of wages and 1.45 percent on all wages exceeding $61,200.

Earned Income Credit

Some employees may be eligible for earned income credit, and these employees may choose to have advance payments of the earned income credit added to their wages at the time the payroll check is prepared.

This tax credit is available to employees who have an adjusted gross income of less than $24,396 in 1995 and who maintain a household for a dependent child. The maximum of advance earned income credit for 1995 is $1,257. To receive the income credit in advance, the employee must fill out Federal Form W-5. Penalties and interest can be imposed on an employer if the advance earned income credit is not paid to an employee who has filed Form W-5.

Employers are required to notify employees who may be eligible for earned income credit. The employer will pay the amount of advance earned income credit from withheld income and FICA taxes. The IRS provides tables for calculating the amount of earned income credit that should be paid to the employee in each payroll period. The employer is required to report the total amount of earned income credit paid in advance on the employee's W-2. Employers that fail to pay the advance earned income credit will be liable for penalties and interest. Penalties are severe.

Tax Deposits

The employer is required not only to calculate the withholding tax obligation but also to deposit the amount of the taxes due, plus the employer's required matching amount of social security and medicare taxes, in a timely fashion in an authorized financial institution or a federal reserve bank. Deposits are due either semiweekly or monthly. If the total tax reported on Form 941 is less than $50,000 for a four-quarter look-back period, the firm is a monthly depositor. If the total tax reported on Form 941 is more than $50,000 for a four-quarter look-back period, the firm is a semiweekly depositor. The look-back period comprises the four quarters beginning July 1 of the second preceding year. Employers must pay careful attention to due dates to avoid the stiff penalties for deposits not made on time. The federal and state governments provide preprinted deposit coupons to all employers.

Deposits for monthly depositors are due by the fifteenth of the month following the month that the taxes are withheld. Semiweekly depositors must make deposits on the Wednesday or Friday of the following week depending on the payment date. If the payment day is Wednesday, Thursday, and/or Friday, the deposit is due the following Wednesday. If the payment day is Saturday, Sunday, Monday, and/or Tuesday, the deposit must be made by the following Friday.

As mentioned earlier, a payroll service can help cut down on some of the firm's IRS obligations. The payroll service will be responsible for all of the regular payroll reporting that must go to the IRS. This can provide relief from the stress of meeting the IRS requirements and give the firm's administrative and professional staff more time to spend running the firm and producing revenue.

Form 941

All employers who are subject to income-tax withholding must file Federal Form 941—the employer's quarterly federal tax return. The first quarter report covering January, February, and March is due by April 30. The next three quarterly reports are due July 31, October 31, and January 31. Penalties for not filing are very steep, and penalties for not withholding or not depositing the income tax, social security, or medicare taxes may be up to 100 percent of the unpaid taxes if the act is deemed to be willful.

Federal Unemployment Insurance

The Federal Unemployment Tax Act (FUTA), together with state unemployment systems, provides for payments of unemployment compensation to workers who have lost their jobs. Most employers pay both a federal and a state unemployment tax. Only the employer pays this tax. It is not deducted from the employee's payroll check. An employer is required to pay FUTA tax if one or more persons are employed on at least some part of one day in each of twenty or more calendar weeks during a current or preceding calendar year, or if wages of $1,500 or more are paid during any calendar quarter in the calendar year or immediately preceding year. The FUTA rate for 1995 is 6.2 percent. Employers are allowed a credit for payments made to state unemployment insurance systems of up to 5.4 percent. This tax, which is also paid entirely by the employer, is paid on only the first $7,000 of wages paid to each employee.

If the FUTA tax liability for a quarter exceeds $100, the amount must be deposited by the last day of the following month. If the FUTA liability is less than $100, it may be carried over to the next quarter to be added to the liability of that quarter to see if the $100 criteria is met. Form 940 or Form 940-EZ is used to report the employer's federal unemployment tax.

Tax Status of Certain Types of Nonwage Payments to Employees

Certain types of payments to the firm's employees may not be considered as wages subject to income-tax withholding or FICA or FUTA taxes. A few common examples of such special payments are fringe benefits, company cars, commuting and moving expenses, group life insurance, meals and lodging, employee expense reimbursements, noncash compensation for services, distributions from qualified pension plans, and employer contributions to 401(k) plans. The business administrators of the landscape architecture office need to be current on the IRS policies regarding payments to employees not subject to income-tax withholding. These policies change regularly. It is helpful to obtain the most current IRS publications relating to these nonwage payments. Whereas two examples of recent policies are discussed below, the business administrators or owners of landscape architecture offices should keep current on all IRS policies regarding nonwage payments.

Company Cars

The first test applied by the IRS is to determine whether the company car is necessary for the employee to perform his or her duties. If the answer is yes, the employee is required to substantiate use by keeping adequate records. Employers must treat the personal use of the company car as wages to the employee unless the employee reimburses the firm, at a rate normally set by the IRS, for the personal use of the car.

Moving Expenses

Reimbursing an employee's moving expenses is not subject to income-tax withholding and FICA and FUTA taxes as long as the expenses are deductible by the employee. Regulations on deducting expenses are likely to tighten in future years.

Information and Year-End Tax Returns

Some of the most common federal tax information returns required to be filed by the landscape architecture office include the following:

1. W-2 forms, used to report wages and other compensation paid to employees.
2. 1099 forms for the following:
   Interest payments
   Dividend payments
   Pension, profit-sharing, and IRA distributions
   Rent and royalty payments
   Mortgage interest
   Real estate transactions
   Payments to nonincorporated vendors and subconsultants
3. Form 5500, filed by sponsors and administrators of the firm's qualified pension and profit-sharing plans.
4. Form 8300, used for reporting cash received for any business transactions.

Backup Withholding

In almost all cases that require the filing of an information return, the employer is required to make backup withholding on the amount paid unless the person receiving the payment provides his or her tax identification number to the employer. Payments that are subject to backup withholding are generally tied to the requirements for filing the 1099 information return. 1099 forms are not required to be sent to corporations. If backup withholding is required because the payee is an individual without a tax number, the backup withholding is calculated at 31 percent. The 1099 forms must be filed by January 31 of the following year.

Filing Information Returns

All W-2 forms must be provided to employees by February 1. Copies of the W-2 forms and the transmittal form, the W-3 form, must be filed by March 1.

All 1099 form summaries must be filed with the IRS by March 1.

If a firm is large and will be filing more than 250 information or W-2 forms, the federal government may require magnetic media filing.

The penalties for not filing correct and timely information forms are severe, and the landscape architecture office administrator must be sure to comply with the IRS requirements.

State Requirements

Each state will also have its own taxing and filing requirements. In most cases, the state withholding tax requirements are expressed as a percentage of the federal amount withheld. Information returns that are required to be filed for the federal government are usually also required by the state government. Because it would be impractical to reiterate the rules and regulations for all fifty states here, the business managers of landscape architecture offices must be aware of the state's requirements.

Resources and Information

The IRS is one of the most helpful of federal agencies. It provides a wide variety of assistance via toll-free numbers and publications aimed at helping the taxpayer. Each year, the IRS publishes the *Tax Guide for Small Business* to help firms comply with the federal tax requirements. Another good IRS reference is the *Guide to Free Tax Services*. The tax administrator in every landscape architecture office should obtain these handy references.

REFERENCES

Diamond, Susan Z. 1991. *Records Management.* 2d ed. New York: AMACOM, a Division of American Management Association.

Gill, Suzanne L. 1988. *File Management and Information Retrieval Systems.* 2d ed. Englewood, Colo.: Libraries Unlimited.

Health Insurance Association of America. 1991. "Health Insurance: It's Everybody's Business: What You Need to Know; Checklist for Comparing Plans; and Holding Down Costs." Washington, D.C.: Health Insurance Association of America.

Internal Revenue Service Publications. 1994. Washington, D.C.: U.S. Government Printing Office.

Publication 334: Tax Guide for Small Business

Publication 937: Employment Taxes and Information Returns

Publication 535: Business Expenses

Publication 553: Highlights of 1994 Tax Changes

Publication 505: Tax Withholding and Estimated Taxes

Publication 917: Business Use of a Car

Publication 463: Travel, Entertainment, and Gift Expense

Publication 501: Exemptions, Standard Deductions, and Filing Information

Publication 583: Taxpayers Starting a Business

Publication 502: Medical and Dental Expenses

Publication 590: Individual Retirement Arrangements (IRAs)

Guide to Free Tax Services

Leimberg, Stephan R., and John J. McFadden. 1990. *The Tools and Techniques of Employee Benefit and Retirement Planning.* Cincinnati, Ohio: National Underwriter Company.

Lundgren, Terry D., and Carol A. Lundgren. 1989. *Records Management in the Computer Age.* Boston: PWS-Kent Publishing Company.

Office of Federal Register, National Archives and Records Administration. 1989. *Guide to Record Retention Requirements.* Washington, D.C.: Superintendent of Documents, U.S. Government Printing Office.

Spencer, Charles D., & Associates. 1991. *SEC. 401(k) Plans: An Employer's Guide to Sponsoring Cash or Deferred Plans.* Chicago, Ill.: Charles D. Spencer & Associates.

Tweedy, Donald B. 1986. *Office Records Systems and Space Management: A Guide for Administrative Services Managers.* New York: Quorum Books.

STUDY QUESTIONS AND ASSIGNMENTS

1. Contact landscape architecture firms and other A/E firms in your community and research the types of job numbering systems that the firms use. Write a paper discussing your findings and summarizing the different job numbering systems your research uncovers.

2. Divide your class into three-to-five-person teams. Obtain blank copies of Standard Forms 254 and 255. Each team is to function as a design office and prepare an SF254 and an SF255 form. Use your studio design projects and your imagination as a basis for completing the forms.

3. Using this chapter and other references, write a paper that illustrates your understanding of an effective and organized office filing system. Describe a system that you would implement if you were starting an office.

4. Divide your class into three-to-five-person teams. Each team is to function as a design office. Develop a complete system of administrative forms that would be used in the office. Consider forms for the following uses:

   - Time cards
   - Phone message forms
   - Call records forms
   - Photocopy records
   - Blueprint records
   - Travel report forms
   - Transmittal letter forms
   - Fax transmittal forms
   - Reimbursable expense forms
   - Mileage report forms
   - Petty cash forms
   - Supply requisition forms
   - Routing forms

5. Using this chapter and other references, write a paper that illustrates your understanding of the insurance obligations of a typical landscape architecture office.

6. Using this chapter and other references, write a paper that illustrated your understanding of why a landscape architecture office provides retirement benefits for its employees. Research, discuss, and evaluate various retirement plans.

7. As individuals or the class as a whole, develop a filing category system for product literature and technical references. Contact product manufacturers and obtain product information. Implement your filing system.

8. Using this chapter as a reference and also by obtaining the current IRS booklets for calculating withholding taxes, work through the process of writing payroll checks as if you were the owner of a landscape architecture office. Set up three employees with different salary levels. Calculate the federal and state tax deductions and prepare sample payroll checks for the employees.

CHAPTER EIGHT

Marketing

Marketing is a social and business management process that landscape architects use to obtain clients and projects. The need for a marketing program and careful attention to the firm's marketing process have become important to the survival and success of the landscape architecture office. A marketing program and sophisticated marketing materials will continue to be important not only for obtaining work but also for elevating the quality of projects that a firm will have an opportunity to work on. Landscape architecture firms that are effective at marketing will obtain and keep more clients and work on more interesting and high-profile projects.

Years ago, the marketing of professional services was hardly discussed in the conference rooms of landscape architecture offices. The firm obtained a client, provided quality service resulting in the successful completion of a project, and word of mouth was all that was necessary to obtain further work. Today the business environment of providing landscape architecture services is more complex and competitive. Providing quality services that result in successfully completed projects remains important, but other marketing procedures and techniques have become standard operating procedure in most landscape architecture offices.

The people, corporations, and governments that need professional landscape architecture services represent the firm's client market. The full range of professional planning and design needs represents the firm's market opportunities. If a landscape architecture firm provides professional services primarily in park planning and design, for example, its client market will center on those agencies, at all levels of government, that develop and manage parks. The types of parks to be developed represent market opportunities.

The landscape architecture firm that is able to differentiate itself from its competitors will be a market leader as long as the external market for the firm's services remains strong. Differentiation can be created in many ways. The firm can win design awards. It may employ one or more recognized leaders in a specialty area, such as visual resource analysis. It may have completed a significant number of projects in a specific market segment, such as waterfront design, becoming a leader by experience. Minority or disadvantaged classification has been a way for some firms to differentiate themselves from other firms. The fact that a firm can differentiate itself is important, and the firm needs to capitalize on the differentiation by proper marketing, promotion, and publicity.

Successful marketing also depends on managing the quality of the professional services delivered by the firm. Quality management is a direct responsibility of the firm's principals and staff who carry out the professional services of the office and interface with clients. The firm's marketing personnel are responsible for publicizing the quality of the firm's work and coaching staff to maintain the highest possible quality in the delivery of the firm's services. The marketing staff are advocates for attaining the highest possible quality of design in the firm's completed projects. In the long term, the market leaders will be the landscape architecture firms that nurture the reputation for high quality of service, as well as high quality of the designed and built environment or planned and preserved natural resources. Indeed, the fashionable notion of total quality management (TQM) that pervades the corporate world in the United States is a concept that is very applicable to the professional services firm. In the TQM philosophy, everyone in the company is empowered to be responsible for the quality of the product or service. Nowhere is quality management by all members of a firm more important than in the professional landscape architecture office.

Without marketing and the development of clients and jobs, there will be no opportunities for talented design and technical staff to fulfill their potential. Marketing must be a central component of the business plan of today's landscape architecture firm. The keys to effective and productive marketing include the following:

- The firm has a written strategic business plan and a marketing plan that are prepared and updated annually.
- The firm is aware of its competitors and regularly analyzes their marketing maneuvers.
- The firm develops and utilizes the best possible marketing tools.
- The firm develops effective methods for producing proposals and carrying out interviews.
- The firm regularly identifies new market opportunities and evaluates market expansion possibilities.
- The firm nurtures its present clients.
- The firm manages its services and products for the highest possible quality.
- The firm strives for high design and technical excellence in its completed projects.
- The firm constantly tries to differentiate itself from its competitors.
- The firm designs and implements a public relations program.
- The firm accepts the need for marketing and integrates client development and client maintenance in all of its endeavors.
- The firm regularly obtains feedback from its clients about its delivery of services.

The Strategic Plan

To be effective at marketing, the owners and principals of the landscape architecture firm must develop and continually update a strategic business plan. The business plan includes a marketing plan that identifies the firm's target markets. Without such a plan, the evolution of the firm is subject entirely to the forces of the market and the whims of the firm's top managers.

The Mission Statement

The mission statement, which is a part of the strategic business plan, is a declaration of the firm's competitive strategy. The mission statement describes the specific philosophy the owners of the firm wish to adopt in delivering the landscape architecture services. The firm's mission and the firm's efforts at strategic planning are shaped by three main factors:

1. The interests, education, and cultural background of the firm's founders, owners, and principals.
2. The internal environment of the firm, including physical, intellectual, technical, and financial resources of the owners, principals, and staff.
3. The external environment of the firm, including the regional geography and national economic trends.

Interests, Education, and Cultural Background

If a landscape architect is trained in Arizona, he or she is not as likely to head off to Massachusetts to begin professional practice as to stay in the Southwest or move to another desert region to practice. If a landscape architect receives an M.L.A. degree from a university program specializing in behavioral research and environmental psychology, he or she is less likely to go out and begin a private practice that focuses on design and preparing construction documents. A landscape architecture graduate who grew up in an inner-city area may have nurtured a strong desire to return to the city and dedicate his or her practice to improving the quality of the urban environment. The landscape architect with an M.L.A. degree and a Ph.D. in biological sciences will be more likely to become a college teacher or be part of a professional firm with a strategic plan focused on environmental assessment and research.

There is little doubt that the interests, education, and cultural background of each landscape architect and of the firm's leaders play a central role in the mission of each landscape architecture firm. Expressing the interests and background is an important part of the firm's mission statement. Finding a good fit between the interests of the firm's owners and principals and the type of work the firm secures increases the firm's productivity. Disaster can occur if the fit can't be found.

The Internal Environment

The number of professional staff, their educational background, their interests, the equipment, the computer capability, work attitudes, financing capability, and all other elements of the internal makeup of the firm are key considerations of the firm's strategic plan. The internal environment is the part of the firm that the owners have the most control over. They have the greatest opportunity to manipulate and direct these internal elements in order to support the firm's objectives and market orientation.

The External Environment

There are two major parts to the external environment that influence the development of a landscape architecture firm's strategic planning. The first is the immediate operating environment, including the firm's competition, the client base, and the geographic region. A shift in the local economy because a factory stops production, for example, would depress the local housing market and impact the elasticity of the pricing of landscape architecture services, driving fees down. A number of spin-off firms that begin at the same time in a local landscape architecture market would also affect landscape architecture fees negatively because the new firms would be likely to compete by lowering fees to capture market share. Conversely, a local boom in industrial growth might impact the landscape architecture firm in other ways, such as a competitor's attempting to steal staff by offering higher wages. Whereas the external operating environment can be influenced to some degree by the actions of the owners of the landscape architecture firm, the more likely course of action is reactionary management. The better the firm's managers become at forecasting changes in the external operating environment, the greater the chances of counteracting the effects on the firm.

The second external influence is the remote or national environment, which the landscape architecture office can do little or nothing to influence. The national environment includes influences such as the trends in the national economy; impacts of the international economic climate, such as the price of oil; and philosophies of the national political party in control of Congress and the executive branch of government. Is the national economy on the upswing, or is the country in a recession? Are social programs in vogue, or is the federal government tightening its belt and reducing social spending programs? Are there technological forces at work that may shape the practice of landscape architecture? The introduction of the personal computer into the everyday operations of the landscape architecture office in the early 1980s is an example of a national external force that has dramatically affected the practice of landscape architecture. The oil embargo of the mid-1970s and the concern for oil self-sufficiency caused a focus on mass transit, creating many design and environmental assessment opportunities for landscape architects. Remote external forces are always at work changing the political, social, economic, and technological environment and causing the possibility of change in the strategic plans of the landscape architecture office.

National disasters, unfortunate as they may be, are a type of external force that cannot be anticipated but often results in market opportunities for landscape architects. The eruption of Mount Saint Helens volcano in Oregon in 1980 is an example of an unpredictable natural occurrence that created numerous natural-resources analysis and design opportunities for landscape architects, including the design of a new access road and a new visitor center. The devastation of Hurricane Hugo brought the need to rebuild cities and towns along the southeastern coast of the United States.

Based on the background and interests of the firm's principals, analysis of the internal and external environments, and formulation of strategy, the owners of each architecture office will develop a mission statement for the firm—an ideological and competitive strategy. The firm's mission statement, as set down by the owners and the principals, will shape the firm's strategic posture. The mission statement should accomplish a number of important goals:

1. Specify the types of services to be provided by the landscape architecture office and the markets the firm seeks to serve.

2. Specify the immediate external environment in which the firm intends to operate.

3. Provide the motivational focus of the firm, fostering allegiance and camaraderie among the firm's employees.

4. Specify the technology that the firm will use to carry out its professional services.

5. Address the organizational parameters of the firm.

6. Spell out the management philosophy of the firm, as well as planning and design ideologies.

7. Differentiate the firm and reinforce its strengths.

8. Identify profitability and survival as a business priority of the firm. After all, the firm that does not prosper and survive will not be around to worry about it.

Strategic Business Planning

After the firm's founders have laid out the mission statement, they should develop a strategic business plan that defines the firm's target market. A target market for a landscape architecture firm could be all of the architects and engineers in a given geographical area; parks and recreation departments and agencies of local, state, and federal levels of government; multi-family housing developers; or conservation and environmental protection public agencies. A firm might target several markets, emphasizing versatility and attempting to be a jack-of-all-trades. In the latter case, the firm should address the process of strategic planning and make a conscious decision to have a generalist orientation.

Strategic business planning is the ongoing process of developing a niche for the landscape architecture firm in the changing marketplace. The aim of strategic planning is to constantly shape the firm's ability to provide landscape architecture services, to produce profits, and to maintain the firm as a viable entity in the external environment. Strategic planning is a relatively new concept in the corporate and industrial world, and even newer in the world of service professions. As the external environment continues to become more and more competitive, however, the need for strategic planning will continue to be more and more important.

Analyzing the external environment is the most important part of strategic business planning. The external environment is made up of the forces that are beyond control of the firm's managers but which constantly impact the nature and profitability of the firm's practice of landscape architecture. These political, economic, social, and technological factors present opportunities, as well as threats, to the firm's business health. Political factors include changes in the tax code that may affect the business structure of the firm; the taxing structure of local, state, and federal branches of government; the social orientation of the national party with the most power in the congressional and executive branches of government; and the current political attitudes toward conservation, urban renewal, highway development, and other government programs. Economic considerations include factors such as the availability of credit for expansion, the cost of credit as related to the prime interest rate, the rate of inflation, and the economic expansion of the national economy as measured by the gross domestic product. Social considerations involve the values, attitudes, and mores of potential clients in the firm's external environment. One of the most significant social impacts on the practice of landscape architecture has been the large number of women entering the workforce in general and the landscape architecture profession specifically. This social change has further impacted the professional practice of landscape architecture due to national and local programs that give preference to minority and women-owned firms. A shift in population is another social trend that may affect the regional practice of landscape architecture. After 1950, national shifts in population from the Rust Belt to the Sun Belt created many landscape architecture opportunities in Texas, Arizona, and California. Technological change is another external force that is constantly at work shaping the practice of landscape architecture. Who can deny the impact that the computer and software applications have had on the profession?

The third and most manageable part of the strategic planning equation is analyzing and formulating the makeup of the internal environment. The process involves constantly assessing the firm's realistic ability to respond to the professional-practice opportunities that it encounters. One of the best ways to analyze the landscape architecture firm's internal environment is to carry out a regular review of the firm's strengths and weaknesses. A number of categories should be analyzed:

1. Design capability and expertise represented in the firm's principals and staff
2. Technical capability and expertise represented in the firm's principals and staff
3. Technical and production resources of the firm
4. Marketing capability and expertise of the firm's principals and staff, and marketing resources
5. Financial resources of the firm
6. Business management abilities and support staff capabilities of the firm
7. Track record of completed projects
8. Desire to take on challenges and break new professional ground

The results of the internal analysis will identify if the firm has competitive advantages, meets only the basic competitive capabilities, or has competitive vulnerabilities. Obviously, the firm should maintain and strengthen its competitive advantages. The firm that has only basic competitive capabilities should at least maintain its competitiveness and also try to develop competitive advantages. The firm that diagnoses competitive vulnerabilities should attempt first to remedy the vulnerable aspects of its internal environment, then continue to move into the basic competitive level, and even work on developing competitive advantages.

The strategic planning process ends in action statements that drive the firm forward. These goals and objectives are the strategic plan itself and provide direction in a number of areas:

1. market and clients
2. revenue and profit
3. staff and personnel
4. resources
5. geography

The Marketing Plan

The Marketing Process

Managing the marketing process requires a number of tasks including, but not limited to, the following:

1. Analyzing marketing opportunities
2. Identifying and selecting target markets
3. Developing marketing strategies
4. Planning, implementing, and controlling marketing efforts

The first task facing owners, principals, and managers of a landscape architecture office is analyzing the short- and long-term opportunities for the firm to compete in the market or markets the firm has identified in its strategic plan. For example, a landscape architecture office may have a long-term goal to engage in master planning, site design, and landscape architecture for commercial projects, corporate facilities, and corporate headquarters. At the present, however, the firm will be able to enter the desired market only by serving as a subconsultant to architecture firms because the landscape architecture firm does not have direct experience as a prime consultant in the planning and design of large commercial facilities or corporate projects. If there is strong market demand for the subconsulting services, the landscape architecture firm can set a short-term goal of providing the best possible subconsulting services to nurture its architecture clients while trying to develop the ultimate client the firm wishes to serve—the commercial developer or corporate executive. Working as a subconsultant provides a good opportunity for the landscape architects to acquire experience and to home in on the types of services desired by the prospective commercial and corporate clients. Working as a subconsultant gives the landscape architects the opportunity to identify key players such as planning and zoning officials, financiers, and real estate brokers. Moreover, working as a subconsultant provides the opportunity to become aware of what the firm's competitors, including the prime consultant, are doing. All of the education and experience gained by the landscape architects while serving in a subconsulting role provides market research for penetrating the desired market.

After subconsulting for a while, the landscape architects will have developed a track record of completed commercial and corporate projects. They will have identified several potential commercial or corporate clients whom the landscape architects could approach with the proposal that they serve as the prime consultant on a future project. The commercial and corporate clients are targeted by the landscape architects; the target market has been identified. The landscape architect's potential clients represent a segment of the market that can be focused on in order to achieve the firm's long-term goal of master planning, site design, and landscape architecture for large commercial or corporate projects.

Next the firm develops a marketing strategy that consists of the time commitment and financial resources the firm will spend in developing the target market. The strategy may address the following questions:

- How will prospective clients be contacted?
- What marketing and promotional material will be most useful?
- Are the marketing and promotional materials already available, or will the landscape architecture firm have to develop new materials or expand presently available materials?
- What are the prospective client's previous projects? Could the landscape architects have improved on the previous projects?
- What is the prospective client's next project? What research must be carried out to become familiar with the new projects?
- What other contacts, such as real estate brokers or lenders, could the firm approach as helpful contacts for its landscape architects?
- Is the prospective client price or fee sensitive?
- How can a social relationship and a friendship be developed and nurtured with the prospective client?
- Which people in the landscape architecture firm are best suited for making contact with the prospective client in terms of personality, mutual interests, and available time?
- What financial resources are available or can be budgeted for developing the prospective client?
- What is the value of the landscape architect's services to the prospective client?

The marketing and client-development strategy will be set based on the firm's responses to the issues and questions about the prospective client and the market opportunity. Developing a written strategy, if only a memorandum of the main efforts to be made in marketing and client development, is the best way to culminate the marketing strategy efforts. The most important element of the written marketing strategy is a time line that identifies when key steps of the marketing effort should be completed and when the land-

scape architecture firm hopes the efforts will culminate in a contract.

Sometimes the marketing efforts do not produce the desired results, and it becomes evident to the firm's marketing manager or principal in charge of the marketing and client-development effort that a successful conclusion is unlikely. In such cases, the firm should cut its losses and return to the beginning of the marketing process, to analyzing its short- and long-term marketing opportunities.

Once implemented, the firm's marketing effort should be evaluated regularly. The firm should evaluate the success of its marketing efforts with the marketing budget and monitor the time line for achieving the market penetration.

The Marketing Plan

The culmination of the planning efforts is the written marketing plan, which might include the following main sections:

I. *Executive Summary.* This is an abbreviated overview of the marketing plan.
II. *The Marketing Environment.* This section presents relevant information about the size of the market in which the firm wants to capture market share. The commercial development market in the landscape architecture firm's region, for example, might be projected as $100 million per year with an expected increase of 20 percent per year for five years. The total of project fees might be 8 percent, or $8,000,000, the first year.

This section also discusses the competitive environment. Who are the landscape architecture firm's main competitors? What is the firm's strategy for competing (i.e., fees, better experience, snag-free approvals with local government officials)? What percentage of market share is held by each of the competitors? What is the quality of services provided by each competitor? Generally, what are the intentions and behaviors of the competitors? This section would present a summary of the internal and external environment factors that might impact the landscape architecture firm's marketing capabilities.

III. *Analysis of Issues: Opportunities and Threats.* Here the plan spells out the main opportunities and threats facing the landscape architecture firm.

A. *Opportunities*

1. The firm can penetrate the market and obtain 5 percent market share by securing one project with a specific client.

2. The client has indicated a strong interest in the landscape architecture firm because of the excellent services and award-winning landscape architecture on the client's two previous projects.

3. The architecture firm that served as the prime consultant on the client's last project has been criticized for taking too long to complete the planning and design phase of the last project.

4. The landscape architecture firm has a well-established working relationship with another architecture firm that is willing to serve as the landscape architecture firm's subconsultant if the client awards the prime contract to the landscape architecture firm for the next project.

B. *Threats.* The landscape architecture firm is likely to lose as a client the architecture firm it served as a subconsultant on previous projects for the developer. This architecture firm provided $40,000 in revenue per year for the previous two years to the landscape architecture firm. The landscape architecture firm may impact its subconsulting relationship with other local architecture firms if it is viewed as taking away work that might otherwise be considered the market domain of architecture firms in general.

C. *Issues.* Is the prospective opportunity to serve the commercial developer a one-shot deal, or will it lead to fulfillment of the firm's strategic long-term goals and result in a strong market share?

IV. *Objectives.* Here the plan describes the financial and the marketing goals of the plan. The firm expects to achieve a 5 percent market share in the first year, and 10 percent overall.

If the project is successful, the firm will have gained a significant foothold in the commercial market related to the firm's long-term marketing goals.

V. *Marketing Strategy.* Here the plan outlines the strategies and action programs the firm will need to implement in order to secure the market and develop the client. What will be done? Who will do it? When will it be done? What it will cost?

VI. *Controls.* This section of the plan outlines the controls that will be used to monitor the progress of the plan. A key part of this section is the schedule or time line associated with the marketing plan. This section might also include a contingency plan to cut losses if adverse developments occur.

VII. *Potential Revenue and Profit.* The last section of the plan is a presentation of the potential revenue that can be achieved by successfully implementing the marketing plan. Revenue of $400,000 in the first year is possible by completing one project for the prospective client. These fees will result in a $24,000 profit for the firm. This section might include a five-year projection of revenue and projected profit-and-loss statements.

Marketing Tools and the Promotion Mix

A wide variety of marketing tools is available to the landscape architecture firm. Developing the tools and selecting the right mix of marketing tools for the firm in general and for a target market or client requires a great deal of time and attention by the firm's owners, managers, and principals. The tools that work for one target market or client may not work for another. The tools that worked for ten years may suddenly become outdated and have to be scrapped. The tools that the firm used for fifteen years may need to be revised when the firm changes ownership.

Selecting the right mix of marketing tools requires that a landscape architecture firm have a variety of tools as part of its marketing arsenal. If the firm's primary marketing tool is a general brochure, the firm may have difficulty competing for a specific target market when the firm really needs a group of specific project cut sheets related to the target market. Selecting the right mix of marketing tools occurs at two levels—first for the firm in general and second as related to a specific target market, client, or project.

The mix of marketing tools may be based on the financial resources of the firm and on the personalities and philosophies of the principals and marketing staff who use the tools. Principals who believe that the quality of the services provided and the quality of the built project are the keys to securing future work may feel that word of mouth is the central component of the firm's promotional mix. They will subsequently select other marketing tools, such as newspaper, journal, and magazine coverage of the firm's work, that support word of mouth as the primary marketing method.

Word of Mouth

The marketing tool used by every landscape architecture firm is word of mouth. Word of mouth refers to the comments made by a former client to friends, acquaintances, and associates regarding the quality of services provided by the landscape architect and the satisfaction with the finished products. Obviously, the landscape architect wants the comments to be positive. The more that is said publicly by satisfied clients, the better the standing of the landscape architecture firm in the community. As potential clients hear more about the landscape architecture firm, the firm may be considered "hot" and have many prospective customers calling.

If negative word-of-mouth comments surface about a landscape architecture firm about a specific project, the firm should meet the criticism head on and be truthful about the issues involved when asked about them. The firm must identify the source of negative word-of-mouth comments and make every attempt to correct the situation and mitigate the negative publicity.

Brochures

The purpose of a brochure is to convey an overview of the landscape architecture firm's philosophy toward planning and design, to showcase the firm's most no-

table projects, and to spotlight the experience of the firm's owners and principals. The brochure paints a broad-brush picture of the firm. Brochures have become less popular in recent times because of their static nature in today's constantly changing business environment and the national landscape architecture market. Brochures tend to be expensive to produce, especially if they include photographs and if they are printed in color. Using high-quality paper, printing at an unusual size, and perfect binding also add substantially to the costs. The design of a high-quality brochure can cost several thousand dollars or more. If the firm can afford the cost of a brochure, it can be a very useful marketing tool. If well designed and printed in a high-quality fashion, the appearance of the brochure itself—in addition to its contents—will make a statement about the firm. The brochure is effective as a general follow-up to cold calling prospective clients.

Brochures can also be produced inexpensively with a reasonable degree of quality. Keeping the artwork or photographs to black and white and producing the layout in house on the firm's laser printer can substantially reduce costs. One type of inexpensive and useful brochure is a one-page flyer that folds to fit in the standard-size business envelope and also fits in the pocket of a sport coat or inside a briefcase or purse. Flyers can be used effectively in a direct-mail marketing campaign if the flyer is targeted to a specific market.

Cut Sheets

Firms today use individual project cut sheets instead of, or as a supplement to, the general office brochure. A project cut sheet is normally produced on 8½-by-11-inch paper so that production is inexpensive. The size is compatible with standard letter and envelope sizes. Any other size is not very practical.

Individual project cut sheets are extremely useful for target marketing because the specific types of projects a firm has completed that relate to the target market can be featured in the firm's marketing approach. For example, the firm could send a selection of cut sheets that illustrates the firm's school project experience with a letter of introduction to a school board that may have a number of projects available in the near future. Or the selection of school project cut

Morris K. Udall Regional Park Master Plan

Ace Landscape Architects developed a comprehensive master plan for the 172-acre Udall Regional Park in Tucson, Arizona. The project included coordinating the work of four subconsultants and working with several public agencies, including the Bureau of Land Management, which operates the Magnetic and Seismological Observatory on the site. The Observatory required that metal objects, such as cars, could not be concentrated on the site because the concentration of metal would affect their instruments. Concentric circles were established where no cars were allowed in the inner circle of 1,200 feet diameter, up to four cars could be parked together in the next concentric circle, up to 8 cars in the next, and any number of cars could be concentrated in the perimeter circle. Up to 406 cars could be parked on the site. This criteria played a central role in the form of the masterplan. Preservation of native vegetation and wildlife habitat was another important planning criteria.

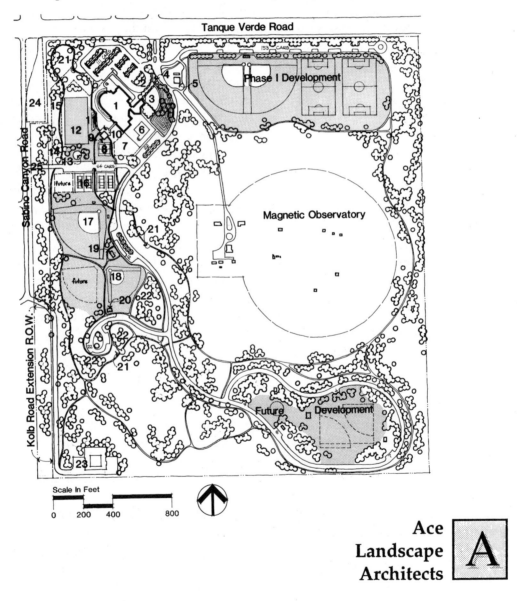

FIGURE 8-1. Black-and-white cut sheets are easy to develop in house using page layout software and reductions of project-related graphics. Photocopying is economical.

sheets could be used to indicate the landscape architecture firm's experience in a response to a request for proposals from a school board.

Cut sheets allow flexibility in target market responses and allow the firm to appear as if it specializes in a particular type of project because the cut sheets can be slanted to the target market. Several different cut sheets can be made for the same project, each with a different slant to be used with a different target market. A housing project that the firm has worked on may have included professional services for environmental assessment, preparation of a master site plan including a large common recreation area, and design of site amenities, landscape, and irrigation systems. This project could be used to develop a cut sheet featuring (1) environmental assessment services, (2) site planning services, (3) housing services, (4) recreation planning and design services, and (5) landscape architecture and irrigation design services. By using different headlines, photographs, or graphics, the firm can produce at least five cut sheets for this project, each for a different target market. A broad selection of individual cut sheets bound in a preprinted folder has taken the place of a general office brochure for most firms today.

Cut sheets are very useful to send to other A/E firms when the landscape architecture firm is asked to participate as a subconsultant on a project team assembled in response to a request for proposals (RFP). The cut sheet method of promotional materials allows the landscape architecture firm to tailor the cut sheet selection, and therefore the firm's experience, to the requirements of the RFP.

Individual cut sheets can be produced in large quantities using offset printing techniques on high-quality paper stock. When the supply is used up, the cut sheet can be updated if desired and additional copies printed. One drawback of this method is that the office will need ample storage if it has a large supply of cut sheets.

Simpler and less costly approaches to the production and use of cut sheets also work. A single, original cut sheet can be prepared from color photographs or black-and-white graphics and kept in a filing cabinet with other original cut sheets. These originals can be duplicated by black-and-white or color photocopying methods when cut sheets are needed for mailings or responses to RFPs.

Using computer and laser printer technology (if the firm can afford the hardware and software) is another way to develop, store, and produce cut sheets. The firm can produce a cut sheet on in-house computers using desktop publishing software and scanners to scan either black-and-white or color photographs onto the cut sheet original, which is stored electronically. When copies are needed, they can be printed on black-and-white or color laser printers.

Standard Forms 255 and 254

If a landscape architecture firm intends to procure federal government projects, an essential part of the firm's marketing toolbox is the capability to respond with completed SF254 and SF255 forms. These forms are used not only by the federal government to screen firms but also by local and state levels of government.

The SF254 is updated once each year and the SF255 is completed specifically for each project. The SF255 is where the firm targets its experience to match the needs of the procuring agency. Proprietary software is available that automatically updates the SF254 and prepares SF255 forms electronically. Some firms also use page composition software to develop electronic files of the SF255 forms and then to prepare actual completed SF255 forms for various categories of potential government work, such as road beautification, military base work, housing, and environmental assessment. The prepared SF255 forms are pulled and put together as needed. They can be stored as hard copy and as electronic files. Having the ability to respond effectively with these standard forms is very important to public works marketing success.

One of the best ways to enhance the firm's SF255 submittals is by using the long form of section 8 of the SF255. The long form allows graphics and photographs of completed projects to be inserted on the full-page section 8 in addition to the verbal descriptions and other information requested on construction costs.

Direct-Mail Marketing

With the integration of computer technology and applications software in today's landscape architecture office, the typical firm is now capable of producing sophisticated direct-mail advertising featuring regular mailings in large quantities. Many people argue—and

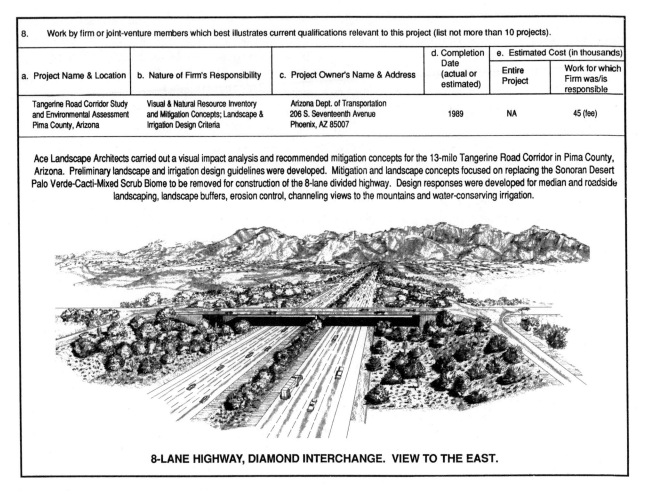

8.	Work by firm or joint-venture members which best illustrates current qualifications relevant to this project (list not more than 10 projects).				
a. Project Name & Location	b. Nature of Firm's Responsibility	c. Project Owner's Name & Address	d. Completion Date (actual or estimated)	e. Estimated Cost (in thousands) Entire Project	Work for which Firm was/is responsible
Tangerine Road Corridor Study and Environmental Assessment Pima County, Arizona	Visual & Natural Resource Inventory and Mitigation Concepts; Landscape & Irrigation Design Criteria	Arizona Dept. of Transportation 206 S. Seventeenth Avenue Phoenix, AZ 85007	1989	NA	45 (fee)

Ace Landscape Architects carried out a visual impact analysis and recommended mitigation concepts for the 13-mile Tangerine Road Corridor in Pima County, Arizona. Preliminary landscape and irrigation design guidelines were developed. Mitigation and landscape concepts focused on replacing the Sonoran Desert Palo Verde-Cacti-Mixed Scrub Biome to be removed for construction of the 8-lane divided highway. Design responses were developed for median and roadside landscaping, landscape buffers, erosion control, channeling views to the mountains and water-conserving irrigation.

8-LANE HIGHWAY, DIAMOND INTERCHANGE. VIEW TO THE EAST.

FIGURE 8-2. Example of an SF255 Section 8 long-form project description with black-and-white graphics.

indeed the marketing literature points out—that the payoff for direct-mail mass marketing is low, but direct mail does serve a useful purpose in the overall marketing efforts of a landscape architecture firm.

Direct-mail marketing has two good purposes:

1. General publicity of the firm (i.e., to keep the name of the firm in front of as many people in the broad market as possible).
2. Target marketing related to a specific request for proposals with the emphasis on a specific consulting opportunity for the firm.

In the first use of direct-mail marketing, the landscape architecture firm keeps its name and its accomplishments in front of the widest possible range of prospective clients. To be effective at general publicity by direct mail, the landscape architecture firm first must develop and maintain a database of its contacts and potential clients—the firm's market opportunities. With the ability to sort the database, the firm can be selective with the mailings, targeting a market and cutting costs. Effective use of mail-merge software also reduces costs.

After computer techniques and administrative methods are in place for quick and effective responses to direct-mail marketing opportunities, the firm should seize opportunities to publicize itself to a broad range of potential clients. Any noteworthy achievement, award received, personal recognition, or other differentiating event for the firm is a reason for a general direct-mail marketing effort. Some professional offices use a newsletter to publicize achievements and to keep in touch with the firm's larger client base. Another very effective direct-mail campaign is the year-end greeting card. Some firms have also used a calendar as a year-end greeting that is mass mailed to the firm's large mailing list. A calendar is a very effective marketing tool, especially if well designed and visually appealing. When the prospective client hangs the calendar on the wall, the calendar will keep the name of the landscape architecture firm in front of the potential client and all of the people who visit the potential client's office for an entire year.

The second good use of direct-mail marketing is to target a selected group of potential prime-consulting firms in response to a specific request for proposals. In this approach, the landscape architecture firm should use its general marketing operations to track a wide range of RFPs for large-scale projects. When the landscape architecture firm receives an RFP for a large and complex project, such as an urban expressway or a mass transit system, a targeted mailing can be made to transportation planning firms and other large A/E firms in the landscape architecture office's database or other firms likely to submit a proposal as a prime consultant. The landscape architecture firm would attempt to be listed by several larger firms as a subconsultant for urban design, environmental assessment, and landscape architecture services. The targeted mailing might include a package of materials such as descriptions of prior related project work, résumés of key staff, cut sheets, and other material that would assist the prime consultant in expediting the production of the proposal. By putting the needed response materials in the hands of the marketing staff of the larger firm, the landscape architecture firm has a better chance of being selected as a subconsultant on the team.

The shotgun response to an RFP can put the landscape architecture firm in the enviable position of being listed by a number of prime consultants, especially if the landscape architecture firm's prior project experience matches the services required for the proposed project particularly well. With effective follow-up calls and a little luck, the landscape architecture firm may find that it is listed with enough prime consultants that it has 100 percent coverage when the shortlist is announced. At this point, the landscape architecture firm is in a no-lose situation, assured of the opportunity to work on the project.

The shotgun effort is useful in a subconsulting market. A key to successful shotgun mailings is the follow-up phone call after the mailing has reached the prospective client to get a commitment from the larger A/E firm. In this direct-mail approach, the mailing comes first, and the call is second.

A rule of thumb with the direct-mail marketing approach is to give something useful to the firms receiving the mailed information. If one merely sends a letter asking the larger firm to consider using the landscape architecture firm as its subconsultant, the response from the prospective prime consultant is likely to be "Why should we?" If the landscape architecture firm's mailing package includes the materials necessary for the larger firm to use in responding to the RFP, and if the materials are eye-catching, the landscape architecture firm will increase its chances of being selected by the larger firm. Always provide something useful in the direct-mail approach.

Direct-Call Marketing

In the same way that direct-mail marketing can be effective, direct-call marketing is effective. Principals and marketing personnel in the firm keep phone numbers on file of the firms they team up with or provide subconsulting services to. As with direct-mail marketing, the principals or marketing staff of a landscape architecture firm make calls when they hear about a project where the firm is competitive. By using the phone, they can quickly cover much ground. Larger firms can be contacted before they are contacted by other landscape architecture firms. In this approach, the landscape architecture firm seeks a verbal commitment from another firm to team up with the landscape architecture firm. If it receives an affirmative response, the landscape architecture firm can follow up by mailing the necessary promotional materials. In this method, the call comes first, and the mailed materials follow.

Many principals and managers of landscape architecture firms keep a regular calls list at their desk. The list includes other professional firms and former and present clients that the principal or manager frequently works with on projects. Keeping in contact with these people is important. At any time during a conversation, a lead can be mentioned if the landscape architect is alert.

Cold Calls

Telephone solicitation is a technique used to introduce a landscape architecture firm to a prospective client with whom no prior relationship exists. Cold calling usually starts with a list of potential clients—a target market—that the landscape architecture firm wishes to penetrate and establish market share. The list may be developed from any number of sources, such as the phone book or a listing of government or nonprofit agencies. Each prospective client is called with a goal of trying to establish common interests resulting in a follow-up call or meeting. The follow-up will be used to expand on the common interests and begin nurturing a relationship with the prospective client.

Cold calling is one of the most unnerving tasks that faces the marketing personnel of the landscape architecture firm (or almost any firm, for that matter). Perseverance is a helpful personality trait for the cold caller. Getting through to a person who has the authority to make decisions about hiring consultants can be difficult, and sometimes it is difficult to get through to anyone even interested in talking to the cold caller. In other cases, the cold caller is headed off by a receptionist or a secretary, who tells the cold caller to send materials in the mail and will not connect the caller to the prospective client (a brush-off). The landscape architect cannot be sure that the materials ever reach the appropriate decision maker, and if they do, the personal touch of presenting the materials is missing.

Another criticism of this method is the low rate of success often attributed to cold calls. Although the success rate is indeed low, the cold call has a definite place in the overall marketing scheme.

There are a number of techniques that can be used by the caller to make cold calling easier and more pleasant. The overall technique should focus on asking questions. By asking questions, the cold caller will uncover information about the prospective client's interests and will be able to keep asking further questions, seeking common interests. Given the opportunity, most people like to talk about their interests. Therefore, if the cold caller can uncover the interests in a few questions, the prospective client may do a lot of talking about his or her interests and feel good about the conversation. By breaking the conversational ice, the cold caller will often end up with an opportunity for a firsthand meeting and interview. The following list of techniques is useful as a guide for making easier and more effective cold calls:

1. Prepare a written outline in advance of cold calling. The outline should include a number of specific questions designed to identify some of the interests of the prospective client. The outline should also include some of the main points about the landscape architecture firm that the cold caller wants to emphasize. But remember, it's better to talk about the interests of the prospective client than to talk about the landscape architecture office and its achievements.

2. Take notes during the conversation and summarize the notes and the actions required for follow-up. Be sure to follow up promptly with any requests of information.

3. Humor is a very helpful element of cold calling. A joke or a funny anecdote can go a long way in keeping a cold call on the lighter side for both caller and the callee.

4. Be upbeat. Don't apologize for calling or act intimidated.

5. Take advantage of the opportunity to leave a specific message on an answering system if the person you're trying to reach is not available.

6. Set a clear goal or outcome desired from the cold call, such as the opportunity for a personal meeting or the opportunity to send some promotional material by mail with another follow-up call after the prospective client receives the material.

7. Try to keep the conversation reasonably brief.

8. Thank the prospective client for his or her time.

9. Make a regular effort at cold calls. The more calls you make, the better you'll be at making cold calls.

Video

A video production about the firm and its prior experience is another marketing tool used more and more by landscape architecture firms. An effective video technique is to produce a videocassette that features a specific project of the firm. Because video production is expensive, the project that is highlighted should be unique, award-winning, photogenic, and interesting.

The video should be professionally produced whenever funding is available.

Tickle Files

One of the oldest sales and marketing tools is the tickle file. Basically, a tickle file is a reminder system comprising two main elements: (1) a calendar in which the names of prospective clients or contacts are entered on future dates when they should be called in order to keep in touch and query about possible project opportunities and (2) an ongoing system of note keeping about each phone conversation held with the contact. These notes are very important because the prospective client or contact may be called (or tickled) only once every three to six months, and the landscape architect needs to remember what was discussed in previous conversations in order to resume the conversation, which may lead to a possible project. Because a large percentage of a landscape architecture firm's work often comes from repeat clients, a tickle file is a particularly useful method for keeping in touch with former clients when there has been a time lag from the previous project executed for the client.

Newspaper, Magazine, Radio, and TV Coverage

Reprints and photocopies of newspaper and magazine coverage make useful marketing tools. These articles impress a prospective client more than promotional literature written by members of the firm because the articles are written by an objective outsider. Prospective clients will normally be impressed by news articles about the landscape architecture firm's work. The more articles that are written about the firm's work, the better. News articles and general-interest pieces written about the firm or its designer make excellent background information when bound into proposals.

The marketing staff, principals, and project managers of the landscape architecture firm need to be aware of news opportunities when they arise and see that newspapers and magazine editors are made aware of newsworthy or interesting story opportunities about the firm. The best way to do this is by engaging the services of a public relations firm, which will write press releases to be sent to the editors of local or other newspapers or magazines. The public relations firm will have a wide variety of newspaper and magazine contacts, and the public relations consultant will be able to press the right buttons, resulting in more articles about the landscape architecture firm hitting the news than if the landscape architecture firm tries to manage its own public relations. If the landscape architecture firm decides to manage its own public relations, it should have a principal and a staff person who take responsibility for the publicity and who regularly write press releases about the firm's work and attempt to get them in the news. Internal management of the landscape architecture firm's public relations can be successful, but it takes a lot of work and time. One question that the smaller firm must answer is whether the time taken by a principal to work on publicizing the firm would be better spent on generating billable time working on projects. The larger landscape architecture firm may have a marketing person or staff who also handle the public relations for the firm.

Radio and TV coverage of the firm's work can also be very useful in keeping the firm in the public eye. As with newspaper and magazine coverage, the firm or its public relations staff must be on the lookout for interesting, newsworthy opportunities. An opening of a new project, a major achievement of the firm's staff, and a significant award for one of the firm's principals are opportunities that may make excellent TV or radio coverage.

Cable TV provides opportunities for TV coverage. Cable TV shows developed and produced locally document human interest stories on a wide variety of topics. Landscape architecture firms working in the areas of ecology, water resource planning, landscape recovery programs, parks and playgrounds, and historic preservation, for example, have excellent material for cable TV stories about the firm's work.

Journal Articles

Like the newspaper or magazine article, the journal article is very useful as a background piece in a proposal or a letter of introduction. The big difference between the two is that newspaper and magazine articles are written by an outside author about the firm, its staff, or its work. Journal articles, on the other hand, are usually written by an insider, a principal or member of the firm. Journal articles usually deal with a technical subject. They are particularly useful if they are written about a new idea, new type of design, or a new way of carrying out the design, planning, or analysis process.

Public Speaking

Giving a talk at a local historic society or a meeting of the AIA or presenting a paper at a conference on Xeriscape principles are examples of public-speaking opportunities available to principals and staff of a landscape architecture firm. Public speaking gets the landscape architect in front of the public, and the landscape architect is remembered as being knowledgeable in the topic area he or she speaks about. If enough speaking opportunities are carried out, the landscape architect may become recognized as an authority on the subject. Word-of-mouth references by audience members at speaking engagements is a client-development by-product of the speaking opportunities.

One of the best ways to find out about public speaking opportunities is by contacting the executive staff—elected or appointed leaders—of local professional or community organizations. These organizations are always looking for speakers and may welcome contact by a landscape architect wishing to speak at a meeting.

In order to be effective, the landscape architect must have the personality for public speaking and enjoy getting up in front of an audience. Having a number of prepared talks including slide presentations, illustration boards, flip charts, handouts, or other supporting materials is very useful. The landscape architect can use the prepared talk as is, or alter it slightly to slant it appropriately for the audience. The prepared talks can be used as a base for developing new presentations. Having several prepared talks ready to use gives the landscape architect the opportunity to make a commitment for a speaking engagement on short notice without the anxiety of having to put together a talk and supporting materials from scratch. Making a commitment to speak on short notice is a good way to endear the landscape architect to the leaders of a professional or community organization, and the resulting goodwill is a valuable public relations payoff.

Community Service

Landscape architecture marketing opportunities can be created by serving on commissions, boards, task forces, and other community service organizations. The local zoning board, the city or county design review committee, the local or regional planning commission, the mayor's task force for downtown redevelopment, nonprofit group fund-raising activities, urban forestry advisory boards, water quality advisory groups, and hundreds of other community service opportunities are available to the landscape architect. Most firms encourage their employees, from principals to entry-level designers, to be active in community service.

The main benefits of community service are

1. visibility and name presence for the landscape architecture firm
2. meeting people and making friends
3. fostering word-of-mouth marketing for the landscape architecture firm
4. personal and professional development of social and political skills
5. development of presentation and group dynamics skills
6. firsthand knowledge of the community's political and social dynamics
7. altruism

Sponsoring Community Events

Similar to contributing time through participating in community service, the landscape architecture firm can achieve visibility by contributing to community events through financial sponsorship and donating time or services. Sponsoring a golf tournament, a children's museum fund-raiser, or a tennis match are some of hundreds of sponsorship opportunities available to the landscape architect on a community-wide basis.

Because opportunities to sponsor local fund-raising events abound, the landscape architecture firm's principals and marking staff may have many more requests for funding than the firm has funds available. Establishing and holding to an annual budget for community events is a good idea. Funds may be spent on a first-come-first-serve basis or on targeted community events that the firms sponsors on an annual basis.

Trade Shows and Conferences

Many landscape architects advocate trade show exhibits and conferences as an effective marketing tool. Obviously, the trade show or conference should be oriented to one of the firm's target markets. The National Recreation and Parks Association (NRPA), for example, holds annual state and national conferences open to landscape architecture exhibitors. Attending NRPA conferences as an exhibitor is an effective method of target marketing for the firm that specializes in parks and recreation planning.

The main criticism of trade show and conference exhibiting is the expense. Preparing the actual exhibit materials, building or purchasing an exhibit system, leasing the exhibit space, traveling to the trade show location, staffing the booth for several days to a week, and paying for the expenses and client entertainment while at the conference add up to a very expensive marketing vehicle. Nevertheless the expense may be worthwhile because trade shows and conferences can result in big marketing payoffs.

If the firm exhibits at trade show or conferences, the firm's marketing staff should pay careful attention to designing and preparing the actual exhibits and the exhibit booth. The firm should also select its most outgoing, people-oriented principals and marketing personnel to staff the booth. The exhibit staff must be comfortable meeting people and striking up a conversation. The work of staffing an exhibit booth can be physically and emotionally demanding. Effective selection of staff will result in a higher degree of success.

Print Advertising

The advertising medium used most by landscape architecture firms is the print medium. Trade journals; local promotional magazines and literature; real estate publications; newsletters published by architecture, engineering, and planning societies; and other print media that generally have a targeted audience represent good advertising opportunities. Other print advertising opportunities prevail but are often associated with some of the other marketing tools discussed in this section, such as advertising related to sponsoring a community event.

Like trade shows, advertising in print media can be an expensive marketing tool. The actual cost of the ad is only one of many expenses including preparing the artwork, photography, copy writing, and using an advertising agent if the landscape architecture firm is not capable of putting the ad together itself.

Professional landscape architecture offices have not traditionally used TV and radio for advertising, although a few opportunities exist. One of the best TV and radio opportunities is advertising associated with supporting a public radio or TV station. Most public TV and public radio stations operate in part on funds raised through listener-supported broadcasts. Some public information broadcasts are related to the professional services of a landscape architecture firm, and the firm may choose to fund all or a part of the specific show. A five-minute daily broadcast of the events held weekly by a city parks and recreation department is a good example of the type of broadcast that a landscape architecture firm might sponsor. Public information broadcasts carry a byline for the sponsoring firm. If the ad is repeated daily, it will result in excellent radio or TV exposure for the firm.

There are many print medium advertising opportunities that do not take a major investment of funds but get the name of the landscape architecture firm into the public eye. Here are a few print advertising opportunities:

1. List the services that the firm provides on the firm's business cards, letterhead, and stationery. A client who receives a letter from the firm about landscape architecture services already under contract may also need environmental analysis services, and if the client sees these advertised on the firm's letterhead it might lead to another contract.

Ace Landscape Architects

Walt Rogers, ASLA, *Principal*

•Landscape Architecture •Park & Recreation Planning•
•Site Planning •Environmental Assessment •Irrigation Design•
•Urban Design •Water Conservation Planning•
•Desert Revegetation Programs•

2440 E. Broadway Blvd., Tucson, Arizona, 85719
(520) 555-2302 • FAX (520) 555-8270• Mobile (520) 555-8974

FIGURE 8-3. Listing the services provided by the landscape architecture firm on the business calling card is an easy way to advertise the firm's capabilities.

2. Advertise tastefully on company cars or vehicles.

3. Insist on a job sign for all projects under construction listing the landscape architecture firm as the designer. A paragraph can be included in the firm's standard contractual terms and conditions that requires a job sign.

4. Always include a cover sheet on the firm's sets of construction documents with the firm's name in large letters and its logo. Request that other firms to which the landscape architecture firm serves as a subconsultant also include a cover.

5. Always advertise in the yellow pages.

6. Always insist that the name of the firm is listed in the literature of community service organizations supported by the firm.

7. Always insist that the name of the firm is used when news or trade journal articles are written about the firm's work.

8. Take advantage of trade publications that provide free listings. These publications list the providers of professional services and related industry companies by type of services or product and are often distributed free to a wide audience that may include a distribution list of as many as 20,000 to 30,000 copies.

9. Be sure that the firm is included in the lists of local firms by categories that are often published by local trade magazines and local business papers.

10. Include the landscape architecture firm's name and logo on all cut sheets and promotional literature. There is no telling when a copy of a cut sheet might be used unbeknownst to the landscape architecture firm. If the firm's name and logo are on the cut sheet, the firm will receive proper recognition.

FIGURE 8-4. A job sign is a great advertising opportunity at no or low cost. If the sign is on a busy street, thousands of potential clients may see it every day.

Slide Files and Photo Archives

Photographic records of the firm's constructed designs or exhibits from completed planning projects are used in developing cut sheets and presentation boards for use in interviews, for journal and magazine articles, for enhancing the office environment, and for a number of other promotional uses. Photographs are the necessary raw materials of the firm's promotional materials, and photo archives are a valuable resource.

Slide files and photo archives must be well managed. Project work should be photographed when the project is completed and updated every other year or so. The firm should delegate responsibility for photography to one or more staff members and should consider using a professional photographer if funds are available, especially for recording the firm's highest-profile projects.

A slide file and photo morgue need to be accessible, easy to use, and up to date. One of the simplest filing methods is to use plastic loose-leaf sleeves, which are designed to hold slides, photographs, and negatives, filed in loose-leaf binders and organized by types of projects and by project numbers. A light table is important for selecting and previewing slides and organizing slide shows. The slides in the slide show can be laid out on the light table in sequence, enabling the presenter to see an overview of the slide show. A handheld slide viewer is useful, and a slide projector in good working order is a necessity.

Photo archives, although important, can be replaced for the most part by a slide file in some offices. Color photocopies can be made from slides, and the quality of the color photocopy, although not as good as actual photographs, is acceptable for many uses. Using color copies from slides may reduce the number of duplicate photo archives required and allow the firm to designate the more expensive color photography for only the most high-profile projects.

Some firms use video records to provide a photographic record of the firm's projects. Undoubtedly, video records will be used more as time goes on. Video records will also be used with interactive computer technology as it becomes more widely used. The greatest drawback to using video for marketing and promotion is that video requires a VCR and CRT or video playback unit. This equipment is expensive and somewhat difficult to move around.

Display Boards

Photographic and photocopy records of the firm's work can be enlarged and mounted on display boards to be used for marketing. These are useful in interviews, at trade shows, and for displays in the office. One of the most common ways to display a project is to dry mount the photographic work on large pieces of foam-core boards. Having a number of key boards available in the office can be very useful when a call is received for an impromptu interview and no time is available to develop a presentation.

The Physical Environment of the Office

One marketing tool that is often overlooked is the physical environment of the office. An attractive, well-designed office environment can reflect the design talents of the firm's owners, principals, and design staff. Although subtle, the environment can definitely leave an impression with a prospective client. The office environment may even be intentionally designed and furnished to feel comfortable to representatives of the market segment targeted by the landscape architecture firm. If the firm's clients are primarily A/E firms doing public-sector work, the landscape architecture firm's

owners may intentionally keep the office environment tasteful but toned down and comfortable to the firm's clients. If the firm has primarily upscale corporate clients, the office environment may intentionally be representative of high design. Always consider the design and furnishing of the office environment as a part of the firm's marketing plan.

Answering the Telephone

Last but not least, all members of the firm should be trained to answer the phone in a pleasant and welcoming manner. Phone skills are exceptionally important for the receptionist or whoever answers the phone on a regular basis. The receptionist is the first point of contact with the landscape architecture firm, and the way that the receptionist answers the phone and directs the call can leave a big impression on the caller. The receptionist must always be cheerful, helpful, and knowledgeable about the firm's services and who does what in the office. The receptionist should be capable in dealing with the irate caller and the cold caller. This first point of contact with the firm should represent the corporate culture or personality of the firm itself. That first point of contact can be a continuing important detail in why a client continues to stay with a landscape architecture firm for project after project. If it is a pleasure every time a client calls the landscape architecture firm, that client is more likely to keep on calling.

The Marketing Payoff— The Proposal and the Interview

Successful marketing efforts of the landscape architecture firm result in the opportunities to submit statements of interest, statements of qualification, or proposals. Each of these—the statement of interest (SOI), the statement of qualifications (SOQ), and the proposal—is a different initial response to a prospective client.

A statement of interest (SOI) confirms the firm's interest in a project and is a response to a request for interest (RFI) issued by a public- or private-sector client. Submitting an SOI is a prerequisite to receiving further information, such as a request for proposals (RFP). An SOI is usually a letter sent on the firm's letterhead. A statement of interest may include a very brief statement about the landscape architecture firm's previous experience or the background and experience of the firm's principals or key staff.

A statement of qualifications (SOQ) is a response to a request for qualifications (RFQ). The SOQ is a lengthier document than the SOI. The SOQ will include information about the firm's prior experience, staff capabilities, and resources.

A proposal, which responds to a request for proposals (RFP), may include the same information as an SOQ, but will also include a scope of work and scope of services to be provided by the landscape architecture firm. The scope of work and scope of services are likely to become part of the contract if the firm is selected to carry out the services. In general, effective marketing will result in more SOI, SOQ, and proposal opportunities.

The Statement of Interest and the Statement of Qualifications

The landscape architecture firm writes and assembles SOIs and SOQs in response to an RFI or RFQ. The RFI is used as an initial screening process. It describes the project and the services required in general terms so that the marketing staff or principal of the landscape architecture firm can decide if the firm has the prior related experience, track record, manpower, staff expertise, and other requirements necessary to carry out the project. After receiving the SOI from the landscape architecture firm, the agency that issued the RFI will send a package of information outlining the next step in the process—either submittal of an SOQ or a proposal.

The request for qualifications is a further screening device to determine which of the firms responding to the RFQ are most qualified to provide the solicited professional services. The RFQ may ask for information that will prequalify landscape architecture firms in terms of the firm's financial stability, availability of insurance, proximity of the firm's office to the project site, and other considerations. The agency or prospective client will evaluate all of the SOQs received and take one of several different actions, including the following:

1. Screen the firms to a shortlist of several firms invited to write competitive proposals.
2. Screen the firms to a shortlist of several firms invited for competitive interviews.
3. Rank the firms and select one for further discussion and negotiation of a scope of work and a contract.
4. Start the selection process over because the SOQs received did not provide an adequate pool of qualified firms.
5. Abandon the project.

The SOQ process normally requires a great deal of effort for a firm to be successful. The firm is competing with a wide variety of other firms and must write and put together an SOQ that is detailed and graphic. The process is expensive in terms of time and out-of-pocket costs.

Sometimes a public agency will use the RFQ format to prequalify a select list of landscape architecture firms capable of providing services for a specific type of project or a specific range of services. The agency will then draw upon the prequalified list of firms as specific project needs arise, selecting first one firm, then another, and revolving through the list of prequalified firms.

The Written Proposal

There are two general types of written proposals. The first responds to a request for proposals (RFP) where a private client or a public agency solicits proposals from any and all firms for a specific project. The RFP process usually results in a shortlist of firms to be interviewed for the project or direct selection of a firm. The selected firm goes on to negotiate a contract for professional services. The second type of RFP is received by a landscape architecture firm directly from a prospective private or public client without going through a competitive selection process. This direct selection process would be made by a prospective client that has done its homework and evaluated a number of different landscape architecture firms through means such as word of mouth and discussions with former clients.

A proposal written in response to an RFP must be carefully conceived and produced because the firm will be eliminated from the selection process if it is not either awarded the contract based on its written proposal or short-listed for a personal interview. Writing proposals is expensive, and landscape architecture firms need to have a reasonable success rate. None of the firm's costs are reimbursed by the public agency or private company, and most landscape architecture firms cannot afford to continue submitting proposals unless they succeed at least some of the time.

Typically, the response to RFPs will include some of the same information provided in a response to an SOQ, including examples of prior related experience, expertise of the firm's key staff (résumés), and financial and insurance data. The RFP response also includes a written understanding of the project or problem, how the landscape architecture firm will approach the project, an employee-hours estimate, and a cost proposal.

Preparing a response to an RFI, RFQ, or RFP is an important capability required of landscape architecture firms because a large number of private projects and even more public works projects are obtained by engaging in the RFI, RFQ, and RFP process. Preparing standardized materials such as résumés, project lists, cut sheets, and lists of references, along with word processing for electronic cut and pasting, makes the response process easier and faster. The following general guidelines may be applied to the preparation of SOIs, SOQs, and proposals:

1. Always respond specifically to the questions asked in the RFI, RFQ, or RFP. Use the same headings. Address each of the specific items of information requested.

2. Always ask what specific criteria will be used in evaluating the SOQ or proposal. The evaluation criteria will usually be directly related to the information requested. If the evaluation criteria are available, always address each criterion.

3. Make phone calls or personal visits to the contact persons identified in the RFI, RFQ, or RFP. Before making contact, review the RFI, RFQ, or RFP and develop a list of questions to ask the contract person. The list of questions should be expanded by a brainstorming session in the landscape architecture office attended by key project staff, consultants, and other staff with experience in the specific type of project. Once the questions have been formulated, make contact with the contact person. Take notes during the conversation. The phone calls or personal contact with the contact person will accomplish three things:

A. Provide clarification about the project and alert the landscape architecture firm to nuances that are not covered in the written RFI, RFQ, or RFP.

B. Show interest in the project to the people who are on the selection committee.

C. Begin the process of getting to know the people who have made the request for services and become friendly with them.

4. Visit the site of the proposed project. Carry out research and a site analysis to the extent possible within the marketing budget set for the project. While visiting the site, take photographs that will be useful in the written response. The photographs will be evidence that the landscape architect has visited the site and will reinforce the landscape architecture firm's interest in the project with the selection committee.

5. Set a time or dollar budget for the job-development effort needed to prepare an SOI, SOQ, or proposal for the prospective project. Set the budget prior to starting the response effort. Many firms use a 10 percent rule of thumb as a budget-setting guideline. In other words, job development should not exceed 10 percent of the anticipated professional fee. Set the budget and level of effort commensurate with the fee. If a project will have a fee of $20,000, the job-development budget and level of effort will be small compared to a project that will have a fee of $200,000. Be prepared to exceed the marketing budget if the chances of being selected appear to increase throughout the process of preparing the SOI, SOQ, or proposal.

6. Always illustrate the SOI, SOQ, or proposal. The photographs taken during the initial site visit are excellent for illustrating the section of the response dealing with understanding of the project. Cut sheets or photographs of the landscape architecture firm's prior related experience can enhance the section of the response dealing with prior experience. Photographs of the firm's principals or key staff are effective for humanizing the résumés or descriptions of

prior experience and expertise of the key staff who will be dedicated to the project.

7. Determine if there is a political agenda behind the scenes related to the RFI, RFQ, or RFP. Sometimes, even though the selection process is open to all firms, there is a political agenda that may make some firms unacceptable. If the firm appears to be unacceptable, don't spend the time, effort, and costs to go through the SOI, SOQ, or proposal process.

8. Use the best typographic and illustrative methods available to the firm unless specifically required to respond in a certain way. Page layout software and laser printers are indispensable for effective proposal production.

9. Consider how the landscape architecture firm's competitors may respond to the RFQ or RFP. Factor this consideration into the landscape architecture firm's response.

10. Create a cover for the firm's response that will stand out from the other proposals. There may be a large number of proposals submitted, and the proposals that have covers that attract the reviewers may get reviewed first and remembered more by the selection committee members. In the competitive process, the landscape architecture firm should take advantage of every option to come out the winner.

11. Always include a transmittal letter or cover letter that provides an opportunity for a brief recap of the most salient points of the SOQ or proposal.

12. Minimize the use of lengthy statements of philosophy. Most prospective clients are more interested in what the landscape architect's experience is and what the landscape architect can do to solve the client's needs or problems.

The Interview

If the landscape architecture firm is successful in the SOQ or proposal process, the next step is usually an interview. In most cases, the interview is also a competitive process engaged in by the firms selected for the interview shortlist. The interview may also be noncompetitive. If the landscape architecture firm is fortunate to have been selected directly through the RFQ or RFP process, the personal interview is carried

out only to confirm the selection committee's decision. The selected firm enters directly into the negotiation phase with the client. When a direct selection is made, the interview and contract negotiation should be an upbeat process. The landscape architecture firm should do whatever is necessary to meet the administrative requests of the prospective client and keep the process on track, resulting in a signed contract.

The Competitive Interview

In the RFI, RFQ, and RFP process, a shortlist of firms is arrived at by a selection committee. The shortlisted landscape architecture firms will be invited for a competitive interview, which is the last phase of the selection process and the most stressful for the participating professionals. No matter how well prepared the firm's proposal is or how qualified the firm and its subconsultants may be, all can be lost if the personal interview is unsuccessful.

When the landscape architecture firm is notified that it has been short-listed, the firm must take this last part of the selection process very seriously. Time will be a limiting factor. There may be only a week or two from the time that the firm is notified of its selection to the shortlist and when it must appear at the interview. During the time that is available, the landscape architecture firm should rehash all of its efforts in the selection process in order to come up with its interview strategy. The following considerations are useful:

1. Touch base with the client's representative or key contact person and ask further detailed questions about the project based on further information gained by being short-listed for the interview.

2. Prepare an interview outline and assign personnel to specific speaking parts. Set time allotments for each speaker.

3. Discuss the pros and cons of who is best able to represent the firm in the interview. Choose the best speakers whose personalities are most closely aligned with the interview committee. Choose knowledgeable staff to participate. Many interview committees prefer to meet the firm's project manager at the interview.

4. Limit the number of representatives of the firm and its subconsultants who are allowed to attend the interview. Too many people can overwhelm the interview committee. The ex-

ception to this rule is when a number of specialized subconsultants are members of the team and it is important for them to be present to explain unique concepts or answer specialized questions.

5. Visual presentation materials are almost always a good idea. Slide shows, videos, photographs, copies of project cut sheets, overhead projector acetates, flip charts, illustration boards, models, and many other types of visual props are useful in interviews. The type of visual prop will depend on the makeup of the interview committee, the topic itself, the shape and size of the room, the comfort range of the selection committee, and the physical characteristics of the room. (Can it be darkened to show slides effectively?)

6. Check out the interview room beforehand, if possible. At a minimum, find out the physical characteristics, size, and shape of the room prior to the interview.

7. Rehearse the interview and go through as many dry runs as time permits. Practice makes perfect.

8. Always leave time to answer questions. If the members of the interview committee do not ask questions of the firm, the interview team should have a number of questions prepared to ask the interview committee in order to get them involved in a dialogue.

9. Involve the selection committee in conversation.

10. Always try to differentiate the firm from the other firms during the interview.

11. Always be honest. Don't be afraid to admit that you don't know the answer to a question, and if you don't know, offer to find out and get back to the interview committee.

12. Don't criticize the competition.

Market Expansion— Entering New Markets

There are several ways for a landscape architecture firm to enter a new geographic market. One of the first considerations, however, is whether the landscape architecture firm has a service that is marketable in the

new region. Does the firm provide a higher-quality service than landscape architecture firms in the region? Does the firm provide a unique service not yet offered in the region—landscape restoration and wetlands reconstruction, for example? Does the firm have a management system or production method that allows it to be significantly more competitive than firms existing in the region? Has the firm won widespread acclaim for its planning and design projects, including numerous national, state, and local awards? Does the firm employ a number of ambitious and talented staff who are looking for opportunities to advance their careers by developing a branch office? These are considerations for assessing whether the firm has opportunities to expand in the new geographic market.

Entering a new geographic market will be easier and less costly if the firm has a marketing edge on the firms already practicing landscape architecture in the region. Another important part of the decision to expand into the region is an analysis of the strengths and weaknesses of the existing competition in the region. The capabilities and services provided by each existing firm should be tabulated, and a summary of strengths and weaknesses prepared for each firm. This process has a secondary benefit of identifying possible merger or acquisition candidates if the landscape architecture firm is considering this approach to establishing its new office. This process will also be useful in determining the economic size of the existing landscape architecture market.

If the landscape architecture firm determines that it has a marketable service and can fill a niche market or capture general market share in the new geographic region, the firm should assess the revenue potential. The firm should determine the size of the market, as well as what percentage of the existing market the firm will be able to capture.

A number of different methods and techniques can be used to assess the revenue potential of the new geographic market. The first decision, however, is whether to hire a professional business marketing analyst to carry out the market assessment or do it in house. The following techniques can be used if the firm decides to do the assessment in house.

Multiplier of Landscape Architecture Salaries

One way to assess the size of the landscape architecture market in any region is to identify the number of landscape architects practicing there, multiply by a salary and overhead factor, and convert to a yearly statistic. The number of registered landscape architects practicing in a city or region may be obtained from statistics available from the state board of technical registration, the yellow pages, or the local chapter of ASLA. If the region does not have licensure, professional registration, or an ASLA chapter, another option is to identify the number of registered architects or civil engineers practicing there. As a rule of thumb, there are ten architects and fifteen civil engineers practicing in every region for each landscape architect. Thus if the numbers of these related professions are available, the firm can estimate the potential number of landscape architects by using the numbers from the allied professionals. Next, the firm can determine the number of nonregistered landscape architects by assuming three nonregistrants for each registrant. Assuming that registrants would be in positions such as principals and project managers, and that nonregistrants would be in positions such as draftspersons and designers, an average pay rate can be set for each category. Average pay rates can be determined by using a number of different national publications of annual salary surveys, such as that published by Practice Management Associates, Ltd., of Newton, Massachusetts, or by using the firm's current pay rate categories. Last, an overhead and profit multiplier, such as 150 percent of the pay rate, should be established. To determine the size of the market, multiply the number of landscape architects in each category by the pay rate per hour, add the overhead and profit amount, and multiply by 2,080 hours per year to arrive at the annual amount. Totaling the amount will result in an approximation of the economic market size:

(50 registrants × $30 per hour)
+ (50 × $45 per hour) × 2,080   = $ 7,800,000

(150 nonregistrants × $14 per hour)
+ (150 × $21 per hour) × 2,080 = $10,920,000

Total $18,720,000

The total market figure should be adjusted down because every hour of the yearly work week will not be available for producing revenue due to time spent in job development, overhead activities, vacations, and sick leave. Seventy percent of registrants' time and 85 percent of nonregistrants' time would be a more likely scenario of time available for producing revenue, resulting in an adjusted total market of $14,742,000. The total market figure may be adjusted up or down based on the national or regional economy or other factors deemed relevant. If the local market has a higher-than-average number of practicing architects and engineers, the total market potential may be reduced because these professionals are likely to control a part of the market that would otherwise be available to landscape architecture firms. Economic adjustments are somewhat arbitrary, but it may be better to err on the conservative side. In the preceding example, the landscape architecture firm might apply a 20 percent reduction due to a large number of allied professionals working in the expansion market, resulting in an adjusted total market of $11,793,600 for the expansion market.

Public Records Method

Virtually all cities, counties, and states make forecasts and projected budgets for public spending. These projections are often made five years in advance. Thus the city or county parks and recreation department will have a five-year projection of park development that will require planning and design efforts. The city or county transportation department will have a five-year budget projection of new roads and public works spending. Sometimes the projections will include categories for landscape architecture and environmental assessment associated with the transportation and public works improvements. Other times only total line item amounts will be available for the transportation and public works improvements. If only the total is available, a percentage of the cost, such as 5 percent, can be assumed for the landscape architectural work.

By researching the public records and budget projections, the landscape architecture firm can identify a total of public funds that will be spent in construction of public projects in the landscape architecture market. The total can be multiplied by a percentage such as 6 percent or 8 percent to determine the magnitude of fees that may be available (see table 8-1).

As a rule of thumb, the public works market in the expansion area can be estimated to be 50 percent of the private-sector market under normal economic conditions. Thus in the first year shown in table 8-1,

TABLE 8-1   **Estimating Landscape Architecture Fees by Using Public Spending Forecasts**

Public Agency	Year 1	Year 2	Year 3	Year 4
County transportation department	$5.0[a]	$5.5	$5.8	$6.0
City engineering department	2.0	2.3	2.5	2.7
City housing authority	1.0	1.5	2.0	2.5
County parks department	10.0	12.0	15.0	18.0
City parks department	8.0	9.0	5.0	5.0
Other	1.0	1.1	1.2	1.3
Total	27.0	31.4	31.5	35.5
Landscape architecture				
Fees @ 6%	1.62	1.88	1.89	2.13
Landscape				
Arch Fees @ 8%	2.16	2.51	2.52	2.84

[a] Fees in millions of dollars.

the landscape architecture firm can assume a total market of $4.32 million if 8 percent is used as the public-fee percentage likely and 50 percent is used as the public/private market split. Further adjustment can be based on local conditions. If the targeted expansion area is experiencing a boom in industrial growth and housing, the private-sector market may be estimated as being twice as large as the public-sector market, resulting in an estimated total market of $6.48 million in fees.

Local or Regional Statistics on Niche Markets

There are many sources of information about niche markets. Housing is a good example. Local chapters of the National Association of Home Builders (NAHB) produce statistics on the number of houses built by category, such as single-family and multifamily. The landscape architecture firm can assess the size of the housing market by using the statistics available on housing starts and information from the firm's own archives.

Let's assume that housing information for the target city or region indicates that five thousand new homes will be constructed annually. This number can be multiplied by an average price per home of $100,000, for example, to arrive at the total housing market of $500 million. The actual average price per home is another statistic that is available from local and national sources. By studying the records of the firm's current housing market, the percentage of the

market that utilizes the services of a landscape architecture firm can be determined. Let's say that the firm estimates that 50 percent of the housing projects in the firm's current market use the services of a landscape architect for environmental assessment, site planning, and landscape design. The expansion market can be expected to represent a similar percentage, or $250 million, of landscape architecture services. Of the total market, the landscape architecture firm estimates that 5 percent of the housing costs, or $12.5 million, are for environmental assessment, site planning, and landscape design. If fees for the private sector work average 10 percent, the landscape architecture housing niche market is $1.25 million.

Making an estimate of the market potential is an important element of deciding whether to expand into a new geographic area. The process should be carried out in the most defensible manner possible. Having a reasonably good estimate of the market potential is much better than blindly entering a market.

How to Get Established in the New Market

If the landscape architecture firm determines that it has a marketable service, has evaluated the revenue potential of the market, and has decided that it is feasible to capture enough market share so that future profits will pay back expansion costs, the firm must decide how it will establish its presence in the new geographic market and how it will compete with the existing firms in the market.

There are five basic ways to establish the firm's presence in the new geographic market and open an office:

1. Merger/acquisition with an existing firm
2. Hiring away a principal or key person from a firm in the existing market
3. Relocating a principal or key staff person from the firm to the new market
4. Shuttling a principal or key staff person to the new market
5. Associating with a local firm to secure a large project

Merger/Acquisition

Often a firm in the expansion market can benefit as much by a merger as the landscape architecture firm desiring to enter the new market. The greatest difficulty with this method of expansion is finding a candidate that is interested in merging and is compatible with the parent landscape architecture firm. Merger/ acquisitions are time consuming if a willing partner is not readily found. Even if a willing partner is found, a merger/acquisition can take a year or more to work through and complete. Merger/acquisitions are not always successful. They require a considerable investment of management time. Regardless, merger/acquisition should always be considered as a means of expansion in the new geographic area.

Hiring Away

One of the best ways to speed up the expansion process and the local learning curve is by hiring away a locally successful principal or key staff person from another firm to serve as the principal in charge of the expansion office. The main downside is training the principal in the policies and practices of the landscape architecture firm. One other problem that can occasionally occur is that the new principal can use the opportunity to establish a private practice and then jump ship after the office is established. In most cases the new principal in charge of the expansion office will excel if empowered to develop the local market drawing on the expertise and marketing capability of the parent firm. When looking to hire away the talent for the new expansion office, the landscape architecture firm should look not only toward the private sector, but also to public employees who may be looking to move into the private market. Hiring an employee of

the local parks department, for example, can provide opportunities to obtain park work through the knowledge and contacts of the new hire.

Relocating a Principal or Key Staff Person

Developing an expansion office may be a timely opportunity for professional development and personal growth for one of the principals in the landscape architecture office or an ambitious associate or project manager. Starting a new office anywhere is a challenge that may provide a career opportunity for someone from the parent office. This is a good way to challenge and retain valuable staff if there is nowhere for them to move upward in the parent office.

Shuttling to the Expansion Location

Many firms have used this approach successfully to reduce some of the overhead costs associated with expansion offices. A principal is assigned the job of shuttling back and forth between the main office and the expansion office, staying perhaps two or three days a week in the expansion location to carry out job- and client-development tasks. Firms often use an executive suite type of office with a secretarial pool and an answering service in the expansion location, reducing the overhead costs until enough jobs have been developed to allow a fully staffed, permanent office location. This method of geographic expansion is economical and allows the landscape architecture firm to cut its losses and exit from the expansion attempt if it does not appear to be a profitable venture.

Associating with a Local Firm

Another way that some firms have initiated expansion into a new geographic area is by associating with a local firm to obtain one or more large contracts. This method usually works well when the landscape architecture firm has expertise or resources that can be instrumental for a smaller local firm to secure the large project. If there is to be a steady stream of similar projects, the landscape architecture firm can use the first project as a stepping stone to obtaining further work and ultimately to establishing the expansion office. This method can often result in an opportunity for merger/acquisition with the smaller local firm. Having developed work in the expansion location will also expedite expansion by the other means discussed, such as shuttling a principal back and forth.

The Marketing Staff

The size and makeup of the landscape architecture firm's marketing staff depends on the size of the firm, its financial resources, and the marketing attitude of the principals and owners of the firm, or how accepting they are of the need for a proactive marketing program. In one sense, the marketing staff is the entire firm, all of its staff, no matter how large the firm. Making all of the firm's staff sensitive to marketing and market opportunities is goal number one of the firm's lead marketing personnel.

Notwithstanding the fact that all of the firm's staff play a role in marketing the firm's services, job development, and client maintenance, the greater the number of the firm's staff that is able to take on sole and specific functions of marketing, the more effective and

---

I.   Occupational classification: marketing production coordinator
II. Organizational relationships
   A. Reports to: director of marketing
   B. Supervises: none
   C. Coordinates with
      1. Design and production staff
      2. Secretarial and administrative staff
      3. Project managers
      4. Director of human resources
      5. Business and finance director
      6. Principal in charge of corporate planning and marketing
      7. Principal in charge of production
      8. Director of landscape architecture
      9. Director of planning
      10. Director of information systems
      11. Public relations director
III. Primary duties: Produces proposals and marketing and advertising materials. Implements the firm's public relations program. Manages photo archives and slide file. Annually updates all SF254 and SF255 materials. Annually updates mailing lists and agency procurement data. Manages the data systems for marketing information and public relations.
IV. Work performed
   A. Principal duties
      1. Work with principals and staff and generate final copies of proposals.
         a) Produce proposals.
         b) Assist technical staff in gathering data for technical aspects of proposal production.
         c) Prepare graphics and insert materials for proposals.
         d) Write descriptions and promotional material for proposals.
         e) Coordinate production of proposals with technical staff.
      2. Develop and carry out public relations plan in coordination with director of marketing, principals, and management staff.
         a) Design and produce annual calendar.
         b) Design and produce at least twenty-four new project cut sheets each year.
         c) Update the firm's general brochure every two years.
         d) Identify national, regional, and local awards programs and submit for at least two national and four regional and local programs each year.

FIGURE 8-5. Job description for a marketing production coordinator.

3. Develop, maintain, and improve data input and retrieval systems for marketing and management information.
   a) Develop and maintain an efficient workstation.
   b) Create and maintain hard-copy and electronic master files of project descriptions, staff résumés, SF254, SF255, qualifications, firm history, and other information pertinent to proposals.
   c) Update the firm's SF254 annually and mail to appropriate agencies and clients by February 1 of each year.
4. Train new employees about the firm's past project experience. Develop a project information packet that is included in the initial information given to new employees.
5. Assist principals in formulating an effective public relations program for effective firm participation in community service.
   a) Identify community service opportunities.
   b) Maintain contact with representatives of community service groups.
   c) Develop and administer the annual budget for community service.
   d) Publicize the firm's participation in community service events.

B. Coordinating duties
   1. Coordinate with the marketing director.
   2. Remain in close contact with principals for public relations opportunities.
   3. Coordinate with administrative staff for filing space needs.

C. Subsidiary duties
   1. Develop and maintain slide files.
   2. Update project information files.
   3. Create graphics and coordinate reproduction services for proposal submittals.
   4. Manage the firm's job-site sign program.
   5. Perform other related duties as requested.
   6. Coordinate with directors of marketing, landscape architecture, and planning to identify and select most promising projects for PR value.
   7. Support directors of marketing, landscape architecture, and planning, as well as principals and project managers in their individual marketing and public relations efforts.
   8. Assist in the development and updating of the firm's marketing program.
   9. Provide technical staff with support in their individual marketing and public relations efforts.

V. Education, experience, and job requirements
   1. Good writing skills
   2. Macintosh computer skills
   3. Proficiency in page-layout, word-processing, spreadsheet, and database software applications
   4. Skills in management, planning, and coordinating work activities
   5. Sensitivity to interpersonal relations
   6. Photography skills
   7. Ability to establish and maintain effective working relationships with staff and the general public
   8. Competent and current with technology applied to marketing and public relations such as print media, TV, and internet marketing
   9. Three years minimum experience in marketing and public relations

VI. Measurement of performance
   1. Timely and accurate submittal of proposals
   2. Exceptional graphic design and visual quality of proposals, marketing, and public relations materials
   3. Harmony, happiness, and cooperation between co-workers

FIGURE 8-5. (Cont'd.)

successful the firm's marketing endeavors are likely to be. Most firms can not afford to delegate full-time staff responsibility or hire full-time marketing staff until the firm has reached a considerable size and revenues are large enough to support the overhead of full-time marketing efforts. Typically, a firm needs to have fifteen to twenty employees and have revenue of approximately $750,000 before it can begin to think about full-time marketing staff. Until such time, marketing functions are handled by one or more principals working with assistance from the firm's planning and design staff and its secretarial staff. The principals are responsible for contacts; following up on leads; responding to RFIs, RFQs, and RFPs; and leading the firm in its interviews. Secretarial staff, aided by computers and page layout software, are normally indispensable in the production of proposals. The downside is taking principals away from revenue production.

If the economy (the external economic environment) is expanding or is particularly conducive to landscape architecture work, the firm will most likely be on a growth path and will eventually need full-time marketing staff. The first marketing person normally hired is a marketing coordinator responsible for producing proposals, coordinating the efforts of the technical staff who write the technical core of proposals, producing marketing materials, and managing the firm's public relations. Hiring a full-time marketing coordinator may coincide with one of the firm's principals devoting full time or nearly full-time to marketing. When this point is reached, the landscape architecture firm must be able to set an overhead rate high enough to generate revenue as much as $40,000 in overhead costs just for salaries.

If the firm continues to grow, it might add a proposal production assistant, and a second and third principal might devote more time solely to marketing, job development, and client maintenance. At some point, the firm might consider a full-time marketing person at the principal level. Marketing support staff may be hired to manage photo archives and the production of marketing materials. Another option is hiring outside consulting firms to carry out some of the marketing functions, such as producing marketing materials.

The largest landscape architecture firms, which have multiple offices in several states and foreign countries, will not only have marketing staff in each individual office, but also have a corporate marketing department working out of the headquarters office.

The corporate marketing staff will study market trends and develop marketing strategies to tap the trends. They will meet with the top management of the firm and see that the firm's marketing direction is in line with firm's corporate goals. They will assist local offices with different marketing problems and in developing important clients. They will also develop cross-office marketing tools and make each office aware of the human resources available in the other offices. They may develop the firm's most high-profile marketing materials, such as a corporate brochure, video, or book describing the history and achievements of the firm.

REFERENCES

Birnberg & Associates/The Profit Center. 1985. *Small Design Firm Marketing Manual.* Chicago: Charles Grant Pederson.

Kotler, Philip. 1988. *Marketing Management: Analysis, Planning, Implementation, and Control.* 6th ed. Englewood Cliffs, N.J.: Prentice Hall.

STUDY QUESTIONS AND ASSIGNMENTS

1. Interview principals of landscape architecture firms in your area to find out how they obtain clients and contracts. Do they have a marketing plan? Do they follow it? What methods does the firm use to differentiate itself from other firms? What role does quality of services and completed design projects play in the marketing of the firm's professional services? Identify what the principals believe are the keys to marketing and obtaining clients and contracts. Discuss your findings in a paper.

2. Using this chapter and other references, write a paper that illustrates your understanding of the keys to successful marketing for a landscape architecture firm.

3. Divide your class into three-to-five-person teams. Each team is to function as a design office. Develop a strategic plan for your office.

4. Divide your class into three-to-five-person teams. Each team is to function as a design office. Develop a marketing plan for your office.

5. Divide your class into three-to-five-person teams. Each team is to function as a design office. Using projects you have completed in design studios or elsewhere, develop a series of project cut sheets for your work.

6. Develop an outline and techniques that you would use to make cold calls to prospective clients. Practice making cold calls to your classmates or to actual prospective clients so that you can fine-tune the outline and techniques.

7. Find a public-speaking opportunity in your community and carry out the speaking engagement.

8. Design a trade-show or conference booth for presenting the work of a landscape architecture firm. Present your design graphically. Consider building a model of the booth to a size of 10 feet by 20 feet.

9. Develop a slide and photo, video, or digital archive system for the work you have completed in school or in your practice of landscape architecture design.

10. Find an RFP advertising the need for professional landscape architecture service in your community. Obtain the RFP. Divide your class into three-to-five-person teams. Each team is to function as a design office. Each team is to develop a proposal in response to the specific guidelines of the RFP. Take the process to the point where each of the teams in the class is hypothetically shortlisted and prepare for an interview. Hold a mock interview.

11. Using this chapter and other references, try to determine the dollar size of the landscape architecture market in your region.

CHAPTER NINE

Contracts

Writing a contract for professional services is one of the most important skills a landscape architect must acquire. A contract is the foundation for providing professional services to a client. It is the legal document that sets forth the obligations of each party to the contract. It specifies the duties and responsibilities of the entities that sign the contract and should leave as little as possible open to interpretation.

Landscape architects enter into contractual agreements with at least four entities: clients, allied professionals, credit agencies, and employees. The contract formats are different for each entity. The landscape architect also has a different type of contractual relationship with the client or owner of a project that will be constructed or implemented based on the professional's instruments of service. The landscape architect has an agency relationship and serves as the owner's agent.

When the landscape architect enters into a contract with a client, the professional should be cautious about entering into a professional services agreement without a written contract. Although landscape architects use oral agreements, the precise terms of an oral agreement are difficult to prove in the event of a contract dispute. Both written and oral contracts are binding, but written contracts that are explicit and thorough are far superior to oral contracts.

The landscape architect also enters into contracts with allied professionals where the landscape architect serves as a prime consultant and the allied professional serves as a subconsultant. Again, a written contract is preferable. The agreement between the landscape architect and the subconsultant is frequently tied to the

agreement between the landscape architect and the client. The terms that bind the landscape architect to the client are typically incorporated into the agreement between the landscape architect and the subconsultant.

The landscape architect enters into contracts with creditors, including vendors such as blueprinting companies, long-distance phone service providers, office cleaning services, computer technicians, and others that carry out business transactions with the landscape architect under specified payment terms.

Banks or lending institutions also use contracts to bind the terms by which they will provide financing to the landscape architect. These lenders use tightly written contracts that tie security interests to accounts receivable, real property, real estate, or another form of collateral. In both vendor and lender contracts, the landscape architect's ability to negotiate and understand the terms is an acquired skill. This chapter will discuss some of the elements of negotiating a contract that is favorable to both parties. The landscape architect should always seek legal assistance, however, if the terms of a contract with a vendor or a lender are difficult to understand or negotiate in a successful manner.

The last type of contract that will be discussed is the landscape architecture firm's agreement with its employees. Most firms today use an employment agreement that spells out the terms of employment and gives the firm the right to discharge the employee with or without cause.

Most of this chapter will focus on the development of the contract for professional services, covering the key terminology and the main elements of a contract, as well as the proposal process, the cornerstone of forming a contract for professional services. A section of this chapter also covers the important elements, or clauses, of a contract that are favorable to the professional, and another section covers the skills and attitudes helpful in negotiating a contract.

Contract Terminology

Enforceable Contract. For a contract to be enforceable, where the parties have the legal obligation to perform the duties specified by the contract, it must have the elements required to bind the parties.

The elements of an enforceable contract include

1. voluntary agreement
2. consideration
3. lawfulness
4. legally competent parties
5. enforceable form

Voluntary Agreement. When the landscape architect makes an offer to provide specific professional services, the contract contains half of the first enforceable element. When the client accepts the offer for professional services, the second half of the first enforceable element occurs. Agreement exists when an offer is voluntarily made *and* accepted. The description of the scope of professional services to be provided by the landscape architect, including all of the qualifying clauses of the agreement, spells out the terms of the agreement that will be executed for consideration.

Consideration. When the landscape architect promises to prepare construction documents and the owner promises to pay the landscape architect, consideration is consummated in the agreement. Consideration is the pledge to exchange something of value in order to bind the contract.

Lawfulness. A contract between a landscape architect and a client should be for a lawful purpose. One should not enter into a contract for illegal activities because the contract would not be enforceable in a court of law.

The lawfulness of contracts is more important than one would think due to professional licensure laws. An unlicensed professional, for example, must be careful not to break the law by offering landscape architecture services if the licensure law in his or her state is a practice law requiring that only a registered landscape architect may legally provide landscape architecture services.

Legally Competent Parties. A contract must be signed by legally competent parties. If the landscape architect and the client are representing business entities, such as corporations, each person must have the authority to make legal commitments for his or her company. When in doubt about the authority of a client's representative, the landscape architect can request that the contract be signed by a corporate officer or suggest to the client's representative that the corporate seal be affixed to the contract and signed by an officer. Another way to handle this issue of competency is to suggest that the client include a written clause in the contract indicating that the person who signs the contract has the legal authority to act on behalf of the corporation. Legally competent parties are needed to sign contracts not only for private-sector work but also for public-sector projects.

Enforceable Form. The landscape architect must ensure that the contract will remain in force in the event that some part of the contract violates the law. The entire contract may be judged unenforceable or void if only one of its clauses is found to be unlawful.

Contracts should include a severability and survival clause in order to avoid nullifying the entire contract if a small part of it is found to be invalid and to ensure that some of the contract's provisions, such as a limit-of-liability clause and terms covering dispute resolution, will continue in force after the landscape architect has completed the scope of services and has been paid. The following is an example of a severability and survival clause:

> In the event that any term or terms of this contract are found to be unlawful, all other provisions of this contract shall remain in full force and effect. The following Articles of the contract shall survive the termination of the scope of services and shall continue to be enforceable between the parties to the maximum legal extent (Dixon and Crowell 1993).

Both the landscape architect and the client may wish to have contract provisions providing for the severability and survivability of certain elements of the contract.

Unenforceable Contract. A clause, a provision, or some element of the execution of the contract that is illegal may cause the contract to become impossible to enforce. For example, a contract with a public-sector client for a project that was approved, but for which no funding was authorized, is likely to be an unenforceable contract. A contract may also be unenforceable because it has become invalid under the provisions of the statute of limitations.

Void Contract. When one of the elements required to bind a contract (agreement, consideration, lawfulness, legally competent parties, enforceable form) is missing, the contract may be considered void. When a contract is voidable, either the landscape architect or the client has the legal right to terminate the contract. An example of when a landscape architect would consider voiding a contract is if the client used fraud as an enticement for the professional to sign a contract (Dixon and Crowell 1993).

Arbitration. The method of settling a contract dispute by agreeing in advance in the contract to accept the decision of an impartial person (an arbiter) based on evidence and argument presented by the parties to the contract is the process of arbitration (Wehringer 1969).

Mediation. Settling a contract dispute by facilitated negotiation is the process of mediation (Kovach 1994).

Litigation. The process of settling a contract dispute through legal proceedings and a lawsuit is called litigation. In litigation, one or both of the parties feel the other is 100 percent responsible for the contract dispute, and neither is willing to assume any responsibility. An adversarial situation usually exists.

Breach of Contract. A contract is said to have been breached if one of the parties to the contract reneges on performing the terms of the contract. The injured party may seek relief and damages from the party that breached the contract.

Contracts with Clients— Professional Services Contract Formats

There are three formats most often used by landscape architects for the professional services contract:

1. Professional association standard contracts
2. Landscape architect–developed contracts
3. Client-developed contracts

Professional Association Standard Contracts

Sometimes landscape architects use a standard contract developed by professional associations. The association standard contract most frequently used is published by the American Institute of Architects (AIA). The document is covered by copyright laws, which protect unauthorized photocopying of the document. The landscape architect can purchase original copies from the local AIA chapter or from the American Institute of Architects, 1735 New York Avenue, NW, Washington, DC 20006.

The association standard contracts provide blank areas to fill in the elements specific to the firm, the client, and the project. The contracts also include general-purpose articles, terms, and conditions that have been developed to cover the work that typifies a design and construction contract. The user should review the general articles, terms, and conditions and adapt or strengthen them to suit the needs of each specific project.

The 1993 edition of the AIA *Standard Form of Agreement Between Owner and Architect with Descriptions of Designated Services and Terms and Conditions* includes the following table of articles:

PART 1—FORM OF AGREEMENT
Article 1.1   Schedule of Design Services
Article 1.2   Compensation
Article 1.3   Payments
Article 1.4   Time and Cost
Article 1.5   Enumeration of Documents
Article 1.6   Other Conditions or Services

PART 2—DESCRIPTIONS OF
                DESIGNATED SERVICES
Article 2.1   Designated Services
Article 2.2   Phases of Designated Services
Article 2.3   Descriptions of Designated Services
Article 2.4   Descriptions of Supplemental
                Services

PART 3—TERMS AND CONDITIONS

Article 3.1 Architect's Responsibilities
Article 3.2 Owner's Responsibilities
Article 3.3 Contract Administration
Article 3.4 Use of Project Drawings,
            Specifications and Other Documents
Article 3.5 Cost of the Work
Article 3.6 Payments to the Architect
Article 3.7 Dispute Resolution
Article 3.8 Miscellaneous Provisions
Article 3.9 Termination, Suspension
            or Abandonment

Source: AIA (1993)

The AIA also produces a standard form agreement for special services used when project design and construction are not the focus of the scope of work. Landscape architects may find the special services standard form agreement, AIA Document B727, well suited to their projects.

Landscape Architect–Developed Contracts

All landscape architecture firms, in one way or another, develop their own form of agreement to be used as a professional services contract with a client. The most common format is probably a letter agreement. The tedium of customizing a standard letter contract format to meet the needs of each individual project has been made easy and quick by using word-processing and spreadsheet software. Figure 9-1 is an example of a letter agreement format. Figure 9-2 is an example of a scope of services, hours projection, and derivation of fee written as an attachment to the letter agreement.

The landscape architect–developed contract form usually evolves over a number of years. As the professionals in the design firm come across different contract forms received from other professionals, for example, or that are generated by their clients, the landscape architects amend their own standard contract form with new or improved clauses. A landscape architecture firm should have an attorney review the firm's standard contract form both when the contract form is created and periodically throughout the firm's life. Keeping the firm's standard contract form legally current and ensuring that it contains adequate language to protect the interests of the firm's landscape architects is an important business practice.

Client-Developed Contracts

When a landscape architecture firm is asked to sign a contract developed by a client, the need for careful review is even more important and the firm's attorney should review any parts of the contract unclear to the landscape architect. Client-developed contracts, particularly contracts used by public-sector and corporate clients, are usually written to favor the client.

The most disagreeable provision found in client-developed contracts is the *hold-harmless clause,* where the intent is to transfer to the landscape architect all of the exposure and liability for any and all claims related to the project. The landscape architect is asked to indemnify the client and assume the client's legal liability in the event of a claim or a lawsuit. The validity of hold-harmless language in contracts varies from state to state; but some states vigorously support and uphold the indemnification clauses used by governmental jurisdictions. Local and state governments rely upon indemnification as a form of legal defense in the event of a lawsuit related to a landscape architecture project.

Cities and other government bodies will ask the landscape architect to accept unlimited liability in the contract for professional services. The hold-harmless clause will even ask the landscape architect to defend the city, too, covering all of the legal costs for defense before there is proof that the firm even has liability for negligence. Cities insist that the landscape architect sign a contract with the hold-harmless clause or the city will not award the contract to the firm. The best approach for countering the hold-harmless provision in a client-developed contract is to request firmly that the client delete the clause from the contract. The landscape architect can explain that he or she is already obligated by law to perform professional services with the standard of care practiced by other landscape architects, and that professional licensure and tort law also require the landscape architect to practice in a nonnegligent manner.

If persuasion is not effective in having the hold-harmless clause removed, the landscape architect can attempt to change the wording of the clause so that

Ace Landscape Architects

Landscape Architecture
Site Planning
Park & Recreation Planning
Urban Design
Environmental Assessment
Irrigation Design
Water Conservation Planning
Desert Revegetation Programs

ACE #96110-00

Mr. Bill Jones
The Architects Group, Inc. AIA
2552 N. Alvernon Way
Tucson, AZ 85712

Subject: Agreement by and between Ace Landscape Architects, Inc. ("ACE") and The Architects Group, Inc. ("Client") for the RV Park, Casino, and Convenience Mart on the Tohono-O'Odham Indian Nation, near Why, Arizona

Dear Bill:

This letter will serve as our proposal and agreement to provide the professional landscape architectural services that you requested for the above referenced subject. We are pleased to have the opportunity for providing these services and assure you of our interest and best professional effort consistent with the normal standard of care practiced by professional landscape architects.

If this proposal does not meet your scope of services or fee expectations, please call me so that we will have an opportunity to negotiate and resolve any issues that you may have.

Scope of Work

ACE will develop a master plan for an RV Park of approximately 90 spaces. The master plan will include a connection to the Casino and Convenience Store. ACE also will prepare design development plans and construction documents for the site amenities, landscaping, and irrigation. We will coordinate with the Client, the Owner, and other consultants as indicated in the scope of services. The construction budget for our work has been established at $125,000.

2440 E. Broadway Blvd.
Tucson, AZ 85719
(520) 622-2302
FAX (520) 622-8270

FIGURE 9-1. Example of a letter agreement.

We see a key part of our role on this project as being environmental advocates to see that the RV Park, access road, septic systems, pedestrian circulation and common and recreation facilities are sensitively developed in relation to the outstanding natural resources of the site. We are very excited about having the opportunity to prepare a master plan for the RV Park, siting it softly in the landscape and enhancing the relationship with the arroyo that bisects the site.

Scope of Services

ACE will provide the professional landscape architectural services described in attachment A. We have included an estimate of hours and a derivation of fees for your information.

The Scope of Services is divided into three phases as follows:

Phase 1: Master plan and schematic design
   A. Site visit and analysis, master plan, and coordination
   B. Schematic plan of the RV Park

Phase 2: Design development and construction documents
   A. Design development plans
   B. Landscape and site construction documents

Phase 3: Services during construction

Additional and Excluded Services

Additional services, including but not limited to the following, are not provided under the terms of this agreement but will be provided at your request or concurrence.

1. Presentation renderings, perspectives, models.
2. Changes to approved concepts or plans necessitating redoing the design, plans, or specifications.
3. Soil, or other materials, testing; engineering services, including structural engineering.
4. Any services not included in or in excess of the scope and fee proposal, attachment A, that are provided by ACE at your request or concurrence.

FIGURE 9-1. (*Cont'd.*) Example of a letter agreement.

Professional Fee

ACE will provide the Landscape Architecture Services for the fees itemized in attachment A.

Hourly Services

All services provided on an hourly basis will be billed at the following hourly rates:

Project landscape architect $80.00/hour
Project designer/drafter $40.00/hour

The General Terms and Conditions set forth on the attached pages are incorporated herein and made a part of this agreement.

We are very interested in working with you on this project and are pleased to submit this proposal and agreement to you. If you concur with this agreement, please return a signed copy for our files.

Sincerely,

Robert Anderson, ASLA
Principal, Ace Landscape Architects, Inc.

This Agreement accepted this _____ day of _____, 1996

By: _____

FIGURE 9-1. (*Cont'd.*) Example of a letter agreement.

Hickiwan District Casino, Convenience Store and RV Park Landscape Architecture Services Scope and Fee Proposal

Scope of Services Item	Project Land. Arch.	Drafts-Person
Phase 1: Master Plan and Schematic Design Phase		
A. Site visit and analysis, master plan, and coordination		
1 Visit the site and carry out a thorough reconnaissance with aerial photograph in hand. Analyze site character and develop site concept.	16	
2 Prepare a master plan base plan for ACE's use at a scale of 1″ = 100′–0″. Client to provide aerial with topography.		8
3 Develop a master plan of the RV park as connected to the casino and convenience store for review and approval by the client and owner.	16	
4 Project administration, meetings with client and owner, coordination, and project management.	10	
Total hours	42	8
B. Schematic plan of the RV Park		
1 Develop a schematic plan of the RV park at a scale of 1″ = 40′–0″.	20	8
2 Meet with the client and owner to review the schematic plan.	4	
3 Project administration, meetings with client and owner, coordination, and project management.	4	
Total hours	28	8
Phase 2: Design Development and Construction Documents		
A. Design development plans		
1 Carry out design development for the site improvements, landscaping and irrigation.	16	
2 Prepare design development plans.	4	56
3 Meet with the client and owner to review design development plans.	4	
4 Prepare an estimate of probable construction costs for site improvements, landscaping, and irrigation.	1	8
5 Project administration, meetings with client and owner, coordination, and project management.	10	
Total hours	35	64

FIGURE 9-2. The scope of services, hours estimate, and derivation of fee (attachment A to the letter agreement, Figure 9-1).

Hickiwan District Casino, Convenience Store and RV Park Landscape Architecture Services Scope and Fee Proposal

Scope of Services Item	Project Land. Arch.	Drafts-Person
B. Landscape and site construction documents		
1 Prepare construction document base plans for TAG's use.		12
2 Develop and prepare landscape construction bid documents including revisions necessary from Client and Client review as follows:		
1. RV and Casino/Conv. Store site improvements and landscape plans	8	20
2. Irrigation plans & schedules	2	12
3. Landscape & irrigation installation details	1	8
4. Site improvement construction details	6	12
5. Camera-ready specifications in CSI format	4	6
3 Submit 90% complete plans to the Client for Client and Owner review and approval. Make revisions as requested.	2	4
4 Meet with the Client and Owner to review the 90% construction plans.	6	
5 Prepare an estimate of probable construction costs for site improvements, landscaping & irrigation.	1	6
6 Check plans, make final corrections, and transmit 100% complete, sealed construction documents to the Client.	6	8
7 Project administration, meetings with Client and Owner, coordination, and project management.	10	4
Total hours	46	92

Phase 3: Services during Bidding and Construction

	Project Land. Arch.
1 Provide services during bidding including attending a prebid meeting and clarification of documents.	4
2 Make 5 visits to the site for observation of workmanship and clarification of construction documents; prepare a report for each visit. (8 hours each)	40
3 Review and approve submittals.	8
4 Phone coordination with contractor and Owner.	2
5 Carry out a punch list review and prepare a written punchlist.	8
6 Provide project administration and management during construction.	4
Total hours	66

FIGURE 9-2. (*Cont'd.*) The scope of services, hours estimate, and derivation of fee (attachment A to the letter agreement, Figure 9-1).

Fee Proposal

Phase 1: Master Plan and Schematic Design Phase

A. Site visit and analysis, master plan, and coordination

42 hours project landscape architect	$3,360.00
8 hours draftsperson	$320.00
Fee	$3,680.00

B. Schematic plan of the RV park

28 hours project landscape architect	$2,240.00
8 hours draftsperson	$320.00
Fee	$2,560.00
Phase 1 fee	$6,240.00

Phase 2: Design Development and Construction Documents

A. Design development plans

35 hours project landscape architect	$2,800.00
64 hours draftsperson	$2,560.00
Fee	$5,360.00

B. Landscape and site construction documents

46 hours project landscape architect	$3,680.00
92 hours draftsperson	$3,680.00
Fee	$7,360.00
Phase 2 fee	$12,720.00

Phase 3: Services during Bidding and Construction

66 hours project landscape architect:	$5,280.00
Fee	$5,280.00
Extra per trip construction observation services	$600 Ea.

FIGURE 9-2. (*Cont'd.*) The scope of services, hours estimate, and derivation of fee (attachment A to the letter agreement, Figure 9-1).

both the landscape architect and the client indemnify each other for their own negligent acts. *The Contract Guide: DPIC's Risk Management Handbook for Architects and Engineers,* by Sheila A. Dixon and Richard D. Crowell, has an excellent model paragraph for the equitable sharing of liability between the landscape architect and the client:

The Design Professional agrees, to the fullest extent permitted by law, to indemnify and hold harmless from any damage, liability or cost (including reasonable attorneys' fees and costs of defense) to the extent caused by the Design Professional's negligent acts, errors or omissions in the performance of professional services under this agreement and those of his or her subconsultants or anyone for whom the Design Professional is legally liable.

The Client agrees, to the fullest extent permitted by law, to indemnify and hold the Design Professional harmless from any damage, liability or cost (including reasonable attorneys' fees and costs of defense) to the extent caused by the Client's negligent acts, errors or omissions in the performance of professional services under this agreement and those of his or her contractors, subcontractors or consultants or anyone for whom the Client is legally liable, and arising from the project that is the subject of this Agreement.

The Design Professional is not obligated to indemnify the Client in any manner whatsoever for the Client's own negligence (Dixon and Crowell 1993, 161).

Proposals—The Process of Forming a Contract

The contract for professional services is a direct evolution of the proposal. In most cases, the client develops the general scope of the project as a statement of the client's needs. The client is just as likely to also develop the proposal format. In other cases, the scope of the project is mutually developed by the landscape architect and the client. When the landscape architect develops the scope, he or she first meets with the client to discuss the client's aims at length, then attempts to translate the client's goals and objectives into a precise description of the needs and a scope of services.

Most public-sector clients, such as city or state agencies, have well-developed proposal formats that the landscape architect must follow explicitly as a requirement of pursuing the design commission. Public-sector clients often establish the fee, too, which may or may not be commensurate with the client's aims.

The scope of work, the scope of services, and the fee are spelled out generally in the client's request for proposals (RFP), and the landscape architect is asked to elaborate on them. The landscape architect's elaboration of the scope and the fee proposal is the beginning of the contracting process regardless of which contract format is used. A specific and well-thought-out proposal is necessary for engaging the contract process. The proposal is the first element that is negotiated with the client, and the landscape architect and the client must first agree that the scope of work and scope of services are appropriate for the project and can be adequately completed for the client's proposed fee. Upon agreement, the remainder of the terms and conditions of the contract for professional services will be negotiated.

A specific and well-thought-out proposal is the cornerstone of the agreement. The client's aim is often to keep the scope to a minimum—hoping, of course, to keep the fee to the lowest possible amount commensurate with the proposed scope of services. The landscape architect, on the other hand, has a professional obligation to identify and call to the attention of the client the full gamut of professional services and scope of work that he or she deems appropriate for the project. The landscape architect should not hesitate to be thorough in the proposal process so that all of the work necessary to complete a thoroughly professional services obligation is detailed. If the client's proposed fee is inadequate, the landscape architect must have the courage and assertiveness to inform the client. Doing so transfers the onus to the client to make decisions about what services the client absolutely needs and what services are not within the funds budgeted for the project. In cases where the funding is not commensurate with the scope of the project, the landscape architect should be very cautious. If the client wants the full range of services proposed by the professional but is not able or willing to pay for them, the landscape architect must be careful to negotiate a realistic scope if additional funding is not available. If the scope does not match the perceived needs and budget of the client, the landscape architect may find that the project cannot be properly completed with the standard of care practiced by landscape architecture professionals. In cases where the scope and budget cannot be effectively matched, the landscape architect may wish to forgo working on the project because the work may compromise the professional's standard of care or the professional may end up providing more services than the client is willing to pay for and losing money on the project.

Proposals are presented in a letter format that often doubles as the agreement if the client concurs with the proposal, or they are presented in the client's prescribed format. The scope of work and scope of services that are written in the proposal are frequently appended to the final contract format, so great care and attention must be paid to the proposal-forming process.

One last benefit of the proposal-forming process is the opportunity to glean how open the client is to negotiating the contract. If the client is stubborn or not willing to make compromises on the scope of work and the scope of services in order to bring project expectations in line with available fees, the client may be equally unwilling to negotiate terms and conditions of the contract that put extreme risk, responsibility, and liability on the professional.

Elements of a Successful Written Proposal

The quality of the landscape architect's proposal is a key determinant in whether the client becomes interested. There are a number of elements of a written proposal that enhance its success:

- *Accuracy.* Are the facts, figures, and grammar accurate? What is a client to think of the landscape architect's professional and technical capability if the proposal includes spelling errors, errors of fact, or you've spelled the client's name wrong?
- *Completeness.* A complete proposal is essential, but it should not include a lot of extraneous material. Eliminate fluff. Deciding the right degree of completeness is often one of the more difficult aspects of preparing a proposal, particularly for large, complex, and big-fee projects. Win or lose, one of the best compliments a landscape architect can receive about a proposal is that it is concise and to the point.

   Proposals written in response to an RFP must pay careful attention to presenting in the proposal the answers to the specific questions asked.
- *Be persuasive.* The landscape architect's proposal must convince the client that he or she can do what the client asks. The proposal must be persuasive. It should come across as confident.
- *Address the problems.* If there are serious problems to be overcome in the project, do not ignore them. Address the problems and suggest possible ways to resolve them. How you intend to handle problems associated with a project is one element of a proposal that makes for good discussion during an interview (if you make it to that stage of a selection process).
- *Solve the "right" problem.* Avoid presenting a proposal that includes everything but the kitchen sink. Avoid thinking that you can cover the problem if you tell the prospective client that you know everything about everything related to even the most remote or potential aspects of the client's project.
- *Be creative.* Successful proposals stand out from the others by their presentation, their graphic quality, and their creative response to the project.
- *Be selective.* You don't have to go after every RFP that comes across your desk. Evaluate each project and how it fits your expertise, experience, and office goals. Don't waste your efforts.
- *Make the proposal readable.* Delegate proposal writing to people in the office who can write. The readers of your proposal may not understand technical terms, so avoid jargon unless it is appropriate for the expected evaluator (Fuller 1991).

The Elements of a Professional Services Contract with a Client

Regardless of the format used, the professional services contract normally includes the following elements:

- Agreement
- Project description
- Scope of work
- Scope of services
- Responsibilities of the parties to the contract

- Fees
- Terms and conditions
- Signature lines

Agreement

A professional services contract should start by stating that it is an agreement by and between the owner and the landscape architect. The correct name and address of each should be used to precisely set forth the parties to the contract.

Project Description

The professional services contract should identify the name of the project and its location. The legal description of the property is the best way to describe the location, but an address will also work.

Scope of Work

The scope of work is different from the scope of services. The scope of work describes what the project is or is not about; the scope of services describes the actions that the landscape architect will carry out.

The scope of work describes what elements the owner wants the landscape architect to plan or design. It is a short version of the client's program and should include a statement of the client's budget, if known. The scope of work can be used to describe the components of the project and any specific construction materials or elements that define the level of quality the client desires in the design of the project and in the types of materials to be used. If the project is an ordinary commercial project, the scope of work can specify that the design professional will use construction materials such as standard concrete walks and asphalt paving. If the project is upscale, the scope of work can identify the types of materials, such as unit pavers, integrated-color concrete, or marble finishes, that will be used to achieve the high design quality the client desires. The scope of work is the section of the contract where the landscape architect spells out any of the qualifying elements of the planning or design project that the client has indicated are desired.

If the project is a site-planning project for a mixed-use housing development, for example, the scope of work might be stated as follows:

> The landscape architect will develop a plan that will locate on the 925-acre site approximately 500 single-family lots of 1 acre each, four apartment blocks of 15 acres each, two 30-acre blocks for patio homes, and one 10-acre commercial parcel with six 10,000-acre pads. The site plan will locate the major streets and the common open space, which will comprise approximately 200 acres of land. The common open space will include the high-quality riparian habitat that exists on the site.

If the project is a small commercial landscape design project for a branch bank office building, the scope of work might be stated as follows:

> The landscape architect will prepare design plans and construction documents for the 2-acre site including parking areas, sidewalks, entry plaza and site amenities including outdoor furniture, lighting, landscaping, and irrigation. The client has indicated that high-quality construction materials such as granite and marble stone should be used in the entry plaza. A fountain is also desired as a focal point of the entry plaza. The client desires large plant materials to be used in order to create an "instant" landscape effect. The client's construction budget for the site improvements and landscaping is $200,000.

Scope of Services

The items included in the scope of services are the specific actions or activities the landscape architect will carry out in order to accomplish the scope of work. The estimate of the hours needed to complete the project, as well as the fee, is based on the scope of services. Thus thoroughness is an important ingredient of developing the scope of services to ensure that all of the activities are identified. The landscape architect may be embarrassed if he or she has to go back to the client to ask for additional fees because one or more important or time-consuming tasks were omitted from the scope of services. The professional also runs the risk of having the client be unwilling to pay additional fees for services that must be carried out but were forgotten by the landscape architect when the design services contract was signed.

The scope of services may be divided into a number of headings as needed for clarity. In many standard contract formats, the scope of services is typically divided into *basic services,* which include the specific activities the landscape architect will carry out for the fees indicated, and *additional services,* which include any services not provided in the basic services.

Typical categories of standard basic services itemized for project design work include

- pre-design/programming
- site planning
- schematic design
- design development
- construction documents
- bidding and construction contract negotiation
- construction administration
- project administration, management, and co-ordination

A number of recommended services may be listed under the category of additional or excluded services so the client is clear that certain services are not provided under the terms of the contract for basic services. The following two items are catchall phrases that are typically listed as standard additional services in a landscape architecture contract:

1. Changes by the owner or client to approved concepts or plans necessitating redoing the design, plans, or specifications
2. Any services not included in or in excess of the scope of services—basic services that are provided by the landscape architect at the client's request or concurrence

I like to use a spreadsheet computer program for the scope of services and to include an hours estimate by category of professional staff. By taking advantage of the spreadsheet software capabilities, the hours by category can be automatically totaled, multiplied by the billing rates for each category, and added together to derive the total fee. The spreadsheet software allows effortless manipulation of the scope and the hours estimate until the right combination of hours is achieved to bring the proposed fee in harmony with the scope of services and the client's construction budget. The entire spreadsheet printout, including the hours estimate, if desired, can be attached to the contract, and the scope of services paragraph in the agreement can simply refer to attachment A, for example.

Using a spreadsheet to itemize the scope of services and hours estimate has another advantage. The spreadsheet software allows the landscape architect to make changes easily when the client reviews the scope of services and desires changes such as more or fewer services resulting in either a higher or lower fee. See figure 9-3 for an example of a scope of services, hours estimate, and derivation of fee for a single-family residential landscape architecture project.

Responsibilities of the Parties to the Contract

In many contracts, the landscape architect and the client have responsibilities pertaining to the successful completion of the project. Many of these responsibilities are related to providing information or access to information or resources. The client, for example, is responsible for providing a site boundary and topographic survey, soil tests and reports, a design program, a construction budget, and access to other information that is germane to successful completion of the project. The landscape architect is responsible for identifying the applicable codes and generally recognized planning and design principles necessary for completing the work. The professional is responsible for satisfying the requirements necessary for the project to be approved by public agencies and for obtaining necessary permits. The landscape architect is also responsible for carrying out the professional services in a manner that is reasonable, prudent, and consistent with the standard of care ordinarily practiced by other landscape architects.

Robinson Residence Professional Landscape Architecture Services Scope of Services and Derivation of Fee

Scope of Work Item	ESTIMATE OF HOURS	
	Project Landscape Architect	Draftsperson
Base Plan		
1 Prepare a site base plan for the Landscape Architect's use at a scale of 1/8" = 1'–0" using the architect's house plan and topography provided by the owner in the form of a boundary and topographic survey.	1	6
2 Visit the site. Carry out a field survey of existing conditions and locate significant existing trees on the base plan.	3	4
Subtotal	4	10
Master Landscape Plan		
1 Meet with the client regarding existing conditions, drainage, and to identify the client's desired site uses, construction, and plant materials.	2	
2 Develop a preliminary master landscape plan for review and concurrence. The plan will illustrate a grading and drainage solution, layout of site improvements, and plant and construction material selections.	12	
3 Prepare a preliminary estimate of probable construction costs for site improvements, landscaping, and irrigation.	1	3
4 Review the preliminary master landscape plan with the client.	2	
5 Incorporate changes desired by the client in the preparation of landscape construction bid documents.	4	
Subtotal	21	3
Construction Bid Documents		
1 Prepare construction documents, including		
A. Landscape and site improvement plan with spot elevations	2	6
B. Planting plan	2	6
C. Irrigation plan	1	5
D. Landscape, irrigation, and site improvement construction details	2	6
E. Specifications	1	3
2 Prepare an estimate of probable construction costs.	1	3
3 Meet with the client to review the construction bid documents.	2	
4 Make changes in the construction bid documents based on the review meeting with the client.	2	4
5 Provide project administration and coordination.	4	
Subtotal	17	33
Total hours	42	46

FIGURE 9-3. Example scope of services, hours estimate, and derivation of fee for a single-family residential project.

Derivation of Fee

Base Plan

4 hours project landscape architect	$320.00
10 hours draftsperson	$400.00
Fee	$720.00

Master Landscape Plan

21 hours project landscape architect	$1,680.00
3 hours draftsperson	$120.00
Fee	$1,800.00

Construction Bid Documents

17 hours project landscape architect	$1,360.00
33 hours draftsperson	$1,320.00
Fee	$2,680.00
Total fee	$5,200.00

FIGURE 9-3. (*Cont'd.*) Example scope of services, hours estimate, and derivation of fee for a single-family residential project.

Fees

The fee for professional services may be calculated and stated in many ways. The following are the most commonly used ways to present a professional fee:

- Hourly
- Fixed fee
- Multiplier of direct pay rates
- Percentage of construction

Of all the ways to present a fee in a contract, the fixed fee is used most often. The fixed fee allows the landscape architect to budget the work on the project in such a way as to cover costs and make a profit. Clients prefer fixed fees because they know exactly how much to budget for the professional services and what to expect for the fee. Clients often add a contingency in their budgets to cover the possibility of additional services materializing during the course of the project.

In some cases, the landscape architect cannot clearly estimate the amount of work and quotes an hourly fee that is agreed to by the client. An upset maximum amount may be specified so that the client has a ballpark idea of the fees that will be required and can budget for the fees.

Using a multiplier fee, the landscape architect estimates the number of hours required for the services and multiplies by the hourly pay rates of the employees who will carry out the services to arrive at a total of direct personnel costs. The total direct cost is then multiplied by a multiplier that covers the costs of overhead. Profit and the costs of reimbursable expenses are added to arrive at a total fee, usually expressed as a fixed fee.

A fee based on a percentage of construction is arrived at by multiplying the construction budget by a percentage rate, usually 6 percent to 12 percent. In this method of calculating the fee, the landscape architect may add a clause that sets the final fee based on the actual construction cost, using the budget estimate as the basis for setting the initial fee parameter.

Whatever approach is used, the contract should include the method for establishing fees for additional services. Typically, the landscape architect carries out additional services on an hourly basis at billing rates specified in the contract.

The fee section of the contract may also specify other related information, such as when invoices will be sent to the client and on what basis the landscape architect will submit for partial payments. The fee section of the contract can also specify those expenses that are to be considered reimbursable in addition to the professional fees. If a reimbursable multiplier is used, it should be specified. Professional design consultants typically specify a multiplier of 10 percent to 35 percent for handling reimbursable expenses and engaging the services of subconsultants.

Terms and Conditions

The elements of the professional services contract that deal with the business and legal understandings are called the *terms and conditions*. Many professional consulting firms have developed a separate contract attachment itemizing the terms and conditions. Professional association standard contracts, as well as contracts developed by clients, devote entire sections to terms and conditions. Some of the contract elements typically covered by the terms and conditions include who has ownership of documents and how they may be used, liability limitations, timeliness and schedule, cancellation and termination, warranties, liability limitations, insurance coverage, legal jurisdiction and court costs, assignment, dispute resolution, authority to enter into the agreement, covenants and conditions, publicity, and payment terms including cost of living adjustments. Figure 9-4 is an example of the terms and conditions contract attachment.

Signature Lines

Every contract should include signature lines for the parties signing the contract. As mentioned earlier, the person or persons signing for an entity must have the authority to bind the contract and commit the resources of each party to carrying out the terms of the contract.

Agency

Landscape architects serve as agents to their clients as part of the contract for professional services. In the agency relationship, the client authorizes the landscape architect to represent the client and make binding decisions in the client's business with a third party, usually the contractor. The authority is granted by the client under the terms of the contract. The agent is given the power to act with discretion on behalf of the client. There are normally three partners in the agency relationship: the client, the landscape architect, and the third party.

The landscape architect serves an agency role throughout the contract for professional services, but the role is more prominent when the landscape architect is carrying out construction administration and construction observation services. While serving as the client's agent, the landscape architect is empowered to do anything the client can do, and the landscape architect's agency actions should be guided by a few important guidelines:

- Act only in the client's best interest.
- Keep the client informed and seek concurrence of agreement for all agency decisions.
- Act only within the agency powers provided for under the terms of the contract.
- Do not act illegally or immorally.
- Do not act to further personal gains.
- Remember that any and all actions on behalf of the client will bind the client to the actions you have taken. Avoid actions that might bind the client to detrimental consequences.

During construction administration and observation, the landscape architect must take care to act judiciously and perform services that fall within his or her expertise. For example, do not provide construction observation services for a building that was designed by an architectural subconsultant under the design phase of the contract. Engage the architect, as part of the construction services, to perform the necessary building construction observation and make reports to the client through you. Misrepresentation of professional ability, such as the capability to inspect building construction, may cause the landscape architect to be accused of breaching the contract or even fraudulent representation of his or her professional capability. If the landscape architect attempts to perform construction services outside his or her expertise, and if damages occur, the landscape architect may be held liable for negligent acts (Hinze 1993).

General Terms and Conditions
Between Client and Ace Landscape Architects (ACE)

GENERAL

1. *Cooperation and client's obligations.* Client agrees to cooperate and to give all reasonable assistance to ACE in providing information and access to resources for expediting services to be performed on this project. The Client shall provide ACE with a program that sets forth the Client's objectives, schedule, a project budget, and other criteria necessary for ACE to perform the professional services. The Client shall designate a representative to act on behalf of the Client.

    The Client shall provide ACE with a site survey, a legal description of the property, and information about utilities.

    The Client shall engage the services of all specialty consultants and engineers deemed necessary by ACE to complete the professional services.

    The Client shall provide for testing or provide existing evidence that the site is clear of hazardous materials.

2. *Ownership of documents.* All sketches, drawings, tracings, computations, notes, reports, plans, and other original documents are instruments of service and shall remain the property of ACE subject to the requirements of public agencies. These instruments of service are to be used solely for this specific project. ACE shall retain all legal rights to the use of the instruments of service and shall retain full protection under U.S. copyright law.

FIGURE 9-4. Standard terms and conditions used as an attachment to the letter agreement, contract, or proposal.

3. *Timeliness.* All the terms of the letter agreement and this addendum shall be performed in a timely manner. ACE shall not be responsible, however, for delays in performance caused by Client, or any of Client's agents or employees or any other avoidable delays or causes beyond the reasonable control of ACE. If ACE is delayed at any time by any of the foregoing events, then the time of completion shall be extended for a period equal to the number of days the work has been prevented, interrupted, or delayed. If the interruption is in excess of ninety (90) days, ACE will charge an additional fee of 35 percent of the total fee for the restart-up of the project.

4. *Professional services liability.* ACE's responsibilities in performing services hereunder shall be limited to the scope of work and scope of services to be performed as set forth in the agreement, and ACE, its agents, and/or employees, shall have no liability of any kind to Client, its agents or any persons having contractual relationships with Client for any acts, errors, and omissions of ACE, its agents, and employees, which does not fall within the scope of work and scope of services to be performed. Client further agrees to limit ACE's liability to the Client due to ACE's negligent acts, errors, or omissions, such that the total aggregate liability of ACE to all those named shall not exceed $50,000 or ACE's total fee for services rendered on this project, whichever is greater.

5. *Cancellation.* This agreement may be canceled by ACE if Client has become delinquent in the payment of amounts due ACE hereunder over ninety (90) days. This agreement may also be canceled by ACE or the Client, with or without cause. In either instance, the canceling party shall give seven (7) days written notice prior to termination and specify the date of termination. In the event of cancellation, ACE shall be paid for services

FIGURE 9-4. (*Cont'd.*) Standard terms and conditions used as an attachment to the letter agreement, contract, or proposal.

rendered and costs incurred hereunder through the date of cancellation including the costs of terminating the work.

6. *Warranties.*

   A. ACE makes no representations concerning soil conditions unless specifically included in this agreement and is not responsible for the accuracy nor for any liability that may arise out of the use of information furnished by the Client, its agents, or other persons with whom the Client has contracted, including but not limited to plans, specifications, reports, or any other data.

   B. ACE warrants that its services will be performed with the usual standard of care practiced by landscape architects.

   C. No other warranty or representation, either expressed or implied, is included or intended in ACE's proposals, contracts, plans, surveys, or reports, either written or oral.

7. *Additional or excluded services.* Other services available from ACE and applicable to the project have been discussed with the Client. Where ACE has deemed a service to be needed or advisable, ACE has made its opinion known to the Client, and the Client has confirmed his opinion that the services are not requested of ACE or the Client has made arrangements to obtain those services from a source other than ACE. The additional or excluded services are itemized in the agreement.

8. *Invalid provisions.* Any provision that shall prove to be invalid, void, or illegal shall in no way effect, impair, or invalidate any other provision of this agreement, and such other provisions shall remain in full force and effect. In the event of any dispute, venue shall be the Superior Court in and for Pima County, Arizona, United States of America,

FIGURE 9-4. (*Cont'd.*) Standard terms and conditions used as an attachment to the letter agreement, contract, or proposal.

and service of process of a legal document against Client shall be effective seventy-two (72) hours after depositing in the United States of America Certified Mail, return receipt requested, postage prepaid.

9. *The laws of the State of Arizona* shall govern the validity, performance, and enforcement of this agreement.

10. *Dispute resolution.* In the event of a dispute arising out of the terms hereunder, the dispute shall be resolved through formal mediation.

11. *Assignment.* This agreement shall not be assigned by either party without prior written consent of the nonassigning party.

12. *Authority to enter into agreement.* Each party represents by signing this agreement that they have the authority to enter into the same and bind each and every party, their heirs, successors, assigns, fellow beneficiaries in trust, and/or partners, to the terms and conditions as herein set forth.

13. *Opinion of probable construction costs.* In providing an opinion of the probable construction cost, the Client understands that ACE has no control over the contractor's method of pricing nor the cost of labor, equipment, or materials. The opinion of probable construction costs provided by ACE under the terms of this contract is made on the basis of ACE's professional qualifications and experience. ACE makes no warranty, expressed or implied, as to the accuracy of its opinion of probable construction costs as compared to bids or actual costs.

14. *Publicity.* Client agrees to include ACE's name on the job sign at the construction site and in any publication or press coverage relating to ACE's work.

FIGURE 9-4. (*Cont'd.*) Standard terms and conditions used as an attachment to the letter agreement, contract, or proposal.

PAYMENT

1. *Statements* will be issued every four (4) weeks, are due and payable upon receipt and shall be deemed delinquent after thirty (30) days from the date of the initial statement. If statements are not paid in full prior to delinquency, Client agrees to pay interest on the unpaid amount at the rate of 1.5 percent per month (annual percentage rate of 18 percent) from the delinquency date until paid in full. All payments received shall first be credited to the payment of delinquent interest and then to the principal balance due.

2. *Reimbursable expenses.* Client shall pay the cost of all reimbursable items such as charges, fees, permits, bond premiums, delivery charges, postage, fax transmissions, long-distance telephone calls, reproductions and copies, photographic enlargements and reductions, film processing and supplies, mileage, and any other charges and expenses not specifically covered by the foregoing. In the event that such reimbursable items are paid directly by ACE, then the charges and expenses shall be invoiced at the direct cost plus 35 percent for handling. Subconsultant and testing services arranged for and managed by ACE will also be invoiced at the direct cost plus 35 percent.

   Client shall pay the cost of all expenses incurred for out-of-town travel required to perform the services in this agreement. Expenses shall be invoiced at their direct cost to ACE. Automobile mileage shall be invoiced at thirty cents ($0.30) per mile. Out-of-town travel shall be made at the request or concurrence of the Client.

3. *Prompt payment.* Client shall promptly review invoices and notify ACE of any objection thereto. In the event Client fails to notify ACE of any ob-

FIGURE 9-4. (*Cont'd.*) Standard terms and conditions used as an attachment to the letter agreement, contract, or proposal.

jection, in writing, within ten (10) days of receipt of invoice, the invoice shall be deemed accepted by the Client.

4. *Cost of living adjustment.* In the event the services hereunder are not completed within six (6) months from the date of this agreement, ACE reserves the right to adjust its fee for the uncompleted portion of services to reflect any cost-of-living increases of wages or salaries to be paid by ACE to its employees in the performance of this agreement.

FIGURE 9-4. (*Cont'd.*) Standard terms and conditions used as an attachment to the letter agreement, contract, or proposal.

In practicing the agency relationship, the landscape architect must always be concerned about whether his or her acts require impartiality or fidelity to the client. Many times on the job site of a project under construction, the landscape architect is faced with making decisions that require impartiality, such as approving pay requests, evaluating the percent complete of the project, or evaluating claims made by the contractor, client, or both. Other times the landscape architect must be faithful to the client's interests to see that the construction is carried out expressly in terms of the construction documents. For example, if the landscape architect observes the contractor taking a shortcut or compromising construction activities in any way, the landscape architect must be faithful to the client's interests and require the contractor to carry out the construction activities properly in accordance with the specifications and plans. The landscape architect must maintain a high degree of integrity and the courage to insist that the construction is carried out properly so that no questions can be raised about negligence or improper activities.

Agency relationships may be most tested by change orders during construction activities. Changes to the scope during construction can be caused by a number of reasons. The client may voluntarily want some aspect of the construction changed, enhanced, or reduced. Unexpected conditions may arise, typically unknown subsurface conditions that require changes from the plans. Government agents may require changes due to their interpretation of codes. Design errors may have occurred. In the case of design errors, the cause of the change usually determines who is responsible for paying for the change.

If the client requests a design change, he or she will be responsible for the additional costs. The client is responsible for changes caused by hidden or unknown conditions, particularly if the landscape architect and the subconsultants acted within the standard of care during the design process to identify all conditions, such as existing subsurface conditions, that should be relevant to the construction project. The client also usually pays for code issues that occur during construction. When the landscape architect has followed the codes to the best of his or her ability, but a government inspector sees things differently during construction, the landscape architect would not normally be considered negligent for not anticipating the government agent's on-site interpretation (Samuels 1996).

Design errors, if they occur, must be dealt with by the landscape architect in an honest way with the client. With some clients, such as a municipality or a developer that are construction savvy, a contingency of 5 percent to 10 percent of the construction budget is set aside in the construction budget to cover change orders that may occur due to design omissions or errors. The client with construction experience will expect that some changes during construction will be necessary and will benefit the project. The owner is entitled to recover from the landscape architect extra costs caused by apparent design error. In practice, however, if the costs are within the acceptable contingency range, the client may not attempt to recover them.

Where a contingency is not available, the landscape architect must rely on the relationship of trust established with the client and try to reach a conciliatory position for any extras that may arise from design error. A good approach is to have a candid discussion with the client before the construction starts. State that the landscape architect has done his or her best to consider all of the necessary design elements during the design phase, but the landscape architect hopes the client will understand that changes may be necessary during construction and will be open minded to paying for any necessary changes. In most instances, properly presented, the client may be willing to pay for design changes that result from design errors. If the landscape architect has clearly made a design error and the client refuses to pay for the change, the landscape architect must be willing to do what is necessary to correct the situation, including paying for the change.

Last, while working as the client's agent, the landscape architect needs to take each issue of possible design error as part of a continuum of many changes that are likely to occur during the course of construction. Don't get upset, angry, or afraid of monetary impact if one change appears to be caused by design error. There are likely to be changes caused by each of the three parties to the agency relationship. Keep tabs on the changes like a running balance sheet. They all may offset each other over the course of construction. Trade-offs and compromises can be structured and summed up at the end of construction such that no one feels he or she has been treated unfairly regarding extra costs. Each party will be satisfied that fair decisions have been made and the project ends up being successful for all of the participants.

Contracts with Allied Professionals

Similar to contracts with the client for professional services, the landscape architect uses three formats for contracts with allied professionals:

1. Professional association standard contracts
2. Landscape architect–developed contracts
3. Allied professional–developed contracts

Professional Association Standard Contracts

As with the contract for professional services with the client, many landscape architecture firms use an association-developed standard contract for the agreement with subconsultants working under the direction of the landscape architect acting as the prime consultant. Firms most frequently use the AIA standard contract.

The standard contract covers elements germane to the relationship between the prime consultant and the subconsultant including the subconsultant's scope of services, compensation, and terms and conditions of the contract.

Provisions for clarifying additional services are an important part of the agreement with a subconsultant. Without tight control on additional services, a subconsultant may provide services that are known to be needed but not a part of the agreed-upon scope of services. After the services are complete, the subconsultant may feel the prime consultant is obligated to pay for the unanticipated services. Additional-services terminology in the standard association contracts usually includes the specific services that may be considered additional. The additional services are itemized so there is no question that if they are deemed necessary by the subconsultant, they will be authorized in advance by the landscape architect. The standard contract requires that the landscape architect authorize additional services in writing before they are executed by the subconsultant.

The standard contract specifies the responsibilities of the prime consultant, including providing all available information to the subconsultant, such as a survey and a soil report. The prime consultant also agrees to designate an authorized contact to act on behalf of the prime.

The standard agreement includes language regarding construction costs, particularly related to a fee that is based on a percentage of construction, and de-fines reimbursable expenses and the terms of payment to the subconsultant. The standard agreement also covers ownership of the documents, provisions for terminating the contract, insurance requirements, assignment provisions, governing law, dispute resolution provisions, and signature lines. When using a standard association-developed contract, keep in mind that it should be adjusted as necessary to accommodate specific requirements of the project.

Landscape Architect–Developed Contracts

When landscape architects develop their own contracts for use with a subconsultant, the contract should include the elements necessary for proper formation of the agreement so that it is enforceable. It must represent a voluntary agreement for consideration. It should be for a lawful purpose, be signed by legally competent parties, and it must have an enforceable form.

There are a number of elements that should be considered in the landscape architect's favor when developing a contract for agreements with subconsultants:

- Reference the landscape architect's contract with the client so that the subconsultant is bound by the same terms and conditions that bind the landscape architect contractually to the client.
- Include a clause specifying that the subconsultant will receive payment when and if the prime consultant receives payment. As a matter of money management, the clause might specify that the subconsultant will be paid within fifteen to thirty days after the prime consultant is paid by the client. The contract should also cover the acceptable method of billing if the landscape architect requires specific billing procedures and receipt of invoices at specific times of the month.
- Require that the subconsultant furnish proof of insurance coverage including professional liability insurance. Request copies of insurance certificates for the landscape architect's file.
- Clarify ownership of the drawings and other instruments of service, including copyright protection.
- Include a provision covering changes to the documents prepared by the subconsultant and

prohibiting changes made by the prime consultant, the owner, or the contractor without the consent of the subconsultant.

- Include a mutual indemnification provision by which the landscape architect and the subconsultant agree to hold each other harmless for any liability for damages except liability arising from their own individual negligence.

The landscape architect–developed contract used with subconsultants is often created by referring to other subconsultant contracts (such as association-developed contracts and contracts received from other prime consultants when the landscape architect serves as the subconsultant) as models. These sometimes cover elements beyond what may be necessary with less verbiage. They are useful references, however, to serve as a starting point. The contract created by the landscape architect should be reviewed by the firm's attorney. Figure 9-5 is a sample of a subconsultant agreement that can be used as a starting point.

Allied Professional–Developed Contracts

There is no good reason for a landscape architect to sign a subconsultant agreement developed by the subconsultant. If the landscape architect is too lazy to take charge of the subconsultant's contract, the landscape architect's role as prime consultant should be questioned. As the prime consultant, the landscape architect has the opportunity to directly manage and control the language of the agreement and should exercise this opportunity.

When the landscape architect serves as a subconsultant on a project, the landscape architect will be obligated to sign a contract developed by the prime consultant. The landscape architect should review the contract in detail, looking for fairness and equitable treatment in the provisions of the agreement. The list of elements discussed above can be used to identify if the proposed agreement is fair.

Contracts with Credit Agencies

Generally speaking, contracts with credit agencies are based on either unsecured credit or secured credit. Credit, which involves the quality or state of being trustworthy, is used in businesses where goods are sold, services are rendered, or money is loaned in exchange for the promise to pay for them in the future.

In some business transactions, usually with vendors that supply goods or services that have a small relative economic value, the vendor is willing to rely on the debtor's word that payment will be forthcoming. These business transactions are based on unsecured credit. The business, firm, or person extending the unsecured credit has a high degree of risk. If the debtor does not pay for the goods or services, the creditor has more limited options than if the debt were secured by something of tangible value.

Landscape architects are on both sides of unsecured credit transactions. They obtain trade credit from their suppliers, and they give trade credit to most, if not all, of the clients for whom they work.

Unsecured Credit

When unsecured credit is given and the debtor does not meet the obligation to pay for the goods, services, or money loaned, the creditor can rely on a few measures to seek repayment by the debtor. First is persuasion and persistence. There is an old business proverb, "the squeaky wheel gets the grease." There have been many times during the life of my landscape architecture business practice when I have been late on payments to unsecured creditors because of cash-flow problems, slow business, or pressing financial needs that must be met before money can be directed to unsecured credit obligations. I can tell you from experience that I have been more likely to pay those unsecured creditors who have persistently called me and asked for payment, sometimes in a nicely persuasive way, other times in anger. I can also attest to the benefits of persistent persuasion when my firm has been owed money by a slow-paying client and it has seemed like the only way to assure payment was to hound the client until a check was received. Another good old saying to remember is "the best clients are the ones that pay."

The second course of action is to bring a lawsuit against the debtor and obtain a legal judgment. Lawsuits should not, however, be entered into lightly. Even if the creditor wins the suit, the debtor may be broke, near or in bankruptcy, or have no property that can be used to pay the debt. Lawsuits are expensive

Subconsultant Agreement in the Performance of Services for (*Insert Project Name*) Ace Project No. (*Insert Project No.*)

This document shall serve as the AGREEMENT, made this _____ day of _____, 1996, between Ace Landscape Architects, the Landscape Architect (ACE), and (*insert subconsultant's name*), an independent contractor (the CONSULTANT), to provide _____ services for the above-referenced project.

1.0 **Scope of Services**

1.1 Consultant shall provide the following services: See attachment A.

1.2 CONSULTANT shall provide the personnel, materials, and equipment necessary to perform all services, and shall not delegate or subcontract the work to anyone without the written approval of ACE. CONSULTANT shall also perform all work in accordance with established professional standards, procedures, and regulations.

1.3 ACE shall administer all professional and other services for the project, and shall assist in the coordination of information among consultants retained by ACE for the project as necessary.

1.4 All communication between the CONSULTANT and the Client or contractor shall be forwarded through ACE, except as approved by ACE.

FIGURE 9-5. Ace Landscape Architects subconsultant agreement.

1.5 Services additional to those specified in paragraph 1.1, and which shall result in additional fees, will be provided by the CONSULTANT only upon written consent from ACE prior to beginning any work related to such additional services.

2.0 **Project Schedule**

2.1 CONSULTANT will perform the above services according to the schedule to be provided by ACE.

2.2 Failure to meet the proposed project schedule without prior written approval shall result in the reduction of compensation, at the sole discretion of ACE, in an amount sufficient to allow ACE to complete the work.

3.0 **Compensation**

3.1 CONSULTANT shall be compensated for its services in accordance with the following payment amount, schedule, and terms:

3.2 Amount: *(insert amount)*

3.3 Invoicing schedule: monthly

3.4 Reimbursables: Reimbursable expenses shall be included in above fee. ACE shall remit payment to CONSULTANT within ten (10) days after receipt of payment from the Client. In the event that retention monies are withheld from ACE by ACE's Client, retention monies will also be withheld from the CONSULTANT, at the same percentage as withheld from ACE, and will be released to the CONSULTANT within ten (10) working days of the remittance of retention monies to

FIGURE 9-5. (*Cont'd.*) Ace Landscape Architects subconsultant agreement.

ACE from ACE's Client. ACE shall exercise reasonable and diligent efforts to obtain payment from a client on a timely basis.

3.5 CONSULTANT shall be compensated per the same terms as in paragraph 3.5 for any approved additional services as agreed upon in writing with ACE.

3.6 Records of services performed and reimbursable expenses shall be kept on the basis of generally accepted accounting principles, and shall be available to ACE or ACE's representative during the term of work on the project for three (3) years from the date of final payment to the CONSULTANT.

4.0 **Ownership of Documents**

4.1 All drawings, specifications, and calculations prepared by the CONSULTANT as part of the professional services shall be the property of ACE, whether the project is executed or not. The CONSULTANT shall be permitted to retain copies for reproduction, information, and reference.

4.2 Neither ACE nor the CONSULTANT may make changes in the other's drawings or specifications without the written permission of the other party. ACE shall not use the drawings or specifications for any other projects, except by agreement in writing and with appropriate compensation to the CONSULTANT.

5.0 **Mutual Understanding of the Parties**

5.1 CONSULTANT understands that he/she is employed solely as an independent contractor and not as an employee of ACE.

FIGURE 9-5. (*Cont'd.*) Ace Landscape Architects subconsultant agreement.

Also, this Agreement shall not be interpreted to create a joint venture between the parties herein. In accordance with this relationship, ACE shall report all payments made to the CONSULTANT during the calendar year to the Internal Revenue Service on the appropriate Form 1099. CONSULTANT shall provide ACE, at the commencement of this agreement, a Form W-9, indicating the CONSULTANT's personal or corporate tax identification number. CONSULTANT shall thus meet all federal and state tax obligations including the payment of the CONSULTANT's own F.I.C.A. liability, as well as any health or general liability insurance and worker's compensation payments relative to CONSULTANT's work.

5.3 The parties agree that the CONSULTANT shall be responsible for correcting all errors and omissions of work for services and that such corrections shall be performed at no extra cost to ACE.

5.4 The laws of the State of Arizona shall govern all matters pertaining to the performance of both parties under this agreement. If the CONSULTANT violates any terms of the agreement, and ACE as a consequence seeks legal remedies in order to enforce any provisions contained in this agreement, then the CONSULTANT shall be responsible for any reasonable attorneys' fees and court costs incurred by ACE.

5.5 ACE or CONSULTANT may terminate this Agreement upon ten (10) days written notice, with or without consent. CONSULTANT shall receive compensation for all work completed up to the date of termination of the agreement per the terms in paragraph 3.5. ACE may at its sole discretion terminate the agreement for unacceptable performance at any time.

6.0 **Insurance Requirements**

6.1 CONSULTANT shall procure and maintain at its own expense insurance protection under worker's compensation and comprehensive general liability from

FIGURE 9-5. (*Cont'd.*) Ace Landscape Architects subconsultant agreement.

claims for bodily injury, personal injury, sickness, disease, or death of any and all employees, and from any claims or damages because of injury to or destruction of property. Also, CONSULTANT shall procure and maintain at its own expense professional liability insurance for protection from any claims arising out of performance of professional services for which the insured is legally liable, with coverage in the amount of $1,000,000 during and for seven (7) years after the date of completion of professional services on the project as agreed by ACE and the CONSULTANT.

6.2 CONSULTANT shall provide ACE with certificates of insurance for worker's compensation, comprehensive general liability insurance, comprehensive automobile liability insurance, and professional liability insurance prior to initiating work on this project.

7.0 **Successors and Assigns**

7.1 ACE and the CONSULTANT bind themselves, their partners, successors, assigns, and legal representatives to the other party to this agreement with respect to all covenants of this agreement. Neither ACE nor the CONSULTANT shall assign or transfer any interest in this agreement without the written consent of the other.

With the following signatures by their respective duly authorized officers, the parties hereby enter into this Agreement as of the day and year first above written.

CONSULTANT: LANDSCAPE ARCHITECT:

(*Insert firm's name*)   Ace Landscape Architects, Inc.

By: _____   By: _____

                                             Robert Anderson, ASLA

Title: _____   Title: <u>President</u>

FIGURE 9-5. (*Cont'd.*) Ace Landscape Architects subconsultant agreement.

and the courts may not rule in favor of the creditor. I have always avoided lawsuits if at all possible and have been guided by another old proverb—no lawsuit is a good lawsuit. In many cases, I've weighed the cost of attorney's fees and court costs against what is owed the firm and concluded that writing off the debt was more cost-effective than bringing a lawsuit against the debtor.

If the debt is a small one, a creditor has another option of seeking relief in small-claims court. There are debt ceilings on the amount that can be sought under small-claims court criteria. The limit and the process varies on a state-by-state basis. For example, the maximum amount of a claim in Arizona is $1,500. I have used this process to make several demands for payment for small amounts owed to my firm. The threat of a small-claims court claim is often enough to nudge the debtor into paying the debt.

Small-Claims Court Process

The process of filing a small-claims court complaint, using Arizona's procedure as an example, follows these steps:

1. A plaintiff, the entity or person bringing the suit, files a complaint on a form provided by the court. The complaint is filed with the clerk of the small-claims court division. The complaint must be filed under the justice court jurisdiction of the defendant. The information in the complaint includes the names and addresses of plaintiff and defendant, the reason for filing the complaint, and the amount of money disputed.
2. When the complaint is filed, the clerk will issue a summons ordering the defendant to appear in court. In Arizona, the summons must be served by registered mail, return receipt requested.
3. The defendant has twenty days to file a written response. If the defendant fails to respond, the court may rule in favor of the plaintiff. The defendant may also make a counterclaim that alleges other facts and demands a monetary award from the plaintiff.
4. A trial is scheduled because all small-claims court claims are heard by a judge. Both plaintiff and defendant prepare for the trial.
5. On the day of the trial, both parties appear before the judge and testify. After both plaintiff and defendant have presented their testimony, evidence, and witnesses, the judge will make a judgment and record the decision in the court's records. Sometimes the judge may take up to ten days to reach a judgment.
6. In some cases, the defendant fails to appear. Under these circumstances, the judge is likely to rule in favor of the plaintiff.
7. The judgment in Arizona's small-claims court cannot be appealed. If the plaintiff gets a favorable judgment, he or she must still collect the money owed.
8. Upon being notified in writing of the court's judgment, the parties make arrangements for payment. If the defendant does not make full payment, the plaintiff may request that the court issue a Writ of Execution or Writ of Garnishment. If the writs are not successful, obtaining an attorney may be necessary for further legal action against the defendant. In Arizona's small-claims court, the court does not have the responsibility to enforce collection of the judgment on behalf of the plaintiff.

Secured Credit

Contracts with credit agencies that are based on secured credit carry significant obligations to repay the debt. Creditors use a security interest or a lien on the debtor's property as a means of mitigating the credit risk. When a landscape architect purchases a vehicle and obtains a loan from a leasing company or a bank, a contract for repayment of the loan is executed between the lender and the landscape architect. The vehicle is used as the security for the loan.

When a landscape architect negotiates an operating line of credit from a bank, the lender will require the landscape architect to pledge the firm's accounts receivable or other assets as the collateral or security for the loan. The lender may also require additional security such as a personal guarantee. The loan document, contract, or promissory note clearly spells out the security interest. If the landscape architect defaults on the loan, the creditor has the contractual right to go after the security. If the security is a vehicle, for example, the creditor has the right to repossess the vehicle and sell it to recover the monetary interest. If the security is the accounts receivable, the creditor can collect the money tied up in the accounts receivable.

The landscape architect must be familiar with and understand the ramifications of performance of a contract for an operating line of credit or a business loan used for capital equipment. This type of contract will typically include a loan agreement and a promissory note:

LOAN AGREEMENT

1. The names and addresses of the parties to the agreement.
2. The term of the loan (e.g., one year).
3. The definitions of terms used in the agreement.
4. A definition of the type of loan (e.g., a line of credit) and the conditions related to advances or borrowing amounts on the loan. When the loan is tied to a specific formula establishing a borrowing base on the accounts receivable, the definitions will require mandatory repayment of any amounts that exceed the borrowing base.
5. The collateral and the terms of the collateral. If receivables are used as the primary form of collateral, the lender will require that the borrower make financial reports available to the lender on demand. Records such as financial statements and aged accounts receivable reports will be required documentation. As the borrower, the landscape architect will be required to warrant or guarantee that the accounts are eligible for use as collateral and will always remain eligible under the terms of the loan agreement.
6. The loan agreement will contain a clause of representations and warrantees in which the borrower warrants that the firm is a duly organized and lawful business and that the loan document has been signed by an authorized representative of the firm. For a sole proprietorship, authorization will be by the individual owner. For a partnership, authorization will be by a partner or all of the partners. For a corporation, the loan agreement will be signed by a corporate officer, and the lender

will likely ask for a corporate resolution authorizing the loan.

The borrower will also be asked to warrant other elements, such as clear title to real property, that may be used as security for the loan and that no hazardous substances have been used, generated, manufactured, stored, or released related to the real property. The borrower will warrant that there are no liens on any property used as security for the loan. The borrower will also guarantee survivability of the loan until it is repaid in full.

7. The borrower will agree to a number of covenants and other terms. The borrower may be required to notify the lender if the borrower's financial condition changes due to litigation or other legal claims against the borrower. The borrower will promise to furnish financial statements and other information deemed important to the lender. The lender is likely to require evidence that the borrower has complied with financial ratios and maintained acceptable levels of working cash and liquid assets. (See chapter 6 for a discussion of financial ratios.)

The loan agreement will include insurance obligations and requirements to submit insurance certificates to the lender. The borrower may be required to maintain its present operation, including owners, executives, and other management personnel. The borrower will also be required to maintain operation as it is at the time the loan is granted; for example, the borrower may not be allowed to engage in any business activity that is different from landscape architecture without the agreement of the lender. The lender will request inspection rights at any time to review the status of any property or accounts receivable, as well as all records and books.

The covenants will also include a personal guarantee naming those persons responsible for the debt.

8. The terms for cessation of advances will be spelled out if the loan is for an operating line of credit. The terms will normally include conditions such as the borrower defaulting on any terms of the loan agreement, insolvency, bankruptcy, or voluntary admission by the

borrower that the business is in jeopardy for one reason or another.

9. The loan agreement will include a right-of-setoff clause in which the borrower grants to the lender the right to offset any amounts owed under the loan by using other accounts, such as checking, savings, IRA, Keogh, and trust accounts, to the extent permissible by law.

10. The loan agreement will define the events of default. They will include failure to make payments when due, making false statements, defects in the collateral, insolvency, foreclosure on real property, and change in ownership of at least 25 percent.

11. The loan agreement will also include a number of miscellaneous provisions. These provisions include defining the applicable law, such as the state law where the loan is executed; the right for the lender to sell the loan to another; payment terms for any costs associated with the preparation, execution, enforcement, and collection of the loan; terms for official notices; a severability clause; and a clause binding all successors and assigns.

PROMISSORY NOTE

1. The promissory note will identify the parties to the contract.

2. The promissory note includes the borrower's pledge or promise to pay any amount of the loan outstanding, including interest on or before the due date of the loan. Payments are always applied first to the accrued interest and then to the unpaid balance.

3. The promissory note will define the interest rate and the index, such as the prime rate, used by the bank. If the interest rate is 2 percent, for instance, and the prime rate is 7.5 percent, the total interest charge will be 9.5 percent. When the interest rate is indexed, it provides for the 2 percent interest rate always to be added to the selected index rate. Therefore, if the prime rate goes down to 7 percent during the term of the loan, the total interest payment will go down to 9 percent. Usually a minimum total interest also will be specified, 8.75 percent, for example. If the prime rate were to drop to 6 percent, result-

ing in a total interest of 8 percent, the loan's minimum interest of 8.75 percent would be effective.

4. If the lender requests a late charge, it will be identified in the promissory note.

5. The promissory note will spell out in detail the provisions for defaulting on the loan. They may be repeated from the loan agreement.

6. Lender's rights to collect on a defaulted loan will be spelled out in detail. Sometimes the lender will have a provision that allows the lender to increase the interest to the maximum allowed under law if the loan is in default.

7. The note may repeat the setoff rights.

8. The note will clearly set out the name of the person or persons who are eligible to make requests for advances on the line of credit.

9. The note will specify the total amount or upset maximum amount of money that can be borrowed under the loan or line of credit.

The most important point to remember when entering into a credit contract where security interest is sought by the lender is to review the contract in great detail and question any points not understood or agreed to. The following are some of the key points to look for and negotiate in the written agreement:

- *Personal guarantee.* Try to eliminate the personal guarantee if the landscape architecture firm is a corporation.

- *Interest rate.* Try to obtain the lowest interest rate above the index rate. Firms that have good credit should be able to obtain a rate of .5 percent to 1 percent above the prime rate. Firms with poor credit may be lucky to obtain 3 percent to 4 percent above the prime rate.

- *Late charge.* Try to negotiate a late charge out of the agreement. If not possible, negotiate the longest length of time possible before the charge is applied and the lowest charge possible.

- *Loan amount.* Carefully determine the maximum amount of the loan so that it is adequate to cover the expected borrowing needs but not so high that it might tempt the borrower to borrow more than needed.

- *Collateral.* Try to limit the collateral to only accounts receivable or a specific interest in some other real property. Try to eliminate the lender's rights to any and all security owned personally by the borrower.
- *Hidden fees.* Ask the lender to identify up front all of the fees associated with the loan. There may be a document preparation fee, an annual renewal fee, a late payment fee, an account maintenance fee, a fee for payments made when the borrower's account has insufficient funds, and a whole host of other fees that are now charged by banks and lending institutions. Remember that everything is negotiable, and if the bank wants to give you credit, especially if your firm has established excellent credit, the bank may be willing to waive some of the fees.

Default on a Secured Loan

When the landscape architect enters into a loan agreement to purchase business equipment, vehicles, or real property, the creditor will obtain a security interest in the property. The creditor wants to ensure that the security interest is superior to others that may have an interest in the property, usually referred to as being in first position. Establishing a security interest is covered by Article 9 of the Uniform Commercial Code, and the code must be followed explicitly for the security interest to be secure and not revert to a general interest in the event that a firm becomes bankrupt. The security agreement must describe the collateral, require the debtor to pay certain amounts on a regular basis, and specify the events that constitute default.

If the borrower (the landscape architecture firm) defaults, the secured creditor has two main options:

- Forget about the collateral and sue the landscape architecture firm based on the terms of the loan agreement and the promissory note. If the collateral can be obtained peacefully, the creditor will attempt to do so. If not, the creditor must take legal action to repossess the security. If the collateral is intangible, such as the landscape architecture firm's accounts receivable, the creditor will seek to have performance on the loan carried out through the courts.

- Repossess the collateral, foreclose on the loan agreement, and keep the collateral in payment for the remaining debt.

If the collateral is not valuable enough to cover the remaining debt, the creditor may also sue the debtor for amounts outstanding. Many lenders do not want to take back the collateral, and this becomes a negotiating point for the borrower to renegotiate the terms of the loan. If the security is sold, the lender must act in good faith and the sale must be for fair market value. The proceeds of the sale are distributed first to cover the expenses of repossessing and selling the collateral, second to cover attorney's fees, third to cover the debt, and fourth to pay any creditors that may not be in first position. Last, any remaining amounts go to the debtor. The creditor is allowed to sue for any deficiency that is not covered by the sale of the collateral.

Employee Agreements

When a landscape architect hires his or her first employee, or when a landscape architecture firm adds new hires, an employment agreement is one of the best ways to consummate the new employer-employee relationship. An employment agreement is a contract with the employee spelling out the terms of employment. The agreement should deal with a number of topics covering the employee-employer relationship.

- The employment agreement should define the entire legal agreement between the employer and the employee.
- The agreement should cite the initial salary or hourly wage rate and may also define how or when future wage increases will take place.
- The agreement should spell out the term of employment.
- The agreement should state that the employer may at its sole discretion terminate the employee's employment at any time with or without cause.
- The agreement may point out that the firm adheres to all federal employment laws including nondiscrimination as described in Title VII of

the Civil Rights Act of 1964, the Occupational Safety and Health Act of 1970, the Employee Retirement Security Act of 1974, the Equal Pay Act of 1963, and others as desired.
- The agreement should include a statement that the new employee has read the agreement and has read the firm's employee manual and understands both.
- The employee contract should have signature lines for the employee and an authorized representative of the firm.

An example of an employment agreement is illustrated in figure 9-6.

Negotiating a Contract

I have often heard people say there are only two sure things in life—death and taxes. If there is another sure thing in life, both professional business life and personal life, it is negotiation. To be sure, the art and skill of negotiating is a landscape architecture business fact of life.

Successful negotiating is paramount to the successful development of agreements and contracts for professional services. More and more in the daily practice of landscape architecture, negotiating with clients and special-interest groups has become a necessary skill for completing a project. Reaching consensus with public-interest groups for the design of a park, a highway, or any other public improvement project is a common component of almost every public project today. Reaching consensus with a client on how to bring an overbudget design solution into conformance with the client's budget happens all too frequently. Negotiating a fee, a schedule, and contract terms that are acceptable to both the professional landscape architect and the client is a regular occurrence. When the negotiations are acceptable, and both parties to the professional services contract are comfortable with the agreement, the relationship is likely to get off to a good start. This section emphasizes negotiating a professional services contract, but the principles discussed carry over into other negotiating circumstances, such as negotiating with an employee for a raise during an annual work review or negotiating with a lender for an operating line of

credit. Indeed, many professional landscape architects spend a substantial part of their professional time negotiating.

A professional landscape architecture practice is built around the cornerstone of trust. Successful landscape architects build long-term and meaningful relationships with their clients. Negotiating within a well-developed long-term business relationship may require more flexibility than negotiating in a business relationship that is perceived to be a probable short-term business relationship. If the landscape architect perceives a potential client as a one-project client, the landscape architect may be inclined to present a proposal and negotiate firmly without budging on the price and terms of the agreement. The professional is willing to take the project or forget about it. A word of caution: If the probable one-project client acquiesces to contract terms that favor the landscape architect, the landscape architect should carry out the project with the highest professional standards aimed at creating a highly satisfied client. The project deserves the same care, attention to detail, and development of trust and mutual respect as a project for a long-term, well-established client. The landscape architect should carry out the practice of developing trust and providing meaningful professional services in every project regardless of the client relationship. By always practicing with the highest standards of ethics, honesty, and quality of services, the landscape architect will never compromise his or her reputation. One never knows how many friends—other potential clients—the one-time client has, and word-of-mouth references from a one-time client can pay off just as handsomely as the follow-up projects received from a trusting long-term client.

The Fundamentals of Negotiating

Preparation

The first step in negotiating is being prepared. This starts with a well-thought-out and thorough initial proposal for professional services. Some of the negotiating often occurs in conversations with the client before the proposal is written and delivered. Asking as many questions of the prospective client as you possibly can is the way to start fleshing out the client's position on a wide range of elements related to the project.

Another key element of preparation is doing your homework. Before writing the proposal, research as

Ace Landscape Architects

EMPLOYMENT AGREEMENT

This Employment Agreement, hereinafter called the "Agreement," between Ace Landscape Architects, Inc., hereinafter called the "Employer" and _____ , hereinafter called the "Employee," is effective as of the following date: _____.

1. The Employer will employ the Employee in the initial position of _____ at the initial wage rate of $_____ per _____.

2. The Employee's future wage rate and position shall be determined by the Employer in its sole discretion.

3. The Employee's employment with the Employer is not for any specified term and may be terminated by the Employee or by the Employer at any time for any reason, with or without cause.

4. Paragraphs 1, 2, and 3 above constitute the complete agreement between the Employer and the Employee regarding the matters referred to in said paragraphs and supersede any and all prior written or oral agreements or understandings on employment of the Employee. The Employee understands that no representative of the Employer has been authorized to enter into any agreement or commitment with the Employee that is inconsistent in any way with the terms of paragraphs 2 and 3 above.

5. The terms set forth in paragraphs 2 and 3 above may not be modified in any way except by a written addendum to this agreement signed by the Employee and by an authorized representative of the Employer that expressly states the intention of the parties to modify the terms of the Agreement.

Dated: _____   Dated: _____

_____   _____
Employee   Employer

FIGURE 9-6. Ace Landscape Architects employment agreement.

much about the client's background, the site, the locale, the laws, the design process, the design principles, and the preliminary costs of the project as you can. Research the client and the client's company in the public records at the library. Information will be more readily available if the company is a publicly traded corporation. Obtain an annual report of the company if one is available.

If the client is a public agency, research the previous types of projects it has completed. Find out what the client's administrative procedures are. Talk to other members of your firm who have worked with the client before. If no one in your firm has worked with the client, call up a friendly allied professional who might have done work for the client and query your friend about the prospective client. Is the client easy to work with? Is the client fee sensitive? Does the client have pet prejudices? Does the client pay in a timely fashion? What is the quality level of the client's previous projects? Which of your competitors has the client used in the past? Any and all information that you can assemble about the prospective client will help you properly slant your proposal for professional services, negotiate a contract that you are comfortable with, and be prepared.

Being prepared with the greatest amount of information possible about the prospective client will help alleviate one of the greatest detriments to successful negotiation—uncertainty. Being prepared will enable the landscape architect to write the most responsive proposal possible.

Create Room to Maneuver

There are several aspects of creating room to maneuver during your negotiations with a client:

1. Ask for more than you're willing to settle for.
2. Have alternatives in mind and be flexible.
3. Decide what you can concede to and what your bottom line is.

The main elements of a professional services contract that has room to maneuver in and is negotiable are

- the scope of work
- the scope of services
- the fee
- reimbursable expenses
- the terms and conditions of the contract
- the schedule

For each of these elements, the landscape architect can develop a position more than might ultimately be settled for. The scope of work can be written to include everything that the landscape architect wants to be involved with in the project. The scope of services can include the maximum range of services that would be possible. The fee can be based on the greatest number of hours deemed necessary. The terms and conditions can be written in favor of the professional. The schedule can be made extra comfortable.

The professional should assume that the client will want to reduce, eliminate, and scale down all aspects of the proposed contract. If the landscape architect has built in room to maneuver, the professional can give on all of the items or will able to negotiate by give-and-take so that some of the elements of the contract provide a good comfort level for completing the work with a favorable conclusion. If the initial proposal includes the scope, fee, and terms that the landscape architect expects to end up with, the landscape architect will have no room to negotiate, and will in effect have to assume a take-it-or-leave-it attitude. Furthermore, if the landscape architect does make concessions on a proposal that represents his or her bottom line, then he or she may feel cheated and the professional relationship will get off to a bad start. The client will perceive the landscape architect as presenting a take-it-or-leave-it position. The client will get no satisfaction out of obtaining some negotiating achievements. The client may present his or her alternatives to the landscape architect's proposal and assume the same take-it-or-leave-it attitude. Negotiations may break down, and the client and the project may be lost.

Having alternatives in mind during the negotiating process is a way to enhance the landscape architect's room to maneuver. By developing alternatives to the scope of work or the scope of services, for example, the landscape architect can present the alternatives and be willing to give away the original position if the alternative is acceptable. Here's an example: On a residential site planning and landscape architecture project, you require that the client provide a boundary and topographic survey by a registered surveyor. The client gets quotes from three surveyors of $2,500,

$2,400, and $2,600 for the work. The client is reluctant to engage the service at the cost. Here are some alternatives that you may have at hand:

1. You research the city engineer's files and find that a plat plan of the subdivision is available with topography at a one-foot contour interval. You indicate that you can enlarge the plat plan to be used as an acceptable site plan. If the design is one that can float reasonably well inside the lot lines, and the topography is not severe, you can indicate that you are willing to develop the base plan for a fee of $1,000 and reserve the right to revisit the need for an accurate boundary and topographic survey if the need presents itself after the preliminary plan is completed.

2. You call the local aerial photographic company and establish that a very recent blanket flight has been made of the area and the aerial company's photos include topography superimposed on the photo. You obtain a boundary plan from a recent appraisal of the property and find that you can match the aerial and the boundary to create a reasonably accurate base plan for a fee of $900. Again, you reserve the right to revisit the need for an accurate boundary and topographic survey if the need presents itself after the preliminary plan is completed.

3. You find that city road improvements have been recently completed adjacent to the site, and a site plan with accurate boundaries and topography are available from the roadway improvement project. You ask the city engineer if you can use the survey information and agree to compensate the original surveyor with a fee of $500 for using the work for your project.

The client is likely to be impressed that you have done your homework and have these creative and less expensive alternatives at hand. This alone may create a trusting relationship that will make easier going of the rest of the negotiation on the proposed contract.

Before you start negotiating any contract, establish your bottom line on everything that is negotiable. The final agreed-upon scope, fee, and terms must be something you can live with. If you go below your bottom line, you'll resent it, you may be tempted to cut corners, the project may suffer, and the relationship may deteriorate.

When you establish your bottom line, or what you are willing to concede in the negotiating process, you also will want to prioritize the concessions you are willing to make. By initially presenting your maximum position, such as the maximum scope of work you would like to carry out, and by establishing a minimum scope you are willing to settle for, you will have the upper and lower limits of your negotiating position. You then allow yourself a great deal of flexibility to agree on a scope that is somewhere between the maximum and the minimum, and one that you have predetermined you can live with.

Don't Give Up Too Much Too Soon

In negotiating, concessions are the key points of the give-and-take process. Concessions give each side leverage. If one side gives up one thing, that side is likely to want the other party to give up something. Never give up something without getting something. The best approach is to exchange negotiating points with your client, rather than forcing points from the client.

One of the downfalls of being willing to give up too much too soon is that the landscape architect's client may feel that the proposal is altogether overwritten. The client may become leery that the scope is overwritten, the fee is too much, and the terms and conditions are too heavily in favor of the landscape architect. If the client senses this, he or she may feel that the landscape architect is not trustworthy and is not presenting a fair deal from the start.

Time is one of the elements that works in the landscape architect's favor when making concessions. Let the client think about some element of the proposal or contract that the landscape architect is not willing to give up. The client is often willing to acquiesce to the landscape architect's point of view if the client has time to consider it.

Be Willing to Say No and Mean It

Knowing when to use the word *no* and being able to say it with meaning is one of the most difficult but important skills in the negotiating process. If the landscape architect really believes that he or she cannot make a concession, such as reducing the fee below a certain level, the landscape architect must be willing to say no and live with the consequences. The key to saying no in the negotiating process depends upon the landscape architect's beliefs. Ethical compromise, for example, is definitely a time to say no and mean it. If the landscape architect really believes that saying no to a client's request is important, the landscape architect should have the courage to say no and have the hard facts and the infallible rationale to defend the position.

No is a powerful word in the landscape architect's negotiating arsenal. When used in the right circumstances, it can provide a great deal of negotiating leverage.

Don't Renege on What You Agree To

The easiest way to lose face and a client's trust is to renege on an agreement.

If the landscape architect makes an honest mistake in the proposal or the contract, or agrees to something in the client's interest that he or she is not sure of, only to find out after further study that the agreement is deleterious to the landscape architect, the first thing to do is assess the seriousness of the mistake. If the mistake is not too serious, decide if you can live with it and continue negotiations in a positive manner. If the mistake is honest, and the landscape architect can't live with it, try to retract the error. If the client is reasonable, there may be no problem. If the client insists that the landscape architect hold to the agreement, the landscape architect will have to decide if it is a deal breaker.

If you make a mistake and decide to honor it, let the client know you are aware of the mistake and are willing to live with it. Doing so will retain as much goodwill in the negotiating process as possible, and your client will respect you for it. The client may even soften and ultimately restructure the element of the agreement to be favorable to both parties as long as the landscape architect is honest and credible. Besides, there may come a time when you are working with the same client and the client makes a mistake and wants to renege. You can get in the very gracious position of returning the favor.

Getting the Fee You Want

One of the toughest negotiating points for landscape architects in the contract for professional services is the fee. Getting the fee you want can be exasperating at times. Regardless of everything one hears about not negotiating on fees, it is done on a regular basis. Competition on a fee basis has increased in recent years among professional landscape architecture firms, as well as among allied professionals. Clients are for the most part fee sensitive and want to know that they are getting the best services for the lowest price. The landscape architect can incorporate some helpful measures into his or her approach to contracting professional services and negotiating contracts to get the desired fee.

To start with, the landscape architect should be very aware of the scope of work and the scope of services that the fee is based on. It is difficult to defend a proposed fee if the landscape architect is not clear about the scope of services and the hours estimate that the fee is based on. This is one of the reasons I am a strong advocate of including a thorough, accurate, and step-by-step scope of services, as well as the actual hours expected to be used on each item of the scope, in the agreement with the client. This type of scope is illustrated in figure 9-2. Writing a general paragraph that says the landscape architect will carry out the services necessary to produce a site plan leaves a great deal to the imagination of both the professional and the would-be client. Because landscape architects are selling intangible services, they need to make the services seem as real and definable to the client as possible. In the client's eyes, the landscape architect's price is too high unless proven otherwise.

Remember some of the following points when presenting and negotiating a fee:

- *Sell experience.* A good way to sell experience is to recapitulate your experience with the same or similar projects. This establishes a confidence level in your client.
- *Sell benefits.* Similar to experience, you can tell your client the benefits of engaging your services. You may have an excellent track record of successful rezoning projects and a good rapport with the local planning and zoning staff. The benefit to a client with a rezoning project is that you are likely to get his or her project rezoned without a hitch.
- *Sell value of services.* One of the best arguments for selling value of services is that your client can use the construction documents to receive

competitive bids. You can point out the success other clients have had with bidding your plans. You can illustrate how detailed your plans are, which allows contractors to bid your plans more competitively.

- *Sell the quality of your completed projects.* A good way to convince your client of the quality of your completed projects is by mentioning the awards you have won. Another way is to obtain and use letters of reference from satisfied clients.
- *Sell pride.* Let the client know how proud of your work you are. Present your proposal with enthusiasm and gusto. Tell the client how your design work and the completed project will enhance his or her pride in ownership.
- *Sell uniqueness.* Every project for a landscape architect is different. Each has unique design criteria and design responses. Tell your client that he or she will have a one-of-a-kind project—a project that no other client has.
- *Sell service.* Let the client know that you will stand by your work and will make right any problems that may occur. Always remember that service is what the landscape architect sells, and attention to serving the client is a primary motivation (Fuller 1991).

Because you know that most clients are fee sensitive, you should invariably request a fee that is the maximum amount you would like to receive for the project within reason and based on general prevailing professional services rates. At the same time, have a bottom-line fee in mind that you are not willing to go below. If you have this range in mind, then somewhere between the high and the low fee will work for you.

One way to counter the issue that your client feels your fee is too high is to advance the notion that your fee, if anything, is too low. People love bargains, and if you can convince your client that he or she is getting a bargain, your fee may stay intact as quoted. One approach is to let the client know that your firm is contemplating a raise in hourly billing rates. By signing the agreement for professional services now, the client can avoid the increase in fees that would occur with the increase in hourly billing rates. You might also indicate that your competitors have raised their fees. You might be able to base your argument on the fact that inflation is driving up fees and costs, therefore the client is getting a good deal at the fee you have quoted (Fuller 1991).

Another important element to remember in negotiating with a client who has received more than one proposal for the same project is to remind the client to compare apples with apples. Make sure that the client carefully matches your scope of services, hours estimate, and fee with your competitors'.

You also can brainstorm the client's project, trying to identify ways to save the client money in construction costs while not reducing the quality level of the project. This approach is called *value engineering* and is frequently carried out after a project has been bid and the contract for construction has been let or is imminent. The process is valuable in the fee-negotiating process because the landscape architect shows an interest in the client's costs, and everyone wants to save money. If you can come up with several ways to save money without compromising quality or safety, the client may be happy to pay the fee you have requested.

Become Knowledgeable on Negotiating

Recognize the importance of negotiating to the business aspects of landscape architecture. Read books on negotiating and obtaining consensus. Attend negotiating seminars and workshops. Develop standard responses to negotiating tactics and have them at hand for use in negotiating situations.

Negotiating Strategies

When negotiating with a client, an employee, a lender, or any other person in the course of professional practice, being aware of tactics that may be used in negotiating with you and how to counter them can be very useful to the landscape architect. The following sections discuss some of the more common tactics.

Winner Takes All

Some negotiators take the position of giving as little as possible and taking as much as they can get. They establish points that they want at all costs and are not willing to budge an inch. They stick to their position. If any alternatives are presented, the alternatives are merely the same points they initially presented, repackaged in a different way to achieve the same end result.

If you are negotiating a renewal of your operating line of credit and the lender wants to increase your interest rate from 1.5 percent over prime to 2.5 percent over prime, the lender may say that the bank wants your business, but the proposed rate increase says otherwise. The lender may have a number of reasons why the bank wants to raise the rate. You counter that times are good for the banking industry and record profits are being made because the interest rates banks are paying are low and the interest rates they are charging are high. The bank counters with an alternative proposal that you pay the rate of 2.5 percent over prime on a balance of $25,000 or below, and the rate will drop to your present rate of 1.5 percent over prime on balances over $25,000. The alternative is their final offer. If you agree, the bank will have successfully negotiated a .5 percent average increase in your lending rate in spite of the claims you have made. You may have to recognize, however, that this is the best deal you can negotiate. Knowing when you've reached the best point in the negotiating process is a skill, somewhat like a sixth sense, that the landscape architect must cultivate.

In this case, you must be aware of your alternatives. You would probably shop around and obtain quotes from other banks to develop ammunition for further negotiation to try to retain your present terms with the bank. If all else fails and the bank continues to maintain its winner-take-all attitude, you can elect to move your account to another lending agency that is willing to match your present interest-rate charges. Under the winner-take-all approach to negotiating, the landscape architect must know when to walk away, but be sure to cover his or her bases and have a reasonable alternative to move on to (Economy 1994).

Win/Win

Almost everyone has heard of the win/win strategy to negotiating. This approach is used by two parties intent on working together to resolve any issues that need to be negotiated so that each leaves the negotiating table feeling good. Win/win tactics in negotiating involve creating mutual gain in the negotiating process, or at least giving minimal or no cost concessions.

Establishing a win/win philosophy up front with your negotiating partner is the initial posture that must be agreed to by both parties. Problems occur if negotiations break down or one of the negotiators perceives that the other has abandoned the win/win strategy during negotiations and becomes stubborn on one or more points resulting in a winner-take-all or a take-it-or-leave-it attitude.

A key to win/win negotiating is honesty and open communication. If the landscape architect lays all of his or her cards on the table in negotiating a contract for professional services and the prospective client deals only half of his or her deck, the landscape architect will be playing with half a deck in negotiating with the prospective client. Both parties in a win/win approach to negotiating must work together with mutual trust.

There is no real counter to a win/win approach to negotiating because both parties endeavor to end negotiations satisfied that they have won everything they wanted or made low-cost or no-cost concessions in exchange for obtaining all they wanted (Fuller 1991).

Good Guy/Bad Guy

This negotiating method involves teamwork. The scenario starts with the opposing negotiator's bad guy suddenly going ballistic, slamming the table, and saying that the proposal being offered by the landscape architect is totally unrealistic and that the fee is way out of line. The bad guy raises his voice and rants and raves about every aspect of the proposal or the terms of the contract. He storms out of the room, saying there is no way that his side will sign the agreement.

After the bad guy has carried on and made the landscape architect feel like he or she should have stayed home, the good guy on the opposing negotiating team enters and is sympathetic to the landscape architect's position. The good guy apologizes for the actions of the bad guy. The good guy informs the landscape architect that he feels an agreement can be reached. He suggests a number of compromises that usually benefit the opposing negotiating team and suggests that if the landscape architect can agree, they will be able to wrap up negotiations and get on with the project. The landscape architect may have been intimidated by the explosive actions of the bad guy and acquiesce to the points offered by the good guy.

There are two ways to counter the good guy/bad guy approach. The first is to adopt the good guy/bad guy posture yourself. Counter the bad guy with your own brow beater so that the good guy's entrance is tactically blunted. You may then be able to bring on your own good guy and obtain the negotiating points you want from your opponent because you have outmaneuvered him.

The second way to defuse the good guy/bad guy approach is to listen to the bad guy, announce that it is clear the opposition is not willing to negotiate in a calm and nonadversarial approach, and insist on negotiating with another representative of the opponent. If the opponent refuses, the landscape architect must be willing to break off negotiations until a reasonable negotiator is found to represent the opponent.

Team Approach

The team approach is used in an effort to overwhelm the opposition. I have actually seen landscape architects use this tactic effectively when arguing for a major development project that has a great deal of controversy associated with it. The firm will bring in a team of specialists, each with a string of credentials a mile long. Each will tell of the benefits of the project and how the plan will benefit the city or neighborhood.

Team tactics are also used when the landscape architect is on the other side of the line. Negotiating a big contract with a large corporate client is a typical situation when team tactics can be used against a landscape architect. The landscape architect may first run the gamut of lower middle managers, each with a small vested interest in the project. During the interviews, the landscape architect may feel he or she is being tested and scrutinized to see if he or she fits the corporate mold and if the landscape architect's prior experience and completed projects meet the image the corporation is seeking. If the landscape architect makes it past the middle managers, he or she will go higher up the corporate ladder to vice presidents, and ultimately up to the CEO and possibly the board of directors. This team tactic is spread out over time, but one can be sure the interviewers are talking together and constantly evaluating the personalities representing the landscape architecture firm and how the landscape architects handle themselves.

Confronted with team tactics in the negotiating process can be overwhelming to the landscape architect. There are two ways to effectively counter the team-tactic approach. One way is to prepare your own team of experts and use them wisely. Match your team and its specialties carefully to counter the opponent's team of experts.

The second approach is to take the heroic approach, facing the team alone. In this approach the landscape architect must be well prepared and exude a considerable degree of confidence. If the landscape architect can keep winning the confidence and approval of the opponent's specialized team, negotiating victory will be sweet, if it occurs. In this approach, try to space out the negotiations, taking on only one or a small group of the opponent's specialists at a time. By spacing out the negotiations, you will have time to prepare between each negotiating session (Economy 1994).

Use Time as a Weapon

Using time as a negotiating tactic is a very old and often-used approach. Time can be used in a number of ways, but the most common ways are to limit time, creating a short deadline to the negotiating process, or to use the technique of stalling or delaying a decision.

Salespeople often use the time limit as an effective tactic. In this approach, the salesperson says that an offer is good only for a certain length of time and lets you know that at the end of the time period the offer will no longer be good. A classic example is the phone call by a salesperson who wants to let you know that a product that you may use in bulk or volume, such as blueprint paper, is available for a limited time at a deep discount—but of course you will probably be required to purchase a supply large enough to keep your firm in blueprint paper through the next century.

Your best bet for countering the time-limit tactic is to call the salesperson's bluff. The time limit may be real or may not be real. It may apply to the volumes the salesperson has said must be purchased, or you may be able to negotiate a substantially smaller volume for the same or a slightly higher price. A factor that enters your consideration is cash flow and your own projections of how much of the product you will need in the near future or how important the purchase is to the operations of your firm at the time.

The other technique for using time as an advantage is to stall, obstruct, delay, or ignore. The landscape architect may encounter this technique after presenting a proposal for professional services. It is one way to gauge how serious a client is about the proposal. It can also be used by the prospective client to get concessions or additional work for the proposed fee because the landscape architect gets nervous and believes that by making concessions he or she will ultimately secure the contract. Stalling should alert the landscape architect that the prospective client may be fishing for concessions, obtaining competitive proposals from other landscape architects, is unsure of the project or its funding, or the client's representative may not have the authority to make decisions on behalf of the client (e.g., if it is a corporation or a government agency).

The stalling technique works best when the person using it has leverage. If the project a landscape architect is seeking is a real plum, an exceptional design project, and if the prospective client knows it, the client has leverage. On the other hand, if the landscape architect has an excellent reputation for a particular type of project and is busy at the time, the landscape architect can use stalling as leverage if he or she perceives the client really wants the firm to do the project.

To counter the stalling technique, the leverage must be removed as a negotiating weapon. The landscape architect prepares as many alternatives and options as possible to counter the delay tactics. If the client says there is an interest in using the firm but the contract can't be let for six months, the landscape architecture firm may counter with the fact that it needs to start the work immediately because it has another large project coming on line in six months. If the client wants to delay because funds won't be available for six months, the landscape architect may suggest that a small initial phase of the project for a low fee can be initiated immediately and the bulk of the work can take place later when the client's funding comes on line. The more counters to the delay tactics, the better. If the landscape architect's countertactics don't seem to be working, the landscape architect also needs to know when to cut the losses and move on to other job-development opportunities (Economy 1994).

Take It or Leave It

One of the most unpalatable negotiating approaches is the ultimatum—take it or leave it. No one likes a gun held to his or her head. "It's my way or the highway" has made the hair on more than one person's back bristle with resentment. In the take-it-or-leave-it approach, one party presents a proposal or an offer and indicates that the offer must be accepted exactly as it has been presented or the deal is off. This approach is used by a winner-take-all negotiator. Even if the loser accepts the take-it-or-leave-it deal, resentment and even anger is likely to color the relationship throughout the duration of the contract.

There are ways to counter the take-it-or-leave-it offer. First and foremost you must be willing to walk away from the potential contract in a clear and decisive manner. You may want to evaluate the take-it-or-leave-it offer in several ways before you walk away. For example, your firm may need the work, and the reality of staying alive may be an incentive to take the offer. Another approach is to call the bluff to see how inflexible the prospective client really is. You may ask yourself if your competitors would be willing to engage the take-it-or-leave-it offer (Economy 1994).

Another approach is to talk through the ultimatum and ignore it. If the client stays in the game, you may realize that the client is not as hard and fast as implied in the take-it-or-leave-it offer. Real negotiating might ensue, and you may be able to negotiate a win/win approach to the contract. You must be in a position to walk away from an ultimatum. If you take the position to walk away, your prospective client may often engage in realistic negotiations. One of the rewards of walking away from the my-way-or-the-highway negotiator is the self-respect gained by knowing that you won't be bullied into a lopsided agreement. You may even gain a reputation of being a hard-nosed and honest negotiator with a high degree of integrity in your landscape architecture business community (Fuller 1991).

Forming an Agreement

The best part of negotiating a contract is coming to the realization that an agreement is imminent. Knowing when you've reached the point where both sides feel comfortable with the outcome of the negotiating process can be very exhilarating. It has brought a big smile to many a face and given rise to many high fives. When you know you've reached an agreement, especially a win/win agreement, the project can get off to an auspicious start on a firm foundation of mutual respect and trust.

Defining Areas of Mutual Agreement

One of the first things you can do when negotiating a contract for professional services (or any other contract, for that matter) is to identify the areas of mutual agreement that you share with your negotiating partner. When the going gets tough in the process of negotiating those points that you don't agree on, you can regularly come back to those areas where you agree. The points you agree on are a foundation upon which to build the rest of the agreement point by point until you concur on all of the points that need to be negotiated in the proposal or contract. Establishing the areas of agreement and building on them is a great way to build the trust and appreciation of the other party as you negotiate a contract. By adding to the points you agree on and by reiterating these points, you will be able to build momentum that will help to carry you and your negotiating partner through the process.

In addition to building the points you agree on, you should keep track of concessions made by each of you, because the act of making a concession is in effect agreeing with the other person.

Another important point to agree on is that you both have a goal of forming an agreement that is mutually beneficial to each party. You might also have a common goal of establishing and fostering a long-term professional relationship. Long-term relationships with clients are highly valuable to a landscape architect because the majority of work a landscape architect obtains is from callbacks and referrals by satisfied clients with whom the landscape architect has nurtured a successful and trusting long-term relationship. The professional-client relationships that have the greatest value and pay off with a steady stream of projects are the long-term relationships.

A cornerstone to successful negotiation is agreeing to agree. After you identify those points that you agree on and those points you or your negotiating partner are willing to concede to, you may want to consent to and affirm your desire to reach an agreement by agreeing to agree on the remaining points. Avoid focusing on any conflict or fears that you may have by orienting your focus on agreement and mutually beneficial negotiation (Economy 1994).

Identifying Areas of Disagreement

When you and your client or negotiating partner have identified all the areas where you agree, you may find that you have evolved into a mutually agreeable posture. You may also find that you have some points that you disagree on. Turning these points of disagreement into agreement is always the most demanding part of the negotiation process.

To resolve disagreement, the first step is identifying the areas where you disagree with your negotiating partner. You carry out this step of the process alone and independent of your negotiating partner. Consolidate the areas of disagreement. Write them down. Rank them and prepare an arsenal of options to offer that you are willing to live with. This process of brainstorming alternatives to the areas of disagreement can be facilitated by discussing them with your partners and managers if you work in a large office. If you are a one-person office, you may want to ask a trusted friend, your spouse, or another professional, such a your attorney or insurance broker, to allow you to bounce your ideas off of him or her. Outside input can be extremely beneficial.

By ranking the areas of disagreement, you may determine that there are one or more points that you cannot compromise on or concede to. You may feel, for example, that the fee you are asking for the proposed services represents the true value of the services and you are not willing to reduce the fee unless significant reductions in the scope of work or scope of services are negotiated.

Armed with your ranking of the areas you disagree on, your alternatives, and your resolve to hold firm on those areas in which you cannot compromise, you reinitiate the negotiation process with a give-and-take frame of mind. You use your alternatives and approach the areas of disagreement with proposals aimed at achieving agreement so that both you and your prospective client are willing to accept the negotiated alternative and be able to live with it. During this process, you must remain alert to the concessions that your opponent is willing to make. You may find that he or she wants a concession that is palatable to you, and by giving the concession, you are setting up a frame of mind for your negotiating partner to give you concessions that you want.

One thing that can always get in the way at this point in the negotiating process is your ego. At all costs, avoid ego battles. You must keep your focus on the goal of obtaining a mutually agreeable agreement. If your ego gets in the way, it can lead to a serious breakdown in communication and threaten the trust you have built up in the negotiating process.

Dealing with Deadlock

After you have established areas of agreement and both sides have made concessions, if one or more points remain in deadlock, there are several approaches that you can take to deal with the stalemate. If you cannot break the deadlock, all the hard work at negotiating, all the anticipation of reaching agreement, and the potential reward of working on a new project or achieving a loan you very much need may fall in vain.

You may use some or all of the following tactics to resolve the deadlock:

- Determine what is causing the deadlock. Your negotiating opponent may be required to maintain a position that is mandated by some higher authority, for example. The cause may be an ego element: your opponent may just have to have the last word. The better you are at determining what is causing the deadlock, the more likely you are to find a way around it. If all else fails, you might simply concede to the last remaining point that your negotiator is interested in if it won't be a significant compromise for you.

- Keep talking. The chances of completing negotiations and solving a deadlock are nil if you break off communications. This is not to say that you cannot use the time tactic as a ploy to resolve the issue. Keeping communication channels open, however, keeps alive the possibility of reaching an agreement.

- Turn the deadlock into significant other gains for you if you acquiesce to the point that your negotiating opponent is standing firm on. If a negotiator has a certain limit placed on the deal by a higher authority, you may decide to agree to the point but propose significant concessions in other areas that your opponent agrees to in order to maintain the win solution to the deadlocked point.

- Revisit the points that you have agreed on. Summarize all the points you've successfully negotiated. This process will hopefully reinvigorate the negotiations and allow the negotiating partners to come to terms on the deadlocked point or points.

- Offer a new point that may make the deadlocked agreement more attractive to your negotiating partner without making any further concessions.

- Attempt to engage your negotiating partner in a discussion that brings a different or new perspective to the deadlock. Use logic, intellect, objectivity, analysis, meeting of the minds, and other techniques designed to deal with the deadlock in a mature and intelligent way.

- Use some of the negotiating techniques mentioned earlier. Bring in a surprise specialist who is prepared for the deadlock with a compromise backed up by hard facts and extensive experience in dealing with the deadlocked topic. A neutral third party can often save the day and obtain a successful conclusion to the negotiations. This approach is similar to using a professional mediator for dispute resolution.

- When all else fails, withdraw. Break off negotiations. You can break off negotiations by giving your negotiating partner a deadline. This technique is a gamble. It can test the resolve of your negotiating opponent and may bring him or her back to the table determined to succeed and reach agreement by the deadline you have set. It also can result in negotiations breaking off entirely, the loss of the contract, and the loss of a great deal of time and money involved in the negotiating process.

- Bring in your partner, if you have one. When negotiations deteriorate, the interpersonal relations between you and the person you're negotiating with also tend to fall apart. Substituting new negotiators on one or both sides of the table can sometimes breathe new life into the process and result in an agreement (Economy 1994; Fuller 1991).

Knowing When You Have Reached an Agreement

Once the agreement has been finalized, the first thing to do is shake hands if you've concluded the negotiations in person. Regardless of how legal implications and formal, written contracts have become the cornerstones of today's contracts, there is something about the good old-fashioned handshake that says a lot about the mutual respect, trust, and goodwill that has been created through the negotiating process. To most people, the handshake still signifies a personal bond that the agreement will be executed according to the terms hammered out.

Whether the meeting is in person, on the telephone, or through fax communications, the last step in the process is to confirm any and all concessions or points that are different from the items made in your or your negotiating partner's proposal. You can handle this with a verbal recap and concurrence. Thank your prospective client or the representative of the party you've been negotiating with.

The last step is to confirm the negotiated agreement by drawing up a contract for your client to sign, or to review carefully a contract written and presented by a banker, an employee, or a prospective partner if the negotiations involve something other than a contract for professional services.

If the negotiations are for a professional services contract, I recommend that the landscape architect always offer to be the one who writes the final agreement—the contract. Taking charge of writing the final document allows you to put the items agreed to in your own terms. You can use contract language that is in your favor with the exception that you would never renege on any of the points you have negotiated. Be careful to write any of the negotiated terms so that they truly reflect what you have agreed to.

Submit your contract to your client and let him or her know that you will commence work when you have received a signed contract for your files. If the client has objections to any specific wording, you will find yourself back in a negotiating posture. Usually, the negotiating at this point will be over minor wording, but you still have to remain wary that any proposed changes by your client may alter the meaning of the way you have written the contract. When wording issues occur, they can be focused on intently because they are concrete at this point.

You should keep a very detailed file of the negotiation process as it has occurred, which can help you in resolving issues with your client over wording. If your negotiating file is detailed and thorough, you may be able to go back into your negotiating records and remind your client of exactly what he or she agreed to as you have interpreted it in the written contract. Being able to refer to your notes may not only resolve the problem but also prevent the possibility of losing the contract at the last minute because your client has a problem with the wording (Fuller 1991).

Learning from Your Mistakes

No matter how hard you try, no matter how clearly you negotiate, no matter how much you want a project, there are times when it just wasn't meant to be.

When you don't get the project, the most important thing to do is accept the fact and go on with your professional life. There will be other opportunities, other clients, and a wide range of proposal, negotiation, and contract possibilities. You will learn from proposals that go nowhere, from negotiations that end with no project in hand.

I remember a time that I wanted to design a particular entry feature, open-space areas, and a common recreation center for a high-end, upscale townhouse project. I was asked to submit a proposal and found out that I was competing against only one other landscape architect for this plum of a project. Fifty percent odds seemed good to me. I worked very hard on the proposal. I thought my presentation went well, and the client was receptive. There seemed to be little about my proposal, fee, scope of services, and terms that the prospective client had any problem with whatsoever. I was disappointed and resentful when I didn't get the project. After digging a little deeper into the background of my competitor, I found out that he was married to the client's daughter. From that proposal process, I learned to always find out as much about my competition as possible. That project just wasn't meant for me. The very next day, I was on to another lead that turned out to be one of the most successful design projects my firm has ever completed. I also learned for the first time not to dwell on the negative, but to always try to live in the solution instead of the problem.

One of the worst things you can do is feel sorry for yourself and dwell on the fact that you negotiated poorly or didn't hit it off with the prospective client. Indeed, one of the main reasons why many agreements are not consummated is because there is a personality difference between the landscape architect and the prospective client. Whereas you will undoubtedly have many successes in the business practice of landscape architecture, you will have failures too. Take the time to learn from the process you pursued. Learn from your mistakes and learn from your successes. Make adjustments in your process of becoming aware of a prospective client or a project, submitting a proposal, negotiating an agreement, and writing and consummating a contract.

In summary, here are some of the best rules of thumb gleaned from years of private practice and from several excellent references on negotiating:

- The lower your expectations about getting the project, the better the agreement you'll negotiate.
- Always know your negotiating goals.
- Always plan your proposal, negotiating, and contracting process.
- Always assess your opponent's strengths and weaknesses, as well as your own.
- Anticipate your client's position to your proposals.
- Always negotiate with the right person.
- Identify all the points where you agree in the proposal, negotiating, and contracting process so that the negotiating process is focused ultimately on resolving areas where you don't agree.
- Make your word your bond. Develop trust with a client.
- When you are developing a client and negotiating for a project, always keep your emotions in control.
- Be confident. Prospective clients have confidence in confident professionals.
- No matter what your asking price, you can ultimately obtain only the fee that the client is willing to pay.
- To counter a client's negotiation tactics, you first have to be able to recognize them.
- Always negotiate out services when a client wants you to reduce your fee.
- Avoid agreeing to a contract that holds your client harmless for any and all damages that may occur with the project.
- Always do your homework.
- Always write the contract if the option is open.
- One of the best ways to handle a take-it-or-leave-it ultimatum is to ignore it.
- Use time wisely in the negotiating and contracting process.
- Always strive to create and nurture trust, cooperation, and honesty in the proposal and contracting process.
- Remember that almost everything is negotiable.
- Be aware of general market and economic conditions and how these might affect your proposal, the negotiations, and the development of the contract.
- Successful negotiators neither avoid conflict nor encourage it. They manage conflict.

- Always write a thorough and complete scope of services.
- Be up front about the hours estimate you make in the proposal.
- For every concession you make during the negotiating process, always get something in return.
- Don't make concessions easily.
- Don't let your ego get in the way of negotiating a successful deal.
- Always expect to make concessions, even if you end up making none.
- Make it easy for your prospective client to say yes.
- Have a flexible attitude when negotiating.
- If you are confused about a contract point or a negotiating position, take time to study it and seek knowledgeable counsel. Never commit to something you do not understand.
- Anticipate your prospective client's objections to your proposal or contract.
- Always have alternatives and options ready when negotiating a proposal or a contract.
- Read and study negotiating literature. Make yourself a negotiating expert.
- Always think of the negotiating process as developing a relationship.
- Nonverbal communication, both yours and your negotiating opponent's, is important.
- Timing can be everything in the proposal, negotiating, and contracting process.
- Negotiating is a listening process.
- Use technology. For example, the fax machine has become a terrific aid to the proposal, negotiating, and contracting process.
- Win/win negotiating means finding ways to create mutual gain or give low-cost or no-cost concessions.
- Bargaining is the process of exchanging one element of the proposal or agreement for another.
- Never be afraid to say you don't know how you feel about a negotiator's proposal and that you need time to think about it.
- Don't underestimate the power of team tactics in negotiating. Bring your partner if you have one.
- Keep good notes throughout the proposal, negotiating, and contracting process. Put everything in writing.

- Agreements are the result of both sides realizing it is in their best interest to agree rather than not to reach an agreement.
- Smile. It can be contagious. (Economy 1994; Fuller 1991; Schoenfield 1991)

Important Elements and Useful Contract Clauses

You've made your proposal. You've negotiated the agreement. Now you must write the contract.

There is a wide range of contract elements and clauses that the landscape architect can use to prevent or mitigate problems that may and do occur in carrying out professional services.

There are a number of excellent guides that are useful and meaningful to the landscape architect in preparing a contract for professional services. The standard association contracts, such as the AIA contracts and their accompanying instruction sheets, are very helpful. As mentioned earlier, these standard contracts and other contract reference sources are available from the local chapter of the AIA or from the Washington, D.C., headquarters office of the AIA. One excellent summary of the options available for dispute resolution is *The Architect in Dispute Resolution,* written by John Timpson and published by RIBA Publications.

One of the most helpful guides is published by the DPIC Companies, which specialize in professional liability insurance. The DPIC Companies, which are represented by local insurance agents, are a proactive organization that seeks to mitigate claims made involving landscape architects and other professionals. The organization insures for problems related to professional errors, omissions, and negligence. The DPIC Companies sponsor and provide discount incentives for professionals to take part in educational programs aimed at increasing the professionals' awareness of issues about contract liability and other professional endeavors.

Although most professional liability insurance companies also offer guidance in developing contract language (such as the professional liability insurance program geared specifically to landscape architecture practice available from Leatzow & Associates), I have found *The Contract Guide: DPIC's Risk Management*

Handbook for Architects and Engineers, written by Sheila A. Dixon and Richard D. Crowell, to be the most comprehensive resource available. It not only provides suggested clauses covering over seventy topics germane to the preparation of contracts and contract activities, but also includes a discussion of the problem and solution to the contract topics, giving the professional a clearer understanding of the background related to the topic.

In the remainder of this chapter, I have attempted to concentrate on those contract elements and clauses that I feel are of paramount importance to the successful development of landscape architecture contracts for professional services.

Dispute Resolution

The longer a landscape architect stays in practice, the greater the chances he or she will inevitably be involved in a dispute related to execution of the contract for professional services, a construction incident, or a third-party lawsuit after a construction project has been completed. No matter how careful the practitioner is in carrying out professional landscape architecture services, the law of averages favors a dispute occurring sooner or later.

There are a number of methods for resolving disputes, and the specific method that is to be used can be written into the contract for professional services. The principal methods of dispute resolution are (1) *legal, adversarial methods* (these include litigation and arbitration) and (2) *paralegal, nonadversarial methods* (these include voluntary discussions to reach mutual conciliation and mediation).

Legal, Adversarial Methods

Litigation is the legal process of suing another party. Litigation is frequently chosen when the parties are in a seriously adversarial dispute that may involve significant loss in millions of dollars or bodily injury and where significant legal matters may be an issue. In adversarial cases, a judge may be the only person with the power to handle the case and the binding authority to bring forth a reasonable and fair decision.

Litigation should be elected as the method of dispute resolution only if other less adversarial options cannot be engaged. The landscape architect may not have a choice in the matter. If a lawsuit is brought against the landscape architect, he or she will be obligated to make a defense. Litigation is said to be the most costly method of dispute resolution. It also tends to be a long and time-consuming process, often involving years of interrogation, depositions, legal maneuvering, and legal costs that may be beyond the financial capability of the landscape architect. The legal fees ultimately may become a moot point if the landscape architect wins a judgment and receives legal fees as part of the judgment. The capability to assess the likelihood of winning a case and recovering attorney's fees is a decision that needs to be made early in the litigation process.

In most cases, lawsuits are settled out of court before the case is ever heard by a judge. Decisions in lawsuits are often economic in nature, made to minimize legal fees and other costs, especially if the case appears to be one that will be settled by all parties to the lawsuit, each having some culpability and responsibility for contributing to the loss.

Another fact of life in a lawsuit is deep pockets. All too frequently, the participant with the deepest pockets—with the most assets available in economic resources or insurance protection—is the one that contributes the most to an award resulting from litigation. My rule of thumb is to avoid lawsuits if at all possible.

Arbitration is the method of settling a contract dispute by agreeing in advance in the contract to accept the decision of an impartial person (an arbiter) to resolve the issue after hearing the facts of the parties to the dispute. Arbitration was at one time the favored way of settling contractual and technical disputes. The AIA standard form of agreement includes an arbitration clause that specifies that the arbitration be carried out in accordance with the Construction Industry Arbitration Rules of the American Arbitration Association.

The complexity of disputes and contractual or technical issues, as well as the cost and length of time associated with arbitration, have increased over time. However, arbitration continues to be an effective method of dispute resolution. One of the main reasons arbitration is effective is because the precise methods and rules are set down in writing in the contract in advance.

Paralegal, Nonadversarial Methods

Increasingly, what are now called *alternative dispute resolution methods* are being advocated by professional liability insurance companies, construction industry representatives, and professional practitioners. There are two basic approaches. The first approach is to agree to talk through the problem, coming to mutually acceptable conciliatory terms. You may be surprised to learn that many disputes, large and small, can be resolved in a reasonable way if you first agree to talk and approach the problem with the notion of agreeing to agree. Thus the first position to take when a problem occurs, such as a wall or sidewalk or bench that you feel is improperly constructed, is to use your powers of clear thinking and persuasion to come to terms in an amicable way.

The second approach, mediation, uses a mediator or facilitator, who is usually a member of the legal or business professions, to focus and direct the dispute negotiations toward an agreeable resolution. Formal mediation is not binding unless and until the parties involved agree to the outcome and sign a formal, binding letter of agreement.

The most important point for the landscape architect to remember in approaching alternative dispute resolution is to be constructive and take a nonadversarial, positive attitude into the discussions. One of the biggest rewards of alternative dispute resolution is lower cost. Another is the self-esteem that accompanies successfully working through a tough situation, even when you know it is likely to cost you or your firm a monetary loss.

I can personally attest to the effectiveness of successfully mediating a construction contract dispute. My firm was sued by a city because 500 feet of a sanitary sewer line was installed in such a way as not to drain properly. My firm clearly had some of the responsibility for the mishap. We believed, nevertheless, that the city, our civil-engineering subconsultant, the contractor, and the contractor's on-site layout surveyor had also contributed to the errors resulting in the sewer line being installed incorrectly. In this case, the city sued my firm to collect the costs of reinstalling the sewer line properly. With a great deal of help from the firm's professional liability insurance company, which at the time happened to be DPIC, and after a year and a half of negotiating with the parties involved, I was able to obtain agreement by all parties to engage in nonbinding mediation, hoping to avoid litigation.

The monetary stakes were large. Although the actual costs to replace the sewer line correctly were about $50,000, the contractor countersued the city for various other costs associated with the work, primarily downtime for construction equipment. The contractor was asking for approximately $350,000 in damages. Through my personal perseverance, the agreement to mediate meant huge potential savings for my firm. Furthermore, a clause in my professional liability insurance contract provided for cutting my deductible amount in half if successful mediation was used to resolve the dispute. Because the deductible amount that my firm would be responsible for was $25,000, saving $12,500 was in itself a big incentive for me to negotiate with the parties involved to mediate a resolution.

A considerable amount of time and effort went into finding and organizing documents for the disclosure process that was part of the nonbinding mediation, because each of the three main parties, our firm, the contractor, and the city, were represented by legal counsel. The disclosure and posturing took another one and one-half years. When the big day came, the mediation process was facilitated by an attorney, and it was concluded in one long day. What could have been a $350,000 award under litigation procedures—not to mention another $100,000 in attorney's fees—ended up being resolved so that my firm was responsible for $18,000 and the city was responsible for $37,000 in mediated awards to the contractor.

The intangible results were significantly more important to my firm than the impact of the $18,000 loss, half of which was paid for by the firm's insurance company. None of the parties to the dispute, including the city and its legal department, had ever worked through a dispute using mediation as the preferred approach. As a result of my personal efforts and my positive attitude throughout the process, my firm gained in stature with the city. I was viewed as a catalyst working toward a nonadversarial decision and willing to accept my firm's part in the payout without pointing fingers or harboring negative feelings toward either of the other parties involved. Later that year, when I thought that we would never get another contract with the city department under which the construction problem had occurred, our firm was awarded one of the largest contracts we ever received from the very city department that we had successfully led through the mediation process. The point is that there can be both financial and other intangible rewards of successfully using alternative dispute resolution methods.

We now include a nonbinding mediation clause in all of our contracts as the preferred method of dispute resolution. Mediation is a less adversarial way to resolve disputes, and as attested by my lesson with the city agency, if you ever have a significant contractual dispute, you too may emerge with your client intact and continue to have a healthy landscape architectural business relationship with that client.

Billing and Terms of Payment

A landscape architecture contract for professional services should include billing and payment terms. The more precisely the terms are spelled out in the contract, the greater the likelihood of being paid within a reasonable period of time and without disputes related to the fee. One of the business facts of life related to providing landscape architecture professional services—services that are intangible in nature—is that one must trust that the client will be satisfied and will pay the fees. This is not always the case, however, and collecting the fees owed to the landscape architect can be arduous at times. Separating the professional-client relationship from the business practice of getting paid for the services is one of those touchy areas where ethical, business, and interpersonal relationships cross over and can sometimes become muddled.

In order to have a greater sense of security about being paid, the landscape architect's contract must take advantage of legal contractual options available. By including specific billing and payment terms in the contract, the landscape architect can remain as impartial a businessperson as possible while trying to nurture the interpersonal relationship with his or her client. The key elements that should be included in the contract include the precise fee itself, the frequency of billings, retainer, costs of collection, interest charges on overdue accounts, suspension of work for nonpayment, payment of reimbursable expenses, and any rights available to the firm (such as lien rights) if they are available to professionals in the state where the contract is executed. By defining the terms of payment and billing, the landscape architect's contract will have the necessary elements to enforce payment from an unwilling client.

The contract should include a clause specifying how and when statements will be sent to the client and when amounts owed are overdue. My firm's clause says that invoices will be issued every four weeks and that they are payable upon receipt. Amounts owed are deemed delinquent after thirty days. The clause indicates that interest is due and payable on amounts outstanding after thirty days, and that payment received will be credited first to the payment of delinquent interest and then to principal amounts owed.

Sometimes the landscape architect needs or wants a retainer, a part of the fees due and payable prior to initiating work on a project. Retainers are typically used for the following circumstances:

- The client is new to the firm, and there is some question as to the reliability of receiving payment.
- The work of the contract requires an initial outlay of funds for equipment, supplies, or additional employees, such as temporary help required to complete the services. The retainer is used to cover the initial outlay of funds.
- The firm has worked for the client in the past, and receiving payment has been difficult or the client has paid very slowly.
- The landscape architect is cash poor at the time and really needs the retainer to carry on the services in a professional manner.

The retainer clause can be worded as follows:

The client shall make an initial payment of $_____ as a retainer upon executing this contract. The retainer will be applied against the first (or final) invoice for services rendered.

The contract can include a clause regarding collection costs or court costs if the landscape architect finds it necessary to enforce the payment provisions of the agreement or any other terms of the contract. The clause normally includes language that entitles the landscape architect to collect from the client any sums due, reasonable attorney's fees, court costs, and expenses in connection with collection activities. The clause should also spell out that the laws of the state in which the agreement is executed shall govern the validity, performance, and enforcement of the agreement.

My firm always tries to collect reimbursable expenses over and above ordinary overhead expenses. The clause in our contract states that the client will pay the cost of all reimbursable items such as fees, permits, delivery charges, postage, fax transmissions, long-distance phone calls, reproductions, photocopies, photographic work, mileage, film, film processing, and other costs directly related to performing the professional services. The clause states that a service charge of 35 percent will be charged as a handling fee for all reimbursable items, including the cost of managing subconsultants. We also specify that the client will pay for all out-of-town travel required to perform the professional services.

Another good clause to include is that services may be suspended if the client fails to make payments for the professional services or otherwise breaches any terms of the agreement. The clause should state that the client will be notified in writing if the landscape architect intends to suspend services. The clause should also state that the landscape architect will have no liability to the client for any costs or damages that may result from the suspension of professional services as a result of nonpayment or a breach of the agreement by the client.

A cost-of-living adjustment may be included in the contract to cover restarting work in the event that work is stopped by the client for a specific length of time such as six months or more. The landscape architecture firm would state in the agreement that the firm reserves the right to enforce a cost-of-living adjustment to the fee to restart the project and to cover such costs as increases in salaries of staff assigned to the project.

Last, my firm's standard contract terms call for prompt payment by the client. We ask that the client review invoices and notify the firm of any objection within ten days of receiving the invoice. If the client has no objection within the grace period, the invoice is deemed to be accepted by the client. Another measure similar to the prompt payment clause is a statement dealing with the client's satisfaction with the services rendered. The agreement can state that payment of the firm's invoices by the client will be deemed as an indication that the client is satisfied with the services performed by the landscape architect and is not aware of any deficiencies in the services.

Client's Obligations

The landscape architect's contract must clearly point out any and all responsibilities or obligations of the owner in connection with the requirements of the project. Some of the typical responsibilities of the client set forth in the agreement are as follows:

- The client shall provide the landscape architect with a program that sets forth the client's objectives, schedule, and other criteria necessary for the landscape architect to perform the professional services.
- The client shall provide a budget for the project.
- The client shall designate a representative to act on behalf of the client.
- The client shall provide the landscape architect with site surveys, legal descriptions of the property, and information regarding utilities.
- The client shall engage the services of a geotechnical engineer if the services are requested by the landscape architect.
- The client shall engage the services of other consultants, such as structural, mechanical, and electrical engineers, deemed necessary by the landscape architect.
- The client shall provide for testing and evidence that the site has been tested and cleared for hazardous material.

Compliance with Codes and Standards

The landscape architect's contract may state that the professional will provide the customary care associated with landscape architecture services to comply with codes, regulations, and laws related to the execution of the contract. The professional should avoid stating that he or she will comply with all codes, regulations, and laws. By agreeing to comply with *all* codes, regulations, and laws, the landscape architect is putting himself or herself in a difficult situation. A professional is bound to design to the codes and standards set by local building and zoning codes, as well as to practice the profession with the standard of care practiced by other reasonably competent landscape architects. These are the reasonable assurances a landscape architect can provide the client regarding codes, regulations, and laws.

Excluded Services or Additional Services

My firm works with clients to develop a scope of services that is, to the best of our ability, directly related to the client's needs. If we determine the need for specialty consultants is appropriate to the scope of work, we request these services be included as a part of our contract. We attempt to develop a thorough scope of work, and our first proposal to the client includes all of the services that we believe to be necessary and helpful to culminate in the best possible planning or design process and completed project.

After the client reviews our first proposal, and if the client decides to reject some of the services that we have recommended, we will revise our proposal and may insert the services the client has decided not to engage or to engage with another party in a paragraph titled "Excluded or Additional Services." In doing so, we ensure that the client cannot accuse our firm of being negligent because we have not informed the client of services that may be needed.

Some of our clients have tried to reject services during construction and construction administration. When we find a client that refuses construction services, we always include these in our standard paragraph that specifies those services that are additional or excluded from the contract.

The contract clause can be as simple as the following:

> The following professional services have been discussed with the client and are excluded from the scope of services. They are considered additional services and will be carried out at the concurrence of the client for additional fees under the terms for additional services covered by this contract.

The specific excluded services would be listed after this opening paragraph.

The Contract Guide, published by DPIC, has a similar clause emphasizing that the landscape architect has made the services known to the client and explained the need for them to the client:

> Other services available from the Design Professional and applicable to the project have been made known and explained to the client. Where the design professional has deemed a service needed or advisable, the design professional has made this opinion known to the client and the client has confirmed his or her opinion that such services are not requested of the Design Professional and/or that the Client has made or shall make arrangements to

obtain those services from a source other than the Design Professional. These excluded services included:

(List the services excluded by the client)

(Dixon and Crowell 1993, 140)

The DPIC guide further suggests that the professional consider coupling a hold-harmless clause with the above paragraph to relieve the design professional from liability associated with the services the client has rejected.

Ownership of Documents

Landscape architects prepare construction documents that the client specifically uses to construct the landscape architect's design. The landscape architect usually wants to retain the ownership and rights to the construction documents so the client does not use the landscape architect's instruments of service to build another identical or similar project using the documents prepared for the first project, at least not without justly compensating the landscape architect for reusing some or all of the design plans.

The landscape architect has some protection under U.S. copyright laws, which were amended in 1990 by the Architectural Works Copyright Protection Act. The act not only enforces ownership of copyrighted drawings but also protects the actual construction.

In addition to the landscape architect's rights to the design for a specific project, the rights to use spin-offs of the design in future projects need to be protected. If the landscape architect gives away his or her rights to the plans to a client, the landscape architect is not only giving up the rights to use the plan itself, but also may be giving up rights to using derivations of the plan at a later date.

The landscape architect's contract should contain a clause specifying that the plans, specifications, and other documents, which are the instruments of service, are to be used solely for the specific project. The instruments of service will remain the property of the landscape architect and the landscape architect will retain all legal rights to the use of the plans and full protection under the U.S. copyright law.

The landscape architect should also mark the plans with a copyright symbol. The simple act of marking the plans and other documents with a copyright symbol will protect the landscape architect under U.S. copyright law. Registering the documents with the United States Copyright Office, however, will provide the maximum protection under the law. For small offices, registering the copyright for every project may be too much of an administrative task. Many projects are ordinary in nature, and the basic protection under copyright law may be all that is warranted. A unique design may be worth the administrative chore of filing copyright registration. Larger offices with greater resources and those offices that focus their practice on unique and upscale design may decide to register almost all of the firm's plans with the Copyright Office. Further information about registering copyrights can be obtained from the U.S. Library of Congress, Washington, D.C.

Indemnities

Landscape architects usually face indemnity clauses in contracts that have been prepared by their clients. In the case when a sewer line designed by a subconsultant to my firm was installed improperly, the city's contract with my firm included an indemnity clause. The clause effectively indemnified the city and held them harmless for any and all damage, liability, or costs associated with my firm's performance under the terms of the contract. When the problem was discovered, this clause provided the city's main line of defense, and the state allows cities to broadly apply and rely upon mutually agreed-upon indemnity clauses as a form of defense. (Some states, on the other hand, do not allow indemnity clauses as a form of defense.)

What should you do when you are faced with an indemnity clause in a contract presented by your client? The best approach is to negotiate the provision out of the contract. If you cannot, then try to make the indemnity clause as fair as possible. The approach here is to adopt a mutual indemnity where both the landscape architect and the client agree to indemnify each other for their own negligent acts. The landscape architect should not indemnify the client for the client's negligence.

In the landscape architect's contracts generated in house, references to indemnification should generally be avoided except in situations where the project has a high risk potential, such as hazardous environmental conditions. There are projects that a landscape architect may face where the environmental risks, especially from third-party lawsuits, are so high that indemnity by the client has to be considered very carefully, and without receiving indemnity, the landscape architect may elect to forgo working on the project (Dixon and Crowell 1993).

Insurance

The landscape architect should include in the contract a paragraph that indicates both the firm and the client will maintain appropriate insurance coverage, including coverage required by law, with reasonable limits of insured protection, and list the coverage and the limits of liability in the paragraph. If the client wants additional coverage, the terms may be dealt with while negotiating the agreement. The landscape architect must learn to rely on the various insurance agents for all assistance with insurance matters. If the landscape architect is using subconsultants on the project, the contracts with the subconsultants should include insurance requirements similar to those identified in the contract with the client.

The main types of insurance that the landscape architecture firm will be concerned with in contracts for professional services include the following:

- Commercial general liability insurance
- Worker's compensation insurance
- Vehicle liability insurance
- Professional liability insurance

Commercial general liability insurance insures the firm for damages and liabilities that may result from the landscape architect's general business activities. The insurance covers liabilities that may arise if a person is injured on the firm's business property or if office equipment is stolen. Many firms carry a commercial umbrella policy that provides additional coverage over and above the limitations set in the general liability insurance policy.

Frequently the client will request that the landscape architect have the firm's general liability insurance company name the client as an additional insured under the terms of the agreement. This is a typical request of insurance companies, and is normally provided by requesting an additional insured form be completed and sent to the client for their files.

Worker's compensation insurance is required by law and protects the landscape architecture employer and the firm's employees against injuries that may occur on the job. Worker's compensation insurance primarily covers medical benefits and wages lost due to the job-related injury. Most clients may require proof that you have met the legal requirements of providing worker's compensation insurance.

Vehicle liability insurance covers damages and liability arising from accidents that occur while office vehicles are in use. Most clients may only want to have certificates of vehicle insurance coverage in their files as part of the agreement. Again, these are easy to obtain from the firm's vehicle insurance agent.

Professional liability insurance protects the landscape architect from claims based on negligent acts, errors, or omissions that may arise from the performance of professional services. Clients usually want to know that the landscape architecture firm has professional liability insurance coverage and that it is adequate to cover the potential loss that could result from work on the specific project. The client will request a certificate of insurance. A problem can arise if the landscape architect's professional liability coverage does not seem adequate to the client. The adequacy of coverage may become a negotiating point during contract deliberations. The landscape architect can attempt to persuade the client that the coverage is adequate or may decide to increase the coverage if the contract is important and the client is reluctant to accept a lower level of coverage (Dixon and Crowell 1993).

The main insurance considerations to be dealt with in contract negotiation include the following:

- The dollar amounts of coverage
- Any exclusions that may limit or otherwise affect coverage related to the professional services contract
- Applying coverage requirements to the client, as well as the landscape architect, and the landscape architect's subconsultants
- Providing for the transmittal of certificates of insurance from the landscape architect to the client and from the client to the landscape architect

Limit of Liability

The landscape architect's contract should include a limit-of-liability clause, which is intended to put a cap on the dollar extent of the liability arising from a construction problem that occurs on the project. The clause attempts to allocate the appropriate amount of risk associated with the landscape architect's performance of services on the project.

Our firm's contracts always include a limit-of-liability clause. Our clause limits our liability to a maximum of $50,000, or to the total of our firm's fee, whichever is greater. Here is the standard clause that our contract includes:

> **PROFESSIONAL SERVICES LIABILITY**
>
> The firm's responsibilities in performing the professional services hereunder shall be limited to the Scope of Work and the Scope of Services to be performed as set forth in the agreement. The firm, its agents and/or employees, shall have no liability of any kind to the Client, its agents or any persons having contractual relationships with Client for any acts, errors and omissions of the firm, its agents and employees, which does not fall within the Scope of Work and the Scope of Services to be performed. Client further agrees to limit the firm's liability to the Client due to the firm's negligent acts, errors or omissions, such that the total aggregate liability of the firm to all those named shall not exceed $50,000 or the firm's total fee for services rendered on this project, whichever is greater.

There have been some times when we have not been successful at keeping the limit-of-liability clause in our contract; there been other times when we have agreed to increase the limit from $50,000 to $100,000. However, we always present the limit-of-liability clause in our agreements as a starting point.

Opinion of Probable Construction Costs

For reasons that are not clear to me, landscape architects are regularly asked to include estimates of construction costs as a normal element of the scope of services to their clients. This is not to say that architects and engineers are not asked to provide the same service; they frequently are. In the case of landscape architects, however, the request is either made by the client or even volunteered by the landscape architect.

In my experience, when architects or engineers are asked to provide estimates of construction costs, they almost invariably are authorized to use the services of a professional cost estimator, or they may have an in-house specialist who does nothing but construction cost estimating and functions as an in-house consultant to the design and production staff of the firm.

When clients ask the landscape architect to provide an estimate of probable construction costs, they may be implying that the landscape architect must guarantee that the project will not exceed the cost projection. In some public works contracts my firm has agreed to, the public agency insists on language that requires the firm to redesign and adjust construction documents if the bids are more than 10 percent over the established construction budget and keep making revisions at the firm's cost until the project is successfully brought in line with the construction budget. Such provisions ultimately may lead to repressed and uncreative design solutions as the landscape architect tries to develop a plan that will not jeopardize the budget and cost the firm losses in time and money redesigning the project.

With a contract clause that limits the liability for the landscape architect's construction cost projection, the professional can have some assurance that the client will view the cost projection as the best-informed opinion of probable costs that the professional is able to prepare. The landscape architect wants to avoid a client's claim that critical financing and schedule decisions were made based on the landscape architect's design approach and construction cost projection, resulting in a dispute. With a properly worded contract clause, the landscape architect is on somewhat safer ground that a dispute will not end up in litigation initiated by the client.

One way to approach the requirement of providing an estimate of probable construction costs is not to provide the service as an in-house service, but to recommend to the client that the construction cost projection be carried out by a professional estimating firm. If your client rejects this idea, you may decide to list the cost projection as one of the excluded or additional services rejected by the client.

Another approach is to put the project out for bid estimates carried out by contractors when the construction documents have been assembled at the conclusion of the design development stage of the project or at about 75 percent complete. This set of 75 percent complete documents is often referred to as a pricing package. The contractors may be willing to execute the preliminary pricing estimates for the privilege of getting a head start on the ultimate bidding documents. There is also the option to pay the construction companies a fee for providing the service. The contractors can be very helpful in coming up with ways to bring the costs down if it appears that the documents will result in an overbudget project.

If the client prefers that the landscape architect provide the construction cost estimate as part of the scope of services, a contract clause should be used to achieve two purposes. First, the clause should use the terminology that the landscape architect is providing an opinion of probable construction costs and not an estimate. The clause might further explain that the landscape architect has no control over the pricing methods and the costs associated with a contractor's constructing the project. The clause can also state that the landscape architect is not willing to guarantee that the opinion of probable costs will accurately reflect the actual bids for construction (Dixon and Crowell 1993).

Termination

Last, the landscape architect's contract should include a clause that provides for both the professional and the client to terminate the contract. Typically such a clause can be handled very simply by saying that either party may terminate the contract with or without cause. The clause should provide that notification of termination should be in writing with a reasonable time period such as five or ten days notice.

As the professional, you want to have the option to terminate the contract for a variety of reasons including breach of contract, fraud, nonpayment of professional fees, extreme changes in the scope, discovery of hazardous site conditions that the client is unwilling to rectify, or a client who is unwilling to pay for recommended special consulting services or additional services not covered under the terms of the contract for professional services.

The termination clause should also contain language that requires the client to pay for the landscape architect's services provided up and to the notice of termination, including the actual costs of terminating

work and archiving the project. The clause would indicate that the client would receive a complete set of all documents and other design products that have resulted from the landscape architect's involvement on the project.

REFERENCES

AIA. 1993. *Standard Form of Agreement between Owner and Architect with Descriptions of Designated Services and Terms.* Washington, D.C.: American Institute of Architects.

Dixon, Sheila A., and Richard D. Crowell. 1993. *The Contract Guide: DPIC's Risk Management Handbook for Architects and Engineers.* Monterey, Calif.: DPIC Companies.

Economy, Peter. 1994. *Business Negotiating Basics.* Burr Ridge, Ill.: Richard D. Irwin.

Fuller, George. 1991. *The Negotiator's Handbook.* Englewood Cliffs, N.J.: Prentice Hall.

Hauf, Harold D. 1968. *Building Contracts for Design and Construction.* New York: John Wiley & Sons.

Henry, James K., and Jethro K. Lieberman. 1985. *The Manager's Guide to Resolving Legal Disputes.* New York: Harper & Row.

Hinze, Jimmie. 1993. *Construction Contracts.* New York: McGraw-Hill.

Karner, Gary A. 1989. *Contracting Design Services.* Washington, D.C.: American Society of Landscape Architects.

Kovach, Kimberlee K. 1994. *Mediation: Principles and Practice.* St. Paul, Minn.: West Publishing.

Metsger, Michael B., Jane P. Mallor, A. James Barnes, Thomas Bowers, and Michael J. Phillips. 1989. *Business Law and the Regulatory Environment.* Homewood, Ill.: Richard D. Irwin.

Poage, Wallace. 1987. *Plans, Specs and Contracts for Building Professionals.* Kingston, Mass.: R. S. Means Company.

Samuels, Brian M. 1996. *Construction Law.* Englewood Cliffs, N.J.: Prentice Hall.

Sharkey, Bruce G. 1994. *Ready, Set, Practice: Elements of Landscape Architecture Professional Practice.* New York: John Wiley & Sons.

Schoenfield, Mark K., and Rick M. Schoenfield. 1991. *The McGraw-Hill 36-Hour Negotiating Course.* New York: McGraw-Hill.

Timpson, John. 1994. *The Architect in Dispute Resolution.* London: RIBA Publications.

Tirella, O.C. "Russ," and Gary D. Bates. 1993. *Win-Win Negotiating: A Professional's Playbook.* New York: American Society of Civil Engineers.

Wehringer, Cameron K. 1969. *Arbitration: Precepts and Principles.* Dobbs Ferry, N.Y.: Oceana Publications.

STUDY QUESTIONS AND ASSIGNMENTS

1. Using this chapter and other references, write a paper that illustrates your understanding of the elements that make up an enforceable contract for professional services.

2. Obtain a copy of the current AIA *Standard Form of Agreement between Owner and Architect.* Complete the fill-in portions of the standard form contract using a design project from your studio courses.

3. Based on your experience completing the AIA standard form contract in question 2, and using the same project as a base, create a self-developed contract for professional services using this chapter and other references for the landscape architect–developed contracts. Include specific terms and conditions as part of the contract terminology or as a separate attachment.

4. Using this chapter, chapter 10, and other references, and a design project from your studio courses, develop a proposal for professional services including a specific and thorough scope of services.

5. Using this chapter and other references, write a paper that illustrates your understanding of the agency relationship between a landscape architect and a client.

6. Obtain a copy of the current AIA *Standard Form of Agreement between Architect and Consultant.* Complete the fill-in portions of the standard form contract using a design project from your studio courses that would require a consultant's services.

7. Based on your experience completing the AIA standard form contract for engaging the services of a consultant, and using the same project as a base, create a self-developed contract for the services of a sub-consultant, using this chapter and other references for the landscape architect–developed contracts.

8. Using this chapter and other references, write a paper that illustrates your understanding of the differences between unsecured credit and secured credit.

9. Obtain a copy of the information necessary to submit a small-claims court claim in your legal jurisdiction. Complete the forms and go through a mock process of submitting a small-claims court claim.

10. Interview a bank representative about how a landscape architect would apply for an operating line of credit. Obtain copies of the bank's loan agreement, promissory note, and any other terms of borrowing funds. Develop a proposal for an operating line of credit. Ask the bank representative you interviewed to evaluate your proposal for a loan.

11. Using this chapter and other references, write a thorough and in-depth paper that illustrates your understanding of how to negotiate a contract. Address the fundamentals and techniques of negotiating.

12. Using the paper you wrote about your understanding of how to negotiate a contract, and the proposal you wrote for question 11, carry out a mock contract negotiation. Pair off in twos. One person should play the role of landscape architect. The other should play the role of the owner. Each role player should negotiate a contract representing the two parties. You may also wish to involve other classmates to role-play the "good guy/bad guy" and the "team" approaches to negotiating.

13. Use this chapter as a reference and obtain a copy of the DPIC Contract Guide. Write a paper that illustrates your understanding of the contract elements that are strategic to successfully developing landscape architecture contracts for professional services.

14. Contact three providers of professional liability insurance. Obtain the information that describes the coverage and limitations of coverage provided by the insurance companies for private practice of landscape architects. Write a paper that illustrates your understanding of professional liability insurance coverage and limitations.

CHAPTER TEN

Project Management

The most popular way to organize a landscape architecture office for the delivery of professional services is the project-manager approach, in which the firm designates a project manager (PM) for each project the firm engages. The PM is given full responsibility for managing the project to its successful completion. The project manager occupies a pivotal position in the landscape architecture office and functions for the most part as a jack-of-all-trades. To be successful, the PM must be technically competent and have good interpersonal skills. Indeed, many owners and principals of landscape architecture firms spend a great deal of their time developing their own project-management abilities and nurturing their key project-management staff.

What Is Project Management?

Project management involves the following key elements for effective practice of landscape architecture:

1. Planning, organizing, and scoping the elements of a project so they can be managed and controlled.
2. Setting up tracking systems to monitor and control the flow of work, the hours utilized, the money spent, and other resources used to complete a project.
3. Tracking and monitoring a project and developing strategies when a project is over budget.
4. Managing the work flow, the hours utilized, and the costs to maximize profit for the firm on every project.
5. Selecting and organizing staff for successful completion of projects.
6. Directing and motivating staff for successful completion of projects.
7. Serving the client and developing a friendly relationship that results in a satisfied client.
8. Providing technical supervision for the project staff.
9. Inspiring the professional staff. Nurturing the staff and promoting professional development opportunities.
10. Coordinating with the firm's top management, clients, client representatives, and representatives of public and private agencies.
11. Attaining high quality in the planning and design output of the office, including constructed projects. Advocating quality in all phases of project work.
12. Marketing the firm by doing a good job with existing clients and selling additional services when opportunities arise.
13. Managing the planning or design effort so that it meets the client's implementation or construction cost expectations.
14. Taking part in performance reviews of technical staff and peers.
15. Assisting in writing and preparing proposals.
16. Closing out projects.
17. Managing construction observation services.

This chapter describes each of these elements in greater detail.

Planning, Scoping, and Organizing the Project

Scope of Services and Work Plan

A project cannot be easily managed unless it is organized into manageable parts. The first step in managing all landscape architecture projects is defining all of the tasks in the scope of services and preparing a detailed work plan so that the number of hours needed to complete each task can be estimated and the execution of each task can be monitored and managed.

Establishing the scope of work and the scope of services starts with writing the proposal. Many legal experts and business managers prefer the scope of work and scope of services to be as detailed as possible in the proposal and in the contract. A detailed scope provides not only a good understanding of exactly what services the client is to receive, but also a good starting point for the project manager to understand the tasks necessary for organizing the work and completing the project.

The *scope of work* included in the proposal is a written explanation or a description of the actual project in terms of its elements and its budget. The *scope of services* is a list of the actual tasks and specific services that will be provided by the landscape architecture firm. The scope of services will include all tasks requiring time utilization so that an estimate of hours can be made for each in order to establish the fee.

When the work plan is developed, the PM may need to break the scope of services down into smaller tasks for effective management and control of the project. The work plan is usually developed after the scope of services and the proposal have been accepted by the client and the firm is under contract, because developing the work plan is a time-intensive task that is usually considered to be part of the actual services provided. In some cases, the work plan may be developed before the scope of services is written and the proposal is presented to ensure that all of the tasks and subtasks have been identified and that enough hours are estimated for completing the work. For examples of the scope of work, scope of services, and work plan, see figures 10-1 and 10-2.

Once the scope of services and work plan have been written, the project manager estimates the hours required for each worker category needed on the project, including principal, project manager, project landscape architect, designer, CADD technician, draftsperson,

---

Scope of Work

The landscape architecture firm will provide professional services for the Stoneybrook Apartment Complex, which will include approximately 120 units on 8 acres. The firm will be responsible for designing the site amenities, hardscape, landscape, and irrigation system. We anticipate a probable construction cost of $2,000 per unit for the exterior site improvements, landscaping, and irrigation for a total budget of $240,000.

Scope of Services

The firm will provide the following professional landscape architectural services.

Preliminary Design

1. Visit the site and carry out a visual reconnaissance to serve as a basis of design.
2. Prepare a base plan of the project site for the firm's use in developing the plans.

FIGURE 10-1. Example scope of work and scope of services for an apartment project.

3. Develop a preliminary landscape plan that meets city codes and ordinances. Submit the preliminary plan to the Client for review and comment.
4. Coordinate with the Client, the Owner, and the other consultants.

Construction Bid Documents

1. Develop and prepare construction bid documents for hardscape, softscape, and irrigation including
   a. hardscape grading and layout plans
   b. landscaping and planting plans, notes, and schedules
   c. irrigation system plans, notes, and schedules
   d. landscape and irrigation system construction details
   e. hardscape detail plans and construction details
   f. specifications
2. Submit construction documents to the Client for review and comment.
3. Prepare final construction bid documents. Check and seal the plans.
4. Coordinate with the Client, the Owner, government agencies, and the other consultants during preparation of construction bid documents for completion of the project.

Construction Services

1. Provide assistance during bidding including selection of contractors, clarification of construction documents, and bid analysis.
2. Provide assistance in awarding a construction contract.
3. Provide in-the-field review and observation of plants, materials, and the contractor's workmanship for compliance with the construction documents and the design intent.
4. Prepare field reports regarding the acceptance or rejection of materials or workmanship.
5. Review for approval or rejection field changes in the design.
6. Review for compliance with the construction documents all required submittals, shop drawings, and tests by the contractor.
7. Provide a final walk-through for final acceptance and prepare a punch list for the Client.

Additional Services

Additional services, including but not limited to the following, are not provided under the terms of this agreement but will be provided at your request or concurrence.

1. Presentation renderings or perspectives.
2. Changes to approved concepts or plans necessitating redoing the design, plans, or specifications.
3. Soil or other materials testing, engineering services, including structural engineering, lighting, and electrical engineering.
4. Any services not included in or in excess of the scope of services above that are provided by the firm at your request or concurrence.

FIGURE 10-1. (*Cont'd.*) Example scope of work and scope of services for an apartment project.

Draft Work Plan

I. Project Mobilization
   A. Hold an initial meeting with City Task Force.
   B. Develop and computerize the project mailing list for public involvement in the planning process.
   C. Initialize in-house project administrative and project management systems.
   D. Assemble and catalog all available project-related data and resource documents.
   E. Prepare a base map of site area (16 acres) from available aerial photographs, topographic maps, and assessor's parcel maps.
   F. Generate the base map on GIS.
   G. Prepare, coordinate, and distribute initial newsletter for public participation.

II. Site Analysis
   Carry out an in-depth analysis of the historic site and its urban context including but not limited to the following elements. Document the site analysis in graphic and written formats.
   A. Carry out a visual reconnassaince of the site and its context and fix the site's boundary.
   B. Identify and map the layout of cultural features on the site, including written descriptions of the following historic periods:
      1. Late Archaic Era: 2,500 to 3,000 years ago
      2. Late Hohokam Era: 500 to 1,000 years ago
      3. Initial contact: 300 years ago
      4. Mission period: 180 to 300 years ago
      5. Mexican period: 135 to 180 years ago
      6. Early American period: 110 to 135 years ago
      7. Late nineteenth century: 90 to 110 years ago
      8. Early twentieth century: 50 to 90 years ago
      The cultural resource inventory also will include
      1. Location on the site base map of all known historical and archaeological features
      2. Description and location of all known historical routes through the site
      3. Description and location of all known irrigation canals serving the site
      4. Sources of historic photographs, maps, and documents
      5. Linkages to other nearby historic resources
      6. The potential for excavation of the site's historic resources, stabilization, or reconstruction to contribute to interpretation of the site's history
   C. Existing land use and ownership of adjacent and nearby strategic parcels.
   D. Existing zoning in study area.
   E. Issues related to the solid waste landfill over part of the site's historic resources, including
      1. Mapped extent of the landfill in relation to known archaeological resources
      2. Depth of landfill
      3. Soil conditions
      4. Constraints
   F. Circulation and access to the site.
   G. Utilities and easements.
   H. Flood control and drainage.

FIGURE 10-2. Work plan submitted with a proposal for a schematic plan for a Southwest United States Mission Cultural Park. This draft work plan would likely be further refined by the project manager if the firm is awarded the contract.

> I.   Vegetation and wildlife habitat.
> J.   Visual resources and qualities.
>
> III. Draft Plan
> > A.   Prepare a preliminary draft report and concept plan.
> > B.   Prepare a final draft report and concept plan for public review and comment. The final draft shall be developed based on review comments from the advisory task force and city staff. The draft concept plan shall illustrate phasing with the ultimate goal of reconstructing the site's significant historic resources. The plan shall include locations of reconstructed buildings and gardens, park facilities, recreation facilities, management and maintenance facilities, access control, circulation, and parking.
> > C.   Develop a projection of probable costs by phase.
>
> IV. Public Participation and Public Relations
> > A.   Monthly meetings will be held with the project task force for the duration of the project.
> > B.   Three public meetings will be held.
> > > 1.   Initial meeting, during site analysis phase, to review the scope of the project and receive public input.
> > > 2.   Second meeting to present the draft concept plan and receive public comments using a feedback questionnaire.
> > > 3.   Third meeting to present the final plan.
> > C.   Prepare and distribute monthly news releases to proactively articulate the progress of the planning effort.
> > D.   Questionnaire mailing: The draft concept plan feedback questionnaire will be mailed to the public and to all contact groups identified on the project mailing list. Analysis of the questionnaire and effected changes on the plan will be documented and included as part of the final plan report.
> > E.   Prepare a public information video presentation about the planning process and the final concept plan.
>
> V.   Final Plan
> > A.   Based on the task force, staff, and public review, a final plan and report will be developed. The final plan will be executed in presentation-quality graphics suitable for public presentation. The final report shall include
> > > 1.   A summary report of sixteen pages
> > > 2.   A working document report of the entire project
> > B.   The consultant will submit camera-ready copy for both the summary report and the working document report.

FIGURE 10-2. (*Cont'd.*) Work plan submitted with a proposal for a schematic plan for a Southwest United States Mission Cultural Park. This draft work plan would likely be further refined by the project manager if the firm is awarded the contract.

clerical, secretarial, and others who actually will work on the project. The estimate of hours is multiplied by the billing rate for each category of worker to arrive at the labor fee required for the proposal. Other elements are included in the actual fee quote to cover reimbursable expenses and the costs of subconsultants. The project manager must also track these costs.

The final work plan and hours estimate by worker category is one of the project manager's main tools for setting up tracking systems and managing the flow of work. For example, if a specific task such as preparing a base plan of existing conditions is budgeted at two hours of the project manager's time and sixteen hours of a draftsperson's time, the project manager must see that only the budgeted time or less than the budgeted time is actually spent on the task.

A note of practicality, however, should govern the preparation of the scope of services and the work plan. Most project managers do not have time to track too many minor tasks or activities. On a regular basis, the PM needs the overall big-picture information about the utilization of time and materials for a project. Detail information, on the other hand, is most useful when a specific problem occurs, such as spending too much time on a task versus the time budgeted.

Developing a Budget

When the scope of services and work plan are complete, the next step is to set the project budget so that the PM can track actual versus budgeted costs in addition to the time and materials spent versus time and materials budgeted.

Commonly used methods for developing a budget include the following:

1. Hours budgeted times the standard office billing rates charged for each category of worker assigned to the project
2. Number of sheets of drawings times an office cost to produce a sheet
3. Percent of time required for each task related to the entire project

In the first method, the PM estimates the dollar costs for each task and then monitors the actual costs required to complete the task. In the second, the PM determines how many sheets will be needed and multiplies by the cost per sheet to determine the total cost. The PM then monitors the actual cost spent in relation to the percentage of sheets completed for the entire project. In the third method, the PM determines the cost as a percentage of the total costs based on the percentage that each task is of the total project. The PM then monitors expenses versus budget based on the percentage completed for each task.

The hours budgeted times the office billing rate is the best method for tracking the budget because it can be coordinated easily with the time spent on each project.

Setting Up Tracking Systems

Monitoring Time and Materials

Starting with the final work plan, hours budget, and cost budget, the project manager develops the required

tracking systems to monitor the actual time and expenses on a project versus the time and costs budgeted. This can be done by hand for a small project, but normally requires the aid of computer spreadsheets or job-costing software for complex projects. The PM constantly monitors the actual time spent, as measured by project time cards or project summary printouts by task, and compares it to the amount of time budgeted. Project summary printouts prepared on a weekly basis either by office administrative staff or by the project manager are vital sources of information for larger projects. A large, complex project may have a fee of $250,000 or more, several thousand hours of time in various categories of labor, a half-dozen subconsultants, and a schedule of eighteen months. Without a fairly sophisticated tracking method, a project manager would not be able to effectively manage time and materials spent versus time and materials budgeted. The project manager must be computer literate and comfortable with spreadsheet software to be effective at monitoring time spent versus time budgeted.

There is a variety of project costing and tracking software systems available and a number of spreadsheet programs that are very adaptable for project tracking. One of the simplest methods is to use a spreadsheet to develop a work plan that has columns for hours estimated by worker category and a set of parallel columns for the actual time spent on each task. By adding columns for subtotals and percentages, as well as using the graphing function of most spreadsheet programs, the project manager can develop very useful tools for monitoring any project. In most larger offices, a standard system will be in place and available for each project manager to use. Many offices have computer systems and software that integrate job costing and monitoring systems with financial operations so that the project manager has available a wide variety of printouts of job costs versus job estimates. Some integrated financial and project-management systems provide so many variations of printouts in such detail that the project manager may be overwhelmed with unnecessary information. The bottom line, however, is the need for some type of spreadsheet monitoring method. For an example of a project progress report, see figure 10-3.

Controlling the Flow of Work

Besides monitoring the time and materials spent versus the time and materials budgeted, the project

FIGURE 10-3. Example project progress summary report.

No.	Project Billing Period	Estimated % Complete	Actual % Complete	Fee Budgeted ($)	Fee Spent ($)	Reimb. Expenses Budgeted ($)	Reimb. Expenses Spent ($)	Sub-consultant Fees Budgeted ($)	Sub-consultant Fees Spent ($)	Total Budgeted ($)	Total Spent ($)	Estimated Total % Complete	Actual Total % Complete	% Over (+) or Under (−) Budget
1	January 1 to January 26	7.1%	7.1	4,500.00	4,200.00	225.00	250.00	2,500.00	2,200.00	7,225.00	6,650.00	7.0	6.4	8.0
2	January 27 to February 22	20.0	21.2	8,200.00	8,400.00	400.00	500.00	3,000.00	4,000.00	11,600.00	12,900.00	18.3	19.0	−11.2
3	February 23 to March 22	43.6	42.3	15,000.00	12,500.00	650.00	600.00	8,000.00	7,300.00	23,650.00	20,400.00	41.2	38.7	13.7
4	March 23 to April 19	72.8	69.2	18,500.00	16,000.00	750.00	700.00	18,000.00	16,800.00	37,250.00	33,500.00	77.3	71.2	10.1
5	April 20 to May 17	86.9	84.7	9,000.00	9,200.00	200.00	225.00	3,000.00	4,200.00	12,200.00	13,625.00	89.1	84.4	−11.7
6	May 18 to June 14	87.6	85.5	400.00	480.00	40.00	25.00	500.00	500.00	940.00	1,005.00	90.0	85.4	−6.9
7	June 15 to July 19	89.9	88.1	1,500.00	1,520.00	75.00	75.00	0.00	0.00	1,575.00	1,595.00	91.6	86.9	−1.3
8	July 20 to August 16	90.4	88.6	300.00	280.00	0.00	25.00	0.00	0.00	300.00	305.00	91.9	87.2	−1.7
9	August 17 to September 13	90.9	89.0	300.00	280.00	0.00	0.00	0.00	0.00	300.00	280.00	92.1	87.5	6.7
10	September 14 to October 11	91.3	89.7	300.00	360.00	0.00	0.00	0.00	200.00	300.00	560.00	92.4	88.1	−86.7
11	October 12 to November 8	94.5	93.2	2,000.00	2,100.00	100.00	125.00	1,000.00	900.00	3,100.00	3,125.00	95.4	91.1	−0.8
12	November 9 to December 6	97.6	97.0	2,000.00	2,240.00	100.00	125.00	500.00	400.00	2,600.00	2,765.00	98.0	93.8	−6.3
13	December 7 to December 31	100.0	100.0	1,500.00	1,800.00	100.00	150.00	500.00	500.00	2,100.00	2,450.00	100.0	96.1	−16.7
	Total			63,500.00	59,360.00	2,640.00	2,800.00	37,000.00	37,000.00	103,140.00	99,160.00			−3.9

manager must also control the flow of work and the project schedule. The PM typically uses several good schedule-tracking tools depending on the complexity of the project. In order to track the schedule of a simple project, the PM may need only a list of key dates, such as due dates. To track the schedule of a complex project, the PM may need to use a sophisticated system. The four most commonly used schedule-tracking tools are a list of milestone dates, a bar chart, a wall chart, and the critical path method.

Milestone lists are the simplest method of tracking the project schedule. They are easy to prepare and useful for any size project. They consist simply of a list of project tasks and the targeted due date for each task. The PM must ensure that the milestone list includes key dates for subconsultants' submittals, as well as time for the client's review of the project work at its various stages of completion. The list of activities should also be arranged in a more-or-less ordered sequence from the start of the project to its completion.

Milestone lists are most useful on small projects, but they can be very helpful for larger projects that have a number of participants and complex interrelationships of tasks because milestone lists help the PM simplify and summarize the key project requirements. For the larger, more complex projects, milestone lists should include less detail and stick to the major proj-

ect due dates. The PM may break down the major tasks into the necessary subtasks and create separate milestone lists to manage the subtasks.

Adding the starting dates to the list of targeted due dates for each task provides the PM with even greater control over the flow of work. By coordinating a calendar that can be marked up with colorful symbols for start and due dates, the PM will have another useful tool for controlling the flow of work.

Bar charts are commonly used to manage the flow of work for both simple and complex projects. A bar chart consists of the tasks listed on the left side of the chart and weeks or months listed across the top of the chart. Lines indicate the starting and stopping points of each activity for the duration of the project. The same list of activities that is developed for the milestone chart can also be used for the bar chart. Organizing the list of activities by sequence from the start of the project to its completion is even more important than on the milestone chart to help the PM visualize the relationship between activities and the flow of the tasks.

Wall charts are a project-scheduling technique that involves participation of the project staff. If the chart is displayed on the wall of the landscape architecture office, the chart provides a highly visible daily reminder of the flow of work for the project team.

Tasks	SCHEDULE	
	Start Date	End Date
1. Initial start-up meeting	Dec. 15	Dec. 15
2. Research the literature	Dec. 16	Jan. 15
3. Meet with resource people	Jan. 6	Feb. 15
4. Identify all known trails	Jan. 6	Mar. 15
5. Develop a typology of trails	Mar. 15	Mar. 22
6. Develop a statewide base map	Jan. 6	Jan. 7
7. Map the location of trails	Mar. 8	Mar. 22
8. Identify National Register eligibility	Mar. 8	Mar. 29
9. Prepare preliminary outline	Dec. 16	Dec. 23
10. Prepare first draft	Mar. 1	Mar. 29
11. Prepare final draft	May 1	May 30
12. Prepare final report, camera-ready copy	June 15	June 30
13. Provide project administration	Weekly	

FIGURE 10-4. Milestone chart for a project to identify and develop an inventory of historic trails in the state and create a statewide typology of historic trails.

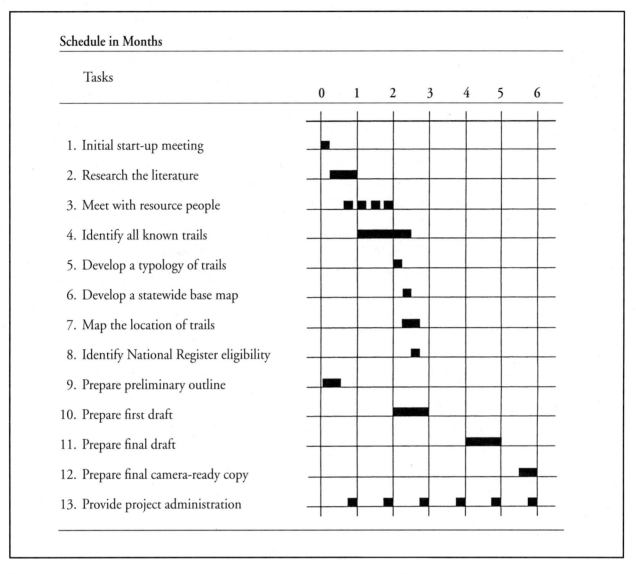

FIGURE 10-5. Bar chart for a project to identify and create a statewide typology of historic trails.

Wall charts are commonly made up of three-by-five-inch index cards pinned to a prominent wall in the office. The weeks or months for the duration of the project are listed across the top of the chart. The left side of the chart is normally organized in one of two ways. The left side consists of either the sequence of tasks in the project or a list of the participants on the design team. The project manager will normally create the wall chart by having a participatory meeting with the team, including subconsultants, at the start of the project. If the chart is organized by task, one three-by-five-inch card bearing the name of the responsible participant is tacked to the wall at the task's starting date, and another card at the completion date. If the chart is organized by participants, each card will bear the description of a task, and one card will be tacked to the task's starting date and the other card to the completion date.

The participatory nature of the wall chart method is one of its main values. During the initial charting meeting, the PM can obtain the concurrence of each participant that he or she will be able to meet or exceed the schedule. The meeting also provides a good forum for discussing coordination and interrelationships of the project tasks. All participants in the project can work out conflicts and develop satisfactory resolutions. The initial meeting establishes a team spirit and camaraderie.

It is valuable to leave the wall chart on the wall for the duration of the project. If the project gets off schedule, or if there are problems with coordination of participants or interfacing of tasks, the PM can call a meeting and the participants can rework the wall chart so that everyone is part of the problem's solution. If the wall chart must be removed, it can be duplicated at a smaller scale in a written format so that the schedule of tasks, participants, and start and due dates remain available to the project team.

The fourth method of controlling the project schedule is the *critical path method* (CPM). The critical path method is used for the most complicated projects, where it is important to be able to see and manage the interrelationships among tasks.

The first step in developing a CPM schedule is to identify all of the project tasks chronologically and their time requirements in days, weeks, or months. The second step is to diagram the relationships between the tasks. There are only three main relationships and methods of showing these relationships graphically:

1. The task must be completed before the next task can begin.
2. The task must be partially completed before the next task can begin.
3. The task must be completed before the next task can be completed.

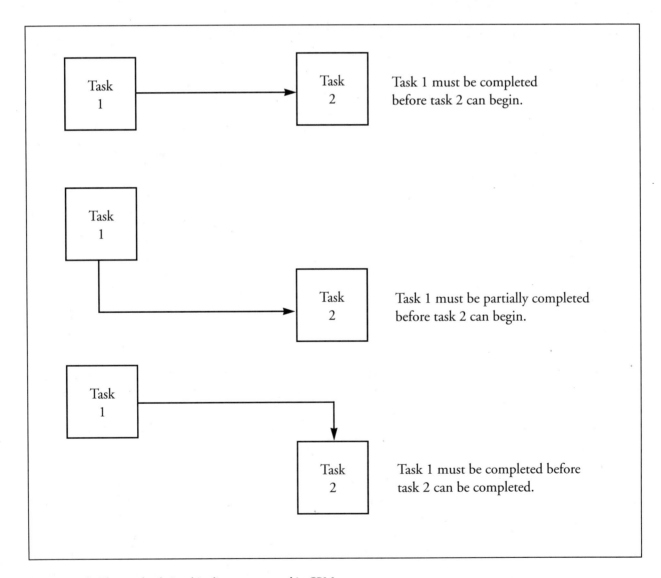

FIGURE 10-6. Three task relationship diagrams are used in CPM.

Tasks	Time Required
1. Have an initial meeting with the client.	1
2. Visit the site.	1
3. Develop a preliminary landscape design plan.	4
4. Review the preliminary plan with the client.	1
5. Prepare a base plan to be used for construction documents.	2
6. Prepare construction documents.	
A. Planting plan	3
B. Irrigation plan	3
C. Construction details	2
D. Specifications	3
7. Prepare a construction cost projection.	2
8. Check and seal the construction documents.	3
Total days required	25

FIGURE 10-7. The first step in developing a CPM schedule is identifying all of the project tasks chronologically and the time requirements of each task in days.

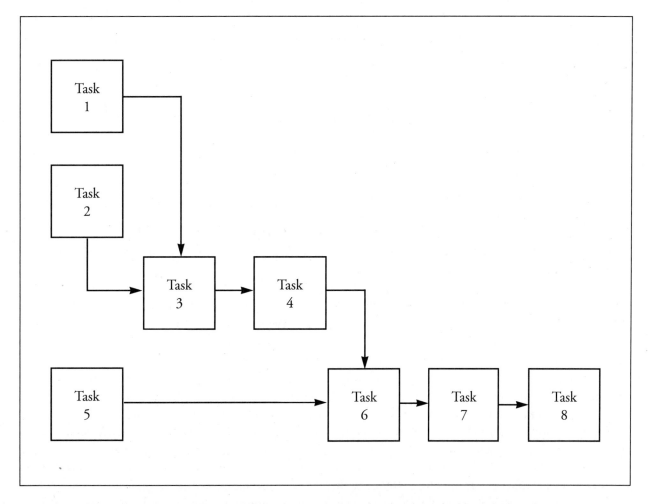

FIGURE 10-8. The second step in developing a CPM schedule is diagramming the relationships between the tasks. See Figure 10-6.

FIGURE 10-9. The third step in developing a CPM schedule is casting the tasks in a time/task duration diagram.

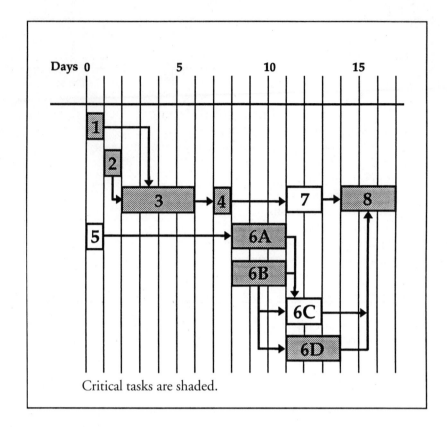

Critical tasks are shaded.

The third step in the CPM scheduling system is to reconfigure the tasks in a project schedule based on steps one and two.

Last, those tasks that are critical to meeting the schedule are identified and graphically differentiated in the critical path diagram. Critical tasks are defined as those tasks that will affect the completion date of the project.

Critical path method of project scheduling is somewhat difficult to understand and apply and might make an already-difficult project even more difficult for all but the experienced users of CPM scheduling. Computers have made the process of developing CPM scheduling much easier in recent years, but the method still remains complicated. Unless the project manager in the landscape architecture firm has experience with CPM, or can involve someone with experience, simpler schedule-control techniques such as milestone lists and bar charts may be more effective.

Tracking a Project and Developing Strategies When a Project Is Over Budget or Off Schedule

To track and monitor a project, the project manager uses the tools discussed in the previous section, referring to them frequently. The PM must review and inspect the work carried out by the project staff on a daily and weekly basis, estimating the percentages complete of each task. If a task appears to be 50 percent complete, for example, and the technical staff also agrees that the task is 50 percent complete, the PM refers to the time-management tools developed for monitoring the time and materials spent. If the task being monitored has a total of 200 hours budgeted for its completion, and the project summary printout indicates that only 80 hours, or 40 percent of the time budgeted, have been spent on the task to date, the task is ahead of schedule.

The project manager must constantly check and update the schedule-monitoring tools. Using the same example, the PM checks the list of milestone dates and observes that the 200-hour task began on the first day of the month and is to be completed on the fourteenth day of the month. The PM knows that only four people are working on the task, and the PM sees that it is already the twelfth day of the month. Although the task is ahead of budgeted time and materials costs, it is behind schedule and needs to be completed in two days to be on schedule. The PM knows that 50 percent of the project remains to be completed, requiring 100 hours, but that only eight person-days, or 64 hours, are available in order to remain on schedule. The project manager notes that the fourteenth day of the project schedule is a Friday and all four of the project staff are willing to work a full day on Saturday, or 32 hours of time, in order to get the project back on schedule. The project manager receives the approval of the principal in charge of the project to authorize the overtime because the PM was under budget for the first half of the time budgeted for the task. The project is completed on time and under budget because of the PM's effective schedule and budget management. This scenario is typical of the balancing routine used by project managers throughout the duration of a project. However, the result is not always a positive conclusion. More often than not, a project that gets into schedule or budget problems remains in schedule or budget problems despite the most clever project management.

What to Do When a Project Is Over Budget

If the project manager notices that a project is beginning to be over budget, he or she should first analyze why the project is over budget so the right corrective actions may be taken. Here are some examples of the reasons why a project may be over budget:

1. The initial budget of time and expenses was set too low because the firm had not had a great deal of experience with the project.
2. Some of the project staff had filled out time cards incorrectly and had charged time to a current phase of work that should have been charged to a later phase.

3. A clerical mistake was made, charging time to the PM's project that should have been charged to another project.
4. The staff selected to work on the project were not experienced with the specific tasks required.
5. The client increased the scope of work without the firm adjusting the fee to cover the additional work.
6. The design solution created by the firm's designers requires extensive research and design development of construction details, far more time and costs than were envisioned when the fee was set.
7. Because of a heavy office workload, drafting staff were used on other projects in the office, causing the PM's project to be worked on by senior staff with higher billing rates than originally intended.

There are many other reasons why projects can be over budget, so it is important to analyze the situation first. The problem may be a clerical error that will be resolved easily and quickly. If the problem is serious, however, and requires corrective action, here are some approaches to consider:

1. Study the figures carefully. Examine in detail time cards, project progress reports, and expense records to determine whether the project is in fact over budget.
2. If the project is over budget, discuss the situation with the principal in charge and other managers in the firm to see if they can recommend any solutions.
3. Reconfigure the remaining hours and adjust the staffing so that as much as possible of the future work will be carried out by staff with lower billing rates.
4. Reevaluate the remaining scope of work, scope of services, and work plan to look for alternative ways to complete the project by adjusting the scope.
5. If work is being completed that is not in the initial scope of work, discuss the need for the work with the client and request a fee adjustment.
6. Renegotiate the subconsultants' contracts. Eliminate subconsultants' tasks if possible.

7. Regularly send memos to your client identifying the work performed by the firm that was not considered during the scoping process but has been provided by the firm at no cost (NC). If the PM needs to go back to the client for a fee adjustment on a project that is over budget, the NC memos that have been sent to the client may help negotiations for additional fees.

What to Do When a Project Is Off Schedule

Budget problems go hand in hand with schedule problems. If the PM begins to have a schedule problem on a project, he or she should first analyze why the project is not on schedule. The schedule may have been thrown off because the client has taken longer than anticipated to review the plans and documents. The staff selected to work on the project may be inexperienced and take longer to complete the work. The project may have been targeted by the firm as an important key to future job-development efforts for similar projects. The project may have been targeted as an award opportunity. If so, the firm's leaders may be willing to contribute extra time to a project that will have future marketing potential. Here are some corrective actions for schedule problems:

1. Make staff changes so that more experienced people are working on the project and can get the job done quicker. For example, using principals combines production of the drawings with checking the drawings at the same time.
2. Meet with the principal in charge and other project managers in the firm to see if they have any suggestions for overcoming the schedule problem.
3. Get a commitment from the project staff to help in resolving the schedule problem. When staff are made aware that a schedule problem exists, they feel more involved with the solution. The project staff may be willing to help in many ways to resolve the problem, including putting in overtime or even contributing time without pay to the project.
4. Work overtime.
5. Reevaluate the significance of the project to the firm's track record and future job-

development and marketing potential. For an ordinary project, shortcuts for completing the scope of services may be more palatable than if the project is a highly visible project for the firm. If the project has been targeted as a high-impact project, the firm's principals and owners and even the firm's client may be willing to accept that the project will take more time than originally estimated.
6. Pull out a part of the scope of services and hire a subconsultant to complete the tasks concurrently with the firm's remaining tasks.
7. Ask the client for help. See if the client can provide greater input or even help complete the remaining tasks. The client is often very willing to help if the project is behind schedule.

Long-Term Management of Budgets and Schedules

Every project manager should keep records and statistics of previous projects, tracking key numbers such as profitability on each project, so that the PM's performance can be evaluated. If the statistical trends indicate that the PM is having difficulty with profitability, the firm's owners and other project managers may be able to analyze the statistics and find a corrective action that will result in greater profitability for the PM. For an example of a project manager's profit report, see figure 10-10.

Managing the Work Flow and the Costs to Maximize Profit on Every Project

The key word in the heading above is *every*. Whereas the project manager needs to be effective in all components of managing projects, making a profit on every project is the most important part of the PM's job. Without profits, resources such as computers, software, and other technological advances will not be available to develop the professional capability of the firm.

The weekly project manager's meeting is a method used by almost all firms large enough to have

FIGURE 10-10. Project manager's profit report.

Project Number	Project Name	Budgeted Fee	Budgeted Reimb.	Budgeted Subconsultants	Total Budget	Actual Fee Expense	Actual Reimb. Expense	Actual Subconsultants Expense	Total Expense	Profit or Loss	% of Total Budget
93102-19	Washington Ave. and 4th Ave. Apartments	$125,000	$6,500	$60,000	$191,500	$115,000	$6,500	$58,500	$180,000	$11,500	93.99%
93155-10	Big Sky Park master plan	65,000	5,000	15,000	85,000	64,500	4,800	12,000	81,300	3,700	95.65
94168-14	Grace Chapel	5,000	500	0	5,500	5,200	400	0	5,600	(100)	101.82
94172-17	Home Depot code compliance	10,000	650	0	10,650	9,800	650	0	10,450	200	98.12
94185-10	First National Bank landscape and irrigation	8,000	600	0	8,600	8,200	350	0	8,550	50	99.42
94198-11	Riverside Linear Park master plan	75,000	6,200	45,000	126,200	70,000	6,000	46,500	122,500	3,700	97.07
94220-15	Davis Parkway landscape and irrigation	150,000	10,000	25,000	185,000	140,000	10,100	25,000	175,100	9,900	94.65
95102-17	Stop and Shop Center	8,500	600	0	9,100	8,500	500	0	9,000	100	98.90
	Totals				$621,550				$592,500	$29,050	95.33%
93105-10	Big Sky Park phase 1 CDs	$140,000	$12,000	$100,000	$252,000	$125,000	$11,900	$102,000	$238,900	$13,100	94.80%
94150-19	Seaside Condominiums site planning and CDs	60,000	3,000	0	63,000	59,900	2,950	0	62,850	150	99.76
94175-15	Aviation Parkway landscape and irrigation	200,000	16,000	0	216,000	190,000	16,000	0	206,000	10,000	95.37
94178-18	Hyatt Hotel	36,000	3,000	0	39,000	38,550	2,900	0	41,450	(2,450)	106.28
95109-10	Kentucky Fried Chicken code compliance	8,500	500	0	9,000	8,500	750	0	9,250	(250)	102.78
	Totals				$579,000				$558,450	$20,550	96.45%
93106-12	County Water Dept. env. assessment	$20,000	$2000	$15,000	$37,000	$19,100	$1,900	$15,000	$36,000	$1,000	97.30%
94120-19	Paradise Valley Patio Homes	65,000	4,000	0	69,000	60,200	3,800	0	64,000	5,000	92.75
94151-15	Eastside Expressway	190,000	15,000	15,000	220,000	175,000	14,900	15,000	204,900	15,100	93.14
94197-10	Big Sky Park phase 2 CDs	100,000	6,000	25,000	131,000	98,000	5,800	24,500	128,300	2,700	97.94
94206-11	County open-end landscape and irrigation	250,000	0	0	250,000	250,000	0	0	250,000	0	100.00
	Totals				$707,000				$683,200	$23,800	96.63%

several principals and project managers. The project manager's meeting is often held on Monday mornings and is attended by all of the firm's principals and project managers. A firm will set an agenda every week for the meeting. A typical agenda might cover the following tasks and issues:

1. *Project Progress Reports.* Each project is reviewed and discussed regarding its schedule, profitability, and other issues related to the successful conclusion of the work.
2. *Marketing and Job Development.* The status of marketing and job-development efforts are discussed. New leads are discussed and staff assigned to develop the new project or client opportunities.
3. *Administrative Issues.* Insurance coverage, professional-development opportunities for members of the firm, financial items, and other issues may be discussed.
4. *Staffing Needs and Issues.* Demands on the firm's staff pool are discussed, and the staffing needs of each project are discussed. Staff assignments are made.

The status of each project should be discussed at each meeting, and project managers should make project progress reports. The PM will use computer printouts to detail the progress of projects.

The *workload forecast,* prepared by the office management and administrative staff, is indispensable for managing the flow of work in the office. The purpose of the workload forecast is to illustrate the amount of work in progress and in job development that is likely to become an actual project in the future. The work in progress and in job development can be compared to the firm's workload capacity to determine whether the firm has an adequate future workload or needs to lay off or hire staff.

Landscape architecture firms have different ways of illustrating workload forecasts. The ways used most often are either by fee capacity or by hours assigned to staff. Because there is much emphasis on billable time and profitability in the competitive landscape architecture office, the billing capacity method may be the most popular method. In the billing capacity method, all of the firm's work in progress and very high job-development opportunities are listed with the fee remaining on each project assigned to present and future billing periods. The forecast is illustrated for at least six billing periods, six months or longer. The remaining fee for each project is broken down into the likely amounts of fee that will be billable in each of the projected periods. The fees are totaled up by month and evaluated in relation to the firm's fee capacity in a billing period. The firm's fee capacity is generated by assigning a percentage of billable time to each member of the firm and multiplying by the number of staff in each billing category and by the number of hours available per staff category in each billing period. Table 10-1 shows an example of setting the fee capacity for a firm that bills for time spent on a four-week basis.

The fee capacity is the amount of revenue that the firm's managers think the staff can produce by working at estimated realistic capacities. The capacity, or percent billable, for each category must be reevaluated regularly. Many factors have an influence on capacity. The firm may be in an expansion mode where the capacity will probably increase. Or the firm may be downsizing due to a work shortfall. The capacity, or percent billable, should not be confused with the amount of revenue needed to keep the firm operating—these are likely to be two different amounts.

TABLE 10-1

Staff Category and Number of Staff	% Billable	Total Hours Billable	Billing Rate	Amount Billable
2 principals	33	160	$90/Hr	$14,400
2 project managers	85	272	65/Hr	17,680
3 project designers	95	456	45/Hr	20,520
3 draftspersons	100	480	35/Hr	16,800
1 secretarial	20	32	30/Hr	960
Total capacity				70,360

Work in Progress

Project Number	Project Name	Fee Rem.	7 6/21–7/18	8 7/19–8/15	9 8/16–9/12	10 9/13–10/10	11 10/11–11/07	Future
92162-15	South Side Parkway	$114,500.00	$20,000.00	$28,000.00	$30,000.00	$24,000.00	$12,500.00	$0.00
93126-15	South Side Parkway phase 1 constr. services	37,500.00	8,000.00	8,000.00	8,000.00	6,000.00	5,000.00	2,500.00
93121-11	Chiller Plant Landscape Buffer	4,500.00	3,000.00	1,200.00	300.00			0.00
94162-15	South Side Parkway at Euclid Ave. add services	15,000.00	15,000.00					0.00
94148-14	Grace Chapel landscape and irrigation	3,500.00	3,000.00	500.00				0.00
95143-15	Biggs AFB roads	26,520.00	1,000.00	1,000.00	12,000.00	6,000.00	820.00	5,700.00
95133-19	B'nai Brith Elderly Housing	14,000.00	8,000.00	3,500.00	2,500.00			0.00
95148-14	City Schools open end contract	73,000.00		5,000.00	10,000.00	12,000.00	12,000.00	34,000.00
95166-14	Biggs Dorm landscaping	3,600.00	3,000.00	600.00				0.00
96116-17	Biggs AFB Maintenance Facility EIS	750.00		750.00				0.00
96119-17	Home Depot CDs	3,500.00	3,500.00					0.00
96130-10	Target rezoning, site plan, landscaping	6,800.00	3,400.00	3,400.00				0.00
96138-10	Kennedy Park master plan	45,000.00		5,000.00	10,000.00	10,000.00	10,000.00	10,000.00
96157-00	City Water Booster pump site analysis	2,000.00	2,000.00					0.00
96166-10	City Water open-end contract	48,000.00						48,000.00
	Subtotal	398,170.00	69,900.00	56,950.00	72,800.00	58,000.00	40,320.00	100,200.00

Very High Job Development

Project Number	Project Name	Fee Rem.	7 6/21–7/18	8 7/19–8/15	9 8/16–9/12	10 9/13–10/10	11 10/11–11/07	Future
96154-00	Pantano-Seneca Apartment Project	$16,000.00		$5,000.00	$6,000.00	$5,000.00		$0.00
96114-00	Downtown Park	20,000.00			5,000.00	5,000.00	5,000.00	5,000.00
96101-00	Army Corps Rillito River Park Design	50,000.00				5,000.00	10,000.00	35,000.00
96151-00	City Schools District Middle School	20,000.00			2,000.00	5,000.00	2,000.00	11,000.00
96132-00	TKE Fraternity House landscaping	3,000.00		1,500.00	1,500.00			0.00
96158-00	Statewide bank code compliance	6,000.00	3,000.00	3,000.00				0.00
96170-00	State License Center	8,500.00			1,500.00	4,000.00	3,000.00	0.00
	Subtotal	107,500.00	3,000.00	4,500.00	10,000.00	19,000.00	20,000.00	51,000.00
	Total WIP and JD	505,670.00	72,900.00	61,450.00	82,800.00	77,000.00	60,320.00	151,200.00
	Capacity corp.		70,360.00	70,360.00	70,360.00	70,360.00	70,360.00	70,360.00
	Surplus or shortfall (–)		2,540.00	(8,910.00)	12,440.00	6,640.00	(10,040.00)	80,840.00

FIGURE 10-11. Workload projection by fee capacity for work in progress and very high job development.

The second method of forecasting workload is organized by hours of billable time projected for each of the firm's staff in billing periods. Using the same percent billable and hours billable in table 10-1, the firm has a capacity of billing 1,480 hours per revenue period. By tracking the amount of time that each member of the firm is projected to be billable, the firm can determine if it is meeting its capacity. A workload capacity forecast organized by billable time also shows which of the firm's staff are light on work or overworked.

By carefully examining the projection of billable time, the firm's managers can see who needs work and how much lead time is available for scheduling work

for each staff person. If all the staff are at or approaching 100 percent billable time and a surplus of billable time remains, the firm may have to consider overtime, expanding the schedule of projects where possible (moving them ahead), or hiring additional staff.

The workload capacity projection by billable time should be used together with a projection of billable time by projects for both work in progress and very high job-development opportunities. This approach is the same as the workload capacity projection by revenue except that billable time is projected instead of revenue. Using both projections will give the firm's managers a good picture of short- and long-term staffing needs.

Work in Progress

Project Number	Project Name	Total Rem. Hours	7 6/21–7/18	8 7/19–8/15	9 8/16–9/12	10 9/13–10/10	11 10/11–11/07	Future
92162-15	South Side Parkway	1760	240	400	500	400	220	0
93126-15	South Side Parkway phase 1 constr. services	930	150	160	160	120	100	240
91121-11	Chiller plant landscape buffer	135	60	60	15			0
92162-15	South Side Parkway @ Euclid—add services	300	300					0
93148-14	Grace Chapel landscape and irrigation	250	150	100				0
93143-15	Biggs AFB roads	610	60	20	240	140	50	100
92133-19	B'nai B'rith elderly housing	250	120	80	50			0
92148-14	City Schools open-end contract	640		100	120	140	160	120
92166-14	Biggs Dorm landscaping	220	100	120				0
93116-17	Biggs AFB Maint. facility EIS	200	60	140				0
93119-17	Home Depot CDs	60	60					0
93130-10	Target rezoning, site plan, landscaping	140	60	80				0
93138-10	Kennedy Park master plan	580	60	140	140	120	120	200
93157-00	City Water booster pump site analysis	40	40					0
93126-10	City Water open-end contract	0						
	Subtotal	5655	1,460	1,400	1,225	920	650	660
	Capacity corp.		1,480	1,480	1,480	1,480	1,480	1,480
	Surplus or shortfall (−)		−20	−80	−255	−560	−830	−820

FIGURE 10-12. Workload projection by hours capacity for work in progress and very high job development.

Very High Development

Project Number	Project Name	Total Rem. Hours	7 6/21–7/18	8 7/19–8/15	9 8/16–9/12	10 9/13–10/10	11 10/11–11/07	Future
93154-00	Pantano-Seneca apartment project	400		100	100	80		0
93114-00	Downtown Park	500			90	80	100	100
93101-00	Army Corps Rillito River Park design	1,000				100	100	350
93151-00	City Schools District Middle School	500			40	100	40	200
93132-00	TKE fraternity house landscaping	60		40	30			0
93158-00	Statewide bank code compliance	125	60	60				0
93150-00	State License Center	200			30	60	60	0
	Subtotal	2,785	60	200	290	420	300	650
	Total WIP and JD	440	1,520	1,600	1,515	1,340	950	1,310
	Capacity corp.		1,480	1,480	1,480	1,480	1,480	1,480
	Surplus or shortfall (−)		40	120	35	−140	−530	−170

FIGURE 10-12. (*Cont'd.*) Workload projection by hours capacity for work in progress and very high job development.

Selecting and Organizing Staff

Selecting staff to work on each project is based on availability and matching experience with the expertise needed to carry out the scope of services. In many cases, key staffing assignments have already been worked out in the proposal and contract negotiation process.

Principals and project managers usually work out staffing assignments at the weekly project-management meeting. Staffing patterns, workload projection reports, and project progress reports are some of the key management reports reviewed by principals and project managers in order to select staff for each new project and to plan for staff assignments on very high job-development projects. A management report illustrating the long-term projection of billable time assigned to staff is useful for visualizing long-range staffing patterns. For an example of projecting billable time by staff person, see figure 10-13.

At the time of project start-up, the project manager assembles the project staff for a start-up meeting. At the initial meeting, the PM discusses the scope of work, the scope of services, schedule, budget, and other salient points related to successfully completing the project. Every task in the scope of services should be reviewed in detail. Each staff person, including principals, should be clear on his or her role in the project and on his or her billable time budget. The project manager should review the project work plan, hours, and fee budget with each staff person working on the project team. The PM should discuss other project goals at the initial meeting: Is the project an ordinary project where the goal is high profitability? Is the project a high-profile project that will require extra effort? Is the project one that the firm will submit for an award? Is the project on a fast-track schedule?

The initial meeting is very important for organizing the staff. Additional staff meetings will be needed during the course of work to keep the project on schedule and to communicate with the project staff, keeping them informed of progress.

Directing and Motivating Project Staff

Selecting the project staff is an easier project-management task than directing and motivating the staff. Directing and motivating the staff takes constant

FIGURE 10-13. Projection of billable time by staff person.

Staff Category	Staff Number	Revenue Period 1				Revenue Period 2				Revenue Period 3				Revenue Period 4				Revenue Period 5				Revenue Period 6				Future
		Weeks 1	2	3	4	Weeks 1	2	3	4	Weeks 1	2	3	4	Weeks 1	2	3	4	Weeks 1	2	3	4	Weeks 1	2	3	4	
Principals	01RW	30	40	40	40	30	30	30	30	30	40	40	30	20	20	10	10	10	20	20	10	10	0	0	0	30
	02GR	30	40	40	40	30	30	30	30	30	30	20	30	30	30	30	30	30	30	30	30	20	20	20	20	180
Project managers	04JH	35	35	35	35	35	35	35	35	35	35	35	35	35	35	35	35	20	20	20	20	20	20	20	20	80
	05MN	35	40	40	40	35	40	40	40	35	35	35	35	35	35	35	35	35	35	35	35	0	0	0	0	0
	07AW	40	40	40	40	40	40	40	40	30	30	30	30	20	20	20	20	20	20	20	20	10	10	10	10	40
Designers	08KN	40	40	40	40	55	55	55	55	30	30	30	30	20	20	20	20	20	20	20	20	20	20	20	20	120
	14TE	40	40	40	40	40	40	40	40	40	40	40	40	40	40	40	40	40	40	40	40	40	40	40	40	180
Draftspersons	12RW	40	40	40	40	40	40	40	40	40	40	40	40	40	40	40	40	40	40	40	40	40	40	40	40	160
	36TM	40	40	60	60	60	60	60	60	40	40	40	40	40	40	40	40	20	20	20	20	40	40	40	40	160
	39AB	45	45	45	45	60	60	60	60	60	60	60	60	45	45	40	40	40	40	40	40	40	40	40	40	80
Secretarial	64CA	10	10	10	10	15	15	15	15	15	15	15	15	20	20	10	10	10	10	10	10	10	10	10	10	40
TOTAL BILLABLE		385	410	430	430	440	445	445	445	385	395	385	385	345	345	320	320	285	295	295	285	250	240	240	240	1070
Billable Capacity		370	370	370	370	370	370	370	370	370	370	370	370	370	370	370	370	370	370	370	370	370	370	370	370	370
Difference		15	40	60	60	70	75	75	75	15	25	15	15	−25	−25	−50	−50	−85	−75	−75	−85	−120	−130	−130	−130	700

attention to detail. The project manager must constantly refer to project progress reports while watching the staff production on the project. Communication with each staff person assigned to the project is vital for staying on schedule and under budget.

The project manager must have good people skills for motivating staff. Motivational skills are one of the intangible qualities of an effective project manager. Project managers need natural, people-oriented abilities. They should be friendly and caring, and should be respected by the office staff. The PM combines abilities to manage, schedule, and complete the tasks at hand with sensitivity to the personal problems, desires, and needs of each staff person. Motivational skills, although complex, can be learned and can be enhanced by the following suggestions:

1. The project manager should be interested in each staff person assigned to the project. Each member of the project team is an important resource to the PM. The staff assigned to the project will be like a family for the duration of the project. If the PM takes the time to learn about the interests of each person assigned to the project team, each person will feel like the PM cares about him or her as a person.

2. The project manager must be personally sensitive to each member of the project team. People have up days and down days. The up days coincide with positive happenings in the person's life; down days indicate personal problems such as family emergencies, personal health concerns, and sleepless nights. There are many times when the PM may be able to lend a helpful ear to the person—resulting in a more effective worker.

3. Honesty and sincerity are desirable qualities of every project manager. People appreciate both. Honesty and sincerity help the project manager gain the respect of each member of the project team.

4. Smile a lot and be friendly. Most people respond favorably to a positive outlook.

5. Be concerned about the professional interests of each person assigned to the project. For example, friction may occur if a staff person is assigned to production and drafting but is more interested in design. The PM may need to point out the learning opportunities on all phases of the project in order to motivate staff. The PM must be sensitive to the professional growth opportunities for everyone working on the project. The PM may need to find ways to challenge each member of the team with the work at hand. There may be construction details, for example, that require research and design development and can provide a project challenge for inexperienced design staff. There may be client-contact opportunities. Junior staff can be asked to attend high level meetings. There may be graphics or computer challenges. There may be presentations that provide unique professional-growth opportunities. The project manager needs to be sensitive to each team member and create professional-development opportunities for all members of the project team.

6. The project manager also needs to be sensitive to limitations of staff if project demands seem to be beyond the expertise level of an individual team member. Productivity may decline if a staff person is unsure about how to proceed with a task. When limitations are detected, the PM may need to coach team members through the work.

In the final analysis, the project manager must see that project staff are motivated, schedules are met, products are delivered, and work is completed. One of the all-time best sources of motivational and people skills, *How to Win Friends and Influence People,* was written by Dale Carnegie in 1930. This book is recommended reading for all project managers. The references at the end of this chapter also provide additional sources for directing and motivating the members of the project team—the project manager's key resources.

Serving the Client and Developing a Friendly Relationship

There's an old saying in the retail business: The customer is always right.

Why should it be different in a service business? For the most part, it isn't.

The project manager should accept the fact that the client has needs, desires, and ideas. Reinforcing the client's needs is central to the success of the project. There are times when the client's needs, desires, or ideas may clash with the PM's professional experience. When a clash occurs, the PM should query the client about the request and express an opinion or alternative to the client's request. Issues must be worked out. Most people are pleased when their needs are met, and pleasing the client is an important part of the PM's job. The only time the PM should seriously question a client's wishes is when the client makes an unethical or illegal request.

If a client requests a service that appears to be unethical or illegal, the PM should immediately discuss the request with the firm's owners, principals, or managers in order to develop a strategy for dealing with the request or to consider terminating the relationship with the client if the request involves serious ethical compromises.

In most cases, however, the relationship between the PM and the client is guided by the notion that the client is always right. The PM must be responsive to the scope of services agreed to with the client and sensitive to the client's needs that arise during the course of the project. Client needs that surface during a project often lead to opportunities for an expanded scope of work and additional fees. The PM needs to establish a business relationship with the client from the start of the project. Then, if the client makes significant requests for additional services, the PM will be in a position to request additional fees. If the client truly desires the services, there will be no problem with approving the PM's request for additional fees. If the PM establishes a good business relationship, the client will be less likely to seek work outside of the scope of services without paying for it. If the PM allows the client to secure free work, reversing the situation will be difficult.

In addition to maintaining a professional and business relationship with the client, developing a social relationship often enhances the consultant/client relationship. Getting to know a client and developing a friendship is one of the most rewarding opportunities available to a project manager. The best client/project manager relationships combine business, ethical, and social elements.

Providing Technical Supervision for the Project Staff

Above all, the project manager must be technically competent. Technical expertise is important when discussing the project and alternatives with the client and for monitoring the progress of the staff's work on each project. The PM must know the technical requirements of each project task—what work needs to be completed, when and how. In most cases, the project staff will be experienced with the work at hand. With experienced staff, the PM's role focuses more on monitoring the costs and schedule while observing that technical requirements are completed. In cases where the project staff are less experienced or have no experience, the PM may be required to closely direct the technical work. The PM may even recommend that project staff put in extra time to research other similar projects and develop the skills needed to complete the work. If adequate research time is not provided in the contract, outside library research and networking usually turn up useful examples of prior similar projects that can be used as a starting point for the firm's current project. The project designers and drafting staff can be very helpful in carrying out research in an effort

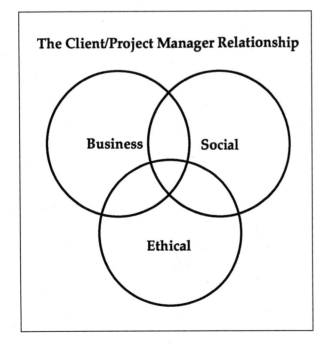

FIGURE 10-14. The client/project manager relationship.

The Client/Project Manager Relationship

Business

Social

Ethical

to make the project as successful as possible. Every aspect of project landscape architecture can benefit from research, and the research process will provide the education and experience needed by inexperienced staff.

In many offices, the project manager is responsible for sealing construction documents and other professional documents, which provides incentive for the PM to direct the project staff to complete a technically competent project. Checking and back checking at each stage of a project is the main vehicle the PM uses to provide quality control on each project. Submittals should be thoroughly checked throughout the schematic, design development, and construction document phases. After corrections have been made by project staff, the PM should back check the corrections to verify that they have been made correctly.

Every landscape architecture firm has developed checking systems for internal quality control and technical supervision. Commonly used techniques include some of the following:

1. *Dual Principal Review.* A project principal is assigned to oversee the project, and a second reviewing principal is assigned to serve only to check the work.
2. *Ladder Approach.* Checking starts at the lowest level of the project team and proceeds up the project ladder of command to the project manager and finally to the principal in charge.
3. *Outside Peer Review.* Once in a while, the perspective and objective viewpoint of an outside expert is the best way to enhance the quality level of a project. Outside peer review often works well for research and planning projects.
4. *Designated Reviewing Principal.* Some firms designate a certain principal to be the bottom-line reviewer on every project that leaves the office. By specializing in reviewing work, the principal develops better and better skills at finding errors or omissions before they actually become a problem.
5. *Client Review.* Most clients are very interested in reviewing the plans, reports, and other project output. The project manager needs to be sure that the client is providing the office with thorough review comments at

each stage of the project. The client's review is very important and assures the PM that the client understands what he or she is getting in the way of a design or planning product.

Inspiring, Nurturing, and Promoting Professional Development Opportunities for Staff

Every employee wants to succeed. Sometimes coaching is one of the project manager's most useful talents. The PM should want each staff person to get as much professional development as possible out of each project. The personal professional growth of each individual in the office creates a synergistic effect on the firm as a whole.

Some staff will let the PM know in no uncertain terms where they would like to go with their personal professional development. Other staff will be less vocal but equally appreciative of professional-development opportunities made available to them. The project manager has many options available for individual professional development opportunities:

1. Speaking opportunities for principals, project managers, or marketing staff.
2. Submitting projects for awards.
3. Training sessions for staff on topics of interest to the individual's and the firm's needs (e.g., computer software training, time-management seminars, irrigation equipment show-and-tells.
4. Supporting memberships in professional organizations.
5. Firm-sponsored classes at universities and colleges.
6. Opportunities for client contact, especially for junior staff.
7. Opportunities to represent the firm at public meetings or project interviews.
8. Speaking engagements.
9. Publication opportunities for articles about the firm's projects.

10. On-site reconnaissance, especially out-of-town travel.
11. Representation on commissions, boards, committees, and other community service opportunities.

Coordinating with the Firm's Top Management and Clients

Coordination is a constant activity of a project manager. A complex project will require coordination with the firm's principals, owners, and top management, as well as a web of public agency representatives when dealing with codes, code compliance issues, and other regulatory requirements. Client representatives, whether public or private, will require ongoing coordination. Even small projects may require a great deal of coordination with public and private agencies.

The PM needs to develop a list of the key players in each project, their roles, phone numbers, addresses, and other important information. Developing a written list of who needs to be coordinated with on each project, when and with what information or deliverables, will help the PM's coordination process go smoothly. Meeting with key individuals early in the project is a useful way to establish a relationship and define the necessary coordination requirements. Many cities and counties have ordinances that require initial, as well as follow-up, meetings with agency representatives.

The weekly project-management meeting is one of the best ways for the project manager to coordinate with the firm's top management. Informal methods work, too. Lunch meetings, after-work get-togethers, and office social events and activities are other good ways for the PM to coordinate with the firm's other management staff. Weekly project staff meetings can be used to coordinate the project team, and desktop crits can be used in between the weekly staff meetings.

Attaining High Quality in Planning and Design Output

Quality should be a goal of every project—quality in the planning and design process, quality in the service to the client, quality in the drawings or reports, quality of construction administration, quality of the finished project, attention to stewardship and environmental ethics, and quality of planning and research documents (contents and presentation). Nothing advances the reputation of a landscape architecture office more than a constructed project that achieves acclaim and high visibility in the community, or a planning effort that breaks new ground and is praised by professional peers. A successful project keeps the client happy and satisfied and retains the client.

The project manager is a central force for positioning each project to attain the highest quality possible. The effort can sometimes be trying. Many projects are lackluster, everyday projects. Trying to find ways to strive for quality when working on an ordinary project can be tedious. Bumping up the quality level of an ordinary project, however, may give the project manager a rewarding sense of professional achievement.

Marketing the Firm

Every professional practitioner will tell you that repeat work from the firm's existing client base is the best source of new projects. The project manager plays a central role in maintaining existing clients, keeping them satisfied, and obtaining additional work from them.

The project manager's first goal is satisfying the client, ensuring that the scope of services is carried out in a timely fashion, and producing a competent professional product with the highest quality possible. A satisfied and pleased client is the first step to an ongoing professional relationship and securing future work from the client. The importance of developing a social relationship with the firm's clients cannot be stressed enough. The project manager is usually the firm's lead contact with the client on a day-to-day basis and may have the best opportunities to develop a social relationship with the client. The firm's principals also play a strategic role in client maintenance.

Looking for both new job opportunities and additional services that a current client may need is a high-priority goal for each project manager. The PM starts by memorizing the contractual scope of services agreed to with the client and then observing when or if the direction of the project changes and a change of scope becomes necessary. There are times when a project changes so that the scope is actually reduced. Whereas a reduction in scope and fees may cause a short-term reduction in fees, the long-term outcome may have a very positive effect on the client. Generally, a client would be pleased with the savings and develop respect for the project manager. A client who has benefited from competent, high-quality services at lower costs will definitely keep the savings in mind when thinking about hiring a consultant for a future project.

In many cases, a change in the scope of a project usually means that the firm can renegotiate the fee to cover the additional work. The PM should meet with the firm's principals and top managers, review the change in scope, and determine what adjustments in scope and fee will be necessary to complete the project. When changes in scope occur after a project has been partially completed, there is often a corresponding reduction in the original scope of services. Presenting to the client both the additional scope and fees needed, as well as the scope that has been eliminated and fees that have been deducted, is a practical way to make the presentation.

The project manager also needs to be aware of the upcoming planning, design, or environmental services the client may be considering and offer to help the client clarify new project consulting needs and even draft a scope of services for the client—a good way to get the PM's foot in the door for securing the new work. The PM also needs to be aware if the client is considering using the firm's competitors for future work. By knowing that the client may have other firms in mind, the PM can help the firm develop a competitive strategy aimed at retaining the client.

Managing the Planning or Design Effort to Meet Construction Cost Expectations

Holding a project's construction cost to the client's budget is one of the best ways to satisfy a client. The PM must make a focused effort throughout the duration of the project to keep the output in line with the client's implementation budget. If a need arises for a

change in scope that will likely impact the client's implementation or construction budget, the PM should notify the client and discuss the situation as soon as possible.

Making construction or implementation cost projections for each key phase of the project is the only way to effectively monitor the design effort to keep it in line with the client's budget. If the project is a typical design project, the PM should make construction cost projections at each of the following phases:

1. *Contract Negotiation.* Assess whether the budget established by the client is realistic in terms of the client's expectations and the firm's prior experience with similar projects. If the budget is not realistic, the budget needs to be discussed with the client before a contract for professional services is agreed on. Starting work on a project that a client has severely underbudgeted will inevitably result in problems further along in the design process.

   Initial budgetary cost projections are normally made on a unit-cost basis for broad-brush areas of the site plan or the client's design program. Initial projections are completed only to the level of detail to satisfy the design firm that the implementation or construction budget is adequate.

2. *Schematic Design.* The next construction cost projection should be made after the first phase of design—the schematic design phase—has been completed, normally when the project is about 35 percent complete. This is the point at which the PM is concerned with verifying that the firm's design effort is in line with the agreed-upon construction budget. This is the point at which the PM must scale back the firm's design effort or reduce the design complexity of the detail design work if necessary to get the project on budget. If the PM does not get the project on budget at the schematic phase, budget problems will continue to plague the project as it progresses through the design and construction documentation process, and budget adjustments will be more difficult to make.

   Once in a while, the project is over budget at the schematic design phase, but the landscape architecture firm is convinced that its design plans are in the client's best interest. In this case, the project manager and the principal in charge of the project will meet with the client and present the plans that the firm knows are over budget, letting the client decide whether the firm's recommendations should be implemented at the higher budget projection. If the client needs to hold the line on the budget, the firm will get a clear indication of it and can reduce its design effort accordingly.

3. *Design Development.* The cost projection at the design development (DD) phase may be the most important of all. The DD cost projection takes place when the design has been fairly well cast in stone in the eyes of the client and the design firm. Making changes in the project to reduce construction cost in order to hold the line on the budget is harder to do as the design process proceeds. For example, changes can be made at the DD phase in materials to lower the projected costs, but major changes in the site plan are normally not made unless the project is radically over budget.

At the DD phase, usually 75 percent complete, the project plan is set and the details are for the most part worked out. At this point, a fairly accurate cost projection can be carried out. Most firms complete the DD construction cost projection in house using quantity takeoffs multiplied by a unit cost.

Another approach, used on complex projects, is to have one or more general contractors prepare a preliminary, or pricing, bid on the DD package of drawings. This serves two good purposes: First, the general contractor is more likely to cover all of the costs, some of which might not be picked up by the landscape architecture firm, because the general contractor is viewing the project impartially. Second, if the project appears to be over budget, the general contractor may have some very good ideas to help the landscape architecture firm reduce costs by using alternative methods, materials, or quantities.

When the landscape architecture firm uses an outside estimating firm on a project, the estimating firm may be brought into the loop at each phase of the work, including initial budget verification and schematic design. Frequently, outside estimating firms are not engaged until the design development phase has been completed and the design is fairly well set.

4. *Construction Documents.* The final construction cost projection is made using a quantity takeoff on the final construction documents (CDs) at 90 percent to 100 percent complete. The client will use this final cost projection for comparing bids or negotiated construction contract amounts. The final cost projection must be as accurate as possible. If a general contractor were used to provide construction quotes at the DD phase, the same contractor or contractors may be asked to provide final construction quotes at the 100 percent CDs phase. If the project is to be released for general bidding, the client will use the final cost projection as a guide for evaluating the bids received.

Managing a project so that it meets a client's implementation cost expectations requires different approaches for planning projects, environmental assessments, and environmental research. These types of nonconstruction projects normally result in the landscape architecture firm's setting a future implementation budget for the client's project rather than working toward a fixed budget for a construction type of project. In a planning or environmental project, the landscape architecture firm's effort focuses on identifying all future implementation costs so that the client will have the most realistic budget numbers possible. If a landscape architecture firm carries out a visual impact assessment, for example, and reports to the client that mitigation efforts should be budgeted at $1.5 million, the budget needs to hold up when the project goes into the design and construction documents phases. The landscape architecture firm has another incentive to make accurate estimates for planning and environmental projects: In many cases the firm will continue with design and construction documentation. Therefore the firm wants to make the most realistic and healthy budget projection it can make in order to make the later phases of the project go more smoothly.

Sunnyside Middle School Landscape Construction Cost Projection

Playing Fields Area

Item No.	Item	Quantity	Unit	Unit Cost	Cost
1	6″ × 10″ concrete header	2,010	LF	$6.00	$12,060.00
2	Open 7′ fence (type B)	580	LF	32.00	18,560.00
3	Opaque 7′ fence (type A)	872	LF	40.00	34,880.00
4	Open 6′ fence above 12″ CMU wall (type D)	304	LF	36.00	10,944.00
5	Pilasters	5	EA	250.00	1,250.00
6	Low CMU bollard with cable	24	EA	250.00	6,000.00
7	28′ auto access gates	2	EA	1,500.00	3,000.00
8	Patterson Williams backstop	1	EA	4,500.00	4,500.00
9	Players benches	6	EA	300.00	1,800.00
10	Planting:				
	A. 36″ box trees	10	EA	450.00	4,500.00
	B. 24″ box trees	36	EA	225.00	8,100.00
	C. 5 gal. shrubs	89	EA	18.00	1,602.00
	D. 1 gal. shrubs	513	EA	8.00	4,104.00
	E. Hybrid Bermuda sod over 6″ imported topsoil	171,544	SF	0.55	94,349.20
11	Decomposed granite:				
	A. Stabilizer red infield mix (4″ depth)	17,514	SF	0.65	11,384.10
	B. ¼″ minus stabilized red DG (3″ depth)	85,778	SF	0.60	51,466.80
12	Turf irrigation	171,544	SF	0.35	60,040.40
12	Drip irrigation	1	LS	9,000.00	9,000.00
	Subtotal				337,540.50
	Contingency (5%)				16,877.03
	Total				354,417.53

Building Area

Item No.	Item	Quantity	Unit	Unit Cost	Cost
1	6″ × 10″ concrete header	1,007	LF	$6.00	$6,042.00
2	Open 7′ fence (Type B)	739	LF	32.00	23,648.00
3	Open 4′ fence above 28″ CMU wall (Type C)	420	LF	46.00	19,320.00
4	Open 6′ fence above 12″ CMU wall (Type D)	647	LF	36.00	23,292.00
5	Pilasters	22	EA	250.00	5,500.00
6	Retaining wall at retention basin	152	EA	40.00	6,080.00
7	28′ auto access gates	1	EA	1,500.00	1,500.00
8	Bike racks	63	EA	75.00	4,725.00
9	Planting:				
	A. 36″ box trees	46	EA	450.00	20,700.00
	B. 24″ box trees	67	EA	225.00	15,075.00
	C. 5 gal. shrubs	120	EA	18.00	2,160.00
	D. 1 gal. shrubs	781	EA	8.00	6,248.00
	E. 84″ box specimen tree	1	EA	2,000.00	2,000.00
10	Drip irrigation	1	LS	15,000.00	15,000.00
11	Decomposed Granite:				0.00
	A. ¼″ minus stabilized red DG (3″ depth)	1,600	SF	0.60	960.00
	B. 1½″ graded	12,093	SF	0.45	5,441.85
	C. ½″ minus non-stabilized DG (2″ depth)	127,550	SF	0.25	31,887.50
12	River run rock	5,825	SF	0.40	2,330.00
13	Basketball courts	4	EA	12,500.00	50,000.00
13	Central courtyard and inner bldg. areas	1	LS	20,000.00	20,000.00
	Subtotal				261,909.35
	Contingency (5%)				13,095.47
	Total				275,004.82
	Project total				**$629,422.34**

FIGURE 10-15. Example of a construction cost projection prepared on a spreadsheet program at the design development phase of a middle school project.

Taking Part in Performance Reviews of Technical Staff

The project manager may be the most qualified person in the office to assess the performance of the firm's technical staff. The PM works with all of the staff and is normally well aware of successful and unsuccessful performance.

Peer review is important for each employee of the firm to establish professional development goals. Salary increases are normally tied to peer reviews. Most firms have a set approach and frequency for carrying out performance reviews. In most cases, the ap-proach involves a meeting with the staff person attended by the project manager with whom the staff person has had the most contact in the office. A principal and the personnel manager, if the firm is large enough to have one, will also attend the peer review meeting. The frequency of peer reviews varies from firm to firm. Six-month reviews are common, but up to a year may also be satisfactory to provide proper direction for technical staff. Peer review meetings should be kept upbeat and informal, making the staff person feel as comfortable as possible. Most firms use a personnel review form that is normally filled out in advance of the peer review meeting. For an example of a work review form, see figure 10-16.

Work Review Form

To Be Completed by Firm

Employee's name:

Reviewer's name:

Date of the work review:

Employee's anniversary date:

Date of last review:

Note: Work review forms must be completed within five days of the date of the work review.

Action to be taken:

FIGURE 10-16. Work review form.

To Be Completed by Employee

1. Please describe and evaluate your professional development and achievement since your last work review. Consider the following:
   - What have you done to develop your skills?
   - What have you done to enhance your productivity?
   - Has your professional attitude changed?
   - How have you helped the firm develop?
   - How has the firm helped you develop your skills, productivity, and professional attitude?

Employee comments:

Reviewer comments:

2. Please describe your work relationships within the firm. Consider the following:
   - Do you find your supervisors and co-workers friendly and easy to work with? Have you had any problems relating to your supervisors or co-workers?
   - Describe your reliability since your last work review.
   - Has the firm given you opportunities for independent action, initiative, and self-improvement?
   - Have you been encouraged to succeed? To learn by experience? To extend yourself?
   - Describe instances of leadership you have taken since your last review.

Employee's comments:

Reviewer's comments:

3. What are your professional development goals for the next year? For the next five years? Describe how you intend to achieve the goals and how the firm can support your efforts. Consider the following:
   - What can be done to improve my professional development?
   - What are my chances for advancement in the firm?
   - What is expected of me and how will I be evaluated?
   - What is your wildest dream that the firm can help you fulfill?

Employee's comments:

Reviewer's comments:

FIGURE 10-16. (*Cont'd.*) Work review form.

4. Provide a brief summary of your self-evaluation and conclude with your request for action, promotion, and change in compensation.

5. Are there any topics you would like to discuss in your work review?

6. What do you think of this self-evaluation form?

Signatures

_____   _____
Employee   Date

_____   _____
Reviewer   Date

FIGURE 10-16. (*Cont'd.*) Work review form.

The project manager should take time between peer review dates to make notes on the performance of each staff person he or she works with. Notes to the staff person's personnel file are very helpful to remind the project manager of successful performance of the staff person since the previous review.

Assisting in Writing and Preparing Proposals

The responsibility for writing and preparing proposals differs among professional landscape architecture firms, based on the number of employees in the firm and firm's operational structure. If the firm is large enough to employ a marketing manager or marketing coordinator, he or she will prepare proposals with only technical input from the project manager. In many landscape architecture firms, the principals are the lead marketing points of contact, and they manage the proposal process. In some firms, the project manager may be asked to spearhead the proposal process. In any case, the PM's role is most often to develop the scope of work, hours, and fee estimate, or review and check these after they have been developed by a principal who has had direct contact with the prospective client. The PM may also help by defining the technical requirements of the proposal. If the PM does not have direct responsibility, the principal or proposal coordinator should ask the PM to review the scope of services, hours projection, and fee. Being the firm's lead point of contact for carrying out the work, the PM needs to feel comfortable that the work can be done for the fee that will be quoted to the prospective client. What could be worse than not involving the PM, then handing over a project to be completed that has been underestimated? The PM will start out in a hole and may never have the opportunity to complete the project on or under budget. The project will be a money loser from the start. If too many underestimated projects are given to the PM, sooner or later friction will develop between the PM and the proposal writers.

Another excellent way to involve the PM in the proposal process is during the interview stage. Because the project manager will have day-to-day contact with the client, the PM normally participates in interviews for projects. The PM's experience with the technical requirements of the prospective client's project will be helpful in the event that questions of a technical nature come up in an interview. In addition, interview panels usually like to meet the project manager because of the central role that he or she will play. A project manager who is a good speaker and is able to contribute technical input in an interview can help the firm be selected for the project.

Involving the project manager in preparing proposals is important, and the minimum involvement should include (1) reviewing the scope of work, scope of services, hours estimate, and fee; and (2) attending interviews.

Closing Out a Project

Every landscape architecture office has some type of project close-out system. Files and drawings must be archived. Computer files must be stored on floppy disks, magnetic tape, compact disc, or hard drives. Project materials must be sorted through and organized so that only one copy of all information is being archived and so that information can be easily retrieved from the archived materials if the need arises. New construction details developed for the project need to be added to the office general files so they are available for future reference and reuse.

Photographs or videos of the completed project need to be taken and archived. In most cases, the job of closing out and archiving a project is the responsibility of the project manager. The PM may delegate much of the actual close-out work, but the PM will manage the process.

Closing out a project is an important part of keeping an office environment organized. Administrative time should be estimated in the scope of services and fees provided for project close-out so that the cost of archiving the project information is covered. Attention to proper archiving of materials will pay off in time savings when there is a need to refer to the project information in the future. Most landscape architects are surprised at the amount of back referencing of completed projects that actually occurs in the regular operations of a typical landscape architecture office.

PROJECT CLOSE-OUT LIST

1. Review the material in all of the project files. Delete material that is a duplicate or is not necessary to keep for future reference. Organize the files.
2. Send a letter notifying the client that the project is complete and ask if the client wants copies of any project materials in addition to the deliverables provided for under the terms of the contract.
3. Physically move all of the hard-copy files and drawings into the office archive storage area.
4. Clean up all computer files and store project electronic data in the office computer archive system.
5. Update the office standard details files, both hard copy and electronic, with any new or revised and updated construction details developed for the project.
6. Update the office construction estimating files with new information received during the estimating and bidding of the project.
7. Update the office specifications files if new specifications have been written for the project or old specifications have been revised.
8. Make recommendations to the firm's lead marketing staff for photo opportunities and other opportunities to develop marketing materials such as a new cut sheet on the project.

9. Prepare a memorandum for general office distribution regarding any problems that occurred on the project and solutions developed by the project team to resolve the problems. This memo will help other PMs and office personnel avoid making a similar mistake in the future. If there are positive outcomes of the project, share them with office personnel.

10. Review the project financial records, progress reports, profitability reports, and summary reports that will help the PM in future project management.

Managing Construction Observation Services

When a project enters the construction stage, the project manager may remain involved or turn the project over to office staff who specialize in services during construction. In smaller firms, the PM may actually be the lead staff person who carries out the services during construction, including construction observation. Larger offices may have full-time staff who specialize in construction services. Either approach works, and there are many variations of staffing used by landscape architecture offices for carrying out services during construction.

Every project will have its own specific scope of services that has been developed for the firm's services during construction. The following list provides an overview of the services typically provided during construction.

EXAMPLE OF SERVICES PROVIDED DURING CONSTRUCTION

1. Printing, preparing, and disseminating construction bid documents.
2. Contacting potential bidders.
3. Providing clarification of construction documents during bidding.
4. Attending a prebid meeting.
5. Evaluating bids and recommending the selection of the contractor.
6. Assisting the client in developing a contract for construction and awarding the contract.

7. Developing a filing system and project manual to use in keeping accurate records and filing information received during construction.
8. Attending preconstruction meetings.
9. Attending regular weekly construction meetings.
10. Reviewing the product and materials submittals for construction of the project.
11. Reviewing the shop drawings for construction of the project.
12. Preparing construction observation reports.
13. Following up on all construction-related problems until each is resolved.
14. Reviewing all requests for information (RFIs) developed by the contractor and making recommendations to the owner. Requests for information often lead to change orders.
15. Reviewing requests for construction change orders.
16. Reviewing the contractor's pay requests.
17. Developing and preparing a punch list at completion of the construction.
18. Checking that all items on the punch list have been completed by the contractor before recommending final acceptance to the owner.
19. Establishing a date for final acceptance, a date when the landscape establishment period begins, and the date when guarantees end.
20. Notifying the owner that the firm's services during construction have been completed.
21. Carrying out a postoccupancy review of the project. A postoccupancy review is sometimes covered under the scope of services. If it is not, the landscape architecture firm should carry out this service for its own benefit to identify if any problems exist with actually using the facility. A postoccupancy analysis is usually very helpful for improving the design ability of the office staff who worked on the project. If the evaluation is done by the firm at its own cost, the process can be made into a fun event, such as having a bag lunch meeting at the project site, shared by many members of the office. Sometimes carrying out a postconstruction evaluation can also lead to additional work on the project.

Most landscape architecture firms have prepared a construction services manual used by office staff as an aid in carrying out services during construction. The manual includes the duties and responsibilities of the staff person carrying out the construction services, ways to achieve quality compliance, requirements for proper and thorough documentation, and copies of forms used by the office during construction services, such as field report forms and forms used to review submittals and shop drawings. The forms are normally also available on the office computer system. Professional organizations such as ASLA and AIA have a wide variety of preprinted forms that many landscape architecture offices use during construction. These forms may also be included by reference in the office's construction services manual. A complete copy of a typical office manual for services during construction is included in the appendix.

Summary

In summary, the project-management approach to organizing the landscape architecture office is the most frequently used way of structuring the firm's technical operations. The PM is the hub of the office wheel. The project manager must be able to handle all phases of a project and all aspects of project management. The PM must be technically competent. Ability to use computer technology for developing project control systems and supervising office CAD production is a requirement for every project manager. The PM should be friendly, sociable, and inspirational. The PM must be willing to manage and not meddle. The PM must be a good coordinator, a good listener, and have good time-management skills. For an example of a typical job description for a project manager, see figure 10-17.

JOB DESCRIPTION

    I.   Occupational classification: Project Manager
   II.   Organizational relationships
       A. Reports to: principal in charge of production
       B. Supervises: design and production staff
       C. Coordinates with:
          1. Design and production staff
          2. Project managers
          3. Director of human resources
          4. Business and finance director
          5. Principal in charge of corporate planning and marketing
          6. Principal in charge of production
          7. Director of landscape architecture
          8. Director of planning
          9. Director of information systems
         10. Public relations director
 III. Primary duties: Responsible for profitability. Responsible for managing projects. Responsible for writing proposals, establishing the scope of services, and deriving fees. Coordinates with principals during contract negotiation. Responsible for job scheduling, project staffing, project design, production and client maintenance from initial contact through project close-out. Keeps abreast of job development and new client development opportunities while maintaining good relations with existing clients.
 IV. Work performed
       A. Principal duties
          1. Initiates client contact. Maintains clients. Develops new clients and job leads while fostering sound relationships with existing clients by frequent client contact and regularly reporting to the client on the progress of the project.

FIGURE 10-17. Job description for a project manager.

2. Develops proposal content, scope of work, and scope of services. Derives fees based on the project scope. Analyzes fee alternatives and assists with fee negotiation. Establishes project hours and fee budgets. Establishes project-management tools using spreadsheet and other software. Uses office job costing reports and other financial reports to manage projects for profitability.

3. Coordinates and supervises the design and production staff for timely and accurate completion of projects.

4. Coordinates with the principal in charge of production to develop short- and long-term staffing schedules and specific staffing needs.

5. Sets the planning and design direction of projects in coordination with the director of landscape architecture, the director of planning, and project planning and design staff. Monitors completion of the project in line with planning and design intent.

6. Reviews design, design development, and planning output and is responsible for quality control.

7. Reviews construction documents, specifications, and other documents for technical competence. Responsible for quality control of project documents, construction documents, correspondence, reports, field notes, phone notes, construction cost projections, and any other project-related documents.

8. Tracks the project hours and fee budget on at least a weekly basis. Reviews and approves invoice to the client for each billing period.

9. Works with the director of landscape architecture and the director of planning to ensure that the high standards of the firm and the needs of the client are met for every project.

10. Responsible for managing all projects for a goal of 15 percent profit.

11. Develops and nurtures high morale among the planning and design technical staff by being responsive to needs, concerns, and professional goals.

12. Strives to utilize all professional staff in the most efficient and productive capacity. Provides opportunities for personnel to acquire new skills and broaden responsibilities. Encourages staff in professional development opportunities.

13. Keeps current on trends in landscape architecture and planning professions by reading books and journals, attending seminars and workshops, and participating in continuing education.

14. Attends weekly project-management meetings.

15. Reviews staff time cards for accuracy.

16. Participates in staff work reviews.

17. Monitors and organizes project hard-copy and computer files for thorough and proper documentation of all job-related activities.

18. Maintains a photographic record of projects for archive and marketing purposes.

19. Sharpens management skills through reading books and journals, attending seminars and workshops, and participating in continuing education.

20. Performs other duties as required.

B. Coordinating duties

1. Coordinates with the director of human resources for reviewing the work of planning, design, and technical staff, and for carrying out work staff reviews.

2. Coordinates with the public relations director to identify opportunities for publicity in print, video, and multimedia outlets.

FIGURE 10-17. *(Cont'd.)* Job description for a project manager.

3. Remains in close contact with principals for business development and marketing opportunities.
4. Coordinates with the director of corporate planning and marketing and with other project managers to develop incentive programs to challenge and reward technical staff.
5. Coordinates with the directors of business and finance and information systems to determine time-management reporting needs, billing methods, and billing dates. Coordinates with the director of business and finance for timely and accurate invoicing of clients.

V. Education and experience
  A. Landscape architecture degree
  B. Professional registration
  C. A minimum of three years experience in landscape architecture
  D. Strong skills in management, planning, assigning, supervising, and coordinating work activities
  E. Sensitivity to interpersonal relations
  F. Able to express information and ideas clearly and precisely both verbally and in writing
  G. Ability to establish and maintain effective working relationships with staff, clients, contractors, and the general public
  H. Technically competent and current with technology and techniques applied to the design and construction of landscape architecture projects

VI. Personal qualities
  Motivates people. Is well organized, creative, and a problem solver. Communicates well. Is sensitive to people. Is innovative and open to new ideas. Is a self-starter.

FIGURE 10-17. (Cont'd.) Job description for a project manager.

REFERENCES

Burstein, David, and Frank Stasiowski. 1991. *Project Management for the Design Professional.* Rev. ed. New York: Whitney Library of Design.

Stasiowski, Frank. 1991. *Staying Small Successfully: A Guide for Architects, Engineers, and Design Professionals.* New York: John Wiley & Sons.

Stasiowski, Frank. 1985. *Negotiating Higher Design Fees.* New York: Witney Library of Design.

Drucker, Paul F. 1974. *Management: Tasks, Responsibilities, Practices.* New York: Harper & Row.

STUDY QUESTIONS AND ASSIGNMENTS

1. Using this chapter and other references, write a thorough and in-depth paper that illustrates your understanding of project management in the landscape architecture office.

2. Using a design project from your studio courses and this chapter, chapter 9, and other references, develop a proposal for professional services including a specific and thorough scope of work and scope of services. Develop an hours projection and a project budget. Develop a work plan for the scope of services that would be used as the project-management guideline for the project. Include a list of milestone events and a bar chart as part of the work plan.

3. Using the proposal developed in question 2, develop a critical path diagram for completing the professional services. Use this chapter and other reference sources to obtain a thorough understanding of the critical path method of organizing the flow of work in a professional design project.

4. Using this chapter and other references, write a thorough and in-depth paper that illustrates your understanding of tracking, monitoring, and managing a project. Your paper should cover what you will do, in a descending order of priorities, if the project were to become over budget and off schedule.

5. Using spreadsheet software, develop a project progress report format as a tool for project management.

6. Using this chapter and other references, write a thorough and in-depth paper that illustrates your understanding of quality control in the landscape architecture office. Include methods such as dual principal review, the ladder approach to checking documents, outside peer review, designated principal review, and client review. Identify and discuss other methods based on your research.

7. Using a design project from your studio courses and this chapter as a reference, develop a construction cost projection using spreadsheet software.

8. Using this chapter and other references, develop a personnel work review form. Pair off in twos and carry out a mock work review using the form you created. After completing the mock work review, combine the separate work review forms you and your partner created into a single form that includes the best part of each form.

9. Using this chapter and other references, develop a project close-out checklist.

10. Using this chapter and other references, write a paper that illustrates your understanding of the services provided by landscape architects during construction. Develop your own version of the key forms that are useful during construction observation activities.

CHAPTER ELEVEN

Business and Personnel Law

The Legal Environment of Professional Practice

Landscape architects use legal rules and laws on a daily basis. They rely on, react to, make plans in accordance with, and at times may violate laws. The legal environment of professional practice can be a harsh reality for landscape architects, and the more knowledge each landscape architect has about laws, regulations, and the legal system affecting professional practice, the more likely he or she will be to avoid legal hassles and practice in a legally acceptable fashion.

In its broadest sense, *law* refers to the general code of conduct set down by the controlling authority with binding legal consequences. Law is the collection of rules and regulations intended to control business and social behavior. The enforcement of laws creates a level of predictability and uniformity in our society. Laws are used by members of society to resolve disputes, whether through informal dispute resolution or through formal methods that apply laws through the legal and justice system. Law creates structure for society and the world of professional practice.

The landscape architect can use law to counteract dishonest, unethical, or fraudulent business practices. Law can also be used to encourage practices that further the opportunities of landscape architects.

To be effective, law must be enforceable. It must have teeth. Deviation from generally acceptable legal behavior, whether defined by formal laws and regulations or by ethical considerations, will inevitably result in reactions to the practice of landscape architecture.

Law enforcement can take many forms related to the practice of landscape architecture. Illegal actions related to professional regulation may result in restrictions, fines, or the loss of a landscape architect's license to practice. A landscape architect's client may be polluting a river, causing ethical or legal actions to be taken against the client or even the landscape architect. An employee who believes he or she has been discriminated against or harassed can allege discrimination or sexual harassment, and the landscape architect will face legal defense costs and a possible judgment against the landscape architect resulting in financial loss.

Enforcement of laws can become a stark reality to the landscape architecture firm engaged in illegal or unethical practice. Law enforcement is the incentive for the landscape architecture firm to carry out its practice in conformance with behavior that is lawful and acceptable to society. Every landscape architect and landscape architecture firm must monitor its practice of the profession to maintain its reputation and goodwill in the community and avoid the impact of law enforcement. Fines, insurance losses, and other consequences of violating the law are seriously detrimental impacts to professional practice.

No single chapter in a book can begin to provide in-depth coverage of all the laws and rules that can and will impact a landscape architecture firm. The goal of this chapter is to provide an overview of the laws and regulations that are likely to apply to the business practice of landscape architecture.

An overview of the origin of law is discussed first. The remainder of this chapter, however, will cover areas pertinent to the lawful practice of the profession:

1. licensure law
2. government regulatory law and agencies
3. tort law
4. labor relations
5. discrimination law
6. protection of the general public and the consumer

Last, let me say to every landscape architect who is in, or wants to be in, private practice: Find a good attorney and develop a relationship with him or her. At some time, probably when you least expect it, you will need legal advice. Having an established relationship with an attorney will make easier going of any legal complications you find yourself in.

The Origin of Law

The source of law in the United States is called *common law* and is made and applied by judges as they resolve disputes between entities. Under common law, change is very slow and methodical as the resolution to each dispute is carefully made consistent with previous cases brought before judges and that together build up the legal tradition surrounding decisions by judges in the resolution of similar disputes.

The historical roots of our legal system in the United States have their origin in English common law. After William the Conqueror and the Normans conquered England in 1066, they began the task of unifying the country under their rule. With the establishment of the King's Courts, uniform rules and laws were set out for the country, marking the beginning of English common law.

Under the practice of English common law, important cases were recorded, and judges began using recorded cases as the basis for decisions on situations that were similar to past disputes, developing in the process precedent for settling future similar cases. This practice of deciding legal problems by referring to prior case decisions is the foundation of both the English and the American legal process. This process forms the doctrine called *stare decisis,* which means to stand on decided cases—to use precedent. The importance of using precedent in dispute resolution is that it creates consistency in the legal system and provides stability for businesses as long as they act within the established boundaries of preceding cases (Meiners, Ringleb, and Edwards 1988).

American Law Today

Case law, or judge-made law, is not the only source of law in the United States today. The executive, legislative, and judicial branches of federal and state government all have the authority to make laws. In addition, Congress at the federal level and legislatures at the state level of government use powers granted to them to establish wide-ranging laws and regulations, called statutory laws, that have wide bearing on the daily lives of citizens and the business practice of landscape architecture. The legislative process of forming laws originates with the over 20,000 items of legislation brought up for consideration in each session of Congress and hundreds of thousands of items brought before state legislatures every year.

The legislative branches of government create administrative agencies and give them the authority to implement statutory law. Agencies that we are all familiar with include federal and state departments of agriculture, commerce, defense, education, energy, housing, labor, transportation, environmental protection, health, and human services. The regulations and administrative orders issued by government administrative agencies have daily impacts on the business practice of landscape architecture. The impacts of statutory law enforced by government agencies will be discussed later in this chapter.

The legal environment of the professional practice of landscape architecture is therefore defined as the collection of laws that guide and influence the behavior and conduct of the practitioner's activities. These laws include the legal rights, duties, and responsibilities associated with professional practice, establishing the boundaries of lawful relationships between the landscape architecture firm and its clients, personnel, and business contacts. The legal environment, if not adhered to by the landscape architect, will result in the law being enforced by a wide variety of legal sanctions including fines, liability for damages, and even imprisonment (Meiners, Ringleb, and Edwards 1988).

Licensure Laws

Professional registration, or licensure of landscape architects, is regulated at the state level of government. Over forty states have adopted licensure laws.

Generally, there are two types of landscape architecture licensure laws:

1. *Practice law,* which allows only qualified individuals to practice landscape architecture.
2. *Title law,* which prevents individuals from using the title or calling themselves a landscape architect without being licensed. Title laws normally allow unlicensed individuals to carry out landscape architecture work using a different title or designation, such as *landscape designer.*

The premise of licensure laws is the protection of public health, safety, and welfare. Work properly performed by the landscape architect under the standard of care practiced by reasonably competent professionals can have a definite impact on the public's physical health and safety. The following is a cross-section of situations where public health, safety, and welfare are at risk:

- Relationships between water supply and water drainage facilities might result in the contamination of a water supply system.
- Improperly designed outdoor lighting systems could result in fire or injury from electric shock.
- Improperly designed outdoor structures, such as park shelters or stadium bleachers, could result in significant injury to people due to structural collapse.
- Failure and collapse of a retaining wall could lead to serious property damage.
- Unsafe playground design might result in the lifelong impairment or even death of a child.
- Improperly designed walks, steps, ramps, and railings can expose the public to hazardous injury.
- Roads, streets, and driveways designed too steeply can result in accidents, particularly in mountainous terrain subject to severe winter weather conditions.
- Poorly designed storm drainage may result in flooding or damage to building foundations.
- Lack of care in designing irrigation systems adjacent to building foundations can cause undermining of the footings and structural damage. Standing water caused by overspray on sidewalks can lead to slipping and falling accidents.
- Misunderstanding the functional characteristics of plant materials can result in some of the following hazards to human health:

   A. Improper irrigation of the root systems of trees can cause instability and the possibility of blowdown and injury to property or people.
   B. Root systems can cause upheaval of foundations and walkways, resulting in structural failure and tripping hazards.
   C. Being unaware of the toxicity of some plant materials can cause health injury if plant parts are ingested by children, adults, or pets.
   D. Improper placement of trees can obstruct roadway visibility.
   E. Placing thorny plants where pedestrians may come into contact with them can result in dangerous conditions.
- Improper planning of open space and inattention to the selection of plant materials can lead to fire hazards or unstable slope conditions.
- Poorly designed cut-and-fill grading can lead to soil instability, slides, and erosion, causing property damage and possible loss of life.
- Unsafe pool deck conditions and lack of adequate deck space can cause safety hazards, slippery conditions, and even the possibility of drowning.
- Lack of construction knowledge can jeopardize the safety of the built environment and the welfare of the general public, who are dependent on professionals such as landscape architects to be aware of how the built environment is safely constructed.

Licensure benefits the general public by ensuring a minimum level of qualifications, minimum education requirements, and demonstrated competency through examination and continuing education. Licensure, through a technical board of registration, also provides the general public with an avenue of consumer protection for inadequate or incompetent professional services that cause injury or impacts to the public health, safety, and welfare. Censure, fines, or even removal of the landscape architect's license to practice can result from grievances brought before a state board of technical registration (Bowman).

There are a number of other considerations related to licensure that would impact landscape architects and their profession if professional registration were jeopardized. Loss of licensure would decrease the consumer's options for design services.

Three professions—landscape architecture, engineering, and architecture—often compete for the opportunity to provide similar services such as site planning. The loss of licensure would impact landscape architects' capabilities to compete with engineers and architects, decreasing choices for the general public and possibly causing fees to increase among the other professions. Landscape architects also have an important interdisciplinary relationship with architects and engineers, bringing their specific educational and training background into a synergistic role with the other professions for project planning and design. Loss of landscape architecture licensure would limit consumer opportunities and possibly increase consumer costs.

Licensure of landscape architects puts them on an equal basis with other professionals licensed to perform activities that landscape architects also perform. Licensure is important to clients when it is specified as one of the criteria required for working on a project. When public agencies request licensed landscape architects as the professional of choice for a specific type of design project, a park project, for example, they are making an informed decision to target the professional expertise they believe to be most suitable for the project's requirements.

Licensure also provides economic opportunity for landscape architects. Lack of professional registration may prohibit landscape architects from forming business alliances with other licensed professionals. Without professional registration, landscape architects may not be allowed to form professional corporations (PCs). Landscape architects would be limited to forming business organizations only on a full-corporation basis. They might also be denied or not be able to obtain professional liability insurance coverage. Other opportunities such as licensure reciprocity with other states could be jeopardized. Last, loss of licensure would severely restrict opportunities for landscape architects to perform public services for municipalities, counties, and states (Bowman).

To sum up, licensure may be the best form of regulation to protect public health, safety, and welfare by ensuring a level of competency and qualifying the standard of care practiced by landscape architects. Licensure is important to the profession of landscape architecture, providing a degree of equality with other allied design professionals and a validation of the relevancy of the profession.

Historical Precedent of Landscape Architecture Licensure

According to Dr. Samuel C. Miller (1978), a decline in the quality of medical services resulting from the practice of more apprentice-trained than university-trained doctors led to the first American professional regulatory statute in 1639, designed to control medical profession fees. It was not until 1772, however, that New Jersey became the first state to implement a comprehensive medical practice act, regulating the practice of physicians. By the end of the 1700s, thirteen states had medical licensing laws.

By the mid-nineteenth century, most regulatory statutes had been repealed due to prevailing sentiment in the United States. In the nineteenth century, the spirit of the free marketplace flourished in America, and the distant and wild frontier of the West made enforcing regulations very difficult. The fragmented regulations implemented by states needed the development and evolution of binding national organizations of professional interests to adopt professional practice guidelines and singleness of purpose. Not until a number of national professional organizations were in place by the mid-nineteenth century was there the overall organization and commitment of purpose for professional organizations such as the American Medical Association (established in 1847) to form an ethical code for professions and address criteria such as educational requirements, training, and competency. After national associations were established to guide their respective professions, the impetus and implementation of state licensure picked up momentum again (see table 11-1).

The growth in licensure of professionals developed further impetus after World War II, when credentials and the need to define various areas of professional specialization picked up momentum with the emergence of new forms of technology. The information and knowledge growth that has occurred since the middle of the twentieth century brought with it a realization that we could no longer rely on simplistic or undefined measures of professional and occupational competency. Nevertheless, the significance of national associations to bring uniformity and purpose to their professionals remained a powerful force behind the willingness of states to pass legislation regulating various professions.

TABLE 11-1. Early Formation of National Professional Organizations

Organization	Year Formed	Years during Which 80% of States Adopted Professional Licensure
American Medical Association	1847	1871–1915
American Pharmacists Association	1852	1871–1910
American Institute of Architects	1857	1897–1939
American Dental Association	1859	1881–1930
National Society of Professional Engineers	1934	1921–1950

Source: Miller 1978

Since about 1975, professions have experienced another move toward less government intervention in regulation of professionals. States have increasingly supported sunset review of professional licensure with the aim of reducing costs to administer professional licensure and reducing restriction on fair market competition. Arguments have been advanced that licensure is restrictive and discriminatory and may even be monopolistic in nature. The new emphasis on sunset regulation, if looked at positively, will provide landscape architects with opportunities to strengthen licensure regulation in their own states (Miller 1978).

Legal Considerations of Licensure

Licensure laws have a bipolar nature. They prohibit practice for those who do not qualify for licensure and at the same time provide the basis for making legitimate professional practice available for those who are capable of meeting the licensure requirements.

Licensure boards have the responsibility for policing the professional activities of licensees. Boards have an adjudicatory function as a part of their policing activities. They serve to provide judicial inquiry and legal resolution to allegations of professional wrongdoing or malpractice. They serve as judge and jury in applying adjudicatory power by using peers to evaluate peer activity to determine if wrongdoing has indeed occurred. Licensure boards are obligated to function within constitutional limits in exercising enforcement and police power over the profession. Boards must function within the Fourteenth Amendment rights of individuals for due process. Due process allows a landscape architect accused of professional malpractice the right to be present before peer evaluators and provide evidence on his or her own behalf in defense against the allegations.

The establishment and policing of professional licensure resides legally with states, and the precedent of state sovereignty has been preserved under the Ninth and Tenth Amendments of the U.S. Constitution. The licensing and police power maintained at the state level reinforces the direct relationship between the activities of professions such as landscape architecture and the health, safety, and welfare of the public. One of the most important legal cases that reinforced the applicability of licensure for landscape architects is *Patterson v. The State of New York*. In this case, the court ruled that the "regulation and practice of landscape architecture is clearly related to the public health and welfare, and, as such, constitutes a valid exercise of the police power" (Miller 1978, 18).

One of the issues dealt with by licensure is the concept of relative ignorance, or the capability of a consumer, a landscape architect's client, to make an informed decision about the quality and performance of the professional's services. The landscape architect provides intangible professional services, for which it is difficult to establish standards and objectively measure the quality of the services. The general public is vulnerable to professional practice by landscape architects because the general public may not be able to make an informed decision about the quality of the performance of the services. The client may not become aware of the consequences of poor professional services until some time after the services have been delivered. Licensing provides a level of protection for the consumer—the client—by setting competency levels, removing incompetent practitioners, and providing a body—the technical registration board—to bring grievances to if and when they occur.

State Boards of Technical Registration

Typically, membership on state licensure boards consists of professionals, usually appointed by the governor of the state, of the same profession as is licensed by the board. If the board functions only for landscape architecture registration, the board will comprise landscape architects. If the board governs the professional activities of several professions, such as the state board of technical registration in Arizona, which administers professional registration for architects, assayers, engineers, geologists, land surveyors, and landscape architects, the board will include representatives of each of the professions governed. It is also common to have members of the general public appointed to state registration boards to provide balance and refute arguments that a board might have a conflict of interest if it is made up solely of landscape architects or other professionals trying to govern themselves.

The powers and duties of a state licensure board normally include some or all of the following:

- Adopt rules of conduct of its meetings and performance of the duties spelled out in the enabling legislation.
- Elect a chairperson and other officers of the board.
- Employ staff for board administration as necessary and provided for within authorized funding. The staff may rent office space as needed to carry out the board's mission.
- Adopt an official seal for registered individuals to use on their plans and other documents.
- Set competency, education, and training requirements for professional registration.
- Conduct registration examinations.
- Consider and pass candidates for registration.
- Hear and rule on complaints or charges that a professional has not practiced in accordance with the state registration law.
- Provide for due process in hearing complaints and charges that a professional has not practiced in accordance with the state registration law.
- Keep records of proceedings and other statistics and information about professional registration in the state.
- Administer the regular renewal of individual professional registration.

- Adopt rules and regulations for professional conduct.
- Require evidence of continuing competency of registrants, such as setting provisions for continuing education.

State boards set the regulatory provisions for professional practice. They may require that all public works projects executed in the state, for example, be stamped by the various registrants required to provide the full range of professional expertise needed on the project. The boards will set the limitations, if any, on professional practice, and they will establish classifications of violations. Violations may include some or all of the following, which by law are usually considered misdemeanors:

- Practicing, or offering to practice, landscape architecture without being registered
- Advertising or displaying a card or other device that indicates to the public that one is a landscape architect who is not duly registered
- Assuming or using the title *landscape architect* without being registered
- Using an expired or revoked landscape architecture license
- Presenting false evidence to the technical board of registration with the intent to obtain a license to practice landscape architecture

Each state board will have a review process regarding complaints. In Arizona, the state board of technical registration appoints standing enforcement advisory committees made up of at least four registrants and public members. These committees are used by the board's staff to provide technical assistance in evaluating the disposition of complaints. Members are selected from lists of volunteers and letters of interest and résumés. During the preliminary informal investigation of a complaint, registrants named as respondents are offered an opportunity to appear before an advisory committee for an informal conference related to the complaint. Respondents may elect to appear with or without counsel. The committee attempts to assess the complaint and discuss the complaint with the respondent and others, if deemed necessary, and prepares a recommendation for disposition of the complaint. Respondents can elect not to participate in the informal conference, and no inference will be drawn from a respondent's decision not to attend. The respondent will be advised of the committee's recommendation and will be offered the opportunity to attend an informal compliance conference as part of the informal investigation. After the informal investigation has been completed and the committee recommendation supports a determination that the complaint is unfounded, the committee forwards the recommendation to the board for review and final disposition. In cases where the advisory committee finds probable cause to believe that disciplinary action is warranted, the staff will attempt to obtain a signed consent order for review by the board. The board will be presented with a report of the committee's recommendation, a staff recommendation, and a counterproposal from the defendant.

When the state board receives a report concerning a possible violation, the board will conduct its own investigation. The investigation reports, the advisory committee's recommendations, and any other documents and materials relating to the investigation remain confidential until the matter is closed, a hearing notice is made, or until the matter is settled by consent of the registrant. The registrant will be notified, and the public is allowed to obtain information that an investigation is being conducted and about the general nature of the investigation. After notification, subpoenas may be issued to possible witnesses regarding the complaint. Thereafter a hearing before the board will be scheduled according to the adjudicative rules of the state's Administrative Procedures Act. At any time, either before or after formal disciplinary proceedings have been instituted against a registrant, the registrant may submit to the board an offer of settlement whereby, in lieu of formal disciplinary action by the board, the registrant agrees to accept certain sanctions such as suspension, civil penalties, enrolling in continuing education courses, limiting the scope of his or her practice, submitting his or her work product to professional peer review, or other self-recommended sanctions. If the board determines that the proposed action will adequately protect the public welfare, the board can accept the offer and enter a decision for the record incorporating the proposed settlement.

During the formal hearing process, the board may grant a rehearing by specifying the grounds on which the rehearing is to be granted. The rehearing will deal only with the particular elements specified. If the board determines that a rehearing is impracticable, unnecessary, or contrary to the public interest, the board may issue its decision as final without the opportunity for a rehearing. The registrant may seek judicial review of the decision as a last resort.

Boards also initiate inquiries into malpractice claims. In Arizona, the attorney who files a malpractice claim must file a copy of the complaint with the state board, containing the following information:

1. The name and address of the defendant (e.g., the landscape architect)
2. The name and address of the plaintiff
3. The name and address of each registrant providing services to the plaintiff
4. A statement specifying the nature of the occurrence resulting in the malpractice action

The report is not discoverable and not admissible as evidence. Upon receipt of the report, the board initiates an investigation into the matter to determine if the registrant against whom the complaint is filed is in violation of any provision or rule promulgated by the board.

Government Regulatory Laws and Agencies

Government regulatory laws are enforced by federal and state agencies, which have the power granted by legislative authority to take actions affecting individuals and the practice of landscape architecture. Agencies are created through enabling legislation that spells out the makeup and powers of the agency. Legislative bodies create agencies when a societal problem becomes important enough for legislative leaders to believe that supervisory processes and expert leadership are necessary to regulate and control the problem.

In the 1930s, for example, there was a need to bring the country's workforce out of the underemployment and substandard wages caused by the Great Depression. The United States Congress, at the urging of then-President Franklin Delano Roosevelt, enacted the Fair Labor Standards Act (FLSA), establishing a minimum wage for employees. Congress established regulatory powers for the FLSA under the Department of Labor. The act has been amended many times since then to the point where virtually every employee in the private sector is covered and receives at least the minimum wage, as well as rights involving working hours, overtime pay, and work breaks.

In 1946 Congress enacted the Administrative Procedures Act (APA), which defined and systematized the basic procedural rules for all federal agencies. The APA is the cornerstone of administrative law for federal agencies. The act sets forth the requirements for agencies to publicize their rules in the Federal Register and make documents available to the general public upon request. The APA established rule-making procedures and procedures for review of agency decisions made by each agency. The act also established the scope of judicial review of agency decisions.

The first federal regulatory agency to be established was the Interstate Commerce Commission, which was authorized by Congress in 1887 primarily to regulate railroads. Shortly thereafter, the Food and Drug Administration (1907) and the Federal Trade Commission (1914) were established. A significant introduction of federal agencies occurred in the 1930s as part of President Roosevelt's New Deal. The Securities and Exchange Commission (SEC), the Civil Aeronautics Board (CAB), and the Federal Deposit Insurance Corporation (FDIC) are a few of the federal agencies established in the 1930s. The New Deal agencies tended to target controls needed on specific industries.

The next boom of federal agencies came in the 1960s and 1970s. The agencies established at this time targeted the broader need for social reform and the environmental and health protection of the general public. The Environmental Protection Agency (EPA) was established to control pollution of the environment. The Occupational Safety and Health Administration (OSHA) was established to provide a safe and healthy workplace for the general public. Other federal agencies established in the 1960s and 1970s included the following:

- Consumer Product Safety Commission
- Department of Housing and Urban Development
- Council of Environmental Quality
- Council of Consumer Affairs
- Department of Energy
- Department of Transportation

- Equal Employment Opportunity Commission
- Federal Maritime Commission
- Federal Energy Regulatory Commission
- National Railroad Passenger Corporation
- Nuclear Regulatory Commission
- United States Postal Service

(Meiners, Ringleb, and Edwards 1988)

There are two basic types of administrative agencies: executive agencies that fall under the Executive Office of the President and independent agencies.

Executive agencies include the Food and Drug Administration, the Nuclear Regulatory Agency, the Internal Revenue Service, and the Occupational Safety and Health Administration. The heads of executive agencies are appointed by the president.

Independent agencies have been created by Congress to act in a more politically impartial fashion. Membership and leadership are controlled by the enabling legislation to spread out the makeup of the agency among the political parties. The independent agencies are normally headed by a board or commission that allows only a slight majority to be of the same political party. The independent agencies are very active, and a great deal of federal regulations originate with them.

The powers of regulatory agencies generally fall under three categories: investigative power, rule-making power, and adjudicatory power.

Each regulatory agency needs information to control and regulate the agency's administrative area of responsibility. The agencies need information about the industries and activities they are charged with regulating so they can identify violators, and so they can identify areas where the regulations need to be modified or strengthened. Much of the information needed by regulatory agencies must come from the industries, businesses, and individuals the agencies regulate. One can imagine that industries, businesses, and individuals may be reluctant to provide information, especially if an infraction of the regulations may be in question. Industries, businesses, and individuals normally desire to protect their privacy and avoid costs associated with providing information to regulatory agencies. If a regulatory agency requests information, and the information supplied is inadequate or suspicious, the agencies have the powers of subpoena and search and seizure as means to obtain information from industries, businesses, and individuals unwilling to provide information. These powers give the agencies the teeth they need to enforce their areas of responsibility. All investigations of industries, businesses, and individuals must be for a relevant and lawful purpose based on a suspicion of some infraction of the regulations governed by the regulatory agency. Requests for information must be specific and not unreasonably burdensome. The Requests must also not violate the Fifth Amendment rights of the industry, business, or individual (Metzger et al. 1989).

The rule-making power of agencies is governed by the enabling legislation that established the agency. Rules generally take three forms: substantive, interpretive, or procedural.

Substantive rules have the same effect as legislation enacted by Congress. In establishing a substantive rule, the agency must follow the rules set down by the APA. The agency is required to conduct a hearing where interested parties and experts have the opportunity to present background information and arguments either in favor of the proposed rule or against it. The APA does have a provision for allowing an agency to develop a rule without going through the public hearing process if there is good cause that the rule is necessary and the public hearing process would be impractical or unnecessary. Reasons for an agency to develop a rule without going through the public hearing process include expediency and urgency of the need for the rule where the time needed for the public hearing process may not be in the public interest.

Interpretive rules are set out by the agencies to guide and interpret the responsibilities of the agencies. The rules may be general policy statements or strict regulations that have binding effects on industries, businesses, and individuals. The agency is not required to follow the public hearing process when setting interpretive rules. The rules are usually based on the expert opinions of the staff and consultants working for the agency. However, laws allow industries, businesses, and individuals that would be adversely affected by the interpretive rules to legally challenge the rule. If the rule is successfully challenged, the agency is usually required to go through a public hearing process regarding the proposed rule.

Procedural rules are developed by agencies to make the industries, businesses, and individuals aware of the operations and practices of each agency. The authority to set procedural rules is governed by the enabling leg-

islation that establishes each agency (Meiners, Ringleb, and Edwards 1988).

Agency Processes and Procedures

Agency processes and procedures fall under two general categories: day-to-day, informal procedures and formal procedures including investigations and adjudicatory hearings.

Informal, discretionary procedures are developed by each agency to cover day-to-day operations including activities such as processing regulatory applications and permits; advising industry, business, and individuals; negotiating resolution to regulatory issues; and providing for the ongoing supervision of industry, business, and individuals as related to the agency's regulatory responsibility.

Publicity is one of the informal procedures used by agencies to pressure industry, business, and individuals to conform with regulatory procedures. If an industrial plant is polluting the groundwater by discharging harmful chemicals, the EPA may use publicity in the local media as part of the corrective measures, in addition to using the agency's full regulatory powers. The publicity is coercive in nature and also designed to build public support for the EPA's regulatory actions, which could include the plant's paying fines and the costs of remedying the pollution.

The agencies' formal procedures include investigations and adjudicatory hearings. Investigations are carried out through the public hearing process, following rules established under the APA. The hearing results in rules or regulations that will be used by the agency in exercising its authority over industry, business, and individuals. The APA requires the agency to publish a proposed rule that results from an investigation and hearing in the Federal Register. Under the APA's informal policies for developing rules, interested parties may comment on the proposed rule. A full hearing involving testimony and expert witnesses is not usually carried out. Under formal APA procedures, on the other hand, the agency *is* obligated to engage a formal investigative hearing with proceedings on the record. Public-interest groups and other concerned individuals may bring forth expert witnesses to testify regarding the proposed rule. The witnesses will be cross-examined. The process also allows for appeals if the affected industry, business, or individuals are unhappy with the outcome of the hearing and the rule. The industry, business, and individuals also have the opportunity to seek review through the federal courts.

Adjudicatory hearings also follow APA procedures. Such hearings are used to initiate a ruling against an entity or individual as opposed to an industry-wide or broader audience. To initiate an adjudicatory hearing, the agency files a complaint against a specific business believed to be violating an agency rule or regulation. The decision reached in the adjudicatory hearing is applicable only to the specific business and not to the industry as a whole.

If a complaint is filed, the business must respond to the allegations. The agency will research the alleged rule infractions and develop a case against the specific business. The business, of course, will develop its defensive posture. The hearing will be presided over by a judge who is a civil servant of the agency holding the hearing. The hearing is carried out very much like a trial, including the presentation of evidence and the examination and cross-examination of witnesses. Upon completion of the hearing, the agency law judge will render an opinion. If the decision is acceptable to the specific business, the decision is implemented by the agency. If the business is not satisfied with the decision, the business may appeal to the commissioners of the agency and then the federal court system (Meiners, Ringleb, and Edwards 1988).

Legal and Legislative Restrictions

The checks and balances on the powers of agencies are provided by both the federal courts and the legislature.

Industries, businesses, and individuals affected by agency rules may appeal decisions and rules in federal courts. The process is called *judicial review* and is intended to see that agencies follow appropriate legal procedures and uphold the constitutional and legal rights of industry, business, and individuals. In order to challenge an agency decision in federal court, the industry, business, or individual must have *standing*— a ruling that is entitled to protection under the law. Without standing, the industry, business, or individual is not entitled to seek judicial review. The criteria for determining if an industry, business, or individual has standing is whether the agency's action or rule has caused legitimate injury to the industry, business, or individual seeking judicial review.

The judicial review will look at three areas of the agency's regulatory power. First, the court will examine the agency's approach with regard to its substantive determinants. Have the facts been thoroughly explained? Do the facts have some basis in the agency's record? Do the facts present a logical explanation such that a reasonable person would reach a similar conclusion?

Second, the court will examine the agency's statutory interpretation. The court will look at the agency's implementation of the congressional statutes that authorize the power of the agency.

Third, the courts will examine the agency's procedures to see if the agency has acted fairly and has not violated its own established procedures.

Congress also serves as a watchdog on agency actions. Congress can revoke agency power and use its funding authority to cut or support agency programs. In order to keep abreast of agency activities, Congress requires agencies to make reports on their activities. Congress also holds veto power over any agency regulation and uses the veto power if it finds the regulatory agency's actions inconsistent with the power and objectives of the agency (Meiners, Ringleb, and Edwards 1988).

Last, Congress has used sunset laws as a control over agencies. Sunset laws require the agency's need, effectiveness, value, and procedures to be reviewed on a periodic basis, such as every ten years. If the agency is found to serve no further public value, it is abolished, or the sun is allowed to set on it. Landscape architects are particularly familiar with sunset laws related to professional licensure. Many states have adopted sunset laws that require review of landscape architecture professional registration and its value to serving the public needs. Many groups of landscape architects throughout the country have been involved in defending the value of technical registration of landscape architects to their state legislatures.

Tort Law and Negligence

Tort law frequently has the greatest impact on the professional practice of landscape architecture. This does not mean that other branches of law, such as contract, administrative, or regulatory law, do not affect professional practice. They do. Tort law, however, is a civil wrongdoing against another entity or person where there is a breach of a legal obligation to the entity or person resulting in a legally defined harm to the entity or the person. The courts will provide a remedy for the wrongdoing in the form of payment of actual or compensatory damages, and in cases of particularly repulsive wrongdoing, the courts may also award punitive damages.

Tort law is important to the professional landscape architect because claims of negligence, strict liability, and intentional tort fall under this section of the law. Under tort law, landscape architects have a duty, simply put, not to injure or damage another person by negligent acts.

Negligence

Michael B. Metzger et al. give the following definition in their text *Business Law and the Regulatory Environment:* "Negligence essentially involves an unintentional breach of a legal duty owed to another that results in some legally recognizable injury to the other's person or property" (Metzger et al. 1988, 95).

The injured party that sues a landscape architect for negligence must prove that the landscape architect had a duty not to injure the party, that the landscape architect actually breached the duty, and that the landscape architect's breach was the actual and legal cause of the injury to the party.

If the professional conduct of a landscape architect is carried on below the expected standards established to protect the public, a lawsuit for negligence may inevitably be brought against the landscape architect. In addition to the elements of proof discussed in the previous section, the courts apply the concept of the standard of care in assessing whether a landscape architect has carried out professional practice negligently. The standard of care is the obligation of the landscape architect to provide professional services with the ordinary degree of skill that would be expected of other reasonably competent landscape architects under the same set of conditions.

Duty Not to Injure the Party

In proving that a landscape architect has been negligent, the courts will rely on the standard of care and attempt to prove that the landscape architect has not acted with reasonable care. The initial question facing the courts is whether the landscape architect has a

duty to protect his or her client from the harm that has occurred. The legal duty can be established by the contract between the landscape architect and the client. Professional licensure provides another basis for determining the duty of the landscape architect to his or her client. Statutes and codes provide other reasons for determining that the landscape architect has a specified duty to be aware of the statutes and codes and not act negligently in relation to the areas of service covered by the statutes or codes. If a landscape architect violates a statute or a code, he or she may be guilty of negligence if the statute has been designed to protect the client or the general public. The courts usually find that violating a statute is conclusive evidence that a landscape architect has acted negligently. The bottom line applied by the courts is the consideration of whether the risk caused to the injured person is unreasonable. In reaching a conclusion, the courts will assess whether the risk caused to the injured party could have been easily avoided by the landscape architect against the possibility that injury might have occurred and how serious the injury is. As the risk of injury to the general public increases, the duty of the landscape architect to act without negligence also increases (Metzger et al. 1989).

Did the Landscape Architect Actually Breach the Duty?

In determining if the landscape architect has breached his or her duty, the courts must find that the landscape architect's actions were in fact the actual cause of the injury or damage to the person. Courts apply the concept that the landscape architect's actions are the actual cause and the injury would not have occurred but for the landscape architect's breach of duty. The landscape architect's responsibility will be for the actual results of the harmful act.

One of the courts' interpretations of actual cause is also one of the main defenses to claims of negligence. The courts may determine that if the landscape architect could not have reasonably foreseen an injury to a party, the landscape architect may not owe a duty or remedy to the injured party. In other words, if the landscape architect has followed all of the statutes and codes by designing a safety railing, and a person sues the landscape architect because he or she fell over the railing and was injured, the courts may find that the landscape architect acted with the proper standard of care and may drop the charge of negligence. On the other hand, courts will not side with the landscape architect if the injured party can prove that he or she was truly seeking to avoid an injury that was caused by the landscape architect's negligence.

Another way that a landscape architect can be relieved of negligence is by *superseding* or *intervening causes*. In certain situations, an intervening cause occurs in addition to or after the fact of an allegation of a landscape architect's negligent act. If a tree branch above a bench in a courtyard falls on a person and seriously injures the person, a suit may be brought against the landscape architect for negligence. If the landscape architect can prove that the cause of the tree branch falling off was improper maintenance, pruning, and watering of the tree, the court may decide that this intervening cause is the real reason the tree branch fell off, and the landscape architect would be absolved of the responsibility for negligence. If the intervening actions are the primary cause to the injury, courts are very likely to agree and the landscape architect would be exonerated (Metzger et al. 1989).

Another situation is *contributory negligence*. In this case, if the landscape architect proves that the injured party caused or contributed to the harm done, the landscape architect may not be liable even though his or her negligence was a contributing factor. The concept of contributory negligence means that the injured person also has a responsibility for acting within his or her own standard of care to avoid injury. Attempting to prove contributory negligence is a proactive defense against negligence that must be initiated by the landscape architect (Schoumacher 1986).

In today's litigious world, the notion of contributory negligence is one of the other defenses against accusations of negligence. If a landscape architect is part of a design team and a lawsuit is brought due to an injury on the project site, the courts may find that several of the consultants contributed to the cause and distribute the damages among the design consultants. A landscape architect's attorney often uses this type of defense position to spread out the financial responsibility in cases of alleged negligence where a design team of a number of consultants worked on the project (Schoumacher 1986).

The Landscape Architect's Negligence Is the Actual and Legal Cause of the Injury

The third element of a negligence case brought against a landscape architect is the burden of proving that the landscape architect actually broke a law. Unfortunately, this is normally the easiest part of the alleged negligence to prove. If an injury occurs, it is relatively easy to prove. Shades of gray occur when the injuries are claimed to be emotional in nature. The courts are much more reluctant to award claims based on emotional injury. To be successful, the injured party must prove the emotional injury was the result of a landscape architect's negligence. Although this may be difficult, the courts have evolved into a slightly more lenient stance regarding emotional injury if the plaintiff can prove that the emotional injury was a foreseeable consequence of the landscape architect's negligence (Metzger et al. 1989).

Strict Liability

"Strict liability means that defendants who participate in certain harm-producing activities may be held *strictly liable* for any harm that results to others, even though they did not intend to cause the harm and did everything in their power to prevent it" (Metzger et al. 1989, 113). Strict liability is less likely to be a legal problem for the landscape architect, but it may enter into unique situations such as zoo design. If a wild animal escapes and causes injury to a party, regardless of how careful the zookeeper may have been in keeping the animal confined or how carefully the landscape architect designed the enclosure to prevent the wild animal from escaping, both the zoo and the landscape architect may be sued and held strictly liable for the injury (Schoumacher 1986).

Intentional Torts

The last type of tort violation that a landscape architect could be involved in is a case where the injured party contends that the landscape architect intended to cause harm. Examples of intentional torts are trespassing, libel, slander, defamation, invasion of privacy, battery, and assault. Although these activities are less likely to result from the day-to-day practice of professional landscape architecture, people, being people, can and do get themselves into situations where they are accused of intentionally harming another person.

Trespassing is a good example of an intentional tort that a landscape architect may be accused of while carrying out a site analysis. The landscape architect may plead that he or she was not aware of straying onto property clearly posted with Do Not Trespass signs, but if a particularly angry or litigious landowner doesn't agree that the trespassing was unintentional and wants to press charges, he or she is well within legal rights to do so.

Libel and slander are two other intentional torts that may enter into a landscape architect's realm, if anger over a client or another professional occurs. *Defamation* is the tortious act of injuring a person's reputation thorough false and defamatory statements. *Libel* is written or printed defamation. *Slander* is verbal defamation. There may be times in the professional practice history of a landscape architect where he or she feels deeply wronged by a client or another allied professional. If the landscape architect says or writes something defamatory about the client or the allied professional, the landscape architect may be opening up himself or herself to a lawsuit based on defamation. The best word for the wise here is to control your temper, because if you can't, you may have to face the rather ugly allegation of defamation.

Most landscape architects who carry out their professional practice honestly and with a high degree of respect for the personal rights of their fellow citizens should be able to avoid intentional torts.

Labor Relations

This section covers many of the key laws affecting employer/employee relations. Because almost all landscape architecture firms become employers, the laws and issues concerning the rights and responsibilities of the employees play an important role in the legal environment of business.

A number of federal laws have affected labor and management relationships in the twentieth century. These laws include the Norris–La Guardia Act, the Wagner Act, the Taft-Hartley Act, the Landrum-Griffin Act, and the National Labor Relations Act. These laws generally relate to employees' rights to organize in unions and how unions must legally carry out their business of organizing and collective bargaining. Federal laws also cover labor considerations such as right-to-work, minimum wage, and worker's compensation laws. Federal laws also cover worker's safety, health, retirement rights, and whistle-blower protection. In general these laws do not significantly impact landscape architecture firms and relations with their employees.

The National Labor Relations Board (NLRB) is the governing board with the responsibility to administer the National Labor Relations Act. Five board-members and a general counsel are appointed by the president and confirmed by the U.S. Senate.

The NLRB has statutory jurisdiction over all employers where interstate commerce is carried on. The NLRB generally does not get involved with jurisdiction over small employers with a local business orientation. As such, the NLRB would be unlikely to exercise authority over the practice of most landscape architecture firms. The remainder of this section covers those federal and state laws that have more of a bearing on landscape architecture private practice.

Employment-at-Will

Under common law, employees serve employers at will. Employers may discharge employees for any cause or reason at their will and discretion, and employees may leave their employment at any time for any reason. Specific terms of an employment contract can alter employment-at-will law by containing employment terms such as a specific length of time the employee will be employed or the specific tasks that the employment contract covers.

Most states have laws that prevent discharging an employee for refusing to carry out acts that are illegal, unethical, or against public policy. In most states, employees cannot be fired at will for the following reasons:

- Refusing to carry out an illegal act
- Serving a public duty such as jury duty
- Seeking a right governed by law, such as filing a worker's compensation claim

Some states also include what has become known as whistle-blower protection. Whistle-blowing occurs if an employee is aware of an illegal act and tells authorities about it. The whistle-blower may not be terminated by the employer for his or her actions (Meiners, Ringleb, and Edwards 1988).

Minimum Wage

The Fair Labor Standards Act (FLSA) passed by Congress in 1938 set the first federal minimum wage standards. The first minimum wage was set in 1938 at $.25 per hour. In 1996 the minimum wage is $4.25 per hour.

As a general rule, employees must be paid for all of the time they are at work when that time is not used for personal reasons. An employee must be paid at least the minimum wage for each hour worked in the work week. If the average hourly earnings, not including overtime, in each work week equal the minimum wage rate per hour, the minimum wage requirement is considered to be met. Hourly employees must be paid at least the current minimum wage rate per hour. Salaried employees' pay must also meet the minimum wage rate for the hours worked. The salary, divided by the hours worked in the work week, must meet minimum wage requirements.

The FLSA allows employers some latitude to employ interns or trainees at an hourly rate below the prevailing minimum wage. The rate can be as low as 85 percent of the minimum wage. There are a number of requirements, however, that must be met:

- The trainee and the employer must be aware that the trainee is not entitled to full compensation during the training period.
- The trainee understands that the employer is not obligated to provide a job at the conclusion of the training period.
- The training is not unique and is like an extension of school.
- The training period is for the benefit of the trainee.
- The trainee does not replace regular employees.
- The employer does not receive a business advantage by employing the trainee.
- The employer has not laid off regular employees in order to employ the trainee.
- The proportion of hours worked by trainees cannot exceed 25 percent of the hours worked by all employees.
- The employer must provide the trainee with a written notice of the requirements of the training program.
- The training period cannot exceed ninety days (London 1991).

Worker's Compensation Laws

Under worker's compensation laws enacted by state governments, employers are required to pay a benefit to an employee or an employee's heirs for injuries or death that occur on the job. Individual states set the level of benefits. The premiums are paid by all employers and relieve the employer from damage suits related to job injuries.

There are five typical benefits paid under worker's compensation laws: death, total disability, permanent partial disability, temporary partial disability, and medical expenses.

Worker's compensation insurance rates are set by category of employee and the degree to which the category of employment may be hazardous. In a landscape architecture firm, a person who goes out to sites for construction observation activities will have a higher insurance rate than a draftsperson or secretary. Rates are also lower overall if a firm has a good safety record and low or no claims.

Claims made against worker's compensation insurance are generally cut and dried. The worker must be injured from an accident that occurred in the course of employment. As employers, landscape architecture firms must be sensitive to any and all worker's compensation claims. The firm must inform employees of their worker's compensation insurance rights. If an injury occurs, the welfare of the employee must be of immediate concern to the employer (Meiners, Ringleb, and Edwards 1988).

OSHA and Workers' Personal Job Safety

All landscape architecture firms have an obligation to provide a safe and healthful work environment. Workers' rights to a safe workplace were legalized when Congress passed legislation establishing the Occupational Safety and Health Administration. That year, the National Safety Council published the startling facts that over fourteen thousand workers die on the job each year and over two million workers suffer disabling injuries (Meiners, Ringleb, and Edwards 1988, 207).

The act establishing OSHA requires employers to comply with workplace safety standards and to keep records of work-related injuries, illnesses, and death due to job-related accidents. Employers are obligated to provide a work environment free from recognized hazards that may cause death, injury, or hardship. OSHA's regulations also encourage employers to implement safety and health education programs. OSHA compliance is required of every employer, and the law encompasses virtually all employers, including landscape architecture firms. Self-employed individuals are exempt.

OSHA's standards are developed by the National Institute of Occupational Safety and Health (NIOSH). One of NIOSH's main purposes is carrying out research related to work-environment safety in occupations prone to job-related injury. An advisory committee consisting of a representative from industry and public members establishes and amends standards governing workplace safety. Proposed OSHA standards are published in the Federal Register, at which time the public and interested parties have the opportunity to comment on the proposed regulations. A public meeting may be held. After receiving public and industry input, the secretary of labor approves the standard and it becomes law (Meiners, Ringleb, and Edwards 1988).

OSHA has the authority not only to set workplace safety standards but also to make inspections to see that the standards are being met. OSHA inspectors may issue citations and fines for conditions believed to violate OSHA regulations. Because OSHA's staff of inspectors cannot possibly inspect all of the five million businesses in the United States, OSHA has prioritized the categories of businesses to inspect. The first priority is workplace environments that present imminent danger situations. There are workplaces where it is reasonably certain that dangerous working conditions may prevail. The steel industry is an example. The second priority focuses on fatalities and catastrophes resulting in five or more workers being hospitalized. Again, in an attempt to avoid similar accidents in the future, OSHA staff will make inspections to determine if OSHA regulations have been violated.

An OSHA inspection will begin with the inspector's meeting a representative of the employer and a representative of the employees. The inspector will review the workplace conditions and the employer's records of health problems, noise, ventilation, and use of hazardous materials. The workplace inspection will include looking for signs of possible health safety risks such as odors, dust, fumes, excessive noise, chemicals, and other dangerous substances.

After reviewing possible hazards, the inspector will take samples, make measurements, and use equipment designed to determine levels of noise, dust, and other hazards. These measurements will be used as evidence if a citation is made.

The OSHA inspector will also determine if the employer has implemented engineering or administrative measures to control workplace injury and if personal protective devices are provided by the employer and properly used by employees. The inspector will ascertain if the employer monitors health hazards, provides regular medical exams to identify possible health problems, and if the employer conducts safety training programs.

At the end of the inspection, the OSHA inspector will meet with both the employer and employee representatives. If a citation is issued, employees have the right to refuse work assignments that may present hazardous working conditions. Employees also have the right to oversee the employer's correction of hazards within the schedule set by the OSHA inspector.

Another of OSHA's important activities is issuing Hazard Communication Standards, with which all employers must comply. Hazard Communication Standards deal primarily with the hazards of chemicals produced or imported by chemical manufacturers. The standards require all employers to inform their employees about the hazardous materials they might be exposed to. Employers must develop and implement a written hazard communication program describing procedures for using the materials safely and providing information about safety precautions and what to do if accidents occur.

Restricting smoking in the workplace is another consideration, although not expressly covered by OSHA regulations, that employers such as landscape architecture firms must be sensitive to. Most firms develop a nonsmoking policy that limits smoking to certain areas in the workplace. The main consideration in developing a nonsmoking policy is that it must withstand legal challenge based upon discrimination.

Video display terminals (VDTs) are another work-related concern that has become significant since 1980 with the rapid advancement of the use of computers in the workplace. Again, OSHA has no regulatory authority over VDTs, but state and local levels of government have made attempts to regulate the impact of VDTs on users of computers. Some of the recommendations include introducing ergonomically designed equipment to reduce eye and wrist strain, adjustable chairs, glare shields, and effective lighting conditions (London 1991).

Firing an Employee

One of the most traumatic events that can occur in a landscape architecture firm is the firing of an employee. It is not easy for either the employer or the employee. For the employer, there is the ever-present possibility that firing an employee may lead to a lawsuit for unjust termination or wrongful discharge.

The concept of employment-at-will, discussed earlier, generally prevails in workplace law. Wrongful termination is a recent legal development that generally works in favor of employees and provides a legal basis whereby employees may be dismissed only for just cause because they have a right to their job. Wrongful discharge is big news nowadays. There is hardly a newspaper printed that doesn't sooner or later carry stories of cases where employees have been legally exonerated for wrongful termination and have been awarded large sums of money for back pay and punitive damages. The employer also may be required to reinstate the employee who has been wrongfully terminated.

How do the managers of a landscape architecture firm go about firing an employee if the need arises? First, the termination should be planned. Avoid spur-of-the-moment actions perhaps brought on by anger or frustration at a perceived lack of proper performance. Most authorities on this matter agree that a paper trail is important documentation should an employee need to be terminated. The documentation should be specific and filed in the employee's personnel file. It should describe specific cases of improper performance, such as insubordination, tardiness, lack of qualifications to carry out duties, or harassment of other employees. The reason may also be because of a decline in business or the termination of a major contract, requiring a reduction in office staff. Each written incidence with regard to the employee's performance should also be accompanied by a sit-down talk with the employee to discuss the improper behavior and to inform the employee that a report will be filed in his or her employee file.

The following considerations should be used as a guide in handling the actual termination of an employee:

- The landscape architecture firm's managers or owners should review the need to fire an employee and obtain concurrence.
- Clearly understand the reasons for terminating the employee. Be clear that the reasons are not discriminatory.
- Check out the situation and reasons for firing the employee with the firm's attorney.
- Make sure that the firm has an established policy for firing employees and that it is followed for each dismissal.
- When the decision is final, set a private, personal meeting with the employee being terminated.
- During the meeting, state the reasons for the termination. Be brief, because the termination will be traumatic for both employer and employee. Stick to the facts.
- Allow the employee to respond, but keep in control of the meeting and do not hesitate or waver in the decision to let the employee go. Let the employee know that the decision is final and irrevocable.
- Keep the decision discreet and keep the reasons for firing the employee to yourself and the managers who have made the decision.
- Prepare in advance and have ready to give to the employee all final paychecks, vacation pay, other benefits, and severance pay if it is firm policy and possible financially. If severance pay is provided, the firm may request the employee to sign an agreement not to file a lawsuit for wrongful termination.
- Request that the employee remove all personal property from the office and leave by a set time.
- Notify the employee during the termination meeting of his or her rights to legal employment benefits such as health protection under COBRA laws.
- Let the employee know that you will assist him or her in any way possible with the transition and seeking new employment.
- After the meeting, the manager may wish to take a brief period of time alone, away from

the office setting, to regroup emotionally. During this time, review the facts leading to the dismissal and accept the facts as they are. Avoid remorse.

The legal basis for firing an employee is strengthened by having well-planned company policies, including employment agreements, employee handbooks, performance evaluation forms, and a standard letter format for termination. The importance of the paper trail cannot be emphasized enough. The firm should practice a progressive disciplinary policy that includes a sequence of warnings about the employee's performance. At each step, let the employee know that if the employee does not make corrective measures, he or she will face dismissal. Refer to chapter 3 to see how some of the firms' employment policies set up the progressive sequence of reprimands (London 1991).

Employee Retirement Income Security Act (ERISA)

In 1974 the federal government enacted the Employee Retirement Income Security Act (ERISA) to regulate private employee retirement plans. The legislation was enacted as a countermeasure to growing concerns over employers who set up employee retirement benefits programs only to go out of business and leave employees without the retirement benefits they had planned on.

Employee retirement plans are voluntarily set up and maintained by landscape architecture firms for the benefit of the owners and employees. Pension plans are established specifically to provide income at retirement. ERISA also covers other employee benefits such as health insurance, disability insurance programs, vacation benefits, day care provisions, scholarship funds, prepaid legal services, deferred income programs, apprenticeship, and training benefits.

ERISA sets uniform standards to ensure the equitable character of employee benefit plans and the financial soundness of the plans in order to provide employees with the benefits promised by the landscape architecture firm. The statutory and regulatory authority to implement ERISA is the Pension and Welfare Benefits Administration (PWBA) under the U.S. Department of Labor, as well as the Internal Revenue Service (IRS). The PWBA carries out Title I

administration of the act, which requires employers who manage and control pension plan funds to

- carry out duties in a prudent manner and refrain from conflict-of-interest transactions expressly prohibited by law, for the exclusive benefit of participants and beneficiaries;
- comply with limitations on investments in employer securities and properties;
- fund benefits in accordance with the law and plan rules;
- report and disclose information on the operations and financial condition of plans to the government and to participants;
- provide documents required in the conduct of investigations to assure compliance with the law.

Part I of Title I requires the administrator of an employee benefit plan to furnish participants and beneficiaries with a summary plan description, describing in understandable terms their rights, benefits, and responsibilities under the plan. Plan administrators are also required to furnish participants with a summary of any material changes to the plan or to the information contained in the summary plan description. Each year, the plan administrator must file an annual report (Form 5500) containing financial and other information concerning the operation of the pension plan. Plans with 100 or more participants must file Form 5500 every year. Plans with fewer than 100 participants must file the form at least every third year. The forms are filed with the IRS, which furnishes the information to the Department of Labor. Plans with fewer than 100 participants that are fully insured are not required to file annual reports. Plan administrators are required to furnish participants and beneficiaries with a summary of the information contained in the annual report. ERISA guarantees that some retirement benefits will be received by participants in a pension plan, largely by overseeing that plans are adequately funded to meet the pension payout requirements.

Part 4 of Title I includes the standards and rules governing the conduct of pension plan fiduciaries—those persons who exercise the discretionary authority in managing the investments of the pension plan and disposition of its assets. Fiduciaries are required to discharge their duties solely in the interest of the plan's participants and beneficiaries and for the exclusive purpose of providing benefits and defraying reasonable expenses of administering the plan. In discharging their duties, fiduciaries must act prudently and in accordance with documents governing the plan, to the extent such documents are consistent with ERISA.

ERISA gives substantial law-enforcement authority to the Department of Labor. The law gives the Department of Labor investigatory powers and the authority to bring a civil action to correct violations of the law. Criminal penalties will be imposed on any person who violates the law.

The PWBA has a wide range of general publications designed to assist employers and employees in understanding their obligations and rights under ERISA. A listing of publications available can be obtained by writing to: Publications Desk, PWBA, Division of Public Affairs, Room N-5511, 200 Constitution Avenue NW, Washington, DC 20210. The PWBA also has a public disclosure center where materials such as examples of summary plan descriptions may be reviewed. Copies of materials may also be obtained by writing to the center.

Consolidated Omnibus Budget Reconciliation Act (COBRA)

Passed in 1985, COBRA covers group health plans of employers with twenty or more employees on a typical workday in the previous calendar year. COBRA provides an employee the opportunity to continue health coverage under the landscape architecture firm's health insurance program at the employee's own expense at a cost comparable to what it would be if the employee were still a member of the group plan. In 1989 COBRA was amended to require employers to provide coverage for former employees who may have a medical condition that precludes them from getting coverage under a new plan. Spouses and dependent children of employees are covered due to death of the employee, divorce, or legal separation. Coverage must be provided for at least eighteen months. The employer may stop coverage if the employee does not pay the premium or if the individual becomes covered under another health plan.

COBRA requires employers and health plan administrators to determine specific rights of beneficiaries with respect to election, notification, and type of health plan coverage. Plans must give individuals an initial general notice informing them of their rights under COBRA and describing the law.

The Department of Labor and the Internal Revenue Service have regulatory and interpretive responsibility for COBRA. If a landscape architecture firm qualifies for meeting COBRA requirements and fails to comply with the law, the following penalties may be assessed:

- Loss of federal income-tax deduction for the health plan.
- Cost of coverage for highly compensated individuals would become taxable.
- The plan fiduciary and the administrator are liable for $100 per day personal damages for failure to give notice of the plan if requested by an employee.
- Attorney's fees and court costs may be awarded for mishandling fiduciary responsibility.

One last note about COBRA: Although the law applies to firms that employ twenty or more people, the concept of providing continuing health insurance coverage to employees who may leave the smaller landscape architecture firm is a good idea. If the employee is willing to pay for the coverage, many firms might consider adopting the terms of COBRA as a goodwill gesture to persons leaving the firm.

Family and Medical Leave Act

The Family and Medical Leave Act (FMLA) became public law in 1993. The act is intended to provide a means for employees to balance their work and family life by taking reasonable unpaid leave for certain reasons. The act is intended to promote the stability and economic security of the family unit and the national interests in preserving the integrity of family life.

The FMLA is applicable to any employer that has fifty or more employees for each working day during at least twenty calendar weeks or more in the current or preceding calendar year. All public agencies of state and local governments, some federal agencies, and local education agencies (schools) are covered by the law.

In order to eligible for FMLA leave, an employee must be employed by a covered employer and work at a site where at least fifty employees are employed, must have worked at least twelve months for the employer, and must have worked at least 1,250 hours during the twelve months immediately preceding the FMLA leave. The FMLA provides an entitlement of up to twelve weeks of unpaid leave during any twelve months for the following reasons:

- Birth of a child or placement for adoption or foster care of a child
- To care for an immediate family member (spouse, child, or parent) who has a serious health condition
- For the employee's own serious health condition

Employers must maintain group health benefits that an employee was receiving at the time family leave begins. An employee may elect or the employer may require the use of any accrued paid leave time (vacation, sick, or personal) for periods of unpaid family leave. Employees may also take family leave in blocks of time less than the full twelve weeks on an intermittent or reduced leave basis.

When family leave is foreseeable, such as for birthing or child care after the time of birth, an employee must provide the employer with at least thirty days notice of the need for the leave. If the leave is not foreseeable, the employee must give notice as soon as is practicable. An employer is allowed to require medical certification of a serious health problem with the employee. Periodic reports on the status of the health condition may also be required in relation to the employee's status and intent to return to work, as well as fitness for duty upon return to work.

When the employee returns from family leave, the employee is entitled to be restored to the same job that he or she left when the family leave time commenced. In the event that the same job is not available, the employer must place the employee in an equivalent job with equivalent pay, responsibilities, and benefits. The employee is not entitled to accrue benefits during periods of unpaid family leave.

Employers are required to publish and post a notice for employees that outlines the basic provisions of FMLA and are subject to a civil penalty and fine for willfully failing to post the notice. Employers are prohibited from discriminating against or interfering with employees who take family leave.

FMLA is administered by the U.S. Department of Labor, Employment Standards Administration's Wage and Hour Division. Employees may file complaints with this division, usually through the nearest office of the Wage and Hour Division. Employees also have private legal rights of action under the law without involving the federal department. The secretary of the department of labor, however, may file suit to ensure compliance with FMLA and recover damages if a complaint cannot be resolved administratively.

A number of states have family leave statutes. Nothing in the FMLA, however, supersedes a provision of state law that is more beneficial to the employee, and employers must comply with the more beneficial provision. Under some circumstances, an employee with a disability may have rights for similar leave time under the Americans with Disabilities Act.

The American with Disabilities Act (ADA)

In 1988 Congress passed the Americans with Disabilities Act. The act has been considered landmark legislation that is hoped to end discrimination for more than forty million physically and mentally handicapped persons.

There has been some controversy about the law and the huge sums of money that will be required over time to retrofit existing facilities and plan new facilities for accessibility. Another concern has been the term used in the legislation to describe accessibility as *reasonable accommodation*. The term is not precise, and it will be left to the courts over a long period of time to decide by case law what facility adjustments indeed provide reasonable access. The legislation itself provides some guidance on what Congress intended as reasonable accommodation. The main intent is to remove any physical barriers that might jeopardize a person's right to employment.

The ADA provides that no employer may discriminate against a qualified individual with a disability with regard to job application, hiring, advancement, compensation, training, and any other conditions of employment. If the qualified individual with a disability can perform the necessary work duties with reasonable accommodation, he or she can not be discriminated against.

The ADA describes discrimination as follows:

- Limiting, segregating, or defining job requirements to adversely affect employment opportunities of disabled persons
- Participating in a contract or other business arrangement that would affect an employee with a disability and discriminate against the employee with the disability
- Using administrative standards or methods that cause discrimination
- Not making reasonable accommodations for known disabilities of an otherwise qualified employee unless the business can demonstrate that the accommodation is an undue hardship
- Denying employment to an otherwise qualified person who has a disability
- Using qualifications or job testing that would screen out individuals with a disability
- Failing to develop job screening tests that are fair to the otherwise qualified person who has a disability

An employer is not required to accommodate a disabled person if doing so poses an undue hardship that is significantly difficult or very costly to implement. In determining if the accommodations would cause undue hardship, the factors to be considered include

- the extent and cost of the accommodation,
- the financial resources of the business,
- the number of people employed at the business,
- the type of operation of the facility.

In short, businesses that are more able to finance accommodations will be required to fund more significant handicap accommodations than small businesses.

The ADA prohibits employers from inquiring about the existence and extent of an individual's disability prior to making a job offer. Preoffer medical exams are prohibited by the law. One may query the handicapped individual about his or her ability to perform the tasks associated with the job, but one may not ask questions regarding the disability. The law does allow employers to have the handicapped prospective employee complete a physical examination after a conditional job offer has been presented, as long as the exam is given to all employees, handicapped or not, applying in the same work category. The results of the exams cannot be used in a discriminatory way. The exam indicates that the disabled person is either qualified or not. The doctor's report will spell out whether the handicapped person can safely perform the functions of the job with reasonable accommodation.

The ADA allows an employer to dismiss a handicapped employee who uses illegal drugs. Rehabilitated persons and those in treatment for the use of illegal drugs are included in the category of a person with a disability. They may not be discriminated against. Employers have the right to conduct drug testing to determine whether or not an employee is using drugs. A prospective employee who is not hired because of a positive drug test or an employee who tests positively for the use of drugs may be dismissed and will not be able to take action against the employer under the provisions of the ADA. An employer may prohibit drugs to be used in the place of employment and can require that employees not be under the influence of drugs or alcohol while working.

The ADA is enforced by the Equal Employment Opportunity Commission.

Discrimination

Discrimination is one of the major considerations when dealing with labor relationships. Discrimination is dealt with here as a separate topic because of its pervasiveness in American culture and because of the impact of discrimination on the workplace and working conditions among co-workers.

The laws that provide for equal employment opportunity and prevent discrimination in the workplace represent an area of business law that landscape architecture firms must pay a great deal of attention to. Because landscape architecture private practice is a people-oriented business in relation to a firm's clients and staff, nondiscriminatory relationships with clients and staff must prevail in all landscape architecture firms. There are many ways to get into discrimination difficulty today because of a plethora of federal laws covering every possible aspect of discrimination. For example, one may not discriminate against another by law for any of the following reasons: race, color, sex, religion, national origin, age, pregnancy, handicaps, physical disabilities, mental disabilities, drug dependency, alcohol addiction, or carrying a contagious disease such as AIDS.

In the United States and in most other countries and cultures, employment problems caused by discriminatory practices are real considerations of daily business operations. Differences between male and female employment characteristics and between white male versus black male or Native American employment characteristics are well documented. Statistics indicate that the earnings of men are about 20 percent to 40 percent higher than the earnings of women. White males dominate higher-paying managerial and professional jobs in professions such as medicine, law, and landscape architecture, whereas women have historically been cast into lower-paying jobs such as secretarial, clerical, nursing, and elementary-level teaching positions. White male workers have generally earned more than black males for comparable positions. White males typically have half the unemployment rate that black males do at any given time.

Those who fight for antidiscrimination point out that without legislation making discrimination illegal, workplace discrimination including stereotyped assumptions about worker productivity, capability, and preferences for associating in the workplace with persons of similar race, sex, or age would continue unchecked.

The social forces at work to counteract discrimination in America picked up momentum with the civil rights movements in the 1950s and 1960s. The Equal Pay Act of 1963 was one of the first federal laws to address discrimination by prohibiting discrimination in pay based on sex. The law prohibits paying women less than men for a job that requires the same level of effort, skill, and responsibility. The law does allow pay differentiation for the following conditions:

- Using a seniority or merit system. Here, men *or* women may be paid more than other men *or* women because they have a greater amount of seniority.
- Using a work system where compensation is based on the quantity or quality of worker output.
- A pay differential based on any other criteria other than sex.

The law is enforced by the Equal Employment Opportunity Commission (EEOC). Employers are required to keep records of wages, job classifications, and whether the job classifications are filled by male or female employees. Employers found to be in violation of the Equal Pay Act by government agents will be required to compensate employees who have been discriminated against with an award equal to the amount of wages they should have received. Punitive awards may also be granted to the employees discriminated against. Attorney's fees are recoverable if employees need to rely on legal counsel and bring a lawsuit against the employer to obtain just compensation if discrimination is proved (Meiners, Ringleb, and Edwards 1988).

Title VII of the Civil Rights Act of 1964

No other legislation has set as much precedent and as many statutory provisions for counteracting discrimination in employment as Title VII of the Civil Rights Act of 1964, which was amended in 1972 by the Equal Employment Opportunity Act. The civil rights act specifically prohibits discrimination based on race, color, religion, sex, or national origin. Congress sought through the civil rights act to protect classes of people, such as blacks, Hispanics, and women, that have had a history of discriminatory treatment regarding employment. The EEOC, which was established under the Equal Employment Opportunity Act, has the authority and responsibility for enforcing Title VII.

The EEOC is made up of five members appointed by the president. The EEOC attempts to solve cases of discrimination that are brought to it or that it becomes aware of through its investigatory powers by administrative means and persuasion before taking action to file a lawsuit in federal court regarding discriminatory allegations. To fall under the provisions of Title VII, an employer must employ fifteen or more persons.

It has been relatively easy for the EEOC and the courts to identify discriminatory behavior against race and color as a protected Title VII class. In addition to whites, there are four other racial groups in the United States: Blacks, Native Americans, Hispanics, and Asians. These are the protected classes under the civil rights act. Whites are not protected under the act.

Regarding religion, an employer is required under the civil rights act to make reasonable accommodations for the religious practices of all employees. The employer has the right to reduce the degree of religious accommodation if the accommodations would impose an undue hardship on carrying out the business operations.

In relation to sex discrimination, Congress did not provide very clear guidance on how sex discrimination is defined. As a result, the courts have taken more of a role through case law to define the limits of sex discrimination under the civil rights act. Over the years, the courts have upheld cases of discrimination based on whether a person was male or female. On the other hand, the courts have held that discrimination based upon sexual preference is not protected under the civil rights act.

National origin refers to the country where a person is born or from which the person's ancestors came. The civil rights act prohibits discrimination against U.S. citizens based on national origin. The law does not protect aliens or noncitizens.

Another protected class was added in 1978 when Congress amended Title VII by passing the Pregnancy Discrimination Act. This amendment extends sex discrimination to include pregnancy and childbirth. Women who are pregnant are protected and may not be discriminated against. Sexual harassment is also covered under Title VII. If an employee is asked for sexual favors by a supervisor with a promise of career advancement as a reward or that the employee's job or career will be jeopardized if sexual requests made by a supervisor are not met by the employee, sexual harassment can be claimed. Repeated, unsolicited verbal comments or sexually explicit actions are also considered sexual harassment under the law.

Although the discrimination is not explicitly defined in the Title VII legislation, the U.S. Supreme Court has identified a number of areas of discrimination in case law since the passage of the civil rights act. One area of the Court's rulings is differential standards. If an employer sets standards for employees, the standards must be applied equally to all employees of both sexes. If an employer decides to hire only married people because the employer feels they are more stable, then the standard must be applied to *all* employees hired by the employer. For example, the employer cannot hire married women and hire single men. This would be a differential standard and the

courts would define this as discrimination. The courts have also upheld cases of discrimination where differences in pay are based on sex or other personal characteristics. Another area of case-law support for Title VII has revolved around segregation. The courts have indicated that discrimination occurs if an employer segregates workers into specific jobs based on race, sex, or national origin. Any separation of treatment of workers, such as assigning a Hispanic employee to a Hispanic client, could be considered segregation. Another area of case law has dealt with what has become known as *harassment with constructive dismissal*, that is, a person in a protected class may be hired and then harassed to the point where the employee quits because the work environment is intolerable.

Employers have three main defenses against allegations of discrimination.

The first is to use ability tests to determine if job applicants have the knowledge, training, skills, and other attributes necessary to carry out the job. The tests should be developed by a professional testing company to hold more credibility with the courts and ensure impartiality in the event the tests are challenged.

The second defense against allegations of discrimination is to implement a seniority system. The courts have upheld seniority systems as long as the intention is not to discriminate based on race, color, religion, sex, or national origin.

The third defense involves bona fide occupational qualifications where discrimination is necessary for the particular job or business operation. Race is excluded from this defense, but hiring based on sex, religion, or national origin is permitted if it passes the test as a bona fide occupational qualification (Meiners, Ringleb, and Edwards 1988).

Affirmative Action

The EEOC also has responsibility for encouraging affirmative action programs and assisting employers in developing voluntary affirmative action programs. An affirmative action program is a good-faith effort by an employer to reverse any real or apparent discriminatory practices in hiring and promoting employees in a protected class.

Affirmative action programs may be implemented voluntarily by an employer, or the employer may be required to implement an affirmative action program as a result of a court ruling against the employer or as a direct result of Executive Order 11246 issued by President Lyndon Johnson in 1965.

Executive Order 11246 requires that companies doing business with the federal government include affirmative action hiring in their business practice as related to the government contract. State and local governments also enforce affirmative action hiring guidelines for companies doing business with state and local governments. The executive order requires large companies to analyze their workforce and set affirmative action workforce goals by type of job classification for utilizing protected classes in the job categories. Executive Order 11246 applies to all federal government contractors, and an affirmative action goal is frequently applied to government contracts and directly affects the private practice of landscape architects who carry out professional services for federal, state, and local governments.

Age Discrimination

Milestone legislation was passed by Congress in 1967 when the Age Discrimination in Employment Act (ADEA) was enacted, prohibiting employment discrimination based on age. The point of this legislation is to uphold the civil rights of workers based on their ability to perform their job at any age. The EEOC enforces the ADEA, which focused on persons aged forty to sixty-five under legislation passed in 1967.

In 1978 Congress amended the ADEA and raised the upper age limit to seventy years old. Congress also included language in this amendment to prevent forced retirement of persons below the age of seventy. A further amendment in 1986 removed the mandatory retirement age of seventy.

The ADEA applies to all employers with twenty or more employees, to all government employers, employment agencies serving the public sector, and labor unions or organizations with at least twenty-four members. The law defines the following discriminatory practices as illegal:

- Practicing any type of employment discrimination based on age
- Segregating or classifying workers based on age
- Paying someone less than others based on age

- Practicing age discrimination related to employee benefits

Two areas watched by the EEOC are help-wanted advertisements and job application forms. Help-wanted ads cannot contain descriptions of desirable employee characteristics that would discriminate by age. Advertisements should not refer to specific age ranges (e.g., twenty to thirty-five years old desirable). They cannot use phrases such as "college student desired" or "young woman/jack-of-all-trades desired." Likewise they cannot use phrases that discriminate against younger employees, such as "this job is perfect for retirees," or "persons over forty years old should apply." Application forms should not include requests for date of birth or request the age of the applicant. All job application forms should include the following sentence: "The Age Discrimination in Employment Act prohibits discrimination on the basis of age with respect to individuals who are over forty years old."

An employee may allege a violation of the ADEA and submit a charge of wrongdoing to the EEOC. The charge would include

- the name, address, and telephone number of the person filing the complaint;
- the name and address of the employer;
- a concise statement of the facts and dates of the alleged age discrimination violations.

The complaint must be filed within 180 days of the alleged discrimination. The EEOC notifies the employer upon receiving a complaint and will first attempt to resolve the issue through administrative procedures. If the conciliatory efforts are unsuccessful, the employee is entitled to file a lawsuit against the employer. The EEOC is also likely to investigate the employer if an age discrimination charge is brought forth by an employee.

The EEOC requires employers to keep employee records to comply with the ADEA. The following information is required to be kept in personnel files for all employees for at least three years:

- Name
- Address
- Date of birth
- Occupation or job classification

- Pay rate
- Amount of pay earned each week

Other information should be kept for one year, including

- job application, résumé, and letters submitted by an employee in response to a job opening or advertisement;
- records of promotions, demotions, transfers, layoffs, or firing of employees;
- job announcements submitted to employment agencies, labor unions, or organizations;
- results of ability tests;
- results of physical exams;
- copies of ads relating to job opportunities (London 1991).

Protecting the General Public, the Environment, and the Consumer

The landscape architect is in a unique situation regarding a wide range of federal, state, and local legislation designed to protect our air, water, and land for the general public. Legislation such as the National Environmental Policy Act of 1969 requires that landscape architects comply with the laws in carrying out their business and the business of their clients. The laws also provide a source of clients and job opportunities for landscape architects.

Landscape architects are a broad group of professionals whose professional code of conduct includes efforts to preserve and protect our nation's natural resources. As a group, landscape architects have adopted a general social and environmental responsibility aimed at reconciling the needs of the general public with minimal disruption to social and natural systems. Landscape architects are imbued with a strong environmental ethic.

A hallmark of landscape architecture private practice is an awareness of and sensitivity to the intent, scope, and requirements of the environmental legislation passed by federal, state, and local governments and designed to protect the environment for the present and future generations.

This section is an overview of the significant federal environmental legislation. The intent is to identify a broad environmental ethic for landscape architects based on the core intent of the federal legislation that has been passed to protect the environment, the general public, and the consumer.

The National Environmental Policy Act

In 1970 the Environmental Protection Agency (EPA) was created when Congress passed the National Environmental Policy Act (NEPA) to centralize and coordinate the government's environmental responsibilities. The legislation was passed in response to the growing awareness that environmental problems such as air pollution, water pollution, and overuse of pesticides and other chemicals are interrelated and would be more appropriately addressed by an integrated approach. The EPA's initial emphasis was on pollution problems that are directly discernible to people, such as the visual degradation of the environment caused by smog. As time has passed, the EPA has placed additional emphasis on scientific research and dealing with environmental problems caused by chemical pollution and other types of pollution that cannot be seen, tasted, or smelled.

NEPA requires an environmental impact statement to be prepared for all federal action that significantly affects the environment. The gist of the environmental impact statement is akin to a landscape architect's site analysis process. The requirements for an environmental impact statement include

1. a description of the environmental impact of the proposed action,
2. a description of unavoidable impacts,
3. a discussion of alternatives to the proposed action,
4. identification of short- and long-term environmental impacts,
5. identification of any irreversible impacts on environmental resources.

Whereas some landscape architects prepare environmental impact statements under professional contracts, all landscape architects can practice the aims of environmental protection by directly responding to a personal and professional environmental ethic.

The Clean Air Act

Enacted in 1963, the Clean Air Act was originally intended to help states deal with interstate air pollution, and includes subsequent amendments that deal with controlling automobile emissions. The act was amended in 1970 and 1977 to develop a comprehensive approach to air pollution that is enforced by the EPA. The act requires the EPA to develop and set ambient air-quality standards that are applied nationally for the major air-polluting elements. The standards are set at two levels: (1) primary standards that protect human health and (2) secondary standards designed to protect the general environment, including forest resources, and visible air quality. EPA regions throughout the country must develop plans that meet the ambient air-quality standards set and adjusted for each region. The law covers stationary sources such as factories, automobile and vehicle air pollution, indoor air pollution such as from household chemical use and from the use of stoves and fireplaces. The law also sets standards for radioactive emissions from nuclear power plants.

Landscape architects are sensitive to the issues of air pollution in their everyday practice through a wide variety of planting applications, preservation of natural vegetation resources, revegetation efforts, preservation and management of open space, and other uses of plant materials for air purification.

Clean Water Act

The Federal Water Pollution Control Act (FWPCA) passed by Congress in 1948 was amended several times through 1970 to provide greater federal control over water pollution. In 1972 Congress again amended the FWPCA. These amendments are known as the Clean Water Act, and are parallel in intent and enforcement characteristics to the Clean Air Act. The Clean Water Act sought to achieve nonpolluted water throughout the country for human recreational activities such as swimming and boating, for productive fisheries resources, and to eliminate polluting discharge into the nation's rivers. Similar to the ambient air-quality standards of the Clean Air Act, the EPA sets water-quality standards under the Clean Water Act. The act requires all city and industrial dischargers to obtain permits for discharging into the nation's waterways.

An element of the Clean Water Act that many landscape architects are familiar with is the 404 provisions requiring permits for filling or dredging wetlands or other waterways.

The environmental ethic and educational training of the landscape architect is developed to be in tune with the legal provisions of the Clean Water Act. Landscape architects are sensitive to storm water runoff issues, wetlands protection, careful development and sensitive use of shorelines, and scientific analysis and management plans for aquifers. The provisions of the Clean Water Act enhance an already sensitive landscape architecture profession in carrying out protective planning and design applications related to our nation's water resources.

Resource Conservation and Recovery Act

Passed in 1974 and amended in 1985, the Resource Conservation and Recovery Act (RCRA) regulates the generation, treatment, storage, and disposal of hazardous waste. Generators of hazardous waste are required to obtain permits and meet stringent requirements for handling hazardous waste. The law focuses on operators of sanitary landfill operations. They are required to monitor the impacts of landfill operations on groundwater resources and protect underground water resources, including taking responsibility for any costs that may be associated with protecting groundwater.

Individual states are required to enforce standards set by the EPA regarding resource conservation and recovery. Noncompliance can bring about civil and criminal penalties. State and local governments are generally responsible for proper siting and operation of sanitary landfill operations. The RCRA has encouraged a shift in dealing with waste toward recycling waste, a practice that has become more prominent in the 1980s and 1990s. Other emphases such as focusing on changes in packaging and type of waste materials, as well as adoption of deposits on recyclable materials, have grown out of the RCRA.

Another result of the RCRA is the Comprehensive Environmental Response Compensation Act (CERCA), which expanded the RCRA to deal with wildcat dumping of hazardous waste and with abandoned hazardous waste sites. Hazardous waste sites throughout the country have been identified and prioritized to receive federal spending for cleanup. CERCA also provides the funding for quick federal and state response to cleanup of hazardous waste emergencies such as oil spills or probable contamination of water resources. The entity responsible for the hazardous waste emergency also bears the responsibility for the cost of the cleanup. The EPA has the authority to legally recover costs from the polluter if federal money is needed to respond to the emergency. Further amendment to CERCA in 1986 requires public notification of accidental spills of chemicals and other hazardous waste emergencies.

The federal government has also passed a wide range of other regulations covering protection of the public's drinking water supplies (Safe Drinking Water Act, 1974), protection of marine resources (Marine Protection, Research, and Sanctuaries Act, 1972), regulation of the use of agricultural chemicals and pesticides (Federal Insecticide, Fungicide, and Rodenticide Act), and prevention of chemical pollution directly affecting public health (Toxic Substances Control Act, 1976) (Metzger et al. 1989).

Landscape architects, serving in their self-proclaimed ethic of stewards of the environment, continue to orient their private-practice goals to comply with the wide range of federal laws designed to protect our nation's natural resources. As a profession, landscape architects provide leadership across the country in advancing the values of open-space protection and management for the public good. Landscape architects advance the concepts of reclaiming landscape that has been mined or quarried. They urge the protection of drinking water resources and advocate water conservation in their landscape architecture design practice. They are involved with the careful planning of coastal zones and coastal zone ecosystem management. They support the critical function of wetlands in protecting wildlife habitats and human quality of life. They seek to be of service to the general public by thoughtful planning and design efforts related to wetlands protection and use. The role of the landscape architect will inevitably complement the federal, state, and local laws designed to protect our nation's natural resources.

Environmental Commitment

There are many professions that have a commitment to protecting our nation's natural resources. Landscape architecture is preeminent among these professions.

Caring for the land and its people is a hallmark of the education and practice of the profession and is central to the environmental ethic practiced by individual landscape architects and the profession as a whole.

As each landscape architect matures in the practice of this sensitive and much-needed profession, the country will benefit from the well-being endowed on the landscape by those individuals who have selected this inspired profession. Landscape architecture offers its practitioners a professional framework to prosper and be of great service to the people of this country by creating useful, safe, aesthetic, and enjoyable environments for the good of all.

As you go forward in this profession, practice with honesty, integrity, and happiness. Good luck. You have chosen a wonderful way to work and live that encompasses a concern for our land and the people who use it.

REFERENCES

Arizona Department of Economic Security, Unemployment Insurance Administration. *Unemployment Insurance, What You Should Know About Unemployment Insurance in Arizona.* Phoenix, Ariz.: Arizona Department of Economic Security.

Bowman, Stan L. *An Overview of the Case for Licensure.* Washington, D.C.: American Society of Landscape Architects.

Cihon, Patrick J., and James O. Castagnera. 1988. *Labor and Employment Law.* 2d ed. Boston, Mass.: PWS-Kent Publishing Company.

Greenstreet, Bob, and Karen Greenstreet. 1984. *The Architect's Guide to Law and Practice.* New York: Van Nostrand Reinhold.

London, Sheldon I. 1991. *How to Comply with Federal Employee Laws.* Washington, D.C.: London Publishing Company.

Meiners, Roger E., Al H. Ringleb, and Frances L. Edwards. 1988. *The Legal Environment of Business.* 3d ed. Saint Paul, Minn.: West Publishing Company.

Metzger, Michael B., Jane P. Mallor, A. James Barnes, Thomas Bowers, and Michael J. Phillips. 1989. *Business Law and the Regulatory Environment.* 7th ed. Homewood, Ill.: Richard D. Irwin.

Miller, Samuel C. *Professional Licensure of Landscape Architects: An Assessment of Public Needs and Private Responsibilities.* 1978. Washington, D.C.: American Society of Landscape Architects.

Schoumacher, Bruce. 1986. *Engineers and the Law: An Overview.* New York: Van Nostrand Reinhold.

State of Arizona. *Code and Rules of the State Board of Technical Registration for Architects, Assayers, Engineers, Geologists, Landscape Architects and Land Surveyors.* 1991. Phoenix, Ariz: State Board of Technical Registration.

U.S. Department of Labor. 1993. *Small Business Handbook: Laws, Regulations and Technical Assistance Services.* Washington, D.C.: Government Printing Office.

STUDY QUESTIONS AND ASSIGNMENTS

1. Using this chapter and other references, write a thorough and in-depth paper that illustrates your understanding of the origin of law in the United States.

2. Using this chapter and other references, write a thorough and in-depth paper that illustrates your understanding of professional licensure laws for landscape architects. Obtain a copy of the code and rules of regulations governing the practice of landscape architecture in your state as part of your research.

3. Using this chapter and other references, write a thorough and in-depth paper that illustrates your understanding of the powers of regulatory agencies. Discuss processes and procedures, legal restrictions, and legislative restrictions on the powers of regulatory agencies.

4. Using this chapter and other references, write a thorough and in-depth paper that illustrates your understanding of tort law and negligence. Discuss the three main elements of proof of negligence:

   • Proof that the landscape architect has a duty not to injure a party
   • Proof that the landscape architect actually breached the duty not to injure the party
   • Proof that the landscape architect's breach is the actual and legal cause of the injury to the party

5. Using this chapter and other references, write a thorough and in-depth paper that illustrates your understanding of the concept of employment-at-will.

6. Obtain a copy of the Occupational Safety and Health Act (OSHA) from your congressperson.

Using the act, this chapter, and other references, write a paper that illustrates your understanding of OSHA and its effect on the practice of landscape architecture.

7. Using this chapter and other references, write a thorough and in-depth paper that illustrates your understanding of how to fire an employee. Develop a procedure for the disciplinary action and the actual process of terminating an employee.

8. Using this chapter and other references, write a thorough and in-depth paper that illustrates your understanding of the Employee Retirement Income Security Act (ERISA). As part of your research, obtain a copy of the act from your congressperson.

9. Using this chapter and other references, write a thorough and in-depth paper that illustrates your understanding of the Consolidated Omnibus Budget Reconciliation Act (COBRA). As part of your research, obtain a copy of the act from your congressperson.

10. Using this chapter and other references, write a thorough and in-depth paper that illustrates your understanding of the Family and Medical Leave Act (FMLA). As part of your research, obtain a copy of the act from your congressperson.

11. Using this chapter and other references, write a thorough and in-depth paper that illustrates your understanding of the Americans with Disabilities Act (ADA). Obtain a copy of the act from your congressperson.

12. Using this chapter and other references, write a thorough and in-depth paper that illustrates your understanding of Title VII of the Civil Rights Act of 1964 and later amendments. Obtain a copy of the act and amendments from your congressperson.

13. Using this chapter and other references, write a thorough and in-depth paper that illustrates your understanding of Executive Order 11246. Obtain a copy of the executive order from your congressperson.

14. Using this chapter and other references, write a thorough and in-depth paper that illustrates your understanding of the landscape architect's obligation to protect the general public, the environment, and the consumer.

Ace Landscape Architects Construction Services Manual

Summary of Major Items

1. Prepare a budget of all time and expenses allocated for Ace's construction services contract. Monitor time and expenses on a weekly basis and keep the project manager or principal advised on the progress and problems.

2. Be thoroughly familiar with the plans, specifications, and contracts, including all requirements for the construction schedule, quality of work, and coordination between contractor, owner, and Ace.

3. Visit the site to determine the nature and extent of existing improvements. Note in writing any preexisting conditions that do not match the survey, as well as any damage or vandalism.

4. To the extent permitted in Ace's agreement with the owner, conduct a prebid meeting to clarify the plans and specifications, form of contract, schedules, and other important items. Require each bidder to document acceptance of existing site conditions in the bid submittal.

5. To the extent permitted in our agreement with the owner, conduct a preconstruction meeting after the bid award, on the site with plans and specifications, to confirm the requirements pertaining to quality and schedule. Require the contractor to verify that all specified materials and products have been located and that the contractor has covered all required labor, taxes, permits, fees, inspections, and tests.

6. Prepare a complete checklist of all construction activities and product submittals that will have to be reviewed for acceptance by Ace on behalf of the owner.

7. Develop and follow a direct and logical communication process. Communicate directly with the contractor's project manager and site superintendent. Get twenty-four-hour telephone numbers.

8. Develop and practice good communication and documentation techniques. When in doubt, write it down as a field report, memo, or transmittal. Anticipate, think out, and express yourself clearly and thoroughly. Go beyond the immediate issue and consider its impact on the project as a whole.

9. Make prompt and fair decisions. Consider alternatives when possible. Stand by your decisions when you are right. Be honest and correct your decisions when you are wrong.

10. Write up all discussions, meetings, and telephone conversations clearly and completely, send copies to all concerned parties, and file a copy in the project file or project manual. Make a photographic record to back up observations when you believe a photographic record may be important. If the budget does not allow recording every conversation or communication in a formal way, keep a detailed journal and send out routine correspondence weekly or biweekly.

11. Promptly review all change orders submitted by the contractor. Review your approval or disapproval with the owner, and if the changes are accepted, process and incorporate the changes into the contract documents.

12. Follow and document a legally acceptable trail whenever you are considering stopping work.

13. Prepare a postconstruction follow-up report. Document crisis events and changes to Ace's procedures. Review guarantees, operations, and maintenance instructions with the owner. Photograph the project for public relations efforts and discuss its award potential with the project manager.

14. Always act with the highest degree of honesty, integrity, and fairness as a representative of Ace.

Construction Services Manual

I. Key Issues
   A. Design: construction reflects design intent.
   B. Responsibility: to Ace, to the client, and to the contractor
   C. Professionalism: knowledge, decision, fairness
II. Duties and responsibilities
   A. Ace Landscape Architects
      1. Preconstruction planning
         a. Prepare a budget of all time and fees allocated in the construction services contract. Review the budget with the project manager. Monitor the schedule weekly and review progress with the project manager.
         b. Check the plans and specifications thoroughly. Get corrective action by the project manager if there are discrepancies or problems.
         c. Verify existing site conditions with those shown on the plans.
         d. Review the construction contract between the owner and the contractor. Verify that the contract includes the authority for Ace's services during construction.
         e. Obtain all phone numbers of key people involved with the construction contract.
         f. Obtain a list of all subcontractors.
         g. Obtain a construction schedule from the contractor.
      2. Construction compliance with the contract documents
         a. Observe and inform. Avoid using works such as *supervise, inspect,* or *control.* They imply Ace's responsibility for the contractor's work.
         b. Be thoroughly familiar with the construction documents.
      3. Make prompt decisions. Avoid delays unless unavoidable.
      4. Schedule site review visits as much as possible. Reduce extra visits. Be sure that the contractor is prepared for your visit. Use a weekly meeting format whenever possible.
      5. Develop cooperation and mutual respect with the contractor. Mutual respect improves communication and facilitates negotiated compromises.
      6. Be decisive.
         a. Stand by the decision.
         b. Anticipate decisions. Avoid spending time in research or deliberation, but do not hesitate to let the contractor know that you will get back to him or her if you do not readily know the answer to a question.
         c. Offer alternatives to the contractor.
      7. Suggestions for effective construction review communication:
         a. Establish a contact person for client and contractor.
         b. Approach all situations with an open mind.
         c. Resolve the problem for the good of the project.
         d. Maintain design integrity.
         e. Anticipate anxiety in both yourself and others. Do not deal from emotions at any time. Never lose your temper. Be professional, fair, and understanding at the same time.
         f. Strive to have all situations clearly stated, properly and promptly documented, and provide correspondence to all concerned.

g. Be specific and do not deal in wide-ranging generalities.

h. Refer to current work and do not bring up past negative experiences.

i. Be sure you talk to the right person. Is he or she in a decision-making capacity?

j. Be sure that the time is right to discuss a particular situation.

k. Make sure that the proposed solution is doable.

l. Be extremely patient. You may have to discuss, evaluate, or even reword communications at various times.

m. Be sure that both you and your listener are paying attention to the problem at hand and that you are not wandering from the subject.

n. Do not pass on incomplete information, and do not accept incomplete information.

o. Make sure that both you and the person you are dealing with are interpreting words and phrases of construction jargon in exactly the same way.

p. If at any time a sketch or drawing can be used to clarify the situation, use one. Enter the drawing in the project file or project manual.

q. Do not carry out an obviously foolish or questionable interpretation. Check out the information and ask for clarification from a principal, project manager, or other experienced person at Ace. Be sure that the interpretation makes sense before you act on it.

r. Be sure that it is clearly your responsibility to act and not someone else's.

s. Keep the owner and client informed and current on all construction activities and decisions.

t. Thoroughly think out all proposed changes and how they will affect other construction elements not yet completed.

B. Owner

1. Government or institutional clients may require their representative to be frequently involved. They can expedite approvals and resolutions.

2. Limit direct contract between owner and contractor.

3. You may have to educate an owner who is unfamiliar with construction practices.

4. The owner always has the right to make changes in the project.

C. Contractor

1. Must fulfill the contract requirements.

2. Provides on-site review and continuous supervision of his work.

3. Coordinates with all trades and subcontractors.

4. Has bottom-line accountability.

5. Has direct participation with Ace's landscape architects during site visits.

6. Receives and distributes all of Ace's communication.

7. Resolves conflicts between subcontractors.

D. Regulatory agencies

1. Are involved as required by laws and codes.

2. Ensure code compliance.

3. Make note of any special inspections that may be required.

III. Quality compliance

A. Have scheduled project site meetings.

B. Bidder prequalification, prebid conferences, preconstruction conference

C. Have a preconstruction site review to

1. Verify existing conditions.

2. Record damages that may have been previously made to existing facilities.

3. Identify changes to the base conditions used for our design work and determine the impact to the contractor and our construction services contract. Advise the project manager.

D. Performance, payment, and other types of bonds are supplied by the contractor to the owner.

E. Site visit verification letter

1. The letter shall be included in the bid documents and signed by the bidder.

2. The letter attests that the bidder has visited the site and is familiar with all visible site conditions and these conditions are covered by the bid.

F. Bid award letter

1. Sent to the contractor selected for his signature.

2. Contractor has located all specified materials, products, and equipment and has covered all required labor, taxes, permits, inspections, and tests.

G. Develop a checklist of construction and coordination required for on-site reviews.

1. Obtain written construction schedule from the contractor.

2. Timeliness of being on site is critical, so become involved in preconstruction meetings and progress meetings with the contractor and subconsultants. Keep informed about the work, decisions, changes, and schedules of the contractor and how these decisions may impact our work.

3. Inform other subconsultants when they need to review construction activities.

4. Include the names and phone numbers of all subcontractors.

5. List major work items and materials to be approved and determine when they will be ready for review. Include the following topics:
   a. Site clearing and preparation
   b. Grading and drainage
   c. Paving
   d. Walls, steps, ramps, edges, and other hardscape elements
   e. Irrigation
   f. Planting
   g. Layout
   h. Other construction

6. Note: Under each heading, include the points of construction requiring review, e.g.:
   Walls
   a. Footings
   b. Steel
   c. Masonry, etc.
   d. Finishes

H. Review for approval samples and shop drawings. Use the Ace form for approval.

1. Review all items required by the specifications.

2. If an item submittal is not required by the contract documents, and it is critical to the design, request a sample from the contractor. The contractor does not have to provide it; however, you should try to convince the contractor that prior sample approval could be helpful to you and the project owner and may result in a better project.

I. What to do when you observe a compliance problem:

1. Discuss it on site with the contractor and verbally notify the contractor that the item is not in compliance. Ask the contractor what he or she is going to do to bring the item into compliance.

2. Follow up promptly with written documentation.

3. Distribute a copy of the documentation to all concerned parties and the project file.

4. Obtain a resolution for compliance.

5. Involve the appropriate Ace project manager or principal.

IV. Construction documentation

A. Clear communication and accurate records

1. Maintain a construction services manual. (Who's who, phone numbers, project written records.)

2. Keep records in chronological order. Follow the policies and procedures of the client or owner.

3. Be concerned for any item that may result in additional costs or in a legal situation.

B. Meeting notes, conversation notes, and correspondence

1. Take minutes of all construction-related meetings and distribute promptly. Use the Ace forms provided in this manual.
   a. The notes do not have to be elaborate, but they should be accurate and succinct.
   b. Ask for concurrence of information.
   c. Correspondence must follow up verbal communication. Distribute copies to all appropriate persons.

2. Essential information
   a. Date and location of meeting; starting and ending times; name, position, and employer of all those in attendance; distribution list for copies; a complete record of the substance of all important statements.

3. Telephone records: same information as for minutes

C. Field reports
1. Summarize, document, and communicate on-site observations. Use the Ace forms provided in this manual.
2. Interpret or clarify work.
3. Evaluate completed work prior to final acceptance review.
   a. Acceptable workmanship and materials
   b. Unacceptable workmanship and materials
4. Content
   a. Brief and to the point
   b. References to plans and specs (sheet, page numbers)
   c. Diagrams and sketches
   d. Weather conditions
   e. Standard reference information
   f. Who did what
5. Distribute ASAP after site visit.
6. Consider tape recording followed by transcription. Keep all tapes on file.
7. Consider using a camera for documenting observations and problems. Take before-and-after shots.

D. Change orders
1. Modifies plans or specifications.
2. Becomes a legally binding part of contract.
3. Owner must approve.
4. Process
   a. Initiation of request for change order.
   b. Proposal of changes and cost changes by contractor.
   c. Review by Ace with recommendation.
   d. Owner reviews and signs. Contractor reviews and signs.
5. Can be standard form or by letter. Public clients normally have a specific form. Ace frequently uses the appropriate AIA standard form.
6. Include supplementary drawings if needed.
7. The basic information usually contained on a standard change order includes the following:
   a. The change order number (most often sequential to enhance the chronological record of the project); date; project name and reference number; owner; contractor and original contract reference date; description of contract changes, cost effect (addition or deduction); time effect; previous original contract amount; and signature lines and dates for owner and contractor.

E. Field orders
1. Field orders are used for minor changes that may or may not affect the cost. Use the Ace forms provided in this manual.
2. Field orders are made by landscape architect as the owner's agent. If possible, always seek authorization by the owner before making a field change.
   a. Limited by a maximum cost overrun allowed by owner.
   b. Use carefully, for immediate decisions.
3. Are usually verbal, and must be followed by a letter or memo.
4. May eventually be incorporated into a change order and included in the contract documents.
5. If minor changes do not affect the price, cost, or completion time, the Ace representative can authorize by letter, memo, or bulletin.
   a. Notify owner and contractor.
   b. Copy to file.

F. Inspection and certification reports
1. The requirements for these reports must be specified in the contract documents or by public reviewing agents.
2. All reports are entered in the construction file.

G. Punch list
1. Itemizes work to be done or corrected to complete the project. Use the Ace forms provided in this manual.
2. Usually made to verify a request for payment or for completion.
3. Contractor to request five days in advance.
4. The punch list usually includes the following information:
   a. Project name and reference identification; date of the review; date and reason for the punch list (final acceptance review, substantial completion, start of the maintenance period, etc.); brief descriptive statements that identify the nonconforming items or workmanship

(each should be separately identified); and copy distribution.

H. Stopping the work for unacceptable work by the contractor.

   1. *Warning 1:* Inform the contractor verbally that the work as installed will not be approved. Follow promptly with a written document.

   2. *Warning 2:* If the unsatisfactory work continues, inform the contractor verbally that the work is still not acceptable. Follow promptly with a written document. Discuss the situation with the owner. Request the owner's input and concurrence regarding the questionable work.

   3. If there is no change in the situation, prepare a letter to stop the work of the contractor. Advise the contractor that any further work from the time of the receipt of the letter will not be approved for payment; nor will the unsatisfactory work previously performed be approved for payment. It is very helpful if the letter is signed by Ace and the owner. The owner's concurrence is required.

   4. Resolve the issue. Involve the appropriate Ace project manager or principal.

V. Project completion

   A. Process

      1. Prefinal review and punch list

      2. Final review to confirm satisfactory completion

      3. Landscape architect sends written notice to owner indicating that the project has been completed in compliance with the contract documents.

      4. Owner writes his formal acceptance of the project.

      5. Final payment is recommended.

   B. Certificate of substantial completion

      1. Minor work needs to be done.

      2. Owner must occupy the project.

      3. Must have all regulatory requirements met.

         a. Code compliance

         b. Agency certificate of occupancy

      4. Ace uses the appropriate AIA standard form for certificate of substantial completion.

C. Review of record drawings—as-builts if our contract documents require as-built preparation and submittal by the contractor

   1. Accuracy is critical.

   2. Important for owner's operation and maintenance of project.

   3. Contractor to record, on a plan set, all amended items or changes at the time of the construction change.

   4. Landscape architect reviews record drawings periodically.

   5. Must be complete before final review and acceptance.

D. Submittal of required documents

   1. Lien waivers

   2. Bonds

   3. Operation and maintenance manuals

   4. Warranties and guarantees

VI. Postconstruction follow-up

   A. Under contract—landscape architect/owner

      1. Evaluation of establishment, maintenance, and monitoring periods

      2. Recommendations for improvement

      3. New job development

   B. Informal review—not under contract

      1. Notify owner of project status.

      2. Not billable.

      3. Good PR.

   C. Write a construction wrap-up report

      1. Identify all crisis events and how they were resolved.

      2. Describe necessary changes to plans, details, specifications, and design concepts for future use on other projects. See that the changes are implemented.

      3. Describe procedures developed on the project that will streamline future design and construction operations.

   D. Maintain a photographic record of construction.

      1. Documentation of unacceptable work

      2. Public relations and promotional photographs

   E. Evaluate the project in a meeting with the Ace project manager, principal, and designers in terms of the project's award potential.

ACE CONSTRUCTION FORMS

BIDDERS VERIFICATION OF EXISTING SITE CONDITIONS

To be submitted with the Contractor's bid for the following project:

PROJECT: _____

BID DATE: _____

_____

Bidder (Name of Bidder)

Attests that bidder has visited the project site prior to the bid submittal and is thoroughly familiar with all visible, existing site conditions pertaining to this project. This bid includes all material, labor and other costs associated with and required for the completion of all work on the project site.

By: _____

_____

Contractor

_____

Address

Date: _____

CONTRACTORS VERIFICATION OF BID

To be submitted to the Landscape Architect prior to signing a contract for construction.

PROJECT: _____

BID DATE: _____

_____
Contractor

Attests that he has located all specified or approved substitutions of materials, products and equipment and that the total cost for the materials, products, equipment, labor, permits, fees, inspections, tests and other associated costs, as required by the contract documents, are included in his bid.

By: _____

_____
Contractor

_____
Address

_____

Date: _____

ACE LANDSCAPE ARCHITECTS

PROJECT:_____

PROJECT NO:_____

LOCATION:_____

OWNER: _____

CONTRACTOR: _____

PRESENT: _____

_____

_____

FIELD REPORT

DATE:_____

TO:_____   FROM:_____

_____   _____

THE FOLLOWING WAS NOTED:

DISTRIBUTION: _____   BY: _____

_____

_____

ACE LANDSCAPE ARCHITECTS

PROJECT: _____

PROJECT NO: _____

REVIEW OF SUBMITTALS & SHOP DRAWINGS

DATE:_____

FROM:_____   TO:_____

_____   _____

APPROVED ( )
APPROVED AS CORRECTED ( )

If checked above, fabrication MAY be undertaken or product MAY be purchased. Approval does not authorize changes to the Contract Sum unless stated in separate Change Order.

If checked below, fabrication may NOT be undertaken nor may the product submitted be used. Resubmit corrected copies for final approval. Correction shall be limited to the items noted.

REVISE AND RESUBMIT ( )
NOT APPROVED ( )

REVIEWING IS ONLY FOR CONFORMANCE WITH THE DESIGN CONCEPT OF THE PROJECT AND COMPLIANCE WITH THE INFORMATION GIVEN IN THE CONTRACT DOCUMENTS. THE CONTRACTOR IS RESPONSIBLE FOR DIMENSIONS TO BE CONFIRMED AND CORRELATED AT THE SITE; FOR INFORMATION THAT PERTAINS SOLELY TO THE FABRICATION PROCESSES OR TO THE MEANS, METHODS, TECHNIQUES, SEQUENCES, AND PROCEDURES OF CONSTRUCTION; AND FOR THE COORDINATION OF WORK OF ALL TRADES.

ACE LANDSCAPE ARCHITECTS

PROJECT:_____

PROJECT NO:_____

PRESENT:

_____

_____

_____

PUNCH LIST

DATE:_____

TO:_____   FROM:_____

_____   _____

ITEMS TO BE COMPLETED:

DISTRIBUTION:_____   BY:_____

_____

_____

ACE LANDSCAPE ARCHITECTS

PROJECT:_____

PROJECT NO:_____

CONTRACT DATE:_____

CONTRACTOR: _____

FIELD ORDER NO. _____

DATE:_____

You are hereby authorized and directed to effect the following modifications of the contract for the project identified above:

MAXIMUM COST: $_____

A duly authorized Change Order with appropriate reference will supersede this Field Order.

_____

CONTRACTOR'S AUTHORIZED REPRESENTATIVE

_____

OWNERS AUTHORIZED REPRESENTATIVE

DISTRIBUTION: _____

_____

_____

ACE LANDSCAPE ARCHITECTS

PROJECT NAME:_____

ADDRESS: _____

_____

OWNER:_____

CONTRACT DATE: _____

CHANGE ORDER NO._____

INITIATION DATE:_____

CONTRACTOR NAME AND ADDRESS:_____

_____

_____

You are directed to make the following changes in this contract:

ITEM	NET ADD	NET DEDUCT	TIME ADD	TIME DEDUCT
	$	$	(days)	(days)
TOTAL	$	$		

Original Contract Amount: $_____
Prior Change Orders: _____
This Change Order: _____

Revised Contract Amount: $_____

The Contract time will be (increased) (decreased) (unchanged) by_____ days.
The Date of Substantial Completion as of the date of this Change Order is _____.

_____   _____   _____
LANDSCAPE ARCHITECT   CONTRACTOR   OWNER

BY: _____   BY: _____   BY: _____

DATE: _____   DATE: _____   DATE: _____

ACE LANDSCAPE ARCHITECTS

PROJECT:_____

PROJECT NO:_____

OBSERVATION DATE:_____

LOCATION:_____

WEATHER:_____

PRESENT:_____

FIELD REPORT

DATE:_____

OBSERVATIONS:

ACTION REQUIRED:

DISTRIBUTION:_____   BY:_____

_____

_____

ACE LANDSCAPE ARCHITECTS

PROJECT: _____

PROJECT NO: _____

FROM: _____

TALKED TO: _____

TELEPHONE MEMORANDUM

DATE: _____

SUBJECT:

DISCUSSION:

ACTION REQUIRED:

DISTRIBUTION: BY: _____

Index